Encyclopedia of
Weird Westerns
SECOND EDITION

Encyclopedia of Weird Westerns

Supernatural and Science Fiction Elements in Novels, Pulps, Comics, Films, Television and Games

Second Edition

PAUL GREEN

Introduction by CYNTHIA J. MILLER

McFarland & Company, Inc., Publishers

Jefferson, North Carolina

LIBRARY OF CONGRESS CATALOGUING-IN-PUBLICATION DATA

Names: Green, Paul, 1955– author.
Title: Encyclopedia of weird westerns : supernatural and science fiction
elements in novels, pulps, comics, films, television and games /
Paul Green ; introduction by Cynthia J. Miller.
Description: Second edition. | Jefferson, North Carolina :
McFarland & Company, Inc., Publishers, 2016. |
Includes bibliographical references and index.
Identifiers: LCCN 2016002635 | ISBN 9781476662572
(softcover : acid free paper) ∞
Subjects: LCSH: Western films—Encyclopedias. |
Western stories—Encyclopedias. | Western comic books,
strips, etc—Encyclopedias. | West (U.S.)—In motion pictures—
Encyclopedias. | West (U.S.)—In literature—Encyclopedias. |
West (U.S.)—In popular culture—Encyclopedias.
Classification: LCC PN1995.9.W4 G74 2016 | DDC 791.43/6587803—dc23
LC record available at http://lccn.loc.gov/2016002635

BRITISH LIBRARY CATALOGUING DATA ARE AVAILABLE

ISBN (print) 978-1-4766-6257-2
ISBN (ebook) 978-1-4766-2402-0

Front cover: Paul Bettany as the title character in the 2011 film *Priest*
(Screen Gems/Photofest)

Printed in the United States of America

*McFarland & Company, Inc., Publishers
Box 611, Jefferson, North Carolina 28640
www.mcfarlandpub.com*

Table of Contents

Acknowledgments

I would like to thank the following for their help in my research for this second edition: popular culture and Weird Western authority Cynthia J. Miller for writing a fascinating and comprehensive Introduction; administrative director Cathy Dougherty and chief creative officer C. Edward Sellner at Visionary Comics; Robert E. Howard aficionado Jeffrey H. Shanks; and authors James Reasoner and Edward J. Erdelac.

My thanks to Jean-Marc Lofficier, Bill Black, Mike Hoffman, Enrico Teodarani, Alex Sheikman, Walter Venturi, Clément Calvet, Jackie Smith, Chris Ryall, Dan Forcey, Scott Bieser, Bill McLoughlin, Paul Guinan, Fred Berney, his wife Ellen, Roy Steffensen (1914–2012) and Madeline Baker.

Preface

In December 1932, Hugo Gernsback, the creator of the first science fiction magazine, *Amazing Stories,* wrote an editorial for *Wonder Stories* titled "Reasonableness in Science Fiction."

> When science fiction first came into being, it was taken most seriously by all authors. In practically all instances, authors laid the basis of their stories upon a solid foundation. If an author made a statement as to certain future instrumentalities, he usually found it advisable to adhere to the possibilities of science as it was then known.
>
> Many modern science fiction authors have no such scruples. They do not hesitate to throw scientific plausibility overboard and embark upon a policy of what I might call scientific magic, in other words, science that is neither plausible, nor possible. Indeed it overlaps the fairy tale, and often goes the fairy tale one better.
>
> This is a deplorable state of affairs, and one that I certainly believe should be avoided by all science fiction authors, if science fiction is to survive.

Times change and our literary sensibilities evolve for better or for worse. What once was considered "a deplorable state of affairs" becomes accepted by the public and critics alike. Weird Western fiction immersed in a magical setting includes *The Dark Tower* series by Stephen King, the *Frontier Magic* series by Patricia C. Wrede and the *Hexslinger* series by Gemma Files.

This second edition expands on my extensive history of the Weird Western in dime novels, pulp magazines, comic books, novels, film, animation, television and games. Some might argue the Weird Western is merely an umbrella term for stories involving the supernatural and science fiction. But there can be no doubt that the Weird Western has its own distinct style within the broader genre of the Western. The Weird Western continues to evolve and move further away from its traditional genre roots.

Since the publication of the first edition in 2009 Weird Westerns have had mixed fortunes. The Steampunk Western novel has become increasingly popular, and zombies have conquered cable TV thanks to the success of *The Walking Dead,* while the mash-up formula has extended to Abraham Lincoln becoming both a slayer of zombies and a vampire hunter. But big-budget films such as *Jonah Hex, Priest, John Carter* and *The Lone Ranger* all failed to ignite the box office and lost significant amounts of money. *Cowboys & Aliens* competed with *The Smurfs* for the no. 1 spot much to the consternation of Harrison Ford on the *Conan O'Brien* chat show, where Ford ripped the head off a Papa Smurf figure in disgust. In contrast, the groundbreaking Space Western *Avatar* proved to be a huge worldwide success for director James Cameron, who embraced new technology to tell a story of the brutality of human colonization on a distant planet.

The main body of this book uses a simple A–Z encyclopedia format. Cross-referenced subjects are in bold type within an individual entry. An appendix lists the entries under their respective subheadings. The entries are divided into various sub-genres according to their subject matter. In the case of comic book series, radio shows and television series, only the specific issues or episodes that can be classified as Weird Westerns are listed.

The quality of work ranges from top-class and innovative to repetitive and formulaic. From work that lifts the spirit to work that revels in the sewer of human actions and emotions. The purpose of any encyclopedia is to document the subject and not to exclude any work. The weird by definition attracts the weird.

It is impossible to include every Weird Western ever published or filmed. My apologies for any titles I've missed during extensive research.

The definitions below will explain my reasoning concerning the exclusion of certain titles or characters. For example, some people have classified *The Terror of Tiny Town* (1938) as a Weird Western. But, according to my definition, any film featuring little people isn't weird, because little people aren't weird, unless you cast them in a Weird Western setting as aliens, zombies, demons, ghosts, vampires, or werewolves, for example.

Weird Western [WW]

A Western story incorporating horror, supernatural or fantasy elements and themes and usually including one or more of the following subjects: vampires, werewolves, mummies, man-made monsters, mythological beings, mutants, zombies, ghosts, haunted buildings, demons, witchcraft, Satanism, possession, demonic or possessed animals, mentalists, shamans, visions, restless or wandering spirits, damned souls, enchantment, shape-shifters, angels, goblins, faeries, sirens, flying horses, psychopathic killers, torture, psychological terror, dismembered moving body parts, spirit guides, the occult, hexes and curses, rising from the dead, talking animals, superhuman abilities and magical potions.

Weird Menace Western [WM]

Popular in 1930s Western films and serials and crime pulp fiction, the Weird Menace story explores supernatural and horror themes but always concludes with a rational explanation for events.

Science Fiction Western [SFW]

A traditional Western setting with science fiction elements or themes, often involving future technology or extra-terrestrials. The Science Fiction Western can sometimes be a clumsy mix of genres given the fact that modern technology didn't exist in the Old West. This is usually solved with plot devices including time travel, aliens from outer space and alternate histories.

The sub-genre also incorporates the post-apocalyptic Western with its back story elements of lawlessness, gang warfare, survival in a hostile environment and the alienated lone hero attempting to make sense out of the chaos. The post-apocalyptic Western often includes Cyberpunk elements with surviving technology being a factor in many stories.

Space Western [SW]

A science fiction story set in outer space that contains Western genre elements or themes. These are usually disguised within a space opera or science fiction format. The hero can at times be little more than a cowboy with a ray gun. Early science fiction pulp magazine cover art sometimes emphasized the similarity in genres by adopting the same poses it used for its Western titles.

Space Westerns became more sophisticated with age but some still blatantly pay homage to their source of inspiration with thinly disguised Western genre plots. In many contemporary Space Westerns, the lines can become increasingly blurred between Western and military genre influences.

Steampunk Western [SPW]

Steampunk Westerns are tales set in the Old West, although Western genre characters can be transported to Victorian England or other non–Western environments.

Stories incorporate Victorian technology and invention, often placing characters at odds with the Old West culture and forcing them to either expand their horizons, shrink in fear or react with violence.

Steampunk has its roots in Cyberpunk with the transforming and corrupting influence of a rampant technology that erodes society. The viewpoint is usually dystopian. While Steampunk often incorporates actual historic events, its world is mainly alternative history involving fantastic machines that might have existed in another timeline.

Weird Western Romance [WWR]

The Weird Western Romance is a traditional romance novel set in the modern day or the Old West that involves time travel or supernatural elements including ghosts, spirit guides, demons, vampires or guardian angels. The romantic male lead character is usually an idealized outlaw, rancher, cowboy or American Indian.

Introduction

by Cynthia J. Miller

Steam men ... Dinosaurs ... Aliens ... Vampires ... Airships... Decidedly not the stuff of traditional Westerns, but if you look closely, the frontier comes alive with figures and themes drawn from horror, science fiction, steampunk, and more. Known collectively as Weird Westerns, these tales weave elements of the fantastic into traditional Western plots, characters, and settings to create stories that complicate, reinforce, and comment on our understanding of Westerns and the West, both as a reinvention of one of our most tradition-bound genres and as a spectacular reaffirmation of one of its central premises.

While such tales may have only begun receiving attention comparatively recently, they are, in fact, a nearly 150-year-old subgenre of the Western; somewhat modest in numbers, but vividly memorable in their mingling of the familiar and the fantastic. In August 1868, dime novel publisher Irwin Beadle's independent publication, *Irwin P. Beadle's American Novels*, featured Edward Sylvester Ellis' imaginative tale *The Huge Hunter or The Steam Man of the Prairies* (reprinted as *Baldy's Boy Partner or Young Brainerd's Steam Man* in 1888). Ellis' novel spins the story of two friends who, in "horrified amazement," encounter a gigantic steam-powered robot and his young creator in the Western prairies. In its day, Ellis' novel was viewed as little more than a wild tale of adventure, but it would lay the foundation for what is today known as "Edisonade"—extraordinary dime novel stories of young inventors and their fantastic inventions—as well as for the entire Weird Western subgenre, which would emerge slowly, one genre mash-up at a time. As Jeff VanderMeer explains:

> The Edisonade was the science fiction form of the dime novel and typically featured a young boy inventor escaping his stagnating environment and ... heading West using a steam vehicle built from scratch. Ellis' tale would inspire many, but among those, it was Luis Senarens whose dime novel stories expanded the domain of the Weird Western, as he chronicled the inventions and adventures of Frank Reade, and the two generations of descendants that would follow him: "distinguished inventors of marvelous machines in the line of steam and electricity." Senarens' fantastic tales of the Age of Invention featured the globe-trotting Reades and their spectacular array of futuristic creations: all-terrain vehicles like the *Thunderer*, an eight-wheeled tank-ship hybrid heralded as the "New Electric Terror;" Steam Horse, "a new method of rapid travel without need of rails;" submarines; flying boats; and so much more.

Roughly half a century later, in 1923, *Weird Tales*, "The Magazine of the Bizarre and Unusual," would extend these imaginings in the pulps, drawing in both supernatural horror, with Robert E. Howard's vampire Western "The Horror from the Mound," and science fiction fantasy, with "Shambleau" (1933), the first of C. L. Moore's Space Western adventures featuring Northwest Smith.

As the landscape of entertainment evolved, the pulps, which flourished in the first half of the twentieth century, significantly influenced the growing industries of film, television, and comics. Early films had already established a tradition of drawing their storylines from the pulps, and as the popularity of both horror and science fiction grew, films such as *Forbidden Planet* (1956) and *Creature from the Black Lagoon* (1954); television programming such as *Tom Corbett, Space Cadet* (1950–55) and *Tales of Tomorrow* (1951–53); and comics such as *Adventures into the Unknown* (1948–67) and *Weird Horrors* (1952) took their lead from the popular literary format, responding to and fueling their largely young male audiences' fascination. For the Western genre, this trend began as early as the 1920s, and by midcentury, had already yielded numerous films, both serial format and feature-length, following the pulps' popular Weird Menace template. Here, in titles such as *The Phantom Empire* (1935) and *Ghost Patrol* (1936), threatening, phantomlike figures flirting with supernatural identities plagued individuals and communities until being unmasked by the hero in the final scenes. The pulps ultimately began to give way, in the post–World War II era, to other media that presented writers, publishers, filmmakers, and producers with new opportunities for genre-blending spectacle.

The Western sun, however, was also beginning to dip beneath the horizon of popular entertainment. The youth market had been overtaken by Space Fever, and children across the country were trading in their Stetsons and six-shooters for helmets and ray guns, and soon, the moral complexities of the 1960s were calling into question the genre's tradition of moral absolutes for adult audiences. Rapid social change in perceptions of gender, race, sexuality, and indigenous groups combined to call the Western's relevance into question in the second half of the twentieth century. The Western was dead, or so many critics said; until the Weird Western revived it.

It happened slowly at first—a vampire here, a mystic orb there—but by the 1990s, the Western, and in particular, the Weird Western, found a new life and a new audience. *Billy the Kid Versus Dracula* and *Jessie James Meets Frankenstein's Daughter* had provided popular teenage double-feature fare at the drive-in in 1966, while *Valley of the Gwangi* pitted cowboys against prehistoric dinosaurs in 1969, and both achieved cult status over the next several decades as those teens became adults. DC Comics launched its successful long-running *Weird Western Tales* in 1972 for youthful and adult readers, alike, and after the popular comic ceased publication in 1980, those issues became cherished collector's items. Soon, the Weird West made its presence felt in mainstream media. Viewers and readers may not have had a name for the new subgenre, but horror, science fiction, and the fantastic technologies of steampunk each brought new spectacle to the Old West in their bids for popular acclaim. *The Adventures of Brisco County Jr.* introduced the novelty of a science fiction Western into living rooms across the country in 1993-94; and Quentin Tarantino's 1996 chiller, *From Dusk Till Dawn* opened the door for countless "undead Westerns" with its vampire-infested roadhouse. Low-budget, direct-to-video titles like *Undead or Alive* (2007), *Dead Noon* (2007), and *The Quick and the Undead* (2006) brought a pulp sensibility back to Western adventures with a supernatural twist, while at the opposite end of the entertainment spectrum, *Cowboys and Aliens* (2011) aimed for blockbuster status. The role-playing game *Deadlands: The Weird West* and *Red Dead Redemption* introduced gaming fans to the Weird West, and the comic book-turned-television series *The Walking Dead* (2010–) turned the Weird West into a multiseason transnational pop culture phenomenon.

Harkening back to the subgenre's literary roots, work by mainstream authors, such as Joe R. Lansdale's *Zeppelins West* (2001) and Mike Resnick's *Weird West Tales* series (2010–13) have drawn the horror, science fiction, and steampunk themes begun by early Weird West authors into the twenty-first century. Given their impact on contemporary viewers' relationships with the Western genre, each of these thematic branches of the Weird West warrants a brief but focused introductory discussion.

Weird Western Monsters: Horror

The messages and meanings of frontier tales take on new significance as supernatural threats put the "wild" back in the Wild West—gunslingers walk out of hell to once again besiege dusty towns; Indians rise from the grave to right ancient wrongs; vampires, mummies, and zombies ensure that human sins are, in fact, deadly; and ghostly cowboys guide the living from atop fire-breathing steeds.

At first glance, the supernatural presents vicious, repugnant threats to humanity, terrorizing good and evil alike. On closer examination, however, their existence in the West, in relentless pursuit of the living, calls into question basic assumptions regarding the nature of humanity, the power of the moral order, and long-cherished notions of national identity. And often, the presence of the supernatural on the frontier creates a lens that allows tales with narrative roots in the nineteenth century to speak to and shed light on the complexities of the modern era.

This careful positioning of the supernatural in the West is no accident. Technology, industry, and infrastructure are all absent, permitting these unearthly entities to attack humanity in one of its most elemental regions, at a time when rapid social change has called all fundamental elements of existence into question. The vampires, zombies, mummies, and ghosts of horror Westerns make our inner demons and social plagues visible, and lay siege to a frontier tied to myths of freedom, independence, strength and ingenuity that serve as building blocks of our identities, both individual and collective. And while the hero and his villainous counterpart traditionally make visible the dual nature of the Old West—the rugged wildness and unbridled freedom of the frontier, on one hand, and the moral order of civilization, on the other—the menace presented by the supernatural complicates this duality and threatens the very context in which earthly good and evil exist.

Once only the purview of writers and filmmakers in the realms of horror and fantasy, the supernatural has become part of the everyday and accessible to all, from children's literature, such as Gery Greer and Bob Ruddick's *Billy the Ghost and Me* (1997) and John R. Ericson's "Hank the Cowdog" series, to video games such as *Red Dead Redemption* and internet blogsites, such as Words of Giants. They have been adapted to live theater, in stage shows such as Adam Scott Mazer's comedy *Death Valley* (2011)—described by one reviewer as "*High Plains Drifter* meets *Shaun of the Dead*"—and in verse, such as Andy Rash's "Ten Little Zombies." In role-playing games, such as *Deadlands* (1996), players become the marshal and his posse to vanquish undead gunslingers, hostile Indian spirits, and other deadly creatures that have risen up to overtake the West.

The supernatural first invaded the imaginary West during the years of uneasy peace between the First and Second World Wars. They came furtively, sporadically at first: stalking, shambling, and flitting their way through short stories and serialized novels that saw print in the literary ghettoes of the pulp magazines. Many of the writers behind these early stories—Max Brand (Frederick Faust) and Robert E. Howard among them—were, or would become, towering figures in the pulp-fiction universe, but the stories themselves were diversions and experiments.

Even the most prolific writers of them produced only a handful, and their heroes faced down rustlers, robbers, and renegades far more often than reanimated corpses. If the stories *were* a conscious attempt to create a new pulp subgenre, they failed. Tales that mixed elements of mythology, dark fantasy, and Gothic horror with traditional Western motifs cut against the grain of the genre-bound pulps, drawing rejection slips from skeptical editors and letters of complaint from fans who preferred to take their genre fiction straight-up.

Westerns, fantasy, and horror continued to flourish on newsstands—at least until wartime paper shortages sent the pulps into slow decline—but under separate covers. A short-lived postwar revival of undead Western themes, played out in comic books in the late 1940s and early 1950s, focused on costumed heroes who were—or pretended to be—spirits returned from beyond the grave to seek justice, protect the righteous from the wicked, and uphold the Code of the West. By the mid–1950s, however, the pulps were dying, comic books had been purged of dark and violent themes, and the supernatural Western was, itself, all but dead.

While the supernatural first began to menace the West on screen in the late 1950s, with Edward Dein's *Curse of the Undead* (1959), they did not truly begin to proliferate until the close of the twentieth century. Meanwhile, the subgenre's literary revival began, in the fall of 1978, with a deceptively simple sentence: "The man in black fled across the desert, and the gunslinger followed." Published in the October issue of *The Magazine of Fantasy and Science Fiction*, Stephen King's short story "The Gunslinger" told the story of Roland, "the last gunslinger," who pursued his dark nemesis across the wastelands of "a world that had moved on." First in a series of five linked stories that King, in 1982, knitted into the first in a cycle of novels collectively known as *The Dark Tower*, its abundant literary and mythological overtones signaled a level of ambition that simultaneously revived the moribund undead Western and transcended its pulp roots. The publication of Joe R. Lansdale's short novel *Dead in the West* in 1986, and the release of King's second *Dark Tower* novel, *The Drawing of the Three*, in 1987 edged the undead Western further into the realm of serious literature.

The supernatural Western film underwent a similar maturation in the late 1980s. Clint Eastwood's *Pale Rider* (1985), for example, smuggled an avenging spirit from beyond the grave into what was, otherwise, a straightforward revisionist Western, and Kathryn Bigelow's *Near Dark* (1987) followed an itinerant vampire "family" as it preyed on the residents of a dusty, desolate town in the present-day Southwest. Robert Rodriguez's *From Dusk Till Dawn* (1996) and John Carpenter's *Vampires* (1998) also helped lay the groundwork for the supernatural's twenty-first century invasion of the frontier. In the years that followed, films such as *Bubba Ho-Tep* (2002), *Western Zombie* (2006), *7 Mummies* (2006), *The Quick and the Undead* (2006), *Dead Noon* (2008), *Deadwalkers* (2009), and *Devil's Crossing* (2010) created a convergence of twenty-first century moral panics, situated in the heartland, in order to critique and comment on the Western tradition and the norms and values it promotes and maintains.

Joe Lansdale, who ended the 1980s by winning an Edgar Award for his short story "On the Far Side of the Cadillac Desert with Dead Folks," began the 1990s by reviving the undead Western comic book. His limited series *Jonah Hex: Two-Gun Mojo* (1993) sent DC Comics' scarred, cynical ex–Confederate bounty hunter into battle against zombies, while *Jonah Hex: Riders of the Worm and Such* (1995) pitted him against a monster borrowed from H. P. Lovecraft's Cthulu mythos. Robert Rodriguez's film *From Dusk Till Dawn* (1995) offered a similar blend of extreme violence, grotesque imagery, and dark humor, while revisiting and adapting Robert E. Howard's pulp formula of hardened frontier heroes in hand-to-hand combat with the undead. The spectacular success of *From Dusk Till Dawn* inspired two direct sequels and a steady stream of low-budget imitations. It also completed the transformation of the undead Western into an established—indeed, flourishing—hybrid subgenre firmly positioned in the mainstream of American popular culture.

Buoyed by the growth of a broader popular interest in the undead, the supernatural Western expanded, at the turn of the millennium, into an ever-widening range of media. Long-running comic and graphic novel series such as Garth Ennis and Steve Dillon's *Preacher* (1995–2000) and Robert Kirkman, Tony Moore, and Charlie Adlard's *The Walking Dead* (2003–) moved onto the frontier (re-)opened by Joe Lansdale. The USA network series *Supernatural* (2005–) and AMC's adaptation of *The Walking Dead* (2010–) turned Western heroes and their battles with the supernatural into serial drama. Gaming enthusiasts could, by the first decade of the new century, immerse themselves in the undead-plagued frontier worlds of *Blood* (1998) and *Darkwatch* (2005) or use the *Undead Nightmare* (2010) expansion pack to introduce zombies into the Western-adventure game *Red Dead Redemption*. The tabletop role-playing game *Deadlands*, introduced in 1996 and revised in 2006, invited players not merely to control but to embody traditional Western hero-figures (lawmen, gunslingers, hucksters) as they set out in pursuit of the undead.

These games and serial dramas (whether drawn or televised) exist in media capable of supporting complex fictional worlds, open-ended stories, and greater degrees of audience involvement. Their emergence, and continued popularity, marks a watershed in the evolution of the subgenre. Casually created in the 1920s as a source of spectacle to be consumed and discarded, the undead West has matured into a richly detailed mythological world in which readers, viewers, and players can immerse themselves.

Weird Western Knowledge: Science Fiction

With their shared focus on exploring frontiers and pushing the boundaries of the known, the Western and science fiction often also address similar themes of conquest, identity, humanity, and concerns about progress, and so, are easily blended or hybridized to create tales set both on the Earth and in the wilderness of outer space. In both, hardy individuals journey through hostile landscapes, pausing at isolated outposts of civilization in order to right wrongs and reinforce the moral order. C. L. Moore's spaceship pilot Northwest Smith, an outlaw with the heart of a hero, ventured through the galaxy with his ray gun at his side, like the gunslingers of old. His trusty steed, a spaceship called the *Maid*, and his sidekick, a Venusian named Yarol. Moore's series of stories laid the foundation for numerous tales of "wagon trains to the stars," and Smith, originally written into being as a Western character, is often cited as the predecessor of other interstellar gunslingers, such as *Star Wars'* Han Solo and *Firefly's* Malcolm Reynolds.

While frequently generalized as "Space Westerns" as a result of these origins, not all science fiction-inflected Weird Westerns are set in outer space or feature aliens. As early as 1935, the twelve-part serial *The Phantom Empire* juxtaposed the quirks, chaos, and camaraderie on Gene Autry's Radio Ranch against the sterile dispassion found in the super-scientific city of Murania, located 20,000 leagues beneath the surface, asking audiences to consider the price of progress, as fears about the loss of humanity arose from the midst of the Machine Age. This novel hybrid intermingled the familiar with the strange, combining Western music popularized on radio and the much-loved Western serial format—already a mainstay of American film entertainment—with the novelty and innovation of other-worldly science fiction. Released less than a year before *Flash Gordon*, and a full year before the film version of H.G. Wells' *Things to Come*, *Phantom Empire* takes place in the present but showcases Murania, where technological advances, along with their benefits and consequences, abound. The serial drew much of its futuristic inspiration from the highly popular pulp science fiction magazines of the day, along with strong ties to James Churchward's series of pseudo-factual books about the lost continent of Lemuria, or Mu, as he called it, which began with *The Lost Continent of Mu* (1926).

Murania is a civilization full of wondrous technological advances. Once transported down to the city in a high-speed tubular elevator, the inhabitants of Murania are surrounded by such futuristic scientific marvels as moving sidewalks, robots, video phones, a reviving chamber, ray guns, and television. This was particularly significant, in that while a good deal of experimentation had been done with television in audiences' "real" world, only about 400 sets existed in the United States at the time, and it would be four more years before the beginning of commercial television broadcasting, coinciding with the technology's public debut at the 1939 New York World's Fair.

The popularization of science fiction since the mid-twentieth century has led to a proliferation of Space Westerns and terrestrial futuristic Westerns. Intergalactic marshals, robot horses, human cattle drives, aliens amid the gunfight at the O.K. Corral ... all work to create fantastic frontier sagas that are as strange as they are familiar. Science fiction Weird Western stories have fueled films such as *Westworld* (1973), *The Aurora Encounter* (1986) and *Young Ones* (2014), novels such as Stephen King's *Dark Tower* series (1982–2004), Neal Barrett Jr.'s *Through Darkest America* (1986), and Bruce Boxleitner's *Frontier Earth* (1999), television series such as *The Adventures of Brisco County, Jr.* (1993–94) and *Defiance* (2013–), comic books such as *Preacher* (1995) by Garth Ennis and Steve Dillon, *Iron West* (2006) by Doug TenNapel, and almost all other forms of media. And of course, popular science fiction franchises such as *Star Trek*, *Star Wars*, and *Firefly/Serenity* have been cited as drawing inspiration for themes, characters, and episodes from traditional Western narratives.

Perhaps most notably, Jon Favreau's 2011 *Cowboys and Aliens* attempted to elevate the Science Fiction Weird Western to blockbuster status. Based on the 2006 graphic novel created by Scott Michael Rosenberg, the film attempts to put a new spin on the Old West, featuring a roster of stock Western personalities and starring the well-known Daniel Craig as its disaffected, amnesiac anti-hero, former outlaw Jake Lonergan.

While criticized as a failed Western by frontier fans, and paced too slowly for those accustomed to the spectacular interplanetary warfare of the twenty-first century delivered by science fiction blockbusters, *Cowboys and Aliens* nonetheless successfully merges the two genres in a high-budget format designed for mainstream audiences. Its hybridity introduces the Weird Western—and the Western, in general—to a new generation of viewers unfamiliar with the genre's traditions.

The film's hybridity opens up the storyline for a shift in portrayals of Western women, as well. Its heroine, Ella Swenson (Olivia Wilde), serves as a lightning rod for tropes of both the Western and science fiction genres. One part Rancher's Daughter, one part Ancient Alien, and one part Mystic Ancestor, Swenson is, herself, a hybrid character who bridges the gap between self and Other, past and future, wisdom and instinct, faith and action. She is, in effect, a futuristic spirit guide, with ties to "ancient astronaut" tales in Indian folklore, such as "The Woman Who Fell from the Sky," who journeyed to Earth, like Swenson, from "a place beyond the stars."

Midway through the film, Swenson transforms in fire—in a blinding explosion of light. She dies, sheds Western character stereotype, and is reborn in her true alien nature. Her "resurrection" signals her character's primary genre orientation moves from Western to science fiction, but that shift serves as a pivot point for the genre orientation of the film, as well. Standard science fiction tropes dominate the film's second half, as the entire cast unites in a battle to save the planet, guided by her advanced knowledge, Lonergan's futuristic weapon, and the Apaches' faith in unexplainable phenomena. This transition across genres regenerates the story *and* the characters. In classic Western fashion, humanity, the ultimate "good," wins the day and the moral order is restored.

Weird Western Technology: Steampunk

Western steampunk uses fantastic images of technology—out-of-time to create critical commentary on the genre's notion of progress and the inherent tension between "civilization" and nature. As a hybrid subgenre, it employs the steampunk aesthetic to introduce technology-as-spectacle—breathtaking, larger-than-life; focus, rather than backdrop—and traffics in fetishism, making technology the stuff of fantasy and obsession. Through the steampunk Western, we see the working out of the tension between popular fascination and fear in relation to technology and the Machine Age—a commentary on the loss of wildness, independence, and freedom of the frontier West.

Steampunk Westerns juxtapose elements of the frontier West—characters, technologies, concepts, and ideologies—with elements of the Machine Age. Lasso-swinging cowboys partner with scientists who can juggle lightning in their bare hands, steam-driven cars pass stagecoaches on dusty roads, and dreams of machines used to master nature coexist with nightmares of them used to subjugate men. Only one or two significant examples of technology-out-of-time appear in a typical steampunk Western, and they are depicted (along with their creators) as intrusions into the familiar, recognizable Western setting rather than as part of the fabric of an alternate West. In "Wild Card," an episode of *The Adventures of Brisco County, Jr.,* the bounty-hunter hero rides into a dusty Nevada town one night in the mid–1890s to find the storefronts festooned with strings of incandescent bulbs and a neon sign glowing above the swinging doors of a saloon. Later in the series, he uses the Orb, a mysterious device sought both by his robber-baron employers and their shared nemesis John Bly, to manipulate time and space in order to save a friend's life. Concealed, miniaturized gadgets—cutting torches, power saws, and smoke bombs—abound in both the television and film versions of *The Wild, Wild West.* Albert Wickwire and Janos Bartok, scientist-sidekicks to our traditional Western heroes, are latter-day wizards who brew explosive potions and summon phantom horsemen from amid clouds of swirling fog. Outlaws are mounted on stolen government motorcycles in *Brisco County* ("Steel Horses") and battle the forces of good with bulletproof suits of armor and a "machinery gun." Exotic vehicles—an airship in the short-lived television series *Legend* (1995), a rocket-powered rail car in *Brisco County,* and a steam-powered wheelchair in the film version of *Wild Wild West*—abound.

This introduction of fantastic technology into the lives and landscapes of the West is far more than just a clever collision of genres and tropes. In the steampunk Western, progress, and its fair-haired child, technology, are both used to reflect Machine Age fears, while also serving as the agents of a twenty-first century assault on assumptions fundamental to western expansion and Manifest Destiny.

The spectacular machines given form in steampunk Westerns present powerful and elegant illustrations of the Janus-faced nature of progress and technology, both in their relationship to the West and with humanity-at-large. During the heyday of the classic Western, American audiences, struggling with economic crisis and global unrest, searched for a future with more certainty, more prosperity, and more strength. It was the Machine Age, a period that heralded the dominance of the machine and forecasted the coming of a culture that would be shaped by its influence. For some, science and technology seemed to hold the promise of the brave new world they sought; for others, they represented a universe grounded in invention and innovation: sterile, controlling, and void of the compassion and optimistic ingenuity that had come to characterize the national identity. Traditional Westerns, with their emphasis on progress at its most positive, largely failed to engage with its complexities, and often downplayed, naturalized, or provided facile resolutions to the "collateral damage" to lifeways and landscapes that ensued. Even as Western narratives developed their own critical stance, the inherent commentary was subtle—more lament for a lost golden age than critique or direct engagement.

Steampunk Westerns, however, make the complexities of progress impossible to ignore, turning technology into spectacles of light, sound, and power. They grasp what George Orwell viewed as "the central problem of the Machine Age"—to be in control of the world, but displaced from it—and trouble that notion further, not merely suggesting humanity's potential alienation from the world of concrete experience, but creating a West where nature is conquered by civilization, and civilization is in turn, conquered by technology. Progress, along with its inevitability and outcomes, thus becomes the central problem of the steampunk Western.

The steampunk aesthetic turns Machine Age fascination with technology into a larger-than-life parody of technology fetishism. Exploding the era's frenetic race to advance and expand civilization's reach and capacity through mechanization, steampunk Westerns introduce the fantastic—brilliantly colored zeppelins dominating the Big Sky and casting shadows across the desert; rocket-powered bicycles that beat the fastest horses; extraordinary engines powered by gleaming gears and billowing steam—all portrayed through long, lingering camera shots. These images pander to obsessions with Progress as an end unto itself, creating sacred icons in the image of the Machine. Breathtaking innovation fills the screen, and then, making mockery of its human worshippers, spins out of control. The results are often nightmarish—a product of what Susan Sontag has termed "the imagination of disaster," wherein the consequence of advancement is calamity.

Progress, in the form of extraordinary transportation, weaponry, and invention, simultaneously—and visibly—positions humanity on the brink of triumph or disaster. At the same time, however, technology's morally neutral status is also made apparent, its great power yielding outcomes determined by its context and the hand that sets it in motion. Thinking again about the hybrid serial *Phantom Empire*, which carefully separates the elements that steampunk Westerns draw together, the cautionary tale is not one of the evils of technology so much as in whose hands, and at what speed, it arrives.

A West where destiny is challenged by fantastic technology also complicates the driving force behind western expansion and the conquest of the frontier: the ability of man to reign supreme, and "to overspread and to possess the whole of the continent which Providence has given us." Nineteenth century ideologies of exceptionalism, independence, democracy, the domination of nature, and the West as a site of unfettered pursuit of ambition and inspiration, rest on the notion of

(Anglo-American) Man as Master—of his social universe, his environment, and his technology. These themes are visible in the rhetoric of Manifest Destiny and national identity, as well as in countless oral, literary, and cinematic narratives of traditional American history. Railroads, dams, mines, farms, stagecoach lines, and telegraphs all give testimony to man's ability to harness science and nature in pursuit of a dream. Progress gone awry—fantastic technology out of control—problematizes not only the dreams and ambitions of humankind, but man's ability to maintain control over his environment, to fulfill his destiny, and to embody his national identity. His ability to conquer is compromised, and he is Master no more. Steampunk Westerns, then, through their transgression of long-accepted relationships between Man and Machine, play with notions of control, call into question centuries-old assumptions about the destiny of humankind, and prod at the soft underbelly of American national identity. Only when destroyed or safely locked away does steampunk technology return dominion of the West to the traditional Westerner, and allow humanity to ponder the questions that its presence has raised. The intrusive technologies that drive their plots are always reined in by the end of the story, and never left loose in the world. The doomsday gun in *Jonah Hex* is blown up along with the ironclad that carries it, and the giant steam-powered spider in *Wild Wild West* strides into the sunset under the heroes' control. The Orb is eventually carried away by a time-traveler to its proper home in the twenty-fifth century. Steampunk Western heroes forced, by circumstances, to use advanced technology readily give it up in favor of more traditional tools like and horses and six-shooters.

The introduction of these fantastic elements into familiar Western plots and settings makes visible what remains invisible in traditional Westerns: themes and ideas that, precisely *because* they are so ubiquitous, are taken for granted. Heroism ... morality ... humanity ... justice ... freedom... Weird Westerns shine a spotlight on these themes and make them central to the story. When aliens invade the Old West, bent on subjugating its inhabitants and stripping it of natural resources, they invert the traditional narrative of conquest on which the genre implicitly depends. When Western towns are beset by hordes of the undead—vampires, zombies, or animate mummies—bent on revenge for past wrongs, traditional notions of good, evil, and frontier justice are all called into question. Steampunk tales such as *Wild Wild West* move technology—pervasive, yet rarely remarked on, in traditional Westerns—to center stage, and highlight its double-edged quality: shaping civilization even as it destroys the frontier. Weird Westerns are, by their very nature, exercises in spectacle, and they reassure viewers that the West is vast and full of wonders and marvels ... that the cinematic frontier is never truly closed, and that there is always more to be discovered, just over the next ridge.

BIBLIOGRAPHY

Ellis, Edward Sylvester. *The Huge Hunter; Or, The Steam Man of the Prairies.* 1868. http://www.gutenberg.org/files/7506/7506-h/7506-h.htm.

Goulart, Ron. *Cheap Thrills: An Informal History of the Pulp Magazines.* New Rochelle, NY: Arlington House, 1972.

Green, Paul. *Encyclopedia of Weird Westerns.* Jefferson, NC: McFarland, 2009.

Guinan, Paul, and Anina Bennett. *Frank Reade: Adventures in the Age of Invention.* New York: Abrams Image, 2012.

Gunnels, Jennifer. *The New York Review of Science Fiction Film* 22, no. 6 (issue 282, February 2012), 20.

Lilly, N. E. "The Women of Space Westerns." 2008. http://www.spacewesterns.com/articles/51/.

Marubbio, M. Elise. *Killing the Indian Maiden: Images of Native American Women in Film.* Lexington: University of Kentucky Press, 2006.

McCrisken, Trevor B. "Exceptionalism: Manifest Destiny." *Encyclopedia of American Foreign Policy*, vol. 2. New York: Charles Scribner's Sons, 2002, 68.

Miller, Cynthia J. "The Woman Who Fell from the

Sky: *Cowboys and Aliens' Hybrid Heroine."* In *Heroines of Film and Television.* Norma Jones, Maja Bajac-Carter, and Bob Batchelor, eds. Lanham, MD: Rowman & Littlefield, 2014.

Miller, Cynthia J., and A. Bowdoin Van Riper. *Undead in the West: Vampires, Zombies, Mummies, and Ghosts on the Cinematic Frontier.* Lanham, MD: Scarecrow, 2012.

_____, and _____. *Undead in the West II: They Just Keep Coming.* Lanham, MD: Scarecrow, 2013.

Orwell, George. *1984.* New York: Signet, 1981.

Sampson, Robert. *Yesterday's Faces: A Study of Series Characters in the Early Pulp Magazines.* Bowling Green, KY: Bowling Green University Popular Press, 1993.

Skrymir. "Zombies in the Old West." *Words of Giants,* November 20, 2012. http://skrymir.word press.com/2012/11/20/zombies-in-the-old-west-2/.

Smith, Erin A. *Hard-Boiled: Working-Class Readers and Pulp Magazines.* Philadelphia: Temple University Press, 2000.

Sontag, Susan. *Against Interpretation and Other Essays.* New York: Farrar, Straus and Giroux, 1966.

Telotte, J. P. *A Distant Technology: Science Fiction Film and the Machine Age.* Hanover, NH: Wesleyan University Press, 1999.

VanderMeer, Jeff. *The Steampunk Bible.* New York: Abrams Image, 2001.

Vincent, Bev. *The Road to the Dark Tower: Exploring Stephen King's Magnum Opus.* New York: New American Library, 2004.

Wright, Bradford W. *Comic Book Nation: The Transformation of Youth Culture in America.* Baltimore: Johns Hopkins University Press, 2001.

Cynthia J. Miller is a cultural anthropologist specializing in popular culture and visual media. She is the editor or co-editor of eight volumes, several of which are focused on Westerns and Weird Westerns. She teaches in the Institute for Liberal Arts at Emerson College in Boston.

THE WEIRD WESTERNS

Abraham [Comic book character; Italy; WW]

First appearance: *Bad Karma* #0/1, 1999; Story: Roberto Recchioni; Art: Walter Venturi; Publisher: King Comics.

The adventures of Abraham Van Helsing, vampire and demon hunter in the Old West of the 1880s. Artist Walter Venturi described the two-part, 16-page story as "a mix between Sergio Leone, John Woo and the Wild Weird West."

Abraham Lincoln, Vampire Hunter (2012) [Film; WW]

Premiere: June 22, 2012; Main Cast: Benjamin Walker as Abraham Lincoln, Dominic Cooper as Henry Sturges, Anthony Mackie as Will Johnson, Mary Elizabeth Winstead as Mary Todd Lincoln, Rufus Sewell as Adam, Jimmi Simpson as Joshua Speed, Erin Wasson as Vadoma, Robin McLeavy as Nancy Lincoln, Joseph Mawle as Thomas Lincoln; Executive producers: Seth Grahame-Smith, John J. Kelly, Simon Kinberg, Michele Wolkoff; Screenplay: Seth Grahame-Smith, based on his novel; Director: Timur Bekmambetov; 105 min.; Tim Burton Productions, 20th Century–Fox; 3-D; Color.

Pigeon Creek, Indiana, 1818. Following an altercation with plantation owner and vampire slave trader Jack Barts young Abraham Lincoln witnesses an attack on his mother that leads to her death. Nine years later Henry Sturges teaches Lincoln about the reality of vampires and how to hunt them. Lincoln, a former rail splitter, chooses an ax with a silver plated blade as the weapon of his choice as he seeks revenge for his mother's death. Lincoln

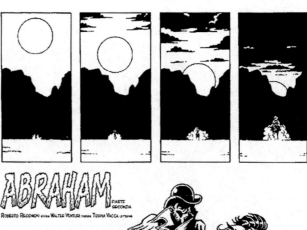

Abraham artwork © Walter Venturi. Used with permission.

eventually tires of hunting vampires and decides to enter law and politics where he fights "with words and ideals before the ax."

Lincoln wants freedom for blacks from their vampire slave owners. But vampire leader Adam has other ideas and arms the Confederate troops with vampires. When Lincoln's young son is attacked by the vampire Vadoma he decides to tackle the problem head-on by melting all the silver and turning it into ammunition for the Union army. Adam learns of the plan through an informant but he is purposely giving the wrong information and led into a trap while attacking the train to Gettysburg.

With the vampire problem defeated for now Lincoln heads for a relaxing night at the theater with his wife, Mary.

Peter Bradshaw of *The Guardian* (June 21, 2012) commented that the film is "Cheerfully subversive post-steam punk fantasy... It's a joke which some will find in sacrilegious bad taste. For me, the self-aware craziness is the whole point."

The film underperformed at the box office with an opening weekend of $16,306,974 against an estimated budget of $69 million.

Abraham Lincoln vs. Zombies (2012) [Film; WW]

Premiere: May 29, 2012; Main Cast: Bill Oberst Jr. as Abraham Lincoln, Kent Igleheart as Thomas Lincoln, Rhianna Van Helton as Nancy Lincoln, Brennen Harper as Young Abe Lincoln, Debra Crittenden as Mary Todd Lincoln, Bernie Askas Edwin Stanton, Joshua Sinyard as Aide, Chris Hlozek as Major John McGill, Richard Schenkman as Dr. Malinoff, Jim E. Chandler as Eckert; Executive producer: David Rimawi; Screenplay: Richard Schenkman; Story: Karl T. Hirsch, J. Lauren Proctor; Director: Richard Schenkman; 96 min.; The Asylum; Color.

Perry County, Indiana 1818. Young Abe Lincoln has to decapitate his parents after they are attacked and infected by zombies. Decades later President Lincoln is on a mission to destroy the Confederate walking dead.

This low budget film was released to coincide with **Abraham Lincoln, Vampire Hunter**. Both films failed to excite audiences.

Absalom [Comic book character; SFW]

First appearance: *X-Force* #10, May 1992; Creators: Fabian Nicieza, Rob Liefeld, Mark Pacella; Publisher: Marvel Comics.

Absalom first discovered his mutant power for regeneration in 1896 when he was being hanged for the murder of Caleb Hammer in Wyoming. Bone-like spikes erupted from his body and shred the rope around his neck but an angry crowd shot him to death as he tried to escape. Two days later he awoke inside his coffin and fled the small town in the dead of night. He later joined the mutant immortals known as the Externals but discovered that even self-regenerating immortals could die when female immortal Selene drained his life.

Aces and Eights [RPG sourcebook; WW]

Author: Micah Jackson; Art: Thomas Biondiolillo, Gerald Brom, Paul Daly, Alex Nunis; First publication: 2001; *GURPS Deadlands* Dime Novel series #1; Publisher: Steve Jackson Games Inc.

In a story that includes Hexslingers, voodoo magic and the undead, Jim Wright is pursued from Denver to New Orleans by someone who wants him dead.

Across the Great Barrier (Frontier Magic book #2) [Novel; WW]

Author: Patricia C. Wrede; First publication: New York: Scholastic Press, 2011

Young Eff Rothmer is a seventh daughter and reluctant magician with a talented twin brother, Lan, a powerful double seventh son, practiced in the art of Avrupan, Aphrikan and Hijero-Cathayan magic. When Professor Jeffries and Professor Torgeson of Northern Plains Riverbank College invite her to accompany them to the Western settlement country beyond the Great Barrier Spell she encounters a world of magic and danger. Predatory saber cats and Columbian sphinxes threaten the settlements scattered through the West. But a new threat is turning animals and people to stone as it moves in from the wilds of the West: fifteen-foot-long medusa lizards. Lan sets himself as bait using his magic to attract the creatures.

Action Comics [Comic book]

This long-running title was the first to feature Superman. The popularity of the Western in the 1940s and 1950s ensured that comic book writers would include a few storylines where Superman would be involved with cowboys and Indians. The light-hearted approach of the Golden Age stories are in marked contrast to the 1971 two-part story which sees Superman being taken hostage as a bargaining tool for the return of Native American land.

"Super Cowboy" [SFW]

First publication: #134 (July 1949); Story: William Woolfolk; Art: Wayne Boring; Publisher: DC Comics.

"Yipee! New Thrills In The Old West When Superman Becomes A Super-Cowboy!"

"Superman, Indian Chief" [SFW]

First publication: #148 (September 1950); Story: Edmond Hamilton; Art: Al Plastino; Publisher: DC Comics.

"An Amazing Adventure of the Past—"

"The Covered Wagon of Doom" [SFW]

First publication: #184 (September 1953); Art: Wayne Boring, Stan Kaye; Publisher: DC Comics.

Can Superman prevent history from repeating itself in the Old West?

"The Test of a Warrior" [WW]

First publication: #200 (January 1955); Art: Wayne Boring, Stan Kaye; Publisher: DC Comics.

This story of Superman helping an aged Indian complete the three tests of a warrior was adapted into an episode of the TV series *The Adventures of Superman* later in the year.

"The Day Super-Horse Became Human" [WW]

First publication: #311 (April 1964); Story: Leo Dorfman; Art: Jim Mooney; Publisher: DC Comics.

In this truly weird tale, Supergirl falls in love with her super-horse Comet after he magically transforms into dashing rodeo cowboy "Bronco" Bill Starr. The strip was reprinted in *Adventure Comics* #390 (March-April 1970) as "Supergirl's Cowboy Hero!"

"Invaders Go Home" [SFW]

First publication: #401 (June 1971); Story: Leo Dorfman; Art: Curtis Swan, Murphy Anderson.

When industrialist Frank Haldane builds a missile-manufacturing site on Navarro Indian land, the Navarros stake their claim to ownership of their land. As part of a plan to remedy the situation, Navarro leader Don Red Hawk takes Superman hostage after rendering him helpless with a red jewel that drains his powers.

"This Hostage Must Die" [SFW]

First publication: #402 (July 1971); Story: Leo Dorfman; Art: Curtis Swan, Murphy Anderson.

Superman discovers Frank Haldane's real motive for acquiring Navarro land is Montezuma's buried treasure. When Superman recovers his powers by blocking the light from the nearest red sun to Earth, he gives Montezuma's treasure to the Navarro Indians and sends Haldane on his way.

The Addams Family (1973) [Animated TV series]

Voice cast: Leonard Weinrib as Gomez, Janet Waldo as Morticia, Jackie Coogan as Uncle Fester, Ted Cassidy as Lurch, Jodie Foster as Pugsley, Cindy Henderson as Wednesday; Creator: David Levy; Executive Producers: William Hanna, Joseph Barbera; Director: Charles A. Nichols; Hanna-Barbera Productions; 16 × 30 min.; Color.

Based on the Charles Addams cartoons, with Jackie Coogan and Ted Cassidy reprising their roles from the 1960s live-action TV series.

"Ghost Town" (1:10) [WW]

Air date: November 10, 1973

When the Addams Family visits the land of the Old Prospector, they enjoy the challenge of scaring the ghosts of Ghost Town.

"The Addams Family Goes West" (1:15) [WW]

Air date: December 15, 1973

The Addams Family goes West and comes up against Wyatt Burp, Silly the Kid and Badmouth Ben.

Adios, A-Mi-Go! [RPG book; WW]

Authors: John Wick with Hal Mangold; First publication: 1998; *Deadlands: The Weird West* Dime Novel series #8; Publisher: Pinnacle Entertainment Group.

The *Deadlands* characters meet the horrors of H.P. Lovecraft's Cthulhu and become involved in a race against time with their lives at stake in this crossover story with the *Call of Cthulhu* role-playing game.

Adventures into the Unknown [Comic book]

Horror anthology title that survived Fredric Wertham's moral crusade against comic books.

"The Haunted Cane" [WW]

First publication: #168 (October-November 1968); Story: Ace Aquila [Richard E. Hughes]; Art: Steve Ditko, Sal Trapani; Publisher: American Comics Group (ACG).

A dead man's cane haunts local townsfolk in the Old West.

The Adventures of Brisco County, Jr.
(1993) [TV series; SFW]

Premiere: August 7, 1993; Main Cast: Bruce Campbell as Brisco County Jr., Julius Carry as Lord Bowler, Christian Clemenson as Socrates Poole; Creators-Executive Producers: Jeffrey Boam, Carlton Cuse; 1 × 90 min., 26 × 45 min.; Boam/Cuse Productions, Warner Bros. Television; Color.

A combination of 1890s Old West traditional action and humor as Harvard-educated bounty hunter Brisco County Jr. (Bruce Campbell) is hired by the robber barons of the Westerfield Club in San Francisco to track down John Bly (Billy Drago) and the gang of outlaws who killed his father.

This short-lived series introduced an eccentric element in the form of Professor Albert Wickwire's (John Astin) forward-looking inventions and took a Weird West diversion with the introduction of a story arc concerning a mysterious Orb from the future with the power to heal and give those who possess it tremendous strength.

Season One
[Weird Western–Steampunk episodes]

"PILOT" (1:01)

Air date: August 27, 1993; Special Guest Stars: Billy Drago as John Bly, John Astin as Professor Albert Wickwire; Story: David Simkins, Jeffrey Boam, Carlton Cuse; Director: Bryan Spicer.

Brisco Jr. first learns of the supernatural powers of the Orb and its importance to John Bly, who seeks its powers.

"THE ORB SCHOLAR" (1:02)

Air date: September 3, 1993; Special Guest Stars: Robert Picardo as Puel, Billy Drago as John Bly; Story: Carlton Cuse; Director: Andy Tennant.

Brisco Jr. tracks the Bly Gang to Poker Flats and comes into contact with the Orb.

"NO MAN'S LAND" (1:03)

Air date: September 10, 1993; Special Guest Stars: John Astin as Professor Albert Wickwire, Denise Crosby as Sheriff Jenny Taylor; Story: Tom Chehak; Director: Kim Manners.

Professor Albert Wickwire's "Amazing Rocket Car" comes to the rescue when the all-female town of No Man's Land is threatened by the Swill Brothers and the armored Mobile Battle Wagon.

"SOCRATES' SISTER" (1:05)

Air date: September 24, 1993; Special Guest Stars: John Astin as Professor Albert Wickwire, Judith Hoag as Iphigenia Poole, John Pyper-Ferguson as Pete Hutter, William Russ as Jack Randolph; Story: Chris Ruppenthal; Director: Greg Beeman.

Counterfeiters use Professor Wickwire's "Inner Space Suit" to retrieve lost treasury plates from the bottom of a lake before Brisco and Socratres' sister come to the rescue.

"SENIOR SPIRIT" (1:08)

Air date: October 15, 1993; Special

The Adventures of Brisco County, Jr. (1993), a television series starring Bruce Campbell (Boam/Cuse Productions, Warner Bros. Television).

Guest Stars: John Astin as Professor Albert Wick-wire, R. Lee Ermey as Brisco County, Sr., Billy Drago as John Bly; Story: John McNamara; Director: Michael Lange.

Requiring an orb rod owned by Brisco to complete his orb, John Bly kidnaps a boy whom he will exchange for the rod. Meanwhile, Brisco meets the spirit of his dead father, who gives him advice on how to confront Bly and rescue the boy.

"STEEL HORSES" (1:13)

Air date: November 19, 1993; Special Guest Stars: John Astin as Professor Albert Wickwire, Don Michael Paul as Juno Dawkins; Story: Tom Chehak; Director: Kim Manners.

Brisco and Lord Bowler are hired to capture motorcycles stolen by Juno Dawkins and his gang but find themselves foiling an attempt to capture the Orb for John Bly on its journey to a government research laboratory in Nevada.

"FOUNTAIN OF YOUTH" (1:17)

Air date: January 14, 1994; Special Guest Star: Billy Drago as John Bly; Story: Kathryn Baker; Director: Michael Caffey.

Brisco Jr., Bowler and Lillian Coles find themselves involved in a tangled web devised by John Bly in an effort to locate the Orb.

"BYE BLY" (1:20)

Air date: February 18, 1994; Special Guest Star: Billy Drago as John Bly; Story: Carlton Cuse; Producer: Paul Marks; Director: Kim Manners.

A naked female time traveler named Karina (Melanie Smith) tells Brisco Jr. the truth about the mysterious Orb. Brisco Jr. finds himself travelling through time in order to reverse the death of Bowler and finally exacts revenge on John Bly for the death of his father.

"BAD LUCK BETTY" (1:25)

Air date: April 29, 1994; Special Guest Star: Jeff Phillips as Whip Morgan; Story: Tony Blake, Paul Jackson; Director: Joseph L. Scanlan.

Socrates Poole's birthday celebrations take a spooky turn after he is kidnapped and finds himself in the small town of Midnightville. This episode incorporates the Bates house from *Psycho*.

The Adventures of Buckaroo Banzai Across the 8th Dimension (1984) [Film; SFW]

Premiere: August 15, 1984; Main Cast: Peter Weller as Buckaroo Banzai, John Lithgow as Lord John Whorfin/Dr. Emilio Lizardo, Ellen Barkin as Penny Priddy, Jeff Goldblum as New Jersey/Sidney Zweibel, Christopher Lloyd as John Bigboote, Clancy Brown as Rawhide; Executive Producer: Sidney Beckerman; Screenplay: Earl Mac Rauch; Director: W.D. Richter; 103 min.; Sherwood Productions; Color.

Multi-talented Buckaroo Banzai and the members of his music band, the Hong Kong Cavaliers, tackle the evil Red Lectroids from Planet 10 in the 8th dimension.

Western influences include the backstory of Buckaroo Banzai, who was raised in the American West by his Japanese father (who named his son Buckaroo out of his affection of the Old West). Jeff Goldblum plays Sidney Zweibel alias New Jersey, a surgeon who plays the piano and loves to dress up as a cowboy. This was described by *Time* magazine as "the first sci-fi western action adventure rock-'n'-roll melodrama farce."

See: *Buckaroo Banzai*

The Adventures of Mendy and the Golem [Comic book]

"HOME ON THE S-SST—RANGE!" [WW]

First published: *The Adventures of Mendy and the Golem* #9 (March, 1983); Story: Leibel Estrin; Art: Dovid Sears; Publisher: Mendy Enterprises.

Advertised as the "The World's Only Kosher Comic Book," this Western-themed issue features the adventures of the Klein Gang alias Rabbi Klein, his family and the living clay creature Sholem the Golem as they journey west to find out what has happened to the local butcher's source of meat, the cattle.

The Adventures of Oky Doky (1948) [TV series; WW]

Premiere: November 4, 1948; Main Cast: Dayton Allen as Oky Doky voice, Wendy Barrie, Burt Hilber; 30 min; DuMont Television Network; b/w.

Cowboy Oky Doky relies on his magic milk pills to give him the strength to fight his enemies. A mixture of live action and puppetry as children play and perform on Oky Doky's dude ranch.

See: *Oky Doky Ranch*

The Adventures of Superboy (1988) [TV series]

Main Cast: Gerard Christopher as Clark Kent/**Superboy**, Stacy Haiduk as Lana Lang, Ilan Mitchell-Smith as Andy McAllister, Sherman Howard as Lex

Luthor; 30 min. × 100; Alexander Salkind, Lowry Productions, Color.

Live-action adventures of Superman as a teenager in Smallville.

"THE HAUNTING OF ANDY MCALISTER" (2:22) [WW]
Air date: April 21, 1990; Guest Cast: Tom Schuster as Billy the Kid, Fred Ornstein as Uncle Nate; Story: Michael Carlin, Andrew Helfer; Director: David Nutter.

On a weekend stay at the home of Andy McAllister's Uncle, Superboy, Lana and Andy become trapped on the other side of a wall that contains outlaws from the Old West. When Superboy discovers he has no powers, he must think of a way to return himself and his friends to the other side of the wall before the outlaws take revenge for being trapped by Andy's ancestor.

The Adventures of Superman [TV series]
Main Cast: George Reeves as Clark Kent/Superman, Noel Neill as Lois Lane, Jack Larson as Jimmy Olsen, John Hamilton as Perry White; 30 min. × 104; MPTV; b/w, Color.

Live-action adventures of the DC Comics superhero from the planet Krypton.

"THE TEST OF A WARRIOR" (3:06) [WW]
Air date: May 28, 1955; Guest Cast: Maurice Jara as Red Hawk, Ralph Moody as Medicine Man, Francis McDonald as Great Horse, George J. Lewis as John Tall Star; Story: Leroy H. Zehren; Director: George Blair.

Superman—the Great White Bird—assists an aging Indian chief who must complete the three tests of a warrior to become the new chief of his tribe.

See: *Action Comics*

"BULLY OF DRY GULCH" (3:10)
Air date: September 24, 1955; Guest Cast: Myron Healey as Gunner Flinch, Martin Garralaga as Pedro, Raymond Hatton as Sagebrush; Story: David T. Chantler; Director: George Blair.

Lois Lane and Jimmy Olsen find themselves stranded in the Western town of Dry Gulch where Olsen attracts the attention of Gunner Flinch (Myron Healey) and ends up in jail. Lois Lane seeks help from Superman who arrives to teach the town bully a lesson.

The Adventures of the Galaxy Rangers [Animated TV series; SW]
Premiere: September 14, 1986; Voice cast: Jerry Or-

bach as Zachery Foxx, Laura Dean as Niko, Doug Preis as Doug "Goose" Gooseman, Hubert Kelly as Walter "Doc" Hartford; Creator: Robert Mandell; Animation: Tokyo Movie Shinsha; 65 × 30 min.; Gaylord Productions, Transcom Media; Color.

Space Western adventures from the elite Series-5 Galaxy Rangers as they protect the Earth and its allies from the Crown Empire with the help of alien hyperdrive technology in the final decades of the 21st century.

With stories and character design originating in America and traditional and computer generated animation from Japan, this joint production combined the space opera with the Western.

Season One
Phoenix (1:01); *Tortuna* (1:02); *Mindnet* (1:03); *Queen's Lair* (1:04); *Chained* (1:05); *One Million Emotions* (1:06); *Space Sorcerer* (1:07); *Wildfire* (1:08); *Space Moby* (1:09); *Shaky* (1:10); *The Power Within* (1:11); *Renegade Rangers* (1:12); *Psychocrypt* (1:13); *The Ax* (1:14); *Traash* (1:15); *Edge of Darkness* (1:16); *Armada* (1:17); *Smuggler's Gauntlet* (1:18); *Ghost Station* (1:19); *Games* (1:20); *Stargate* (1:21); *Birds of a Feather* (1:22); *Showtime* (1:23); *Heart of Tarkon* (1:24); *Murder on the Andorian Express* (1:25); *Lady of Light* (1:26); *Tune-Up* (1:27); *The Magnificent Kiwi* (1:28); *Mistwalker* (1:29); *Progress* (1:30); *Natural Balance* (1:31); *Mothmoose* (1:32); *Bronto Bear* (1:33); *New Frontier* (1:34); *Shoot-Out* (1:35); *Scarecrow* (1:36); *In Sheep's Clothing* (1:37); *Invasion* (1:38); *Rogue Arm* (1:39); *Round-Up* (1:40); *Aces and Apes* (1:41); *Scarecrow's Revenge* (1:42); *Badge of Power* (1:43); *Boomtown* (1:44); *Super Troopers* (1:45); *Galaxy Stranger* (1:46); *Lord of the Sands* (1:47); *Buzzwang's Folly* (1:48); *Promised Land* (1:49); *Marshmallow Trees* (1:50); *Westride* (1:51); *Rainmaker* (1:52); *Changeling* (1:53); *Battle of the Bandits* (1:54); *Horsepower* (1:55); *Don Quixote Cody* (1:56); *Ariel* (1:57); *Rusty and the Boys* (1:58); *Trouble at Texton* (1:59); *Tortuna Rock* (1:60); *Fire and Iron* (1:61); *Tower of Combat* (1:62); *Gift of Life* (1:63); *Sundancer* (1:64); *Heartbeat* (1:65)

The Adventures of the Masked Phantom (1939) [WMW]
Premiere: October 1, 1939; Main Cast: Monte "Alamo" Rawlins as Alamo/The Masked Phantom, Betty Burgess as Carol Davis, Art Davis as Larry Mason, Sonny Lamont as Dumpy, Dot Karroll as

Grandma Mary Barton, Boots the Wonder Dog as Boots; Producer: B. F. Zeidman; Story: Joseph O'Donnell, Clifford Sanforth; Director: Charles Abbott; 56 min.; Equity Pictures Inc.; b/w.

The Miracle Gold Mining company foreman's crooked gold smuggling is curtailed by the mysterious Masked Phantom (Monte Rawlins), a death-headed knife, a couple of sidekicks and Boots the Wonder Dog. A failed attempt to imitate the Three Mesquiteers formula with the "Roving Buckaroos." Lew Porter and Johnny Lange provided the songs.

After Sundown (2006) [Film; WW]

Premiere: July 11, 2006; Main Cast: Susana Gibb as Shannon, Reece Rios as Mikey, Natalie Jones as Molly; Executive Producers: Christopher Abram, Keith Randal Duncan; Story: Christopher Abram, Michael W. Brown; Director: Christopher Abram; 90 min.; Wood Entertainment; Color.

When a vampire gunslinger from the Old West is exhumed from his grave, he and his undead zombie slaves join forces in modern-day Texas.

The Agency: Men in Black Dusters [RPG sourcebook; WW]

Author: John Goff; Art: John Goff, Joyce Goff, Zeke Sparks; First publication: 1999; Setting: *Deadlands: The Weird West*; Publisher: Pinnacle Entertainment Group.

This sourcebook reveals the secrets of the shadowy Union government organization known as the Special Services Agency, including training manuals and Agency-designed special equipment.

Aguila Solitaria [Comic book character; Mexico; WW]

First appearance: 1976; Creator: Héctor González Dueñas aka Víctor Fox; Publishers: Editora Ra-Ca-Na, Editora Cinco.

Native American Aguila Solitaria has the power to fly alongside the eagle in this Mexican comic book series that also enjoyed success in Colombia.

Alferd Packer: The Musical (1996) [Film; WW]

Premiere: 1996; Main Cast: Juan Schwartz (Trey Parker) as Alferd Packer, Toddy Walters as Polly Pry; Executive Producers: Alexandra Kelly, Andrew Kemler, Jason McHugh; Story-Director: Trey Parker; 95 min.; Cannibal Films Ltd., Troma Entertainment; Color.

A bizarre mixture of cannibalism, Japanese Indians, a Confederate cyclops and a musical set in the Old West. Happy-go-lucky gold prospector Alferd Packer (Trey Parker) denies accusations that he ate his fellow pioneers to survive a winter in the Rocky Mountains. From the co-creator of the animated television series *South Park* (1997).

New York Times critic Anita Gates (July 24, 1998) concluded: "It's all pretty stupid, but at times, there are refreshingly ludicrous notes that even people old enough to see this movie without a guardian can appreciate. One approach: Imagine the film taking place in 'South Park' animation. If Cartman were ripping the man's arm off and eating it, it might be cute."

See: *Cannibal! The Musical*

Alien Outlaw (1985) [Film; SFW]

Premiere: 1985; Main Cast: Lash La Rue as Alex Thompson, Stephen Winegard as Wes, Kimberly Mauldin as Girlfriend, Sunset Carson as Sunset, Kari Anderson as Jesse Jamison; Executive Producer: George B. Walker; Story-Director: Phil Smoot; 90 min.; Color.

An aging cowhand (Lash LaRue) and a group of beautiful girls help fight an invasion of aliens who plan to enslave humans and take over the world.

Aliens in the Wild, Wild West (1999) [Film; Canada-Romania; SFW]

Premiere: August 17, 1999; Main Cast: Taylor Locke as Tom Johnson, Carly Pope as Sara Johnson, Barna Moricz as Johnny Coyle, Gerry Quigley as Bloody Bob, Gloria Slade as Elizabeth, George Ilie as Jiffyvawa "Jiffy" Zudo; Story: Alon Kaplan; Director: George Erschbamer; 90 min.; Canarom Productions, Castel Film Romania, Chesler-Perlmutter Productions; Color.

Tom and Sara Johnson, bored with life in the present-day American West, are transported back in time to the Old West where they befriend an alien baby.

All Flesh Must Be Eaten: Fistful o' Zombies [RPG book; WW]

Author: Shane Lacy Hensley; First publication: 2003; Game: *All Flesh Must Be Eaten*; Publisher: Eden Studios.

This supplement to the *All Flesh Must Be Eaten* role-playing game includes background on the Old West (1830–1865), the Wild West (1865–1900), and the New West (1900–1930), plus seven Western Deadworlds settings and conversion notes for the *Deadlands* role-playing game.

All-New Booster Gold [Comic book]

First publication: #3 (October 2007); Story: Geoff Johns, Jeff Katz; Art: Dan Jurgens, Norm Rapmund; Publisher: DC Comics.

A comic book about a time-traveling superhero and former member of the **Justice League**.

"52 Pick-Up Chapter 3: Hexed" [SFW]

Booster Gold travels back in time to the Old West where he encounters **Jonah Hex**.

All-Star Western [Comic book; WW]

First issue: August-September 1970 (2nd series); Publisher: DC Comics.

This revival of the original 1950s title saw the beginnings of DC Comics' Weird Western lineup with the introduction of **El Diablo** in issue #2 and **Jonah Hex** in issue #10 (February-March 1972). The numbering continued into *Weird Western Tales* after the final issue #11. DC Comics' decision to update its Western lineup and introduce supernatural elements coincided with the decline of the traditional Western in films and television.

First issue: September 2011 (3rd series); Publisher: DC Comics.

In September 2011, DC Comics re-launched its entire line under the banner "The New 52" with each issue beginning with #1. Under the creative talent of writers Justin Gray and Jimmy Palmiotti **Jonah Hex** was transferred from his own title to the new **All-Star Western** where he was relocated from his familiar western environment to Gotham City in the 1880s. Hex was essentially a fish-out-of water in a Victorian steam punk inspired world populated with all forms of insanity under the watchful eye of criminal psychologist Dr. Amadeus Arkham.

All-Star Western also featured back-up strips featuring familiar characters such as **Bat-Lash**, **El Diablo**, **Madame .44** and **Tomahawk** and introduced new Weird Western characters, **Barbary Ghost**, **Master Gunfighter**, **Haunted Highwayman** and **Dr. Terrence Thirteen**. Jonah Hex Weird Western stories included cross-overs with **Superman** and **Batman** and time travel to the Old West.

The series concluded with issue #34 in October 2014 and Jonah Hex heading out to sea with his companion Tallulah Black.

The Alloy of Law: A Mistborn Novel [Novel; WW]

Author: Brandon Sanderson; First publication: Tor Books 2011.

In his twenty years spent in frontier lands known as the Roughs, Twinborn Waxillium Ladrian has used the old magics of Allomancy and Feruchemy to good effect, but now he must face new dangers as he adapts to the dangerous metropolis of Elendel as head of a noble house.

Alone in the Dark: Ghosts in Town [Video game; WW]

A 1996 release of *Alone in the Dark 3* for the Windows 95 platform.

Alone in the Dark 3 [Video game; WW]

Release date: 1994; Executive Producer: Emmanuelle Perigault-Vigier; Story: Hubert Chadot, Christain Nabais; Director: Bruno Bonnell; Third-person perspective (POV); Platform: PC; Developer: Infogrames Entertainment; Publishers: Infogrames, Interplay.

When a film crew disappears in the Mojave Desert ghost town of Slaughter Gulch, only paranormal investigator Edward Carnby can save his friend Emily Hartwood from harm by the restless spirits and zombie cowboy outlaws.

Alter-Nation [Comic book; SFW]

First issue: February 2004; Creator-Story: F. G. Haghenbeck; Publisher: Image Comics

An alternate history storyline where Germany has invaded America. Featuring Samuel Clemens, Annie Oakley, the automated Tin Man and her Rebel group, Billy the Kid, General Custer's Imperial Army and his T-Rex and a dinosaur stagecoach.

The American Astronaut (2001) [Film; SW]

Premiere: October 12, 2001; Main Cast: Cory McAbee as Samuel Curtis/Silverminer, Rocco Sisto as Professor Hess, Gregory Russell Cook as The Boy Who Has Seen a Woman's Breast, Annie Golden as Cloris, James Ransone as Bodysuit; Producers: Bobby Lurie, William "Pinetop" Perkins, Joshua Taylor; Story-Director: Cory McAbee; 91 min.; BNS Productions, Artistic License Films, Commodore Films; Color.

Low-budget, surreal Space Western musical. Samuel Curtis must provide the women of Venus with a suitable male for mating, while being pursued by his old enemy, Professor Hess.

New York Times critic Elvis Mitchell (October 12, 2001) commented: "'Astronaut' has moments of inspired dementia. An early song-and-dance number that starts like a showdown out of a Sergio Leone movie and somersaults into what can only be described as slapstick Brecht is phenomenal. In such musical sequences 'Astronaut' smashes its claustrophobic parameters of science fiction and makes the numbers an organic part of the vision. It's a terrifically enjoyable piece of filmmaking that demands you laugh while your jaw drops."

American Eagle [Comic book character; SFW]

First appearance: *Marvel Two-in-One Annual #6* (October 1981); Creators: Doug Moench, Ron Wilson; Publisher: Marvel Comics.

When Navajo Indian Jason Strongbow is exposed to uranium and a sonic blast while exploring a mine on Indian tribal lands in Arizona, he gains super-strength, agility, speed and endurance and adopts the identity of American Eagle to protect his people.

American Gothic [Comic strip; UK; WW]

First publication: *2000 A.D.* #1432 (2005); Creators: Ian Edginton, Mike Collins; Publisher: Rebellion.

A vampire cowboy helps a hunted group of outcasts in the Old West.

The American Gun Club [Comic book characters; SFW]

First appearance: *Planetary* #18 (February 2004); Story: Warren Ellis; Art: John Cassaday; Publisher: Wildstorm Productions.

When a cannonball-shaped object containing two skeletal figures crashes to earth in modern-day America, the history of the American Gun Club is finally revealed. A journal tells of a group of like-minded individuals with the aim of traveling to the moon. A signature in the journal reveals one of the American Gun Club members to be Jules Verne. Photographs show a group of cowboys and "astronauts" posing before the launch of their "spaceship" from a huge metal tube in 1851.

The concept of *The American Gun Club* was inspired by Jules Verne's "Baltimore Gun Club" from his classic novel **From the Earth to the Moon** (1866).

American Vampire [Comic Book; WW]

First issue: May 2010; Publisher: DC Vertigo.

Skinner Sweet is an outlaw with a taste for blood after he is infected by vampire banker and railroad owner Bram Percy as he attempts to escape his hanging in New Mexico. Pursued by Pinkerton agent James Book the first American vampire is powered by the sun, making him stronger, fiercer and more powerful and brutal than any European vampire. The individualism and independence of the first American vampire is in stark contrast to the decaying aristocratic world of the European vampires who only thrive in a world lacking sunlight. Acclaimed horror author Stephen King and Scott Snyder scripted the Western based tales of Sweet.

"Bad Blood" [WW]

First publication: #1–5 (May–September 2010); Story: Stephen King; Art: Rafael Albuquerque.

Will Bunting chronicles the tale of Skinner Sweet beginning in Sidewinder, Colorado, 1880 where he is buried and presumed dead.

"Strange Frontier" [WW]

First publication: #12 (April 2011); Story: Scott Snyder; Cover art: Rafael Albuquerque; Art: Daniel Zezelj.

Idaho, 1919. As Skinner Sweet watches Colonel Seldom French's Wild West Show his memory takes him back to his encounters with all of the "living legends" on display, including former lover Kitty Banks who betrayed his trust and led the authorities to Pinkerton agent James Book.

"The Beast in the Cave" [WW]

First publication: #19–21 (September 2011-January 2012); Story: Scott Snyder; Cover art: Rafael Albuquerque; Art: Jordi Bernet.

Skinner Sweet's background as a U.S. Army soldier in the brutal Indian Wars, fighting alongside the friend who would later hunt him down, James Book.

American Vampire: Second Cycle [Comic Book; WW]

First issue: March, 2014; Publisher: DC Vertigo.

In the year 1965 Skinner Sweet robs smugglers and drug runners along the Mexican border. America is changing and a new menace lurks in the form of the Gray Trader. Pearl Jones and Skinner Sweet join forces in an atmosphere of mutual distrust as they confront the Gary Trader's legions.

"THE MINER'S JOURNAL" [WW]
First publication: #5 (November, 2014); Story: Scott Snyder; Cover art: Rafael Albuquerque; Art: Matias Bergara.

Nevada Desert, 1954. Gene Bunting, West Coast bookkeeper for The Vassals of The Morningstar, an organization dedicated to the eradication of abominations arrives at the site of the Royal Forkes drift claim, mined in the 1850s. Bunting has in his possession the original hand written journal of William Dodgeman telling the horrific story of the mine and its other-worldly secrets but still decides to enter the "hole" at his own peril.

American Wasteland: Blood and Diesel [Comic book; Canada; WW]

First publication: March 2007; Story: R.D. Hall; Art: Mark Kidwell, Andrew Mangum; Four-issue mini-series; Publisher: Arcana Studios.

In this bloody modern horror Western, truck driver Cletus McCoy battles vampire monsters in an apocalyptic America where hell is reserved for both the living and the undead.

Among the Brave [RPG; WW]

First publication: 2014; *Deadlands Tall Tales #6*; Protocol Game Series; Story: Jim Pinto; Art: Rick Hershey; Publisher: Pinnacle Entertainment Group.

The residents of a small tribe near the Coyote Confederation have vanished with only empty tents and teepees remaining in the eerily silent village. A story role-playing game set in *Deadlands: The Weird West*.

And God Said to Cain (1970) [Film: WW]

U.S. release title for *E Dio disse a Caino*.

Anomaly [Graphic Novel; SW]

Author: Skip Brittenham; Art: Brian Haberlin; First publication: Vol #1, October 2012; Publisher: Anomaly Publishing.

Earth 2717 is a dying world ruled by the Conglomerate, a ruthless merging of corporations, nations and technologies whose Enforcer Battalions now conquer planets. With resources depleted humans live in "Terrrarium Cities," off-world colonies or orbiting space stations.

Dishonorably discharged from the Conglomerate's elite Enforcer Corps. Jon is assigned to a first contact mission to a peaceful world, but finds himself marooned on the hostile planet Anomaly, where technology is redundant and flesh-eating mutants, synthetics-eating viruses and deadly magic threaten the existence of Jon, Jasson and Samantha, the daughter of a powerful Conglomerate executive.

The story by fantasy author Skip Brittenham offers comparisons to tales of the Old West frontier and encountering hostile natives in a new land. The 368-page hardcover graphic novel employed a unique printing process featuring high-end, wide gamut inks and stochastic screening and encompassed new technology including Ultimate Augmented Reality.

Readers downloaded an Anomaly companion app for compatible iOS and Android devices featuring over 50 interactive 3D models with sound and animation and over 100 pages of additional material detailing the Anomaly universe. A cast of 15 actors brought 90 speaking roles to life.

The Angel and the Outlaw [Novel; WWR]

Author: Madeline Baker; First publication: New York: N.Y. Leisure Books, 1996.

Following his death by hanging in the 1870s, half-breed outlaw J.T. Cutter is given a second chance by his guardian angel who returns Cutter's soul to his body. Meanwhile a teacher from the present day finds herself back in the Old West when she touches Cutter's body hanging at a gallows. The revived Cutter thanks the woman for rescuing him from the gallows by kidnapping her. But their mutual attraction soon leads to further problems.

El Ánima de Sayula (1978; Mexico; WW)

Main Cast: Antonio Aguilar as Máximo Hernández, Susana Kamini as Lolita, Víctor Alcocer as Don Pascual Alemán, Eleazar García "Chelelo" as Chelelo, Humberto Elizondo as Humberto Ortiz, Delia Magaña as Doña Zoila; Executive Producer: José Aguilar; Producer: Antonio Aguilar; Screenplay: Jorge Patiño; Story: Raúl Ugalde; Director: Javier Durán; Spanish; Águila, Color.

The small town of Sayula is plagued by the spirit of a man who in life had no sexual interest in females. As his spirit wanders through the town, he touches males and transforms them into homosexuals. A surreal Weird Western sex comedy.

El Ánima del Ahorcado contra el Latigo Negro (1959) [Film; Mexico; WW]

Premiere: October 22, 1959; Main Cast: Luis Aguilar

Cover of *The Angel & the Outlaw* by Madeline Baker (1996). Cover art by Pino. Courtesy Madeline Baker.

as El Latigo Negro, Rosita Arenas, Consuelito Frank, Rosa Elana Durgel, Federico Curiel, Fernando Celis Belina; Producers: Aurelio García Yévenes, Luis Enrique Vergara; Story: Federico Curiel "Pichirilo"; Director: Vicente Oroná; 80 min.; Películas Rodríguez; Spanish; Color.

In this variation on **Zorro**, El Latigo Negro fights the spirit of a man hanged for a crime he may not have committed. This was the third film in the *El Latigo Negro* series.

Apache Chief [Animated TV series character; WW]

First appearance: *The All New Super Friends Hour* (1977); Hanna-Barbera Productions.

Able to increase his body to great size by saying "Inyuk-chuk," this Native American Indian character was created specifically for the *Super Friends* animated cartoon series featuring DC Comics characters. Apache Chief never appeared in a DC Comic book.

See: **Justice League**

Appaloosa Rising: or, The Legend of the Cowboy Buddha [Novel; WW]

Author: Gino Sky; First publication: Doubleday, 1980, Garden City NY.

Contemporary Western set in Idaho, Montana and Wyoming fusing American frontier and Buddhist ideals including psychic travel between Montana and Tibet.

Cowboy Buddha is kind of a state of mind, he's never a real character, but it's this evolution from the cowboy consciousness as everyone knows it in the West, with all the stereotypes, to the Buddha consciousness.... And so you have outer space and inner space coming together.—*Boise Weekly*, Jennifer Parsons, August 10, 2005.

See: **Coyote Silk**

Arizonan Kukka [Novel; Finland; SFW]

Author: L. Martin; First publication: 1945, Finland.

Science fiction Western tale of a lost land in the Arizona desert. L. Martin was a pseudonym for prolific Finnish pulp writer Martti L'Fberg (also known as Marton Taiga).

The Arrivals [Novel; WW]

Author: Melissa Marr; First Publication: New York: HarperCollins, 2013.

The Wasteland is awaiting a select few who find themselves inexplicably transported to an alternate world populated with monsters living in a rugged landscape under a two-moon sky. One fact the Arrivals share in common is they were all killers in their previous existence. In the new world death can be followed by resurrection for the Arrivals or can be defeated forever by working for the destructive, greed driven Ajani—the person responsible

Cover of *Arizonan Kukka* by L. Martin (Finland, 1945).

for opening the portal through time and space to the Wasteland.

The Arrivals try to stay within the confines of a fenced tent city that protects them from the monsters and Wastelanders awaiting them in the surrounding Gallows Desert. Arrivals Jack and his sister Kitty, who previously lived in the Old West of 1870, are joined by the latest Arrival, recovering alcoholic Chloe Mattison from 2013, as they struggle to survive in a world they barely understand.

Astonishing [Comic book]

Weird horror anthology title that continued the numbering from the short-lived *Marvel Boy* title.

"The Rainmaker" [WW]

First publication: #39 (June 1955); Art: Doug Wildey; Publisher: Atlas/Marvel.

A rainmaker gets revenge on a Western community suffering from drought after they refuse to pay him for his work.

The Aurora Encounter (1986) [Film: SFW]

Premiere: March 1986; Main Cast: Jack Elam as Charlie Hankins, Carol Bagdarsarian as Alain Peebles, Mickey Hays as Aurora Spaceman, Peter Brown as Sheriff, Dottie West as Irene, Spanky McFarland as Governor Colverson; Executive producers: Fred Kuehnert, M. Sanousi; Story: Melody Brooke, Jim McCullough Jr.; Director: Jim McCullough Sr.; 90 min.; New World Pictures, Jim McCullough Productions; Color.

When school teacher Miss Peebles takes over her late father's newspaper the *Aurora Sentinel* she asks Charlie Hankins if he knows of any "hot selling stories" as "nothing exciting ever happens around here." But unknown to them on the outskirts of town widower Irene encounters an "airship" and a strange-looking person at her window.

Meanwhile a schoolgirl sees the airship and a small, bald alien take off and leave behind a large diamond-like jewel. The airship then lands at the home of Charlie Hankins, where the alien is greeted by a lonely Hankins and invited to play a game of checkers before leaving.

Newspaper editor and publisher Peebles visits Austin, Texas, to inform the Governor of "flying ships from another world" but is met with disbelief. The Governor decides to send a Texas Ranger Phillip Sheridan to Aurora to discover the truth behind the story, but his actions lead to tragedy.

This light-hearted Sci-Fi Western featured Mickey Hays as the alien. Mays suffered from progeria that resulted in premature aging and gave him an unusual appearance. The story emphasizes the kind nature of the alien that is eventually betrayed by an act of human violence. Actor Jack Elam formed a close friendship with Hays during filming that continued until Hays' death on his 20th birthday in 1992.

Avatar (2009) [Film; SW]

Premiere: December 10, 2009; Main cast: Sam Worthington as Jake Sully, Sigourney Weaver as Dr. Grace Augustine, Stephen Lang as Colonel Miles Quaritch, Zoe Saldana as Neytiri, Michelle Rodriguez as Trudy Chacon, Joel David Moore as Norm Spellman, CCH Pounder as Moat, Wes Studi as Eytuykan, Giovanni Ribisi as Parker Selfridge; Story-Director: James Cameron; 163 min.; Twentieth Century–Fox; 3D; Color.

James Cameron's film about a native race facing extermination at the hands of colonists-invaders is a theme central to many Westerns. The year is 2154. Twelve-foot tall, blue skinned, golden-eyed Na'vi (substitute Native Americans), inhabitants of the idyllic planet Pandora, come under threat from the military (substitute the U.S. Cavalry) working for an American mining corporation from Earth, intent on mining a precious, rare mineral with no regard for the Na'vi's sacred tropical environment. Paraplegic war veteran Jake Sully (Sam Worthington) initially agrees to work with the corporation, with the tempting promise of the restoration of his ability to walk, and the novelty of inhabiting an avatar body while wired up in a trance-like state in a pod. But he finds himself sympathizing with the Na'vi after he falls in love with the beautiful native girl Neytiri while in his avatar form and witnesses the wanton destruction of their beautiful natural habitat with its bioluminescent flora and fauna and the mystical gigantic Edenic tree that literally connects them to their ancestors. Ultimately he takes sides with the Na'vi and joins the fight against his fellow invaders from Earth.

The late film critic Roger Ebert (December 11, 2009) stated: "'Avatar' is not simply a sensational entertainment, although it is that. It's a technological breakthrough. It has a flat-out Green and anti-war message. It is predestined to launch a cult. It contains such visual detailing that it would reward repeat viewings. It is an Event, one of those films you feel you must see to keep up with the conversation."

Manohla Dargis of *The New York Times* (December 17, 2009) commented: "If a story of par-adise found and lost feels resonant, it's because 'Avatar' is as much about our Earth as the universe that Mr. Cameron has invented. But the movie's truer meaning is the audacity of its filmmaking."

Peter Bradshaw of *The Guardian* (December 17, 2009) said: "Strip away from this movie the director's massive reputation, and you have a truly weird story about an aggressive future world corporation bankrolling avatar-technology so that human beings can insinuate themselves into the lives of aliens to seduce them. What an indie-freaky idea that is—and that is what makes it an experience."

Sukhdev Sandu of the UK *Telegraph* (December 17, 2009) was less impressed than his fellow film critics. "The start has too much talky exposition, the middle section meanders, and the final hour, while it manages to avoid the Transformers-style mayhem it threatens to ape, doesn't do enough to convince you that all you've been watching is a tricked-up, digitally sophisticated mash-up of Pocahontas, Dances With Wolves and Last of the Mohicans. It's an achievement to make 3D look as good as it does here, but that counts for little if the characters are all in 1D. The film is a triumph of effects over affect."

The Oscar winning film was a major box-office success, grossing almost $3 billion worldwide.

The Avengers [Comic book]

The Marvel superhero group title featured a two-part time-travel story starring Marvel's Western lineup.

"Go West Young Gods"; "Right Between the Eons" [SFW]

First publication: #142–143 (December 1975-January 1976); Story: Steve Englehart; Art: George Perez, Vince Colletta, Sam Grainger; Publisher: Marvel Comics.

Thor, Moondragon and Immortus, Master of Limbo, search for Hawkeye, who is lost in the time stream. They find themselves in Tombstone in 1873 where they meet **Rawhide Kid**, **Two-Gun Kid**, **Kid Colt**, **Night Rider** and Ringo Kid. Reunited with Hawkeye at the office of Matthew J. Hawk, they

Avatar (2009), starring Sam Worthington as the avatar of Jake Sully (left) and Zoe Saldana as Neytiri (Twentieth Century–Fox Film Corporation).

learn that Kang the Conqueror has enslaved the town.

Ayers, Dick (1924–2014) [Comic book artist]

Born in Ossining, New York, on April 28, 1924, Richard "Dick" Ayers began his professional art career in late 1947 penciling Joe Schuster's *Funnyman* strip after first meeting Schuster at Burne Hogarth's Cartoonist and Illustrators School. With *Funnyman* being a Magazine Enterprises publication, Schuster recommended Ayers to M.E. publisher **Vincent Sullivan** and editor Ray Krank in 1948. After an initial start on a Western strip for *Cowboys and Indians* issue #6 ("Doc Holiday–Doctor of Death!"), Ayers provided the artwork for the short-lived *Jimmy Durante* title. Ayers soon found his niche working on Western strips including Calico Kid, **Ghost Rider**, *Bobby Benson and the B-Bar-B Riders* and **The Presto Kid**.

Ayers' primary work in the mid– to late 1950s was for Atlas, where he worked on Western strips such as **Rawhide Kid, Two-Gun Kid, Kid Colt**, Outlaw Kid and *Wyatt Earp*. With the advent of the superhero boom in the 1960s, Ayers contributed to many Marvel titles including *Captain America*, **Fantastic Four**, *The Avengers* and Incredible Hulk. He also contributed pencils to the revamped *Rawhide Kid* and *Ghost Rider* for Marvel and **Jonah Hex** and **Scalphunter** for DC Comics.

In later years Ayers worked for Archie Comics, returning to his roots in the 1980s and 1990s when he produced new **Haunted Horseman** and **Black Phantom** art for **Bill Black** at AC Comics.

Apart from his Western strips, Ayers is best remembered for his collaboration with **John Severin** on the World War II comic book *Sgt. Fury and His Howling Commandos* and cites this as his favorite work for Marvel Comics.

Back East: The North [RPG Book;WW]

Authors: Rick Dakan, Jack Emmert; First publication: 1999; Game: **Deadlands: The Weird West**; Publisher: Pinnacle Entertainment Group.

Location sourcebook for the Eastern Union (North-Eastern United States).

Back East: The South [RPG Book; WW]

Authors: Steven S. Long, Christopher McGlothlin, Kenneth Hite; First publication: 1999; Game: **Deadlands: The Weird West**; Publisher: Pinnacle Entertainment Group.

Location book for Eastern Confederacy including the Okeefenokee swamps of Florida and haunted Kentucky.

Back to the Future (1991) [Animated TV series]

Animated sequel to the film series.

"CLARA'S FOLKS" (1:16) [SFW]
Air date: December 14, 1991; Voice Cast: David Kaufman as Martin Seamus "Marty" McFly, Dan Castellaneta as Dr. Emmett L. Brown, Troy Davidson as Verne Brown, Thomas F. Wilson as Bill Tannen; Story: Bob Gale; Director: Peyton Reed; 30 min.; Universal Cartoon Studios, Amblin; Color.

Travelling back in time to the Oregon Trail, Verne's future grandmother Martha falls in love with Marty, thus threatening to alter history. Doc Brown must put things back in place.

Back to the Future Part II & III [Video game; SFW]

Release date: September 30, 1990; Developer: Beam Software; Publisher: LJN Ltd.; Perspective: Side-Scrolling; Platform: Nintendo Entertainment System (NES).

A game based on the movies *Back to the Future Part II* and **Back to the Future Part III**; the challenge is to retrieve objects trapped out of time and return them to their correct time and place.

Back to the Future, Part III (1990) [Film; SFW]

1—Premiere: May 25, 1990; Main Cast: Michael J. Fox as Marty McFly/Seamus McFly, Christopher Lloyd as Dr. Emmett Brown, Mary Steenburgen as Clara Clayton, Lea Thompson as Maggie McFly/ Lorraine McFly, Thomas F. Wilson as Buford "Mad Dog" Tannen/Biff Tannen, Elisabeth Shue as Jennifer Parker; Executive Producers: Steven Spielberg, Kathleen Kennedy, Frank Marshall; Story: Robert Zemeckis, Bob Gale; Director: Robert Zemeckis; xxx min.; Amblin Entertainment, Universal Pictures; Color.

Marty McFly travels back in time in the DeLorean to the Old West of 1885 to save Dr. Emmett Brown from death at the hands of Buford "Mad Dog" Tannen. The final entry in the highly successful **Back to the Future** trilogy.

Hal Hinson of *The Washington Post* (May 25, 1990) stated: "When Marty crosses the plane of the fourth dimension and moves into the past, the picture becomes a kind of surrealistic western."

2—Video Game; Title: **Back to the Future Part III**

Release date: 1991; Designer: Hugh Riley; Developer: Probe Software; Publisher: Image Works, Mirrorsoft Ltd.; Perspective: Side-Scrolling, Top-Down; Platform: Sega Genesis.

A collection of four arcade games based on scenes from the movie.

The Backwater Gospel [Animation short; WW]

Premiere: September 23, 2011; Voice Cast: Zebulon Whatley as the Tramp, Lucien Dodge as the Minister, Philip Sacramento as Bubba, Laura Post as Townswoman; Animation director: Arthur Gil Larsen; Director: Bob Mathorne; 9 min.; Animation Workshop; Color.

When the winged undertaker visits Blackwater the townsfolk live in fear of who he will claim next for death. The church minister only adds to the pervasive gloom and seeks a scapegoat in the form of a singing tramp. But his death only serves to escalate the fear to the point of mass slaughter.

Bad Moon Rising [Comic Book; WW]

First publication: 2004; Story: Brian Pulido; Art: Wellington Alves; Publisher: Avatar Press.

A hyper-violent supernatural slasher Western set in Hope, Arizona, featuring murderous Black Jack Hatchet and his bloody ax, Mabel, as he searches for his lost love Wynona Mullins across time into the 21st century.

Bad Wind Blowing [Novel; WW]

Author: Peter Brandvold; First publication: Western Trail Blazer, 2010.

Clay Carmody and Nathan Laroque hope to dig for gold in Poudre Canyon, little knowing an ancient Indian demon preys in the remote Colorado river canyon. But as Clay waits for his partner to arrive he encounters the paranormal for the first time at Camp Hawkins and decides to go on a demon hunt with Claudine Bridger, sheriff of Camp Hawkins. A young schoolteacher and an old Indian Shaman join them on their journey through the cursed canyon.

Badlands [Video game; WW]

Release date: 1984; Platform: Arcade, MSX; Developer: Konami; Publishers: Konami, Centuri.

An Old West shooter where players press a button to kill the attacker. If the players miss or are too slow they are killed themselves, and if the players shoot too soon they are found guilty of murder and hanged.

The theme of the game is revenge for the death of Buck's wife and children by a gang of outlaws led by Landolf. Buck ventures through different animated landscapes in his quest to kill the outlaws, including a Weird West environment of a cave leading to a jungle inhabited by prehistoric monsters and dinosaurs. Another scene features a young maiden turning into a mystical monster as Buck approaches her cabin.

The player-Buck has three lives. When these are lost the game is over and Buck becomes an angel who goes to heaven. If Buck succeeds in killing Landolf in the final showdown he rides off into the sunset.

Bakuretsu Tenshi: Angel's Adolescence [Manga; Japan; SFW]

First appearance: 2003; Story: Gonzo, Murao Minoru; Art: Gonzo; Serialized in *Dengeki Comic Gao!*; Publisher: Media Works.

Timid Takeru's life changes when he encounters Megumi and Jo, two beautiful girls he hides from pursuing thugs in his Tokyo home. This Manga prequel to the anime **Burst Angel** is set in a futuristic Tokyo where law and order has been replaced with "guns and strength." Red-haired Megumi wears a revealing Western cowgirl outfit.

The Ballad of Sleeping Beauty [Comic Book; WW]

First publication: July 2004; Story: Gabriel Benson; Art: Mike Hawthorne, Jeff Amano; Eight-issue mini-series; Publisher: Beckett Comics.

Gunfighter Cole Jarrett runs from his past while learning of a woman cursed to spend the rest of her life trapped in sleep for sins she did not commit.

The Ballad of Utopia [Comic Book; WW]

First publication: March 2000; Story: Barry Buchanan; Art: Mike Hoffman; Eight-part mini-series; Publisher: Black Daze Publishing.

A murder in sun-baked Utopia is investigated by Deputy Sam David and occultic bounty hunter Brigham Love, who attempt to uncover dark secrets. This gothic Western has been described as a horse-opera *Twin Peaks*.

Mike Hoffman recalling the creation of the project stated, "*The Ballad of Utopia* is one of my few collaborations. I volunteered to draw it for writer Barry Buchanan, who was having trouble finding a suitable artist. My Western kick had just started then, so I was a-champin'."

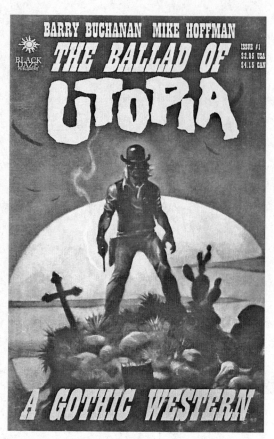

Left: The Ballad of Utopia #1 (March 2000), page 1. Art by Mike Hoffman. *Right:* Cover of *The Ballad of Utopia* #1. Art by Mike Hoffman. © Barry Buchanan and Mike Hoffman. Used with permission.

"Barry is a film school graduate, which explains a lot about the cinematic style and naturalistic dialogue. It took us about three years to complete the story. I think his goal was to create a Western Mystery that wasn't so much a shoot-'em-up and had some gothic horror overtones."

See: **Western Gothic: Ballad of Utopia**

Bang Bang Kid (1967) [Film; Italy-Spain; SFW]

Premiere: November 19, 1967; Main Cast: Guy Madison as Bear Bullock, Tom Bosley as Merriwether T. Newberry, Riccardo Garrone as Killer Kossock, Sandra Milo as Gwenda Skaggel; Producers: Sidney W. Pink, Mirko Purgatori; Story: José Luis de las Bayonas, Luciano Lelli; Directors: Stanley Prager [Giorgio Gentili], Luciano Lelli; 87 min.; Domino Films, L.M. Films; Color.

Inventor Merriwether T. Newberry claims his robot can be trained to be a gunslinger to protect the Western frontier town of Limerick against the notorious crime lord Bear Bullock and his hired gun Killer Kossock.

Bang! Howdy [Strategy game; SPW]

Release date: 2006; Developer-Publisher: Three Rings Design; Platform: Java-enabled Linux, Windows, Mac OSX.

This online tactical strategy game is a combination of cowboys and steampunk robots in a wacky Old West setting. Various gameplay scenarios include Gold Rush where players compete to collect Gold Nuggets and return them to their Steam Tank before being shot from attack Units such as the Steam Gunman.

Banshee Screams [RPG Book; WW]

Authors: Clay and Susan Griffith; First publication: 1999; Game: **Deadlands: Lost Colony**; Publisher: Pinnacle Entertainment Group.

Temptation, the largest colonial settlement on Banshee, is under threat from dark powers.

Colonial Ranger Debbi Dallas and her fellow Rangers must protect the outpost from a renewed Reaper menace.

"The Banshee Singer" [Pulp fiction; WW]

Author: **Lon Williams**; Story character: **Lee Winters**; *Real Western Stories* (April 1957).

They said that the Bodep Opera House in Forlorn Gap was haunted, that a murdered opera singer awaited the man who had slain her there. And that man was believed to be Jason Inbred— the very gent whom Lee Winters had been assigned to track down!

"Bat Durston, Space Marshal" [Magazine fiction; SW]

Author: G. Richard Bozarth; First publication: *Isaac Asimov's Science Fiction Magazine* (September-October 1978).

> Satisfied with the proton blaster, Bat Durston returned it to the holster and stood up with a lethal, yet moral, agility. He strapped the weapon onto his narrow hips, his thin lips in an even straighter line than usual. He did not like to carry a proton blaster, but he knew someone had to if these parsecs were ever to be safe for decent, respectable folks.

A cowboy is surrounded by high technology on an alien landscape but still remains a cowboy in a traditional genre plot. This light-hearted Space Western story has been called lazy, unimaginative writing by ex–*Galaxy* editor H. L. Gold.

Bat Lash [Comic book character; WW]

First appearance: *Showcase* #76 (August 1968); Creators: Joe Orlando, Carmine Infantino, Sheldon Mayer, Sergio Aragones; Publisher: DC Comics.

Bartholomew Alouysius Lash alias Bat Lash was never an official Weird Western character but a light-hearted, vain cowboy with an eye for the ladies and good taste in cuisine and music. With the failure of his own title he was bunched together with **Jonah Hex**, **Scalphunter** and **El Diablo** in *Weird Western Tales* and ultimately became linked with them in various time travel adventures and other Weird Western storylines.

Bates, Harry (1900–1981) [Author]

A native of Pittsburgh, Pennsylvania, Hiram Gilmore Bates III adopted the pseudonym Anthony Gilmore for his **Hawk Carse** series of stories which he co-wrote with Desmond W. Hall. He also worked under the pseudonyms H.G. Winter and A. R. Holmes. From January 1930 to March 1933, Bates served as the first editor of *Astounding* science fiction magazine.

20th Century–Fox assistant story editor Maurice Hanline purchased the screen rights to Bates' 1940 *Astounding* short story *Farewell to the Master* for $1,000. Bates was never contacted or involved in any negotiations between 20th Century–Fox and his publisher Street & Smith. His story was adapted and filmed as *The Day the Earth Stood Still* (1951) starring Michael Rennie and Patricia Neal. Bates received a mere $500. In 1987 Bates told *Cinefantastique* magazine, "I thought the movie was very good but it had nothing to do with my story." A remake starring Keanu Reeves and Jennifer Connelly was released in December 2008.

Selected works: As Anthony Gilmore with Desmond W. Hall: *Hawk Carse* (1931), *The Affair of the Brains* (1932), *The Bluff of the Hawk* (1932), *The Passing of Ku Sui* (1932), *The Return of Hawk Carse* (1942), *Space Hawk* (1952).

Batman

1. [Comic book]

The early pulp-influenced origins of The Batman as created by Bill Finger and Bob Kane soon gave way to stories aimed at a younger audience with the introduction of Robin the Boy Wonder in 1940. Despite being set in 20th century Gotham City, Batman and Robin did venture out West on a few occasions.

"The Streamlined Rustlers" [WW]

First publication: #21, February-March 1944; Story: Jack Schiff; Art: Dick Sprang; Publisher: DC Comics.

When a cattle rustler feeds an unconscious Batman local loco-weed, he wakes up and thinks he's a cowboy.

"Batman—Frontier Marshal" [SFW]

First publication: #99, April 1956; Story: Edmond Hamilton; Art: Sheldon Moldoff, Charles Paris; Publisher: DC Comics.

Batman and Robin travel back in time to the Old West and discover a case of mistaken identity between Batman and Bat Masterson. This story emphasized Batman's policy of never wearing or using a gun.

2. [TV Series; 1966]

Main Cast: Adam West as Bruce Wayne/Batman, Burt Ward as Dick Grayson/Robin the Boy Wonder, Yvonne Craig as Barbara Gordon/Batgirl, Alan Napier as Alfred Pennyworth, Neil Hamilton as Police Commissioner Gordon.

This live-action series based on the popular DC comic book characters created by Bob Kane and Bill Finger dismayed comic book purists with its camp style but proved to be an international ratings winner.

"COME BACK SHAME" (2:25), "IT'S THE WAY YOU PLAY THE GAME" (2:26) [SFW]

Air dates: November 30, December 1, 1966; Guest Cast: Cliff Robertson as Shame, Joan Staley as Okie Annie; Executive Producer: William Dozier; Story: Stanley Ralph Ross; Director: Oscar Rudolph; 30 min.; 20th Century–Fox; Color.

Batman and Robin find themselves staked to the ground as a herd of stampeding cattle head in their direction. Meanwhile, cunning cowboy Shame and his nefarious gang of outlaws have hijacked the Wayne limousine.

"THE GREAT ESCAPE" (3:21), "THE GREAT TRAIN ROBBERY" (3:22) [SFW]

Air dates: February 1, February 8, 1968; Guest Cast: Cliff Robertson as Shame, Dina Merrill as Calamity Jan, Hermione Baddeley as Frontier Fanny; Executive Producer: William Dozier; Story: Stanley Ralph Ross; Director: Oscar Rudolph; 30 min.; 20th Century–Fox; Color.

Batman and Robin turn into pathetic cowards after inhaling cowboy Shame's Fear Gas. Shame takes advantage by kidnapping Batgirl. Shame was a parody of the famous Western character Shane.

Batman: The Animated Series (1992) [Animated TV series]

"SHOWDOWN" (3:12) [SFW]

Premiere: September 12, 1995; Voice cast: Kevin Conroy as Bruce Wayne/Batman, Loren Lester as Dick Grayson/Robin, William McKinney as **Jonah Hex**, David Warner as Ra's al Ghul; Malcolm McDowell as Arkady Duvall, Senator Patrick Leahy as Governor, William Bryant as Sheriff, Elizabeth Montgomery as Barmaid; Teleplay: **Joe R. Lansdale**; Story: Bruce W. Timm, Paul Dini, Kevin Altieri; Director: Kevin Altieri; 30 min.; Warner Bros. Animation; Color.

The story of criminal mastermind Ra's al Ghul's confrontation with renegade bounty hunter Jonah Hex in the Old West of 1883 as Ghul at-

tempts to destroy the transcontinental railroad with a blimp. This episode featured the final work of *Bewitched* actress Elizabeth Montgomery.

Batman: The Brave and the Bold (2008) [Animated TV series]

Based on the DC Comics comic book featuring various DC Comics superheroes with Batman as the central character.

"RETURN OF THE FEARSOME FANGS" (1:12) [SFW]

Premiere: February 20, 2009; Voice cast: Diedrich Bader as Bruce Wayne/Batman, Phil Morris as **Jonah Hex**, Gary Sturgis as Bronze Tiger, Paul Nakauchi as Wong Fei; Story: Todd Casey; Director: Brandon Vietti; 30 min.; Warner Bros. Animation; Color.

Sentenced to death by the Royal Flush Gang, Jonah Hex is tied to the railway lines at Sergio Station. Four horses wait for the signal to pull him apart until Batman comes to the rescue. The main story features Batman teaming up with Bronze Tiger to tackle Fox, Vulture and Shark after they steal the Wudang Totem and transform into mystical creatures.

Batman: The Return of Bruce Wayne (Comic book)

"DARK KNIGHT, DARK RIDER" #4 (September 2010) (SFW)

Story: Grant Morrison; Art: Georges Jeanty, Waldon Wong; 6-issue mini-series; Publisher: DC Comics.

As **Superman**, **Green Lantern** and the **Justice League** attempt to track down a **Batman** missing in time. The Dark Knight, alias Bruce Wayne, finds himself swept through the time stream, becoming a caveman, witch hunter, pirate, detective and a cowboy in the Old West, where he has a showdown with **Jonah Hex**. Bruce Wayne must find his way back to the present to gather his shattered self, reclaim his identity and stop Darkseid's plan for the apocalypse known as the All-Over.

Battle Beyond the Stars (1980) [Film; SW]

Premiere: September 8, 1980; Main Cast: Richard Thomas as Shad, Robert Vaughn as Gelt, George Peppard as Cowboy, Sybil Danning as Saint-Exmin, John Saxon as Sador; Executive Producer: Roger Corman; Story: Anne Dyer, John Sayles; Director:

Jimmy T. Murakami; 105 min.; New World Pictures; Color.

A group of mercenaries gather to protect the people of the planet Akir from destruction by space tyrant Sador (John Saxon). This successful Roger Corman production borrows from *The Seven Samurai* and the American remake *The Magnificent Seven* to create a Space Western. The film features Robert Vaughn (from the original *The Magnificent Seven*) and George Peppard, who stars as a cigar-chewing space cowboy.

Battlestar Galactica (1978) [TV series]

Main Cast: Richard Hatch as Capt. Apollo, Dirk Benedict as Lt. Starbuck, Lorne Greene as Commander Adama.

The Galactica, led by Commander Adama, crosses the galaxy in search of the mythical thirteenth colony known as Earth.

"The Lost Warrior" (1:04) [SW]

Premiere: October 8, 1978; Guest Cast: Kathy Cannon as Vella, Johnny Timko as Puppis, Claude Earl Jones as LaCerta, Lance LeGault as Bootes, Red West as Marcos, Rex Cutter as Red Eye; Executive Producer: Glen A. Larson; Story: Herman Groves; Teleplay: Donald P. Bellisario; Director: Rod Holcomb; 60 min.; Glen A. Larson Productions-Universal Television; ABC; Color.

Pursued across space by the Cylon fleet, Capt. Apollo lands his starship on the planet Equellus after running short of fuel. Given shelter by a woman (Kathy Cannon) and her young son (Johnny Timko), Apollo learns her late husband, a Colonial Warrior, was killed by a Cylon centurion gunslinger named Red Eye.

At the local saloon Apollo meets Red Eye and the ruthless LaCerta who runs the town. LaCerta's right-hand man Marcos seeks to replace Red Eye and attempts to impress LaCerta when he challenges Apollo to a gunfight. But Red Eye is a formidable foe and has just killed Vella's brother Bootes after daring to question the payment of "tribute" to LaCerta.

Unlike many Space Westerns that disguise their Western roots, this episode comes complete with cowboy hats, horses and a saloon and has similarities to the western classic *Shane*.

Beany and Cecil (1962) [Animated TV series]

Voice cast: Jim MacGeorge as Beany Boy and Captain Huffenpuff, Irv Shoemaker as Cecil, the Sea-Sick Serpent, and Dishonest John; 30 min.; Bob Clampett Productions; Color.

"Dishonest John Meets Cowboy Starr" (1:11)

Air date: March 17, 1962.

Cecil, Little Homer and Twinkle the starfish disguise themselves as movie hero Cowboy Starr as they confront Dishonest John under the ocean.

"Phantom of the Horse Opera" (1:12)

Air date: March 24, 1962

Entering Badman's Land, Beany and Cecil journey through Unpassable Pass to Horrors Heights and Withering Heights where they encounter the invisible Phantom of the Horse Opera.

"Vild Vast Vasteland" (1:15)

Air date: April 14, 1962.

Beany and Cecil and the gang travel by submarine to the underwater Old West town Second Hand Dodge City where they encounter Black Jack a.k.a. the Loan Arranger, Marshal Villain and Slopalong Catskill.

"Dragon Train" (1:20)

Air date: May 19, 1962.

Pop Gunn tells fantastic tales of the Old West as he rides his Dragon Train.

The Beast Master [Novel; Juvenile: SW]

Author: **Andre Norton**; First publication: 1959; Publisher: New York: Harcourt, Brace.

First appearance of Navajo exile and telepathic beast master **Hosteen Storm** as he seeks a new home on the hostile frontier planet of Arzor. With the assistance of his team (Surra, a cunning dune cat, Baku, an African eagle scout, and saboteur meerkats Hing and Ho), Storm is on a mission of revenge to track down the man who killed his father.

See: *Lord of Thunder*

Beast Master's Ark [Novel; SW]

Authors: **Andre Norton**, Lyn McConchie; First publication: 2002; Publisher: New York: Tom Doherty Associates/Tor.

An unknown animal is eating horses and local cattle alive after first paralyzing them. And now it's developed a taste for humans. HosteenStorm teams up with Tani, the daughter of the late fellow Beast Master Bright Sky, despite the fact that she views all Beast Masters as evil. Together they work through hostilities to tackle the problem of the animal with a taste for animal and human blood.

Beast Master's Circus [Novel; SW]

Authors: **Andre Norton**, Lyn McConchie; First publication: 2004; Publisher: New York: Tor.

A circus arrives on Arzor with the enigmatic Laris and her performing cat-like creature Prauo. Laris is invited to the ranch by Storm and his half-brother Logan Quade but trouble ensues when animals are stolen.

Beast Master's Quest [Novel; SW]

Authors: **Andre Norton**, Lyn McConchie; First publication: 2006; Publisher: New York: Tor.

Orphaned Beast Master Laris lives with her foster family of Arzor ranchers and her cat-like companion, Prauo. When she inherits a spaceship, she decides to journey to Prauo's mysterious home planet with her fellow Beast Masters Tani and Hosteen Storm. But Prauo's planet of origin is more dangerous than they ever imagined.

Beast of Fire [RPG Book; WW]

Authors: Bob Gels, Rob Clayton Jones; Art: Robin Elliott, Dan Harding, Rob Clayton Jones; First published: 2005; *Deadlands Dime Novel #1*; System: **Deadlands: Reloaded**; Publisher: Legion Publishing.

The deadly Manitou "He Who Stalks the Pines" is on the loose again in the woods of Oconto County, Wisconsin.

The Beast of Hollow Mountain (1956) [Film; WW]

Premiere: August 1956; Main Cast: Guy Madison as Jimmy Ryan, Patricia Medina as Sarita, Carlos Rivas as Felipe Sanchez; Producers: Edward Nassour, William Nassour; Original Story: Willis O'Brien; Screenplay: Robert Hill; Directors: Edward Nassour, Ismael Rodríguez; 81 min.; Nassour Brothers-Peliculas Rodriguez Productions, United Artists; Color.

Theatrical trailer: "Starring Guy Madison, as the courageous rancher who tried to solve the secret of Hollow Mountain, hiding place of a monster spawned in the dawn of time. He dared to ride where no man had ever set foot before. Patricia Medina. The menace of the beast stood between her and the man she loved...."

A Mexican-based rancher (Guy Madison) discovers his cattle are being eaten by a dinosaur in this first feature to use miniature rear projection in color to combine the stop motion and live ac-

The Beast of Hollow Mountain (1956), starring Guy Madison as Jimmy Ryan and Patricia Medina as Sarita (Nassour Brothers-Peliculas Rodriguez Productions).

tion film. A technique called Regiscope, developed by Edward Nassour, was similar to George Pal's replacement animation process and involved filming several models of the same character in slightly different positions to create the illusion of movement. The mix of cowboys and dinosaurs would be developed to greater effect by Willis O'Brien in *The Valley of Gwangi* thirteen years later.

Becoming Coyote [Novel; WW]
Author: Wayne Ude; First publication: Amherst, Mass.: Lynx House Press, 1981.

Pursued by the law for breaking into an Indian museum, two Native Americans enter the Missouri Breaks a.k.a. Coyote Land where myth and magic intermingle with reality.

"The Bee's Nest" [Pulp fiction; WW]
Author: **Lon Williams**; Story character: **Lee Winters**; *Real Western Stories* (April 1958).

Dardeen Blackwood had loved bees, always had them around her—but Dardeen Blackwood was dead, murdered years ago. But now Lee Winters and Doc Bogannon both heard the sound of bees, and Winters had seen a woman who looked like Dardeen Blackwood get off the incoming stage....

Beetlejuice (1989) [Animated TV series]
Voice cast: Stephen Ouimette as Beetlejuice, Alyson Court as Lydia Deitz; Executive Producers: Tim Burton, David Geffen; 30 min.; Geffen Film Company, Tim Burton Inc., Nelvana, Warner Bros. Television; Color.

Loosely based on the 1988 comedy horror film starring Michael Keaton as Neitherworld ghost Beetlejuice.

"PEST O' THE WEST" (1:08) [WW]
Air date: October 28, 1989; Story: J. D. Smith; Director: Robin Budd.

When Beetlejuice decides to visit a Neitherworld Old West town with Lydia, he is made sheriff to keep Bully the Crud at bay. But Bully takes a romantic liking to Lydia and insists on a wedding.

"PRAIRIE STRIFE" (4:43) [WW]
Air date: November 6, 1991; Story: Julianne Klemm.

A peaceful life on Auntie Em's Old West milk farm is threatened by outlaw Jesse Germs' plan to take over the land. Beetlejuice and Lydia have plans of their own to scare him away.

The Bells of Innocence (2003) [Film; WW]
Premiere: April 6, 2003; Main Cast: Chuck Norris as Matthew, Mike Norris as Jux Jonas, Scarlett McAlister as Dianna, David A.R. White as Conrad Champlain, Carey Scott as Oren Ames, Grant James as Emeritus, Marshall R. Teague as Joshua Ravel; Story: Chris Bessey, Mike Norris; Executive Producer: Mike Norris; Director: Alin Bijan; 110 min.; Norris Films, Media World; Color.

In the small town of Ceres, the children are under the power of satanic forces led by the town elder Joshua (Marshall R. Teague). Local Christian rancher Matthew (Chuck Norris) becomes involved in a spiritual battle that could damn souls for eternity if he doesn't prevail.

"The Bells of San Filipo" [Pulp fiction; WMW]
Author: **Max Brand**; First publication: Serialized in *Western Story Magazine*, 1926.

In the ghost town of San Filipo, a bedraggled young Mexican man named Diego Ramirez tells prospector Jim Gore the story of the nine great church bells of San Filipo. Cast in Barcelona, the bells were transported to America and hung in the bell tower of the church. On the first day they were rung "the canals were opened to water the valley." The people said there would be happiness and wealth as long as the bells could ring. The bells rang for two hundred years until war came to the valley and the church bells fell among the charred ruins of the church. On the same day the dam was broken, the canals ran dry and San Filipo was reclaimed by the desert. But now, one hundred years later on the day of an earthquake, Ramirez and others in the valley have heard the lost church bells ring. The prophecy says San Filipo shall be rich again.

When Jim Gore also hears the distant ringing of the bells he declares to his new prospecting partner Chris Estaban, "I dunno nothing about ghosts and don't want to know nothing. But I'll tell you that them are ghost bells, that you hear down yonder in the valley. Yep, they come from the bells of the old church—dead bells—bells that ain't got no body no more'n a spook has!"

Adding to the mystery of San Filipo is the ghost of a beautiful young nun named Alicia who died when the town burned and the bells were lost in the ruins of the church. The sight of her walking by night between the church and the nunnery, wrapped in a black cloak with a long rosary hung around her neck, is said to strike a person dumb.

But Jim Gore soon discovers the truth behind Diego Ramirez, Chris Esteban, and the source of the ringing bells and the ghost that haunts San Filipo.

The Best Little Hellhouse in Texas [RPG book; WW]

First publication: 2008; Publisher: Talisman Studios.

Supernatural horror in the town of Sweetwater as demon-possessed prospectors and townsfolk along with monsters inhabit the Western landscape. Vampire hookers tempt clients to Hellhouse, the local saloon and brothel owned by the Reverend Rasp.

The second adventure toolkit for the Suzerain multi-genre, multi-world game system in the world of Untamed Empires.

Best of the West [Comic book; WW]

First publication: 1951; Publishers: Magazine Enterprises; AC Comics.

This anthology title which ran to twelve issues between 1951 and 1954 featured Magazine Enterprises' most popular Western strips including **Ghost Rider**, *Bobby Benson's B-Bar-B Riders*, *Tim Holt* as *Red Mask*, *The Durango Kid* and *Straight Arrow*.

In 1998, AC Comics (under the editorship of **Bill Black**) began publishing black and white reprints of the title with Ghost Rider renamed **Haunted Horseman** and subsequently **The Haunter**. The title also reprinted other Golden Age Western comic strips including **Red Mask**, **Lemonade Kid**, *Masked Rider*, **Black Phantom**, *Latigo Kid*, *American Eagle*, *The Lone Rider*, *Rocky Lane*, *Black Diamond*, **Lash LaRue**, *Black Bull*, *Arizona Raines*, *Sunset Carson*, *Monte Hale*, *Wild Bill Hickok*, **Wild Bill Pecos**, *The Whip*, *Calamity Kate* and *Roy Rogers*.

Black introduced new material into the title with work from renowned artist **Dick Ayers** recreating his classic *Ghost Rider* creation. *Best of the West* ran to 71 issues before cancellation in January 2009.

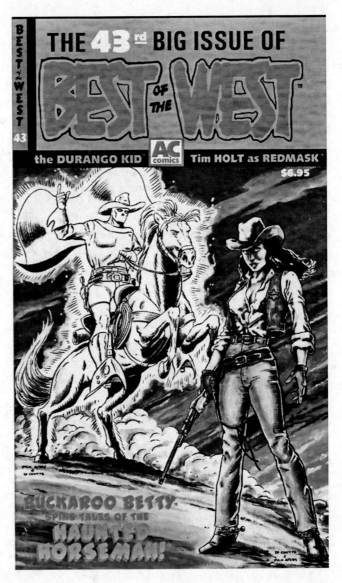

Cover of *Best of the West* #43. Art by Dick Ayers and Ed Coutts. © 2009 AC Comics/Nightveil Media, Inc. Used with permission.

The Best Rootin' Tootin' Shootin' Gunslinger in the Whole Damned Galaxy [Novel; SW]

Author: **Mike Resnick**; First publication: New York: New American Library, 1983.

Galactic carnival entrepreneur Thaddeus Flint arranges a money-spinning showdown between trick shot artist Billybuck Dancer and his enemy, Doc Holliday.

Beyond Belief: Fact or Fiction (1997) [TV series]

The viewer is presented with a series of short dramatized stories with a paranormal twist and is left to decide if they are "Fact or Fiction." The host reveals the answer at the conclusion of each show. Original host James Brolin was replaced by Jonathan Frakes after the first season.

"THE CARD GAME" (2:10) [WW]

Air date: April 24, 1998: Main Cast: Paul Peterson as Lucky, Brandon Cruz, Tony Dow, Barry Livingston, Charlie Dierkop as Judge Roy Bean; Story: Bob Wolterstorff, Mike Scott; Director; Matt Earl Beesley; 7.44 min.; Dick Clark Productions, Maybe Productions, Fox; Color.

A crooked card dealer (Paul Peterson) in an Old West theme bar is given the shock of his life when the ghost of Judge Roy Bean (Charlie Dierkop) and his dog make an appearance at a poker game. Host Jonathan Frakes tells the viewer the story is based on fact.

"THE GHOST TOWN" (3:11) [WW]

Air date: August 4, 2000: Main Cast: Nathan Anderson, Raymond Guth, Wiley Pickett, Charles Gunning; Story: Bob Wolterstorff, Mike Scott; Director; Rachel Feldman; 8.20 min.; Dick Clark Productions, Maybe Productions, Fox; Color.

On August 5, 1998, a traveler stumbles across the small town of Red Ridge. To his amazement he finds himself in the Old West of 1848. Frakes declares the story to be fiction.

The Big Book of the Weird Wild West [Graphic novel; WW]

First publication: 1998; Stories: John Whalen, Deb Picker, Richard Klaw, Ben Ostrander; Art: Russ Heath, Dick Giordano, Joe Staton, Timothy Truman, Marie Severin, Tom Sutton, Gray Morrow, Joe Orlando, Sergio Aragones, Pat Boyette, Charlie Adlard, Sam Glanzman, Chris Shenck, Steve Lieber, Bruce Patterson, Galen Showman, Paul Guinan, Eben Matthews; Publisher: Factoid Books-Paradox Press.

A 196-page anthology of comic strips featuring the strange and weird history of the Old West. Subjects include The James Gang, Butch Cassidy, John Wesley Hardin, Six-Gun Slade, Judge Roy Bean, Joaquin Murieta, scalp hunters, cannibals, tommyknockers, religious festivals, ghosts, wolf men and flying saucers.

Big Calibre (1935) [Film; WMW]

Premiere: March 8, 1935; Main Cast: Bob Steele as Bob O'Neill, Peggy Campbell as June Bowers, Earl Dwire as Sheriff of Gladstone, Bill Quinn as Otto Zenz/Gadski, Georgia O'Dell as Arabella; Producer: A. W. Hackel; Story: Perry Murdock; Screenplay-Director: Robert North Bradbury; 58 min.; Supreme Pictures; b/w.

An unusual early horror Western featuring a disfigured mad scientist (Bill Quinn in a dual role) hunted by rancher Bob O'Neill for murdering his father with poison gas.

Big Thunder Mountain Railroad [Comic book: WW]

First publication: March, 2015; Story: Dennis Hopeless; Art: Tigh Walker; 5-issue mini-series; Publisher: Marvel–Disney Kingdoms.

Abigail Bullion, teenage daughter of feared Big Thunder Mining Company owner Barnabas T. Bullion, moves to Big Thunder following the death of her mother and adopts the alter-ego of a masked bandit.

Based on the popular Disney theme park ride featuring possessed locomotives racing around the sacred and cursed Thunder Mountain.

Bill & Ted's Excellent Adventure (1989) [Film; SFW]

Premiere: February 17, 1989; Main Cast: Keanu Reeves as Ted "Theodore" Logan, Alex Winter as Bill S. Preston, Esq., Dan Shor as Billy the Kid, Jim Cody Williams as Bearded Cowboy; Executive Producers: Robert W. Cort, Ted Field; Story: Chris Matheson, Ed Solomon; Director: Stephen Herek; 90 min.; DeLaurentiis Entertainment Group, Nelson Entertainment, Orion Pictures; Color.

Two dim-witted teenagers travel back in time in a telephone box to do research for their oral history examination. An amusing film that explores the Old West when Logan and Preston meet Billy the Kid and return him to present-day California.

Billy the Ghost and Me [Juvenile book; WW]

Authors: Gery Greer, Bib Ruddick; Illustrator: Roger Roth; First published: 1997; Publisher: Newfield Publications Inc., HarperCollins.

Sarah has a special friend, a practical-joking ghost called Billy that only she can see. When the Cactus Junction Bank is robbed, Sarah and Billy the Ghost decide to catch the robbers in their own unique way.

Billy the Kid Versus Dracula (1966) [Film; WW]

Left: Cover of *Billy the Ghost and Me* by Gery Greer and Bob Ruddick (1997). Illustrated by Roger Roth. *Right: Billy the Kid vs. Dracula* (1966), starring John Carradine as Dracula, Chuck Courtney as Billy the Kid and Melinda Plowman as Betty Bentley (Circle Productions, Embassy Pictures).

Premiere: April 1966; Main Cast: John Carradine as Dracula, Chuck Courtney as William H. Bonney alias Billy the Kid, Melinda Plowman as Betty Bentley, Virginia Christine as Eva Oster; Producer: Carroll Case; Story: Carl Hittleman; Director: William Beaudine; 73 min.; Circle Productions, Embassy Pictures; Color.

The fiancée of Billy the Kid attracts the attention of Dracula, who poses as her uncle.

Carradine resorts to his usual theatrical performance as the vampire Dracula who turns into a bat and can appear and disappear at will. Veteran director William Beaudine was 74 years of age when he filmed his two horror Westerns (this and *Jesse James Meets Frankenstein's Daughter*). Nicknamed "One Shot Beaudine" for his fast turnaround, he retired from directing in 1967.

Billy the Kid's Old Timey Oddities [Comic Book; WW]

First issue: April 2005; Creators: Eric Powell, Kyle

Holtz; Four-issue mini-series; Publisher: Dark Horse.

Billy the Kid is the hired gun of Fineas Sproule, traveling with a group of circus freaks known as "Sproule's Biological Curiosities" as they join forces against Dr. Frankenstein as he searches for the heart of the Golem.

Billy the Kid's Old Timey Oddities and the Ghastly Fiend of London [Comic book; WW]

First publication: September 2010; Story: Eric Powell; Art: Eric Powell, Kyle Hotz; Publisher: Dark Horse.

Billy the Kid, Fineas Sproule and his traveling company of biological curiosities travel to London to meet the Elephant Man but find themselves involved in the Jack the Ripper murders.

Billy the Kid's Old Timey Oddities and the Orm of Loch Ness [Comic book; WW]

First publication: October 2012; Story: Eric Powell, Kyle Hotz, Tracy Marsh; Art: Kyle Hotz; Publisher: Dark Horse.

As Billy and Sproule's traveling "freaks" show search for the alligator man in the gloomy environs of Loch Ness they become guests of Count Dracula at his castle and fall prey to the Mormon brides of Dracula.

The Bird Man [Comic book character; WW]

First appearance: *Weird Comics* #1 (April 1940); Creator: Arnold Mazos; Publisher: Fox Features Syndicate.

> Over the vast wilderness of the great Western canyons swoops the Bird Man, winged hunter of the plains. A descendant of an ancient Indian god, the Bird Man was gifted with the ability to fly and the keen senses of a bird of prey.

Birdman and the Galaxy Trio (1967) [Animated TV series; SW]

The adventures of solar-powered crime fighter Birdman. Although the animation was crude and the stories juvenile, *Birdman* did include an example of the animated science fiction Western decades before the genre gained in popularity.

The Galaxy Trio was a separate show within the 30-minute format of three cartoons per episode.

"THE WILD WEIRD WEST" (1:18)

Air date: December 30, 1967; Voice Cast: Keith Andes as Birdman/Ray Randall, Don Messick as Falcon 7; Executive Producers-Directors: William Hanna, Joseph Barbera; 7 min.; Hanna-Barbera Productions, NBC; Color.

Jesse Jons and his gang use mechanical horses and advanced guns invented by the evil Dr. Kordo to terrorize communities. Birdman and Falcon 7 track these descendants of Old West outlaws to a Western town but fall into a trap.

Bisley's Scrapbook [Comic Book; WW]

First issue: 1993; Stories: Dave Elliott, Simon Bisley; Art: Simon Bisley; Publisher: Atomeka.

Anthology title featuring three supernatural stories including a Western about a zombie riding into the wrong town on his dead horse to seek revenge.

Bizarre Fantasy [Comic book; SFW]

"COWBOYS AND ALIENS" [SFW]

First publication: January 1995 (cover date April);

Story: Steve Busti; Art; Steve Busti, Henry Kujawa; Publisher: Flashback Comics.

This title became the subject of a copyright infringement lawsuit in December 2011 by creator Steven John Busti against Universal Studios, Dreamworks II Distribution Co., Platinum Studios and its chairman and CEO Scott Mitchell Rosenberg. (Busti v Platinum Studios Inc. etal.; case number 1:11-cv-01029 in the U.S. District Court for the Western District of Texas.) Busti claimed his work, created in 1994, had striking similarities to the graphic novel series *Cowboys & Aliens*. Similarities, according to Busti, included an alien spaceship zooming overhead of the main cowboy character, the spacecraft being discovered by Native American warriors (specifically Apache) who are then attacked and the alien commandant being similar to the alien Morguu in the plaintiff's work.

In August 2013 Judge Sam Sparks stated that Busti, "Although reasonable in his claims—failed to muster enough evidence to support the "prior access" requirement for factual copying and lacked suitable evidence showing a "striking similarity" between his 1995 comic book "Cowboys and Aliens" and two subsequent works of the same name owned by the Studios." Additionally, the Judge said the Studios produced evidence that showed "an independent creation" of the later material.

"Black Amazon of Mars" [Pulp fiction; SW]

Author: **Leigh Brackett**; First publication: *Planet Stories* (March 1951); Publisher: Love Romances, Inc.

Eric John Stark is entrusted with a stolen holy talisman that guards the Gates of Death in the city of Kushat. But when Stark is captured by the mysterious masked and armored Ciaran, he learns of plans by the clans of Mekh to attack Kushat. Stark escapes to warn the Kushat leaders but his words go unheeded and Kushat falls to Ciaran and the Mekh. Stark unmasks Ciaran and discovers her to be a beautiful red-haired woman otherwise known as the Black Amazon.

The Gates of Hell are seen as the town's salvation until Stark discovers that evil creatures lurk beyond the gates. The talisman can destroy the creatures but at great risk to Stark.

The story was revised and expanded into the novel ***People of the Talisman*** in 1964.

See: **"Queen of the Martian Catacombs"**

Black, Bill (1943–) [Comic book artist, writer, editor, publisher]

Born in Tarentum, Pennsylvania, Bill Black is a graduate of Florida State University. From 1964 to 1966 he was associate editor of *Charlatan* magazine, a renegade college humor publication. Black worked as an artist for James Warren's *Creepy* and *Eerie* comic book magazines in 1969 and at Marvel Comics in the late 1970s. He also worked for Charlton Comics where he provided cover artwork for *Billy the Kid* and *Gunfighters*, and interior art for *Nightshade*. In the 1990s Black worked for several comic book publishers, including an eight-year run on *Star Wars* at Dark Horse.

Black's desire to be in control of his creations led to the forming of Paragon in 1969, followed by Americomics (later AC Comics) in 1982. AC Comics gave Black an outlet to keep his favorite Western strips from Magazine Enterprises alive after he obtained permission to reprint their entire output including *Best of the West* (71 issues), *The Durango Kid*, **Red Mask**, **Haunted Horseman (Ghost Rider)**, **Presto Kid**, *B-Bar-B Riders* and *Tim Holt*. Other Western titles published by AC Comics included *Roy Rogers*, *Tom Mix*, **Lash LaRue**, *Bob Steele*, *Great American Western*, *TV Western*, *Blazing Western* and *Western Movie Heroes*.

Black also created new strips and characters for AC Comics with **Femforce**, *Paragon*, *Nightveil*, *Bolt*, *Sentinels of Justice*, *Black Diamond*, *Scarlet Scorpion*, *Commando D* and *Fighting Yank*. In total Black has created over 130 comic book titles. He incorporated ME Western characters such as **Black Phantom** into the female superhero comic book *Femforce* and updated her character by introducing supernatural elements. He is currently producing and directing live-action films based on his comic book creations *Nightveil*, *Blue Bulleteer* and *Garganta*.

Black Bison [Comic Book character; WW]

First appearance: *Fury of Firestorm* #1 (June 1982); Creators: Gerry Conway, Pat Broderick; Publisher: DC Comics

The spirit of Bison-Black-as-Midnight-Sky, former shaman of the Bison Cult tribe, possesses the body of Black-Cloud-in-Morning a.k.a. John Ravenhair through a mystic talisman worn around his neck. The talisman used in unison with a wooden coup stick allows Black Bison to control the weather and animate stuffed animals and objects.

Black Blaze [Comic book character; SW]

"Cowgirls in Space"

First publication: *Star Fems* #2 (1982); Story: **Bill Black**; Art: Paul Gulacy; Publisher: Paragon Publications.

Blaze Brand alias Black Blaze is a descendant of Steve Brand alias *The Durango Kid*. The colonization of planets is the new frontier for these cowgirls in space as they combat the natives and seek to expand their version of civilization.

The Black Circle: Unholy Alliance [RPG Book; WW]

Author: John Goff; First publication: 2000; Game: *Deadlands: The Weird West*; Publisher: Pinnacle Entertainment Group.

Plot and background book to Weird West villains Black River, Bayou Vermillion, the Whateleys and their organizations plus an introduction to **the Cackler**.

Black Crow [Comic book character; WW]

First appearance: *Captain America* #292 (April 1984); Creators: J.M. DeMatteis, Paul Neary; Publisher: Marvel Comics.

Navajo Indian Jesse Black Crow, paralyzed after an accident on a construction site, was visited in the hospital by the Earth spirit and transformed into an Indian warrior. Remaining crippled and confined to a wheelchair as Jesse Black Crow, he assumes superhuman strength as Black Crow the warrior. He also has the ability to metamorphose into a black crow, a bolt of lightning or mist, travel to ancestral dimensions, create visions and engage in magic and mysticism.

Black Hills [Novel; WW]

Author: Dan Simmons; First Publication: New York: Reagan Arthur Books, 2010.

In June 1876 on the bloody battlefield of the Little Big Horn 10-year-old Lakota Sioux warrior Paha Sapa is possessed by the spirit of General George Armstrong Custer. Paha Sapa is not only haunted by Custer's spirit, who speaks through him, but also by his ability to see into both the past and the future of men such as Sioux warchief Crazy Horse by simply touching them.

Simmon's novel spans decades, culminating in

the construction of Mount Rushmore in 1936. Paha Sapa signs on as a powder man to the blasting crew with the intention of stopping the desecration to the mountain sacred to the Lakota tribe.

Black Noon (1971) [Telefilm; WW]

Premiere: November 5, 1971; Main Cast: Roy Thinnes as the Rev. John Keyes, Lynn Loring as Lorna Keyes; Yvette Mimieux as Deliverance, Ray Milland as Caleb Hobbs, Gloria Grahame as Bethia; Producer-Story: Andrew J. Fenady; Director: Bernard L. Kowalski; 74 min.; Andrew J. Fenady Productions, Screen Gems Television; Color.

An Old West preacher (Thinnes) and his wife (Loring) are offered refuge in a small town after they become stranded in the desert. But unknown to the reverend, the townspeople are devil worshippers who are practicing voodoo on his wife.

Black Panther [Comic book]

"SADDLES ABLAZE" [SFW]

First publication: #46–47 (October-November 2002); Story: Christopher Priest Art: Jorge Lucas; Publisher: Marvel Comics.

Black Noon (1971), a telefilm starring Roy Thinnes and Lyn Loring (Andrew J. Fenady Productions, Screen Gems Television).

Bizarre time-travel adventure set in the Old West town of Buzzard Gulch featuring Black Panther, Loki, *Thor*, *Kid Colt*, *Two-Gun Kid* and *Rawhide Kid*. In the climax in Asgard, the cowboys do battle with trolls.

The story is a continuation of *Thor* #370 which was also set in the Old West town of Buzzard Gulch but didn't feature Kid Colt, Two-Gun Kid or Rawhide Kid.

Black Phantom [Comic book character; WW]

First appearance: *Tim Holt* #25 (September 1951); Creators: Ray Krank, Frank Bolle; Publishers: Magazine Enterprises, AC Comics.

Masked female partner of Tim Holt's **Red Mask**. She was given her own title in November 1954. In her original Magazine Enterprise adventures she was a standard Western outlaw-turned-good with fighting and gun skills but no supernatural powers.

When **Bill Black** resurrected the character for his AC Comics line, he reprinted her Magazine Enterprise strips before incorporating her in *Femforce* and making her a true phantom.

The Black Range; or, Frank Reade Jr. Among the Cowboys with His New Electric Caravan [Dime Novel; SPW]

Author: "Noname" (**Luis Senarens**); *Frank Reade Library Vol. III* #68 (January 6, 1894)

Black Rider [Comic book character; comic book]

First appearance: *All Western Winners* #2 (Winter 1948); Art: Syd Shores; Publisher: Atlas Comics.

When the infamous Cactus Kid kills the Luke Davis Gang who were holding the town of Jezebel, Texas, hostage, he is granted a pardon for his past crimes. Matthew Masters turns to a peaceful life as a doctor but when one of his patients, foreman Charlie Maddock, is murdered, he is branded a coward for doing nothing to prevent it. Masters decides to adopt the persona of the Black Rider to

Black Phantom in *Femforce* #69 (1994), "Chasing Phantoms," page 1. Story by Bill Black, art by Dick Ayers and Mark Heike. © 2009 AC Comics/Nightveil Media, Inc. Used with permission.

combat evil with the help of his steed Satan. Black Rider was occasionally featured in Weird Western stories.

"The Mystery of the Valley of the Giants" [WW]

First publication: *Black Rider* #8 (March 1950); Art: **John Severin**.

Professor Chalis' invention is capable of turning men into giants and of shrinking cattle.

"The Town That Vanished" [WW]

First publication: *Black Rider* #12 (January 1951); Art: Al Hartley.

A Spanish colonial town reappears through a rift in time populated by Spanish Conquistadors from an earlier era.

"The Spider Strikes!" [WW]

First publication: *Black Rider* #27 (March 1955); Art: Syd Shores.

An "immortal" insane killer named The Spider apparently rises from the grave only to die in flames.

"The Spider Returns" [WMW]

First publication: **Western Tales of Black Rider** #28 (May 1955); Art: Syd Shores; Publisher: Atlas Comics.

The Spider returns from the grave once again only to meet death for the second time at the hands of the Black Rider.

This issue featured a toned-down version of The Spider from his previous appearance due to the newly formed Comics Code Authority's required stamp of approval.

"Specter of Doom" [WMW]

First publication: **Wild Western** #37 (October 1954); Art: Al Hartley; Publisher: Atlas Comics.

Mad Dog Murdock returns from the dead as a glowing specter complete with mask and cape. But it's all down to a can of phosphorous paint.

See: **Strange Westerns Starring the Black Rider**

"Black Thirst" [Pulp fiction; SW]

Author: **C. L. Moore**; First publication; *Weird Tales* (April 1934).

An attractive Minga girl named Vaudir leads **Northwest Smith** into a world where the Alendar feeds on the beauty of women.

Northwest Smith falls prey again to a beautiful young woman leading him astray.

Blackbow the Cheyenne [Comic book character; UK; WW]

First appearance: *Swift* (1961); Creator: Edward Holmes; Story: Edward Cowan; Art: Frank Humphris; Don Lawrence; Publisher: Hulton Press.

Raised by Cheyenne chief Grey Cloud, Blackbow eventually settled in Powder Creek where he was taken under the care of Dr. Tad Barnaby. Adopting the name of Jim Barnaby, he began to practice medicine while secretly trying to maintain law and order as Blackbow, the last of the Cheyenne warriors.

Weird Western elements were introduced into the storylines as the series progressed, including a plot involving an evil "Master Plant" on the rampage in the Old West.

Blackbow was based on the 1953 strip "Strongbow the Mowhawk" featured in *Comet* comic. Each character had the same alter-ego and backstory but the setting was moved forward from the frontier period to the Old West.

Blackfoot Braves Society: Spirit Totems [Children's book; WW]

Author: Christopher E. Long; Illustrator: Michael Geiger; First publication: Boston: Komikwerks, 2006.

Privileged youngster Jackson Brady makes two new friends at the Blackfoot Braves Society Summer Camp. On a treasure map hike, the three take refuge from a storm in a cave and encounter a Ghost Shaman who teaches them to harness their animal spirits to fight hostile supernatural forces.

Blazin' Barrels [Manwha; Korea; SFW]

First publication: June 2005; Creator: Min-Seo Park; Publisher: Tokyo Pop

In a futuristic Wild West, Sting hunts down the all-girl outlaw gang, Gold Romany.

Blood [Video Game; SFW]

Release date: 1997; Voice Cast: Stephan Weyte as Caleb, Jason Hall as The Voice; Executive producer: Jace Hall; Perspective: First-Person; Developer: Monolith Productions, Inc.; Platform: DOS; Publisher: GT Interactive Software Corp.

Resurrected Old West gunslinger Caleb is out for revenge on the dark god Tchernobog and his minions who betrayed his cult "The Chosen."

This excessively violent and gory first-person shooter was originally divided into four episodes. Two extra episodes were released in 1997.

1: The Way of All Flesh (8 levels); 2: Even

Death May Die (9 levels); 3: Farewell to Arms (8 levels); 4: Dead Reckoning (9 levels); 5: Post Mortem (9 levels); Cryptic Passage (10 levels).

Blood and Shadows [Comic book; WW]

First appearance: January 1996; Story: **Joe R. Lansdale**; Art: Mark A. Nelson; Four-issue mini-series; Publisher: Vertigo

East Texas Shamus Chet Daly tracks the demon god of the Razor to his lair and faces his own demons as he unearths secrets from the past and the future.

Blood Drive I: Bad Times on the Goodnight [RPG book; WW]

First publication: 2012; Story: Matthew Cutter, John Goff, Piotr Korys; Art: Thomasz Tworek; Setting: *Deadlands Reloaded;* Publisher: Pinnacle Entertainment Group.

Three-part adventure series that spans one of the longest and most dangerous cattle drives in the Weird West covering two countries, border raiders, major railroads, a land ravaged by the Reckoning and the war parties of the Sioux Nations.

Followed by *Blood Drive II: High Plains Drovers* and *Blood Drive III: Range War!*

Blood Meridian or The Evening Redness in the West [Novel; WW]

Author: **Cormac McCarthy**; First publication: New York: Random House, 1985.

The story of the Glanton Gang, Judge Holden and a fourteen-year-old runaway known as "the kid" as they journey through a nightmarish landscape of violence and horror in the Texas-Mexico borderlands of 1851.

> The men as they rode turned black in the sun from the blood on their clothes and their faces and then paled slowly in the rising dust until they assumed once more the color of the land through which they passed.

Blood Riders [Novel; WW]

Author: Michael P. Spradlin; First publication: New York: Harper Voyager, 2012.

Civil War veteran and former U.S. Cavalry Captain Jonas R. Hollister joins forces with detective Allan Pinkerton, gunsmith Oliver Winchester and European Abraham Van Helsing, among other posse members, as they hunt down "nonhuman, blood-drinking demons" who slaughtered eleven soldiers under Hollister's command.

Blood Rules (A Novel of the Bloodlands #2) [Novel; SFW]

Author: Christine Cody; First publication: New York: Ace Books, 2011.

Mariah Lyander is a were who in desperation to find a cure for her condition crosses the perilous haunted land. Gabriel accompanies Mariah on her journey to a place where monsters are born instead of cured.

This second book in the *Bloodlands* trilogy was followed by *In Blood We Trust*.

Blood Trail (1997) [Film; WW]

Premiere: 1997; Main Cast: Adrian Pasdar as Chase Leonard, Raoul Trujillo as Bloody Hands Spirit, Barry Tubb as Need Hawks, R.J. Preston as Ben Logan; Story: R. J. Preston, Barry Tubb; Producer-Director: Barry Tubb; 81 min.; Color.

Supernatural Western about a group of cowboys possessed by evil spirits after they lay claim to a sacred Indian burial ground.

Blood II: The Chosen [Video Game; SFW]

Release date: October 1998; Voice Cast: Stephan Weyte as Caleb, Jason Hall as The Voice, Lani Minella as Ophelia/Gabriella, Mike Shapiro as Ishmael, Ted D'Arms as Gideon; Perspective: Concept: Jay Wilson; Executive producer: Jace Hall; First-Person; Developer: Monolith Productions, Inc.; Platform: PC, Windows; Publisher: GT Interactive Software Corp.

Sequel to *Blood* set in 2028, featuring the undead gunslinger Caleb who (together with Chosen members Ophelia, Ishmael and Gabriella) attempts to regain leadership of the Cabal which has morphed into a global mega-corporation.

The game is divided into four chapters and includes the extreme graphic violence of its predecessor.

Bloodlands (A Novel of the Bloodlands #1) [Novel; SFW]

Author: Christine Cody; First publication: New York: Ace Books, 2011.

When terrible events create a deadly dangerous society, Mariah Lyander retreats to the western New Badlands to escape the urban terrors. She finds underground shelter in a small community with her genetically engineered dog Chaplin by her side. Mariah forms a relationship with Gabriel when she offers him refuge, but both hide terrible secrets. Gabriel is a vampire seeking his beloved Abby, and Mariah is a were responsible for the death of the woman he loves. Meanwhile Johnson Stamp is tracking down vampires and weres for the kill.

Author Christine Cody stated: "I conceived this series while on a Western movie binge. I thought, 'What if the typical gunslinger who had lost his humanity was actually a guy who slings fangs, not bullets? And what if he had literally lost that humanity because he's a vampire?' Hence, you have what starts out in book one as a paranormal Shane meets Mad Max—an action-adventure futuristic Western with a strong romance at its core."

Bloodlands was praised by *Publisher's Weekly,* which stated it "effectively merges science fiction, horror and the classic western." This first book in the trilogy was followed by *Blood Rules.*

BloodRayne II: Deliverance (2007) [Film; Canada/Germany; WW]

Premiere: September 18, 2007; Main Cast: Natassia Malthe as Rayne, Zack Ward as Billy the Kid, Michael Paré as Pat Garrett; Producers: Dan Clarke, Shawn Williamson; Screenplay: Christopher Donaldson, Neil Every; Story: Masaji Takei; Director: Uwe Boll; 99 min.; Brightlight Pictures; Color.

Billy the Kid and his vampire gang terrorize the town of Deliverance until female vampire hunter Rayne arrives. This poor vampire Western based on the video game character was released direct to video.

Bloodstone: A Jon Shannow Adventure [Novel; SW]

Author: **David Gemmell**; First publication: New York: Random House, 1994.

When a church is razed and its congregation slaughtered, the **Jerusalem Man** returns after an absence of twenty years to fight the evil Deacon and his Jerusalem Riders. But a deadlier foe awaits in another universe.

See: *The Last Guardian*

Bloodsuckers (2005) [Telefilm; Canada; SW]

Air date: July 30, 2005; Main Cast: Joe Lando as Captain Nicholas Churchill, Natassia Malthe as Quintana, Dominic Zamprogna as Damian Underwood, A.J. Cook as Fiona, Aaron Pearl as Roman, Michael DeLuise as Gilles, Michael Ironside as Muco; Story-Director: Matthew Hastings; 99 min.;

Daniel Grodnick Productions, Kandu Entertainment; Color.

In the year 2210, vampires roam the galaxy. Anti-vampire sanitation teams are assigned to put an end to the menace. The Hieronymus Unit comprises of Captain Nicholas Churchill, half-human, half-vampire psychic Quintana, and second-in-command Damian Underwood. But vampire captain, Muco has set a trap for the Hieronymus crew that threatens the future of the galaxy.

Aaron Pearl plays space-cowboy Roman in a graphically violent film that shows influences of writer-director Joss Whedon's *Firefly.* Discussing the film in a promotional featurette, actor Joe Lando declared, "It's like the Old West where around every corner there's something new and dangerous and exciting."

Bloody Ol' Muddy [RPG Book; WW]

Author: Lee Garvin; First publication: 1999; Game: *Deadlands: The Weird West*; Publisher: Pinnacle Entertainment Group.

Strange events are occurring on the Mississippi with mysterious mounds stirring to life.

Blue Bolt Weird Tales of Terror [Comic book]

"THE THING IN THE PIT" [WW]

First publication: #117 (February 1953); Story-Art: Jay Disbrow; Publisher: Star Publications.

An ancient Indian curse brings to life a creature of darkness, evil and total destruction.

Blueberry: L'Expérience Secrète (2004) [Film; France; WW]

Premiere: February 11, 2004; Main Cast: Vincent Cassel as Mike Blueberry, Juliette Lewis as Maria Sullivan, Michael Madsen as Wallace Sebastian Blount, Ernest Borgnine as Rolling Star; Executive Producer: Jean-Michel Lacor; Story: Matt Alexander, Gérard Brach; Director: Jan Kounen; 124 min.; Columbia TriStar (U.S.); Color.

Marshal Mike Blueberry encounters the man who murdered his first love in a search for hidden gold in sacred Indian tribal lands.

Shamanism, mysticism and ancient spirits play a part in an often confused tale that is very loosely based on the comic book series by Jean "Moebius" Giraud and Jean-Michael Charlier.

Director Jan Kounen explained (*The Guardian,* July, 20 2004): "I spent several months with shamans in the Amazon forest. I made more than

100 inner journeys thanks to their visionary plants. Making that feature film, I again met the shamans who have come to play themselves in this strange western where visions link two cultures. So is the film an initiatory western? A mystical western? A science fiction movie that takes place in the west? All three, I guess, and I admit that I am happy that I can't pigeonhole it. For it is above all a voyage. A voyage where the 'other world' is offered up for the traveler's delight."

Jamie Russell, writing for *BBC.co.uk* (July 12, 2004) stated: "The finale owes more to Tron or The Lawnmower Man than any western John Ford would recognize, with Blueberry sucking down some hardcore hallucinogens to battle his nemesis in the dream world. As centipedes, insect larvae, beetles, snakes and scorpions morph into a psychedelic head-trip of CGI graphics, this is one movie that should definitely not be ingested without medical supervision."

See: *Renegade*

Bobby Benson and the B-Bar-B Riders
[Radio show; TV series; WMW]

1. First broadcast: October 17, 1932; Main Cast: Richard Wanamaker as Bobby (Season One), Billy Halop as Bobby (Season Two), Herb Rice as Buck Mason (Season One), Wong Lee, Florence Halop as Polly, Craig McDonnell as Harka, Fred Dampier, Lorraine Pankow; Creator-Director: Herbert C. Rice; Stories: Herbert C. Rice, Peter Dixon; 700 (approx.) × 15 min; Broadcaster: CBS.

The children's radio show about an orphan boy nicknamed "The Cowboy Kid" who inherits a ranch in Texas was originally broadcast on CBS as *The H-Bar-O Rangers*. It began in October 1932, with the first season consisting of 78 fifteen-minute episodes. When the final story aired in December 1936, the show had broadcast over 700 episodes. None have survived to the present day.

The H-Bar-O ranch had originally been based on the sponsor Heckers H-O Cereals. Original creator Rice changed the ranch name to "Bar-B-B" when the cereal sponsorship was cancelled in 1936.

2. First broadcast: November 25, 1949; Main Cast: Ivan Cury as Bobby Benson (1949–1951), Clyde Campbell [Clive Rice] as Bobby Benson (1951), Charles Irving as Tex Mason (1949–1951), Bob Haig as Tex Mason (1951); Don Knotts as Windy Wales, Craig McDonnell as Irish/Harka, Jim Bowles, Athena Lord, Ross Martin, Bill Zuckert, Earl George, Gil Mack; Stories: Jim Shean, Peter Dixon; Producer: Herbert C. Rice; Director: Bob Novak; 350 (approx.) × 30 min; Broadcaster: CBS.

The show was re-launched in 1949. The B-Bar-B riders Irish, Harka, Waco and Windy Wales, foreman Tex Mason and Bobby Benson were featured in Weird Menace storylines including "Ghost Rider" and "The Headless Horseman." A genuine Weird Western adventure broadcast ("The Face of Jebaco," June 8, 1953) involved Bobby Benson, Tex, the Riders and Harka's Indian tribe in a life-threatening encounter with a giant demonic creature known as Jebaco.

Only 17 episodes of the 30-minute series have survived. One episode of an Australian version from 1953 has survived; titled "The Ghost Rustlers," it recounts how Bobby Benson inherited the Texas ranch.

3. A series of five-minute radio shows was produced in 1952 featuring Clyde Campbell [Clive Rice] as Bobby Benson and country & western singer Tex Fletcher. Each singing a song while Windy Wales (Don Knotts) told a short story.

4. Members of the radio cast appeared in two television shows based on the radio show. Ivan Cury starred as Bobby Benson in a live 30-minute show produced by WOR-TV at the New Amsterdam Theater and Channel 9 Studio.

The second series from the 1950s featured a greatly reduced cast consisting of only Clyde Campbell [Clive Rice] as Bobby Benson alongside singer Tex Fletcher and comedian Paul Brown.

Bobby Benson's B-Bar-B Riders [Comic book; WW]

First issue: May-June 1950; Publisher: Magazine Enterprises, Parkway Publishing Company.

The comic book adaptation of the radio series soon included Weird Western themes as the **Lemonade Kid** became involved in storylines involving a spider-man and giant insects. Dick Ayers' **Ghost Rider** joined the comic book starting with issue #13.

"HEADHUNTER OF PIRATE'S PEAK" [WW]

First publication: #14 (1952); Art: **Dick Ayers**; Publisher: Magazine Enterprises.

This classic Weird Western, involving a madman decapitating his victims and stealing their heads, features cover and interior art by Dick Ayers.

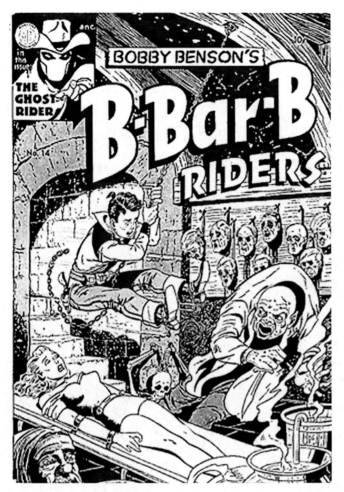

Cover of *Bobby Benson's B-Bar-B Riders* #14 (1952). Cover art by Dick Ayers. © 2009 AC Comics/Nightveil Media, Inc. Used with permission.

Bodas de fuego (1949) [Film; Mexico; WW]

Premiere: April 24, 1951; Main Cast: Pedro Armendáriz as Rodolfo Carrera, Alicia Caro as Leonor Corrientes, Ramón Gay as Federico Losada, Alicia Grau as Marta, José Elías Moreno as Don Antonio, Alejandro Cobo as Dr. Mijares; Producer: César Santos Galindo; Story-Director Marco Aurelio Galindo; 87 min.; Cinematográfica Azteca; b/w.

While a young girl recuperates at her uncle's hacienda with her boyfriend, she meets and falls in love with the enigmatic Rodolfo. Rodolfo's insane mother believes her son is a "beast" who may be responsible for the deaths of animals on the ranch.

Despite her love for Rodolfo, Leonor decides to marry her boyfriend. A jealous and passionate

Rodolfo takes her to his mountain cabin but her poor health and the stress results in her death. Rodolfo sets the cabin alight and willingly perishes in the fire.

Thirty years later the fire refuses to be extinguished and continues to burn as a symbol of their everlasting love and passion.

The Boise Horror [RPG Book; WW]

Author: John Goff; Game: *Deadlands: Hell on Earth*; Publisher: Pinnacle Entertainment Group.

Boise, Idaho, the home of the Templars, is at the mercy of the monster known as the Boise Horror. The posse must stop the creature before it claims further victims and undermines faith in the Templars.

Bonanza (1959) [TV series]

Main Cast: Lorne Greene as Ben Cartwright, Pernell Roberts as Adam Cartwright, Michael Landon as Joseph "Little Joe" Cartwright, Dan Blocker as Eric "Hoss" Cartwright.

1. Adventures of the Cartwright family and life on the Ponderosa Ranch.

"DARK STAR" (1:31) [WMW]

Premiere: April 23, 1960; Guest Cast: Susan Harrison as Tirza, Hugo Haas as Zirko, Lili Valenty as Bruja, Arthur Batanides as Spiro; Producer: David Dortort; Story: Michael Lawrence; Director: Lewis Allen; 60 min.; NBC; Color.

A gypsy girl (Susan Harrison) is shunned by her people who believe she is a witch who can turn herself into a wolf. The young woman is led to believe the devil is in her after being born under a "dark star." Little Joe is attracted to the dark-haired beauty but once again finds himself spurned in love as she undergoes a ritual journey through the underworld to purify her soul. Ben Cartwright concludes, "Sometimes it's possible to see the devil when you're looking for the devil."

"THE SAVAGE" (2:12) [WMW]

Premiere: December 3, 1960; Guest Cast: Anna-Lisa as Ruth Halvorsen/White Buffalo Woman, Hal

Jon Norman as Chief Chato, Victor Millan as Dako; Producer: David Dortort; Story: Joe Stone, Paul King; Director: James Neilson; 60 min.; NBC; Color.

The Shoshone think a Norwegian woman is the White Buffalo Woman or Spirit Woman who lives on the Mountain of the Dead and has supernatural healing powers. The woman nurses a wounded Adam Cartwright back to health after he is attacked by the Shoshone. Adam is fascinated by the mysterious and beautiful Ruth Halvorsen and they fall in love. But she is captured by the Shoshone and threatened into helping them cure their sickness. They are convinced she is the reincarnation of one of their gods. "Only she can save our people from the great sickness." Realizing the responsibility of her spiritual status she feels an obligation to help them. Adam has to accept the loss of the woman who had agreed to be his wife.

"Twilight Town" (5:04) [WW]

Premiere: October 13, 1963; Guest Cast: Davey Davison as Louise Corman, Stacy Harris as Mr. Corman, Doris Dowling as Katie O'Brien, Walter Coy as Masterson; Producer: David Dortort; Story: Cy Chermak; Director: John Florea; 60 min.; NBC; Color.

Ambushed in the desert, Little Joe Cartwright awakens in the bizarre town of Martinville and is asked to take the job of sheriff and stop local gunslinger Felix Matthews (Michael Milker). The cowardly nature of the townsfolk drives Little Joe to anger as he attempts to motivate them to protect themselves. But their actions begin to make sense when he learns of a curse that hangs over the town and its people. An interesting rare excursion into the Weird West for Little Joe Cartwright.

"Hoss and the Leprechauns" (5:12) [WW]

Premiere: December 22, 1963; Guest Cast: Sean McClory as Professor James Aloysius McCarthy, Roger Arroya as Bobby, Frank Delfino as Timothy, Clegg Hoyt as Dorsel; Producer: David Dortort; Story: Robert Barron; Director: John Florea; 60 min.; NBC; Color.

Hoss is convinced he's on the trail of leprechauns after finding their hoard of buried gold dust. A comedy episode that touches on the weird.

2. [Comic book]

"A Ghost Town Speaks" [Text story; WW]

First published: *Bonanza* #9 (August 1964): Publisher: Gold Key.

An interesting one-page story of a Ghost Town personified through the thoughts of a ghost.

"The Witch's Curse" [Comic strip; WMW]

First published: *Bonanza* #21 (August 1966): Publisher: Gold Key.

A woman is accused of being a witch and placing a curse on a wagon train's oxen. But the Cartwrights realize the cattle are suffering from anthrax and placing other cattle in greater danger than any witch's curse ever could.

The Bone Orchard [Novella; WW]

Author: Abigail Roux; First publication: Hillisborough, N.J.: Riptide Publishing, 2014.

U.S. Marshal Ambrose Shaw finally catches up with vicious murderer "Missouri" Boone Jennings in San Francisco. Pinkerton inspector Ezra Johns testifies to Jennings' crimes at the trial and Jennings is found guilty and hanged. But he is far from finished and continues his killing spree from beyond the grave as a romance between Ambrose Shaw and Boone Jennings flourishes.

Bone Wars [Novel; SFW]

Author: Brett Davis; First publication: Riverdale, NY: Baen, 1998

Competing paleontologists dig Montana fossil beds in 1876 with little success but elsewhere a foreign bone digger has uncovered dinosaur bones that he wants taken off the planet. Aliens and Sitting Bull add to the science fiction Western mix.

Based on real-life paleontologists Edward Drinker Cope and Othniel Charles Marsh.

See: *Two Tiny Claws*

Bonelli, Giovanni Luigi (1908–2001) [Comic book writer-publisher; Italy]

Born in Milan, Italy, Bonelli is one of the most influential figures in Italian comics history. His first published work in 1926 was followed by employment at Editrice Vecchi S. A. in the 1930s. In 1939 he became publisher of *L'Audace* and created his most popular and enduring creation, **Tex Willer**, in 1948. His son Sergio eventually took over duties of his publishing house Bonelli which has been responsible for many Western "fumetto" series.

Selected works: *Il Giustiziere Del West* (1947), *Occhio Cupo* (1948), *Tex Willer* (1948), *Plutos*

(1949), *I Tre Bill* (1952), **Yuma Kid** (1953), *El Kid* (1956), *Hondo* (1956), *Kociss* (1957), **Yado** (1957).

Bonelli, Sergio (1932–2011) [Comic book writer-publisher; Italy]

Sergio Bonelli was the son of Giovanni Luigi Bonelli, the creator of **Tex Willer**. Under the pseudonym Guido Nolitta, Bonelli wrote many Tex Willer stories from #183 on and co-created **Zagor** with artist Gallieno Ferri.

Book o' the Dead [RPG Book; WW]

Author: Lester W. Smith; First publication: 1997; Game: **Deadlands: The Weird West**; Publisher: Pinnacle Entertainment Group; Archetype series.

The secrets of the undead Harrowed and the evil manitou who control them are revealed in this sourcebook. Includes the Harrowed adventure "The Dark Canyon."

The Book of Eli (2010) [Film; SFW]

Premiere: January 15. 2010; Main Cast: Denzel Washington as Eli. Gary Oldman as Carnegie, Mila Kunis as Solara, Ray Stevenson as Redridge, Jennifer Beals as Claudia, Evan Jones as Martz, Joe Pingue as Hoyt, Frances De La Tour as Martha, Michael Gambon as George, Tom Waits as Engineer; Executive producers: Susan Downey, Ethan Erwin, Erik Olsen, Steve Richards; Story: Gary Whitta; Directors: The Hughes Brothers; Alcon Entertainment, 118 min.; Silver Pictures, Warner Bros.; Color.

In a post-apocalyptic America, drifter Eli hears a voice telling him to journey across the wastelands to the West with the last copy of a treasured book in existence. Despot Carnegie rules a village Eli comes across on his travels and impresses Carnegie with his fighting skills. Offering Solara, the daughter of blind mother Claudia as tempting bait to persuade Eli to stay, he refuses the girl's advances and walks out of the village. Solara follows, intrigued by the mysterious book and the moral strength and single-minded vision of Eli.

Carnegie and his gang pursue Eli and the woman across the desolate landscape. Carnegie wants the book for the power it will grant him and a gang members desires the woman. Eli feels almost mystically protected whilst the book is in his possession but a meeting with two humans named Martha and George who have resorted to cannibalism to survive ultimately proves to be a turning point. Eli and the woman find themselves trapped in the couple's dilapidated house surrounded by Carnegie and his gang.

The Hughes Brothers pay homage to the Spaghetti Western influences with a gang member humming the music of Ennio Morricone.

A Book of Tongues (Hexslinger Book #1) [Novel; WW]

Author: Gemma Files; First Publication: Toronto: ChiZine Publications, 2010.

Pinkerton detective Ed Murrow infiltrates a gang led by former Confederate chaplain the Reverend Asher Elijah Rook—a spell-casting preacher known as a hexslinger. But when Rook is seduced by the Aztec goddess Ixchel, his lover, sharp-shooter Chess Pargeter, is placed in mortal danger.

Boomtowns! [RPG Book; WW]

Authors: John Goff, Tony Lee, Lisa Smedman and Joseph Wolf, with Hal Mangold; First publication: 1999; Game: **Deadlands: The Weird West**; Publisher: Pinnacle Entertainment Group.

Guide for creating Boomtowns in the Weird West complete with miniature scale maps.

Boos and Arrows (1954) [Animated short feature; WW]

Premiere: October 15, 1954; Story: Izzy Klein; Animation: Myron Waldman, Gordon Whittier; Director: Seymour Kneitel; 6 min.; Famous Studios, Harvey Films Inc., Paramount Studios.

Casper the Friendly Ghost befriends young Little Feather but frightens the Indian tribe who later name him Little White Cloud when he saves a baby from a vulture.

Boos and Saddles (1953) [Animated short feature; WW]

Premiere: December 25, 1953; Story: Larz Bourne; Animation: Myron Waldman, Larry Silverman; Director: Isadore Sparber; 6 min.; Famous Studios, Harvey Films Inc., Paramount Studios.

Casper the Friendly Ghost enters Gun Gulch Saloon and spooks the local cowboys before making friends with the young Billy the Kid. Casper becomes sheriff of Gun Gulch after scaring outlaw Desert Dan out of his boots and into jail.

Border Phantom (1937) [Film; WMW]

Premiere: June 7, 1937; Main Cast: Bob Steele as Larry O'Day, Harley Wood as Barbara Hartwell, Don Barclay as Lucky Smith, Karl Hackett as Obed

Young; Story: Fred Myton; Producer: A.W. Hackel; Director; Roy S. Luby; 60 min.; Supreme Pictures, Republic Pictures; b/w.

With an ancient curse placed on a hacienda owned by Obed Young and shadows lurking in every corner, this Western about a woman (Wood) charged with the murder of her uncle occasionally ventures into horror Western themes.

Boris Karloff Tales of Mystery [Comic book]

Horror and mystery anthology title.

"Legend of the Totem" [WW]

First publication: #50 (October 1973); Story: Arnold Drake; Art: Jack Sparling; Publisher: Gold Key.

"Do you see the horned bear on the totem pole? It's alive and watching!"

Bounty Killer [Comic Book; WW]

First publication: May 2006; Story: Michael Westerman; Art: Erfan Fajar, Donny Hadiwidjaja; Publisher: Americanime Productions.

A mix of American and Manga styles with a hint of the supernatural in a Western featuring a bounty killer known as "BK" and his African sidekick.

Brackett, Leigh (1915–1978) [Author]

The "Queen of Space-Opera" was born in Los Angeles, California. Brackett's first short story, "**Martian Quest**," and her later **Eric John Stark** series (1949–1976) were clearly influenced by **Edgar Rice Burroughs** and the Western genre.

The year 1946 saw the publication of *Lorelei of the Red Mists*, a co-authored story with acclaimed science fantasy writer Ray Bradbury, and marriage to fellow science fiction author Edmond Hamilton. Brackett moved into film and television on a regular basis in the 1940s, contributing to various genres including Westerns, crime and suspense dramas (including work on Alfred Hitchcock's television series). Her final work before her death, the first draft for George Lucas' *The Empire Strikes Back*, won her a posthumous Hugo Award in 1981.

Selected screenplays: *The Vampire's Ghost* with John K. Butler (1945); *The Big Sleep* with William Faulkner and Jules Furthman (1946); *Rio Bravo* with Jules Furthman and B.H. McCampbell (1959); *Gold of the Seven Saints* with Leonard Freeman (1961); *Hatari!* with Harry Kurnitz (1962); *El Dorado* (1967); *Rio Lobo* with Burton Wohl (1970); *The Long Goodbye*, from Raymond Chandler's novel (1973); *The Empire Strikes Back* with Lawrence Kasdan (1979)

Brainburners [RPG Book; WW]

Author: Steve Long; First published: 1998; Game: *Deadlands: Hell on Earth*; Publisher: Pinnacle Entertainment Group.

Recovering from their time on Banshee, the mentally scarred Sykers seek some well-earned rest in the Wasted West. But the Brainburners have other ideas.

Brand, Max (1892–1944) [Pulp author]

Born Frederick Schiller Faust in Seattle, Washington, Max Brand wrote over 300 Western novels and short stories. His prolific career began as regular contributor to *All-Story Weekly* magazine. Under the pseudonym Max Brand he began writing Western fiction in 1918 and achieved early recognition for serialized stories and novels featuring Whistling Dan Barry, his stallion Satan and his wolf dog Black Bart. Although not specifically a Weird Western character, Whistlin' Dan has been described as "more feral than human." An observation verified by such Brand passages as, "the nameless thing which had been Whistling Dan before, sprang up and forward with a leap like that of a panther."

Brand's interest in psychological dramas found expression in stories that explored Weird Western themes. In "**The Garden of Eden**" (1922) Brand presents the reader with a mystical valley. In "'**Sunset' Wins**" (1923) a gunfighter's dreams are haunted by a mysterious girl and those he has killed. The inner journey of a perceived coward is explored in a spirit vision in "**The Werewolf**" (1926). "**The Bells of San Filipo**" (1926) has the ghost of a young nun haunting the grounds of the San Filipo church with its mysterious ringing bells. "**Twenty Notches**" (1932) features a gun perceived as magical by its owner and in "**Lucky Larribee**" (1932) the horse Sky Blue takes on an almost mystical presence.

Frederick Faust died prematurely from a shrapnel wound on May 12, 1944, while working as a war correspondent on the Italian front.

Brautigan, Richard (1935–1984) [Author]

Born in Tacoma, Washington, Richard Gary Brautigan wrote twelve novels in his relatively short lifetime. He is best remembered today for *Trout Fishing in America*. Writing to his agent Robert P. Millson on February 15, 1967 Brautigan stated:

> ... I'm plotting a Western novel that I will write this year, I've always wanted to write a Western and so that's what I'm going to do. I think it will be an interesting novel and I will be starting work on it soon....

The resulting novel was *The Hawkline Monster: A Gothic Western* which received mixed reviews.

On September 14, 1984, Brautigan borrowed a handgun from a friend at a Japanese restaurant in San Francisco. He had been drinking heavily throughout the afternoon after bumping into his former wife Akiko. That evening he returned home and shot himself. His body wasn't discovered until some days later.

Selected works: *A Confederate General from Big Sur* (1964), *Trout Fishing in America* (1967), *In Watermelon Sugar* (1968), *The Hawkline Monster* (1974), *Willard and His Bowling Trophies* (1975), *So the Wind Won't Blow It All Away* (1982).

Brave: The Search for Spirit Dancer [Video Game; WW]

Premiere: August 2007; Developer: Vis Entertainment; Publisher: Evolved Games; Platform: Play Station 2

Brave, a young shaman in training, begins his quest to find the legendary shaman Spirit Dancer before the demonic Wendigo completely destroys his Indian village and its people. On his quest, Brave encounters the Sasquatch, wolves, buffalo, a blizzard, river rapids and evil spirits.

BraveStarr (1987) [Animated TV series; SW]

Premiere: September 14, 1987; Voice cast: Pat Fraley as Marshal Brave Starr, Charles Adler as Deputy Fuzz/Tex Hex, Susan Blu as Judge J. B.; Producers: Norm Prescott, Lou Scheimer; 65 × 30 min.; Filmation Associates; Color.

A shaman bestows animal powers upon the young Native American BraveStarr: eyes of the hawk, ears of the wolf, strength of the bear and speed of the puma. After crashlanding on the frontier planet of "New Texas," BraveStarr grows to manhood and becomes the lone Marshal of New Texas. With the help of his sidekicks, robotic steed Thirty-Thirty, Deputy Fuzz, the beau-

tiful Judge J.B. and his advisor Shaman, BraveStarr maintains law and order in a constant battle with Tex Hex and the Carrion Bunch for the control of the valuable mineral Kerium.

This animated Space Western was the final TV series from Filmation Studios.

Season One

The Disappearance of Thirty-Thirty (1:01); *Fallen Idol* (1:02); *The Taking of Thistledown 123* (1:03); *Skuzz and Fuzz* (1:04); *A Day in the Life of a New Texas Judge* (1:05); *Rampage* (1:06); *To Walk a Mile* (1:07); *Big Thirty and Little Wimble* (1:08); *BraveStarr and the Law* (1:09); *Kerium Fever* (1:10); *Memories* (1:11); *Eyewitness* (1:12); *The Vigilantes* (1.13); *Wild Child* (1:14); *Hail, Hail, the Gang's All Here* (1:15); *Eye of the Beholder* (1:16); *The Wrong Hands* (1:17); *An Older Hand* (1:18); *Showdown at Sawtooth* (1:19); *Unsung Hero* (1:20); *Lost Mountain* (1:21); *Trouble Wears a Badge* (1:22); *Who Am I?* (1:23); *BraveStarr and the Treaty* (1:24); *Thoren the Slavemaster* (1:25); *The Price* (1:26); *Revolt of the Prairie People* (1:27); *Hostage* (1:28); *Tunnel of Terror* (1:29); *The Good, the Bad and the Clumsy* (1:30); *Balance of Power* (1:31); *Call to Arms* (1:32); *BraveStarr and the Three Suns* (1:33); *The Witnesses* (1:34); *Handlebar and Rampage* (1:35); *Runaway Planet* (1:36); *The Bounty Hunter* (1:37); *Buddy* (1:38); *The Day the Town Was Taken* (1:39); *BraveStarr and the Medallion* (1:40); *Legend of a Pretty Lady* (1:41); *Sunrise, Sunset* (1:42); *Call of the Wild* (1:43); *Tex But No Hex* (1:44); *Space Zoo* (1:45); *Tex's Terrible Night* (1:46); *Running Wild* (1:47); *Thirty-Thirty Goes Camping* (1:48); *The Haunted Shield* (1:49); *Ship of No Return* (1:50); *Little Lie That Grew* (1:51); *Brothers in Crime* (1:52); *Sherlock Holmes in the 23rd Century, Part 1* (1:53); *Sherlock Holmes in the 23rd Century, Part 2* (1:54); *New Texas Blues* (1:55); *Jeremiah and the Prairie People* (1:56); *The Ballad of Sara Jane* (1:57); *Brothers Keeper* (1:58); *BraveStarr and the Empress* (1:59); *Night of the Bronco-Tank* (1:60); *No Mad Is on Island* (1:61); *The Blockade* (1:62); *No Drums, No Trumpets* (1:63); *Shake Hands with Long Arm John* (1:64); *Strength of the Bear* (1:65)

BraveStarr: The Movie [Animated film; SW]

Premiere: March 18, 1988; Voice cast: Pat Fraley as Marshal Bravestarr/Thunder Stick; Charles Adler as Deputy Fuzz/Tex Hex, Susan Blu as Judge J. B.; Producer: Lou Scheimer; Story: Bob Forward, Steve Hayes; Director: Bob Tataranowicz; 91 min.; Filmation Associates; Color.

This theatrical sequel to **BraveStarr** the television series tells the story of the discovery of the mineral ore Kerium and the source of BraveStarr's conflict with Tex Hex and Stampede.

Brimstone [Comic book; WW]

First publication: May 2011; Story: Michael Lent, Brian McCarthy; Art: Hyunsang Michael Cho; Publisher: Zenescope.

A dying Indian Shaman unleashes an ancient curse upon his murderers, the miners of Brimstone and their gold stake. His curse appears to take almost immediate effect when Brimstone is overrun by fleshwalkers who leave behind a trail of dismembered corpses. A legendary sullen and callous gunslinger named the Viper leads a posse of outlaws, thieves and killers as they aim to retake Brimstone.

Broken Hearts [RPG; WW]

First publication: 2014; *Deadlands Tall Tales #1*; Protocol Game Series; Author: Jim Pinto; Art: Rick Hershey; Publisher: Pinnacle Entertainment Group.

The western town of Briar Gulch is under attack from fierce winds that threaten to destroy buildings and tombstones in the Boot Hill cemetery. But the winds aren't the result of a storm but are caused by the rage of star-crossed spirits. A story role-playing game set in **Deadlands: The Weird West**.

Bubba the Cowboy Prince: A Fractured Texas Tale [Children's book; WW]

Author: Helen Ketteman; First publication: New York: Scholastic Press, 1997; Illustrations: James Warhola; Juvenile.

A variation on *Cinderella* set in Texas where the fairy godmother is a cow, and cowboy hero Bubba is the stepson of a wicked rancher.

Bubba Ho-Tep (2002) [Film: WW]

Premiere: June 9, 2002; Main Cast: Bruce Campbell as Elvis Presley-Sebastian Huff, Ossie Davis as Jack, Ella Jhoyce as The Nurse, Heidi Marnhout as Callie, Bob Ivy as Bubba Ho-Tep; Executive producer: Dac Coscarelli; Screenplay: Don Coscarelli; Based on the short story by Joe R. Lansdale; Director: Don Coscarelli; 92 min.; Silver Sphere Corp., Vitagraph Films; Color.

Elvis Presley, who switched identities with an impersonator years before his death, is now an elderly resident in an East Texas nursing home. Elvis makes friends with a wheelchair bound African American who thinks he's John F. Kennedy. Together they battle an Egyptian soul-sucking mummy who wears a cowboy hat with a feather and cowboy boots in an offbeat story about redemption, courage and friendship.

Buckaroo Banzai [Comic book; SFW]

First publication: November 1984; Publisher: Marvel; Moonstone.

A two-part comic book adaptation of **The Adventures of Buckaroo Banzai Across the 8th Dimension**. The character was revived by Moonstone in February 2006 when a Preview Edition introduced an ongoing *Buckaroo Banzai* comic book series to a new generation.

Buckaroo Betty [Comic book character; WW]

First appearance: *Femforce* #20, 1989; Creators: **Bill Black**, Rik Levins, Billie Marimon; Publisher: AC Comics.

Sheriff Elizabeth "Betty" Fury alias Buckaroo Betty finds herself traveling through time from 1887 Texas to modern-day Wisconsin where she is revealed as the daughter of the **Haunted Horseman**. Following the death of her husband, Sheriff Mike Bates of Apache, Texas, Betty Bates reverted to her maiden name of Betty Fury. In later adventures Buckaroo Betty takes on the mantle of The Hood together with its supernatural powers.

Buford and the Galloping Ghost (1978) [Animated TV series]

Premiere: February 3, 1979; Executive Producers: Joseph Barbera and William Hanna; Producer: Art Scott; Directors: Ray Patterson, Carl Urbano; 30 min × 13 min.; Hanna Barbera Productions; Color.

Animated series containing two segments per episode: *The Buford Files* featuring a bloodhound and two crime-solving teenagers and *The Galloping Ghost*. The episodes were originally broadcast on **Yogi's Space Race** (1978).

Galloping Ghost segment: Voice Cast: Frank Welker as Nugget Nose, Hal Peary as Fenwick Fuddy, Marilyn Schreffler as Wendy, Pat Parris as Rita.

The Fuddy Dude Ranch is haunted by the ghost of gold prospector Nugget Nose and his invisible horse. Ranch hand Wendy summons Nugget Nose by rubbing on her gold nugget necklace.

Buckaroo Betty in *Best of the West #43*. Art by Ed Coutts. © 2009 AC Comics/Nightveil Media, Inc. Used with permission.

SEASON ONE [*GALLOPING GHOST* segments; WW]

Phantom of the Horse Opera (1:01); *Too Many Crooks* (1:02); *Sagebrush Sergeant* (1:03); *The Bad News Bear* (1:04); *Robot Round-Up* (1:05); *Pests in the West* (1:06); *Rock Star Nuggie* (1:07); *Frontier Fortune Teller* (1:08); *I Want My Mummy* (1:09); *Mr. Sunshine's Eclipse* (1:10); *Klondike's Kate* (1:11); *A Ghost of a Chance* (1:12); *Don't Elmo the Great* (1:13).

Bulls-Eye [Comic Book; WW]

First issue: July-August 1954; Creators: Joe Simon, Jack Kirby; Publisher: Mainline Publications-Charlton Comics

Bedraggled peddler Panhandle Pete is Bulls-Eye, an outlaw pursued by the law and renegade Indian chief Yellow Snake. The comic book entered Weird Western territory with the story "Devil Bird" in issue #3. The Devil Bird being a pterodactyl in Indian country.

The Buntline Special: A Weird Western Tale (Book #1) [Novel; WW]

Author: Mike Resnick; First Publication: New York: Pyr, 2010.

An alternate history tale set in 1881 where U.S. expansion beyond the Mississippi is stalled by Apache magic and the Indian wizard Hook Nose. Following an attempt on Thomas Alva Edison's life that resulted in Edison constructing a cyborg arm to replace his shattered arm he heads a mission to Tombstone, Arizona, working alongside Ned Buntline as they construct motorized stagecoaches and other futuristic devices. Meanwhile Johnny Ringo sets his undead eyes on defeating Doc Holliday in a gunfight and lawman Bat Masterson has vampire tendencies.

Buon funerale. Amigos! ... paga Sartana (1970) [Film; Italy-Spain; WW]

Premiere: 1971; Main Cast: Gianni Garko as Sartana, Daniela Giordano as Abigail Benson, George Wang as Peng/Lee Tse Tung, Antonio Staccioli [Ivano Staccioli] as Blackie, Franco Ressel as Samuel Piggot; Producer: Sergio Borelli; Story: Giovanni Simonelli (as Jean Simon); Screenplay: Roberto Gianviti, Giovanni Simonelli; Director: Anthony Ascott [Giuliano Carmineo]; 96 min.; Elios Film; Color.

Following a massacre whose victims included the owner of a mine, some of the local townsfolk (banker Hoffman, the corrupt sheriff and a

Buon funerale. Amigos! ... paga Sartana (1970), a film starring Gianni Garko as Sartana (Elios Film).

Chinese gambling hall owner) show interest in buying the prospector's property. Sartana discovers the real motive for interest in the mine is gold.

Gianni Garko reprises the role of Sartana in the third film of the series. It marked a return to the dark, mysterious avenging spirit persona first seen in *Se incontri Sartana prega per la tua morte*.

See: *Have a good funeral, my friend ... Sartana will pay*

Burroughs, Edgar Rice (1875–1950)
[Author]

Born in Chicago, Illinois, on September 1, 1875, Burroughs graduated from Michigan Military Academy in 1895. After enlisting in the U.S. Army, Burroughs was assigned to George Armstrong Custer's former regiment the 7th U.S. Cavalry at Fort Grant, Arizona Territory.

Following his premature discharge in 1897 due to a heart murmur, Burroughs failed at a number of jobs including railroad policeman in Salt Lake City, accountant and pencil sharpener wholesaler. Allegedly he was inspired to begin his writing career after he read issues of pulp magazines and decided he could "write something just as rotten."

His short time at Fort Grant in Apache country helped Burroughs create a convincing backdrop for his initial **John Carter of Mars** story **"Under the Moons of Mars"** which he sold to *All-Story Magazine* in 1911. When *Tarzan of the Apes* proved an even bigger success and Hollywood film studios adapted his work, Burroughs knew he could finally lay his past career failures to rest. A series of stories and novels followed, set in various fantastic locations including Venus and the center of the Earth.

The victim of a number of heart attacks in his final years, Burroughs finally succumbed to one final attack on March 19, 1950.

Selected works: *Tarzan of the Apes* (1914), *The Return of Tarzan* (1915), **A Princess of Mars** (1917), **The Gods of Mars** (1918), **The Warlords of Mars** (1919), *Thuvia, Maids of Mars* (1920), *The Mucker* (1921), *At the Earth's Core* (1922), *The Chessmen of Mars* (1922), *Pellucider* (1923), *The Land That Time Forgot* (1924), *The Cave Girl* (1925), *The Moon Maid* (1926), *The Master Mind of Mars* (1928), *A Fighting Man of Mars* (1931), *Apache Devil* (1933), *Carson of Venus* (1939), *Synthetic Men of Mars* (1940), *Llana of Gathol* (1948).

Burroughs, William S. (1914–1997)
[Author]

William Seward Burroughs II was born into an upper-class family and named after his paternal grandfather who had built the first adding machine in St. Louis in 1885. Burroughs studied at Harvard University and worked briefly as a reporter for the *St. Louis Dispatch* before gaining notoriety for shooting and killing his common law wife in Mexico City. From the September 8, 1951, *New York Daily News* account:

> William Seward Burroughs, 37, first admitted, then denied today that he was playing William Tell when his gun killed his pretty, young wife during a drinking party last night.
>
> Police said that Burroughs first told them that, wanting to show off his marksmanship, he placed a glass of gin on her head and fired, but was so drunk that he missed and shot her in the forehead.
>
> After talking with a lawyer, police said, Burroughs, who is a wealthy cotton planter from Pharr, Texas, changed his story and insisted that his wife was shot accidentally when he dropped his newly-purchased .38 caliber pistol.
>
> Mrs. Burroughs, 27, the former Joan Vollmer, died in the Red Cross Hospital. The shooting occurred during a party in the apartment of John Healy of Minneapolis. Burroughs said two other American tourists whom he knew only slightly were present.

Following the initial court hearings, Burroughs abruptly exited Mexico when he found himself without representation. (His lawyer had fired gunshots at a car full of drunken teenagers after they sideswiped his new car. One of the teenagers later died and Burroughs' lawyer fled the country.) Burroughs finally returned in 1953 and was found guilty of homicide and sentenced to two years in prison. He had already served thirteen days and his prison sentence was suspended by the Mexican judge. Burroughs walked away a free man. Rumors circulated of bribery and preferential treatment because of Burroughs' well-to-do background. Nothing was proven.

At the initial hearings, Burroughs claimed Joan Vollmer's death was caused by the accidental firing of his gun. However, in the early 1980s Burroughs admitted to biographer Ted Morgan that he had taken part in a William Tell dare game. "It was an utterly and completely insane thing to do."

Burroughs later earned cult status thanks to his notorious reputation which also included drug addiction, an open homosexual lifestyle and his association with Beat poets Jack Kerouac, Allen Ginsberg and Lawrence Ferlinghetti.

On August 1, 1997, Burroughs suffered a heart attack. He died the following day.

Selected works: *Junkie* (1953), *Naked Lunch* (1959), *The Soft Machine* (1961), *The Ticket That Exploded* (1962), *Nova Express* (1964), *The Wild Boys* (1971), *Cities, of the Red Night* (1981), *Ghost of a Chance* (1991), **The Place of Dead Roads** (1995)

The Burrowers (2008) [Film; WW]

Premiere: September 2008; Main Cast: Doug Hutchison as Henry Victor, Sean Patrick Thomas as Callaghan, Jocelin Donahue as Maryanne, William Mapother as Parcher, Karl Geary as Coffey, Laura Leighton as Gertrude; Executive Producers: Peter Block, John Sacchi; Story-Director: J.T. Petty; 96 min.; Blue Star Pictures; Color.

In the Dakota Territories, a family of settlers are attacked and abducted. But the search and rescue party members have no idea that the menace comes from deep below the ground in the form of a mutated species.

Burst Angel (2004) [Anime; Japan; SFW]

Premiere: April 6, 2004; Creator: Takayasu Hatano; Director: Kouichi Oohata; Story: Fumihiko Shimo, Masashi Sogo; Director: Koichi Ohata; Gonzo Digimation, TV Asahi; 24 × 24 min.; Color. U.S. version: Voice Cast: Monica Rial as Jo, Alison Retzloff as Amy, Jamie Marchie as Meg, Clarine Harp as Sei, Caitlin Glass as Takane, Greg Ayres as Kyohei, Mike McFarland as Leo; FUNimation Entertainment, Gonzo.

Four female guns-for-hire fight underworld crime syndicates and the corrupt organization known as RAPT in a nightmarish Tokyo of the future.

The character of Meg wears a sexy cowgirl outfit complete with holster and hat in an anime that emphasizes sexual imagery, action and violence with themes of Western vigilante justice in a science fiction setting.

Season One

Hell Comes Silently (1:01); *The Heartless Gunfighter* (1:02); *City Where the Beast Howls* (1:03); *The Brothers Die at Dawn* (1:04); *Mansion Where Lurks the Demon* (1:05); *Wash This Garden With Blood* (1:06); *Black Sky* (1:07); *The Wounded Outlaw* (1:08); *Party of the Dragon* (1:09); *Uncharted Cyberspace* (1:10); *Eastern Angel, Western Hawk* (1:11); *Tower of Tears* (1:12); *Showdown in Osaka* (1:13); *Wild Kids* (1:14); *Slingin' Oil* (1:15); *The Man with No Name* (1:16); *Dueling Angels* (1:17); *The Immortal Classmate* (1:18); *24-Hour Strategy* (1:19); *Blood Red Highway* (1:20); *New Sheriff in Town* (1:21); *Genocide Angels* (1:22); *Red Sea Gallows* (1:23); *Angels Explode!* (1:24)

See: **Bakuretsu Tenshi: Angel's Adolescence**

Burst Angel: Infinity (2007) [OVA; Japan; SFW]

Release date (U.S.): November 13, 2007; Animation: Gonzo; Director: Koichi Ohata; Gonzo, Media Factory, FUNimation Studios; 25 min.; Original video animation (OVA); Color.

A cyborg targets Meg after hospitalizing her friend Shierly in New York.

See: **Burst Angel**

Buster Crabbe [Comic Book; SW]

First issue: November 1951; Publisher: Famous Funnies Publications

This Western title based on the actor best known for the *Flash Gordon* serials began crossing science fiction and Space Western genres starting with issue #3 when the cover art showed cowboy Crabbe confronting green, club-wielding aliens.

Buzzard [Comic book character; WW]

First publication: *The Goon* #2 (November 2002); Creator; Eric Powell; Publisher: Exploding Albatross Funnybooks.

Buzzard was formerly a Missouri gunfighter turned sheriff of a Western town where all the townsfolk were turned into zombies. When the sheriff confronted and threatened to kill the charismatic preacher responsible for the zombie spell, the preacher's spell backfired and turned the sheriff into a near-immortal who must consume the flesh of the undead. Buzzard seeks vengeance on the "zombie priest" and to end the threat of the zombies by devouring them.

After rejection by Dark Horse Comics, Powell self-published *The Goon* comic book and introduced **Buzzard** in issue #2. Dark Horse realizing their mistake in rejecting Powell's work published *The Goon*. A three-part **Buzzard** comic book that also included *Billy the Kid's Old Timey Oddities and the Pit of Horrors* as a back-up strip was published by Dark Horse Comics in June 2010. Buzzard is now a lost figure wandering the spirit realm of a forest that leads to a village where villagers live in fear of inhuman creatures that snatch them from their slumber at night.

La Cabeza de Pancho Villa (1957) [Film; Mexico; WW]

Premiere: December 18, 1957; Main Cast: Luis Aguilar, Crox Alvarado, Jaime Fernández, Pascual, García Peña, Flor Silvestre; Producer: Luis Manrique; Story: Ramón Obón; Director: Chano Urueta; 94 min.; Universal; Spanish; B/W.

The second film in the re-edited *Headless Rider* serial features the mysterious Headless Rider, a black-hooded cult interested in a box to place Pancho Villa's head, ghosts, skeletons and a singing cowboy and his comical sidekick.

See: *El Jinete Sin Cabeza, La Marca de Satanás*

Cactoid Jim, King of the Martian Frontier [Comic book character, Podcast character; SW]

First publication: August, 2013; Story: Ben Acker, Ben Blacker; Art: Lar deSouza, Evan Larson, Evan Shaner; Publisher: Archaia Entertainment.

Former professional baseball player turned astronaut, James Lyons finds himself awoken in the twenty-sixth century following a malfunction with his cryo-sleep. Adapting to his new existence Lyons is then transported forward in time once again after entering a black hole. Now in the thirty-first century Lyons becomes Cactoid Jim, keeping law and order on the outlands of Mars.

Published as part of a comic strip anthology collection inspired by the popular live audio theater show and podcast, *The Thrilling Adventure Hour* where Nathan Fillion plays the character.

Cad Bane (*Star Wars* universe character) (SW)

First appearance: *Star Wars: The Clone Wars*; Creators: George Lucas, Dave Filoni, Henry Gilroy.

Inspired primarily by the Spaghetti Western character Angel Eyes (Lee Van Cleef) from *The Good, The Bad and The Ugly* (1967), Cad Bane is a bounty hunter from the planet Duro whose weapons include twin blaster pistols, gauntlets and rocket boots. Working for the highest bidder, Bane has no loyalties. His services have been employed by Darth Sidious, Jabba Desilijic Tiure, the Hutt Grand Council and Count Dooku among others.

George Lucas stated, "When it came to introduce the idea of a ruthless bounty hunter type for the series, it was a natural fit. He's a classic gunslinger—mysterious and also merciless. It's been a thematic part of *Star Wars* since the beginning."

Calamity Jack [Juvenile book; SPW]

Authors: Shannon and Dean Hale; Illustrator: Nathan Hale; First publication: New York: Bloomsbury, 2010.

Young Jack's misguided efforts to help ease his Momma's financial burdens earns him a reputation as a schemer and swindler. When crooked businessman Blunderboar threatens his Momma's bakery Jack attempts to steal Blunderboar's valuables stored in a floating penthouse, but finds himself confronted by giant creatures and a jabberwock. Magical beans provide the answer as a giant beanstalk reaches to the sky. But Jack's plans result in the destruction of his Momma's bakery as the beanstalk crashes down to earth.

Jack decides to head out West to Gothel's

Reach to hide from Blunderboar and his giants and meets up with his friend Rapunzel. He decides to return home to Shyport with Rapunzel only to discover Momma is now a prisoner of Blunderboar and Shyport is living in fear of the man-eating Ant People. Jack, Rapunzel and Prudence the pixie device a plan to free Jack's Momma and find the truth behind the Ant People.

This sequel to **Rapunzel's Revenge** is an alternate version of *Jack and the Beanstalk*.

Caliber [Comic book; WW]

First publication: May 2008; Story: Sam Sarkar; Art: Garrie Gastonny; Publisher: Radical Comics.

Shaman White Feather sees an apocalyptic future for mankind with a savior figure in the form of a man named Arthur and his mystical gun Caliber. The Arthurian legend re-imagined in the Pacific Northwest.

Cannibal! The Musical [Film; Stage Play; WW]

Video release title for **Alferd Packer: The Musical**. The film has also been adapted for the stage as *Cannibal! The Musical* by various theater groups since 1998.

Canyon o' Doom [RPG book; WW]

Author: Hal Mangold; First publication: 1999; Setting: **Deadlands: The Weird West**; Publisher: Pinnacle Entertainment Group.

Reverend Grimme and his cannibal cult seek the elusive City o' Ghouls, rumored to be located in the Grand Canyon.

Captain Ken [Manga; Japan; SW]

First appearance: *Weekly Shonen Sunday*, December 18, 1960; Creator-Story: Osamu Tezuka; Publisher: Shogakukan Inc.

The mysterious Martian-loving Captain Ken has to contend with a lookalike and feuding families in the frontier town of Heden City.

The theme of this Space Western (set on a future Mars where migrating humans are persecuting Martians) parallels 19th century American Western settlers persecuting the Native American population.

Captain Marvel Adventures [Comic book]

When youngster Billy Batson is told by an ancient wizard that he has been chosen to be his successor, he is ordered to say "Shazam!" and is transformed by a bolt of magic lightning into adult superhero Captain Marvel. To turn back into Billy Batson, he just repeats "Shazam!" The comic book featured a few Western stories.

"Captain Marvel and the Last of the Batsons" [WW]

First publication: #51 (January 1946); Story: Otto Binder; Art: Pete Costanza; Publisher: Fawcett Comics.

When Wild Bill Batson claims Billy Batson is his lost grandson and invites him back to his Bar-B-Q Ranch, Captain Marvel looks further into the claim and helps Wild Bill out of trouble.

"Captain Marvel Gets Promoted" [WW]

First publication: #53 (February 1946); Story: Otto Binder; Art: C.C. Beck, Pete Costanza; Publisher: Fawcett Comics.

Thrown by his horse head first into a tree, Colonel Blueridge mistakenly believes the year is 1846 and he is about to come under attack, by American Indians. But when Indians actually attack, Captain Marvel (now Colonel Marvel following a promotion by Colonel Blueridge) pursues the Indians into the depths of a cave. To his amazement, he discovers a lost tribe living in an Indian village.

"Indian Chief"

First publication: #83 (April 1948); Story: Otto Binder; Art: Pete Costanza; Publisher: Fawcett Comics.

Indian chief Captain Marvel proudly stands with arms folded overlooking a snow-capped mountain peak as Indian tribe members watch from a distance.

Captain Marvel Jr. [Comic book]

Wounded by Captain Nazi, Freddy Freeman's life is saved as he is transformed into Captain Marvel Jr. with the help of Captain Marvel and the spirit of the ancient wizard Shazam.

"Captain Marvel Jr., Duels with the Outlaws" [WW]

First publication: #51 (August 1948); Art: Joe Certa; Publisher: Fawcett Comics.

Captain Marvel Jr. (Freddy Freeman) comes up against the outlaw Jesse James, Quantrill and Black Rufe.

"The Outlaw of Crooked Creek" [WW]

First publication: #75 (July 1949); Art: Joe Certa; Publisher: Fawcett Comics.

"The World's Mightiest Boy Battles the Outlaw of Crooked Creek!"

Captain Video and His Video Rangers (1949) [Children's TV series; SFW]

Premiere: June 27, 1949; Main cast: Richard Coogan as Captain Video (1949–50), Al Hodge as Captain Video (1950–55), Don Hastings as The Video Ranger, Bran Mossen as Dr. Pauli, Hal Conklin as Dr. Pauli; Creators: James L. Caddigan, Lawrence Menkin; Producers: Olga Druce, Maurice C. Brock; 30 min.; B/W; DuMont Television Network.

This low-budget children's science fiction show set in the year 2254 was broadcast live, five days a week. The "Remote Tele-Carrier" at Captain Video's secret mountain retreat headquarters transmitted the exploits of Captain Video's Special Agents who were earth-bound cowboys such as Tim McCoy, Bob Steele and Ken Maynard. This strained cost-cutting segue into old film footage provided an early example of the concept of linking the traditional Western with science fiction.

Roy Steffens as Captain Z-Ro and John Trigonis as McGowan face off in "The Pony Express" (3:07), an episode of *Captain Z-Ro* (1951).

Halfway through the show, the scene changes to wild west, which still seems to be wild in the 21st century. By employing good old-fashioned cowboy movies, all the kids are satisfied, and for a few minutes the imagination gets a rest. Baffled adults having cowboy movies thrust upon them in the middle of the 21st century, have been known to leave the room muttering to themselves. But the kids take it all in stride.

—*TV Forecast*, February 9, 1952

Captain Z-Ro (1951) [TV series]

Premiere: November 1951; Main cast: Roy Steffens as Captain Z-Ro, Bobby Trumbull, Bruce Haynes (Season 3) as Jet; Creator: Roy Steffens; KRON-TV San Francisco; 15 min; B/W; W.A. Palmer Films Inc. for Captain Z-Ro Productions Inc.; 26 × 30 min; B/W

Captain Z-Ro and teenage assistant Jet travel through time and space with the help of his time-traveling rocket ship, ZX-99. The original live format made way for new filmed episodes when the show went into syndication on December 18, 1955.

"THE PONY EXPRESS" (3:07) [SFW]

Premiere: January 29, 1956; Guest cast: John Trigonis as McGowan, Bill Sweeney as Higgins, Michael Donn Random as Slade.

Captain Z-Ro and Jet (Haynes) travel through time and space to 1860 to return a Wells Fargo strongbox containing letters to the Pony Express relay station outside of Fort Bridger, Wyoming. But they uncover a plan by the Butterfield Stage Company to destroy the Pony Express.

"SUTTER'S GOLD" (3:17) [SFW]

Premiere: April 8, 1957; Guest cast: Maurice Argent as John Sutter, John Trigonis as Sam Brannon, Bill Sweeney as William Clark, Sydney Walker as James Marshall.

Captain Z-Ro and Jet become involved in the California gold strike of January 1848 when James Marshall struck gold at Sutter's Mill.

Il Cavaliere del Texas [Comic book character; Italy; WW]

First appearance: 1953; Creator-Art: Roy d'Amy; Story: G. L. Bonelli; Publisher: Sergio Bonelli Editore.

Rio Kid and sidekick Whisky Bill journey between Texas and Mexico putting wrongs to right and encountering weird and supernatural events.

See: *Rio Kid*

El Cazador de la Bruja (2007) [Animated TV series; Japan; SFW]

Premiere: April 4, 2007; Story: Kenichi Kanemaki; Director: Kôichi Mashimo; Bee Train, Project Leviathan; 26 × 30 min.; Color.

After capturing murder suspect Ellis, bounty hunter Nadi becomes intrigued by the young girl. A mysterious gemstone and the "Eternal City" of Wiñay Marka act as their guide to uncovering the secrets of Ellis' past.

Taking place in a contemporary Western setting, this anime uses traditional Western motifs in a story involving intrigue, mystery, adventure and mystical powers.

Season One

Running Girl (1:01); *Waiting Girl* (1:02); *Raining Girl* (1:03); *Targeted Girl* (1:04); *Clothed Girl* (1:05); *Man in Love* (1:06); *Working Man* (1:07); *Lying Girl* (1:08); *Digging Woman* (1:09); *Man Who Lives With an Angel* (1:10); *Cursed Woman* (1:11); *Shot Man* (1:12); *Hiding Woman* (1:13); *Maple Leaf* (1:14); *Opposing Woman* (1:15); *Angry Woman* (1:16); *Cornered Woman* (1:17); *Disagreeing Woman* (1:18); *Man Who Protects* (1:19); *Captured Woman* (1:20); *Flapping Woman* (1:21); *Awoken Woman* (1:22); *Puzzled Woman* (1:23); *Dead Man* (1:24); *Saintly Woman* (1:25); *Shining Woman* (1:26)

Chains of Chaos [Comic book; SFW]

First issue: November 1994; Story: Thomas E. Sniegoski; Cover Art: John Estes; Three-issue miniseries; Publisher: Harris Comics.

The Rook and Vampirella team up to defeat the Chaos-child and meet Dracula, Adam Van Helsing and Pendragon along the way.

A cross-over title featuring *The Rook* and Vampirella, this series marked the first Harris Comics appearance of the former Warren Publishing Weird Western character. The revised Rook is a half-cyborg who travels through time and alternate universes known as the "reality stream." The Harris version of the Rook still retains an Old West heritage.

Chambers of Chills [Comic book]

Horror anthology comic book.

"THE MONSTER FROM THE MOUND"

First publication: # 2 (January 1973); Story: Gardner Fox; Adapted from "**The Horror from the Mound**" by Robert E. Howard; Art: Frank Brunner; Cover art: Gil Kane, Tom Palmer; Publisher: Marvel Comics Group.

When rancher Steve Brill learns of possible treasure buried in the local Indian burial ground, he ignores the warning of the legend and releases a vampire.

Champions of the Wild Weird West [Comic book; WW]

First publication: 2012; Story: Eric Hendrix, Michael David Nelsen; Art: George Kambadais; Five-issue mini-series; Publisher: Arcana.

While searching the Old West for his kidnapped wife-to-be and her father, a former samurai encounters a posse investigating a stolen railroad car. Thieves blow up a safe containing a zombie on its way to be dissected by scientists and as the posse arrive on the scene a plague of the living dead is let loose as the train travels over a Native American burial ground.

A scattered group that includes a young Native American shaman, Taro, a fallen samurai, adventurer New York Jack and the masked Grey Gun who possesses supernatural powers form the alliance known as the *Champions of the Wild Weird West*.

Chanbara Beauty [Film; Japan; WW]

International release title for *OneeChanbara: The Movie*.

Charmed (1998) [TV series]

Air date: February 15, 2001; Main Cast: Shannen Doherty as Prue Halliwell, Holly Marie Combs as Piper Halliwell, Alyssa Milano as Phoebe Halliwell, Brian Krause as Leo Wyatt, Julian McMahon as Cole Turner, James Read as Victor Bennett, Michael Greyeyes as Bo Lightfeather, Kimberly Norris as Isabel Lightfeather, Ed Lauter as Sutter; Producer: Jon Paré; Story: Monica Breen, Alison Schapker;

Director: Shannen Doherty; 42 min.; Spelling Television, Paramount Pictures; Color.

Following the death of their grandmother, three sisters discover they have supernatural powers and find themselves under attack from demonic forces in modern-day San Francisco.

"THE GOOD, THE BAD AND THE CURSED" (3:14) [SFW]

Phoebe becomes physically linked to Indian Bo Lightfeather in an Old West town. Only Cole and Prue can save Phoebe from a time loop where she continually suffers Lightfeather's mortal wounds and is destined to die.

El Charro de las Calaveras (1965) [Film; Mexico; WW]

Premiere: July 9, 1965; Main Cast: Dagoberto Rodríguez as El Charro de las Calaveras, David Silva as El Lobo Humano, Pascual García Peña as Cléofas, Alicia Caro as Alvatierra; Producer: Miguel Barragán Angel; Story-Director: Alfredo Salazar; 78 min.; Spanish; B/W.

Three separate stories re-edited from film serials involving the Masked Rider confronting a werewolf (La Lobo Humano), a bat-faced vampire (El Vampiro Sinistro) and a disembodied head in a box demanding it be reconnected with its headless body (El Jinete Sin Cabeza).

Chase the Lightning [Novel; WWR]

Author: Madeline Baker; First publication: New York: N.Y. Leisure Books, 2001.

Escaping from a pursuing posse on a mysterious white "spirit horse" in 1869, Trey Long Walker, a badly wounded half-breed Apache, finds himself in a 21st century corral face to face with Amanda Burkett, a beautiful woman engaged to bounty hunter Rob Langely, the great-great grandson of the man who pursued Trey back in his time.

Chickasaw Adventures [Comic book; SFW]

First issue: March 2005; Story: Jen Murvin Edwards; Art: Tom Lyle; Publisher: Layne Morgan Media.

When Johnny, a modern Chickasaw boy, touches the sacred pole known as the kohta falaya, he travels back in time to witness key events in in Chickasaw history. In "Tears at Fort Coffee" (issue #3) he witnesses the Great Removal of Native Americans from their homelands to the Midwest.

Children o' the Atom [RPG book; WW]

Authors: Rick Dakan, Jack Emmert, Bill King; First publication: 1998; Setting: **Deadlands: Hell on Earth**; Publisher: Pinnacle Entertainment Group.

Facts and information about the Cult o' Doom and their disciples and Vegas, the City o' Sin. Doomsayers will also discover new Edges, Hindrances, and more powers. Includes the adventure "Doom Comes to Frogtown."

Cimarron [Comic book character; SFW]

First appearance: *The Liberty Project* #1 (June 1987); Creators: Kurt Busiek, James Fry; Publisher: Eclipse

Rosalita Vasquez is Cimarron, a feisty but troubled Texan cowgirl possessing super-strength. As a member of a U.S. government group of super-villains, The Liberty Project, she combats various aliens and monsters in return for parole.

Cimarron Strip [TV series]

Air date: November 30, 1967; Main Cast: Stuart Whitman as Marshal Jim Crown, Percy Herbert as Angus McGregor, Randy Boone as Francis Wilde, Jill Townsend as Dulcey Coopersmith, Lola Albright as Stacey Houston, Leslie Nielsen as Rowan Houston, Simon Oakland as Joshua Broom, Royal Dano as Walking Man; Creator: Christopher Knoff; Executive Producer: Philip Leacock; Story: Stephen Kandel, Richard Fielder; Director: Charles R. Rondeau; 72 min.; CBS, Stuart Whitman Corp.; Color.

The adventures of Marshal Jim Crown as he seeks to maintain law and order in land bordering Indian country and Kansas Territory known as the Cimarron Strip.

"THE BEAST THAT WALKS LIKE A MAN" (1:11) [WMW]

When Marshal Crown discovers their butchered bodies of a family of settlers outside of town, the locals believe it to be the work of "The Devil" a mythical creature who growls like a panther. "The Devil" is actually Joshua Broom, an insane one-handed trapper who uses a huge bear claw to kill anyone who enters his territory.

Cinnamon [Comic book character; WW]

First appearance: **Weird Western Tales** #48 (September-October 1978); Creator: Roger McKenzie; Publisher: DC Comics

Kate Manser, determined to avenge her father's death at the hands of bank robbers, hones her gunfighting skills and sets off on her quest. As Cinnamon, she becomes particularly adept with the Japanese throwing star, the shuriken.

Her adventures in **Weird Western Tales** only spanned two issues and displayed no sense that she was a Weird Western character outside of her skills with the shuriken. Subsequent time-traveling stories with the **Justice League of America** and the knowledge she is the incarnation of ancient Egyptian princess Chay-Ara and the reincarnated **Hawkgirl** in the 20th century clearly categorize her as a true Weird Western character.

The Circus of Dr. Lao [Novel; WW]

Author: Charles G. Finney; Illustrator: Boris Artzy-basheff; First publication: 1935; Publisher: New York: Viking Press.

In the Depression years in Abalone, Arizona, the townsfolk flock to a weird traveling carnival. The various sideshows, including a medusa, a fortune teller and a reanimated corpse, serve as window to the soul for the people who dare to enter.

In this exchange a widow named Mrs Howard T. Cassan decides to have her fortune told by Apollonius of Tyana, who claims to be almost two thousand years old.

> ...Now you dream of an oil well to be found on twenty acres of land you own in New Mexico. There is no oil there. You dream of some tall, dark, handsome man to come wooing you. There is no man coming, dark, tall, or otherwise. And yet you will dream on in spite of all I tell you; dream on through your little round of hours, sewing and rocking and gossiping and dreaming; and the world spins and spins and spins...

Despite the prediction of a barren future, Mrs. Cassan refuses to listen and decides to visit the fortune teller again that same evening after recommending him to her friends and telling them he was "frightfully encouraging" about the prospects of an oil strike.

This contemporary Weird Western was the basis of the 1964 film **7 Faces of Dr. Lao**. Most critics agree the connection between the book and the film is superficial.

City o' Gloom [RPG book; WW]

Author: Shane Lacy Hensley; First publication: 1998; Setting: **Deadlands: The Weird West**; Publisher: Pinnacle Entertainment Group.

Location boxed set for Salt Lake City and sourcebook for the City o' Gloom. Salt Lake City resident Six Hundred Pound Sally is the guide.

The City o' Sin [RPG book; WW]

Author: Teller; First publication: 2001; Setting: **Deadlands: Hell on Earth The Wasted West**; Publisher: Pinnacle Entertainment Group.

Silas Rasmussen and his dreaded Doombringers are on the loose in the home to the Wasted West mutants, Lost Vegas.

Cliffhangers (1979) [TV series; SFW]

Each episode featured three 20-minute serials (*Stop Susan Williams*, *The Secret Empire* and *The Curse of Dracula*) broadcast in chapters and each concluding with a cliffhanger.

The show was one of nine mid-season replacement for a disastrous NBC 1978 fall season. The decision to begin each separate serial with chapter numbers Two, Three and Seven added to the confused mix of genres within each show. Ultimately this experiment at reviving the Saturday matinee serial format for network television failed to gain an audience.

THE SECRET EMPIRE (12 × 20 MIN)

Premiere: February 27, 1979; Creator: Kenneth Johnson; Main Cast: Geoffrey Scott as Marshal Jim Donner, Carlene Watkins as Millie Thomas, Tiger Williams as Billy Thomas, Mark Lenard as Emperor Thorval; Producer: Richard Milton; Story: Gene R. Kearney; Director: Joseph Pevney; 20 min.; Universal Television; Color.

When Marshal Jim Donner recovers a mysterious key from the Phantom Riders, he unlocks a door to the secret underground city of Chimera.

The episodes, based on the 1935 serial **The Phantom Empire**, featured scenes based in 1880 Cheyenne, Wyoming, shot in sepia, and scenes taking place in the underground city of Chimera, shot in color.

With the premature cancellation of the show on May 1, 1979, the serial never reached a conclusion on NBC. The two final episodes were only shown on international broadcasts.

Season One

Chapter 3—*Plunge into Mystery* (1:01); Chapter 4—*Prisoner of the Empire* (1:02); Chapter 5—*The Mind Twisters* (1:03); Chapter 6—*Seeds of Revolt* (1:04); Chapter 7—*Attack of the Phantom Riders* (1:05); Chapter 8—*Sizzling Threat* (1:06); Chapter 9—*Mandibles of Death* (1:07); Chapter 10—*The Last Gasp* (1:08); Chapter 11—*Return to Chimera* (1:09); Chapter 12—*Power-*

house (1:10); Chapter 13—*Partisans Unchained* (1:11); Chapter 14—*Escape to the Stars* (1:12)

The Clockwork Century Book #1: Bone-shaker [Novel; SPW]

Author: Cherie Priest; First publication: Tor Books, 2009.

An alternate history series. Stonewall Jackson survived Chancellorsville, Atlanta never burned and England broke the Union's naval blockade and formally recognized the Confederate States of America. The American Civil War still rages after nearly two decades of fierce conflict in a devastated landscape where combat dirigibles, armored vehicles and all manner of new inventions make their presence felt.

Mad inventor Leviticus Blue has built a bone-shaking drill engine to mine through the frozen Klondike in a search for gold. But the test run is a dramatic failure, destroying most of downtown Seattle and unleashing a subterranean vein of blight gas that turns people into zombies. Sixteen years later, Seattle is a toxic, walled city, designed to keep the zombies and various criminals and armed refugees in and outsiders from entering. But Blue's son Ezekiel is intent on clearing his father's name and reputation and enters under the walled city. Zeke's mother, Briar has learned of another mad inventor, Dr. Minnericht, who resembles her dead husband and lives within Seattle. Soon she is attempting a rescue mission to save her son from the man who may be his father in a city inhabited by zombie air pirates.

The Clockwork Century Book #2: Dreadnought [Novel; SPW]

Author: Cherie Priest; First publication: Tor Books, 2010.

Nurse Mercy Lynch is working in a Confederate war hospital in Richmond, Virginia, when she is informed both of the death of her husband in a POW camp and news that her estranged father is dying in the Pacific Northwest. The cross-country journey by dirigible to the Mississippi River and train from St. Louis over the Rockies to Tacoma in Washington Territory turns into a nightmare. The Union steam engine Dreadnought is carrying a mysterious cargo and is pursued by Confederate soldiers and a Mexican legion of zombies as it journeys west. Accompanying Lynch is Texas Ranger Horatio Korman, who has his own agenda.

The Clockwork Century Book #3: Ganymede [Novel; SPW]

Author: Cherie Priest; First publication: Tor Books, 2011.

Air pirate Andan Cly wants to quit being running blight gas because of the damaging effects of its bi-product, the drug sap. But in order to refit his airship he needs to move from Seattle to New Orleans. And by chance, he has a major job waiting for him in the Big Easy: the recovery of the underwater airship and war machine Ganymede in complete secrecy due to martial law imposed by the Texians. But risks are worth taking for a machine that could end the Civil War.

The Clockwork Century Book #4: The Inexplicables [Novel; SPW]

Author: Cherie Priest; First publication: Tor Books, 2012.

Rector "Wreck 'em" Sherman is a drug dealer on a mission. To track down the zombie-like Inexplicables and the remains of his old friend Zeke Wilkes and exorcise the ghost that's been haunting him. Sherman also seeks new sources and revenue for his drug of choice, sap but he discovers there may be greater spoils awaiting him inside the walled city in the form of gold. Standing in his way are a group of sinister gold prospectors.

The Clockwork Century Book #5: Fiddlehead [Novel; SPW]

Author: Cherie Priest; First publication: Tor Books, 2013.

The final book in *The Clockwork Century* series sees genius inventor and former slave Gideon Bardsley creating a calculating engine called Fiddlehead. It determines that if the Civil War doesn't end soon then a plague of zombies, who first surfaced in the walled city of Seattle, will destroy humanity. Bardsley asks former president Abraham Lincoln, who survived an assassination attempt back in 1865, for help in finally ending the war. But someone wants Bardsley and his machine silenced.

The Clockwork Century: Clementine [Novel; SPW]

Author: Cherie Priest; First publication: Burton, MI: Subterranean Press, 2010.

Former actress and Confederate spy Maria Isabella Boyd, now reduced to working for the Pinkerton Detective Agency on behalf of the

Union Army, is assigned to track and capture escaped slave and air pirate Captain Croggon Beauregard Hainey. Hainey has been pursuing the federally sponsored transport dirigible The Clementine—an airship he once stole and now wants back. But events take a strange twist when Boyd and Hainey form an alliance.

This short 208 page novel is set in *The Clockwork Century* universe but wasn't published as part of the official Tor Books series. A 34 page e-book *Tanglefoot* was published by Subterranean Press in 2011 and served as a supernatural spin-off to *Clementine*.

The Clockwork Century: Jacaranda [Novella; WW]

Author: Cherie Priest; First publication: Burton, MI: Subterranean Press, 2014.

The hotel Jacaranda lies off the coast of southeast Texas on the island of Galveston. It is a place of death with two dozen corpses occupying its premises in its the first year of operation. Juan Miguel Quintero, a former gunslinger turned priest with second sight is called upon by a nun to solve the problem of the cursed hotel, while the Texas Rangers send Horatio Korman.

This novella is set in *The Clockwork Century* universe but wasn't published as part of the official Tor Books series.

"The Clockwork Sheriff" [Short story; SFW]

Author: Ken Rand; First publication: *Le shérif mécanique, Sciences et sortileges*, 2002.

When the townsfolk of Cumberland, Wyoming, hire clockwork gunslinger "Bullseye Bixby" to rid them of local road agents, human gun-for-hire Maurice "Lightning" Epstein must show them that the human hand is more accurate.

Cocco Bill [Comic book character; Italy]

First appearance: *Giorno dei Ragazzi* #1, March 28, 1957; Creator: Benito Jacovitti; Publisher: Albi de "Il Giorno"

Surreal Western parody from renowned Italian cartoonist Jacovitti featuring chamomile tea-drinking gunslinger Cocco Bill and his cigarette-smoking horse Trottalemme. Cocco Bill occasionally ventured into Weird Western territory, including a story featuring ghosts that was reprinted as the comic album *Cocco Bill ja kummitukset* (Cocco Bill and the ghosts) in Finland.

See: *Il Corsaro Cocco Bill*

Cocco Bill ja kummitukset [Comic album: Finland; WW]

First publication: 1978; Story-Art: Benito Jacovitti; Translation: Maija Holmen-Bärlund; Publisher: Lehtimiehet Oy.

Finnish reprint of the story that first appeared in the Italian children's comic magazine *Corriere dei Piccoli* #30 (1969).

See: *Cocco Bill*

Coeur Blessé [Comic book character; France; SFW]

First appearance: *Kiwi* #232 (1974); Story: Franco Frescura; Art: Renzo Restani; Publisher: Editions Lug.

A young Native American travels through time to the Old West to come to the aid of his ancestors.

See: **Wounded Heart**

Coffin [Comic book character; WW]

First appearance: *Eerie* #61 (November 1974); Story: Budd Lewis; Art: Jose Ortiz; Publisher: Warren Publishing.

Arizona, 1889. Rifle salesman John Meek a.k.a. Coffin is cursed with immortal life by an elderly Indian medicine man for killing members of his tribe. The Indians proceed to torture Coffin by staking him in the dry heat of the desert and waiting for the flesh-eating ants to feast on his face. Coffin subsequently roams the Old West seeking release from his physical torment and emotional guilt over the deaths of innocent Indians even though he knew he killed them in error.

Coffin's story was told over four issues of *Eerie* (61, 67, 68, 70).

Cold Copper: The Age of Steam (Book #3) [Novel; SPW]

Author: Devon Monk; First publication: New York: Roc, 2012.

The adventures of lycanthropic bounty hunter Cedar Hunt continues as he takes refuge, along with his fellow travelers, from a glacial storm. The frontier town of Des Moines is under the thumb of mayor Killian Vosbrough who is mining cold copper with the intention of furthering his rule to both land and sky. But Hunt and his friends plan to expose Vosborough and his nefarious plans in this mix of the paranormal, mysticism and steam punk.

"The Cold Gray God" [Pulp fiction; SFW]

Author: **C. L. Moore**; First publication: *Weird Tales* (October 1935).

On Righa, pole city of Mars, **Northwest Smith** encounters the beautiful Judai of Venus. Asked to retrieve a mysterious ivory box, Smith discovers it contains a talisman that acts as the key to opening a gateway for the entity known as the Unnamable One to enter the world of Mars. The cold, gray entity had taken control of Judai and now inhabits Northwest Smith as he struggles to regain control of his own body.

> The Spaceman's Rest was crowded. Smith made his way through the maze of tables toward the long bar at the end of the room, threading the crowd of hard-faced men whose wide diversity of races seemed to make little difference in the curious similarity of expression which dwelt upon every face. They were quiet and watchful-eyed and wore the indefinable air of those who live by their wits and their guns.

Cold Harvest (1998) [Film; SFW]

Premiere: 1998; Main Cast: Gary Daniels as Roland/Oliver Chaney, Barbara Crampton as Christine Chaney, Bryan Genesse as Little Ray; Executive Producers: Danny Dimbort, Avi Lerner, Trevor Short; Story: Frank Dietz; Director: Isaac Florentine; 89 min.; Nu World/New Image Films; Color.

Following a lethal meteor strike that brings a plague to Earth, a bounty hunter (Daniels) tracks down the murderer of his twin brother, warlord Little Ray, and protects his pregnant sister-in-law, who is immune to the plague, from harm.

Western action in a post-apocalypse landscape with kung fu–style fighting.

The Collegium [RPG book; WW]

Author: John Goff; First publication: 2000; Setting: **Deadlands: The Weird West**; Publisher: Pinnacle Entertainment Group.

Mad science equipment guide, plot and background book for the town of Gomorra and the Collegium.

Colt the Armadillo [Comic book; WW]

First appearance: *KZ Comics Presents*, August 1985; Story: Tom Zjaba; Art: Dan Berger; Ryan Brown; Publisher: KZ Comics.

This short-lived, independently published comic book featured an Old West armadillo bounty hunter named Colt.

Contract [Comic book; SFW]

First publication: June 2008; Story: Garan Madeiros; 4-issue mini-series; Publisher: First Salvo Productions.

Jessie Garrett, a native of Tropica where she was raised on a ranch, is CEO of the CyberMerc company The Stellar Rangers Inc. In a society where law and order is maintained by the highest bidder, the Stellar Rangers are always available for hire—at a price. When Garret and fellow Mercs Panzer and Tsumi are called upon to rescue a little girl from black market organ dealers, they must first confront and overcome armed combat cyborgs.

Copperhead (2008) [Telefilm; WW]

Premiere: June 28, 2008; Main Cast: Brad Johnson as "Wild" Bill, Billy Drago as Jesse Evans, Wendy Carter as Jane, Atanas Srebrev as Josiah; Executive Producer: T.J. Sakasegawa; Story: Rafael Jordan; Director: Todor Chapkanov; Unified Film Organization (UFO), Universal Television; Color.

Supernatural poisonous snakes terrorize a Western town.

Copperhead [Comic book; SW]

First publication: September 2014; Story: Jay Faerber; Art: Scott Godlewski, Ron Riley; Publisher: Image Comics.

On a distant planet in the 24th century, single mother Clara Bronson is the new sheriff of the dust-laden mining town known as Copperhead, which is in the grips of a crooked mining tycoon. Together with Deputy Boo Clara investigates a multiple murder on the outskirts of town.

Il Corsaro Cocco Bill (2002) [Animated TV series; Italy; WW]

Premiere: 2002; Voice Cast: Gregory Snegoff as **Cocco Bill**, Executive Producer: Pietro Campedelli; Story: Oscar Avogardo, Sergio Crivellaro; Director: Pierluigi De Mas; RAI Radio Televisione Italiana, Raifiction-EM.TV & Merchandising AG; Color.

The animated adventures of Cocco Bill include many Weird Western titles: "Cocco Bill Ritorna al Futuro," "Cocco Bill Jurassic," "Cocco Bill e il Figlio di Moby Dick," "Cocco Bill e il Fratello di Frankenstein," "Cocco Bill e il Mostro del Lago," Cocco Bill e i Fantasmi."

Cosmic Cowboys (2003) [Animated TV series; France; SW]

Premiere: 2003; Creator: Eddy Marx; 52 × 13 min; Producers: Christian Davin, Clement Calvet; Alphanim-France 3, Tooncan Productions VI Inc., Europool; Color.

Comedy Space Western spoof featuring two intergalactic bounty hunters, Curtis the cat-goat mutant and his partner Dook, a humanoid mule who lives by a strict code of honor. They work for the enigmatic Sheriff Mammy who transmits from her cozy home. Their nemesis and public enemy number one is Cereal Bob, a pink rabbit who always finds ways to escape from Deputy Roscoe's jail.

Season One

The Cereal Brothers (1:01); *Vacation Drill* (1:02); *Luck Out Below* (1:03); *Cosmics in the Blizzard* (1:04); *A Cereal Christmas* (1:05); *Spaced Out Momma!* (1:06); *Twiddle Dee Dumb* (1:07); *Star-Strangled Banter* (1:08); *Hot Dog Bob* (1:09); *The Pig Escape* (1:10); *Good Lux Charm* (1:11); *A Shrinking World* (1:12); *Ecomaniac* (1:13); *A Mysterious Tale* (1:14); *Momocop* (1:15); *Grabbit and Run!* (1:16); *Liar's Lair* (1:17); *Space Fan-atic* (1:18); *Friend or Fiend?* (1:19); *Malicious Malicia* (1:20); *Space Castaways* (1:21); *Trading Spaces* (1:22); *Trading Spaces* (1:23); *Debt or Alive* (1:24); *Debt or Alive* (1:25); *Pumpkin Dispatch* (1:26); *Superguy* (1:27); *Split Poisonality* (1:28); *Cosmic Cast* (1:29); *Diploma Dilemma* (1:30); *Spatial Agent* (1:31); *Flying Rodeo Cowboy* (1:32); *Boxing Day* (1:33); *The Ties That Blind* (1:34); *Galactic Voodoo* (1:35); *The Tortoise and the Hare!* (1:36); *Statue of Imitations* (1:37); *So Long Saloon* (1:38); *Hallowed Hologram* (1:39); *Promotion Commotion* (1:40); *Vase That?* (1:41); *Double Trouble* (1:42); *Genie in a Throttle* (1:43); *Heros Tolerance* (1:44); *Psycho Switch* (1:45); *Bad Baby* (1:46); *Guest Work* (1:47); *Pyramid Scheming* (1:48); *Running Joke* (1:49); *The Ghost Ship* (1:50); *Game Over* (1:51); *Mission Implausible* (1:52).

Cosmic Cowboys (2003) promotional artwork. © 2003 Alphanim, France 3, Tooncan Productions VI Inc., Europool. All Rights Reserved.

Cosmo Warrior Zero

(2001) [Animated TV series; Japan; SFW]

Premiere: July 6, 2001; Creator: **Leiji Matsumoto**; Story: Mugi Kamio, Nobuyuki Fujimoto; Director: Kazuyoshi Yokota; AT-X, Tsuburaya Eizo, Vega Entertainment; 30 × 13 min.; Color.

In the late 30th century, Warrior Zero is assigned by the Machine Men to track down rogue pirate Captain Harlock, who still resists the victors of the Earth-Mechanized war.

Season One
[Episodes set in the town of Gun Frontier]

"THE IMMORTAL SAMURAI TOCHIRO" (1:05)
Premiere: August 4, 2001.

Captain Zero sends scouting party members Grenadier, Ishikura, Rai and mechanized soldier Acceluter to the town of Gun Frontier on the planet Heavy Metal to meet with bounty hunter Le Sylviana for information on Harlock. But Tochiro is blamed for an incident that nearly destroys the town and is threatened with death by Le Sylviana.

"MY FRIEND HARLOCK" (1:06)

Premiere: August 11, 2001.

Captain Zero visits Gun Frontier to check on his crew while Captain Harlock rescues Tochiro from Le Sylviana.

Cowboy Bebop [Manga-Anime; Japan; SFW]

1. First appearance: *Asuka Fantasy DX*, 1997; Creators: Hajime Yatate, Shinichiro Watanabe; Story: Dai Saitou, Hajime Yatate, Yutaka Nanten; Art: Yutaka Nanten; Publisher: Kadokawa Shoten—Tokyopop

Intergalactic bounty hunters Spike and Jet roam the solar system in the Bebop spaceship tracking down outlaws and criminals.

2. Animated TV series; Premiere: April 3, 1998; Stories: Keiko Nobumoto, Sadayuki Murai, Dai Sato, Ryota Yamaguchi, Michiko Yokote, Akihiko Inari, Aya Yoshinaga, Shoji Kawamori; Director: Shinichiro Watanabe; 26 × 25 min.; Sunrise Inc.-Bandai Visual; Color.

Based on the manga by Shinichiro Watanabe and the Sunrise animation team under the collective pseudonym of Hajime Yatate.

The series qualifies as a Space Western but owes as much to other genre influences including crime, mystery and film noir. Music and animation are often combined to great effect. The fusion of jazz and rock is by composer Yoko Kanno. Director Watanabe cites *Dirty Harry* and *Enter the Dragon* as the main sources of inspiration for *Cowboy Bebop* with the one-eyed Spike influenced by Western cowboy characters.

Season One

Asteroid Blues (1:01); *Stray Dog Strut* (1:02); *Honky Tonk Women* (1:03); *Gateway Shuffle* (1:04); *Ballad of Fallen Angels* (1:05); *Sympathy for the Devil* (1:06); *Heavy Metal Queen* (1:07); *Waltz for Venus* (1:08); *Jamming with Edward* (1:09); *Ganymede Elegy* (1:10); *Toys in the Attic* (1:11); *Jupiter Jazz: Part 1* (1:12); *Jupiter Jazz: Part 2* (1:13); *Bohemian Rhapsody* (1:14); *My Funny Valentine* (1:15); *Black Dog Serenade* (1:16); *Mushroom Samba* (1:17); *Speak Like a Child* (1:18); *Wild Horses* (1:19); *Pierrot le Fou* (1:20); *Boogie-Woogie Feng-Shui* (1:21); *Cowboy Funk* (1:22); *Brain Scratch* (1:23); *Hard Luck Woman* (1:24); *The Real Folk Blues: Part 1* (1:25); *The Real Folk Blues: Part 2* (1:26)

Cowboy Bebop: Knockin' on Heaven's Door a.k.a. Cowboy Bebop: The Movie (2001) [Animated film; Japan; SFW]

Premiere: September 1, 2001 (Japan); Producers: Masahiko Minami, Minoru Takanashi; Screenplay: Keiko Nobumoto; Director: Shinichiro Watanabe; 115 min.; Sunrise, Bones, Bandai Visual; Sony Pictures Entertainment Japan; Color.

Mars, 2071. Following a deadly chemical terrorist attack that kills and maims hundreds of people the government offers 300 million woolong for the capture of those responsible. The crew of the Bebop, Spike Spiegel, Jet Black, Faye Valentine, Edward "Ed" Wong together with Ein, a cyber-dog with human intelligence, get to work tracking the terrorists. Their enquiries lead them to the source of the biological weapon—a nanomachine developed by a pharmaceutical company. An antivirus must be found before more people are killed.

The events in the film version take place between episodes 22 and 23 of the TV series.

Cowboy Gorilla [Comic book character; WW]

First appearance: *Megaton Man* (1984); Creator-Story-Art: Don Simpson; Publisher: Kitchen Sink Press.

Texas-born Cowboy Gorilla was originally a member of the crimefighting Metropolis Quartet led by Megaton Man. He later joined the VW Gang. After an initial run in the superhero parody title *Megaton Man*, Cowboy Gorilla resurfaced in **Don Simpson's Bizarre Heroes** comic book.

Cowboy Heaven [Novel; SFW]

Author: Ron Goulart; First publication: Garden City, NY: Doubleday, 1979.

Published as part of the *Doubleday Science Fiction* series.

Cowboy Zombies (2013) [Film; WW]

Premiere: October 25, 2013; Main Cast: Jarod Anderson as George Rivers, Greg Bronson as Preacher Black, Kiera Crouch as Becky Miller, Paul Winters as Marshal Frank Wilcox, Sandy Penny as Rose Ann, Lee Whitestar as Warrior Chief Datanta; Producers: Paul Winters, Patty Daniels-Winters; Story: Gahan Wilson, Paul Winters; Director: Paul Winters; 88 min.; Winters Film Group; Color.

Low budget Weird Western set in 1870s Arizona Territory and the town of Crumpit. Marshal Frank Wilcox, Preacher Black Apache Chief Datanta, a U.S. Buffalo soldier and Double Peach saloon proprietor Rose Ann lead the fight against the living dead in a battle of survival.

Cowboys & Aliens [Web comic; Graphic novel; SFW]

First appearance: 2006; Creator: Scott Mitchell Rosenberg; Story: Fred Van Lente, Andrew Foley; Art: Luciano Lima; Publisher: Platinum Studios Inc.

When hostile aliens crash-land in the Arizona desert in 1873, they make claim on the Earth for the glory of the House of Dar, burn Fort Larrabie to the ground and slaughter the entire garrison. Trail masters Zeke Jackson, Verity and Father Breen join forces with War Hawk and the Apache Indians in order to save the Earth from the invaders who want to make slaves of mankind. A renegade alien female named Kai Chak Ra also joins the fight against the House of Dar but hides a secret.

This online serialized comic strip was published as a graphic novel in 2006 by Platinum Studios. Commenting on it, Dan Forcey, former vice president of Content Development at Platinum Studios, said,

> We are all western fans at Platinum and are of the general opinion that not as much has been done with the genre as is possible. In the early days of western comics (or even going back to the pulp novels of the previous century), while they were great, the boundaries weren't really stretched into what they could be. We're all fascinated with the time of the Old West, so why not push it to the extreme? Why not add an element of science fiction, as we do in *Cowboys & Aliens*? Why not throw the occult in there like we do in ***Gunplay***?

Cover of *Cowboys & Aliens*. Cover art by Dennis Calero and Luciano Lima. © Platinum Studios Inc. Used with permission.

> We think if we keep pushing the edges of what this genre is, we can use it to really tell stories that are going to grab people's attention.

Cowboys & Aliens (2011) [Film; SFW]

Premiere: June 29, 2011; Main cast: Daniel Craig as Jake Lonergan, Olivia Wilde as Ella Swenson, Harrison Ford as Woodrow Dolarhyde, Keith Carradine as Sheriff John Taggart, Adam Beach as Nat Colorado, Sam Rockwell as Doc; Story: Roberto Orci, Alex Kurtzman, Damon Lindelof, Max Fergus, Hawk Ostby, Steve Oedekerk; Based on the graphic novel by Scott Mitchell Rosenberg; Director: Jon Favreau; 119 min.; Universal Pictures; Color.

1873. Jake Lonergan (Daniel Craig) awakens in the New Mexico Territory desert to find a mysterious hi-tech manacle attached to his wrist. Staggering into the nearby town of Absolution, Lonergan soon finds himself in the middle of an attack by aliens who lasso the townsfolk and yank them into their dragonfly-shaped spacecraft. Only a mysterious, attractive young woman (Olivia Wilde) appears to have knowledge of Lonergan's past and the meaning of the manacle.

Adapted from the graphic novel and with an estimated budget of $163 million the film barely broke even, grossing $175 million worldwide. Reviews were mainly negative. *Los Angeles Times* (July 29, 2011) film critic Kenneth Turan stated the film was "A leaden mash-up of western and science fiction elements that ends up noisy, grotesque and unappealing. This Jon Favreau film features five producers ... six executive producers and six credited writers... No wonder the film plays like a business deal more than a motion picture."

Cowboys & Aliens (2011), starring from left, Olivia Wilde as Ella Swenson, Daniel Craig as Jake Lonergan and Harrison Ford as Woodrow Dolarhyde (Universal Pictures).

Claudia Puig of *USA Today* (July 27, 2011) continued the negative critical reaction. "The action is poky and unimaginative, despite rolling explosions and creepy aliens poking and prodding with their three-fingered appendages. There's a fine line between hitting the familiar touchstones of a genre and feeling like a reheated cliché. *Cowboys & Aliens* teeters into tepid convention and never makes its way out."

Cowboys & Aliens II [Web comic; SFW]

First appearance: 2007; Creator: Scott Mitchell Rosenberg; Story: Alana Joli Abbott; Art: Rick Hershey; Publisher: Platinum Studios Inc.

In this sequel to *Cowboys & Aliens,* the tale of trail masters Zeke Jackson and Verity and Chiricahua Apache Chief War Hawk is concluded as the Earth faces new threats from the Angaarans.

Cowboys vs. Dinosaurs (2015) [Film; WW]

Premiere: May 19, 2015; Main Cast; Rib Hillis as Val Walker, Casey Fitzgerald as Sky, Vernon Wells as Marcus, John Freeman as Henry, Sara Malakul as Dr. Sinclair, Eric Roberts as Trent Walker; Executive Producers: Nick Campagna, Mike Gut, Paul Wittazen; Story: Anthony Fankhauser, Rafael Jordan; Director: Ari Novak; The Oracle Film Group; Marvista Entertainment; Color.

A mine explosion releases dinosaurs which have been living underground for millions of years. In a small western town in modern day America gunslingers fight the dinosaurs and defend the townsfolk—mostly young girls in skimpy outfits—from certain death.

Cowgirls from Hell [Comic book characters; WW]

First appearance: *Immortal Iron Fist: Orson Randall and the Green Mist of Death #1* (February 2008); Story: Matt Fraction; Art: Russ Heath (Part Two); One-shot; Publisher: Marvel.

Four short stories with an arc involving John Aman a.k.a. Prince of Orphans in pursuit of seven mystical golden coins stolen by Orson Randall and his Confederates of the Curious. In Part Two, the busty Cowgirls from Hell use their charms to trap some of the Confederates of the Curious in an Old West town. Writer Matt Fraction has stated that he wrote the strip specifically for artist Russ Heath as a tribute to his infamous *National Lampoon* strip *Cowgirls at War*.

Coyote Ragtime Show (2006) [Anime; Manga; Japan; SW]

1. Anime

Air date: July 6, 2006; Director: Takuya Nonaka; Studio: Ufotable, Licensors: ADV, FUNimation; Color.

With ten days left until his release "Mister," a space "coyote" outlaw, breaks out of jail and attempts to locate the Pirate King Blues' treasure with the help of the Pirate King's daughter. Federal investigators Angelica and Chelsea plus the android assassins from the Criminal Guild, Madame Marciano's Twelve Sisters, are on his trail. And to complicate matters further, the planet is about to be annihilated.

The series shows influences of *Cowboy Bebop* with its mix of genres and stylistic approach.

Season One

Jailbreak (1:01); *The Girl of the Pirate Hideout* (1:02); *The Man That Was Like a Right Arm* (1:03); *The Days Gone By* (1:04); *Never Change* (1:05); *Fierce Fighting* (1:06); *Marciano the Traitor* (1:07); *The Road Goes On to Gigabanks* (1:08); *Jupiter* (1:09); *Angelica Burns* (1:10); *Fading Memories* (1:11); *Coyote* (1:12)

2. Manga

First publication: Serialized in *Comic Rush* (November 26, 2005–January 16, 2007); Story: Ufotable; Art: Tartan Check; Publisher; JIVE Ltd.

The Milky Way federation has threatened to destroy the planet Graceland. But an invaluable treasure buried by the late Pirate King Bruce lies hidden on the planet. His daughter Franka decides to search for it along with space pirate Mister and his band of coyotes. But Madame Marciano and her band of 12 Sisters stand in their way.

Coyote Silk [Novel; WW]

Author: Gino Sky; Illustrator: Elia Haworth; First publication: Berkeley, CA: North Atlantic Books, 1987.

Sequel to *Appaloosa Rising: or, The Legend of the Cowboy Buddha*.

Crawling Sky [Comic book; WW]

First publication: January 2013; Story: Joe R. Lansdale, Keith Lansdale; Art: Brian Denham; Publisher: Antarctic Press.

Reverend Jebediah Mercer comes to the aid of Norville and his wife, Sissy, who encounter a demonic spirit residing in a well on their homestead near the town of Wood Tick, East Texas.

Creeping Dread: The Fantastic Journals of Luther Henry [Novel; WW]

Author: Terry Lloyd Vinson; First publication; 2008; Publisher: Double Dragon Publishing.

A decade after the conclusion of the Civil War, Luther Henry finds himself pursued by a supernatural assassin hunting and killing former members of his Confederate unit "The Phantom Rebs."

Creepy [Comic book]

Horror anthology title that escaped the Comics Code Authority seal of approval by adopting a black & white magazine format. Its success spawned *Eerie*, *Vampirella*, **The Rook**, *The Spirit*, *The Goblin* and *1984* before Warren Publishing went out of business in 1983.

"Spawn of the Cat People"

First publication: #2 (April 1965); Story: Archie Goodwin; Art: Reed Crandall.

Todd, a New Mexico cowboy, rescues a girl from a rowdy gang accusing her of inheriting a curse from her father. But Todd soon begins to wonder if the men were correct in saying she could turn into a panther.

"Revenge of the Beast!" [WW]

First publication: #5 (October 1965); Story: Archie Goodwin; Art: Gray Morrow.

"You'll have a real howl as Uncle Creepy digs his spurs into a Weird Western."

A group surveying the route for a stagecoach come across the sacred burial ground of the Wikasha tribe and discover the soil is full of gold. Despite warnings from an elderly Indian, they dig the soil and risk the wrath of the devil-beast Kwi-Uktena.

"The Sands That Change" [WW]

First publication: #16 (August 1967); Story: Clark Dimond, Terry Bisson; Art: Steve Ditko.

Comic book artist Tom Newman, on his honeymoon in the Mojave Desert, shows his new wife his latest "monster" creation only to find it come to life and pursue him thanks to an ancient American Indian curse.

"BUFFALOED" [WW]

First publication: #62 (May 1974); Story: Larry Herndon; Art: **John Severin**.

Buffalo-bagger Hawkins is thrown from his horse and knocked unconscious, awakening in an Indian settlement. But first appearances can deceive.

The Crimson Skull (1921) [Film; WMW]

Premiere: 1921; Main Cast: Anita Bush as Anita Nelson, Lawrence Chenault as Bob Calem, Bill Pickett, Steve Reynolds; Producer: Richard E. Norman; Norman Film Manufacturing Company; B/W.

This early silent Weird Menace Western had the distinction of featuring an African-American cast, the one-legged Steve "Peg" Reynolds and world champion rodeo rider Bill Pickett. It was a companion piece to *The Bull Dogger* (1921), also filmed in Boley and featuring Pickett. The white-owned independent Norman Film Manufacturing Company based in Jacksonville, Florida made films specifically aimed at the black movie audience between 1921 and 1928.

The promotional circular from Norman Film Manufacturing Company provided a detailed synopsis.

> The opening scenes of this epic of Wild Life and Smoking Revolvers shows the peace loving, All-Colored City of Boley, Oklahoma, snuggling itself on the great Oklahoma Prairie. Its peace has been disturbed by a Band of Outlaws. "The Skull," and his "Terrors," have sown mortal fear into the hearts of the less intrepid of the Countryside, and they have the Sheriff in their power. "The Law and Order League" force his resignation and offer $5,000.00 for the capture of "The Skull," Dead or Alive. Lem Nelson, fearless Cattleman and owner of the Crown C Ranch, is persuaded to take the Sheriff's job. Bob Calem, his ranch foreman, is in love with Nelson's daughter, Anita, and he volunteers his aid to help capture "The Skull." In order to effect the capture of "The Skull," Bob joins his "Gang." While a member, Anita and Steve Reynolds, a one-legged cowboy, are captured by "The Skull." Bob aids them to escape and is accused of being a traitor. As there is no definite proof of his guilt, and opinion is equally divided between members of the "Gang," he is tried by the test of "The Crimson Skull." One drop of blood decides his fate, if he shall live or die.

Croach the Tracker [Comic book character; Podcast character; SW]

First publication: August, 2013; Story: Ben Acker, Ben Blacker; Art: Lar deSouza, Evan Larson, Evan Shaner; Publisher: Archaia Entertainment.

Martian (Marjun), Croach the Tracker, rides with **Sparks Nevada** in his hoversaddle and has been described as a cross between Tonto and Mr. Spock. Like all Martians Croach has regenerative powers and enhanced senses which total twenty-eight. Born without emotions, Croach has begun to comprehend emotions over time thanks to his friendship with **Sparks Nevada** and the **Red Plains Rider** from Earth.

Published as part of a comic strip anthology collection inspired by the popular live audio theater show and podcast, *The Thrilling Adventure Hour* where Mark Gagliardi plays the character.

Crota: A Novel [Novel; WW]

Author: Owl Goingback; First publication: New York: D.I. Fine Books, 1996.

Police turn to Indian magic when a monster who eats herds of cattle at a time and tears human bodies to pieces is set free from his underground lair in Hobbs County, Missouri. Sheriff Skip Harding's investigations lead him into the area of Indian legend and the demon beast named Crota. Native American game warden Jay Little Hawk joins the sheriff as they track the beast down with a magic, stone-pointed arrow.

Crux [Comic book; SFW]

Caprica revives fellow Atlanteans Danik, Tug, Zephre, Verityn and Galvan from stasis, 100,000 years into the future.

"COWBOYS & AZTECS"

First publication: November 2002, *Crux* #19; Story: Chuck Dixon; Art: Steve Epting, Rick Magyar; Publisher: Cross Generation Entertainment.

Zephyre and Verityn visit Geromi in the Old West section of theme park Earth. Their visit takes a turn for the worse when the god-like Gannish and Yala assume control in this two-issue storyline.

"The Cuckoo's Nest" [Pulp fiction; WW]

Author: **Lon Williams**; Character: **Lee Winters**; *Real Western Stories* (April 1956).

Deputy Winters is chosen to play the doomed King Charles I by a strange group of Shakespearean actors who might be vicious murderers or ghosts.

"The Curse of Apache Canyon" [Pulp fiction; UK; WMW]

First publication: *Second Round Up with the Riders of the Range* (1953); Story: Charles Chilton: Art: Frank R. Grey; Publisher: Juvenile Productions Ltd.-The Thames Publishing Co.

Jeff Arnold and old cowhand Luke explore deserted Apache Canyon in a quest to discover the truth behind tales of ghosts and an Apache curse on the gold mine.

> [H]e described the ghost town and the deserted adobe huts, but declared there was no sign of any mine. But there were other things few men that saw them lived to tell about. Ghosts! Yes, ghosts! He'd seen 'em and heard their screams and mournful cries. And no wonder, for weren't they the ghosts of the murdered miners, screaming and yelling as the Apaches tortured them to death?

Curse of the Forty-Niner (2003) [Film; WW]

Premiere: 2003; Main Cast: Karen Black as Aunt Nelly, John Phillip Law as Sheriff Murphy, Richard Lynch as Old Man Prichard, Vernon Wells as Jeremiah Stone, Martin Kove as Caleb; Executive Producer: Peter Lupus; Story: Antonio Olivas; Director: John Carl Buechler; 86 min.; Wanted Entertainment LLC; Color.

A group of friends on a camping trip to Suttersville discover buried gold in an abandoned mine. But Old West miner Jeremiah Stone is still possessive of his treasure and returns from the grave to protect it.

See: ***Miner's Massacre***

Curse of the Undead (1959) [Film; WW]

Premiere: May 1959; Main Cast: Eric Fleming as Preacher Dan Young, Michael Pate as Drake Robey, Kathleen Crowley as Dolores Carter, John Hoyt as Dr. John Carter; Producer: Joseph Gershenson; Story: Edward Dein, Mildred Dein; Director: Edward Dein; 79 min.; Universal-International Pictures; B/W.

Gunslinger Drake Robey's thirst for blood is concentrated on beautiful young women. Preacher Dan Young uncovers Robey's secret and attempts to release Dolores from the power of the vampire.

Custer's Last Jump and Other Collaborations [Book anthology; SFW]

Authors Howard Waldrop with Steven Utley; First publication: Urbana, IL: Golden Gryphon Press, 2003.

In the title story of this anthology of science fiction, fantasy and horror, General Custer's cavalry parachutes into an ambush by Crazy Horse and his Sioux-piloted Confederate monoplanes in an alternative history.

Cyborgs [RPG book; WW]

Author: John Hopler; First publication: 1999; Setting: ***Deadlands: Hell on Earth***; Publisher: Pinnacle Entertainment Group.

Rules for creating a Cyborg-soldier and weapons.

Dadgum Martians Invade the Lucky Nickel Saloon [Novel; WW]

Author: Ken Rand; First publication: Alma, Arkansas: Yard Dog Press, 2006.

Three dadgum Martians who resemble chickens with lips invade the Lucky Nickel Saloon in Laramie, Wyoming.

See: ***Fairy BrewHaHa at the Lucky Nickel Saloon***

Daisy Kutter: The Last Train [Comic book; SFW]

First issue: August 2004; Creator: Kazu Kibuishi; four-issue mini-series; b/w; Publisher: Viper Comics.

Retired gunslinger Daisy Kutter is forced out of retirement to fight robots and outlaws in the Western town of Middleton.

The Damnation Affair [Novel; WW]

Author: Lilith Saintcrow; First publication: New York: Orbit, 2013.

Damnation is an Old West town infused with magic and secrets. Boston society lady Catherine Barrow settles into her new life as schoolmarm in Damnation, but her real purpose in leaving Boston for the western wilderness is to find her older brother Robbie. Sheriff Jack Gabriel holds the key to Cat's quest, for he killed her wayward brother. The only trouble is, he won't stay dead.

Dances with Demons [Comic book; UK; WW]

First issue: September 1993; Story: Simon Jowett; Art: Charlie Adlard; Publisher: Marvel Frontier Comics UK.

Nathaniel Great Owl inherits his Hopi ancestral role as Ghost Dancer and a mission to serve as gatekeeper to the spirit realm. The evil trickster god Iktomi and the Clown Demons fight Nathaniel and his son James Owl for domination of the world of spirits.

"The Dancing Trees" [Pulp Fiction; WW]

Author: **Lon Williams**; Character: **Lee Winters**; *Real Western Stories* (August 1957)

Lee Winters encounters the mythological figures of Orpheus and Eurydice in Tallyho Canyon.

> "...Winters, do you see those aspen trees just there?"
>
> Winters looked. He recalled having seen them before. "Yeah," he said. Then his mouth opened in astonishment. "What's happening to them? At first I thought it was only wind that moved them."
>
> "They are dancing to my music," said Orpheus.
>
> Winters stared in awe. Truly they were dancing. Their roots had become twisting, writhing feet. As Orpheus played a more lively tune, they waved their branches, also, and began to go round in a great circle.
>
> At length as spaces opened and closed between tree branches, Winters understood what Orpheus had meant by prison. Before a vine-covered shelter within that circle of dancing trees stood a young woman of exquisite charm. Glimpses revealed by degrees that her hair, adorned with a blue or purple flower, was fastened round her head in silvery braids; that her garments were white and flimsy; that her figure had fawn-like grace and shapeliness; that she was looking in his direction and with a countenance filled with excitement and expectancy.

Danger Girl [Comic book]

The adventures of "Danger Girls" Abbey Chase and Sydney Savage, led by British Secret Service agent Deuce.

"BACK IN BLACK" [WW]

First publication: 2006; 4-issue mini-series; Story: Andy Hartnell; Art: Nick Bradshaw, Jim Charalampidis, J. Scott Campbell; Publisher: Wildstorm.

In South Dakota, a government convoy is hijacked by a gang of outlaws and a mystical Native American Sioux relic known as the Black Seed is stolen. Originally thought to be lost during the massacre at Wounded Knee in December, 1890 the Black Seed generates the power to grant life but feeds off those fearful of death.

Danger Girls Abbey and Sydney are assigned to go undercover as bikers to infiltrate the gang

of outlaws known as the Roadkillers and recover the stolen artifact. They are joined by the Black Widows who are not as friendly as they first appear to be.

Danielle Moonstar [Comic book character; WW]

First appearance: *Marvel Graphic Novel #4* (December 1982); Creators: Chris Claremont, Bob McLeod; Publisher: Marvel Comics.

A Native American Indian of the Cheyenne Nation, raised on a ranch in Colorado, Moonstar began to exhibit strange powers during puberty including the ability to transform the greatest fear of a person into a physical image. Her grandfather Black Eagle was murdered shortly before he had arranged her to meet mutant leader Professor Charles Xavier. She joined the *New Mutants* following the defeat of her grandfather's killer. She subsequently experienced visions of a "Demon Bear" which she believed was responsible for the death of her parents, William and Peg Lonestar.

Moonstar was also entrusted by Odin with Brightwind, an immortal winged horse of Asgard, thus making her a Valkyrie.

See: **Mirage**; **Psyche**

Daredevil, the Man Without Fear [Comic book]

"PROPHESY" [WW]

First publication: #215 (February 1985); Story: Denny O'Neil: Art: David Mazzucchelli.

Lawyers Matt Murdock (Daredevil) and Matt Hawk (*Two-Gun Kid*) find themselves communicating across time as an Indian land-grabbing scheme by the unscrupulous Mr. Keeno in the Old West is mysteriously echoed in the present.

"The Dark Boy" [Magazine fiction; WW]

Author: August Derleth; First publication; *The Magazine of Fantasy and Science Fiction* (February 1957).

See: *Rod Serling's Night Gallery*

The Dark Tower: The Gunslinger [Novel; WW]

Author: **Stephen King**; First publication: West Kingston, RI: Donald M. Grant, 1982; Illustrated by Michael Whelan.

> Naked between the unforgiving sun and the sterile sand, blind in the bowels of the mountains

where no light penetrates, shadowed by dangers both magic and physical, the gunslinger moved steadily on his destined path.

The Gunslingers from Gilead are descendants of Arthur Eid, the ancient King of All-World. Resembling Old West cowboys in appearance they also have commonalities with the legendary knights of King Arthur. But after their defeat at the Battle of Jericho Hill only one remains.

Roland Deschain, Mid-World's last surviving Gunslinger pursues an elusive sorcerer known as the Man in Black across the post-apocalyptic demon-infested Mohaine Desert. On his journey, Roland befriends the youngster Jake Chambers and encounters a speaking demon, an insane preacher woman and her depraved followers. As its guardian, Roland's ultimate goal is to find the Dark Tower located in a field of roses in the fey realm of End-World. Supported by six magnetic beams that hold all the universes together the Dark Tower lies at the nexus of the beams and is the center of the time-space continuum. The future of the Dark Tower and all of existence is in danger of total annihilation by dark forces and Roland must stop them.

Based on a series of short stories originally published in *The Magazine of Fantasy and Science Fiction* from October 1978 to November 1981, the novel was originally confined to a 10,000-hardback print run because King felt it only appealed to a limited audience. It was so successful the adventures of gunslinger Roland Deschain continued across a total of eight novels and numerous Marvel comic book adaptations. Roland's complex story takes him beyond the Old West environment into New York, Maine and a medieval style world centered on Gilead.

In his introduction to the revised 2003 edition of **Dark Tower: The Gunslinger** Stephen King mentioned that in 1970 in a near empty movie theater in Bangor Maine, he saw Sergio Leone's *The Good, the Bad and the Ugly*. King said, "I realized that what I wanted to write was a novel that contained Tolkien's sense of quest and magic but set against Leone's almost absurdly majestic backdrop."

Another major influence on King was Robert Browning's poem "Childe Roland to the Dark Tower Came," which in turn echoed a line from Shakespeare's *King Lear* (Act 3, Scene 4).

The *Dark Tower* novels that follow *The Gunslinger* are: *The Drawing of the Three* (1987); *The Waste Lands* (1991); *Wizard and Glass* (1997); *Wolves of Calla* (2003); *Song of Susannah* (2004); *The Dark Tower* (2004) and *The Wind Through the Keyhole* (2012).

Cover of *The Dark Tower: The Gunslinger* by Stephen King (1988). Illustrated by Michael Whelan.

The Dark Tower: The Gunslinger Born [Comic book; WW]

First publication: February 2007; Five-issue mini-series; Story adaptation:

Peter David, Robin Furth; Art: Jae Lee, Richard Isanove; Seven-part mini-series; Publisher: Marvel

In the town of Gilead apprentice Roland Deschain becomes an official Gunslinger when, after being provoked by his father's sorcerer, he passes the coming-of-age test at only fourteen years-old. Roland is now the target of Gilead's enemy John Farsons and his assassins. To protect his son and his tet-mates Steven Deschain sends Roland, Cuthbert Allgood and Alain Johns to the Outer Arc town of Hambry. But instead of being a safe haven Hambry is in the grip of John Farson's forces.

This first comic book adaptation of King's *Dark Tower* series incorporates aspects of *The Dark Tower: The Gunslinger* and *Dark Tower: Wizard and Glass*.

Followed by *Dark Tower: The Long Road Home; Treachery, The Sorcerer, Fall of Gilead, Battle of Jericho Hill, The Journey Begins, The Little Sisters of Eluria, The Battle of Tull, The Way Station., The Man in Black, Sheemie's Tale, Evil Ground, So Fell Lord Perth, The Prisoner* and *The House of Cards*— published between 2007 and 2015.

Darkwatch: Curse of the West [Video game; WW]

Release date: August 16, 2005; Voice Cast: Peter Jason as Narrator, Rose McGowan as Tala—Stalking Wolf, Jennifer Hale as Cassidy Sharp, Michael Bell as Cartwright, Keith Szarabajka as Lazarus Malkoth; First-person-shooter (FPS); Sammy Studios, High Moon Studios; Publisher: Capcom Entertainment; USA.

Outlaw Jericho Cross is the latest agent to join the vampire-hunting organization known as Darkwatch. He must hunt vampire lord Lazarus Malkoth and his undead minions through the Old West frontier and capture him before turning into a vampire himself.

First-person-shooter that incorporates Vampire, horror and Western genres.

Dawnbreaker (Legends of the Duskwalker book 3) [Novel; SFW]

Author: Jay Posey; First publication: Nottingham, UK: Angry Robot, 2015.

The conclusion to the *Legends of the Duskwalker* trilogy sees Wren living in Greenstone under the protection of Chapel. Meanwhile Wren's mother Cass has survived the fall of Morningside but faces the threat of the Weir and Asher. The man named Haiku offers to help defeat Asher as he and Wren seek the support of what remains of the House Eight.

Dawn's Uncertain Light [Novel; SFW]

Author: Neal Barrett Jr.; First publication: New York: New American Library-Penguin, 1989.

In this sequel to *Through Darkest America*, Howie Ryder continues the search for his sister Carolee at the government run Silver Island. But he discovers the truth of Silver Island and the Chosen ones does not live up to the government propaganda and when Ryder is told his sister has been killed his quest turns to revenge.

Dawnstar [Comic book character; WW]

First appearance: *Superboy and the Legion of Super-Heroes* #226 (April 1977); Creators: Mike Grell, Paul Levitz; Publisher: DC Comics.

Born on the planet Starhaven, colonized by "Amerinds," descendants of American Indians are renowned for their deep space navigation and skilled piloting.

Dawnstar is the result of centuries of inbreeding. A mutant with a highly sensitive tracking sense, she is capable of flying faster-than-light through the vacuum of intergalactic space. After graduating from the Legion Academy, she joined the **Legion of Super-Heroes**.

DC Special [Anthology comic book]
"Behold the Wild Frontier" [SFW]

First publication: *DC Special* #6, January-March 1970; Story: Mike Friedrich, Art: Gil Kane, Nick Cardy; Publisher: DC Comics.

Introductory new strip that leads into conventional Western reprint strips including Daniel Boone, Davy Crocket, Kit Carson, Buffalo Bill, **Tomahawk** and **Pow-Wow Smith**.

This issue features striking Neal Adams cover art of cowboys and Indians watching in awe as a rocketship lifts off in the desert.

The Dead and the Damned a.k.a. Cowboys & Zombies (2011) [Film; WW]

Premiere: July 26, 2011; Main Cast: David A. Lockhart as Mortimer, Camille Montgomery as Rhiannon, Rick Mora as Indian-Brother Wolf, Robert Amstler as The German; Executive Producer: Jill Gibson; Writer-Director: Rene Perez; 82 min.; Mattia Borrani Productions, iDiC Entertainment; Color.

The townsfolk of a Californian mining town in 1949 are turned into ravenous mutant zombies when a meteor lands during the gold rush.

Dead in the West [Novel; Comic book; WW]

1. Author: **Joe R. Lansdale**; First publication: New York: Space and Time, 1986.

An Indian medicine man curses the town and people of Mud Creek as he is lynched by a mob. Zombies rise from their graves and disillusioned Reverend Jebidiah Mercer is the only man who can save the town.

2. Comic book: First publication: October 1993; Original Story: Joe R. Lansdale; Adaptation: Neal Barrett Jr.; Art: Jack Jackson; two-issue mini-series; Publisher: Dark Horse Comics.

Black & white adaptation of Lansdale's novel about a community cursed for their prejudice.

Dead Iron: The Age of Steam (Book #1) [Novel; SPW]

Author: Devon Monk; First publication: New York: Roc, 2011.

Bounty hunter Cedar Hunt is a cursed lycanthrope with a mission—to find the brother he long thought dead. Hunt must confront the ancient Strange to recover the powerful, destructive weapon known as the Holder.

The multi-point-of-view story takes the reader through a steam age American landscape, complete with strange machines, guns, monsters and magic. The story is continued in the second book in the Age of Steam series, **Tin Swift**.

Dead Irons [Comic book; WW]

First publication: February, 2009; 4-issue mini-series; Story: James Kuhoric; Art: Jason Alexander, Jae Lee; Publisher: Dynamite.

The Irons are three undead bounty hunters roaming the Old West who strike fear wherever they go. Only Silas Irons can hope to offer them salvation and put an end the curse that turned the siblings into the walking dead. But Silas is tackling his own demons.

Dead Man (1996) [Film; USA-Germany; WW]

Premiere: May 10, 1996; Main Cast: Johnny Depp as William Blake, Gary Farmer as Nobody, Robert Mitchum as John Dickinson, Lance Henriksen as Cole Wilson, John Hurt as John Scholfield, Gabriel

AMERICA WAS BUILT ON BLOOD, SWEAT, AND GEARS.

"Dead Iron is a relentless Western and a gritty steampunk, bound together by wicked magic....Devon Monk rocks."
—NEW YORK TIMES BESTSELLING AUTHOR ILONA ANDREWS

AUTHOR OF *MAGIC ON THE HUNT*

Cover of *Dead Iron: The Age of Steam* by Devon Monk (2011).

Byrne as Charlie Dickinson; Producer: Demetra J. MacBride; Story-Director: Jim Jarmusch; 121 min.; Pandora Filmproduktion, 12-Gauge Productions, FFA Berlin Filmboard, Berlin-Brandenburg, Filmstiftung NRW; B/W.

William Blake leaves his native Cleveland for a factory job in the frontier town of Machine, and discovers the job has been taken. A comforting one-night stand results in the angry boyfriend (Byrne) killing the woman and Blake killing him in return. Fleeing the town with a bullet lodged next to his heart, Blake encounters an American Indian named "Nobody" who mistakes him for the visionary English artist and poet William Blake and takes him on both a physical and spiritual journey.

A mystical Western from independent film director Jim Jarmusch, noted for his dislike of

Dead Man (1996), a film starring Johnny Depp as William Blake (Pandora Filmproduktion, 12-Gauge Productions, FFA Berlin Filmboard, Berlin-Brandenburg, Filmstiftung NRW).

American pop culture and for his interest in marginal characters and themes.

Dead Man's Hand: An Anthology of the Weird West [Short story anthology; WW]

Editor: John Joseph Adams; First publication: London UK: Titan Books; 2014.

Twenty-three original stories of horror, science fiction and fantasy set in the Old West. "Hell on the High Frontier" by David Farland features a ranger hunting deadly clockwork soldiers; "The Red-Headed Dead" by Joe R. Lansdale sees a preacher track a vampire; Wild Bill Hickok is resurrected in "Dead Man's Hand" by Christie Yant; Orson Scott Card contributes a new Alvin Maker story in "Alvin and the Apple Tree" featuring Johnny Appleseed. Other subjects include dragons, zombies. aliens, shape-shifters, elves,

magic and dinosaurs by authors Jeffrey Ford, Fred Van Lente, Charles Yu, Rajan Khanna, Tobias S. Buckell, Mike Resnick, Hugh Howey, Beth Revis, Walter Jon Williams, Ben H. Winters, Laura Anne Gilman, Tad Williams, Jonathan Maberry, Elizabeth Bear, Ken Liu and Alan Dean Foster.

Dead Man's Hand: Five Tales of the Weird West [Book anthology; WW]

Author: Nancy A. Collins; First publication: 2004; Publisher: Two Wolf Press.

A collection of Collins' novellas **Walking Wolf** and **Lynch**, the short stories "Calaverada" and "The Tortuga Hill Gang's Last Ride," and an all-new vampire Western novella, *Hell Come Sundown.*

Dead Noon (2007) [Film; Australia; WW]

Premiere: 2007; Main Cast: Robert Bear as Frank, Lillith Fields as Grace, Robert Milo Andrus as Stuart, Tye Nelson as Kane; Producers: Marianne Myers, Matthew Taggart; Story: Keith Suta, Matthew Taggart, Andrew Wiest; Director: Andrew Wiest; 85 min.; Australia; Blue Collar Pictures; Color.

An outlaw from the Wild West is resurrected to seek revenge on the town of Weston.

The Dead of Winter [Novel: WW]

Author: Lee Collins; First publication: Long Island City, NY: Angry Robot, 2012.

1883. In the Old West mining town of Leadville, Colorado monster hunters Cora Oglesby and husband Ben are hired by the town Marshal to investigate the cause of two unnatural deaths. The Wendigo may be to blame for the violent deaths but they soon discover other monsters lurking within the mines.

Cora Oglesby's story is continued in the 2013 sequel **She Returns from War**.

Dead Presidents [RPG book; WW]

Author: Christopher McGlothlin; First publication: 2001; **Deadlands: The Weird West** Adventure book series; Publisher: Pinnacle Entertainment Group.

When a posse is hired by the Texas Rangers to investigate the Black Circle in Gomorra, they find themselves traveling Back East.

Dead Reckoning [Juvenile book; WW]

Authors: Mercedes Lackey, Rosemary Edghill; First publication: New York: Bloomsbury Children's Books, 2012.

In 1867 Texas three disparate souls join forces to investigate a zombie invasion. Jett Gallatin is a young woman posing and living as a male gambler and sharpshooter searching the Old West for her twin brother. Honoria Gibbons is a smart inventor investigating invisible airships and White Fox is a young, white U.S. Army scout, raised by native Americans, investigating the disappearance of a soldier's family. As the three youngsters investigate the zombies they learn there is a sinister force behind the undead army terrorizing the West.

"The Dead Remember"
[Pulp fiction; WW]

Author: **Robert E. Howard**; First publication: *Argosy* (August 15, 1936).

Texas, 1877. In an argument over crooked dice when shooting craps Jim Gordon shoots and kills Old Joel and his Negro wife Jezebel. Before she dies, the wife places a curse on the cowboy and tells Gordon, "Before this day rolls around again, you'll be branding the devil's cows in hell. You'll see, I'll come to you when the time's ripe and ready."

Gordon lives in fear of the curse coming true as he experiences a run of bad luck. Teamster Thomas Allison recalls an incident at the Big Chief saloon, "Then I saw a woman standing in front of me. The light was dim that streamed out into the alley through the open door, but I saw her plain enough to tell she was a Negro woman. I don't know how she was dressed. She was not pure black, but a light brown or yellow. I could tell that in the dim light. I was so surprised I stopped short, and she spoke to me and said, 'Go tell Jim Gordon I've come for him.'"

Allison tells Gordon who reacts in terror and runs into the alley screaming. A gunshot is heard. Bartender Mike O'Donnell is the first to witness the scene.

"His right hand was torn practically off, being just a mass of bloody tatters. His head was shattered in a way I had never seen caused by a gunshot."

The coroner's report concludes Gordon's death is by accidental gunshot wounds caused by the "bursting of the deceased's pistol" after failing

I shot him twice

The Dead Remember
By ROBERT E. HOWARD

She had cursed him by the big snake and the black swamp and the white cock. What was it, then, that killed Jim Gordon?

Title page for "The Dead Remember" published in *Argosy* (August 15, 1936). Courtesy Jeffrey H. Shanks.

to remove a cleaning rag from the barrel. A cleaning rag that was originally part of a woman's red and green checkered dress.

The Dead Rider [Comic book; WW]

First publication: 2008; Creator-Story-Artist: Kevin Ferrara; Publisher: Dark Horse Comics.

Jacob Bierce is granted immortality by a witch but it comes with a price. Wounds don't heal and soon he becomes nothing more than an immortal rotting corpse at the mercy of the bog witch.

Kevin Ferrara, describing his creation, stated,

I think the overarching concept behind *The Dead Rider* is that immortality isn't all it's cracked up to be and that the vagaries of life and death consist of iconic irrefutable changes that have to be rolled with, rather than railed against. Each character in the series is dealing with mortality in a different way.

Dead Walkers (2009) [Film; WW]

Premiere: June 24, 2010; Main Cast: Michael Shepherd as Jack Link, Cheryl Hanley as Sepe, Brendan Hunter as Dick, Dale Buchanan as the Zombie Sheriff, Lisa Marie Di-Giacinto as Beth, Adam Sterling as Wilbur, Charlotte Mitchell as the Zombie Prostitute; Producers: Spencer Estabrooks, Greg Jeffs, Adrian Young; Story: Spencer Estabrooks, Keith Lawrence; Director: Spencer Estabrooks; 14 min.; Cedar Boy Pictures, Dead West Productions; Color.

Bounty hunter and gunslinger Jack Link finds himself surrounded by zombies in an Old West frontier town and must break the curse of the undead.

Dead West [Graphic novel; WW]

First appearance: September 2005; Creators: Rick Spears, Rob G; Story: Rick Spears; Publisher: Gigantic Graphic Novels.

The one Indian who survived a massacre vengefully places a curse on the town in which the dead rise from their graves to prey upon the living. Meanwhile, a bounty hunter with no conscience is on the prowl.

Dead West a.k.a. Cowboys and Vampires (2010) [Film; WW]

Premiere: October 9, 2010; Main Cast: Jasen Wade as Johnny Dust, Angelica Celaya as Gloria Valenzuela, Shannon Whirry as Sarah Dust, Ariel Myers as Kim Dust, Emily Peizer as Susan, Clint James as Miles; Executive producers: Douglas Myers, Lisa M. Hilton, Faridah Zainal Bryant; Story-Director: Douglas Myers; 94 min.; Duck Soup Productions, Ghost Town LLC; Color.

Struggling Western movie actor Johnny Dust discovers the truth behind the new management team who take control of a theme park and film studio for a Halloween spectacular.

Deadlands: Ghostwalkers [Novel; WW]

Author: Jonathan Maberry; First publication: Tor, Fall 2015.

Promotional cover art by Aaron Riley for the novel *Deadlands: Ghostwalkers* by Jonathan Maberry (2015) (Deadlands is a registered TM and © of Pinnacle Entertainment. Deadlands fiction is exclusively licensed to and produced by Visionary Comics, LLC. All rights reserved. Used with permission).

A haunted gun-for-hire arrives in Paradise Falls and finds the townsfolk in the grips of a brilliant but evil alchemist who is creating terrifying weapons of mass destruction alongside an army of the living dead.

Deadlands: Hell on Earth [RPG game; WW]

Publication date: 1998; Role-Playing Game (RPG); Writer & Design: Shane Lacy Hensley, B. D. Flory; Publisher: Pinnacle Entertainment Group.

The supernatural Reckoners have left a Wasted West in their path of destruction and walk upon it in mortal form. Conflicting groups that include Gunfighters, Junkers, Sykers, Ravenites, Templars, Toxic Shamans and Doomsayers prowl the irradiated High Plains.

Post-apocalyptic setting for **Deadlands: The Weird West**.

Deadlands: Hell on Earth d20 [RPG game; WW]

Publication date: 2002; Role-Playing Game (RPG); Writer & Design: Fred Jandt with Shane Lacy Hensley, John Hopler; Publisher: Pinnacle Entertainment Group.

Sequel to **Deadlands: The Weird West** in the d20 rules system.

Deadlands: Hell on Earth Reloaded [RPG; SFW]

First publication: 2012; Story: Shane Lacey Hensley; Publisher: Pinnacle Entertainment Group.

In the year 2097 the hellish aftermath of the lengthy Cold War between the United and Confederate States of America sees a grim battle for survival in the post-apocalyptic Wasted West. Vast hordes of the undead claim territory east of the Mississippi and violent winds comprising of tortured, irradiated souls surround bombed cities. The Cult of Doom, centered around their leader Silas Rasmussen seeks the destruction of non-mutants. Time to remake the world and vanquish foes in the Savage Worlds game system.

Deadlands: Hell on Earth: The Wasted West [RPG book; WW]

Designer: Shane Lacy Hensley; First publication: 1998; Publisher: Pinnacle Entertainment Group. Authors: Shane Lacy Hensley, Ron Spencer, Charles Ryan; First publication: 1998; Publisher: Pinnacle Entertainment Group.

Worldbook featuring updates and facts on the Last War, the fate of the Maze and the Cult of Lost Angels, and the inner secrets of the Combine.

Core rules and settings for **Deadlands: Hell on Earth** RPG game.

Deadlands: The Kid: Origins [Comic book; WW]

First publication: 2012; Story: C. Edward Sellner; Art: Oscar Capristo (Pt.1), Alejandro Aragon (Pt. 2-4); Publisher: Pinnacle, Visionary Comics.

A stranger walks into a saloon in Silver City, New Mexico and encounters the cattle rustling Montoya Brothers who discover to their misfortune that you don't upset a werewolf. But Billy the Kid is without fear and shoots the werewolf with a silver bullet to the head. From a jail cell The Kid recalls his origins with a story of werewolves and an a Comanche Shaman named Five Dancer who transports him to the spiritual Great Hunting Grounds, teaching him how to survive and granting him the power to literally smell trouble ahead.

Deadlands: Lost Colony [RPG game; RPG book; WW]

Publication date: 2002; Role-Playing Game (RPG); Writer & Design: Shane Lacy Hensley; Publisher: Pinnacle Entertainment Group. Author: John R. Hopler; First publication: 2002; Publisher: Pinnacle Entertainment Group.

The third and final installment of the Deadlands setting, *Lost Colony* combines science fiction, horror and Western genres.

The Tunnel between Earth and the planet Banshee is no more. Colonists from Earth are trapped on a world of howling winds and warring aliens and the Reckoners are not far behind.

Deadlands: The Battle for Slaughter Gulch [BG; WW]

First publication: 2010; Publisher: Twilight Creations.

Slaughter Gulch was once a quiet western town seen as a safe haven from the terrors of the Weird West. But the discovery of priceless Ghost Rock gave way to Shamans, Mad Scientists, Hucksters and others, all claiming control of the mystical element. Thriving on the new environment of fear and greed are the Reckoners, waiting to create Hell on Earth.

A board game for two to six players whose aim is to seek control of Slaughter Gulch and the Ghost Rock.

Deadlands: The Cackler [Comic book: WW]

First publication: April, 2015; 4-issue mini-series; Story: Shane Hensley; Art: Bart Sears; Publisher: Pinnacle, Visionary Select.

A stagecoach carrying a precious cargo is attacked by a gigantic scorpion and blown up by the Cackler and his lieutenants. The Cackler is an ancient Harrowed in search of a mysterious blood relative called Rachel. Meanwhile the Texas Rangers and Agency have invoked the

Cover of *Deadlands: The Cackler* graphic novel (2015). Art by Bart Sears (Deadlands is a registered TM and © of Pinnacle Entertainment. Deadlands fiction is exclusively licensed to and produced by Visionary Comics, LLC. All rights reserved. Used with permission).

"Twilight Protocol" to try to stop his nefarious plans. Joining the hunt is Rachel's sister, a former Witchita Witch known as Morgan Lash.

Deadlands: The Raven [Comic book: WW]

First publication: 2013; 5-issue mini-series; Story: Matthew Cutter, C. Edward Sellner; Art and Plotter: Greg LaRocque; Publisher: Pinnacle, Visionary Select.

December 14, 1763, in Conestoga Town, Pennsylvania. A young boy awakens, drenched in blood, surrounded by fire and smoke and the sight of his slaughtered family and friends.

December 14, 1869, in the hills of Arizona the young Native American boy is now an old man known as the Raven, the last son of the Susquehannock. After torturing the elderly Anasazi, whose spirit is bound to the mortal form of Francisco Vasquez de Coronado, leader of the Conquistadors, he tells him of his youth under the oppression of the white man. With his tribe ravaged by illness and forced into adopting the white man's customs and religion, Raven falls in love with the Reverend John Elder's beautiful daughter, Elizabeth. But at heart the Reverend is an evil man who seeks the death of the Indian heathens.

Raven has become increasingly embittered and as the immortal Raven Doombringer, sets free evil incarnate in the form of the Reckoners with the intention of cleansing the earth of the white man "in a wave of darkness, determined to extinguish all light."

Deadlands: Volume One: Deadman's Hand [Graphic novel; WW]

First publication: April, 2015; Publisher: IDW Publishing.

A collection of stories from the 2011 *Deadlands: One-Shot* comic book series. The collection also includes two eight page stories:

What a Man's Got to Do; Story: Matthew Cutter; Art: Ulises Roman; Great Rail Wars veteran Lucas Pitt joins a posse in Bisbee to track down Chuckles Ryan and his Laughin' Men. But after the shootout Pitt revives to find Apaches leaning over him telling him of a Manitou that lies within him. He soon learns revenge is sweet when you can stay one step ahead of death.

Vengeful; Story: Shane Lacy Hensley; Art: Sean Lee; Tremane seeks vengeance on the Marshal who imprisoned him, but when Tremane and his gang murder the Marshal's wife they forget that in the Weird West some folks don't stay dead for long.

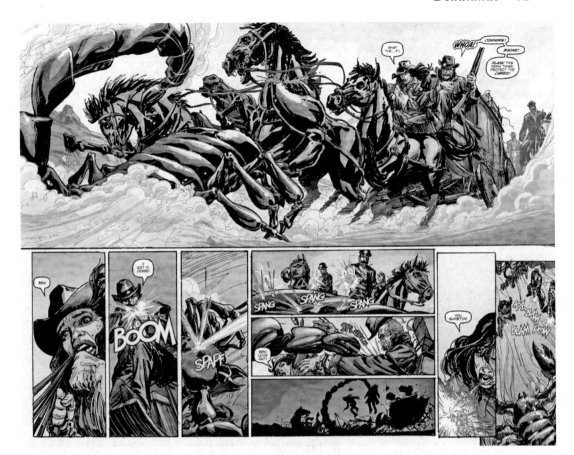

Deadlands: The Cackler graphic novel (2015). Story by Shane Hensly, art by Bart Sears (Deadlands is a registered TM and © of Pinnacle Entertainment. Deadlands fiction is exclusively licensed to and produced by Visionary Comics, LLC. All rights reserved. Used with permission).

Deadlands One Shot [Comic book; WW]

First publication: August 1999; Story: Matt Forbeck; Art: Kevin Sharpe, Richard Pollard; Publisher: Image.

Strip based on the role-playing game featuring Ronan Lynch, Bad Luck Betty and Velvet van Helter against the Weird West's notorious Hangin' Judge.

Deadlands: One-Shot was re-launched in 2011 as a limited series.

Deadlands One-Shot: Black Water [Comic book; WW]

First publication: September 2011; Story: Jeff Mariotte; Art: Brook Turner; Publisher: Pinnacle, Image.

Greenwich Village, New York. Madame Slavatsky, spiritualist, medium and advisor gives a reading to Harmon Rappaport. He is told the woman he is infatuated with is dead, but Rappaport refuses to believe her. Out West Lyle Crumbfine, guide to the channels of the Maze, leads Rappaport and his bodyguard Ian Fairfax into the Maze on a steamboat full of passengers in the hope of finding the woman of his dreams. Awaiting him is the dreaded Black Water. Nobody knows why it's acidic content is lethal to the touch. Some say it's a curse of the Reckoning, while others say it's affected by prolonged contact with Ghost Rock.

Deadlands One-Shot: Death Was Silent [Comic book; WW]

First publication: August 2011; Story: Ron Marz; Art: Bart Sears; Publisher: Pinnacle, Image.

Hoyt Cooper had his tongue cut out by savages who also killed his now Harrowed brother. Now Cooper has the ability to communicate his thoughts with an enchanted chalkboard he wears around his neck. As he rides into a rain drenched

Dandelion Flats he has only one thought in mind—to place all the evil in town unleashed by the Reckoning back into the pit of hell.

Deadlands One-Shot: Massacre at Red Wing [Comic book; WW]

First publication: July 2011; Story: Jimmy Palmiotti, Justin Gray; Art: Lee Moder; Publisher: Pinnacle, Image.

Young warrior woman Clementime was raised by a handmaiden who told her Mahala Two Suns, her mother, had had been sold into slavery. With her faithful dog Hondo by her side, Clementine journeys south to find her but soon finds herself on a quest that will take her through the Deadlands to find Raven, the man who raped her mother.

Deadlands One-Shot: The Devil's Six-Gun [Comic book; WW]

First publication: June 2011; Story: David Gallaher; Art: Steve Ellis; Publisher: Pinnacle, Image.

By the age of twenty young Copernicus Blackburne from Prague has earned a reputation as an inventor and gunsmith. When Copernicus is approached by reclusive inventor Samuel Tygian to meet him in America, Copernicus is intrigued and leaves his family to make the journey across the Atlantic in the spring of 1867.

Tygian enrolls "Perny," as he affectionately calls Copernicus, into university under the agreement he will work for him for a period of no more than three years. But Tygian becomes impatient and takes Perny out of university before graduation to travel out West to Mount Necessity in Salt Lake City in order to tackle the problem of Darius Hellstromme.

Tygian sets Perny the challenge of making a gun that harnesses the power of Ghost Rock that can kill Hellstromme. But the creation of the Devil's Six-Gun brings the effects of Ghost Rock fever and heartache and personal tragedy for Copernicus.

Deadlands One-Shot: Black Water (2011)(Deadlands is a registered TM and © of Pinnacle Entertainment. Deadlands fiction is exclusively licensed to and produced by Visionary Comics, LLC. All rights reserved. Used with permission).

Deadlands: Reloaded [RPG game; WW]

Publication date: May 2006; Role-Playing Game (RPG); Writer & Design: Shane Lacy Hensley; Publisher: Pinnacle Entertainment Group.

Savage Worlds game engine version of **Deadlands: The Weird West**.

Deadlands Reloaded: Coffin Rock [RPG book; WW]

Author: Sean Michael Fish; First publication: 2008; Setting: Deadlands; System: Savage Worlds; Publisher: Pinnacle Entertainment Group

Adventure set in the mining town of Coffin Rock, Colorado. Elements include a posse protecting the town from a serial killer, ghosts roaming the streets, and a troublesome preacher and outlaws.

Deadlands Reloaded: Devil's Night [RPG book; WW]

First publication: 2011; Author: Shane Lacy Hensley; Art: Alberto Froche, T. Jordan Peacock, Richard Pollard; Publisher: Pinnacle Entertainment Group.

Doctor Herbert Langston creates a machine called "the reducer" that extracts ghost rock. But when it explodes and kills 17 workers he flees with his daughter Daphne and flees to Wichita, Kansas.

Deadlands Reloaded: Don't Drink the Water [RPG book; WW]

First publication: 2009; Story: John Goff; Art: Paul Carrick, William O'Connor, Paolo Parente, Jim Pavelec; Publisher: Pinnacle Entertainment Group.

The posse journeys to Mexico where they aid revolutionaries, dodge the Foreign Legion and return the dead to Boot Hill.

Deadlands Reloaded: The 1880 Smith & Robards Catalog [RPG Sourcebook; WW]

First publication: July 2011; Story: Clint Black, Matthew Cutter, John Goff, Shane Lacy Hensley; Art: Doomtown Artists, Joel Kinstle, Ashe Marler, MKultra Studio; Publisher: Pinnacle Entertainment Group, Studio 2 Publishing.

The *1880 Smith & Robards Catalog* includes all the weapons, clothing, armor, elixirs, tonics and various gadgets and supplies a player will require for their *Deadlands Reloaded* Savage Worlds game.

Deadlands Reloaded: The Flood [RPG Sourcebook; WW]

First publication: 2008; Story: Shane Hensley, Matthew Cutter; Art: Beet, Heather Bruton, Leanne Buckley, Ed Cox; Publisher: Pinnacle Entertainment Group, Studio 2 Publishing.

The first Plot Point Campaign begins in 1879 on the Weird West Coast in California, home of the Maze's lucrative ghost rock trade. But standing in your way is Reverend Grimme, ruler of the city of Lost Angels and its surroundings.

Deadlands Reloaded: For Whom the Whistle Blows: Night Train 2 [RPG; WW]

First publication: 2010; Story: John Goff, Simon Lucas; Art: Beet, Hared Blando, Richard Clark, David R. Deitrick; Publisher: Pinnacle Entertainment Group.

Baron LaCroix intends to win the Great Rail War with a revitalized weapon of terror.

Deadlands Reloaded: Ghost Towns [RPG Sourcebook; WW]

First publication: 2012; Story: Ric Byrne Connely, Matthew Cutter, Piotr Korys, Tomasz Z. Majkowski; Art: Chris Bivins, Mike Burns, Mike Chaney, Carly Sorge; Publisher: Pinnacle Entertainment Group, Studio 2 Publishing, GG Studio.

The *Tombstone Epitaph* "Special Report" briefly details sevens town in the Weird West along with locations and major characters. The *Marshal's Section* goes into more detail concerning the history of the towns, local characters and locations of note. A locale generator enables players to create new towns.

Deadlands Reloaded: Grim Prairie Tales [RPG; WW]

First publication: December, 2013; Story: John Goff; Publisher: Pinnacle Entertainment Group.

Nineteen Savage Tales with maps, descriptions and vital statistics plus stats for Weird West cowboys, gamblers, lawmen, bears, boars and cougars.

Deadlands Reloaded: Guess Who's Coming to Donner? [RPG book; WW]

First publication: 2012; Story: John Goff; Art: Aaron Acevedo, Michael Cutter, Joe Kinstle; Publisher: Pinnacle Entertainment Group.

Beware of the party lost in the Sierra Nevadas snow in Truckee Pass. Especially if their name is the Donners. Don't have your neighbors for dinner!

Deadlands Reloaded: The Inheritors [RPG book; WW]

First publication: 2013; Authors: Matthew Cutter, Zach Welhouse; Art: Chris Bivins, Johan Lindroos, Alida Saxon; Publisher: Pinnacle Entertainment Group.

A posse member inherits Aunt Agatha's family farm in Kansas, but old feuds and Black River may ruin the path to Easy Street.

Deadlands Reloaded: The Last Sons [RPG Sourcebook; WW]

First publication: October, 2012; Story: Matthew Cutter, Matt Forbeck, Clint Black, Paul Beakley; Art: Aaron Acevedo, Justin Adams, Paul Daly, Doomtown Artists; Publisher: Pinnacle Entertainment Group.

The second Plot Point Campaign begins in 1880 in the Disputed Territories of the Dakotas, Colorado, Nebraska, Oklahoma, Montana, Wyoming and Kansas.

Deadlands Reloaded: Lone Killers of the Southwest [RPG sourcebook; WW]

First publication: 2015; Story: Matthew Cutter, Steven S. Long; Art: Darnell Johnson, Allen Nunis; Publisher: Pinnacle Entertainment Group.

History, stats and story seeds for Clay Allison, John Wesley Hardin, Deacon Jim Miller, Black Bart and Dave Rudabaugh in preparation for the Deadlands campaign.

Deadlands Reloaded: Marshal's Handbook [RPG Sourcebook; WW]

First publication: 2010; Story: Clint Black, Dave Brewer, Matthew Cutter, B.D. Flory; Art: Aaron Acevedo, Travis Anderson, Chris Appel, Tom Baxa; Publisher: Pinnacle Entertainment Group, GG Studio, Studio 2 Publishing.

The setting book for **Deadlands Reloaded**.

Deadlands Reloaded: Murder on the Hellstromme Express [RPG book; WW]

First publication: 2009; Story: Matthew Cutter, Rick Dakan, Jack Emmert; Art" Justin Adams. Beet, Liz Danforth, Tom Fowler; Publisher: Pinnacle Entertainment Group.

A train full of Mad Scientists is headed for the Kansas Scientific Exposition where they are competing to win a contract with Hellstromme Industries. Warped time and strange elixirs and concoctions await on the perilous train journey.

Deadlands Reloaded: Player's Guide [RPG book; WW]

First publication: January, 2012; Story: Shane Hensley; Publisher: Pinnacle Entertainment Group.

The core rules book players of **Deadlands Reloaded**. Includes new rules for shootouts at high noon, Edges, Hindrances.

Deadlands Reloaded: Return to Manitou Bluff [RPG Book; WW]

First publication: 2012; Story: Matthew Cutter, Patrick Cutter, Shane Lacy Hensley, John R. Hensley, John R. Hopler; Art: Aaron Acevedo, Chris Bivins, Doomtown Artists, Andy Park; Publisher: Pinnacle Entertainment Group, Studio 2 Publishing.

Manitou Bluff is a dumping ground for the outcasts of Maze society where death or something worse can be waiting around the next corner. An adventure for Legendary heroes.

Deadlands Reloaded: Saddle Sore [RPG Book; WW]

First publication: 2010; Story: Paul "Wiggy" Wade-Williams; Art: Aaron Acevedo, Michael Apice, Aaron Boyd; Publisher: Pinnacle Entertainment Group.

Six sinister short stories designed as interludes for the player's journeys.

Deadlands Reloaded: Stone and a Hard Place [RPG Sourcebook; WW]

First publication: March, 2015; Story: Matthew Cutter; Art: Daniel Rudnicki, Mike Burns, James Denton, Carly Sorge, Bryan Syme, Headfirst Studios; Publisher: Pinnacle Entertainment Group.

Sourcebook and Plot Point Campaign for the *Deadlands Rebooted* setting, detailing the *Strange Locales*, the *Marshall's Territory* and new rules for creating characters, including the undead Harrowed in the *Player's Section*. The player is introduced to the *Deadlands* setting in the form of an editorial and newspaper reports from *The Tombstone Epitaph*. The Plot Point Campaign begins in Tombstone, Arizona in 1881, before the gunfight at the OK Corral.

Deadlands Reloaded: A Tale of Two Killers [RPG book; WW]

First publication: 2015; Author: Matthew Cutter; Pinnacle Entertainment Group.

Travelers to Dante's Ferry, Nevada on the banks of Pyramid Lake can get lost in the shadows and encounter the oldest living "Harrowed," the Deathly Drifter, Stone and the Cackler Gang.

Deadlands Reloaded: The Tombstone Seven [RPG Sourcebook; WW]

First publication: 2015; Authors: Clint Black, Jodi Black, Matthew Cutter; Art: Cheyenne Wright; Publisher: Pinnacle Entertainment Group.

Designed for *Deadlands: Reloaded: Stone and a Hard* Place, the Tombstone Seven consist of Luke Pitt—Harrowed, Carmen Valenzuela—Hexslinger, Virginia Ann Earp—Gunslinger, Warren Earp—Texas Ranger, Ned Harkness—Former Outlaw, Matilda Loomis—Shaman and Cooper Grannon—Mad Scientist.

Deadlands Reloaded: Trail Guides Volume One [RPG; WW]

First publication: March 2013; Story: Matthew Cutter; Publisher: Pinnacle Entertainment Group.

Compilation volume of the first three Trail Guides: *South o' the Border*, *The Great Northwest* and *Weird White North*.

Deadlands Reloaded: What a Man's Got to Do [Webcomic; WW]

First publication: 2014; Story: Matthew Cutter; Art: Ulisses Roman; Publisher: Pinnacle.

Death comes in many shapes and sizes.

Deadlands Tall Tales [RPG; WW]

First publication: 2014; Protocol Game Series; Designer: Jim Pinto; Art: Rick Hershey; Publisher: Pinnacle Entertainment Group.

Deadlands Tall Tales is a narrative role-playing game set in **Deadlands: The Weird West** for three or more players. Players assume the roles of directors outside the action and characters inside the action.

Deadlands Territory Guide [RPG book; WW]

First publication: 2004; #1 Newfoundland: Rock of Ages; Setting: **Deadlands: The Weird West**; Publisher: Legion Publishing.

Guide for exploring the Newfoundland area of the Great Weird North

Deadlands: The Epitaph [RPG magazine; WW]

First publication: 2000; Editors: Shane Lacy Hensley, John Goff; Setting: **Deadlands: Hell on Earth**; Publisher: Pinnacle Entertainment Group.

A magazine featuring new dime novels, adventures and rules that ran to four issues.

#1 *Deadlands: Hell on Earth* dime novel "Story's End" by John Hopler; Deadlands adventure "Trouble at Table Rock" by Joseph Wolf; "Ronan Lynch" comic book by Clay and Susan Griffith.

#2 *Deadlands: Hell on Earth* adventure "Biodome 2" by Jay Kyle; "The Medicine Bag" by John Hopler; "A Little Knowledge" by John Goff; "Hellhole" comic book by Clay and Susan Griffith.

#3 *Deadlands: Hell on Earth* dime novel "Devil's Night" by John Hopler; "Guess Who's Coming to Donner?" by John Goff.

#4 *Deadlands: Lost Colony* adventure "High Noon on the High Seas" by Rob Lusk and the Flatlands Game Group; Deadlands: "Range Wars Solo!" by Tony Van.

Deadlands: The Great Rail Wars [MBG game; WW]

Author: Shane Lacy Hensley; First publication: 1998; Miniatures Battle Game; Publisher: Pinnacle Entertainment Group.

Heroes and posses of metal miniatures battle to decide the fate of the Weird West.

Deadlands: The Weird West [RPG game; WW]

Publication date: 1996; Role-Playing Game (RPG); Writer & Design: Shane Lacy Hensley; Publisher: Pinnacle Entertainment Group.

Alternate history RPG set in the year 1876 where the Reckoners have changed time and the South has won its independence. California is a shattered state of flooded sea canyons and the power source known as "ghost rock" fuels steampunk machines and is the cause of war between various factions wanting control of the rock.

Players are gunfighters, sorcerers known as hucksters, shamans, savage braves, mad scientists, and others who attempt to prevent the "Reckoning."

Deadlands: The Weird West d20 [RPG game; WW]

Authors: John Goff, Shane Lacy Hensley, John Hopler; First publication: 2001; Setting: **Deadlands: The Weird West**; Publisher: Pinnacle Entertainment Group.

D20 rules system version updated to the year 1879.

"The Deadly Slowpoke" [Pulp Fiction; WW]

Author: **Lon Williams**; Character: **Lee Winters**; First publication: *Real Western Stories*.

Why should a man be running around on all fours and growling like a dog? Lee Winters found out when he encountered Dr. Mesmer Ludwig....

Deadman's Road [Book anthology; WW]

Author: Joe R. Lansdale; Art: Glenn Chadbourne; First publication: Burton, MI; Subterranean Press, 2010.

This collection of five Weird Western stories featuring the Reverend Jebidiah Mercer includes the previously published **Dead in the West**. "Deadman's Road" sees the Reverend on the trail of a ghoul who feeds on travelers. "The Gentleman's Hotel" features a deserted town populated with ghosts and werewolf Conquistadores. "**The Crawling Sky**" which was also adapted in a comic book mini-series has Reverend Jebediah Mercer coming to the aid of a couple who encounter a demonic spirit residing in a well on their homestead near the town of Wood Tick, East Texas. The final story in the collection, "The Dark Down There" features the Reverend and a 300-pound lady named Flower who tackle cannibals named kobolds who serve a Queen.

The *San Francisco Book Review* commented, "Joe R. Lansdale is the undisputed master of East Texas gothic horror, and his dime novel sensibilities make this marriage of Westerns and horror stories a perfect fit."

Deadshot [Comic book character; SFW]

Creators: Bob Kane, David Vern Reed, Lew Schwartz; First appearance: **Batman** # 59 (June-July 1959); Publisher: DC Comics.

Floyd Lawton turned to crime after years of suffering abuse from his father resulted in Lawton attempting to shoot him. But when he accidentally killed his brother instead Lawton became an assassin-for-hire and eventually joined the Suicide Squad. Although the majority of his adventures have taken place in a contemporary setting Deadshot has adopted a Western outlaw persona in the *Secret Six* comic book and the television series *Smallville*.

Deadshot [RPG book; WW]

Author; Rob Clayton Jones; Art: Robin Elliott, Dan Harding, Andy Park; First publication: 2006; **Deadlands: Reloaded** Dime Novel #2; Publisher: Legion Publishing.

Hoba Hills is home to a deadly competition financed by Fargus O'Driscoll. The price is $5,000 or your life.

Deadwood Dick (1940) [Film serial; WMW]

Premiere: July 19, 1940; Main Cast: Don Douglas as Dick Stanley/Deadwood Dick, Lorna Gray as Anne Butler, Harry Harvey as Dave Miller, Marin Sais as Calamity Jane; Producer: Larry Darmour; Story: Morgan B. Cox, George Plympton, Wyndham Gittens, John Cutting; Director: James W. Horne; 285 min.; Columbia Pictures Corporation; B/W.

Following the death of his star reporter. newspaper editor Dick Stanley alias Deadwood Dick protects the town of Deadwood in Dakota territory from "The Skull" and his gang.

Chapter Titles: 1. *A Wild West Empire*; 2. *Who Is the Skull?*; 3. *Pirates of the Plains*; 4. *The Skull Baits a Trap*; 5. *Win, Lose or Draw*; 6. *Buried Alive*; 7. *The Chariot of Doom*; 8. *The Secret of Number Ten*; 9. *The Fatal Warning*; 10. *Framed for Murder*; 11. *The Bucket of Death*; 12. *A Race Against Time*; 13. *The Arsenal of Revolt*; 14. *Holding the Fort*; 15. *The Deadwood Express*

Deadworld: The Last Siesta [Graphic novel; SFW]

First publication: 2011; Story: Gary Reed, Gary Francis; Art: Mark Bloodworth; Publisher: IDW.

In the supernatural holocaust of Deadworld, outside of Juarez, Mexico civilization has collapsed. The mysterious wanderer known as Raga "The Assassin" is an enforcer in a lawless land. Now he has to contend with the living dead in the form of King Zombie and his hordes of zombies.

Death Collector (1988) [Film; SFW]

Premiere: 1988; Main Cast: Daniel Chapman as Wade Holt, Ruth Collins as Annie Northbride, Loren Blackwell as Hawk, Frank Stewart as Jack Holt; Executive Producers: Gianfranco Galluzzo, Tom Gniazdowski; Story: John McLaughlin; Director: Tom Gniazdowski [Tom Garrett]; 95 min.; Six-Shooter Films Inc.; Color.

Wade Holt seeks revenge on Hawk, leader of the gang who murdered his brother (Stewart), in the Old West town of Hartford City where townsfolk drive 1950s roadsters.

See: **Tin Star Void**

Death Comes to Dillinger [Comic book; WW]

First publication: 2006; Story: James Patrick; Art: Se7enhedd; Two-issue mini-series; Publisher: Spacedog Entertainment

Death is a drifter who rides from town to town claiming souls. When Death rides into Dillinger the local banker is convinced his ill daughter will be Death's next victim and decides to confront Death if it will save the life of his daughter.

Death Valley [Stage play; WW]

Premiere: July 2011; Venue: Bushwick Starr, Brooklyn, N.Y.; Cast: Patrick Harrison as Wilbur, Will Cespedes as Lawrence, Alexandra Arnoldi Panzer as Adele, Jessie Hopkins as Genevieve, James Rutherford as Dr. Oral Crandon; Story: Adam Scott Mazer; Director: Dan Rogers; Production: Anti-Matter Collective.

A confrontation between a jaded, cynical cowboy named Wilbur and the young idealistic Lawrence who is caught going through Wilbur's bag eventually results in Wilbur's premature death. But he doesn't remain dead for long and rises again as a zombie—part of a greater zombie plague infecting the Old West. Adapted from the Vampire Cowboys' *Saturday Night Saloon* episodic serial.

The New York Times (July 3, 2011) theater critic Jason Zinoman stated: "Aiming for the sober, character-driven storytelling of "The Walking Dead," this play tells its story with less humor and sardonic wit than you'll typically see in a Vampire Cowboys production."

Death Walks in Laredo (1966) [Film; Italy, Algeria; WW]

See: *Tre pistole contro Cesare*

Defiance (2013) [TV series; SFW]

Premiere: April 15, 2013: Main Cast: Grant Bowler as Chief Lawkeeper Joshua Nolan, Julie Benz as Mayor Amanda Rosewater, Grahame Greene as Rafe McCawley, Stephanie Leonidas as Irisa, Tony Curran as Datak Carr, Jaime Murray as Stahma Tarr, Mia Kershner as Kenya Rosewater, Trenna Keating as Doc Yewill, Dewshane Williams as Tommy; Creators: Kevin Murphy, Rockne S. O'Bannon, Michael Taylor; 43 min.; Five and Dime Productions, Universal Cable Productions, Syfy; Color.

When the Earth is visited by extraterrestrial alien races, collectively known as Votans, looking for a new home it soon turns to war as negotiations fail. In the year 2046, three decades after the invasion, the Earth has been transformed as humans and aliens share a fragile peace in the border town of Defiance, formerly known as St. Louis. Chief Lawkeeper Nolan is the peacekeeper between the Mayor of Defiance and residents who comprise of powerful humans, military scavengers and ambitious aliens including Irathients and Castithans.

Grant Bowler who plays Chief Lawkeeper Joshua Nolan commented, "We identify with that lone man with a gun making up the rules. It's part of the Western myth. The West is such a strong allegory. I think Defiance is set so much in that small frontier town environment, that it brings it right back to the Western."

Defiance (2013), starring Grant Bowler as Joshua Nolan and Stephanie Leonidas as Irisa.

Demon Gun [Comic book; WW]

First appearance: 1996; Story: Gary Cohn; Pencils: Barry Orkin; Inks: Peter Palmiotti; three-issue mini-series; Publisher: Crusade.

Reverend Howe seeks vengeance on the Comancheros who destroyed his church and congregation by bargaining with evil spiritual powers posing as good.

Demoniaca (1992) [Film; South Africa-UK; WW]

Re-edited Italian version of *Dust Devil*.

The Demons [Comic strip; WW]

First appearance: *Eerie* #72; Story: Bill DuBay; Art: Jose Ortiz; Publisher: Warren Publishing.

Crucifixion Hill, New Mexico territory, 1912. Jedediah Pan reclaims one of two hellbands capable of summoning demons and swears revenge on the townsfolk who murdered his beautiful wife and young daughter in 1892 unless they return the second hellband. Subsequent issues featured Pan's estranged son Jeremiah Cold.

Following a five-issue run in *Eerie,* the story of the hellbands continued into the modern day with demon-possessed Cryssie Collins in *Vampirella* issues #92–93 (December 1980-January 1981).

Denver [RPG book; WW]

Author: Jay Kyle; First publication: 2001; *Deadlands: Hell on Earth: The Wasted West*; Publisher: Pinnacle Entertainment Group.

Location sourcebook for Denver, General Throckmorton's Combine and the resistance to Throckmorton's attempts to dominate the Wasted West. Includes the adventure "Air Force One Is Down."

Derailed! [RPG book; WW]

Authors: Stephen Crane, Shane Lacy Hensley & John Hopler; First publication: 1998; Publisher: Pinnacle Entertainment Group.

Vehicle rules for *The Great Rail Wars*.

"A Desert Hippocrates" [Pulp Fiction; WW]

Author: **Lon Williams**; Character: **Lee Winters**: First publication: *Real Western Stories* (August 1953).

> Winters did not lift his hands. He felt a jab in his back, heard a sixgun click to full cock. He saw Spurlock's right hand move gracefully and swiftly to an under-arm holster.

"And your reason for being here," said Sir Jared, "is your ownership of a lovely head of hair, which of course, you shall give to me. Your predecessors have made their donations. New lips from dear Hodge; new ears from dear Mr. Fuller; a new nose from poor, sorrowful Mr. Winthrop. And now, from you, Mr. Winters—"

Desert Phantom (1936) [Film; WMW]

Premiere: March 10, 1936; Main Cast: Johnny Mack Brown as Billy Donovan, Sheila Manors as Jean Halloran; Producer: A. W. Hackel; Story: E. B. Mann, Earle Snell; Director: S. Roy Luby; 60 min.; Supreme Pictures, William Steiner Productions; B/W.

The Desert Phantom kills in order to gain control of an abandoned gold mine near the Double Bar-A Ranch. This movie has some mild Weird Western elements including a scene of a crippled man able to walk while sleepwalking. A remake of *The Night Rider* (1932), it was later remade as *The Range Busters* (1940).

Desert Punk [Manga; Anime; Japan; SFW]

DVD release title (U.S.A.) for *Sunabozu*.

Desperadoes [Comic book; WW]

First issue: September 1997; Story: Jeff Mariotte; Art: John Cassaday; Five-issue mini-series; Publisher: Image-Homage Comics.

Las Vegas, New Mexico Territory, 1879. Pinkerton detective Race Kennedy is pursuing a killer. Gideon Brood is on the trail of the same killer, with the help of Jerome Alexander Betts and Abby Degrazia. Brood is on a personal quest to avenge the brutal murder of his wife and son. But Leander Peik is no normal killer and each murder serves to increase his supernatural powers.

This five-issue mini-series was published by Homage Comics in graphic novel form in 1998 under the title *Desperadoes: A Moment's Sunlight*.

Desperadoes: Banners of Gold [Comic book; WW]

First issue: December 2004; Story: Jeff Mariotte; Art: Jeremy Haun; Five issue mini-series; Publisher: IDW Publishing.

The Desperadoes become entangled with spiritualist Sarah Williams, murders, messages from beyond the grave and the psychotic Montana Donnie.

Left: Cover of *Desperadoes: Banners of Gold* #3. Story by Jeff Mariotte, art by Jeremy Haun. *Right:* Cover of *Desperadoes: Buffalo Dreams* #1. Story by Jeff Mariotte, art by Alberto Dose. © 2009 Jeff Mariotte and Idea and Design Works, LLC. Used with permission.

Desperadoes: Buffalo Dreams [Comic book; WW]

First issue: January 2007; Story: Jeff Mariotte; Art: Alberto Dose; Four issue mini-series; Publisher: IDW Publishing.

A mystical cave that serves as the gateway for buffalo to enter our world is blocked. Geronimo and Lozen call upon the Desperadoes to discover the cause of the blockage and to remedy the situation.

Desperadoes: Epidemic! [Graphic Novel; WW]

First publication: November 1999; Story: Jeff Mariotte; Art: John Lucas; Publisher: Homage Comics.

Trapped in the town of Naciemento during an influenza epidemic, Gideon Brood, Jerome Alexander Betts, Abby DeGrazia and Race Kennedy encounter demonic priest Padre Montalvo and his minions.

Desperadoes: Quiet of the Grave [Comic book; WW]

First issue: 1997; Story: Jeff Mariotte; Art: **John Severin**; Five-issue mini-series; Publisher: Homage-Image Comics.

Still on the run for accidentally shooting Sheriff Kelton's wife, Gideon Brood seeks to protect his friends from harm. But they are soon in greater danger from a new threat lurking in Luttrel, New Mexico Territory: a gunslinger who refuses to die.

The Devil and Miss Sarah (1971) [Telefilm; WW]

Premiere: December 4, 1971; Main Cast: Gene Barry as Rankin, James Drury as Gil Turner, Janice Rule as Sarah Turner, Charles McGraw as Marshal Duncan, Slim Pickens as Stoney; Producer: Stanley Shpetner; Story: Calvin Clements Jr.; Director: Michael Caffey; 90 min.; Universal Television; Color.

Rankin, demon-possessed outlaw, attempts to possess the spirit of Sarah Turner in order to escape from her husband Gil. But Gil has powers of his own to combat Rankin's.

Devil's Crossing a.ka. *Cowboys vs. Zombies: The Devil's Crossing* (2012) [Film; SFW]

Premiere: 2012 (UK); Main Cast: Michael Sharpe as Shadrach, Patrick G. Keenan as Louise, Kevin L. Johnson as Patrick, Jenny Gulley as Charley; Executive Producer: Paul Reichelt; Writer-Director: James Ryan Gary; 75 min.: Indigo Pictures; Color.

Advertised as a "Post-Apocalyptic Zombie Western," this low budget film takes place in the post-nuclear town of Celestial. "Soul Collector" Shadrach enters town and proceeds his rampage of violence and death. But Shadrach takes no pleasure in death and wants to free his undead soul from the devil. When he refuses to continue his killing spree Satan's minion Louise unleashes zombies on the town. A final gunfight between Shadrach and Louise will determine his fate, along with the town.

Devil's Engine [Novel; WW]

Author: Mark Sumner; First publication: New York: Ballantine Books, 1997.

Magic powers exist in an alternate Old West where Jay Gould is planning to lay the tracks of his railroad through Medicine Rock in order to rob the town of its magic.

Second book in the *Devil's Tower* series.

Devil's Gulch [RPG; WW]

Release date: April, 2012; Author: Troy Williamson; Artists: Stephen Gilberts, Thomas Boatwright; BRP (Basic Roleplaying); Publisher: Chaosium.

Devil's Gulch is an Old West town featuring a cast of characters that includes gunfighters, gamblers, a blacksmith and a prostitute. The player can modify the setting to take place in the Weird West complete with supernatural gunslinger or a steam-punk environment in which the town is an outpost of the British colony on Mars.

The Devil's Mistress (1966) [Film; WW]

Premiere: March 1, 1966; Main Cast: Joan Stapleton as Athaliah, Robert Gregory as Frank, Douglas Warren as Joe, Arthur Resley as Jeroboam, Forrest Westmoreland as Charlie; Producer: Wes Moreland; Story-Director: Orville Wanzer; 66 min.; Holiday Pictures; Color.

Fugitive cowboys go on a rampage of death, destruction and rape in Apache territory but one of the Indian females (Stapleton) they rape has a deadly supernatural secret.

Devil's Tower [Novel; WW]

Author: Mark Sumner; First publication: New York: Ballantine Books, 1996.

The end of the American Civil War unleashes magical powers in the Old West. Sheriff Jake Bird must confront his past and conquer the magic of General George Armstrong Custer.

Followed by *Devil's Engine*.

Devoured: The Legend of Alferd Packer [Film; WW]

Premiere: July 26, 2005; Main Cast: Aarin Teich as Aaron, Evelyn Brewton as barbecue Girl, Patrick Todd as Curtis, Jeff Muzi as Alfred Packer; Director: Kevin Rapp; 85 min.; Troma Entertainment, Color.

A student traces the legend of Alferd Packer and soon believes Packer may still be alive and eating fresh human flesh.

Not to be confused with *The Legend of Alfred Packer* (1980), a dramatization of the Old West cannibal that included no Weird Western elements.

Diamond Gulch [RPG game; WW]

Author: David Garrett; Art: Ed Alexander; First publication: 2006; Setting: Otherwhere; Publisher: Amalara.

Dinosaur-powered trains once crossed the plains of the Old West but in the new era of steamtech only one train remains. Grumbeard Silvertongue wants to kill all the surviving dinosaurs so his steam locomotives can rule the plains and bring renewed prosperity to the town of Diamond Gulch.

Dick Demon [Comic book character; France; WMW]

First appearance: *Zembla* #110 (1972); Story: Franco Frescura; Art: Ivo Pavone; Publisher: EditionsLug.

1. A western avenger with a secret twin brother, Sebastian, enabling him to maintain a double identity and confuse his foes. His friends include life insurance peddler Baratini and undertaker Balmore.

2. First appearance: *Mustang* #309 (2003); Publisher: Semic.

A modern-day version of Dick Demon as a Los Angeles–based private investigator with a demon-like twin brother, and a female cat-like partner who is a descendent of **Jed Puma**.

Django il Bastardo (1969) [Film; Italy; WW]

Premiere: 1969; Main Cast: Anthony Steffen as Django, Paolo Gozlino as Rod Murdok, Lu Kanante [Luciano Rossi] as Luke/Jack Murdok, Teodoro Corra as Williams; Producers: Herman Cohen, Anthony Steffen; Story: Sergio Garrone, Antonio De Teffè [Anthony Steffen]; Producers: Pino De Martino, Tigielle; Director: Sergio Garrone; 107 min.; Italy; SEPAC, Tigielle 33; Color.

Italian gothic horror spaghetti Western in which Django seeks revenge on traitors who were responsible for the death of his Confederate regiment. Django appears on the day of their deaths and places their named cross in the street. Is the stranger man or ghost? Considered by many critics to be the inspiration for Clint Eastwood's *High Plains Drifter* and *Pale Rider*.

See: *The Stranger's Gundown*

Django Kill—If You Live, Shoot! (1967) [Film; Italy; WW]

DVD release title (USA) for *Se sei vivo spara*.

Django Rides Again (1976) [Film; Italy; WW]

Alternate release title (USA) for *Keoma*.

Djustine: Tales from the Twisted West [Comic book; Italy; WW]

First appearance: 1997; Creator: Enrico Teodorani; Publishers: EF Edizioni, Coniglio Editore, Carnal Comics.

The sexually graphic adventures of the large-breasted female gunslinger Djustine and her fight with the supernatural including zombies, vampires and Diabla, daughter of Satan.

"Do Not Hasten to Bid Me Adieu" [Short story; WW]

Author: Norman Partridge; First publication: New York: HarperPrism, 1994.

Quincey P. Morris returns to Texas from Whitby, Yorkshire, with a coffin containing the staked body of his beloved Miss Lucy. A vampire Western partially based on characters from Bram Stoker's *Dracula*.

See: *Love in Vein: Twenty Original Tales of Vampiric Erotica*.

Doc Frankenstein [Comic book; SFW]

First appearance: 2004; Creators: Geoffrey Darrow, Steve Skroce; Story: The Wachowski Brothers; Publisher: Burlyman Entertainment.

The Frankenstein Monster's journey through different eras in world history including his time as a Wild West bounty hunter. This reinvention of Mary Shelley's creation sees an articulate but angry creature at odds with conservative politics and organized religion.

The Doctor and the Dinosaurs: A Weird Western Tale (Book #4) [Novel; SPW]

Author: Mike Resnick; First publication: Amherst, NY: Pyr-Prometheus 2013.

Apache medicine man Geronimo employs the services of the consumptive Doc Holliday for one final time. He promises to restore Holliday to health if he will venture to Wyoming to help keep feuding paleontologists, Edward Drinker Cope and Othniel Charles Marsh from being killed by Comanche warriors and thus threaten a U.S. government treaty. Helping Holliday in his mission are Theodore Roosevelt, Cole Younger and Buffalo Bill Cody as they protect the paleontologists from Comanches and living dinosaurs.

The Doctor and the Kid: A Weird Western Tale (Book #2) [Novel; SPW]

Author: Mike Resnick; First publication: Amherst, NY: Pyr-Prometheus 2010.

After a night of gambling at the Monarch Saloon, the consumptive Doc Holliday loses the savings he intended to cover his final years in a sanatorium. Desperate for money Holliday employs his services as a bounty hunter and sharpshooter. His bounty is Billy the Kid.

Thomas Edison, Geronimo, Oscar Wilde, Pat Garrett, Katie Elder, Ned Buntline and female bounty hunter Charlotte Branson, also looking to earn the considerable bounty on Billy the Kid add to the mix of magic and steam punk in Old West Colorado.

The Doctor and the Rough Rider: A Weird Western Tale (Book #3) [Novel; SPW]

Author: Mike Resnick; First publication: Amherst, NY: Pyr-Prometheus 2012.

Geronimo enlists the services of Doc Holliday to defeat gunfighter John Wesley Hardin. Supernatural medicine man War Bonnet in turn has enlisted the services of Hardin to kill Theodore Roosevelt and Geronimo to keep the United States from expanding west of the Mississippi.

Doctor Saturn [Comic book character; SFW]

First appearance: *Ringo Kid Western* #8 (October 1955); Creator: **John Severin**; Publisher: Marvel Comics.

A mad scientist works out of his laboratory in Conquistador Castle in the Old West. His claim to fame is his alleged connection to British scientist Michael Faraday and Saturn's Black Sunset invention that temporarily blinded his opponents with a highly concentrated flash of light. Ringo Kid was able to defeat Doctor Saturn thanks to an Indian potion that counteracted the blinding effects of the Black Sunset device.

Doctor Thirteen [Comic book character; SW]

First appearance: ***All-Star Western*** #11 (September 2012); Creators: Justin Gray, Jimmy Palmiotti, Scott Kolins; Publisher: DC Comics.

Doctor Terrence Thirteen, an inventor and man of science and reason, is a debunker of the occult and supernatural in 1880s Gotham City.

Doctor Tregan's Collateral Trouble [RPG; WW]

First publication: April, 2014; *Deadlands Tall Tales* #2; Protocol Game Series; Author: Jim Pinto; Art: Rick Hershey; Publisher: Pinnacle Entertainment Group.

Buford Junction is in panic-mode. Doctor Tregan has been abducted and his absence leaves the town open to outlaws who can use his inventions for nefarious means. A rescue attempt is underway but without knowing who kidnapped the Doctor their task is increasingly difficult. A story roleplaying game set in ***Deadlands: The Weird West***.

Doctor Who (1963) [TV series; UK]

Adventures of a Time Lord and his companions as they travel through time and space in a TARDIS (Time and Relative Dimensions in Space) posing as a British police phone box.

"THE GUNFIGHTERS" (3:25) [SFW]
Four-part story; "A Holiday for the Doctor": Air date: April 30, 1966; "Don't Shoot the Pianist": Air date: May 7, 1966; Johnny Ringo: Air date: May 14,

1966; "The OK Corral": Air date: May 21, 1966. Main Cast: William Hartnell as Doctor Who, Peter Purves as Steven Taylor, Jackie Lane as Dodo Chaplet; Guest Stars: John Alderson as Wyatt Earp, Laurence Payne as Johnny Ringo, Anthony Jacobs as Doc Holliday, Richard Beale as Bat Masterson, William Hurndall as Ike Clanton, Maurice Good as Phineas Clanton, David Cole as Billy Clanton, Shane Rimmer as Seth Harper; Producer: Innes Lloyd; Story: Donald Cotton; Director: Rex Tucker; BBC Television; B/W.

The Doctor's desperate need to relieve his toothache takes him to Tombstone in the Old West and a date with Doc Holliday. But a case of mistaken identity leads to his companions Steven and Dodo being sentenced to death. The Doctor must search for a way of saving them and avoiding the gunfight at the OK Corral.

This BBC-TV–produced science fiction Western set in Tombstone pre-dated the **Star Trek** episode "Spectre of the Gun." A Western street was built in the BBC-TV Centre for the four-part episode. Producer Innes Lloyd dismissed the episode's Old West concept for not being in tune with the spirit of the series.

Doctor Who (2005) [TV series; UK]

In 2005 *Doctor Who* was re-launched by the BBC with episodes featuring the ninth incarnation of the Doctor beginning with Season One.

"A TOWN CALLED MERCY" (7:03) [SFW]
Air date: September 15, 2012; Main Cast: Matt Smith as The Doctor, Karen Gillan as Amelia Pond, Arthur Darvill as Rory Williams; Guest Stars: Andrew Brooke as The Gunslinger, Adrian Scarborough as Kahler-Jex; Executive Producers: Steven Moffat, Caroline Skinner; Story: Toby Whithouse; Director: Saul Metzstein; 45 min.; BBC Television; Color.

The Doctor, Amelia and Rory travel to the Old West town of Mercy, Nevada in 1870 where they confront the cyborg gunslinger Kahler-Tek. Tek is the product of experimentation by scientists on his home planet Kahler. He has traveled to Nevada to track and kill the final living "doctor" who experimented on him, Kahler-Jex. With Doctor Who Marshal of Mercy the Gunslinger threatens the town unless they give up Jex but ends up protecting Mercy after Jex commits suicide.

Filmed in Almeria, home to Spaghetti Westerns of the past, this was the first Western-themed **Doctor Who** story since **The Gunfighters** in 1966.

Doctor Who: Peacemaker [Novel; SFW]

Author: James Swallow; First publication: London: BBC Books, 2007.

In the Old West town of Redwater in the 1880s, the Doctor and his assistant Martha investigate the truth behind the patent medicines of a snake-oil salesman that actually cure the patients. They discover intergalactic mercenaries at large searching for "the healer" who are willing to kill or destroy anyone or anything that stands in their way.

This novel based on the BBC-TV series features the tenth Doctor and Martha Jones as portrayed by David Tennant and Freema Agyeman.

Doctor Who: The Gunfighters [Book adaptation; SFW]

Author: Donald Cotton; First publication: W.H. Allen, 1985.

Novelization of the 1966 ***Doctor Who*** storyline from the BBC-TV series.

Dogs o' War: All's Fair [RPG book; WW]

Authors: John Hopler and Shane Lacy Hensley; First publication: 1998; Publisher: Pinnacle Entertainment Group.

Expansion for ***The Great Rail Wars***.

Don Simpson's Bizarre Heroes [Comic book]

First publication: May 1994; Creator-Story-Art: Don Simpson; B/W; Publisher: Fiasco Comics.

Short-lived rebirth of Megaton Man and ***Cowboy Gorilla***.

Don't Touch the White Woman (1974) [Film; France-Italy; WW]

Video release title (USA) for ***Touche pas à la Femme Blanche***.

Doomtown or Bust! [RPG book; WW]

Author: Rob Vaux; First publication: 1999; ***Deadlands: The Weird West***; Publisher: Pinnacle Entertainment Group.

Location book for Gomorra, California, the setting for the *Doomtown* card game.

Dorn, Edward (1929–1999) [Author—poet]

Born in Villa Grove, Illinois, Dorn studied with Charles Olson at Black Mountain College, North Carolina, graduating in 1955. He taught at Idaho State University at Pocatello (1961–1965), the University of Essex, Great Britain (1965–1970), Northeastern Illinois University at Chicago (1970–1971), Kent State University, Ohio (1973–1974), and the University of Colorado (1977–1999).

Dorn was fascinated by the landscape and history of the American West, which he explored in his poetry. His most enduring work is a series of four poems (published between 1969 and 1974) collectively known as "**Gunslinger.**" Dorn died of pancreatic cancer in December 1999 at the age of 70.

Selected works: *The Shoshoneans: The People of the Basin Plateau* (1966), *Gunslinger Book I* (1968), *Gunslinger Book II* (1969), *The Cycle* (1971), *Gunslinger Book III* (1972), *Slinger* (1974), *Recollections of Gran Apacheria* (1974), *Views* (1980), *Yellow Lola* (1981), and *Abhorrences* (1990).

Dove si spara di più (1967) [Film; Italy-Spain; WW]

Premiere: March 2, 1967; Main Cast: Peter Lee Lawrence as Johnny Monter, Cristina Galbó as Giulietta Campos, Andrés Mejuto as Lefty, Executive Producer: Sergio Newman; Story: Maria Del Carmen Martinez; Director: Gianni Puccini; 84 min.; Framer Films, P.C. Hispamer Films; Color.

A traditional Western storyline of the warring Monter and Campos ranch families reaches a Weird Western conclusion when a man dressed in black wanders through the dead and the dying shooting the survivors. He turns to the audience revealing a skull face and his identity as the Grim Reaper.

The stars of the film, German actor Peter Lee Lawrence and Spanish actress Cristina Galbó, became husband and wife in 1969. Lawrence committed suicide in 1974 at the age of 29. He was suffering from a brain tumor at the time.

See: ***Fury of Johnny the Kid***

Dracula Lives [Comic book]

Black & white magazine format title based on Bram Stoker's *Dracula*.

"Bounty for a Vampire" [WW]

First publication: #13 (July 1975); Story: Tony Isabella: Art: Tony DeZuniga; Publisher: Curtis Magazines [Marvel Comics].

An aging former U.S. Marshal working out of the Dakotas in the late 19th century tracks Dracula to his castle and kills him with silver buckshot.

Drago [Comic book character; France; WW]

First appearance: *Dago* #1, July 1966; Art: Carlo Cedroni; Publisher: Editions Lug.

Initiated by Indian shaman Kee-Oh-Kuk, Charles Malden has the power to create illusions by changing his appearance and confusing a person's mind. The blonde and effeminate Malden changes into the dark-haired, dashing Drago to fight crime on the Texas-New Mexico border in the year 1844, with the help of exiled French sailor Tartarin.

Dragonfall 5 and the Space Cowboys [Juvenile book; SW]

Author: Brian Earnshaw; Illustrator: Simon Stern; First publication: London: Methuen Children's Books, 1972.

Tim, Sanchez, Old Elias and Big Mother and pet flying hound Jerk travel through space in their dilapidated spaceship, Dragonfall 5. With their engine in need of repair they drift into a "broken world" of green asteroids that was once a planet. But a war with the Outsiders shattered the planet into asteroids still capable of supporting life. Now space cowboys ride between asteroids and tackle cattle rustlers in the new frontier.

Drago. **Art by Carlo Cedroni. © Mosaic Multimedia. Used with permission.**

The Drastic Dragon of Draco, Texas [Novel; WW]

Author: Elizabeth Ann Scarborough; First publication: New York: Bantam, 1986.

A young woman befriends a fire-breathing dragon who has been terrorizing the Texas countryside and the Old West townsfolk of Draco.

Dreadful Skin [Novel; WW]

Author: Cherie Priest; Burton, MI: Subterranean Press 2010

Three individual stories are connected with a recurring theme and characters. Irish nun Eileen Callaghan is pursuing Jack Gabert, a man infected by a lycanthrope while serving the Queen in India. Now he is on a riverboat in 19th century America in the years following the American Civil War. He escapes the clutches of the nun but not before he infects her.

Years later Sister Callaghan tracks Gabert to a Pentecostal revivalist show when she learns of corpses mauled by an animal. But now Callaghan has unnatural urges of her own and in hunting the killer must come to terms with her own lycanthropic nature.

Drifter [Comic book; SFW]

First publication; November, 2014; Story: Ivan Brandon; Art: Nic Klein: Publisher: Image Comics.

After surviving a crash landing on Ouro, Abram Pollux finds himself on a lawless, barren world in a decrepit town filled with assorted survivors from other wrecks. Marshal Lee Carter attempts to maintain order as Pollux struggles to survive in the hostile, unforgiving environment of an alien world where the Preacher believes the sudden arrival of Pollux is a sign from God.

Drumlin Boiler [Short story; SW]

Author: Jeff Duntemann; First publication: *Issac Asimov's Magazine* (April 2002).

When their starship malfunctions the crew and passengers from Earth have to crash land on the planet Valinor. Here they discover alien manufacturing machines known as Thingmakers capable of producing anything, by drumming several drums in sequence. The artifacts known as drumlins seem to be aware of human thoughts and emotions. Valinor resembles the frontier society in Earth's Old West complete with conflicting interests of the population. The Bitspace Institute seeks to repair the damaged spaceship and limit the power of the Thingmakers. Opposing them are the Grangers and the Tears who want to stay on Valinor and fully incorporate the Thingmakers into society. This proves to be a dangerous alliance as many fear drumlins are not what they appear to be and may prove to be deadly.

Drumlin Circus [Novella; SW]

Author: Jeff Duntemann; First publication: Colorado Springs, CO: Copperwood Media, 2011.

The animal trainer of a visiting circus has been kidnapped by the Bitspace Institute who want her drumlin-made whistle known as the Function Controller. They fear it has the power to enslave animals and will use any means to extract information from her. The Bitspace agents aren't interested in the welfare of the animals but want the whistle so they can create animal assassins. When a circus clown frees Pretty Alice the problems only increase.

Duntemann's novella was published as part of a "Copperwood Double" with another Drumlins universe story *On Gossamer Wings* by James R. Strickland.

"Drumlin Wheel" [Short story; SW]

Author: Jeff Duntemann; First publication: Colorado Springs, CO: Copperwood Press, 2011.

When a man named Roper sells the drum rhythm to a wheel that turns by itself he attracts the attention of Bitspace Industries, The Grange and others seeking to oppress or exploit Roper's drum rhythm constructed wheel.

Published as part of the short story book anthology *Cold Hands and Other Stories*. The collection also included the Drumlin universe short story *Roddie* about an enigmatic drummer of drumlins.

Duckula (1990) [Animated TV series; UK]

Voice Cast: David Jason as Count Duckula, Jack May as Egor, Brian Trueman as Nanny, Jimmy Hibbert as Dr. Von Goosewing; Producers; Brian Cosgrove, Mark Hall; Directors: Chris Randle, Keith Soble; 30 min.; Cosgrove Hall Productions, Thames Television, Color.

Adventures of a vegetarian vampire duck with a dislike of blood and a taste for tomato ketchup. His castle is a time machine activated by Count Duckula in an upright coffin.

"Ghostly Gold" (2:01)

Air date: September 12, 1989; Story: Peter Richard Reeves.

Duckula, Nanny and Egor visit an Old West ghost town and discover it is full of ghosts who don't like vampires.

"Dead Eye Duck" (3:08) [WW]

Air date: December 10, 1990; Story: Peter Richard Reeves

Wanting to escape the bitter cold of his castle, Count Duckula travels in time to the Old West of Colorado.

The Durango Kid [Comic book]

Based on Columbia Pictures' film series starring Charles Starrett. Steve Brand, Secret Service government agent, is the masked Durango Kid, enemy of villains and outlaws in the American West. The majority of stories were standard Western adventures with one standout Weird Western adventure involving the Bakala monster and a science fiction Western involving the "First Atomic Weapon."

"The Ray of Horror" [SFW]

First publication: #7 (October 1950); Art: Joe Certa; Publisher: Magazine Enterprises.

A mad scientist invents an atomic death ray.

'The Curse of the Bakala!" [WW]

First publication: #15 (February 1952); Art: Joe Certa, John Belfi; Publisher: Magazine Enterprises.

The Durango Kid, "The Curse of the Bakala," page 1. Art by Joe Certa and John Belfi. © 2009 AC Comics/Nightveil Media, Inc. Used with permission.

The Durango Kid encounters the Bakala, an 18-foot-tall Native American "monster of the living dead" with the strength of twenty men.

"The Phantom Badhat" [WMW]

First publication: #33 (February 1955); Art: Fred Guardineer; Publisher: Magazine Enterprises.

The twin brother of a deceased outlaw fools people into thinking the latter has returned from the grave.

Dust of the Damned [Novel; WW]

Author: Peter Brandvold; First publication: New York: Berkley, 2012.

Werewolf hunter, Uriah Zane, the beautiful Deputy U.S. Marshal, Angel Coffin and Jesse James are on the trail of the "Hell's Angels"—a group of werewolves whom Abraham Lincoln commissioned to help win the American Civil War. But instead of departing home to Eastern Europe after the end of the war, as promised, the Hell's Angels headed for the American West. Led by an enchanting Mexican witch and her pet dragon they are on the trail of a hidden treasure that will help them conquer humanity and take over the Earth.

Author Peter Brandvold commented, "I really loved Jeff Mariotte's great Weird Western comic book series **Desperadoes**. *Dust of the Damned* is sort of that in prose form."

Dust Devil (1992) [Film; South Africa–UK; WW]

Premiere: August 8, 1992; Main Cast: Robert Burke as Dust Devil, Chelsea Field as Wendy Robinson, William Hootkins as Capt. Beyman; Executive Producers: Paul Trijbits, Stephen Woolley; Story-Director: Richard Stanley; 87 min. [original release], 103 min. [director's cut]; British Screen Productions, Channel Four, Palace Pictures, Shadow Theatre Films; Color.

This contemporary horror Western set in South Africa shows influences of the Italian spaghetti Western in a story centered on the mysterious hitchhiker known as Dust Devil who kills women to feed on their souls.

See: *Demoniaca*

"Dust of Gods" [Pulp Fiction; WW]

Author: **C. L. Moore**; First publication: *Weird Tales* (August 1934).

Eons have passed since three gods from the Lost Planet situated between Jupiter and Mars ruled on Mars. Northwest Smith and his Venusian friend Yarol travel to the Polar Mountains of Mars to recover the remains of the god of the darkness Pharol. But when they encounter his power, they have serious doubts about returning the mound of dust that was once the Great Pharol.

Dusty Star [Comic book; SFW]

First appearance: *Negative Burn* #28, October 1995; First issue: December 2005; Story: Andrew Robinson, Joe Pruett; Art: Andrew Robinson; Publisher: Image/Desperado.

A blend of western, science fiction, adventure and humor that features robot cowboys, flying ships, tattooed horses and Dusty Star as a gunslinger with attitude.

Dynamite Warrior (2006) [Film; Thailand; WW]

U.S. release title for *Khon fai bin*.

...e così divennero i 3 supermen del West (1973) [Film; Italy; SFW]

Main Cast: George Martin as George, Sal Borgese as Sal, Frank Brana as Brad, Pedro Sanchez [Ignazio Spalla] as Navajo Joe; Screenplay: Italo Martinenghi, George Martin; Directors: Anthony Blond [Anthony Blod], Italo Martinenghi, George Martin; 95 min.; Cinesecolo, Rofilm, Roma Film S.p.a., Transcontinental; Color.

On a mission to find a time machine the 3 Supermen accidentally set the machine in operation and travel through time and space to the American Old West of 1867. An entry in the long-running *3 Supermen* series of comedy films.

See: *The Three Supermen of the West*

E Dio disse a Caino (1970) [Film; WMW]

Premiere: February 5, 1970; Main Cast: Klaus Kinski as Gary Hamilton, Peter Carsten as Acombar, Marcella Michelangeli as Maria, Antonio Cantafora as Dick Acombar; Producer-Story-Screenplay: Giovanni Addessi; Screenplay-Director: Anthony Dawson (Antonio Margheriti); 93 min.; D.C. 7 Produzione, Peter Carsten Produktion; Technicolor.

After his release from ten years of hard labor Gary Hamilton seeks revenge on the person who framed him, wealthy land baron Acombar. Hamilton possesses an almost supernatural presence appears to effect both man, animals and the weather as a tornado accompanies his path of vengeance.

See: *And God Said to Cain*

Earp: Saints for Sinners [Comic book; SFW]

First publication: January 2010; Story: M. Zachary Sherman, Matt Cirulnick; Art: Mark Chater, Martin Montiel, Colin Lorimer; 4-Issue Mini-Series; Publisher: Radical Comics.

Set in a dystopian future where lawlessness resembles the Old West, Wyatt Earp and Doc Holliday are re-imagined as former partners for the NYPD Special Case Squad who have since gone their own separate paths. After brother Virgil is killed in a train robbery Wyatt Earp becomes a casino-saloon owner in Las Vegas, the only remaining boom-town in this future landscape. When Morgan Earp is killed by Alan Pinkerton, Wyatt, now a Federal Marshal, hunts him down with the help of former partner Doc Holliday and Jesse James.

In 2010 Dreamworks acquired the screen rights to *Earp: Saints for Sinners*, with Sam Raimi as director. The project was still in development in 2015.

Earth 2 (1994) [TV series; SW]

Air date: November 6, 1994; Main Cast: Debrah Farentino as Devon Adair, Clancy Brown as John Danziger, Sullivan Walker as Yale, Jessica Steen as Julia Heller, M.D., Rebecca Gayheart as Bess Martin, John Gegenhuber as Morgan Martin, Joey Zimmerman as Ulysses Adair, J. Madison Wright as True Danziger, Antonio Sabato Jr. as Alonzo Solace; Executive Producers: Michael Duggan, Carol Flint, Mark Levin; 45 × 22; Amblin Entertainment, Universal TV; Color.

The theme of the frontier settlement of the American West is paralleled in this one-season series about a group of colonists from a dead Earth who attempt to make a new life on a planet with hostile inhabitants.

The Earth Remembers [Novel; SFW]

Author: Susan Torian Olan; First publication: 1989; Publisher: TSR Inc.

Post-apocalyptic tale set in a future American Southwest that resembles the Old West with Comanches and underground mutants fighting the corrupt government of Tesharka.

East of West [Comic book; SFW]

First publication: March 2013; Story: Jonathan Hickman; Art: Nick Dragotta; Publisher: Image Comics.

This alternative history comic book series sees the Seven Nations of America created after the almost mystical conclusion of the American Civil War. Enter the Four Horsemen of the Apocalypse and a supernatural apocalypse that awaits in 2064.

Artist Nick Dragotta stated, "I see this book as science fiction, relying heavily on the attitude of a Sergio Leone western."

Eat-Man [Animated TV series; Japan; SFW]

Air date: January 10, 1997; Animation Directors: Hutoshi Higashide, Norio Matsumoto, Tetsuya Yanagisawa; Director: Koichi Mashimo; Production: Studio Deen, TV Tokyo; 12 × 25 min.; Color.

The strange premise for this limited animation anime loosely based on the manga by Akihito Yoshitomi sees wandering, enigmatic Bolt Crank eating metal objects such as guns, bolts, screws and machinery which he later regenerates in any form from his hand when required. This "power" often serves little purpose in the stories and seems to exist for novelty value. Why not simply carry a gun in a holster instead of regenerating it from metal he has eaten? Does eating the metal serve another function? We are never told in this often frustrating series, which also includes a destroyed flying ship that mysteriously floats in the sky The futuristic frontier setting is in part inspired by the Western genre as is the familiar mysterious, man-of-few-words, loner anti-hero. In this mish-mash of genres *Eat-Man* is part western, part pulp fiction, part fantasy and part science fiction. The series was not well received by fans of the original manga and was revamped for the sequel *Eat-Man '98*.

Season One

Wall of Glass (1:01); *A Person Falling To Ruins* (1:02); *The Promised Room* (1:03); *Trade Friends* (1:04); *Rain, After That* (1:05); *The Window of Genes* (1:06); *The Graveyard of Temptation* (1:07); *Silence of Icicle* (1:08); *Aloof Sky* (1:09); *Fragment of Dreams* (1:10); *Paradise* (1:11); *The Endless Tomorrow* (1:12).

Eat-Man '98 [Animated TV series; Japan; SFW]

Air date: October 8, 1998; Animation: Directors; Akira Shimizu, Haruo Sotozaki, Masahiko Yurata, Mequimi Yamamoto, Yusunao Aoki, Yoshiko Murata; Director; Toshifumi Kawase; Production: Studio Deen, TV Tokyo; 12 × 25 min.; Color.

Season One

Act 1: *Bye, Bye Aimie* (1:01); Act 2: *Bye, Bye Aimie* (1:02); Act 3: *Good Guard* (1:03); Act 4: *Ambrosia Days* (1:04); Act 5: *Ambrosia Days* (1:05); Act 6: *Ambrosia Days* (1:06); Act 7: *Ambrosia Days* (1:07); Act 8: *The World's Greatest Adventure House* (1:08); Act 9: *Mega Mix* (1:09); Act 10: *Mega Mix* (1:10); Act 11: *The Clown's Dream* (1:11); Act 12: *The Clown's Dream* (1:12).

Ehi amico ... c'è Sabata, hai chiuso!
(1969) [Film; Italy; WW]

Premiere: 1969; Main Cast: Lee Van Cleef as Sabata, William Berger as Banjo, Franco Ressel as Hardy Stengel, Nick Jordan [Aldo Canti] as Indio, Pedro Sanchez [Ignazio Spalla] as Carrincha, Linda Veras as Jane; Producer: Alberto Grimaldi; Story: Gianfranco Parolini, Renato Izzo; Director: Frank Kramer [Gianfranco Parolini]; 111 min.; Produzioni Europee Associati (PEA); Color.

When Sabata confronts Banjo in a showdown, Banjo fires three bullets into a bag Sabata has placed in front of his body. But Sabata continues walking as dirt pours out of the bag. Sabata then proceeds to fire from the handle of his gun in another homage to the gimmicky trick shooting of Sartana that is reminiscent of James Bond and **The Wild Wild West** television series.

Sabata reflects director Gianfranco Parolini's other creation Sartana who also appeared to be invulnerable to bullets and relied on gimmicky weapons.

See: **Sabata**

1872—Secret Wars [Comic book; SFW]

First publication: July 2015; Story: Gerry Duggan; Art: Nik Virella, Alex Maleev; Publisher: Marvel Worldwide Inc.

The Western town of Timely is nestled in the Valley of Doom on a patchwork planet composed of fragments of worlds that no longer exist. Battleworld is maintained by Victor Von Doom with each region its own domain. Established in 1872, Valley of Doom is one of those domains.

When gold and silver was discovered near the Savage Mountain Governor Roxonn diverted the Kirby River for his mining concerns. Now the river has dried up and the scorched desert has become a deadly place to cross. But Indian native Red Wolf has other ideas and attempts to blow up Roxonn's dam. In Timely Sheriff Steve Rogers saves Red Wolf from a lynching and places him in jail and at odds with Governor Roxonn and

Mayor Fisk. Meanwhile Tony Stark props up the bar in the local saloon but also has a mechanical trick or two literally up his sleeve.

El Borak [Pulp fiction character; WMW]

Author: **Robert E. Howard**; First appearance: *Top Notch*, December 1934, "The Daughter of Erlik Khan."

The adventures of a former Texas gunslinger turned adventurer in the Middle East in the early decades of the 20th century. While the exploits of Francis Xavier Gordon a.k.a. El Borak the Swift owe more to the swashbuckling genre than the Western, references to his Western past create a link between genres.

El Borak was traditional adventure fiction but he did encounter apparent supernatural forces of the evil djinn in the Weird Menace adventure "The Three-Bladed Doom," which was later adapted by L. Sprague de Camp as a *Conan the Barbarian* adventure and re-titled "The Flame Knife" (1955).

El Diablo [Comic book character; WW]

First appearance: **All-Star Western** #2 (October 1970); Creators: Robert Kanigher, Gray Morrow; Publisher: DC Comics.

After bank teller Lazarus Lane is revived from a near-fatal coma by Apache shaman Wise Owl, he is possessed by a vengeance-seeking demon and becomes feared vigilante El Diablo.

Ellis, Edward Sylvester (1840–1916) [Dime novel author]

Born in Geneva, Ohio, on April 11, 1840, Ellis taught at Red Bank and Raritan, New Jersey, and became vice-principal of the largest grammar school in Trenton.

Ellis was editor of *Public Opinion*, a Trenton daily (1874–75), *Golden Days* (1878–81), where he met his second wife, Clara Spaulding Brown, and *The Boys' Holiday* a.k.a. *The Holiday* (1890–91). In 1887 he received the degree of Master of Arts from Princeton College.

Ellis established the genre labeled as Edisonade and was one of the first writers to introduce science fiction in popular culture through the dime novel with **The Huge Hunter or The Steam Man of the Prairies** (1868). He passed away at Cliff Island, Casco Bay, Maine, on June 20, 1916.

Selected works: *Seth Jones: or the Captives of the Frontier* (1860), *The Rangers of the Mohawk; A Tale of Cherry Valley* (1863), *The Huge Hunter or The Steam Man of the Prairies* (1868), *The Red Eagle* (1901), *Deerfoot in the Forest* (1905), *River and Forest* (1905), *Off the Reservation* (1908), *The Cruise of the Deerfoot* (1915).

Empty Saddles (1936) [Film; WMW]

Premiere: December 20, 1936; Main Cast: Buck Jones as Buck Devlin, Louise Brooks as Boots Boone, Harvey Clark as Swap Boone, Charles Middleton as Cim White, Lloyd Ingraham as Lem Jessup/Jim Grant, Frank Campeau as Kit Kress; Producer: Buck Jones; Story: Cherry Wilson; Screenplay: Frances Guihan; Director: Lesley Selander; 67 min.; Buck Jones Productions, Universal Pictures; B/W.

Buck Devlin converts the Ranch of Empty Saddles into a dude ranch with the assistance of Swap Boone and his daughter Boots, (Boots is played by former silent film sex symbol Louise Brooks). But they soon discover a group of sheep men have plans of making claims on his land. This B Western features a scene involving Buck Devlin and a ghost.

The yarn has plenty of suspense, numerous spooky situations, a good love theme and enough of the western touch to top a western dualer or fill out the action requirements of a mixed bill and leave the cash customers well satisfied.— *Daily Variety*, October 14, 1936.

"Enchantress of Venus" [Pulp fiction; SW]

Author: **Leigh Brackett**; First publication: *Planet Stories* (Fall 1949); Publisher: Love Romances, Inc.

The search for his friend Helvi takes **Eric John Stark** to the Venusian harbor town of Shuruun. Stark's first impressions fill him with apprehension.

> There was a smell about the place he did not like, a damp miasma of mud and crowding bodies and wine, and the breath of the *vela* poppy. Shuruun was an unclean town, and it stank of evil.
>
> There was something else about it, a subtle thing that touched Stark's nerves with a chill finger. Fear. He could see the shadow of it in the eyes of the people, hear its undertone in their voices. The wolves of Shuruun did not feel safe in their own kennel. Unconsciously, as this feeling grew upon him, Stark's step grew more and more wary, his eyes more cold and hard.

The feelings of dread are confirmed when Stark becomes a slave of the Lhari in the city of the Lost Ones.

See: **"Queen of the Martian Catacombs"**; **"Black Amazon of Mars"**

Enton, Harry (1854–1927) [Dime novel author]

Born in Brooklyn, New York, Enton graduated from Long Island College Hospital in 1885 and practiced medicine between his dime novel work.

Enton's creation **Frank Reade** made his debut on February 28, 1876. Enton penned three adventures before an argument with Frank Tousey over the removal of name credit led to his resignation from the series.

He continued writing on the *Old Cap Collier* series for Norman Munro and for the *Boy's Champion* serial "Young Sullivan; or, Knocked Out in Four Rounds." Pseudonyms used by Enton included Mickey Free, Val Versatile, Ironclad and Harry Harrison. He died in March 1927 following a cerebral hemorrhage.

It has been stated that Enton's real name was Harold Cohen but this is disputed by others.

Selected works: *Frank Reade and The Steam Man of the Prairies* (1876), *The Sky Detective; or, A Boy's Fight for Life and Honor* (as Mickey Free, 1883).

Eric John Stark [Pulp fiction character; SW]

First appearance: **"Queen of the Martian Catacombs"** (Summer 1949); Creator: **Leigh Brackett**.

> Civilization had brushed over Stark with a light hand. Raised from infancy by half-human aboriginals, his perceptions were still those of a savage.— **"Enchantress of Venus"**

When Eric John Stark's [Earthborn parents die in a cave-in on one of Mercury's mining colonies, a native aboriginal tribe adopt's him. The young Stark adapts to life in the Mercurian Twilight Belt with his new name of N'Chaka—He With No Tribe. But he finds his life shattered once again when the tribe members who raised him are murdered by Terran (Earth) miners who capture and imprison Stark. Terran official Simon Ashton rescues Stark and becomes his educator and mentor.

Eric John Stark's origins can be viewed in terms of the classic Western theme of the white orphan raised by Indians who feels trapped between opposing cultures as an adult. Brackett explores Western themes of frontier life and of colonial settlers destroying native culture in their quest for domination of natural resources and territory.

Stark's path as an adult takes him along the road of a mercenary outlaw, often working both sides for his own benefit. He lives in a brutal solar system populated by angry Martians and Venusians who feel exploited by the Terran colonizers and their own ruling classes. In many ways Stark is a forerunner of the amoral spaghetti Western anti-heroes of the 1960s and a successor to the earlier pulp fiction space outlaw **Northwest Smith**.

Despite the fact Stark had black skin due to the intensity of the sun on Mercury, pulp artists of the day continued to depict Stark as white or merely tanned.

Escape from High Doom [Juvenile book; WW]

Authors: Hilary H. Milton, Paul Frame; First publication: New York: Wanderer Books, 1984.

Noose City, Texas, is a ghost town where the specters of executed criminals appear on the anniversaries of their deaths. In *Plot-It-Yourself Horror Stories #5*, the readers' choices decide the outcome of the plot.

The Etched City [Novel; SFW]

Author: K. J. Bishop; First publication: New York: Bantam Books, 2004.

Across the wasteland of Copper County gunslinger Gwynn and physician Raule flee the Army of Heroes. Wanted for their part in a war they lost, they head for the Telute Shelf and the sprawling town of Ashamoil where art, magic and violence exist side-by-side. Gwynn becomes an enforcer for the slave trade of the Horn Fan Cartel, while Raule trying to escape the demons of her past seeks to help the poor.

Critics have compared Bishop's dark, fantasy tale to Stephen King's **Dark Tower** and China Mieville's work.

El Extraño hijo del sheriff (1982) [Film; Mexico; WW]

Premiere: 1982; Main Cast: Mario Almada as Dr. Jack Miller, Eric del Castillo as Sheriff Frederick Jackson, Rosa Gloria Chagoyán as Julia, Alfredo Gutiérrez as Jeremías Santos, Luis Mario Quiroz as Fred and Eric Jackson, Alicia Encinas as Mary Jackson; Executive Producer: Armando Duarte; Screenplay: Eric del Castillo, Bárbara Gil; Director: Fernando Durán; 90 min.; ATA, Conacite Dos, Artistas y Técnicos Asociados-Estudios; Spanish; Color.

Supernatural Mexican Western influenced by *The Other*, *The Exorcist* and *The Omen*, set in the American Old West of the 1890s. After giving birth to conjoined twin boys, Sheriff Jackson's wife dies. When Jackson forces the doctor to separate the twins some years later, only one boy (L Quiroz) survives the operation. But the dead son has an evil influence over the surviving twin and guides his thoughts and actions from beyond the grave.

Fairy BrewHaHa at the Lucky Nickel Saloon [Novel; WW]

Author: Ken Rand; First publication: Waterville, Maine: Five Star, 2005.

The patrons of the Lucky Nickel Saloon, Second Avenue, Laramie, Wyoming, confront a gang of faeries who plan to rob the circus of payroll gold.

See: **Dadgum Martians Invade the Lucky Nickel Saloon**

Fallen Cloud Saga [Book series; WW]

Alternate history series by Kurt R.A. Giambastiani where Cheyenne Indians ride dinosaur mounts in a 19th century America ruled by President George Armstrong Custer with an agenda for expansion into the West.

See: **The Year the Cloud Fell; The Spirit of Thunder; The Shadow of the Storm; From the Heart of the Storm**

Fallout: New Vegas [Video game; SFW]

Release date: October 19, 2010; Voice Cast: Ron Perlman as Narrator, Matthew Perry as Benny, Wayne Newton as Mr. New Vegas, Kris Kristofferson as Chief Hanlon, Rene Auberjonois as Robert Edwin House, Michael Dorn as Marcus, Felicia Day as Veronica Renata Santangelo, William Sadler as Victor, Zacharay Levi as Arcade Israel Gannon, Danny Trejo as Raul Alfonso Tejada; Executive producer: Lawrence Liberty; Lead writer: John Gonzalez; Director: Josh Sawyer; Platforms: PlayStation3, Windows, Xbox 360; Developer: Obsidian Entertainment; Publisher: Bethesda Softworks.

In a post apocalypse Nevada the player is Courier Six, assigned to deliver a package to the owner of New Vegas, the mysterious Robert Edwin House. But on his journey across the Mojave Wasteland the courier is shot in the head and buried in an open grave by thugs who steal the package. After the courier is rescued by a robot and attended by a doctor the player sets out on their quest to find the culprits. As the player continues on their quest their choices will determine the final outcome in a war between rival factions in New Vegas.

Fantastic Four [Comic book]

The adventures of Reed Richards (Mr. Fantastic), Benjamin Grimm (The Thing), Susan Richards (Invisible Girl) and Johnny Storm (The Human Torch). Following exposure to cosmic rays, they attain unique superpowers and form The Fantastic Four. One of the key comic book titles that kick-started the superhero boom of the 1960s.

"A Town Called Revelation" [SFW]
First publication: Vol. 3 #33–34 (September-October 2000); Story: John Moore; Art: Salvador Larroca, Art Thibbert: Publisher: Marvel Comics.

The Fantastic Four are forced to land their Fantasti-Car in the Arizona town of Revelation after an atmospheric disturbance. They all have strange experiences, with Sue transported through time to 1873 where she meets *Kid Colt, Outlaw*.

Fantasy Island (1978) [TV series]

Main Cast: Ricardo Montalban as Mr. Roarke, Hervé Villechaize as Tattoo; Executive Producer: Aaron Spelling; Spelling-Goldberg Productions; 157 × 60 min; Columbia Pictures Television; Color.

Fantasy Island is a resort where dreams and fantasies literally come true thanks to the mysterious, charismatic owner Mr. Roarke and his dwarf assistant Tattoo.

Weird Western episodes:

"The Sheriff" (1:03) [SFW]
Air date: February 11, 1978; Story: Robert Hamner; Director: Phil Bondelli; Guest: Harry Guardino as John Burke.

New York detective Burke wants to go back in time to be a sheriff and hand out Old West justice to the man who murdered his partner.

"Butch and Sundance" (1:07) [SFW]
Air date: March 18, 1978; Story: James Schmerer; Director: Cliff Bole; Guest Stars: James MacArthur as Alex Farelli/Sundance Kid, Christopher Connelly as Bill Cummings/Butch Cassidy, William Smith as Wyatt Earp.

Two friends' desire to be Butch Cassidy and the Sundance Kid makes them come to a new appreciation of their present lives.

"Kid Corey Rides Again" (5:02) [SFW]
Air date: October 17, 1981; Guest Stars: Arte Johnson as Ned Plummer, Cameron Mitchell as Sheriff Matt, Jack Elam as Kid Corey; Story: Don Ingalls; Director: Don Chaffey.

Ned Plummer wishes to ride with legendary outlaw Kid Corey in the Old West.

"The Last Cowboy" (5:04) [SFW]
Air date: October 31, 1981; Guest Star: Stuart Whitman as Joel Campbell; Story: Larry Forrester; Director: Don Chaffey.

Joel Campbell's wishes for adventure in the Old West prove to be far different from his fantasy image.

Far West [Graphic novel; WW]

First publication: 2001; Creator: Richard Moore; b/w; Publisher: Nantier Beall Minoustchine Publishing.

Scantily clad elf bounty hunter Ra'Meghan Val'Norium (a.k.a. Meg) and sidekick Phil the bear hunt evil elf Voss. A dragon complicates matters further in this adult Weird Western adventure.

The Far West (*Frontier Magic* book #3) [Novel; WW]

Author: Patricia C. Wrede; First publication: New York: Scholastic Press, 2012.

In the third book in Wrede's *Frontier Magic* series Eff Rothmer is now a 20-year-old woman who joins her twin brother, Lan, among others, in a government-directed expedition into the uncharted wilderness of the Far West. On her journey she matures in her magical skills as she encounters the deadly medusa lizards, rock dragons and creatures new to everyone on the expedition.

A mix of fantasy-action-adventure and Old West pioneer expansion wrapped in a magical 19th century environment.

Farmer in the Sky [Juvenile Novel; SW]

Author: **Robert A. Heinlein**; First publication: New York: Scribner, 1950; Illustrated by Clifford Geary; Originally serialized as *Satellite Scout* in *Boy's Life* (August–November 1950)

A "new frontier" pioneer theme runs through the story of Boy Scout Bill Lerner, his widowed father George, stepmother Molly Kenyon and stepsister Peggy as they strive to survive on one of Jupiter's moons, Ganymede. Heinlein stresses the power of community and the unique nature of mankind's talent for adapting to new situations and environments.

[T]hey had controlled their environment, they weren't animals, pushed around and forced to accept what nature handed them; they took nature and bent it to their will.

The Fast Gun (The Floating Outfit #21) [Novel; SFW]

Author: J. T. Edson; First publication: London: Brown, Watson, 1967.

Dusty Fog falls in love with a beautiful lady he rescued from drunken town bullies as he accompanies the lady and her family cross-country. During the rescue Dusty killed one of the bullies and now they seek revenge as they pursue him. But Dusty has more to worry about when the woman he loves disappears, along with her family. They have been studying the people of Earth and have now returned to their own world.

Captain Dustine Edward Marsden "Dusty" Fog, along with the Ysabel Kid and Mark Counter form the Floating Outfit working out of the OD Connected Ranch. Dusty is skilled in the martial arts and the use of his Army Colts.

"The Fastest Draw" [Short story; WW]

Author: Larry Eisenberg; First publication: *Amazing Stories* (October 1963); Publisher: Ziff-Davis.

A man keeps improving his robot gunslinger to test his gun-shooting skills.

See: *Out of the Unknown*

Fatale [Comic book; WW]

First publication: March 2013; Story: Ed Brubaker; Art: Sean Phillips; Publisher: Image.

This one-shot story, set in the Old West of the 1880s features "Black Bonnie," a femme fatale with supernatural gifts who partners with Native American warrior, Milkfed. A mix of hard-boiled noir and horror in a Spaghetti Western landscape.

Fear Agent [Comic book]

Heath Huston, a Texan with a serious drinking problem, roams the universe exterminating aliens who threaten the security of Earth.

"I AGAINST I" PART 1 & 2 [SFW]

First publication: *Fear Agent* #22 (June 2008); Story: Rick Remender; Art: Tony Moore; Publisher: Dark Horse Comics.

Heath Huston is adrift on a desert world, located in a shadow universe where he is pursued by killers after being shot in the back. But when rescuers come to his aid Huston is split between helping them and returning to Earth.

Fear Itself (2008) [TV anthology series]

Horror anthology series that was cancelled mid-season.

"SKIN & BONES" (1:09) [WW]

Air date: July 31, 2008; Creator: Mike Garris; Main Cast: Doug Jones as Grady Edlund, Molly Hagan as Elena Edlund, Gordon Tootoosis as Eddie Bear; Story: Drew McWeeny, Scott Swan; Director: Larry Fessenden; 40 min.; NBC; Color.

A cattle herder (Jones) returns to his ranch after being lost in a mountain storm for ten days. But the man is now possessed by an evil spirit.

A Feather in the Wind [Novel; WWR]

Author: Madeline Baker; First publication: New York: N.Y. Leisure Books, 1997.

After accepting an eagle feather from an aging American Indian who tells her it will answer her prayers, Susannah awakes in the year 1870. In a South Dakota army camp she meets prisoner Black Wind, whom she recognizes from a photograph she owns. And Black Wind recognizes Susannah as the beautiful woman in his visions.

Felix the Cat (1958) [Animated TV series]

Premiere: 1958; Voice Cast: Jack Mercer as Felix, Poindexter, Vavoom, The Professor, Rock Bottom, The Master Cylinder; Producer: Joseph Oriolo; 30 min.; Trans-Lux Productions; Color.

Joe Oriolo's revisionist version of Felix the Cat complete with his "Magic Bag of Tricks" included episodes set in the American West that often featured surreal imagery involving Felix's magic bag: *Felix Out West; Oil and Indians Don't Mix; Sheriff Felix Vs. the Gas Cloud; Out West With Big Brownie; Chief Standing Bull; Felix and Poindexter Out West.*

Felix the Cat in Eats Are West (1925) [Animated theatrical short; WW]

Premiere; November 15, 1925; Director: Otto Messmer; Pat Sullivan Studios; Silent; b/w.

Felix converts a trolley into an airplane to capture the Pony Express and eats all the sausages on board. But Felix finds trouble with the gang of cowboys whose sausages he ate.

Femforce [Comic book]

First appearance: *Femforce Special*, Fall 1984; Publisher: AC Comics.

The adventures of this female super-team featured occasional Weird Western stories starring the **Haunted Horseman**, **Buckaroo Betty** and **Black Phantom**.

"THE GOOD, THE BAD, AND THE PARANORMAL" [#7; SFW]

First publication: 1987; Story: **Bill Black**, Rik Levins, Don Secrease; Art: Rik Levins, Don Secrease, Bill Black, Tom Grindberg, Howard Bender, Steve Vance, Dan Panosian, Bill Anderson, Dan Davis, Mark Heike.

Femforce travel's through time via the Time Triangle to the town of Apache, Texas, in 1874. Using the aliases Calamity Kate, Black Phantom, Cherokee, and Frenchy King, they attempt to track down Captain Paragon, not aware that Klyness the Kronon have also arrived on the same quest. Guest stars include The Hooded Horseman, *Tim Holt*, **Lemonade Kid**, *Durango Kid*, Angel Eyes Barcroft, Marshal Steve Brand, Chief White Cloud, Bullseye, Old Sure-Shot, Bat Masterson, Rocky Lane, Wild Bill Elliott and Black Diamond.

"FRONTIER JUSTICE" [#8; SFW]

First publication: 1987; Story: Rik Levins, Bill Black; Art: Rik Levins, Bill Black, Dan Davis, John Dell.

As the **Haunted Horseman** tells Nightveil the story of his origin, she comes to realize the Cloaks of Darkness worn by each are identical. But the two Cloaks cannot exist in the same time and space and when Nightveil touches the Haunted Horseman he dies.

The Latigo Kid's showdown with Kronon causes the Kid to confront his own future destiny.

"ARE YOU READY FOR BUCKAROO BETTY?" [#20; SFW]

First publication: 1989; Story: Bill Black, Rick Levins; Art: Bill Marimon, The All-Inker's Squad.

She-Cat persuades Dr. Jimenez to let her travel back in time to visit her Kiowa friends in Apache, Texas. She-Cat meets Sheriff Betty Bates alias Buckaroo Betty, who tells her the story of a Kiowa massacre by the cavalry.

"NIGHTMARE!" [#22; WW]

First publication: 1989; Story: Richard "The Count" Rome; Art: Richard Rome, Mark Propst, Bill Black.

The Black Shroud is the cause of terrifying nightmares for Joan Wayne as she imagines herself fighting old friends. In a nightmare set in the Old West, she is shot by Colt.

"YOU ONLY DIE TWICE" [#28; WW]

First publication: 1990; Story: Bill Black; Art: Norman Hardy Jr., Mark Propst, Marke Heike.

Brother and sister Roger and Laura Wright travel back in time to try to prevent the death of the Haunted Horseman and to fully restore Laura's powers. The Haunted Horseman is lured to Skull Rock by the kidnapping of Dr. Martin Stone; Nightveil tells him he will die if his Cloak of Darkness touches her Cloak.

The Cloak chases after Rex Fury and kills him. This event leads to the ghost of Rex Fury becoming the supernatural **Haunter** as Laura's power is restored.

"TRIAL OF THE BLACK PHANTOM" [#64–68; WW]

Story: Nick Northey, Mark G. Heike, Bill Black; Art: Nick Northey, Nar Castro, Sonny Delos Santos, Chris Allen.

When the Black Phantom is hanged by outlaws, she is rescued from Hell by the Great She-Spirit of the Sky who grants the Black Phantom her powers and returns her to Earth.

Fiction Clemens [Comic book; SFW]

First issue: May 2008; Creator: Josh Wagner; Publisher: Ape Entertainment.

Surreal sci-fi Western featuring gunslinger Fiction Clemens and Tiberius Kitchens, caught in an alien conspiracy by the Clockmaker to bring the Old West into the Space Age.

Fire & Brimstone [RPG book; WW]

Author: John "Salman" Goff; First publication: 1998; Setting: ***Deadlands: The Weird West***; Publisher: Pinnacle Entertainment Group.

Sourcebook for the blessed characters of the Weird West with details of miracles, divine interventions, holy relics and enemies of the faith. Includes the adventure "The Mission."

Fireball XL5 (1962) [Children's TV series; UK]

Space City in the year 2067. The World Space Patrol's *Fireball XL5* spaceship, piloted by Steve Zodiac, patrols Sector 25 of the galaxy. Zodiac and his crew encounter numerous alien races on their patrols and a time-traveling SF Western adventure.

"1875" (1:25) [SFW]

Air date: April 14, 1963; Voice Cast: Paul Maxwell as Colonel Steve Zodiac; Sylvia Anderson as Venus; David Graham as Professor Matthew "Matt" Matic, Lieutenant Ninety, Zoonie the Lazoon; John Bluthal as Commander Zero; Gerry Anderson as Robert the Robot; Producer: Gerry Anderson; Story: Anthony Marriott; Director: Bill Harris; 30 min.; AP Films Production for ATV; Distribution: ITC World Wide; Supermarionation; b/w.

With the often bungling help of Robert the Robot Professor Matic builds a time machine. He tests it on the Robot who travels back in time to the Old West of 1875 before returning to Matic's workshop. Matic orders Lt. Ninety to keep his workshop off limits but Commander Zero orders Ninety to hand over the keys.

As Steve Zodiac, Venus and Commander Zero check out Professor Matic's new invention they see Venus' mischievous pet Zoonie playing with the controls. Before they can stop him they find themselves traveling back in time. As they travel their memory fades and they receive new outfits more suited to 1875. Steve Zodiac becomes sheriff, while Venus is now infamous bank robber Frenchie Lil with her accomplice, gunslinger Zero.

Professor Matic manages to return Zodiac and Commander Zero to the present just as Zero double crosses Frenchie Lil and knocks her unconscious. Venus is trapped in 1875 as Matic overloads and destroys his time machine in his attempt to finally return her to Space City.

Firefly (2002) [TV series; SW]

Premiere: September 20, 2002; Main Cast: Nathan Fillion as Captain Malcolm "Mal" Reynolds, Gina Torres as Zoë Washburne, Adam Baldwin as Jayne Cobb, Alan Tudyk as Hoban "Wash" Washburne, Summer Glau as River Tam, Ron Glass as Shepherd Book, Jewel Staite as Kaylee Frye, Morena Baccarin as Inara Serra; Gina Torres; Creator: Joss Whedon; Executive Producers: Joss Whedon, Tim Minear; Story: Joss Whedon, Tim Minear, Ben Edlund, Jose Molina; Directors: Joss Whedon, Tim Minear, Vern Gillum; 1 × 90 min., 14 × 45 min.; Mutant Enemy, 20th Century–Fox Television; Color.

This science fiction series from *Buffy the Vampire Slayer* creator Joss Whedon features a heavy Western influence including saloon fights, gunfights, covered wagons and herds of cattle transported on the Firefly-class spaceship named Serenity. Former Browncoat resistance fighter against the Alliance in the Unification War, Malcolm "Mal" Reynolds is the owner and Captain of Serenity. He is joined by fellow Browncoat and first mate Zoë Washburne and her husband and pilot of Serenity Hoban "Wash" Wasburne. Shepherd Book serves as preacher and spiritual advisor and Kaylee Frye is the young female mechanic. Mercenary Jayne Cobb has an uneasy relationship with the crew including Dr. Simon Tam and his gifted psychic sister River Tam. Experimentation on Tam's brain by the Alliance has left her with periods of mental instability. The beautiful high society courtesan Inara Serra, otherwise known as a "Companion," completes the crew.

Whedon admits to the influence of Han Solo from *Star Wars* as an inspiration for *Firefly* and the character "Mal" Reynolds. The initial reviews were mixed although some critics saw promise in the series.

Michael Speier of *Variety* (September 18, 2002) stated: "The wild, wild west gets a futuristic transplant in Fox's 'Firefly.' Cheeky and charming, Joss Whedon's attempt to fuse oater with 'Star Trek' is just silly enough to work—and there's absolutely nothing like it on TV."

The Boston Globe (September 20, 2002) critic Matthew Gilbert commented: "'Firefly' the new series from 'Buffy the Vampire Slayer,' is a mess— a wonderful, imaginative mess brimming with possibility. About a dysfunctional family of space cowboys, the sci-fi series arrives not fully formed, like an elaborate photo that's still clarifying in developing fluid."

Following an initial 13-episode order from the Fox network *Firefly* was canceled on December 12, 2002. It remained popular with fans and developed a cult following which led to the film sequel *Serenity*.

Season One
[episodes with a Space Western theme]

"Serenity Pilot"

Air date: December 20, 2002; Story-Director: Joss Whedon.

The feature-length pilot introduces the characters and sets the stage for the series. It is the year AD 2517 and The Alliance controls central planetary systems. Captain Malcolm Reynolds is a veteran of the war against the Alliance.

Reynolds and the crew of the Firefly-class cargo ship *Serenity* eke out a living outside of Alliance control.

Fox Network originally rejected the pilot episode in favor of "The Train Job" and finally broadcast the pilot following the cancellation of the series.

"The Train Job" (1:01)

Air date: September 20, 2002; Story: Joss Whedon, Tim Minear; Director: Joss Whedon.

Hired to rob a train, Reynolds and his crew discover they've been tricked into stealing essential medical supplies intended for the local mining town of Paradiso. This episode begins with a Western-style saloon fight with a science fiction twist.

"Our Mrs. Reynolds" (1:03)

Air date: October 4, 2002; Story: Joss Whedon; Director: Vondie Curtis Hall.

Reynolds finds himself obligated to a gift of a wife named Saffron (Christina Hendricks) as payment for a shipment of livestock. But his wife is leading the ship and crew into a trap.

"Javnestown" (1:04)

Air date: October 18, 2002; Story: Ben Edlund; Director: Marita Grabiak

To his amazement, Jayne Cobb discovers he's become a local folk hero following his last visit to the settlement of Canton.

"Safe" (1:07)

Air date: November 8, 2002; Story: Drew Z. Greenberg; Director: Michael Grossman.

Delivering a herd of cattle to a Western-style town on an outlying planet, Reynolds and his crew find themselves in the middle of a shootout that leaves Shepherd critically wounded. Meanwhile River and her brother Dr. Simon Tam (Sean Maher) are kidnapped and River is accused of being a witch by the townspeople, who decide to burn her at the stake.

"Objects in Space" (1:10)

Air date: December 13, 2002; Story-Director: Joss Whedon.

Bounty hunter Jubal Early (Richard Brooks) seeks River Tam aboard Serenity.

"Heart of Gold" (1:12)

Air date: July 19, 2003 (Fox Latin America); Story: Brett Matthews; Director: Thomas J. Wright.

Reynolds and the crew of *Serenity* respond to a plea for help from the owner (Melinda Clarke) of a bordello on the moon of Deadwood. The bordello is under attack from Rance Burgess (Frederic Lehne), who claims the prostitute Petaline (Tracy Leah Ryan) is pregnant with his son.

See: *Serenity*

Firehair [Comic book character]

First appearance: *Showcase* #85 (September 1969); Creator: Joe Kubert; Publisher: DC Comics.

After the Blackfoot Indian tribe attack's a wagon train on the Great Western Plains, they decide to raise the one survivor as one of their own. Chief Grey Cloud adopts the white infant boy with flaming red hair and introduces him to the culture of the Blackfoot.

Firehair was introduced in a three-issue miniseries in DC Comics' *Showcase* title.

"The Shaman" [WW]

First publication: *Showcase* #87 (December 1969); Art: Joe Kubert; Publisher: DC Comics.

Recovering from an encounter with a cougar, Firehair has various mystical visions as a shaman nurses him back to health.

The First Bad Man (1955) [Animated theatrical short; WW]

Premiere: September 30, 1955; Story: Heck Allen; Animation: Walter Clinton, Michael Lah, Ray Patterson, Grant Simmons; Producer: Fred Quimby; Director; Tex Avery; 6 min.; MGM; Color.

Tex Avery-animated short about dinosaur-riding Texas cowboys, one million years B.C. style, and the first outlaw Dinosaur Dan.

A Fist Full o' Dead Guys [RPG book; WW]

Editor: Shane Lacy Hensley; First publication: 1999; Deadlands anthology with No Name #1; Publisher: Pinnacle Entertainment Group.

Anthology title includes "Hate: Part One" by Shane Lacy Hensley, "Reborn on the Bayou" by Matt Forbeck, "Homecoming" by John R. Hopler, "The Hex Files" by Don DeBrandt, "The Taste" by Clay & Susan Griffith, "A Resurrection, Three Hangings, and an Apache Arrow" by Kevin Ross, "The Drive" by T.G. Shepherd, "Let the River of Death Wash Over Me" by Richard E. Dansky, "Behind Enemy Lines" by Jeff Mariotte, "Comes the Storm" by Ree Soesbee, "The Parker Panic" by Mike Stackpole.

A Fist Full o' Ghost Rock [RPG book; WW]

Author: Shane Lacy Hensley; First publication: 1998; Setting: **Deadlands: The Great Rail Wars**; Publisher: Pinnacle Entertainment Group.

Scenario book for *The Great Rail Wars*. Includes campaigns, *A Fist Full o' Ghost Rock* involving feuding over the rail rights in Trouble, Colorado, *Trail o' Blood* featuring the forces of Ben Stern on the run from Marty Coltrane and *The Many Tasks of Grimme* featuring the City of Lost Angels, the Maze and the Reverend Ezekiah Grimme.

Fistful of Blood [Comic strip; Graphic Novel; WW]

First publication: *Heavy Metal* Vol. 25 #2 (May 2001); Creators: Kevin Eastman, Simon Bisley; Publisher: Kevin Eastman.

The adventures of a mercenary female gunfighter doing battle with zombies and vampire outlaws in a semi-abandoned Western town.

This adult strip features a large-breasted "heroine" who has a preference for very little clothing. A black & white trade paperback-graphic novel edition collecting the previously published strips from *Heavy Metal* magazine was released in 2002.

Fistful of Feet [Novel; WW]

Author: Jordan Krall; First publication: Portland, OR: Eraserhead Press, 2009.

Calamaro enters Screwhorse, Nevada, dragging a wooden donkey named Sartana behind him and carrying a gun that burps. Screwhorse is a small, bedraggled town whose main activity takes place in the brothel, where bizarre fetishes are indulged. Screwhorse is populated by weird characters including gunslinger the Hard Candy Kid, four-footed June who has a small foot growing out of each of her ankles, cattle that have tentacles instead of udders and Cthulhu worshipping Indians intent on killing everyone in the town.

Flaming Star [Comic book character]

First appearance: **Ghost Rider** #1 (February 1967); Publisher: Marvel Comics.

Medicine Man Flaming Star is granted magical powers by the Native American Indian god **Manitou**. He was custodian of the glowing meteorite dust that he passed on to Ghost Rider.

Flesh [Comic strip; UK; SFW]

First publication: *2000 A.D.* #1 (1977); Creator: Pat Mills; Art: Ramon Sola; Publisher: I.P.C. Magazines.

Dinosaur meat is farmed by time-traveling cowboys from the 23rd century. Hunter Earl Reagan and his Rangers have a formidable foe in a Tyrannosaurus Rex named Old One Eye who threatens the sanctuary of domed trading post Carver City.

The Flight of Michael McBride [Novel; WW]

Author: Midori Snyder; First publication: New York: Tor, 1994.

Irish-American cowboy Michael McBride moves West following the death of his mother and secures work as a ranch hand. But he also finds himself pursued by Irish demons.

For a Few Dead Guys More [RPG book; WW]

Editor: Shane Lacy Hensley; First publication: 1999; Deadlands anthology with No Name #2; Publisher: Pinnacle Entertainment Group.

Foreword by **Joe R. Lansdale**; "Hate: Part Two" by Shane Lacy Hensley, "Head Games" by Matt Forbeck, "Providin' the Crick Don't Rise" by Susan Griffith and Clay Griffith, "A Load of Bull" by John Goff, "No Man's Law" by Lucien Soulban, "Some Mercy, Some Justice, Some Magic" by Ginger R. Senter, "Tyrants and Patriots" by Rob Vaux, "Nunna Daul Tsuny" by Zach Bush, "Cold Island" by Chris Snyder, "Hellbent for Leather" by Don DeBrandt, and "Paid in Full" by Hal Mangold.

For a Few Souls More (*Heaven's Gate Trilogy* book #3) [Novel; WW]

Author: Guy Adams; First publication: Oxford UK: Solaris, 2014.

Wormword is a town that travels through time and space and comes to rest for one day only every hundred years. And on that one day the living can escape death by traveling through a portal to Heaven. Each time the location is different but today, September 21, 1889, Wormwood has come to rest in an obscure part of the American Midwest.

Englishman Atherton is on a mission to destroy Wormword and the demons who now inhabit it after Paradise has fallen and Lucifer has become the new governor of Wormwood.

For Texas and Zed [Novel; SW]

Author: Zach Hughes; First publication: New York: Popular Library, April 1976.

Planet Texas, colonized by Texans from the Earth of centuries ago, has retained its independence. But now it finds its civilization and technology under threat from encroaching hostile empires.

"For the Love of Barbara Allen" [Pulp fiction; WW]

Author: **Robert E. Howard**; First publication: *The Magazine of Fantasy & Science Fiction* Vol. 31 #2 (August 1967).

It is love at first sight for Rachel Ormond and Joel beside the Cumberland River in Tennessee. "When Joel saw her standin' there with the morning' sun makin' jewels out of the dew on the bushes, he stopped dead and just stared like a fool. He told me it seemed as if she was standin' in a white blaze of light."

But all too soon the Civil War separates them by distance and finally by death when Joel is killed in battle. Rachel is devastated and never looks at another man again. In her final years she awaits death surrounded by family in Texas and to her great joy finds Joel waiting to comfort her, in the body of another man and "another, different voice, whispering down the ages."

The Forbidden God [RPG book; WW]

Author: Tim Brown; First publication: 1998; *Deadlands: The Weird West* Dime Novel #7; Publisher: Pinnacle Entertainment Group.

Ronan Lynch encounters a Spanish galleon on the dry land of the Great Salt Flats of Utah.

Forbidden Worlds [Comic book]

This successful supernatural and fantasy anthology title from ACG featured tales of specters, demons, monsters, giants, witches, aliens, time travel, dinosaurs, Magicman, Herbie and the occasional Weird Western.

"Where the Redskins Never Fell" [WW]

First publication: #44 (July 1956); Editor: Richard E. Hughes; Art: Harry Lazarus, Tom Hickey; Publisher: American Comics Group (ACG).

"Deadly Peril Looms Out of the Past" as a group of tourists from 1956 are attacked by Indians from the Old West.

"The Vengeance of Coyote Charlie" [WW]

First publication: #82 (September 1959); Story: Kurato Osaki; Art: Ogden Whitney.

An Indian drum defies the laws of nature.

"Soapbox on Wheels" [SFW]

First publication: #95 (May-June 1961); Story: Zev Zimmer; Art: Paul Reinman.

Young Lenny avoid arrows from an American Indian in the Old West when his soapbox ride turns into an adventure through time and space.

Fortress o' Fear: Devil's Tower 3 [RPG book; WW]

Author: Matt Forbeck; First publication: 1998; Setting: ***Deadlands: The Weird West***; Publisher: Pinnacle Entertainment Group.

The final part of the Devil's Tower trilogy.

See: ***Heart o' Darkness: Devil's Tower 2***

"Fountain of Youth" [Pulp fiction; WW]

Author: **Lon Williams**; Character: **Lee Winters**; *Real Western Stories* (December 1952)

When the man who never slept met the stranger who claimed to be three hundred and eighty-seven years old, another gunsmoke headache was building up for the reluctant lawman of Forlorn Gap.

Four Feather Falls (1960) [Children's TV series; UK; WW]

Premiere: February 25, 1960; Voice Cast: Nicholas Parsons as Sheriff Tex Tucker, Kenneth Connoras Dusty/Rocky/Pedro, David Graham as Grandpa Twink/Fernando, Denise Bryer as Ma Jones/Little Jake; Creators: Barry Gray, Gerry Anderson; Producer: Gerry Anderson; Directors: Gerry Anderson, David Elliott, Alan Pattillo; 39 × 15 min.; A. P. Films (APF) for Granada Television UK; b/w.

Sheriff Tex Tucker of Four Feather Falls, Kansas, has been given four magic feathers by Indian Chief Kalamakooya as a reward for sheltering his son. Two feathers give his dog Dusty and horse Rocky the ability to speak and two give his guns the power to swivel and shoot automatically.

The earliest example of Gerry Anderson's Supermarionation work that would reach its peak with *Captain Scarlet and the Mysterons* (1967).

Season One

How It All Began (1:01); *Kidnapped* (1:02); *Pedro Has a Plan* (1:03); *Pedro's Pardon* (1:04); *A Close Shave* (1:05); *Indian Attack* (1:06); *Sheriff for a Day* (1:07); *Dusty Becomes Deputy* (1:08);

Four Feather Falls (1960), a children's television series starring Sheriff Tex Tucker and his magic feathers.

Gunrunners (1:09); *Trouble at Yellow Gulch* (1:10); *Frame-Up* (1:11); *Gold Diggers* (1:12); *Gold Is Where You Find It* (1:13); *Trapped* (1:14); *Best Laid Schemes...* (1:15); *Escort* (1:16); *The Toughest Guy in the West* (1:17); *Ghost of a Chance* (1:18); *Gunplay* (1:19); *A Lawman Rides Alone* (1:20); *Jailbreak* (1:21); *A Little Bit of Luck* (1:22); *Land Grabbers* (1:23); *Once a Lawman* (1:24); *Election Day* (1:25); *Gunfight on Main Street* (1:26); *A Bad Name* (1:27); *Horse Thieves* (1:28); *The Ma Jones Story* (1:29); *Bandits Abroad* (1:30); *A Cure for Everything* (1:31); *Teething Troubles* (1:32); *Buffalo Rocky* (1:33); *Safe As Houses* (1:34); *First Train Through* (1:35); *Happy Birthday* (1:36); *Fancy Shootin'* (1:37); *Ambush* (1:38); *Ride 'Em Cowboy* (1:39)

Four of the Apocalypse (1975) [Film; Italy; WW]

USA DVD release title for *I Quattro dell'Apocalisse*.

Fourth Horseman [Comic book: WW]

First publication: August 2007; Story: Jeffrey Nodelman; Art: Tommy Castillo, Milen Parvanov; Four-part mini-series; Publisher: Fangoria Comics.

This violent and blood-spattered mini-series chronicles the story of how the Riders of the Apocalypse meet and plan to destroy the world.

Stories feature Bear the White Rider, a false Messiah who leads people along the wrong path; former Chinese slave Magog the Red Rider, deliverer of destruction; Prophet the Brown Rider, the fastest gunslinger on Earth and bringer of disease and pestilence; and the Black Rider, the bringer of death.

Fox, Gardner (1911–1986) [Comic book writer]

Born in Brooklyn, New York, Gardner Fox began his professional career as a lawyer before turning to writing for pulp magazines. In 1937 he was employed by **Vincent Sullivan** at National—DC Comics, creating **Hawkman** and the influential Justice Society of America for *All-Star Comics*. In the late 1940s and early 1950s Fox worked for Avon, EC and Magazine Enterprises where he resumed his working relationship with Vincent Sullivan. With the superhero in decline, Fox turned to the Western, working with artist **Dick Ayers** on **Ghost Rider** where he added supernatural elements to the origin story in *Ghost Rider* #1. Fox also worked on **The Lemonade Kid** with artist **Bob Powell** and *Straight Arrow* and created the short-lived **Presto Kid** after Ghost Rider was forced into a premature retirement by the newly formed Comics Code Authority which frowned on supernatural storylines. Fox wrote over 800 scripts during his time at ME.

Returning to National—DC Comics in the mid–1950s, Fox created Adam Strange for *Mystery in Space* and together with artist Carmine Infantino heralded a new Silver Age in comics. In 1961 Fox created the first Western superhero in DC Comics history with the short-lived **Super-Chief** strip. He worked on numerous superhero titles edited by Julius Shwartz including *Justice League of America*, Hawkman, **Batman**, **Green Lantern**, *The Flash* and *The Atom*, throughout the 1960s.

Following a dispute over lack of health care provisions, Fox left DC Comics in 1968 and freelanced for Marvel Comics, including work on the Weird Western title **Red Wolf**. He retired from comics in the mid-970s and concentrated on writing science fiction, sword & sorcery and romance novels. Throughout his career Fox adopted many pseudonyms including Jefferson Cooper (sword & sorcery novels), Lynna Cooper (romance novels), Bart Sommers, Paul Dean and Ray Gardner.

Frag Deadlands [FPS Game; WW]

First publication: 2001; Development: Steve Jackson; Design: Philip Reed; Publisher: Steve Jackson Games.

First-person shooter board game combining Deadlands and Frag game rules in the Weird West setting.

Frank Reade & Frank Reade Jr. [Dime novel characters; SPW]

Writer **Harry Enton**, and publisher Frank Tousey may have been the initial originators of Frank Reade but the credit for the success of the Reade family adventures has to rest with **Luis Senarens**. When Enton quit after four issues, Tousey hired Senarens to replace him.

Senarens had been writing for Tousey since the age of 14 under various pseudonyms. The departure of Enton coincided with the departure of Frank Reade Sr. from the title. His son Frank Reade Jr. replaced him, with "Noname," alias Senarens, penning his nickel library stories. His 179 stories in total would see Reade Jr. and his steam-powered inventions traveling to various locations around the world, including the Old West.

Frank Reade and His Steam Horse. A Thrilling Story of the Plains [Dime novel; SPW]

Frank Tousey's Boys Weekly Vol. 2 #46.

Frank Reade and His Steam Man of the Plains; or, The Terror of the West [Dime novel; SPW]

Author: **Harry Enton**; *The Boys of New York* Vol. 1 #28 (February 28, 1876).

Influenced by the success of **The Huge Hunter or The Steam Man of the Prairies** by **Edward Sylvester Ellis**, Harry Enton wrote of the adventures of a new improved Steam Man equipped with eyes doubling as headlights and the ability to shoot missiles of fire and to travel at 50 miles per hour.

> Charley Gorse beheld a metallic imitation of a man. The figure was about twelve feet high from the bottom of the huge feet to the top of the plug hat which adorned the steam-man's head. An enormous belly was required to accommodate the boiler and steam chest, and this corpulency agreed well with the height of the metallic steam chap. To give full working room to the very delicate machinery in the interior, the old giant was made to convey a sort of knapsack upon his shoulders. The machine held its arms in the position taken by a man when he is drawing a carriage.

> Charlie glanced up at the face of the monster and beheld a huge pair of glass eyes and an enormous mouth.

> "Now then," said Frank, "the lamp will be in his head, and his eyes will be the headlights. His mouth holds the steam whistle. Here, in his belly, we open a door and put in fuel, and the ashes drop down into his legs and are emptied from the movable kneepan, and without injury to the oiled leg-shafts, for they are enclosed in a tube. That is why the fellow's limbs are so large. These wire cords increase the power in one leg, and cause that leg to go much faster, and in that manner we get a side movement and can turn around."

> "Go on," said Charlie, who was intensely excited.

> "Its feet are spiked like a baseball player's are spiked, to prevent the machine from slipping under speed," said Frank. "Then you notice that its legs are very long, and very far apart, so as to give it balance. This stop-cock on the side will let on or shut off steam."

Frank Reade and Sitting Bull; or, White Cunning versus Red [Dime novel; SPW]

Author: "Noname" (**Luis Senarens**); Reprinted: *Aldine Romance of Invention*, Travel and Adventure Library #60 (1894).

Frank Reade Jr. and His New Steam Horse Among the Cowboys; or, The League of the Plains [Dime novel; SPW]

Author: "Noname" (**Luis Senarens**); *Frank Reade Library* #8 (November 12, 1892).

Frank Reade Jr. and His New Steam Horse in the Great American Desert; or, The Sandy Trail of Death [Dime novel; SPW]

Author: "Noname" (**Luis Senarens**); *Frank Reade Library* #9 (November 19, 1892); Publisher: Frank Tousey.

Frank Reade Jr. and His New Steam Horse in the Running Fight on the Plains [Dime novel; SPW]

Author: **Harry Enton**; *The Boys of New York* (July 17, 1876).

Frank Reade, Jr., and His New Steam Man or, The Young Inventor's Trip to the Far West [Dime novel; SPW]

Author: **Harry Enton**; *Frank Reade Library* Vol 1 #1 (September 24, 1892).

Frank Reade Jr. with His New Steam Horse in Search of an Ancient Mine [Dime novel; SPW]

Author: "Noname" (**Luis Senarens**); *Frank Reade Library* #11 (December 3, 1892).

Frank Reade Jr. with His New Steam Horse in the North West; or, Wild Adventures Among the Blackfeet [Dime novel; SPW]

Author: "Noname" (**Luis Senarens**); *Frank Reade Library* #13 (December 17, 1892).

Frank Reade Jr. with His New Steam Horse; or, The Mystery of the Underground Ranch [Dime novel; SPW]

Author: "Noname" (**Luis Senarens**); *Frank Reade Library* #10 (November 26, 1892).

Frank Reade Jr. with His New Steam Man in Texas; or, Chasing the Train Robbers [Dime novel; SPW]

Author: "Noname" (**Luis Senarens**); *Frank Reade Library* #4 (October 15, 1892).

Frank Reade Jr.'s New Electric Invention the "Warrior"; or, Fighting the Apaches in Arizona [Dime novel; SPW]

Author: "Noname" (**Luis Senarens**); *Frank Reade Library* #30 (April 15, 1893).

Frank Reade Library [Dime novel magazine; SPW]

First publication: September 24, 1892; Publisher: Frank Tousey.

This 32-page publication featured the dime novel adventures of young inventor **Frank Reade Jr.** by "Noname" alias **Luis Senarens**. Each issue

Frank Reade and His Steam Man of the Plains; or, The Terror of the West, Boys of New York #28 (February 1876).

featured a black-and-white engraving on the front cover.

Frank Reade with His New Steam Man Chasing a Gang of "Rustlers"; or, Wild Adventures in Montana [Dime novel; SPW]

Author: "Noname" (**Luis Senarens**); *Frank Reade Library* #6 (October 29, 1892).

Frankie Stein: Time Traveller [Comic strip; SFW]

1. First Publication: *Whoopee! book of Frankie Stein 1976*; Art: Robert (R.T.) Nixon; Publisher: Fleetway-IPC.

The British humor comic strip *Frankie Stein* first appeared in *Wham!* # 4 (July 11, 1964). Professor Cube decides to make a playmate for his son from a mixture of formaldehyde, baking powder, Epsom salts and a few nuts and bolts—and Frankie Stein is born. Initially published by Odham's the strip featured Ken Reid's distinctive art. He was succeeded by Robert Nixon and Brian Walker. Frankie Stein made two time travel journeys to the Wild West in soft cover *Frankie Stein* specials published under the *Whoopee!* UK comic book banner.

In the first *Frankie Stein: Time Traveller* strip Frankie travels back to the Wild West of 1860 in a telephone box time machine invented by

Frankie's "Dad," Professor Cube. On arrival he quickly deals with "Black Jake's boys" and becomes the new sheriff. "Meet Sheriff Frankie … the freakiest Sheriff who ever walked the West!" A showdown with Black Jake ends in victory for Frankie after he literally plugs the barrels of Jake's guns with his large index fingers and blows Jake to smithereens after his two six-shooters backfire. Next stop on his travels is 1350 and King Arthur and his Knights of the Round Table.

"Frankie Stein: Time Traveller" [Comic strip; WW]

2. First Publication: *Whoopee! Frankie Stein Holiday Special 1979*; Art: Brian Walker; Publisher: Fleetway-IPC.

Inspired by the **Dr. Who** television show Professor Cube builds a time machine with the intention of finally offloading Frankie Stein who he unkindly refers to as "a big lunk." Instead he finds himself traveling through time with Frankie. First stop, the Wild West. The frustrated Professor is intent on getting rid of Frankie and starts a stampede of cattle to trample him into the ground. But all he succeeds in his getting himself trampled when an Iron Horse scares the cattle. Next attempt at seeing the last of Frankie is a rodeo but as the Professor heads for the time machine Frankie is thrown from his horse high into the air and lands on Professor Cube. Poor, unsuspecting Frankie pulls his "Dad" into the time machine and they await their next adventure—with pirates.

"From Children's Reminiscences of the Westward Migration" [Short story; WW]

Author: Karen Russell; First publication: *St. Lucy's Home For Girls Raised By Wolves*; New York: Knopf, 2006.

A family sells their farm and head out West in a four-thousand pound-prairie schooner. The father is a former rodeo star, stronger than a dozen oxen, who pulls their wagon and also happens to be a Minotaur, a horned, hairy bronco with a human body.

From Dusk Till Dawn 3: The Hangman's Daughter (2000) [Film; WW]

Premiere: January 18, 2000; Main Cast: Marco Leonardi as Johnny Madrid, Ara Celi as Esmeralda/Santanico Pandemonium, Michael Parks as Ambrose Bierce, Sonia Braga as Quixtla, Rebecca Gayheart as Mary Newlie; Executive Producers: Quentin Tarantino, Robert Rodriguez, Lawrence Bender; Story: Álvaro Rodríguez, Robert Rodriguez; Director: P.J. Pesce; 94 min.; A Band Apart; Color.

Escaping from the gallows, Johnny Madrid kidnaps the hangman's daughter Esmeralda. But when Madrid seeks shelter in an inn full of vampires, he discovers Esmeralda is the half-vampire princess Santanico Pandemonium.

Prequel to *From Dusk Till Dawn* (1996). The original film was adapted into a TV series in 2014.

From the Earth to the Moon (1958) [Film; SFW]

Premiere: 1958; Main Cast: Joseph Cotten as Victor Barbicane, George Sanders as Stuyvesant Nicholl, Debra Paget as Virginia Nicholl, Carl Esmond as Jules Verne; Story: Jules Verne (novels); Screenplay: Robert Blees, James Leicester; Producer: Benedict Bogeaus: Director: Byron Haskin; 101 min.; Waverly Productions; Color.

This confusing adaptation of the Verne novel is set in the post–Civil War America of 1868. It's a hybrid of 1950s science fiction, Victoriana, the American frontier spirit and bad special effects; the climax is reduced to a series of flares seen from a distance on the lunar landscape. RKO went bankrupt before the filming was completed.

From the Heart of the Storm [Novel; WW]

Author: Kurt R. A. Giambastiani; First publication: New York: ROC, 2004.

Alternate history where George Armstrong Custer is president of the United States of America, dinosaurs serve as steeds to the Cheyenne Indians and Spain occupies the Southwest.

Final novel in the **Fallen Cloud Saga**.

Frontier Cthulhu: Ancient Horrors of the New World [Short story anthology; WW]

Editor: William Jones; First publication: Hayward, CA: Chaosium, 2007.

A collection of fifteen frontier short stories loosely based on H.P. Lovecraft's Cthulhu mythos. Stories range from Viking settlers to the frightening fate of original English colonists in the East to weird tales set in the Old West.

"Ahiga and the Machine" by Rob Santa has a Native American coming face-to-face with a huge metal object falling from the sky while on a vision quest. "Children of the Mountain" by Stewart Sternberg sees mountain men encountering creatures who are servants of Ithaqua. Other WW short stories include: "Wagon Train For the Star" by Scott Lette, "Incident at Dagon Wells" by Ron Shiflet, "The Deadman's Hand" by Jason Andrew, "Jedediah Smith and the Undying Chinaman" by Chuck Zaglanis, "Snake Oil" by Matthew Baugh, "Cemetery Nevada" by Tim Curran and "The Rider in the Dark" by Darrell Schweitzer.

Frontier Earth [Novel; SFW]

Author: Bruce Boxleitner; First publication: New York: Ace Books, 1999.

Tombstone, Arizona, 1881. Descendants of the 16th century Lost Colony of Roanoke, who were rescued from starvation by aliens of the multispecies Associative, crash land on Earth after coming under attack from the hostile Kra'agh who also crash to earth. The Kra'agh, who plan to invade Earth, gain their sustenance from human fear and their brains. A showdown takes place at the OK Corral between the partially amnesiac alien Macklin and the Kra'agh as Macklin's female companion attempts an off-world rescue.

Frontier Earth: Searcher [Novel; SFW]

Author: Bruce Boxleitner; First publication: New York: Ace Books, 2000.

One year after the events of the first novel Macklin finds himself friends with the Earp brothers and is coming to terms with the fact he is a being from another planet as his memory returns. As an Associative Monitor Corps member he is helping protect Earth from the deadly Kra'agh who are planning an invasion from their hive in the sacred Apache mountains, near Tucson, Arizona.

Frontier Gentleman (1958) [Radio series; WMW]

An English reporter for the *London Times* documents life and death in the Old West.

"Nasty People" a.k.a. "Deadly Homesters" a.k.a. "The Grover Family" (1:39)

Air date: November 2, 1958; Main Cast: John Dehner as J. B. Kendall, Virginia Gregg; Story-Director: Anthony Ellis; 24:50 min; CBS.

Seeking shelter for the night, Kendall is offered lodging by the strange Grover family and a young woman (Gregg) who believes in ghosts. Atmospheric radio production with an undercurrent of sexual tension.

Frontier Secrets [RPG book; WW]

Authors: Phil Brucato, Richard E. Dansky, Robert Hatch, Ian Lemke; First publication: 1997; Setting: **Werewolf: The Wild West**; Publisher: White Wolf Publishing.

A Storyteller Sourcebook for Werewolf: The Wild West. Realm of Texas Tarantulas, Storm Eater spirit minions and the Enlightened Society of the Weeping Moon located in the Savage West.

Frostbite [RPG book; WW]

Author: Dave Blewer; Art: Robin Elliott, Dan Harding, Andy Park, Cheyenne Wright; **Deadlands Reloaded** Dime Novel #3; Publisher: Legion Publishing (POD 2006).

The Posse must discover the truth behind the murders of miners on Mount Frostbite near the town of Overhang.

Fudge: Deadlands [RPG game; WW]

Author: Steffan O'Sullivan; Publisher: Grey Ghost Games.

Fudge conversion of Deadlands RPG game. The Fudge (Freeform Universal Do-it-Yourself Gaming System) roleplaying system, created in November 1992, was borne out of author Steffan O'Sullivan's perceived limitations of writing for GURPS.

Fury of Johnny Kid (1967) [Film; Italy-Spain; WW]

U.S.A. release title for **Dove si spara di più**.

Futurama (1999) [Animated TV series]

A pizza delivery boy, frozen in 1999, wakes up in New York City on New Year's Eve, 2999.

"Where the Buggalo Roam" (4:06) [SW]

Air date: March 3, 2002; Creator: Matt Groening; Executive Producers: David X. Cohen, Matt Groening; Story: J. Stewart Burns; Director: Patty Shinagawa; 30 min.; 20th Century–Fox Television, The Curiosity Company; Color.

The Wong Ranch barbecue on Mars is interrupted by a dust storm. When the storm settles, the Wong family discover their herd of buggalo cattle has been rustled. Amy Wong's boyfriend Kif attempts to come to the rescue and ends up tangling with the Native Martians.

Futureworld (1976) [Film; SFW]

Premiere: August 13, 1976; Main Cast: Peter Fonda as Chuck Browning, Blythe Danner as Tracy Ballard, Arthur Hill as Dr. Duffy, Yul Brynner as The Gunslinger; Executive Producer: Samuel Z. Arkoff;

Story: George Schenck, Mayo Simon; Director: Richard T. Heffron; 104 min.; American International Pictures; Color.

Two reporters investigate the re-opened Delos resort after a colleague is murdered. Yul Brynner reprises his *Westworld* role as the Gunslinger in a bizarre cameo dream sequence where he plays the fantasy lover of Blythe Danner.

Galaxy Express 999 (1979) [Anime; Japan; SW]

International title for the animated TV series. See: *Ginga Tetsudô Three-Nine*

Gallowwalker (2010) [Film; WW]

Premiere: October 27, 2010 (UK); Main Cast: Wesley Snipes as Aman, Riley Smith as Fabulos, Kevin Howarth as Kansa, Steven Elder as Apollo Jones, Tanit Phoenix as Angel, Patrick Bergen as Marshal Gaza; Executive Producers: Andrew Brown, Stephen Hays, Harrison Kordestani; Story: Andrew Goth, Joanne Reay; Director: Andrew Goth; Vantage Media International, Wrekin Hill Entertainment, Boundless Pictures; 90 min.; Color.

Aman, the cursed son of a whore whose victims return from the dead as zombies, enlists the reluctant aid of a young warrior to defeat the albino leader of the undead and his followers. The resurrected Gallowwalkers wear the skins of their victims to periodically rejuvenate their appearance. But the leader has a problem. His son remains lifeless and he seeks the Sisters of San Diablo to learn their secrets of the dead. Meanwhile Aman is headed for a final showdown with the five Gallowwalkers who raped the woman who died in childbirth. The woman he loved. He has killed them before but they all returned from death. As the leader of the Gallowwalkers states, "You never forget the man who killed you for the first time." Now he must rip their heads from their bodies to finally make certain they remain dead.

"The Garden of Eden" [Pulp fiction; WMW]

Author: **Max Brand**; Six-part serialization; First publication: *Argosy All-Story Weekly* (April 15–May 20, 1922).

While hunting up the Girard River near Lukin Junction, Ben Connors' horse and mule go lame. He looks to rest them in the valley known as the Garden of Eden before trekking up the mountainous terrain. Connors is curious to know what lies behind the gated entrance and after initial problems with the guards is granted access to meet the master of the Garden, David Eden.

Eden is a peculiar place inhabited by strange and mysterious characters. As a racehorse gambler Connors is fascinated with the speed of the horses in the valley and the sprightly appearance of the aged servants.

"The hard-hearted Connor was staggered. Back on his mind rushed a score of details, the background of this picture. He remembered the almost superhuman strength of Joseph; he saw again the old servants withering with many years, but still bright-eyed, straight and agile. Perhaps they, too, knew how to stand here and drink in a mysterious light which filled their outworn bodies with youth of spirit, at least. And David? Was this not the reason that he scorned the world? Here was his treasure past reckoning, this fountain of youth."

Seeing an opportunity to make serious money racing the Gray Eden horses Connors suggests to Ruth Manning that she tempt David Eden and his horses out of the valley. But Eden discovers Connors' money making scheme and banishes him from Eden. Ruth follows, disgusted with how low she has sunk.

The dying prophecy of former master of the Garden, Abraham, had come to pass. "He had let the world into the Garden, and the tide of the world's life, receding, would take all the life of the Garden away beyond the mountains among other men."

Eden finds himself alone with his horse Glani as he departs from the Garden with a humble heart, no longer the master of his domain.

Brand leaves the reader with a happy ending and a positive message about the transforming power of God and true love as Eden comes across a tearful Ruth Manning and they leave the valley together.

Garrett a.k.a. *Uccidero Ancora Billy the Kid* [Comic book; Italy; WW]

First publication: 2007; Four-volume mini-series; Story: Roberto Recchiono; Art: Riccardo Burchelli, Werther Dell'Edera, Christian Cook, Massimo Carnevale; Publisher: Edizioni BD, Milan, Italy.

After William Bonney alias Billy the Kid rises from his grave, Pat Garrett, sheriff of Lincoln County, is forced to track his former adversary yet again. Billy the Kid is now the head of a gang of zombies who aim to conquer the world of both the living and the dead.

A Gathering of Widowmakers [Novel; SFW]

Author: **Mike Resnick**; First publication: Decatur, GA: Meisha Merlin, 2006.

The two surviving Nighthawk clones, the seasoned Jason Newman and the younger Jeff Nighthawk, clash as the original Jefferson Nighthawk takes on the role of mediator. In the meantime, Jefferson has plenty to contend with in the form of the villainous alien Younger Brothers, Hairless Jack Bellamy, the Wizard and Cleopatra Rome.

See: *The Widowmaker; TheWidowmaker Reborn; TheWidowmaker Unleashed*

Gemmell, David (1948–2006) [Author]

Gemmell began his writing career in London as a freelance journalist with the *Daily Mail*, *Daily Express* and *Daily Mirror*. He turned to full-time writing in 1986 following the publication of his third novel *Waylander*. Gemmell built his reputation as a writer of heroic fantasy novels. Influences included J.R.R. Tolkien, Louis L'Amour and **Stan Lee**.

Gemmell passed away on July 28, 2006, from a heart attack following quadruple heart bypass surgery two weeks earlier.

Selected works: *Legend* (1984), *Ghost King* (1988), *Last Sword of Power* (1988), **Wolf in Shadow** (1987), *The Last Guardian* (1989), **Bloodstone: A Jon Shannow Adventure** (1994)

General Jack Cosmo Presents [Comic book anthology; WW]

First publication: May 2007; Creator-Story: Aaron M. Shaps; Art: Nate Lovett, Dave Golding, Andrew Froedge, Dave McCaig, Sonny Leader, Gabe Pena; Publisher: General Jack Cosmo Productions.

Anthology title featuring science fiction, horror, action and Western adventures including the Red Ranger fighting werewolves in the Old West.

Generation Hex [Comic book; SFW]

First appearance: June 1997; Story: Peter Milligan; Art: Adam Pollina, Mark Morales; Publisher: Amalgam Comics.

Malforms Jono Hex, Johnny Random, White Whip, Madame Banshee, Skinhunter, Twins Trigger and Retribution are hunted by Malform hunter Marshal "Bat" Trask and his Razormen.

Amalgam Comics combined DC and Marvel Comics characters to create new merged characters in an alternate universe. The one-shot *Generation Hex* merged DC's Western characters and Marvel's *Generation X* mutants.

Get Mean (1975) [Film; Italy; WW]

Premiere: 1975; Main Cast: Tony Anthony as The Stranger, Diana Lorys as Princess Elizabeth Maria, Raf Baldassarre as Diego, Lloyd Battista as Sombra; Executive Producer: Ronald Schneider; Story: Lloyd Batista, Wolfe Lowenthal, Ferdinando Baldi; Director: Ferdinando Baldi; 84 min.; Cee Note, Stranger Productions Inc.; Color.

The Stranger is hired by a gypsy to escort a princess to her throne in Spain but encounters opposition from barbarians.

This bizarre, often violent Western includes unexplained time shifts between the Old West and Medieval Europe, a strange silver sphere that overlooks events, ghosts, Vikings and wild female warriors.

Ghost Busters [RPG book; WW]

Author: Lucien Soulban; First publication: 2000; Setting: **Deadlands: The Weird West**; Publisher: Pinnacle Entertainment Group.

When the head of the Agency's Western Branch in Gomorra is kidnapped, the posse must track down the Ghost to save the Agency.

Ghost Dancers [RPG book; WW]

Author: Paul Beakley; First publication: 1998; Setting: **Deadlands: The Weird West**; Publisher: Pinnacle Entertainment Group.

American Indians of the Weird West sourcebook. Includes the spirits of the Hunting Grounds and new Shamanic powers, Edges and Hindrances.

The Ghost Flyers [Novel; SFW]

Author: Tom Townsend; First publication: Austin, TX: Eakin Press, 1993.

In the late nineteenth century, on a nighttime journey across the Texas countryside, thirteen-year-old Harlin meets the inventor of a strange airship and joins him in his flight from a greedy enemy.

Ghost of Hidden Valley (1946) [Film; WMW]

Premiere: June 5, 1946; Main Cast: Buster Crabbe as Billy Carson, Al "Fuzzy" St. John as Al St. John, Jean Carlin as Kaye Dawson, John Meredith as Henry Trenton, Charles King as Ed "Blackie" Dawson, Jimmy Aubrey as Tweedle; Producer: Sigmund Neufeld; Story: Ellen Coyle; Director: Sam Newfield; 56 min.; Producers Releasing Corporation; b/w.

When Henry Trenton arrives from England to take charge of the Trenton Ranch, cattle rustler Ed "Blackie" Dawson has to make sure the ranch maintains its reputation of being haunted.

Ghost Patrol (1936) [Film; WMW]

Premiere: August 3, 1936; Main Cast: Tim McCoy as Tim Caverly, Claudia Dell as Natalie Brent, Walter Miller as Dawson, Wheeler Oakman as Kincaid, Lloyd Ingraham as Professor Brent; Producers: Sigmund Neufeld, Leslie Simminds; Story: Wyndham Gittens, Joseph O'Donnell; Director: Sam Newfield; 60 min.; Puritan Pictures, Excelsior Pictures Corp.; b/w.

Contemporary story mixing science fiction, gangster and Western genres about a deadly radium tube that causes mail planes to crash in the Shiloh mountains. G-Man Tim Caverly poses as outlaw Tim Toomey to try and capture the gang robbing the mail from the wreckage of the planes.

Special electronic effects for the radium tube were provided by Kenneth Strickfaden, famed for his work on *Frankenstein* (1931).

Ghost Racers: Battleworld Secret Wars [Comic book: SFW]

First publication: August 2015; Story: Felipe Smith; Art: Juan Gedeon; Publisher: Marvel Worldwide Inc.

With the destruction of the Multiverse all that remains is the patchwork planet Battleworld under the control of Victor Von Doom. On the outskirts of the Capital State Doomstadt lies the Battleworld arena—The Killiseum. Ghost Riders Robbie Reyes, Alejandra Blaze, Johnny Blaze, Danny Ketch and Carter Slade compete in the hellish entertainment spectacle known as the Ghost Races. First prize is temporary freedom from the tortures of the arena and the stripping of their supernatural powers until the next race.

The original Marvel Comics *Ghost Rider* a.k.a. Carter Slade appears as a zombie-cowboy-centaur with two Gatling guns on the sides of his horse body. Artist-character designer Juan Gedeon abandons the traditional mask in favor of a skull and blindfold covering his eyes. A Clint Eastwood style poncho replaces the cape.

"Ghost, Ride with Me!" [Pulp fiction; WW]

Author: **Lon Williams**; Character: **Lee Winters**; *Real Western Stories* (June 1953)

His route wound precariously along three miles of precipice and cliff, through shadow and soughing winds. He came to a treacherous turn round jutting rocks, where a misstep could have sent mount and rider plunging in space to a depth of two hundred feet. Cannon Ball, Winters' big, rangy horse, was taking it easy round this turn, when a ghost rose from nowhere and seated itself behind Winters.

The Ghost Rider [Comic book character; Film; WW]

First appearance: *Tim Holt* #11 (October 1949); Creators: **Vincent Sullivan**, Ray Krank, **Dick Ayers**; Art: Dick Ayers; Publisher: Magazine Enterprises; Marvel Comics; AC Comics.

1. The Calico Kid, a strip that began in *Tim Holt* #6, morphed into *The Ghost Rider* in #11. After killing the Calico Kid's faithful steed Ebony, the Calico Kid (alias Federal Marshal Rex Fury) and his Chinese sidekick Sing Song are thrown over a cliff into the "Devil's Sink" whirlpool by Bart Lasher and his Indian renegade friends. They both emerge from the whirlpool into an underground cave. Fury plans his revenge by faking his death and adopting a new identity as his own spirit, the Ghost Rider.

Writer **Gardner Fox** offered a supernatural explanation for his origin in *Ghost Rider* #1 (*A-1 Comics* #27). Clinging to life after his emergence from the whirlpool, Fury is visited by the ghosts of Wild Bill Hickok, Calamity Jane, Marshal Billy Tilghman, Kit Carson and Pat Garrett. After he is taught various survival and shooting skills by the spirits, Hickok introduces Fury to a white stallion whom he names Spectre. When Fury awakes, he considers his ghostly visits merely a dream until he encounters Spectre when he exits the cave.

Co-creator Vin Sullivan's influences for *Ghost Rider* included Walt Disney's Sleepy Hollow-Ichabod Crane, the Headless Horseman and the Vaughn Monroe song "Ghost Riders in the Sky."

2. With the lapsing of the copyright of the Magazine Enterprises character, Marvel Comics decided to re-launch *Ghost Rider* in February 1967 with original co-creator Dick Ayers supplying the artwork and Gary Friedrich and Roy Thomas providing the new storyline. The first version of *Ghost Rider* from Marvel was a throwback to the movie serials where the hooded ghostly phantom was nothing more than a cow-

boy or outlaw wearing a costume. Phosphorescent dust from a meteorite provided by Indian medicine man **Flaming Star** created a ghostly glow to the Ghost Rider's horse, mask, hat and lariat. Marvel's attempt to revive the character was a failure with the title only running to seven issues. In its short run, *Ghost Rider* came up against villains Tarantula, Sting-Ray (originally known as the Scorpion in *Two-Gun Kid*) and the super-strong Indian, Towering Oak.

3. In 1972, Marvel decided to kill the character of Carter Slade and replace him with the **Phantom Rider**. In the same year Marvel updated The *Ghost Rider* to a contemporary setting and re-invented him as demon-possessed stunt motorcyclist Johnny Blaze.

Carter Slade re-surfaced in 1981 in issue #56 of the revamped title as a spirit possessing the Phantom Rider and in the same year as a member of **The Rangers**.

In 1974 Marvel reprinted their original *Ghost Rider* stories under the new title **Night Rider** to avoid confusion with the revamped *Ghost Rider*. With Marvel owning the trademark to *Ghost Rider*, the original 1950s Magazine Enterprise comic book strips were reprinted by **Bill Black**'s Paragon Publications starting in 1971 under the title **The Haunted Horseman**. Original artist and co-creator **Dick Ayers** contributed new material to the AC Comics reprint title in the 1980s and 1990s. The Haunted Horseman was subsequently succeeded by **The Haunter** in the pages of *Femforce*.

4. [Film; 2007]
Premiere: February 16, 2007; Main Cast: Nicolas Cage as Johnny Blaze/Ghost Rider, Eva Mendes as Roxanne Simpson, Sam Elliott as Caretaker, Brett Cullen as Barton Blaze, Peter Fonda as Mephistopheles; Story-Director: Mark Steven Johnson; 114 min.; Columbia Pictures Corporation, Marvel Enterprises; Color.

Although the film is primarily based on the 1970s biker version of *Ghost Rider*, it does include a re-imagined Carter Slade as Caretaker of the local cemetery. The film includes a memorable scene of the Western Ghost Rider (dressed in black instead of the traditional phosphorescent white costume) and the Johnny Blaze Ghost Rider riding side by side.

The end title song "Ghost Riders in the Sky," about the "devil's herd" of cattle being chased endlessly across the sky by damned ghost cowboys on horses "snortin' fire," was composed by park ranger Stanley Davis Jones in 1948 while he gazed at the sky overlooking Death Valley on his 34th birthday.

The following year the song was a number-one hit for Vaughn Monroe on RCA Victor Records. Bing Crosby's version, released by Decca Records one month later (May 1949), peaked at #14 on the Billboard charts. Other versions that have made the Billboard charts were by Burl Ives (the first to be recorded), Marty Robbins and Johnny Cash. In the United Kingdom, The Ramrods peaked at #8 in 1961 and an instrumental version by The Shadows reached #12 in the UK charts in 1980.

Gene Autry featured the song in the movie *Riders in the Sky* (1949). Australian rock band Spiderbait recorded a version of the song for *Ghost Rider* (2007) starring Nicolas Cage.

Ghost Riders (1987) [Film; WW]

Premiere: 1987; Main Cast: Bill Shaw as the Rev. Thadeous Sutton/Prof. Jim Sutton, Jim Peters as Hampton, Cari Powell as Pam; Producers: Thomas L. Callaway, James Desmarais, Alan Stewart; Story: James Desmarais, Clay McBride; Director: Alan Stewart; 85 min.; New World; Color.

Hanged outlaws from the 1880s terrorize the descendants of those responsible for their deaths.

Ghost Town (1988) [Film; Juvenile book; WW]

1. Premiere: 1988; Main Cast: Catherine Hickland as Kate, Franc Luz as Langley, Bruce Glover as Dealer, Penelope Windust as Grace; Producers: Charles Band, Timothy D. Tennant; Story: Duke Sandefur, David Schmoeller; Director: Richard Governor; 85 min.; Empire Pictures; Color.

Officer Langley is stranded in an abandoned ghost town stuck in limbo and haunted by outlaws from the Old West.

2. Author: Annie Bryant; First publication: Lexington, MA.: B*tween Productions, 2007.

While vacationing on a dude ranch in Montana, Beacon Street girls Maeve, Avery, and Charlotte become stranded in an old Montana ghost town during a snowstorm and they encounter a real ghost. Book #11 in the Beacon Street Girls series.

Ghost Town (2009) [Telefilm; SFW]

Premiere: October 24, 2009; Main Cast: Jessica Rose as Jenna, Randy Wayne as Carl, Gil Gerrard as Preacher McCready, Billy Drago as Reb Halland; Producers: Jeffery Beach, Philip J. Roth; Story: Andy Briggs; Director: Todor Chapkanov; 85 min.; United Film Organization, SyFy; Color.

A group of college students stranded in a hostile town are murdered one-by-one. Reb Halland and his gang have controlled the town since the times of the Old West when they gained immortality in a deal with the devil. Only placing five totems around the town in the shape of a pentacle will save the students.

Ghost Town: A Novel [Novel; WW]

Author: Robert Coover; First publication: New York: Henry Holt, 1998.

A small Western town recedes into the horizon as a horse and rider approach. They finally reach the mysterious town as it rolls under the horse. An ever shifting story sees the sheriff become an outlaw, the unnamed cowboy declared sheriff by drunken gamblers and buildings changing position as in a dream.

Ghost Town at Sundown [Juvenile book; SFW]

Author: Mary Pope Osborne; Illustrator: Sal Murdocca; First publication: New York: Random House, 1997.

Jack and Annie travel back in time to the Old West via their Magic Tree House. The tenth book in the "Magic Tree House" series.

Ghost Towns [RPG book; WW]

Authors: Nancy Amboy, Andrew Bates, Derek Pearcy, John Wick; First publication: 1998; Publisher: White Wolf Publishing.

Crossover story supplement for **Werewolf: The Wild West** and *Wraith: The Oblivion*.

Ghost Train [RPG book; WW]

First publication: 2014; *Deadlands Tall Tales* #5; Protocol Game Series; Author: Jim Pinto; Art: Rick Hershey; Publisher: Pinnacle Entertainment Group.

A group of desperados plans to rob a train coming through Bottleneck Falls that's carrying ghost rock and has a high-stakes floating poker game. A story role-playing game set in **Deadlands: The Weird West**.

Ginga Tetsudô Three-Nine (1979) [Anime; Japan; SW]

Premiere: August 4, 1979; Creator: Leiji Matsumoto; Director: Rintaro; 126 min.; Toei Animation Company; Color.

In the year 2121, following the murder of his mother by cyborgs, a young boy travels on a galaxy-hopping steam locomotive in the hope of reaching a planet in the Andromeda Galaxy that offers a free cyborg body and near immortality. A beautiful, mysterious woman named Maetel offers Tetsuro a free pass to travel on the train if he will accompany her.

In the Old West–styled town of Trader's Fork on the planet Heavy Melder, Captain Harlock comes to the aid of Tetsuro in the local saloon. Tetsuro meets Tochiro Oyama, the designer of Harlock's spaceship *Arcadia of My Youth* and is told the Mount Gun Frontier will hold the clue to the mechanized, soulless man who murdered his mother, Count Mecha.

Based on the 1977 *Big Comic* strip by **Leiji Matsumoto** and the subsequent animated TV series.

See: **Galaxy Express 999**

Ginger Snaps Back: The Beginning (2004) [Film; WW]

Premiere: August 27, 2004; Main Cast: Katherine Isabelle as Ginger, Emily Perkins as Brigitte, Nathaniel Arcand as Hunter, Hugh Dillon as Reverend Gilbert, Tom McCamus as Wallace Rowlands, Brendan Fletcher as Finn, J R Bourne as James, David La Haye as Claude, Stevie Mitchell as Geoffrey; Executive producers: Jason Constantine, Donna Sloan, John Fawcett, Noah Segal; Story: Christina Ray, Stephen Massicotte, Director: Grant Harvey; 94 min.; 49 Films, Combustion, Copperheart Entertainment, Lions Gate Films; Color.

In 19th century Canada two sisters are offered shelter in the Northern Legion Trading Company Fort after one of the sisters is caught in an animal trap. Ginger and Brigitte soon become aware that the Fort has many secrets. Wallace Rowland's young son Geoffrey, victim of a werewolf, bites and infects Ginger. An Indian helps Ginger and Brigitte come to terms with their role in the werewolf curse that is passed through the generations by blood.

Brigitte must kill her sister to lift the curse, before Ginger can infect her. But when the infected Ginger returns to the Fort with a pack of werewolves Brigitte discovers her attachment to Ginger is greater than any threat of a curse. The red and the black are united in blood in a bond that cannot be broken.

The Ginger Star [Novel; SW]

Author: **Leigh Brackett**; First publication: New York: Ballantine Books, 1974.

Eric John Stark travels to the lawless planet Skaith at the edge of the universe in search of his foster father and mentor Simon Ashton, who has been kidnapped by the Lord Protectors. Stark is hunted by the corrupt government.

The first in a trilogy of Skaith novels.

See: *The Hounds of Skaith*

The Girl from U.N.C.L.E. (1966) [TV series]

April Dancer and Mark Slate work for the United Network Command for Law and Enforcement, dedicated to protecting the world from its evil nemesis THRUSH.

"THE FURNACE FLATS AFFAIR" (1:22) [SFW]

Air date: February 21, 1967; Main Cast: Stefanie Powers as April Dancer, Leo G. Carroll as Alexander Waverly, Noel Harrison as Mark Slate; Guest Stars: Peggy Lee as Packer Jo, Ruth Roman as Dolly X, Susan Browning as Ladybug Byrd, Percy Helton as Mesquite Swede; Executive Producer: Norman Felton; Story: Archie Tegland; Director: Barry Shear; 50 min; Arena Productions, MGM Television; Color.

THRUSH wants to obtain Titerian crystals from the Utter Anguish gold mine in Furnace Flats for use in a deadly laser ray. April Dancer, races against THRUSH agent Dolly X, and Ladybug Byrd to determine ownership of the mine and the potentially lethal crystals.

Girl in Landscape [Novel; SW]

Author: Jonathan Lethem; First publication: New York: Doubleday, 1998.

Following the death of her mother, 13-year-old Pella Marsh, her ineffectual father Clement and two younger brothers emigrate from post-apocalyptic New York City to the Planet of the Archbuilders. Pella becomes fascinated with an original colonist named Efram Nugent who joins with Pella in her refusal to take a drug that allows her to inhabit mouse like "house deer" and spy on the ruins of the new frontier she now inhabits.

Described by the publisher as a combination of "the tragic grandeur of John Ford's *The Searchers* and the sexual tension of *Lolita*."

Giunse Ringo e ... fu tempo di massacro (1970) [Film; Italy; WW]

Premiere: August 2, 1970; Main Cast: Mickey Hargitay as Mike Wood/Stanton, Jean Louis as Ringo Wood/Stanton, Lucia Bomez as Pilar, Omero Gargano as Don Juan/Alonzo, Anna Cerreto as Witch, Giovanni Ivan Scratuglia as Sheriff Sam Carroll; Producer: Umberto Borsato; Story: Mario Pinzauti; Director: Peter Launders [Mario Pinzauti]; La Volpe; Color.

While investigating a spate of deaths by poisoning, gunslinger Ringo aims to find out the truth behind the murder of his brother and any connection to the wealthy local landlord Don Juan. After Ringo discovers Don Juan has also been poisoned, the clues to the identity of the murderers lead to two diabolical witches.

See: *Ringo, It's Massacre Time*

God Hand [Video game; SFW]

Release date: October 10, 2006; Voice Cast: Beng Spies as Gene, Bettina Bush as Olivia, Sam Riegel, Daran Norris, Jamieson Price, S, Scott Bullock, Susan Chesler, Wally Wingert, Melissa Fahn, Fred Tatasciore; Producer: Atsushi Inaba; Writer: Hiroki Kato; Director: Shinji Mikami; Platform: PlayStation 2; 3rd Person Perspective; Developer: Capcom Entertainment; Publisher: Clover Studio.

In an Old West influenced town a poor drifter named Gene comes to the rescue of Olivia but ends up with his right arm being severed by thugs. But when he returns to consciousness Gene discovers his severed right arm has been replaced with a legendary powerful arm known as the God Hand. Now he is a man on a mission to destroy all the demons who want the God Hand for themselves in order to bring about the end of the world.

The player attacks the enemy with a combination of powerful fist power and the Tension Gauge, which activates the power of the unassailable God Hand.

Godmonster of Indian Flats (1973) [Film: WW]

Premiere: 1973; Main Cast: Christopher Brooks as Barnstable, Stuart Lancaster as Mayor Charles Silverdale, Peggy Browne as Madame Alta, E. Kerrigan Prescott as Professor Clemens; Executive producer: Robert S. Bermson; Story-Director: Fredric Hobbs; 89 min.; Ellman Film Enterprises; Color.

Contaminated gas from an ancient Nevada mine results in the creation of an eight-foot killer mutant sheep that spews inflammable orange gas. The terror of an Old West tourist town is turned into an attraction when it's captured.

The Gods of Mars [Novel; SW]

Author: **Edgar Rice Burroughs**; First publication: Chicago: A. C. McClurg, 1918.

John Carter returns to Mars (Barsoom) after a ten-year separation from his pregnant wife Dejah Thoris. Finding himself in an area known as the Martian heaven, Carter discovers "heaven" doesn't live up to the name as he faces menaces such as great white apes, Black Pirates and an evil goddess of Barsoom.

The second novel in the Barsoom trilogy.

See: *The Warlords of Mars*

"Golden City" [Pulp fiction; WW]

Author: **Lon Williams**; Character: **Lee Winters**; First published: *Real Western Stories* (December 1954).

Eerie hallucinations and encounters with ghosts put thoughts of an early retirement to the back of Lee Winters' mind.

The Golems of Laramie County [Novel; WW]

Author: Ken Rand; First publication: Alma, Arkansas: Yard Dog Press, 2005.

Horace Bixby lives among animated golems, dirigibles and spirit magic in Peaceful Valley, Wyoming, in the late 1800s. But the discovery of an evil undead necrogolem places everyone in danger.

Good News [Novel; SFW]

Author: Edward Abbey; First publication: New York: Dutton, 1980.

Urban and pastoral dwellers clash in a future America where civilization has collapsed. Indians and whites work together in the wilderness of the West to create a new society. But elite urban dwellers remain to impose their order on this emerging society.

Gorilla Gunslinger [Comic book character; WW]

First appeared: *Weird Business* (1995); Creator-Story: Norman Partridge; Art: John Garcia; Publisher MoJo Press.

Simian gunslinger Monjo alias Prince Kilimanjaro has a bounty of $25,000 on his head for the murder of clowns and preachers.

The Good, The Bad and Huckleberry Hound (1988) [Animated Telefilm; WMW]

Air Date: 1988; Voice Cast: Daws Butler as Huckleberry Hound, Yogi Bear, Quick Draw McGraw, Baby Looey, Snagglepuss; Don Messick as Boo Boo, Narrator, B.J. Ward as Desert Flower; Executive Producer: Jayne Barbera; Producers: William Hanna, Joseph Barbera; Directors; Ray Patterson, John Kimball, Bob Goe, Charles A. Nichols, Jay Sarbry; 120 min.; Hanna-Barbera Studios; Color.

Sheriff Huckleberry Hound loses his memory after being attacked by the Dalton Gang while Yogi Bear, Boo-Boo, Quick-Draw McGraw, Baba Luey and Snagglepuss are thrown out of town. Tied to a rocket that crashlands in an Indian reservation, Huckleberry falls in love with the chief's daughter Desert Flower, regains his memory and devises a plan to get his revenge on the Dalton Gang by haunting them as his own ghost.

See: *Quick Draw El Kabong, Yogi's Space Race*

The Good, the Bad, and the Dead [RPG book; WW]

Editor: Shane Lacy Hensley; First publication: 1999; Deadlands anthology with No Name #3; Publisher: Pinnacle Entertainment Group.

Foreword by Bruce Campbell, "Hate: Part Three" by Shane Lacy Hensley, "Talking Heads" by Matt Forbeck, "Out of the Frying Pan" by John R. Hopler, "Dead to Rights" by Philippe R. Boulle, "Playing the Game" by Don DeBrandt, "The Snipe Hunt" by Susan Griffith and Clay Griffith, "Harmony Gap Has a Bad Day" by Angel Leigh McCoy, "No Good Deed" by Timothy B. Brown, "In Search of Mr. Beaseley" by John R. Phythyon Jr., "Boneyard Train" by Lisa Smedman and "From a Fever" by Shane Lacy Hensley.

The Good, The Bad and the Infernal (*Heaven's Gate* Trilogy #1) [Novel; WW]

Author: Guy Adams; First publication: Oxford; Solaris, 2013

Wormword is a town that travels through time and space and comes to rest for one day only every hundred years. And on that one day the living can escape death by traveling through a portal to Heaven. Each time the location is different but today, September 21, 1889, Wormwood has come to rest in an obscure part of the American Midwest.

The town attracts an odd assortment of individuals all looking for a shortcut to Heaven. Patrick Irish posing as explorer and adventurer

Roderick Quartershaft makes the journey with British inventor Lord Forset, his daughter Elisabeth, engineer Billy Herbert and a group of monks known as the Brothers of the Order of Ruth. Traveling preacher Obeisance Hicks and his "messiah" Soldier Joe who suffers from stigmata is accompanied by Joe's nurse Hope Lane. Eyeless gunslinger Henry Jones, his wife and bearded lady Harmonium and other freak show outlaws plus young Elwyn Wallace and an aged fire-breathing gunslinger companion also travel the perilous road to Wormwood.

On their pilgrimage to the town that offers the promise of true Heaven they must first face dangers in the form of monsters, steam punk inventions and a tribe of hybrid Indians with iron limbs and coal-fueled pistons for hearts.

Gorilla Gunslinger: Meet Monjo... [Graphic Novel sampler: WW]

First publication: 1996; Creator-Story: Norman Partridge; Art: Mark Erickson; Publisher MoJo Press.

The proposed 1997 graphic novel project *Gorilla Gunslinger ... The Good, the Bad ... and the Gorilla* didn't progress beyond this nine-page sampler handed out at ComicCon International.

The Grave Doug Freshley [Comic book; WW]

First publication: 2008; Story: Josh Hechinger; Art: mpMann; Publisher: Archaia Studios Press.

Shot between the eyes, Doug Freshley is shocked to find himself still among the living. But tracking down the gang who "killed" him will eventually require him to accept his destiny.

Graveslinger [Comic book; WW]

First publication: October 2007; Story: Shannon Eric Denton, Jeff Mariotte; Art: John Cboins; four-issue mini-series; Publisher: Image Comics.

After undertaker Frank Timmons accidentally releases 117 dead killers from Hell, he tries to avoid damnation by tracking them down across the West.

Greaser's Palace (1972) [Film; WW]

Premiere:1972; Main Cast: Albert Henderson as Seaweedhead Greaser, Michael Sullivan as Lamy "Homo" Greaser, Luana Anders as Cholera, Ronald Nealy as Card Man/Ghost, Toni Basil as Indian Girl, Hervé Villechaize as Mr. Spitunia; Producer: Cyma Rubin; Story-Director: Robert Downey Sr.; 91 min.; Greaser's Palace Ltd.; Color.

Christian satire in a New Mexico Old West setting centering on the saloon Greaser's Palace. This confusing film features a character (Sullivan) who is murdered and repeatedly brought back to life by his Christ-like father (Alan Arbus). Director Robert Downey Sr. finds a place in the film for his young son Robert Downey Jr.

Great Caesar's Ghost [Novel; WWR]

Author: Cynthia Sterling; First publication: New York: Jove Books, 2000.

The spirit of a medicine show owner haunts his son and acts as matchmaker. Weird Western Romance published in the *Haunting Hearts* series.

The Great Maze [RPG book; WW]

Authors: Robin Laws, John Hopler; First publication: 1997; Setting: **Deadlands: The Weird West**; Publisher: Pinnacle Entertainment Group.

Location sourcebook book for California and the City of Lost Angels. Includes a full-length adventure.

The Great Rail Wars [RPG book; WW]

Author: Shane Hensley; First publication: 1996; Setting: Deadlands; Pinnacle Entertainment Group.

Rules for miniature war gaming.

The Great Weird North [RPG book; WW]

Author: Aaron Rosenberg; First publication: 2002; Setting: **Deadlands: The Weird West**; Pinnacle Entertainment Group.

Location book for Canada and Alaska.

Green Lantern [Comic book]

Test pilot Hal Jordan assumes the role of Green Lantern when dying alien Abin Sur gives him his green ring; Jordan is granted the power to replace Sur as a member of an intergalactic peacekeeping force that guards the Earth.

Responding to Marvel Comics' increased sales and socially relevant storylines, DC Comics decided to revamp *Green Lantern* beginning with issue #76.Writer Denny O'Neil teamed Green Lantern with an updated Green Arrow and tackled themes of racial prejudice, poverty and environmental pollution as they traveled across America. Superhero Green Lantern is left to question his own moral character and judgment as he realizes he has avoided dealing with social issues in his career and has viewed the world in black and white.

O'Neil confronted the problems of the Native American in modern America, including signed treaties that have no legal standing under the law, in *Green Lantern* #78 and #79. While issue #78 contained no Weird Western themes, issue #79 included a Weird Menace motif.

"Ulysses Star Is Still Alive" [WMW]

First publication: *Green Lantern* #79 (September 1970); Story: Denny O'Neil; Art: Neal Adams, Dan Adkins; Publisher: DC Comics.

A dispute over land rights takes a spooky turn when the spirit of Chief Ulysses Star demands the departure of white men from Indian tribal land. We later learn that the ghost is Green Arrow in disguise.

Grenadier [Manga; Anime; Japan; SFW]

1. First appearance: 2003; Story-Art: Sousuke Kaise; 7 volumes; Publisher: Kadokawa Shoten—Tokyopop.

Rushuna Tendo is a gunslinger with a difference. She is a large-breasted, golden-haired Senshi who despite her best intentions to create happiness and peace is often forced to display her impressive skills with guns when she joins forces with a samurai.

2. Premiere: October 14, 2004; Creator: Sousuke Kaise; Story: Akira Okeya; Director: Hiroshi Koujina; Studio Live; 12 × 25 min.; Color.

Combined science fiction, fantasy and traditional Western themes in a Japanese setting.

Based on the manga.

Season One

The Smiling Enlightened (1:01); *Rushuna Targeted* (1:02); *Enlightenment of a Demon* (1:03); *The Town with No Smile* (1:04); *Exploding! Kensousen Kurenai Touka* (1:05); *Balloon User. Mikan's Revenge* (1:06); *Well Then, to Tento* (1:07); *An Enemy of Memories Aizen Teppa* (1:08); *Wind Flower, When It Dances* (1:09); *Entering Tento* (1:10); *The Showdown with Tenshi* (1:11); *Things Gained from Travels* (1:12).

Grim Prairie Tales (1990) [Film; WW]

Premiere: 1990; Main Cast: James Earl Jones as Morrison, Brad Dourif as Farley Deeds, William Atherton as Arthur, Lisa Eichhorn as Maureen; Producers: Rick Blumenthal, Larry Huber; Story-Director: Wayne Coe; 90 min.; East-West Film Partners; Color.

A young clerk (Dourif) and a bounty hunter (Jones) exchange four stories over a desert camp-fire; they involve a desecrated burial ground, a pregnant seductress, a lynch mob and a haunted gunslinger.

Grimm Fairy Tales Presents: Dark Shaman [Comic book; WW]

First publication: October 2014; Story: Erica J. Heflin; Art: Sean Hill; 4-issue mini-series; Publisher: Zenescope Entertainment.

Sela Mathers visits a Native American reservation where she learns the story of the Dark Shaman depicted in a tapestry. The Dark Shaman is an ancient evil who seeks power through innocent blood and is targeting anyone who desecrates an ancient American Indian burial ground built upon a campus.

La Guarida del Buitre (1956) [Film; Mexico; WW]

Premiere: 1956; Main Cast: Antonio Aguilar as Mauricio Rosales, Sara Montes as Flora, Lola Casanova as Ana Maria, Agustin Isunza as Emeterio Berlanga, Joaquin Garcia "Borolas" as Timoteo Valdivia, Ignacio Navarro as Rodrigo Rodriguez a.k.a. El Buitre; Producer-Story: Rodolfo Rosas Priego; Director: Jaime Salvador; 86 min.; Rosas Films S.A.; Spanish; Color.

Mexican horror Western featuring witchcraft and a villain called the Vulture (Navarro) who terrorizes the town of Santa Anita until Mauricio Rosales (Aguilar) arrives on the scene.

Gun Blaze West [Manga; Japan; WW]

First appearance: 2008; Story-Art: Nobuhiro Watsuki; Three volumes; Publisher: Shueisha.

Twelve year-old Viu Bannes' desire to be the best gunfighter in the West gets closer to being a reality when renowned gunslinger Marcus Homer takes him under his wing as they journey to the fabled Gun Blaze West.

A Gun for One Hundred Graves (1968) [Film; Italy-Spain; WW]

U.S. release title for **Una Pistola per cento bare**.

Gun Frontier [Manga; Arcade Game; Anime TV series; Japan; SW]

1. First appearance: *Play Comic*, 1972; Creator: **Leiji Matsumoto**; three volumes; Publisher: Akita Shoten.

Tochiro Oyama and gunslinger Franklin Harlock Jr. search for lost Japanese immigrants in the American Western frontier.

2. Arcade game; International title: *Gun & Frontier*.

Released: 1990; Developer: Taito Corporation; Platforms: Arcade, Sega Saturn (home release 1997).

In the year 2120, the planet Gloria has being colonized by exiles from Earth who have created an American Old West–type society. But space pirates known as the Wild Lizards have decided to attack the planet for its rich supply of gold.

This vertically scrolling shooter was re-released in 2006. Packaged as *Taito Legends 2*, it was available on PC, PlayStation 2 and Xbox.

3. Animated TV series.
Premiere: March 28, 2002 (Japan); Creator: Leiji Matsumoto; Director: Soichiro Zen; 13 × 25 min.; Vega Entertainment; Color.

Gunslinger Franklin Harlock Jr. and Tochiro Oyama meet a mysterious woman called Shinunora on the planet Gun Frontier, where law and order does not exist. Based on the manga .

Season One (U.S. titles)
"Departure to Gun Frontier" (1:01); Air date: March 28, 2002

Young Harlock and Samurai Tochiro meet a mysterious woman called Sinunora on the lawless planet Gun Frontier.

"FALL OF A NON-ALCOHOLIC TOWN" (1:02); Air date: April 4, 2002

Sinunora, Harlock and Tochiro are attacked by bandits and rescued by Indians on their journey to a town with no saloons or guns.

"'HANGING' SONG IN THE SAND STORM" (1:03); Air date: April 11, 2002

Traveling to Samurai Creek, Harlock, Tochiro and Sinunora encounter a sandstorm and gunslinger Murigson.

"KILLING IN THE RAIN" (1:04); Air date: April 18, 2002

Tochiro plans to meet Maya in Bourbon Town to discover the secret of his Japanese kinsmen.

"PRAISE FOR THE SHORT-LEGGED!" (1:05); Air date: April 25, 2002

Tochiro, badly beaten by drunken cowboys in Flint Town, receives treatment from Dr. Sulski. His real name is Dr. Madarvic, and he is the man responsible for helping the survivors of Samurai Creek to escape.

"SAMURAI IN THE WILD" (1:06); Air date: May 2, 2002

Newspaper owner Nogson sets a trap for the survivors of Samurai Creek by placing a missing persons list in his Westerners Town newspaper. He is working for the "Organization."

"A BEDROOM IN A MIRAGE" (1:07); Air date: May 9, 2002

Tochiro begins to despair when is arrested and sentenced to hang for urinating in the street, but the beautiful Asaka gives him hope.

"WILD UTAMARO" (1:08); Air date: May 16, 2002

Harlock, Tochiro and Sinunora travel by train to Doji City in an attempt to track the Samurai warrior Utamaro who betrayed Tochiro's kinsmen at Samurai Creek.

"BATTLE IN GRAND CITY" (1:09); Air date: May 23, 2002

When Tochiro rushes toward the body of a woman lying in the street, the townsfolk shoot at him and plan to execute him by hanging.

"RAGE OF A SHORT GUY" (1:10); Air date: May 30, 2002

Tochiro is told he cannot enter Strobe Town to search for his sister Shizuku because he is too short.

"SECRET WEAPON FACTORY IN JAMACITY" (1:11); Air date: June 6, 2002

Tochiro traces his sister and the people of Samurai Creek to a secret factory run by the "Organization" to produce new weapons.

"SITARUNEN AND GATLING GUN" (1:12); Air date: June 13, 2002

Harlock, Tochiro and Sinunora journey to Sitarunen's hideout and the secret factory.

"FOOTPRINTS TO FUTURE" (1:13); Air date: June 20, 2002

Arriving at Sitarunen's hideout, Tochiro must save his sister and the people of Samurai Creek as they board a train carrying the new weapons.

Gun X Sword (2005) [Anime; Japan; SW]

Premiere: July 4, 2005; Producers: Hiroyuki Orukawa, Hiroyuki Saeki; Stories: Hideyuki Kurata; Director: Gorō Taniguchi; Production; 26 ×

25 min.; AIC A.S.T.A. for TV Tokyo (TX), d-rights, Gun Sword Partners; Color.

Van journeys across the "Planet of Endless Illusion" searching for the claw man who murdered his bride. A young girl named Wendy accompanies him in her own quest for her kidnapped brother.

Van can transform his metal sash into a sword and summon a mecha to help him in combat situations. The first episode featured the strongest Space Western theme with the villains, Lucky and the Wild Bunch, dressed in cowboy outfits in a town that mixes modern shopping malls and Old West architecture.

Season One

The Tuxedo That Fluttered in the Wind (1:01); *Funny Stream* (1:02); *The Hero Returns* (1:03); *And then, The Rain Falls* (1:04); *Twin's Guard* (1:05); *Lit the Heart with Fire* (1:06); *Revenge Is Within Me* (1:07); *That Bond Has Its Use* (1:08); *Return to Carmen's Hometown* (1:09); *To the Ocean, Thank You* (1:10); *Cover of Goodbye* (1:11); *The Days of No Return* (1:12); *On the Way to Dreams* (1:13); *Swift Brownie* (1:14); *Neo Original* (1:15); *Electric Fireworks Spark* (1:16); *Pursue Coordinate X* (1:17); *To Pray Like Saudarde* (1:18); *The End of Hope* (1:19); *Wonderful Universe* (1:20); *A Wish to the Sky, Peace to the Earth* (1:21); *For Whose Sake?* (1:22); *Everyone's Song* (1:23); *End of Dreams* (1:24); *Idiots Are those Who Use Armors* (1:25); *Van of Dawn* (1:26)

Gunbreed: Ghost Town Resurrected [Comic book; WW]

First publication: June 2009; Story: Angel Fuentes; Art: AC Osorio; Publisher: Razorblade Apple Studios.

Sheriff William "Powder" Cain returns from the dead to avenge the death of his son. Meanwhile gang leader Henry "Black Cloud" Stevens has made a deal to sacrifice Powder Cain's town in order to resurrect his dead girlfriend. But the wizard Samuel has his own agenda as he intends to take control of the town by using the gang.

Gunfighter (1998) [Film; WW]

Premiere; 1998; Main Cast: Martin Sheen as The Stranger, Robert Carradine as The Kid, Clu Gulager as Uncle Buck Peters, Chris Lybbert as Hopalong Cassidy; Executive Producers: Tom Null, Alain Silver; Story-Director: Christopher Coppola; 94 min.; Plaster City Productions, Citadel Records; Color.

Hopalong Cassidy owns magic gloves that allow him to draw his gun at super-speed. When his girlfriend is abducted by a local cattle rustler, Hopalong seeks justice.

Gunfighters in Hell [Comic book; WW]

First appearance: 1993; Story: David Barbour, Joe Vigil; Art: Joe Vigil; Five-part mini-series; Publisher: Rebel Studios.

The Gunfighter and Anna Sinbuck trade stories with the Keeper in return for the map to the gates of Hell.

Gunman Chronicles [Video game; SW]

Release date: November 20, 2000; First-person shooter (FPS); Developer: Rewolf Software; Publisher: Sierra Studios.

Game set in a frontier outpost at the "Western Spiral of the Galaxy." Colonists fight the genetically enhanced infestation of Xenomes. Western influences include soldiers dressed as U.S. cavalrymen.

Gunman Clive [Video game; SFW]

Release date: December 20, 2012; Platform: Nintendo 3DS; Developer: Horberg Productions; Publisher: Microsoft Studios.

In this side-scrolling action game Gunman Clive is a gunslinger in a futuristic Old West attempting to rescue Mayor Johnson's daughter from a group of bandits.

The single player controlling Gunman Clive jumps, flies a rocket and shoots across sixteen levels. Weapons include laser guns and explosive bullets as Clive tackles giants, robots, bandits and wild animals.

An updated *Gunman Clive 2* with improved graphics and extra levels, environments and characters was released January 29, 2015, by Horberg Productions.

Gunplay [Comic book; Graphic novel; WW]

First publication: March 2008; Creator: Jorge Vega; Publisher: Platinum Studios.

Cursed buffalo soldier Abner Meeks roams the West with a demonic gun that forces him to kill once a day. An adolescent faith healer, with a secret of his own, is Meeks' only hope of salvation.

Guns of the Dragon [Comic book; WW]

First appearance: October 1998; Story-Art: Timothy Truman; Publisher: DC Comics.

Bat Lash joins Enemy Ace and Biff Bradley in

1927 China as they journey to Dragon Island to retrieve two enchanted swords and a living dragon.

"Gunslinger" [Poem; WW]

Author: **Edward Dorn**; First publication: Los Angeles: Black Sparrow Press, 1968.

This four-part comic poem has been described as "an American *Canterbury Tales*" by poet Robert Duncan. The critically praised poem was published in four parts, beginning in 1968 and concluding in 1974. It defies conventional description. A 2,000-year-old gunslinger, a talking horse named Claude Lévi-Strauss, who rolls and smokes marijuana joints, and Lil, the madam of a brothel travel the Southwest in search of Howard Hughes. On their travels they pick up a hitchhiker named Kool Everything who happens to have a five-gallon can of LSD in his possession.

Poet Dorn attempts to shun conventional definitions and to shift boundaries of perception, forcing the readers into new ways of thought. They enter a surreal world where nothing is fixed and floating anxiety and uncertainty is a way of life.

Gunslinger Spawn [Comic book character; WW]

First appearance: *Spawn* #174-175, January 2008; Story; David Hine; Art: Brian Haberlin, Greg Capullo; Publisher: Image.

In the town of Bane, preacher Jeremy Winston is framed for the murder of his family by businessman Ed Kremper who wants Winston's land. Following his execution by hanging Winston returns to life as *Gunslinger Spawn*, thanks to the intervention of a former angel banished to Hell named Mammon, and takes his revenge on the men, women and children of Bane. Only Francis Charles Parker, ancestor of Al Simmons alias Spawn remains alive.

Gunslinger Spawn originally appeared in one panel of *Spawn* #119. The character design by Angel Medina inspired a 7 inch action figure by McFarlane Toys in 2005. In 2008 the story of *Gunslinger Spawn* was told in a two-part story in *Spawn* #174-175.

Gunslingers [Comic book; WW]

First publication: February 2000; Publisher: Marvel Comics.

One-shot title featuring reprints of **Two-Gun Kid**, **Rawhide Kid**, and Caleb Hammer strips.

The *Rawhide Kid* reprint is the Weird Western "Beware!! The Terrible Totem!!" by **Stan Lee**, Jack Kirby and **Dick Ayers**. In Peter B. Gillis' "The Devil's Starry Anvil" starring Pinkerton detective Caleb Hammer, Hammer plays upon the fears and guilt of two desperadoes who think he's an Indian Wolf-Spirit come to seek retribution for defiling their land.

Gunsmith: Bayou Ghosts (#235) [Novel; WMW]

Author: J R Roberts; First publication: New York: Jove Books, 2001.

Clint Adams and a passionate voodoo priestess investigate the apparent death of a Cajun friend whose body is rumored to have been stolen by a priest killer and his posse of ghosts.

The adventures of wandering gunsmith and sharpshooter Clint Adams were published from January 1982 to February 2015 by Jove Books under the pen name J. R. Roberts.

Gunsmith: Magic Man (#388) [Novel; WMW]

Author: J R Roberts; First publication: New York: Jove Books, 2014.

Fascinated with a traveling magician, Clint Adams rides along with him in the hopes of learning a few magic tricks for himself. But someone is stalking the magician, intent on killing him and convinced he is the devil.

Gunsmith: The Ghost of Billy the Kid (Gunsmith Giant #8) [Novel; WMW]

Author: J R Roberts; First publication: New York: Jove Books, 2003.

Billy the Kid has apparently returned from the dead and is walking around the town of White Oaks. Hired gun Clint Adams sets to find out the truth and encounters Billy the Kid himself.

Gunsmith: The Valley of the Wendigo (#317) [Novel; WMW]

Author: J R Roberts; First publication: New York: Jove Books, 2008.

Clint Adams joins a beautiful hunter and an Indian as they pursue a terrifying creature that has been attacking and eating people in and around the town of Roseau, Minnesota.

Gunsmith: The Wolf Teacher (#166) [Novel; WMW]

Author: J R Roberts; First publication: New York: Jove Books, 2001.

A group of Comanche Indians believe Clint Adams is the legendary Dreamwalker after discovering him wounded with a fever from an attack by a grizzly bear. But Adams knows he will need the powers of the mythical Dreamwalker to help the Indians in their plight against the U.S. Cavalry.

Gunsmoke: Blazing Stories of the West [Comic book character; WW]

First published: 1948 (cover date April-May 1949); Publisher: Western Comics Inc., Youthful Publications.

The adventures of the masked gunfighter known as Gunsmoke. All issues also featured the **Masked Marvel** back-up strip. The sub-title of the comic book was later changed to "Blazing Hero of the West." The cover artist for the early issues, Graham Ingels, would achieve greater recognition on the EC horror titles.

"Horrors in the Cave"

First publication: #11 (February 1951); Art: Manny Stallman. [WMW]

A gold mine is guarded by monsters from the depths of the Earth. But on closer inspection they are nothing more than mechanical man-made monsters aimed at keeping people away from the gold.

"Screaming Terrors of Skull Canyon"

First publication: #13 (June 1951); Art: Manny Stallman. [WMW]

The group of skeletons on horseback driving stolen cattle through Indian burial grounds are actually rustlers in disguise.

"The Thing"

First publication: #16 (January 1952); Art: Doug Wildey. [WW]

A beautiful woman turns into a murdering werewolf. A genuine Weird Western story for the final issue.

The Gunstringer [Video game; WW]

Release date: September, 2011; Executive Producer: Mark Coates; Director: Bill Meuhl; Designers: Josh Bear, Dan Teasdale, Sean Riley, Alex Jones, Sean Conway; Third person shooter, Rail shooter; Platform: Xbox 360-Kinect; Developer: Twisted Pixel Games; Publisher: Microsoft Studios.

Buried and left for dead, a skeleton cowboy marionette is on a vengeance quest to track down his betrayers. His trail takes him from the desert plains to the bayou swampland to the Asian mountains to the dark depths of the underworld.

With Kinect there is no gamepad. The player's hand controls the cowboy marionette while the other hand aims and fires his gun. The rail shooter has the character moving along a set path while the player can use both hands to control the guns.

The novelty of the game is its setting. It begins with live-action footage filmed in the Paramount Theater, Austin, Texas. We follow an attractive young woman as she enters a packed theater and sits down. Backstage a stagehand is taking a marionette to the stage where the puppet is buried in a shallow grave, complete with a headstone. Suddenly he rises from his grave and crawls across the stage into a computer generated western landscape. The game begins.

Supporting characters include The Wavy Tube Man, The Oil Baron, The Brothel Madam, The Beard Master, Gator Jack and The Sheriff. The Lady of the Dead is Queen of the Underworld and ruler of the afterlife. In a later add-on to *Gunstringer* El Diablo searches for his Queen in the March 2012 Xbox release *El Diablo's 'Merican Adventure.*

GURPS Deadlands: Hexes [RPG book; WW]

Author: Michael Suileabhain-Wilson; First publication: 2002; Setting: **Deadlands: The Weird West**; Publisher: Steve Jackson Games.

The huckster attempts to control the evil Indian spirit known as a Manitou.

GURPS Deadlands: The Weird West [RPG book; WW]

Adaptation: Andrew Hackard, Stephen Dedman; First publication: 2001; Publisher: Steve Jackson Games.

In the Weird West of 1873, monsters, hucksters, demons, shamans and zombies roam the landscape. **Deadlands: The Weird West** sourcebook for use with GURPS (Generic Universal Role-Playing System).

GURPS Deadlands: Varmints [RPG book; WW]

Author: Michael Suileabhain-Wilson; First publication: 2003; Setiing: **Deadlands: The Weird West**; Publisher: Steve Jackson Games.

New monsters, critters and beasts plus conversions from the original Deadlands game.

The H-Bar-O Rangers [Radio show; WMW]

See: ***Bobby Benson and the B-Bar-B Riders***

The Half-Made World [Novel; SPW]

Author: Felix Gilman; First publication: New York: Tor Books 2010

In an alternate history America the people of the Gun and the people of the Line each fight to become the dominant force. The Gun invokes terror and fear with their demon-possessed guns that grants them supernatural powers and the Line, with the aid of Engine spirits, continues to build factories and enslave the people.

The only hope of putting an end to the never-ending war was the Red Republic, whose free society was quickly squashed by the Line and the Gun decades ago. But psychologist Liv Alverhyusen discovers the General of the Red Republic still lives in a spiritually protected mental institution on the borders of the uncharted West, home to the legendary immortal Hill People. Within the General's fractured mind lies the secret to a weapon that is capable of stopping the war. When the Line and the Gun learn the General still lives each sends out agents to capture him in the hope of obtaining the elusive secret to the weapon that is the key to ultimate power and control.

The Hanged Man (1974) [Telefilm; WW]

Premiere: March 13, 1974; Main Cast: Steve Forrest as James Devlin, Dean Jagger as Josiah Lowe, Sharon Acker as Carrie Gault, Barbara Luna as Soledad Villegas, Cameron Mitchell as Lew Halleck; Creator: Andrew J. Fenady; Producer-Story: Ken Trevey; Director: Michael Caffey; 90 min.; Andrew J. Fenady Productions, Bing Crosby Productions; Color.

Gunslinger James Devlin survives his hanging despite being officially declared dead. A reformed Devlin discovers he now has the ability to read minds and decides to put his new abilities to good use by helping others.

Hank the Cowdog [Juvenile book series; WMW]

Author: John R. Erickson; Illustrator: Gerald L. Holmes; First appearance: *The Cattleman* magazine, 1982; Publishers: Maverick Books, Viking Books.

As Head of Ranch Security on a West Texas ranch, Hank the Cowdog can't keep his nose out of trouble. The long-running series has seen Hank in numerous adventures in and around the M-Cross ranch. The humor comes from seeing everything from Hank's point of view where simple everyday objects can become monsters and cats and children can be mistaken for vampires or ghosts.

Weird Menace Western titles in the series: *The Case of the Halloween Ghost* #19; *The Phantom in the Mirror* #20; *The Case of the Vampire Cat* #21, *The Case of the Black Hooded Hangman* #24, *The Case of the Night-Stalking Bone Monster* #27, *The Vampire Vacuum Sweeper* #29, *The Garbage Monster From Outer Space* #32, *The Secret Laundry Monster Files* #29, *The Case of the Burrowing Robot* #42, *The Dungeon of Doom* #44, *The Case of the Falling Sky* #45

"Hart and Boot" [Short story; WW]

Author: Tim Pratt; First publication; *Polyphony 4*, 2004; Publisher: Wheatland Press.

Pearl meets John Boot the outlaw. But is he real or a spectre from her imagination?

The story was reprinted in *Best American Short Stories: 2005* and in the Tim Pratt anthology *Hart and Boot and Other Stories* (2007).

Haunted Gold (1932) [Film; WMW]

Premiere: December 17, 1932; Main Cast: John Wayne as John Mason, Sheila Terry as Janet Carter, Harry Woods as Joe Ryan, Blue Washington as Clarence Washington Brown; Producer: Leon Schlesinger; Story: Adele Buffington; Director: Mack V. Wright; 58 min.; Warner Bros. b/w.

A 25-year-old John Wayne stars in a story about hidden gold in the abandoned Sally Ann mine. Joe Ryan and his gang's attempts to make a bogus claim on the gold are under scrutiny from a mysterious cloaked phantom who roams the secret passages of the mine shaft. This movie, a remake of *The Phantom City* (1928), utilizes footage from the original film including distant shots of Ken Maynard.

The Haunted Horseman [Comic book character; WW]

See: **Ghost Rider, Phantom Rider, Night Rider, The Haunter**

The Haunted Mesa [Novel; SFW]

Author: Louis L'Amour; First publication: New York: Bantam Books, 1987.

Above: *Haunted Horseman.* Art by Dick Ayers. *Right: Haunted Horseman* in "The Ghost of Longhair John." Reprinted in *Best of the West* #11. Art by Dick Ayers. Adapted from *Best of the West* #10 (October 1953). © 2009 AC Comics/Nightveil Media, Inc. Used with permission.

Responding to a letter from trusted friend Erik Horkart, investigator Mark Raglan uncovers the mysterious and baffling world of the cliff dwelling Anasazi at No Man's Mesa in Southwest Utah. Raglan's investigations lead him to an unexplored frontier that defies the laws of nature and leads to clues about the sudden disappearance of the Anasazi centuries ago.

Haunted Ranch (1943) [Film; WMW]

Premiere: February 19, 1943; Main Cast: John "Dusty" King as "Dusty" King, David Sharpe as Davy Sharpe, Max "Alibi" Terhune as "Alibi" Terhune, Julie Duncan as Helen Weston, Glenn Strange as Rance Austin, Rex Lease as Deputy Rex Lease, Steve Clark as Marshal Hammond; Producer: George W. Weeks; Story: Arthur Hoerl; Screenplay: Harriett Beecher; Director: Robert Tansey; 57 min.; Range Busters, Monogram Pictures Corporation; b/w.

Rance Austin and his outlaw gang search for stolen gold bullion on a supposedly haunted ranch.

The Haunter [Comic book character; WW]

First appearance: *Femforce* #28; Creator: **Bill Black**; Publisher: AC Comics.

When **Haunted Horseman** is killed by the touch of the Mystick Cloak, Rex Fury becomes the supernatural **Haunter**, lawman of the Limbo Realm. He ultimately assumes the identity of Randall Fury, psychic investigator, as he battles supernatural evil on Earth.

Have a Good Funeral, My Friend ... Sartana Will Pay (1970) [Film; Italy; WW]

U.S. release title for *Buon funerale, amigos! ... paga Sartana*.

Hawk Carse [Pulp fiction character; SW]

Authors: Anthony Gilmore (**Harry Bates** with Desmond W. Hall); First appearance: *Astounding Stories* (November 1931).

Space Western with 22nd century adventurer Hawk Carse traveling in his rocket ship the Star Devil. Evil Oriental scientist Dr. Ku Sui and his space pirate cohorts provide the opposition. The fast-draw skills of Carse as he shoots the bad guys cannot disguise the fact this is essentially a Western pulp hero with a ray gun.

Other Hawk Carse stories published in *Astounding Stories*: *The Affair of the Brains* (March 1932); *The Bluff of the Hawk* (May 1932); *The Passing of Ku Sui* (November 1932); *The Return of Hawk Carse* (July 1942).

Hawken [Comic book; WW]

First publication: November 2011; Story: Benjamin Truman, Timothy Truman; Art: Timothy Truman; Six-issue mini-series; Publisher: IDW.

Aging gunman Kitchell Hawken is on a one-man rampage against arms merchants who once employed him, the Tucson Ring. On the trail Hawken rides a blind mule accompanied by a bulldog as he encounters the ghosts of every person he ever killed and is pursued by the person who was once his protege, a psychotic murderer named Sombre.

Hawkgirl [Comic book character; WW]

First appearance: *Flash Comics* #1 (January 1940); Creators: **Gardner Fox**, Dennis Neville; Publisher: DC Comics.

The Golden Age Hawkgirl, Shiera Sanders-Hall has been reborn throughout the centuries in many incarnations, including the Egyptian Princess Chay-Ara and Old West gunslinger **Cinnamon** alias Kate Manser. She is connected in her incarnations to **Hawkman**, Carter Hall, whom she first met as Egyptian Prince Khufu and later in the Old West as Hannibal Hawkes alias **Nighthawk**.

The Hawkline Monster: A Gothic Western [Novel; WW]

Author: Richard Brautigan; First publication: New York: Simon and Schuster, 1974.

In 1902 Oregon in, the twin Hawkline daughters hire professional gunmen Greer and Cameron to kill a monster that lives in the ice caves beneath their Victorian mansion. The monster has transformed its creator Professor Hawkline into an elephant-foot umbrella stand and shrunk their seven-foot butler into a 3-inch dwarf.

The novel came to the attention of director Hal Ashby, who purchased the screen play rights. Brautigan dropped out of the film project when asked to revise his first draft. Ultimately the novel never made the transition to film.

Hawkman [Comic book character; WW]

First appearance: *Flash Comics* #1 (January 1940); Creators: **Gardner Fox**, Dennis Neville; Publisher: DC Comics.

The Golden Age Hawkman, archaeologist Carter Hall, was Old West vigilante **Nighthawk** alias Hannibal Hawkes in a previous incarnation, and boyfriend to **Cinnamon**, the future **Hawkgirl**.

Heart o' Darkness: Devil's Tower 2 [RPG book; WW]

Author: Hal Mangold; First publication: 1998; Setting: *Deadlands: The Weird West*; Publisher: Pinnacle Entertainment Group.

Trilogy of tales featuring Weird West villains Dr. Darious Hellstromme, Reverend Ezekiah Grimme, and the mysterious Stone as they seek to gain possession of the legendary 150-carat black diamond known as the Heart of Darkness. But major obstacles stand in their way: crossing shark-infested Prosperity Bay to reach and break into the impenetrable prison fortress of Rock Island where the diamond is being held.

Heart of the Hawk [Novel; WWR]

Author: Justine Davis; First publication: Memphis, TN: Bell Bridge Books, 1996.

Renowned gun fighter Joshua Hawk is rescued from the hangman's noose in Gambler's Notch by the widow of the abusive husband he murdered in self defense. Hawk feels indebted to Kate Dixon and helps her run her general store. Meanwhile to his amazement a book suddenly appears in his saddlebag. The magical book details the lengthy Hawk ancestry and offers Josh glimpses of his future pointing to how the Hawk line will continue. In this story of new beginnings Kate finds her new life centered on Hawk and an orphan boy named Luke.

Heaven in West Texas [Novel; WWR]

Author: Susan Kay Law; First publication: New York: Harper Paperbacks, 1997.

Joshua West returns from the dead to guide his former love Abigail Grier as she struggles to run the Rolling G ranch amid continuing drought and her father's worsening Alzheimers.

Hector Plasm [Comic book character; WW]

First appearance: April 2004; Creators: Benito Cereno, Nate Bellegarde; Publishers: Hoarse & Buggy Productions, Image.

Hector Plasm, a member of the ancient cult "the benandanti," has been thrust into the world of the supernatural, acting as mediator between humans and spirits the help of colleagues Sinner and Saint.

Hector Plasm was introduced in a contemporary college campus setting in a four-part story beginning with in *Invincible* #10 and later appeared in two issues of **Western Tales of Terror**.

Heinlein, Robert A. (1907–1988) [Author]

Born in Butler, Missouri, Robert Anson Heinlein showed an interest in astronomy from early childhood. This soon extended into science fiction and a fascination with the stories of Olaf Stapledon.

Heinlein graduated from the U.S. Naval Academy at Annapolis, Maryland, in 1929 but was discharged out of active duty in 1934 due to pulmonary tuberculosis which he contracted the previous year. After struggling through various jobs including silver mining and real estate, Heinlein turned to writing and gained early recognition writing for *Astounding Stories*. The year 1947 saw the publication of *Rocket Ship Galileo*, the first of twelve juvenile science fiction novels for Scribner's.

His most widely acclaimed work remains his Hugo award-winning novel *Stranger in a Strange Land* (1961). Health problems curtailed his output in the later years of his life. He passed away during a morning nap on May 8, 1988. His ashes were cast into the Pacific from the deck of a warship.

Selected works: **Farmer in the Sky** (1950), *The Puppet Masters* (1951), **Tunnel in the Sky** (1955), *Starship Troopers* (1959), *Stranger in a Strange Land* (1961), *Glory Road* (1963), **Time Enough for Love, The Lives of Lazarus Long** (1973).

Hell Hole [Novel; WW]

Author: Hunter Shea; First publication: Cincinnati, Ohio: Samhain, 2014.

President Theodore Roosevelt hires former Rough Rider Nat Blackburn, who along with friend and hired gun Teta, investigate the abandoned mining town of Hecla, in the Deep Rock Hills. What they find shocks them as they encounter black-eyed children and savage wild men deep in the mine.

Hell on Earth Reloaded: The Worm's Turn [RPG Book; WW]

First publication: 2014; Story: Clint Black, John Goff, Shane Lacy Hensley, Teller; Art: Aaron Acevedo, Ben Acevedo, Emma Beltran, Tom Fowler; Publisher: Pinnacle Entertainment Group.

A full-length Plot Point Campaign features the aftermath of the huge battle known as The Harvest. The Reckoners have been defeated and banished to the distant planet of Banshee. But the time for celebration is on hold after the Iron Alliance discovers more terrors are waiting to be unleashed.

Hell or High Water [RPG book; WW]

Author: John Goff; First publication: 1998; Setting: **Deadlands: Hell on Earth**; Publisher: Pinnacle Entertainment Group.

Hell or High Water finds the posse in a post-apocalyptic Baton Rouge confronting Mississippi River pirates and an evil presence in the surrounding swamplands.

Hell's Bounty [Novel; WW]

Authors: Joe R. Lansdale, John L. Lansdale; Publisher: Burton, MI: Subterranean Press; 2016.

A man named Quill has sold his soul and has been possessed by a winged demon. Now Quill has a desire to bring about the end of all creation and hand it over to demonic entities. Bounty hunter Smith enters the town of Falling Rock on his near-mystical horse Shadow, armed with a Colt pistol with an endless supply of silver bullets and a magical pack of cards straight out of Hell itself. His mission is to stop Quill.

Helldorado [Comic book; WW]

First publication: October, 2011; 3-issue mini-series; Story: C. Michael Hall; Art: Martin Coccolo, Diego Rodriguez; Publisher: Ape Entertainment.

A supernatural evil overtakes the western town of El Dorado as a vengeful Chinese vampire and his army of undead minions threaten to destroy mankind. Only an heiress, an aging sheriff, his deputy, a gambler and a warrior priest stand in their way.

Heroes Reborn: Rebel [Comic book; SFW]

First publication: January 2000; Creators: Joe Kelly, Matt Haley; Publisher: Marvel Comics.

In a post-nuclear California, Rebel wears a cowboy hat, a poncho, shotgun and Iron Man's damaged armor suit. Paramilitary Pepper Potts, Guinness (a man-salamander) and Michka (a woman with a deadly voice) join him as they attempt to destroy Master Man, a fanatic who claims to be God.

Hex [Comic book; Comic book character; SFW]

1. First appearance: September 1985; Creators: Michael Fleischer, Mark Texeira; Publisher: DC Comics

Jonah Hex finds himself trapped in a post-nuclear future of warring gangs.

Following the cancellation of his regular title with issue #92 (August 1985), this re-imagining of Jonah Hex saw him adopt a new costume, change timelines and cross into the science fiction genre.

2. First appearance: *Superboy* #54 (August 1998); Creator: Karl Kesel; Publisher: DC Comics.

Red-haired former supermodel Hex assumes the persona of **Jonah Hex** down to the scarred face, opaque eye and Southern drawl.

Hex: Escort to Hell [Role-playing module; SFW]

First published: *DC Heroes*, 1986; Story: Matthew J. Costello; Art: Carlos Garzon, Ed Hannigan, Bob LeRose, Mark Texiera; Publisher: Mayfair Games.

In the 21st century you must survive in a hostile, alien environment as an Escort to Hell.

A DC Heroes solo role-playing module based on the science fiction comic book character *Hex*.

Hexarcana [RPG book; WW]

Author: John Goff; First publication: 1999; Setting: *Deadlands: The Weird West*; Publisher: Pinnacle Entertainment Group.

Expanded and collected rules for hexes, miracles, magic, voodoo and martial arts.

The Hidden Goddess (*Venificas Americana* book 2) [Novel: SPW]

Author: M. K. Hobson; First publication: New York: Spectra-Ballantine Books, 2011.

In this sequel to *Native Star* the witch from the Old West settlement of Lost Pine in Sierra Nevada is now part of the magical society of New York City with her warlock fiancé Dreadnought Stanton. In Emily Edwards' new role she has to contend with a future mother-in-law who detests her, nefarious Russian scientists out to possess the artifact and Aztec blood sorcerers intent on destroying the world.

High Moon [Comic book; WW]

First publication: October 2007; Story: David Gallaher; Art: Steve Ellis; Publisher: Zuda.

Bounty hunter and former Pinkerton detective Matthew Macgregor investigates mysterious happenings in the Texan town of Blest. A supernatural detective Western from DC Comics' Zuda webcomic site.

High Plains Drifter (1972) [Film; WW]

Premiere: August 22, 1973; Main Cast: Clint Eastwood as The Stranger, Verna Bloom as Sarah Belding; Executive Producer: Jennings Lang; Story: Ernest Tidyman; Director: Clint Eastwood; 105 min.; The Malpaso Company; Color.

A mysterious Stranger rides into the town of Largo and takes revenge on three outlaws and the townsfolk of Hell while keeping his own identity secret.

The film implies a supernatural origin for Eastwood's character but never explicitly states his real identity. Many critics feel the film was influenced by Sergio Garrone's *Django il Bastardo* (1969).

Vincent Canby of *The New York Times* (April 20, 1973) commented: "High Plains Drifter, with Eastwood as director as well as star, is part ghost story, part revenge western, more than a little silly, and often quite entertaining in a way that makes you wonder if you have lost your good sense."

High Plains Invaders (2009) [Telefilm; SFW]

Premiere: August 30, 2009; Main Cast: James Masters as Sam Danville, Cindy Sampson as Abigail Pixley, Sebastian Knapp as Jules Arning, Sanny van Heteren as Rose Hilridge, Angus MacInnes as Silich Cure, Antony Byrne as Gus McGreevey; Producer:

Spanish language film poster for *High Plains Drifter* (1972), starring Clint Eastwood as the enigmatic Stranger (The Malpaso Company).

Ric Nish; Story: Richard Beattie; Director: K. T. Donaldson (Krisoffer Tabori); 85 min.; Castel Film Romania, SyFy; Color.

Colorado, 1892. Convicted outlaw Sam Danville is about to be hanged when a giant, scorpion-like "bug" attacks. An army of extraterrestrial insectoids are after the uranium being mined by mine-owner Jules Arning. Danville eventually becomes the town savior as he leads the fight against the invaders from another planet.

Highlander [TV series; Canada-France]

Main Cast: Adrian Paul as Duncan MacLeod/Highlander, Stan Kirsch as Richard H. Ryan, Jim Byrnes as Joe Dawson, Alexandra Vandernoot as Tessa Noel; Executive Producers: Peter S. Davis, William

Panzer, Christian Charret, Marlia Ginsburg; 119 × 50 min.; Davis-Panzer Productions, Filmline International Inc., Gaumont Télévision; Color.

Born in Scotland in 1592, Immortal Duncan MacLeod attempts to live the life of a normal mortal in the present day as other Immortals pursue him across time in the hope of destroying him.

"Under Color of Authority" (2:12) [WW]

Air date: February 7, 1994; Guest Cast: Jonathan Banks as Mako, Deanna Milligan as Laura Daniels, Lochlyn Munro as Tim, Howard Storey as Sheriff; Producer: Ken Gord; Story: Peter Mohan; Director: Clay Borris.

Duncan MacLeod recognizes the description of the man pursuing a young woman (Milligan) as Immortal Mako. In flashback we see when MacLeod previously encountered Marshal Mako in the Pacific Northwest of 1882. Despite Mako's methods, MacLeod knows he follows the rules of the law

"Line of Fire" (3:02) [WW]

Air date: October 3, 1994; Guest Cast: Randall "Tex" Cobb as Kern, Chandra West as Donna, Michelle Thrush as Little Deer, Andrew Wheeler as Father Mathew, Peter Bob as Kahani, Richard Leacock as Jamal, James & Mathew Harrington as Jeremy; Producer: Ken Gord; Writer: David Tynan; Director: Clay Borris.

An encounter with Immortal Kern revives painful memories of the murder of the Highlander's Sioux lover and foster son in the Old West.

"Something Wicked" (4:13) [WW]

Air date: February 12, 1996; Guest Cast: Byron Chief-Moon as Jim Coltec, Benjamin Ratner as Bryce Korland, Darcy Laurie as Harry Kant, Carla Temple as Denise; Writer: David Tynan; Director: Dennis Berry.

Native American Immortal Jim Coltec, possessing the special powers of the Hayoka, protected his tribe from evil by absorbing it and taking the hatred from the world. But absorbing evil through the centuries has resulted in Coltec becoming evil himself. Duncan MacLeod must track Coltec and choose between the life or death for his friend.

This episode includes a flashback to Mac-Leod's former life on Lakota Sioux tribal land in 1872, when he planned to marry Little Deer and adopt her son until the entire tribe was brutally slaughtered. A brief flashback following the slaughter of Little Deer was seen in the pilot episode "The Gathering" (1:01).

"COMES A HORSEMAN" (5:12) [WW]

Air date: February 3, 1997; Guest Cast: Peter Wingfield as Methos, Tracy Scoggins as Cassandra, Valentine Pelka as Kronos, Richard Ridings as Silas, Marcus Testory as Caspian, Greg Michaels as Tippet, David Longworth as Paxton, Sotigui Kouyate as Hijad; Story: David Tynan; Director: Gerard Hameline.

The Immortal known as Kronos, leader of the Bronze Age slaughterers known as the Four Horsemen, is hunted across time by Cassandra, who wants to avenge the death of her people. But Duncan MacLeod remembers Kronos as outlaw Melvin Koren, who blazed a path of death and destruction across the Old West.

His Brother's Ghost (1945) [Film; WMW]

Premiere: February 3, 1945; Main Cast: Buster Crabbe as Billy Carson, Al "Fuzzy" St. John as Jonathan "Fuzzy" Q. Jones/Andy Jones, Charles King as Thorne, Karl Hackett as "Doc" Packard, Archie Hall as Deputy Bentley; Producer: Sigmund Neufeld; Story: George Wallace Sayre, Milton Raison; Director: Sam Newfield; 58 min.; Producers Releasing Corporation; b/w.

When bandits kill Fuzzy's twin brother Andy, he poses as his brother's ghost to get his revenge on Thorne and his gang.

Holliday [Comic book; WW]

First publication: November 2002; Story: Dave Samuelson; Art: Jason Wright; Publisher: Saddle Tramp Press.

Doc Holliday deals with the supernatural in the Old West as he teams up with his enemy Johnny Ringo to put a stop to the Horsemen's spree of murder and mayhem.

"The Honey Jug" [Pulp fiction; WW]

Author: **Lon Williams**; Character: **Lee Winters**: *Real Western Stories* (October 1955)

Was it just the after-effects of the slug that grazed his skull, or did Lee Winters really have an utterly strange encounter in ghostly Lowbow Canyon?

Holliday Mountain Madness [Web comic; WW]

First publication: December 2012; Story: Bill Woodcock Jr., Gregory C. Giodarno; Art: Gregory C. Giodarno.

An ongoing serialized graphic novel with occult, horror, steam punk and teslapunk themes. A resurrected Doc Holliday deals out justice to monsters and occult menaces with witchcraft and six-guns. Described as "a weird, psychotronic acid western" by the creators Bill Woodcock Jr. and Gregory C. Giodarno.

Hong on the Range [Juvenile book; SFW]

1. Author: William F. Wu; First publication: New York: Walker, 1989. Juvenile; Illustrated by Phil Hale, Darrel Anderson and Richard Berry.

Cowboy Louie Hong lives in the American West of the future where people and animals are bionic and outlaws and bounty hunters are hot on his trail after his name becomes linked to a bank robbery. Based on the Hugo-and Nebula-nominated short story "Hong's Bluff."

2. Comic book

First publication: December 1997; Story: William F. Wu; Art: Jeff Lafferty; Three-part mini-series; Publisher: Flypaper Press-Image Comics.

The science fiction–Western adventure of Louie Hong and his companions, Prism Chisholm, Chuck, Rusty and Betsy, plus talking and singing cows. Based on the novel.

"The Horror from the Mound" [Pulp fiction; WW]

Author: **Robert E. Howard**; First publication: *Weird Tales* (May 1932)

A search for hidden gold leads West Texas farmer Steve Brill to the disinterment of a notorious Spanish vampire.

At the window a face glared and gibbered soundlessly at him. Two icy eyes pierced his very soul. A shriek burst from his throat and that ghastly visage vanished. But the very air was permeated by the foul scent that had hung about the ancient mound. And now the door creaked—bent slowly inward. Brill backed up against the wall, his gun shaking in his hand: It did not occur to him to fire through the door; in his chaotic brain he

"Brill reeled back against the wall with a choking cry."

The Horror From the Mound

By ROBERT E. HOWARD

A grisly tale of a screaming fear let loose from bondage after having been buried for more than three hundred years

Title page for "The Horror from the Mound" published in *Weird Tales* (May 1932). Illustrated by T. Wyatt Nelson. Courtesy Jeffrey H. Shanks.

had but one thought that only that thin portal of wood separated him from some horror born out of the womb of night and gloom and the black past. His eyes were distended as he saw the door give, as he heard the staples of the bolt groan. The door burst inward. Brill did not scream.

Horror in the West [Comic book; WW]

First publication: 2012; Stories: Phil McClorey, Courtney Joyner, Fred Kennedy, Mike Gagnon, Chris McQuid, AG Pasquella, Ben Truman; Art: Sam Agro, Jeff McComsey, Jason Copland, Kurt Belcher, Simon Dan, Brian Evinou, Shane Heron, Adam Marvin, Graham Law, Antonio Brandao, Ron Gravelle, Andre Fernandes, Jason Ho, Adam Christopher, Chris McFann; Publisher: Alterna Comics.

An anthology of eleven black and white comic strips featuring zombies, aliens, demons and general horror in the Old West. Titles include: Star Calf, Under the Mountain, The Devil's Prome-

nade, Lawson, Brother's Keeper, The Hunters, Pinkerton Express, Sacred Heart of Hell, The Amulet, El Tigre and Captured in a Flash.

Horrors o' the Weird West [RPG book; WW]

Author: Christopher McGlothlin, Shane Lacy Hensley (compilation and editing); First publication: 2001; Setting: **Deadlands: The Weird West**; Publisher: Pinnacle Entertainment Group.

Bestiary and game statistics for the monsters of Deadlands d20 game system. Based on the *Deadlands: The Weird West* books **Rascals, Varmints & Critters** and **Rascals, Varmints & Critters 2: The Book of Curses**.

Horrors of the Wasted West [RPG book; WW]

Authors: Aaron C. Acevedo, Aaron Rosenberg; First publication: 2002; Setting: **Deadlands: Hell on Earth**; Publisher: Pinnacle Entertainment Group.

Revision and adaptation of the book **Monsters, Muties, and Misfits** for the Core D20 conversion game system.

Hosteen Storm [Book character; SW]

First appearance: 1959; Creator: **Andre Norton**; Publisher: New York: Harcourt, Brace.

Navajo born "Amerindian" Hosteen Storm, forced to flee his native Earth, finds a new home on the distant planet Azor. Able to communicate with the animals, he becomes known as the **Beast Master**. Storm's closest animal friends include Baku the eagle, Surra the dune cat and Hing and Ho the meerkats.

Author Andre Norton explores themes of colonization of the American West by European settlers and places them in an alien landscape with the Native Norbies and the Terran settlers placed in an uneasy relationship. By placing Navajo-born Hosteen Storm in a role as the settler in a foreign land, Norton approaches the classic Western formula from a new angle.

The Hounds of Skaith [Novel; SW]

Author: **Leigh Brackett**; First publication: New York: Ballantine Books, 1974.

With the help of a beautiful woman, a group of bloodied insurgents and nine telepathic ferocious hounds with the power to kill with their thoughts, **Eric John Stark** seeks to remove the corrupt Wandsmen from power. But he must also win over the nomadic Hooded Men, the winged Fallarin and the meek populace in his quest to bring freedom to the people of Skaith. The second book in the Skaith trilogy.

See: *The Reavers of Skaith*

Howard, Robert E. (1906–1936) [Pulp author]

Born in the small town of Peaster, Texas, Howard is best remembered today for *Conan the Barbarian* and his association with "sword and sorcery" fiction. But during his short lifetime he was a prolific writer who wrote for many genres including horror, science fiction, fantasy, boxing, spice, detective fiction, historical adventures and the Western.

In correspondence with fellow author August Derleth, Howard wrote, "I don't want to live to be old. I want to die when my time comes, quickly and suddenly, in the full tide of my strength and health."

Howard's wish was self-fulfilled when on June 11, 1936, he calmly walked out of his house, opened the door to his Chevrolet, sat in the driver's seat and shot himself in the head. He survived for eight hours in a state of unconsciousness. His ailing mother, who had been in a coma, died the following day. The mother and son were buried together. Howard was only 30.

Author L. Sprague de Camp was primarily responsible for preserving Howard's work following his death by editing and completing many of Howard's *Conan* stories.

Selected works: *Beyond the Black River* (1935).

Howdy Pardner [Comic book]

The humorous comic adventures of singing cowboy Howdy Pardner, his girlfriend Flower and the Speagle Brothers.

"Howdy Pardner in Ghost Town Glee Club" [WW]

First Published: #1 (1999); Creator-Story-Art: Andrew Brandou; Publisher: Robot Publishing.

Howdy Pardner comes to the aid of a lady haunted by ghosts in her Old West home.

Hucksters & Hexes [RPG book; WW]

Author: John Goff; First publication: 1998; Setting: *Deadlands: The Weird West*; Publisher: Pinnacle Entertainment Group.

Hucksters are natural poker players who use their skills as the gateway to the realm of the demonic manitou. Includes the adventure "Abracadabra and an Arab Cadaver" by Tony Lee and the secret hexes in *Hoyles Book of Games*.

The Huge Hunter or The Steam Man of the Prairies [Dime novel; SPW]

Author: **Edward Sylvester Ellis**; First publication: *Irwin P. Beadle's American Novels* #45 (August 1868)

Johnny Brainerd, a teenage hunch backed dwarf inventor, builds a ten-foot-tall iron Steam Man capable of traveling at 30 miles per hour. Complete with stove-pipe hat, the Steam Man pulls a passenger wagon carrying Ethan Hopkins, Mickey McSquille and Baldy Bicknell as Johnny Brainerd ventures across the prairie fighting off Native Indians and buffalo in their search for gold.

Ellis's "Steam Man" was written in an era when the steam-driven engine was the new wonder of the age with its ability to power steam-ships across oceans. In 1839 the *Sirius* became the first steamship to cross the Atlantic. The age of automation was the new reality. Inventors of steam-driven gadgets saw a new market opening up. Zadoc P. Dederick from Newark, New Jersey, was an entrepreneurial inventor who patented his "Steam Man" on March 24, 1868. *The Newark Advertiser* January 23, 1868, stated:

> [A] Newark machinist has invented a man; one that, moved by steam, will perform some of the most important functions of humanity; that will, standing upright, walk or run as he is bid, in any direction, and at almost any rate of speed, drawing after him a load whose weight would tax the strength of three draught horses...

Ellis was clearly influenced by Dederick's creation. The description of his Steam Man shows similarities:

> Several miles to the north, something like a gigantic man could be seen approaching, apparently at a rapid gait for a few seconds, when it slackened its speed, until it scarcely moved. Occasionally it changed its course, so that it went nearly at right angles. At such times, its colossal proportions were brought out in full relief, looking like some Titan as it took its giant strides over the prairie. The distance was too great to scrutinize the phenomenon closely; but they could see that a black volume of smoke issued either from its mouth or the top of its head, while it was drawing behind it

a sort of carriage, in which a single man was seated, who appeared to control the movements of the extraordinary being in front of him...

The Hunter (*The Legend Chronicles* book 1) [Novel; SPW]

Author: Theresa Meyers; First publication: New York: Kensington Publishing, 2011.

Brothers Winchester, Remington and Colt Jackson have been trained in the family tradition of vampire and demon hunting. Now the time has come for Colt to search for the Book of Legend that's been separated into three parts. A book that can banish demons, but that also requires a demon to locate a vital third of the book hidden by Jacksons' father. When Colt summons a beautiful succubus who longs to become human, Colt strikes a deal that that comes dangerously close to becoming a handshake with the devil.

Followed by book 2 in The Legend Chronicles, *The Slayer*.

Hurricane [Comic book character; WW]

First appearance: *Two-Gun Kid* #70 (July 1964); Creators: **Stan Lee**, **Dick Ayers**; Publisher: Marvel Comics.

Escaping from Two-Gun Kid following a failed train robbery, Harry Kane drinks a potion (brewed by an Indian shaman) that has been struck by lightning. The potion gives Kane superspeed and the ability to outdraw his opponents. Emboldened by his new powers, Kane attempts a daring bank robbery but is foiled by Two-Gun Kid and imprisoned.

Hurricane also came into conflict with Carter Slade alias the **Phantom Rider** and the time-traveling West Coast Avengers.

See: **Western Legends**

I Travel By Night [Novel; WW]

Author: Robert R. McCammon; First publication: Burton, MI: Subterranean Press, 2013.

On the battlefields of Shiloh former Confederate soldier Trevor Lawson entered the realm of the undead. Now a gunslinger, Lawson hunts vampire queen LaRouge by night in the hope that drinking her blood may help him regain his humanity.

If You Meet Sartana, Pray for Your Death (1968) [Film; Italy-France-West Germany; WW]

U.S. release title for *Se incontri Sartana prega per la tua morte*.

In Blood We Trust (*A Novel of the Bloodlands* #3) [Novel; SFW]

Author: Christine Cody; First publication: New York: Ace Books, 2011.

The final book in the **Bloodlands** trilogy Mariah Lyander and Gabriel flee to the Bloodlands after freeing their fellow monsters from captivity. But their return to Bloodlands forces Mariah to face the demons of her past and Gabriel to face his future.

In Nome del Padre, del Figlio e della Colt (1971) [Film; Italy-Spain; WMW]

Premiere: December 3, 1975; Main Cast: Craig Hill as Bill Nolan/Bandido enmascarado, Nuccia Cardinali as Clarissa Nolan, Ágata Lys as Antonieta, Frank Braña as Juez; Story: Arpad DeRiso, Mario Gariazzo; Director: Frank Bronston [Mario Bianchi]; 77 min.; Aldebarán Films S.A., Cooperativa Cine España (Copercines), Copercines, Cooperativa Cinematográfica, New Films; Color.

A gunfighter trails his masked outlaw brother and his gang who are involved in murder, rape and robbery. Meanwhile, in the same village on the night of Halloween, another masked assassin starts his killing spree.

Low-budget film that anticipated John Carpenter's *Halloween* (1978). Filmed in 1971, it had limited Italian distribution in 1975.

In the Name of the Father, the Son and the Colt (1971) [Film; Italy-Spain; WMW]

U.S. release title for *In Nome del Padre, del Figlio e della Colt*.

Independence Day [RPG book; WW]

Authors: Matt Forbeck, Chris Snyder; First publication: 1996; **Deadlands: The Weird West** Dime Novel #2; Publisher: Pinnacle Entertainment Group.

Wyatt Earp hires a posse to maintain law and order during Independence Day and to track down a ruthless murderer.

The Indian in the Cupboard [Juvenile novel; Film; WW]

1. Author: Lynne Reid Banks; First publication: Garden City NY: Doubleday, 1980.

An old cupboard, a toy plastic Indian and a magic key change the life of a nine-year-old boy when the Indian comes to life.

Followed by: *The Return of the Indian* (1985); *The Secret of the Indian* (1989); *The Mystery of the Cupboard* (1992); *The Key to the Indian* (1998).

2. Premiere: July 14, 1995; Main Cast: Hal Scardino as Omri, Litefoot as Little Bear, Lindsay Crouse as Jane, Richard Jenkins as Victor, Rishi Bhat as Patrick, David Keith as Boo-hoo Boone, Vincent Kartheiser as Gillon, Steve Coogan as Tommy Atkins; Producers: Kathleen Kennedy, Frank Marshall, Jane Startz; Original novel: Lynne Reid Banks; Screenplay: Melissa Matheson; Director: Frank Oz; 96 min.; Columbia Pictures, Kennedy/Marshall Company, Paramount Pictures, Reliable Pictures, Scholastic; Color.

Film adaptation of the novel that explores the relationship between two young boys, a Texan cowboy from 1879 and an 18th century Iroquois Indian come to life.

Infestations [RPG book; WW]

Author: Charles Ryan; First publication: 1999; *Deadlands: Hell on Earth* Dime novel #2; Publisher: Pinnacle Entertainment Group.

The continuing *Wasted West* adventures of Teller.

Inn of the Damned (1975) [Film; Australia; WW]

Premiere: November 13, 1975; Main Cast: Judith Anderson as Caroline Straulle, Alex Cord as Cal Kincaid, Michael Craig as Paul Melford, Tony Bonner as Trooper Moore; Producers: Rod Hay, Terry Bourke; Story-Director: Terry Bourke; 118 min.; Terryrod; Color.

In this horror Western variation on the *Psycho* theme, the Australian outback serves as the backdrop to a story of an inn with a history of missing guests and grisly murders.

Interplanetary Lizards of the Western Plains [Comic book; SFW]

First appearance: 1992; Story: J. Allen Cogliette, Glenn Boyd, Alan Jude Summa; Art: Glenn Boyd, Alan Jude Summa; Publisher: Leadbelly Productions.

Humor strip featuring cowboy lizards Doc, Rattler and Tumbleweed, stranded in the Old West by a time probe from an alternate reality.

Into the Badlands (1991) [Telefilm; WW]

Premiere: July 24, 1991; Main Cast: Bruce Dern as T.L. Barston, Mariel Hemingway as Alma Heusser, Helen Hunt as Blossom, Dylan McDermott as McComas, Lisa Pelikan as Sarah Carstairs, Andrew Robinson as Sheriff Aaron Starett, Michael J. Metzger as Red Roundtree; Executive Producers: Josh Kane, Michael Ogiens; Teleplay: Dick Beebe, Marjorie David, Gordon Dawson; Director: Sam Pillsbury; 89 min.; MTE, Ogiens/Kane Company; Color.

Three tales are interwoven into the main story involving the mysterious bounty hunter T. L. Barston and his hunt for wanted outlaw Red Roundtree. Horror Western based on short stories by Will Henry a.k.a. Heck Allen (*The Streets of Laredo*), Marcia Muller (*The Time of the Wolves*) and Bryce Walton (*The Last Pelt*).

Iron Oasis [RPG book; WW]

Author: John Hopler; First publication: 1999; Setting: *Deadlands: Hell on Earth The Wasted West*; Publisher: Pinnacle Entertainment Group.

Location book for the *Wasted West* city of Junkyard, the main setting for *Hell on Earth*.

Iron West [Graphic novel; SFW]

First publication: July 2006; Story-Art: Doug TenNapel; b/w; Publisher: Image.

Outlaw Preston Struck encounters an army of mechanical men. With the help of a shaman and his sidekick Sasquatch, Struck attempts to stop the robots from destroying central California.

Jack Wright [Dime novel character; SPW]

With the continuing success of **Frank Reade Jr.**, Frank Tousey knew he had a successful formula in the traveling boy inventor. **Luis Senarens** was called upon to create Jack Wright, who first appeared in *The Boys' Star Library* #216, July 18, 1891, in "Jack Wright, the Boy Inventor; or, Hunting for a Sunken Treasure" and was later featured in Tousey's *Boys of New York* before ending his run in *Happy Days*. Between 1891 and 1896 he appeared in 121 stories.

Jack Wright and His Electric Stage; or, Leagued Against the James Boys [Dime novel; SPW]

Author: "Noname" (**Luis Senarens**); *The Boys' Star Library.* #344, September 14, 1894.

Swindling Jack Wright out of $5,000, the James Boys are pursued by Wright to Missouri with the help of his electric stage known as the Terror.

"...For a long time I have tried every means to capture those bandits. But they slip away from me with the most remarkable ease every time I feel surest I've got them. There's a reward of $5,000 offered by the governor of the State for their capture, and I and a Pinkerton detective named Carl Greene have been making the most desperate efforts to capture the James Boys, and break up their gang. We have thus far failed to do so."

"Why has it been such a difficult task?" asked Jack.

"In the first place, Jesse James owns a horse named Siroc which is unequaled in speed and intelligence by any horse in the world that I know of, and he can easily outfoot the fleetest animal that ever chased him."

"Well," asked Jack, "suppose an electric overland engine were to chase that remarkable quadruped, don't you think he might be overtaken? The engine I refer to can run at the rate of fifty miles an hour over rough ground."

"Any engine could last longer than a horse, and such a machine as you mention could outspeed that horse. But, of course, such an engine is an utter impossibility."

"You are mistaken," said Jack, quietly.

"How so?" asked Timberlake, with a puzzled look.

"Because I have got such an engine."

Jack Wright and His Electric Stage; or, Leagued Against the James Boys by "Noname." *The Boys' Star Library* 344, September 14, 1894.

Jack Wright and His Prairie Yacht [Dime novel; SPW]

Author: "Noname" (**Luis Senarens**); 1894.

Wright fights Indians with the help of his Prairie Yacht.

Jack Wright's Electric Prairie Car or, Hot Times With the Broncho Buster, Part I [Dime novel; SPW]

Author: "Noname" (**Luis Senarens**); *The Boys' Star Library*.

Jed Puma [Comic book; France; WW]

First appearance: *Pampa* (2nd series) #1, *Bronco* #9 (1966); Art: Annibale Casabianca; Publisher: Editions Lug.

Western crimefighter Jed Puma has superhuman fighting skills and agility and takes pride in never wearing or using a gun. He is accompanied by Asian martial arts master Tashi.

The Jerusalem Man [Novel; SFW]

Author: **David Gemmell**; First publication: New York: Baen Books, 1988.

Variant title for **Wolf in Shadow**.

Jesse James Meets Frankenstein's Daughter (1966) [Film; SFW]

Premiere: April 1966; Main Cast: John Lupton as Jesse James, Jim Davis as Marshal MacPhee, Narda Onyx as Dr. Maria Frankenstein, Steven Geray as Dr. Rudolph Frankenstein, Estelita Rodriguez as Juanita Lopez, Cal Bolder as Hank Tracy/Igor; Producer: Carroll Case; Story: Carl Hittleman; Director: William Beaudine; 88 min.; Circle Productions, Embassy Pictures; Color.

When Jesse James' partner Hank Tracy is shot in a foiled stagecoach robbery, they take refuge in a converted mission belonging to Baron Frankenstein's granddaughter and her brother Rudolph Frankenstein.

A standard "B" Western about spurned love with an over-the-top Frankenstein horror story involving a brain transplant thrown in the mix.

El Jinete sin Cabeza (1957) [Film; Mexico; WW]

Premiere: September 18, 1957; Main Cast: Luis Aguilar, Crox Alvarado, Jaime Fernandez, Flor Silvestre; Producer: Luis Manrique; Story: Ramón Obón; Director: Chano Urueta; 95 min.; Universal; Spanish; b/w.

When a skull-masked gang, attempting to gain control of Herminio González's hacienda, captures him and chops off his hand with an axe, it takes on a life of its own. The Headless Rider appears on the scene to rescue a beautiful girl from the clutches of the ruthless gang and expose their true identities.

The first film in the *Headless Rider* series was originally part one of a three-part serial.

See: *La Cabeza de Pancho Villa, La Marca de Satanás*

Los Jinetes de la Bruja (1966) [Film; Mexico; WW]

Premiere: December 8, 1966; Main Cast: Kitty de Hoyos, Fernando Almada, Dagoberto Rodríguez, Blanca Sánchez; Producer: Mário Almada; Story-Director: Vicente Oroná; 110 min.; Producciones Almada; Spanish; Color.

A witch, a death masked rider and ghost puppets feature in a tale of a rancher who is framed for the murder of a puppeteer.

John Carter (2012) [Film; SW]

Premiere: March 9, 2012; Main Cast: Taylor Kitsch as John Carter, Lynn Collins as Dejah Thoris, Samantha Morton as Sola, Willem Dafoe as Tars Tarkas, Bryan Cranston as Powell, Thomas Haden Church as Tal Hajus, Polly Walker as Sarkoja, Ciaran Hinds as Tardos Mors, Dominic West as Sab Than, Mark Strong as Matai Shang; Producers; Lindsey Collins, Jim Morris, Colin Wilson; Screenplay: Andrew Stanton, Mark Andrews, Michael Chabon; Based on "A Princess of Mars" by Edgar Rice Burroughs; Director: Andrew Stanton; 132 min.; Walt Disney Pictures; 3D; Color.

American Civil War veteran John Carter escapes from prison after refusing to join the U.S. Cavalry and seeks refuge in a cave. Upon discovering a golden amulet with runic occult symbols he suddenly finds himself transported to an alien planet with a landscape resembling Arizona, where he can leap to great heights and distances. Carter soon encounters strange 12-foot tall six-limbed and tusked creatures named Tharks who are allied with the Heliums in a war with the Zodangans. The beautiful Helium Princess Dejah Thoris beguiles Carter as he learns he is on Barsoom also known as Mars.

Based on the Edgar Rice Burroughs story *A Princess of Mars,* the reviews were mainly negative. Peter Bradshaw of *The Guardian* (UK) (March 8, 2012) wrote, "The fantasy-romance adventures of a Civil War veteran transported to Mars made for a giant, suffocating doughy feast of boredom." The late Roger Ebert (March 7, 2012) stated, "The movie is more Western than science fiction." Robbie Collin of *The Telegraph* (UK) (March 8, 2012) concluded his review with, "Stanton has made a movie that is a technical marvel, but it is also armrest clawingly hammy and painfully dated. This is a vision of the future that belongs in the past."

The film was a financial disaster for Disney. The original $263 million budget resulted in a meager opening weekend of a little over $30 million.

John Carter of Mars [Pulp fiction character; SW]

First comic book appearance: *The Funnies* #30 (May 1939); Publisher: Dell Publishing.

The Funnies (Issue's #30–56) was the first of many comic book and comic strip adaptations based on the **Edgar Rice Burroughs** character first introduced in *Under the Moons of Mars*.

United Feature Syndicate Sunday Strip (December 7, 1941-April 3, 1943); Story: Edgar Rice Burroughs; Art: John Coleman Burroughs.

Edgar Rice Burroughs' John Carter of Mars

"The Prisoner of the Tharks"
First publication: *Four Color* #375 (February 1952); Story: Gaylord DuBois; Art: Jesse Marsh; Publisher: Dell Publishing Co.

"Tyrant of the North"
First publication: *Four Color* #437 (November 1952); Story: Phil Evans; Art: Jesse Marsh; Publisher: Dell Publishing Co.

"The Black Pirates of Omean"
First publication: *Four Color* #488 (1953); Story: Phil Evans; Art: Jesse Marsh; Publisher: Dell Publishing Co.

All three Dell issues were reprinted by Gold Key (April-October 1964).

"The Martian"
Sun Weekly #507–537 (October 25, 1958–May 23, 1959); Adaptation: D.R. Morton; Art: Robert Forrest; Publisher: Amalgamated Press UK. *Tarzan* #207–209 (April 1972); DC Comics; *Weird Worlds* #1–7 (August-September 1972); DC Comics; *John Carter Warlord of Mars* #1–10 (June 1977-March 1978); Marvel Comics.

Jonah Hex [Comic book character; Comic book; WW]

First appearance: ***All-Star Western*** #10 (February-March 1972); Creators: John Albano, Tony DeZuniga; Publisher: DC comics.

Sold as a slave to the Apache tribe by his alcoholic father, Jonah Woodson Hex received his "mark of the demon" facial scar from an Apache's red-hot tomahawk following a trial of combat with the chief's son who had previously betrayed him. The embittered and disfigured former Confederate officer became a bounty hunter with weapons including a Winchester rifle, Colt Peacemaker .45, Colt Dragoon .44 and Colt Navy .36. His days of bounty hunting caught up with him in old age when he was killed in cold blood by George Barrow in 1904.

Jonah Hex has proven to be one of DC Comics' most popular and enduring Western characters and has straddled the line between a traditional Western anti-hero and a character moving through Weird Western landscapes that include werewolves and zombies. In addition to his own title, Jonah Hex has also been featured in mini-series and guest-starred in various DC titles including ***All-New Booster Gold***, ***Justice League of America*** and ***Justice League Unlimited***.

Jonah Hex also guest-starred on ***Batman: The Animated Series***, ***Justice League Unlimited*** and ***Batman: The Brave and the Bold*** animated TV series.

Jonah Hex (2010) [Film; WW]

Premiere: June 17, 2010; Main Cast: Josh Brolin as Jonah Hex, John Malkovich as Quentin Turnbull, Megan Fox as Lilah, Michael Fassbender as Burke, Will Arnett as Liutenant Grass, Aidan Quinn as President Grant, Tom Wopat as Colonel Slocum; Producers; Akiva Goldsman, Andrew Lazar; Story: Mark Neveldine, Brian Taylor, William Farmer, John Albano; Director: Jimmy Hayward; 81 min.; Warner Bros.; Color.

Disfigured bounty hunter Jonah Hex is on the vengeance trail for the murder of his wife and son by fellow Confederate veteran Quentin Turnbull. Now Turnbull has turned his attention to destroying the Union and Washington with a super-weapon of mass destruction. Hex is offered amnesty and freedom by President Grant in return for helping stop Turnbull and his renegade army.

Based on the DC Comics character, the film re-imagines Hex's disfigurement, replacing Native Americans with the diabolical Turnbull and giving Hex the power to talk to and resurrect the dead. Reviews were mixed. *The New York Times* critic Manohla Dargis (June 17, 2010) was positive. "Though it has bad word of mouth, 'Jonah Hex' is generally better, sprier and more diverting than most of the action flicks playing, 'The A-Team' included." Claudia Puig of *USA Today* (June 19, 2010) was less generous. "The opening frame of Jonah Hex should say: 'Caution: Made expressly for the male teen demographic. Not suitable for anyone of any age who prefers movies with coherence, an original plot or characters they give a hoot about.'"

Audiences stayed away as the opening weekend ranked a disappointing # 8 with earnings of $5.8 million. Given the estimated $47 million budget and a U.S. gross of $11 million *Jonah Hex* was a major disappointment for Warner Bros.

Jonah Hex: Riders of the Worm and Such [Comic book; WW]

First publication: April 1995; Story: **Joe R. Lansdale**; Art: Timothy Truman, Sam Glanzman; Five-part mini-series; Publisher: DC Vertigo.

Jonah Hex fights the half-worm, half-human albino Autumn Brothers who serve the technologically advanced worms that live underground.

Jonah Hex (2010), starring from left, Michael Fassbender as Burke, John Malkovich as Quentin Turnbull, Josh Brolin as Jonah Hex and Megan Fox as Lilah (Warner Bros.).

In 1996, Texas blues rockers Johnny and Edgar Winter attempted to sue DC Comics, Joe R. Lansdale, Timothy Truman and Sam Glanzman on the grounds the green-tentacled, pale-faced, half-human, half-worm creatures known as Johnny and Edgar Autumn were defamatory, an invasion of privacy and caused "intentional infliction of emotional distress."

Joe Lansdale stated in a Comic Book Legal Defense Fund release, "It was our intent to use the Jonah Hex comic book series as a vehicle for satire and parody of musical genres, Texas music in particular, as well as old radio shows, movie serials and the like. We feel within our rights to parody music, stage personas, album personas, lyrics and public figures."

The Winter brothers appealed the decision by a Los Angeles judge to dismiss the suit. They lost their appeal in June 2003. The unanimous ruling stated that artists and publishers had constitutional right to produce works that include creatively transformed images of actual persons. "The First Amendment dictates that the right to comment on, parody, lampoon and make other expressive uses of the celebrity image must be given broad scope."

However, the Appeals Court ruling didn't hide their distaste for the *Jonah Hex* mini-series. They begrudgingly had to admit, "Vulgar forms of expression fully qualify for First Amendment protection. While it is true that many of the gags and depictions are violent, gross and in bad taste, that is apparently the nature of this type of genre."

Jonah Hex: Shadows West [Comic book; WW]

First publication: February 1999; Story: **Joe R. Lansdale**; Art: Timothy Truman, Sam Glanzman; Three-part mini-series; Publisher: DC Vertigo.

Jonah Hex joins Buffalo Will's Wild West Show and his motley crew including a midget sharpshooter and a washed-up bounty hunter out to prove himself one last time by claiming the bounty on Jonah Hex.

Jonah Hex: Two Gun Mojo [Comic book; WW]

First publication: August 1993; Story: **Joe R. Lansdale**; Art: Timothy Truman, Sam Glanzman; Five-part mini-series; Publisher: DC Vertigo.

Trapped in a barrel by snake-oil salesman and voodoo practitioner Doc "Cross" Williams, **Jonah**

Hex is forced to drink zombie brew. He manages to escape only to find himself face to face again with Williams and his carnival freak show, including the zombie of Wild Bill Hickok, in New Mexico. Jonah Hex surprisingly finds allies in Williams and his zombies as they join forces to repel an attack from Apache Indians.

Jonas: Tales of an Ironstar [Comic book; SFW]

First publication: November 2004; Story-Art: Brian Colin; Publisher: CodeDeco Inc.

Monster hunter Jonas Eightstar returns home to Reedville, Arizona, to find the town deserted. In his search to uncover the truth behind the tragic and violent murder of his son, Jonas joins the Ironstars to protect the people from the mutant animals that populate the ravaged post-apocalyptic West.

Journey into Mystery [Comic book]

Horror and science fiction anthology title from Atlas Comics. When Atlas was succeeded by Marvel Comics, the comic book eventually changed emphasis to a superhero title featuring *Thor* starting with issue #83 (August 1962).

"THOSE WHO VANISH!" [WW]

First publication: #38 (September 1956); Art: Steve Ditko; Publisher: Atlas Comics—Marvel Comics.

Released from prison after a twenty-year sentence, an aging man ponders his gloomy future prospects when Chief Red Dust tempts him with an offer to enter the magic water of Chi-Ha-Nichi and get a new lease on life. But at what price to the man?

Judok [Comic book character; Italy; SW]

First publication: *Collana Rodeo* #8 (1967); Story: Gian Luigi Bonelli; Art: Giovanni Ticci; Publisher: Sergio Bonelli Editore.

Judok has been described as "**Tex Willer** in Space" by its publisher.

"Julhi" [Pulp fiction; SW]

Author: **C. L. Moore**; First publication: *Weird Tales* (March 1935).

A beautiful female Venusian named Apri leads **Northwest Smith** to the mysterious, alluring Julhi and the blood-feeding haunters of the ruined island city of Vonng.

C. L. Moore maintains the interest of the reader through her descriptive and imaginative narrative that incorporates sensuality and eroticism and reads like a subconscious dream-like state.

The Junkman Cometh [RPG book; WW]

Author: John Hopler; First publication: 1999; Setting: *Deadlands: Hell on Earth*; Publisher: Pinnacle Entertainment Group.

Includes new powers for the technical wizardry of the junkers and detailed description of tech spirits.

Just a Pilgrim [Comic book; SFW]

First publication: May 2001; Story: Garth Ennis; Art: Carlos Ezquerra; Five-issue mini-series; Publisher: Black Bull Entertainment.

Set on a post-apocalyptic, scorched Earth following the expansion of the sun, the story centers on religious fanatic Pilgrim who has developed a taste for human flesh. In his search for water, Pilgrim helps a group of refugees and young Billy Shepard as they journey across the dried-up Atlantic Ocean basin.

Creator Garth Ennis has acknowledged the Western influences in the visual appearance of Pilgrim, stating that he is a cross between Clint Eastwood and Lee Marvin. But his personality is more in keeping with a "warrior monk."

Just a Pilgrim: Garden of Eden [Comic book; SFW]

First publication: 2002; Story: Garth Ennis; Art: Carlos Ezquerra; Four-issue mini-series; Publisher: Black Bull Entertainment.

Pilgrim encounters scientists building a spaceship among the few remaining humans left alive in the Atlantic basin. But mutated jellyfish threaten the lives of the few as the spaceship prepares to travel to a new world.

Sequel to *Just a Pilgrim*.

Justice League (2001) [Animated TV series]

Animated adventures featuring the DC comic book characters. The series was revamped for the third season with a new theme tune, new characters and a change of title from *Justice League* to *Justice League Unlimited*. **Vigilante** joined the JLA in the fourth season.

Science Fiction Western episodes:

"ULTIMATUM" (3:09) [SFW]

Air date: December 4, 2004; Voice cast: Gregg

Rainwater as Long Shadow, Tim Matheson as Max Lord, James Sie as Wind Dragon, Grey DeLisle as Downpour/Shifter, Jennifer Hale as Giganta, Susan Eisenberg as **Wonder Woman**, Kevin Conroy as **Batman**, George Newbern as Superman, Scott Rummell as Aquaman, Phil LaMarr as **Green Lantern**/John Stewart, Carl Lumbly as J'onn J'onzz, Robert Foxworth as Professor Hamilton, CCH Pounder as Amanda Waller; Story: Dwayne McDuffie; Teleplay: J.M. DeMatteis; Director: Joaquim Dos Santos; 30 min.; Warner Bros. Animation; Color.

Project Cadmus creates a genetically engineered group of superheroes to counteract the Justice League. The Ultimen include the American Indian Long Shadow, who rebels against Cadmus and his fellow Ultimen members and joins the Justice League.

The character of Long Shadow, who has the ability to grow to gigantic size, was influenced by the animated *Super Friends* character **Apache Chief**. This was the only appearance of Long Shadow in the series.

"THE ONCE AND FUTURE THING PART ONE: WEIRD WESTERN TALES" (3:12) [SFW]

Premiere: January 22, 2005; Voice cast: Adam Baldwin as **Jonah Hex**, Kevin Conroy as **Batman**, Phil LaMarr as **Green Lantern**, Susan Eisenberg as **Wonder Woman**, Nestor Carbonell as **El Diablo**, Ben Browder as **Bat Lash**, Jonathan Joss as Sheriff Ohyesa "**Pow Wow**" Smith, Ed O'Ross as Tobias Manning, Peter MacNicol as Chronos, Peter Onorati as Warhawk; Story: Dwayne McDuffie; Director: Dan Riba; 30 min.; Warner Bros. Animation; Color.

Justice League members are transported to the Old West of 1879 where they discover Tobias Manning is controlling the town of Elkhorn with future technology accumulated through the help of a time machine. The episode features Weird Western characters Bat Lash, Jonah Hex, El Diablo and "Pow Wow" Smith.

"TASK FORCE X" (4:04) [SW]

Air date: May 21, 2005; Voice cast: Michael Rosenbaum as **Vigilante**/Floyd Lawton/Deadshot, Phil LaMarr as Green Lantern/John Stewart, Carl Lumbly as J'onn J'onzz; Adam Baldwin as Rick Flagg, Donal Gibson as Captain Boomerang, Alan Rachins as Clock King, Juliet Landau as Plastique/Tala, Chris Cox as Captain Atom; Story: Dwayne McDuffie; Teleplay: Darwyn Cooke; Director: Joaquim Dos Santos; 30 min.; Warner Bros. Animation; Color.

The Justice League's Watchtower is infiltrated by Captain Boomerang, **Deadshot**, Plastique and Clock King, collectively known as Task Force X.

"HUNTER'S MOON" (4:08) [SW]

Air date: June 18, 2005; Voice cast: Nathan Fillion as Vigilante, Maria Canals as **Hawkgirl**/Shayera Hol, Gina Torres as Vixen, Phil LaMarr as Green Lantern/John Stewart, Carl Lumbly as J'onn J'onzz, Hector Elizondo as Kragger; Story: Stan Berkowitz; Teleplay: Dwayne McDuffie; Director: Joaquim Dos Santos; 30 min.; Warner Bros. Animation; Color.

When they respond to an emergency request for help. Shayera (Hawkgirl), Vigilante and Vixen are led into an ambush by Thanagarians seeking revenge on Shayera.

"PATRIOT ACT" (5:07) [SW]

Air date: February 25, 2006; Voice cast: Nathan Fillion as Vigilante/Spy Smasher, Phil LaMarr as Green Lantern/John Stewart, J.K. Simmons as General Eiling, Michael Beach as Mr. Terrific, Kin Shriner as Green Arrow, Chris Cox as Shining Knight, Giselle Loren as Stargirl, Mike Erwin as Speedy; Story: Matt Wayne; Director: Joaquim Dos Santos; 30 min.; Warner Bros. Animation; Color.

A serum used by the Nazis transforms General Wade Eiling into a superhuman monster who seeks to destroy members of the Justice League including Vigilante, Shining Knight, Stargirl, Green Arrow, Speedy and Crimson Avenger.

Justice League of America [Comic book]

Groundbreaking comic book series that saw DC Comics' line-up of superheroes form a team to keep the Earth safe from harm.

"CRISIS FROM YESTERDAY" [SFW]

First publication: #159 (October 1978); Story: Gerry Conway; Art: Dick Dillin, Frank McLaughlin; Publisher: DC Comics.

Jonah Hex is transported from the Old West by the Lord of Time to battle the Justice League and Justice Society of America in 1978. Fighting alongside him are Viking Prince, Enemy Ace, Miss Liberty and The Black Pirate, who have also been transplanted in time and space by the Lord of Time.

"CRISIS FROM TOMORROW" [SFW]

First publication: #160 (November 1978); Story: Gerry Conway; Art: Dick Dillin, Frank McLaughlin; Publisher: DC Comics.

Jonah Hex and his fellow fighting men and

women confront dinosaurs and lizard men in the year 3786 as they attack the Lord of Time's castle.

"Once Upon a Time in the Wild Wild West" [SFW]

First publication: #198 (January 1982); Story: Gerry Conway; Art: Don Heck, Brett Breeding; Publisher: DC Comics.

The Flash, **Green Lantern**, Elongated Man and Zatanna find themselves in the Old West of 1878 with no knowledge of who they are and meet Jonah Hex, **Bat Lash**, **Cinnamon** and the **Scalphunter**. The Lord of Time is using the amnesiac superheroes as pawns in his plans to capture an anti-matter bubble which will strike the Grand Canyon.

"Grand Canyon Showdown" [SFW]

First publication: #199 (February 1982); Story: Gerry Conway; Art: Don Heck, Brett Breeding; Publisher: DC Comics.

Jonah Hex, Cinnamon, Scalphunter and Bat Lash vanish after successfully stopping the anti-matter bubble from striking the Grand Canyon.

Justice League Unlimited [Animated TV series; Comic book]

1. Third-to fifth-season title for the *Justice League* animated TV series.
2. Based on the animated TV series.

"The Justice Rangers Ride Again" [SFW]

First published: *Justice League Unlimited* #19 (March 2006); Story: Adam Beechen; Art: Gordon Purcell, Bob Petrecca; Publisher: DC Comics.

The Time Commander takes refuge in the Old West but **Wonder Woman**, **Vigilante** and Elongated Man pursue him through time and space and enlist the help of **Jonah Hex**, **Bat Lash** and **El Diablo**.

Justice Riders [Comic book; SFW]

First appearance: January 1997; Story: Chuck Dixon; Art: J. H. Williams III; Publisher: DC Comics.

One-issue *Elseworlds* cross-genre tale set in an alternate DC Universe featuring the **Justice League of America** as Old West marshals.

Kaiju Rising: Age of Monsters [Short story anthology; WW]

First publication: February, 2014; Publisher: Ragnarok Publications.

This collection of 23 short stories on the theme of strange creatures features the Weird Western story "Devil Cap's Brawl" by Edward M. Erdelac. Set in 1880s High Sierra country, Chinese and Shoshone laborers work on the Union Pacific Railroad. But when the blast their way through the Devil's Cap promontory they awaken a long dormant menace.

Karen Memory [Novel; SPW]

Author: Elizabeth Bear; First publication: New York: Tor, 2015.

This alternate history novel takes places in 19th century Rapid City (later named Seattle) in a steam-powered landscape where airships travel the route between Rapid City and Alaska, with its enticing promise of gold. An orphaned young woman makes her living in a bordello with a reputation for quality. One night her world changes when Peter Bantle enters the bordello with a device that can control people's minds. The following night the corpse of a murdered streetwalker is discovered in a garbage dump in the grounds of the establishment.

A mix of steampunk, western, romance and thriller set in the northwest frontier of the late 1800s.

Keller, Jack (1922–2003) [Comic book artist]

Born in Reading, Pennsylvania, Jack Keller sold his first strip in 1941 to Dell Comics. The following year he was offered employment by Quality Comics inking the *Blackhawk* strip. Other assignments included work for Fiction House, Fawcett and Lev Gleason plus supplying backgrounds for Will Eisner's Sunday supplement strip *The Spirit*.

In 1950 he was offered work by **Stan Lee** at Timely-Atlas on their horror, crime, romance and Western titles. He found his niche with *Kid Colt Outlaw* and within a few years was working solely on Western titles.

When Atlas collapsed in 1957, Keller was briefly without work as a comic artist but returned to *Kid Colt* when Atlas changed management and became Marvel Comics. He supplemented his income working freelance for Charlton Comics on their Western and war titles but achieved his greatest success with *Hot Rods and Racing Cars*.

Keller quit *Kid Colt* in 1967 when the comic went over to reprints. He worked briefly for DC

Comics and continued with Charlton Comics until 1973.

Keoma (1976) [Film; Italy; WW]

Premiere: 1976; Main Cast: Franco Nero as Keoma, Woody Strode as George, William Berger as William Shannon, Donald O'Brian as Caldwell, Olga Karlatos as Lisa, Gabriella Giacobbe as The Witch; Producer: Manolo Bolognini; Story: Luigi Montefiori [George Eastman]; Screenplay: Enzo G. Castellari, Nico Ducci, Luigi Montefiori, Mino Roli; Director: Enzo G. Castellari; 105 min.; Uranos Cinematografica; Color.

Halfbreed gunfighter Keoma discovers plague is rampant in his home town. When ruthless landlord Caldwell refuses to accept medical supplies or food, Keoma decides to evict Caldwell and his men from the town and relieve the suffering of the townsfolk.

An often violent and brutal film that includes Weird Western elements of an old hag personifying Death as Keoma's companion.

The Key to the Indian [Juvenile novel; WW]

Author: Lynne Reid Banks; Illustrator: James Watling; First publication: HarperTrophy 1999.

When Omri's father discovers the secret of the cupboard, he decides to journey back in time with his son to attempt to help the Iroquois people and Little Bear. But their goodwill mission becomes fraught with danger.

Khon fai bin (2006) [Film; Thailand; WW]

Premiere: December 21, 2006; Main Cast: Dan Chupong as Zieng/Jone Bang Fai, Leo Putt as Lord Wang, Panna Rittikrai as Nai Hoi Dam, Samart Payakarun as Nai Hoi Singh, Kanyapak Suworakood as E-sao; Producer: Prachya Pinkaew; Director: Chalerm Wongpim; 103 min.; Sahamongkol Film International Co. Ltd.; Color.

Martial arts Western set in Siam in the 1890s. A young Muay Thai warrior named Zieng seeks revenge on the tattooed man who killed his parents.

Cover of *The Key to the Indian* by Lynne Reid Banks (1998).

Only the Black Wizard can reverse tattooed cattle trader Singh's supernatural spells using the menstrual blood of her virgin daughter. With the help of his flying rocket, Zieng sets out to stop Singh's cattle rustling and return them to their owners.

Jim Ridley of *The New York Village Voice* (June 26, 2007) stated: "This wacko Thai import means to annihilate whatever brain cells survived all those sixth-grade viewings of *Infra-Man*. Director Chalerm Wongpim's skull-buster makes up in wild-eyed insanity (and excessive, arbitrary slow motion) what it lacks in acting, pacing and coherence."

See: *Dynamite Warrior*

Kid Colt and the Arizona Girl [Comic book; WW]

First publication: September 2006; Story: Jimmy Palmiotti, Justin Gray, Jim McCann; Art: Federica Manfredi, Jimmy Palmiotti, David Williams.

Escorting a stagecoach through Apache territory, Kid Colt and Arizona Annie quickly come to realize that one town is filled with weird townsfolk.

Kid Colt, Outlaw [Comic book character; Comic book; WW]

1. First appearance: *Kid Colt Hero of the West* #1 (August 1948); Publisher: Timely-Atlas–Marvel Comics.

Blaine Colt's reputation with a six-gun preceded him as he fled from the law rather than face trial for a murder he didn't commit.

Early stories were standard Western adventures with the occasional Weird Menace Western plot.

"Curse of the Chinese Idol" [WMW]

First publication: **Wild Western** #7 (May 1949); Story: Ernie Hart; Art: Russ Heath.

When Kid Colt hears of an accursed Chinese idol that brings death to anyone who comes into contact with it, he investigates.

In the early 1960s with the cross-over from Atlas to Marvel Comics, *Kid Colt* stories became increasingly weird, beginning with:

"The Ghost of Midnight Mountain" [WW]

First publication: *Kid Colt Outlaw* #93 (October 1960); Story: **Stan Lee**; Art: **Jack Keller**.

When Kid Colt encounters three "ghosts" on Midnight Mountain, he quickly discovers they are the cloaked figures of outlaw Caleb and his gang. But when Caleb and his men freeze in terror at the sight before them, Kid Colt wonders if the stories about the mountain being haunted are true.

"When the Witch Doctor Strikes" [WMW]

First publication: *Kid Colt Outlaw* #100 (September 1961); Story: Stan Lee; Art: Jack Keller.

Stage magician Rack Morgan claims he possesses supernatural powers and is a witch doctor. Comanche Indian Black Feather further perpetuates the reputation of Waroo the witch doctor to overthrow Chief Tall Bear. Meanwhile, Kid Colt is hiding out among the Comanche to escape the law.

"The Ghost of Silver City" [WMW]

First publication: *Kid Colt Outlaw* #102 (January 1962); Story: Stan Lee; Art: Jack Keller.

Outlaw Johnny Ringo fakes his death and returns as his ghost in a scheme to trap Kid Colt on a murder charge.

"The Invisible Gunman" [WMW]

First publication: *Kid Colt Outlaw* #116 (May 1964); Story: Stan Lee; Art: Jack Keller.

The "partner" of Doctor Danger, the Invisible Gunman strikes terror into the townsfolk by appearing as a hat and a gun with a disembodied voice. But it is all an illusion of skilled ventriloquist Doctor Danger, who throws his voice and controls the hat and gun with a powerful magnet.

"The Giant Monster of Midnight Valley" [SFW]

First publication: *Kid Colt Outlaw* #107 (November 1962); Story: Stan Lee; Art: Jack Keller.

The Weird Menace plot device with a logical explanation for seemingly supernatural events was common in Western comic books of the period. This issue from the early 1960s stands out as a genuine Science Fiction Western.

A gigantic telepathic and telekinetic alien creature is stranded in the Old West after its spacecraft is struck by a comet and is forced to crashland in the vicinity of Midnight Mountain.

Kid Colt Outlaw also featured borderline Weird Menace villains including hypnotistsBennington Brown and Orville Jones andthe armored and seemingly invulnerable IronMask.

The longest-running Western comic book character spanned 31 years, although the majority of issues from #140 (November 1969) onward were reprints of earlier issues with new cover art. Kid Colt later appeared as a guest star in various Marvel comic books including **The Avengers**, **Black Panther** and **Fantastic Four**.

2. First appearance: *Heroes Reborn: Young Allies* #1 (January 2000); Creators: Fabian Nicieza, Mark Bagley; Publisher: Marvel Comics.

A weird twist on the original Kid Colt character. Elric Freedom Whitemane undergoes government experiments that result in him becoming a humanoid horse! Fascinated by stories of the Old West, Elric decides to name himself after outlaw Kid Colt. In human form, Elric wears a cowboy costume to emulate his hero.

Killer Clowns [RPG book; WW]

Author: John Goff; First publication: 1999; ***Deadlands: Hell on Earth*** #3 Dime Novel series; Publisher: Pinnacle Entertainment Group.

Teller, gunslinger Gabriel Roth and female sniper Brooks enter Dempsey Island amuse-ment park in their search for hostages held by a renegade road gang. But the amusement park has dangers of its own in the form of monsters.

Killjoys (2015) [TV series; SW]

Premiere: June 19, 2015; Main Cast: Hannah Jon-Kamen as Dutch, Aaron Ashmore as John Jaqobis, Luke Macfarlane as D'avin Jaqobis; Creator: Michelle Lovretta; Executive producers: David Fortier, Ivan Scheenberg; 42 min.; Temple Street Productions, Bell Media, Universal Cable Productions; Color.

A trio of reclamation agents tracks criminals throughout a distant planetary system on the verge of war, known as the Quad. Leader of the Killjoys is former assassin Dutch accompanied by technical wiz-kid John and his brother D'avin, a combat tactics expert and elite soldier.

Some critics have compared ***Killjoys*** to ***Firefly***, although Killjoy's Space Western links are basically related to the theme of bounty hunters.

"King Solomon's Throne" [Pulp fiction; WMW]

Author: **Lon Williams**; Character: **Lee Winters**; First publication: ***Real Western Stories*** (October 1952)

Lee Winters encounters a person claiming to be King Solomon in Alkali Flats.

> "Follow us, Winters, to King Solomon's throne. Ride hard, too, or we shall outdistance you."
> They dug with spurs, and their horses pounded away. Winters, cursing himself for a great fool, raced after them, determined to get under this crazy business.
> Meanwhile, he was scared stiff. Sweat popped, and his face began to sting.
> In fifteen minutes they arrived. King Solomon sat upon a rocky throne, a lantern on a ledge beside him, a corpse—Lightning Latimer—stretched at his feet, pointing south.

King, Stephen (1947–) [Author]

A native of Portland, Maine, Stephen Edwin King established himself as a master of horror and fantasy fiction with the publication of his first novel *Carrie* (1974). King has proved to be a prolific writer novels and short stories, including those published under the pseudonym Richard Bachman between 1977 and 1984.

Many of his novels have been adapted into films and mini-series. To date he is the most successful horror author of all time with worldwide sales exceeding 100 million copies.

Selected works: *Salem's Lot* (1975), *The Shining* (1977), *The Dead Zone* (1979), *Misery* (1987), *The Green Mile* (1996), *Dolores Claiborne* (1992). Novel series: ***The Dark Tower*** (1982–2004).

Kingsway West [Comic book; WW]

First publication: November, 2015; Creator-Story: Greg Park; Art: Mirko Colak, Wil Quintana, Simon Bowland; Publisher: Dark Horse.

In an alternate history Old West, Chinese gunslinger and wild man of the frontier Kingsway West is searching for his wife after completing a 13-year prison sentence. On his quest to find her he meets a mysterious Chinese swordswoman and encounters monsters and magic.

Kolchak the Night Stalker [TV series]

Creator: Jeffrey Grant Rice; Main Cast: Darren McGavin as Carl Kolchak, Simon Oakland as Tony Vincenzo; 60 min. × 20; Francy Productions, Universal TV; Color.

Investigative reporter Carl Kolchak pursues supernatural forces, creatures and spirits in Chicago.

"Bad Medicine" (1:08) [WW]

Air date: November 29, 1974; Guest Stars: Richard Kiel as the Diablero, Victor Jory as Charles Rolling Thunder, Alice Ghostley as Dr. Agnes Temple; Creator: Jeffrey Grant Rice; Executive Producer: Cy Chermak; Story: L. Ford Neale, John Huff; Director: Alexander Grasshoff; 60 min.; Francy Productions, Universal TV; Color.

A shape-shifting Native American Indian known as a Diablero walks the earth for eternity gathering valuable jewels. The Diablero's power of hypnotism that results in the suicide of his victims must be turned against itself by Kolchak in order to destroy it.

"The Energy Eater" (1:10) [WW]

Air date: December 13, 1974; Guest Stars: Ruth McDevitt as Emily Cowles, William Smith as Jim Elkhorn, Michael Strong as Walter Green, Elaine Giftos as Nurse Janice Eisen; Executive Producer: Cy Chermak; Story: Arthur Rowe, Rudolph Borchert; Director: Alexander Grasshoff.

Kolchak investigates a hospital built by Native

American Indians where he is told patients are dying from fear. Medicine man Jim Elkhorn tells Kolchak of the legend of the Indian bear-god Matchemonedo and his resurrected spirit that feeds on energy. Kolchak knows he is in trouble when attempts to destroy the spirit only result in it feeding on the energy of the radioactive cobalt in the hospital.

Kung Fu (1972) [TV Series; WW]

Premiere: October 14, 1972; Main Cast: David Carradine as Kwai Chang Caine, Radames Pera as Young Kwai Chang Caine; Keye Luke as Master Po, Philip Ahn as Master Kan; Creator: Ed Spielman; Executive Producer: Jerry Thorpe; 62 × 50 min. + 75 min. pilot; Warner Bros. Television; Color.

Forced into exile following the murder of the emperor's nephew, Kwai Chang Caine (David Carradine) is pursued by bounty hunters and Chinese assassins in the Old West of 1870s America. After learning of a half-brother, Danny Caine, he decides to locate him.

An Emmy Award winning martial arts Western series. David Carradine's performance as Chinese-American Shaolin monk Kwai Chang Caine was in stark contrast to the prevalent Hollywood Western hero of the time. Carradine's unconventional offscreen lifestyle added to the mystique

Kung Fu (1972), a television series starring David Carradine as Kwai Chang Caine.

of the character who preached peace and love but wasn't averse to defending himself in spectacular fashion when required.

While early seasons emphasized traditional Western storylines with a kung fu twist, the third season explored supernatural Weird Western themes.

Weird Western episodes:

"SUPERSTITION" (1:12)

Air date: April 5, 1973; Story: Dave Moessinger; Teleplay: Ed Waters; Director: Charles S. Dubin.

Caine encounters prisoners at a labor camp who are held captive by both their deeds and their belief in an ancient Indian curse. Convinced that uncovering human bones results in death, they live in constant fear.

"THE BRUJO" (2:19)

Air date: October 25, 1973; Guest Star: Henry Darrow; Special Guest Star: Benson Fong; Teleplay: Katharyn Terry & Michael S. Michaelian; Director: Richard Lang.

At the request of his dying mother, Caine escorts a young boy to the village of San Martin where Caine attempts to break the curse of a Brujo that has been cast on the townsfolk and himself.

"BLOOD OF THE DRAGON PART ONE AND TWO" (3:07; 3:08)

Air date: September 14, 1974; 120 min; Special Guest Stars: Eddie Albert, Edward Albert; Teleplay: John T. Dugan; Director: Richard Lang.

Caine's premonition that his grandfather has died comes true. Meanwhile a group of Chinese assassins with the ability to summon demons are tracking him.

"CRY OF THE NIGHT BEAST" (3:01)

Air date: October 19, 1974; Special Guest Star: Stefanie Powers; Story: Abe Polsky, Ed Waters; Teleplay: Ed Waters; Director: Richard Lang.

A distressed baby buffalo and the cry of a young child become joined in time as Caine protects the buffalo calf and its mother from hunters.

"THIS VALLEY OF TERROR" (3:03)

Air date: September 28, 1974; Special Guest Star: Howard Duff; Story: Katharyn & Michael Michaelian; Teleplay: Katharyn Michaelian; Director: Harry Harris.

Caine befriends a young woman who has visions of future events and of the signs of the dragon and the tiger burned into his forearms.

"The Demon God" (3:09)

Air date: December 13, 1974; Story: George Clayton Johnson; Teleplay: George Clayton Johnson, David Michael Korn; Director: David Carradine.

The delirium caused by a scorpion sting takes Caine back to his time as a temple student in China when a member of the royal family poisoned him to discover what awaited his dying father beyond death.

"The Vanishing Image" (3:06)

Air date: December 20, 1974; Guest Star: Lew Ayres; Teleplay: Gustave Field Director: Barry Crane.

An Indian attacks Caine and seeks to kill a photographer for taking a picture of him that he believes has stolen his spirit.

"One Step to Darkness" (3:15)

Air date: January 25, 1975; Story: Gerald Sanford; Teleplay: Robert Sherman, Theodore Apstein; Director: Marc Daniels

A drug addicted Army wife introduces Caine to a demon who makes claims on his life.

"Battle Hymn" (3:17)

Air date: February 8, 1975; Special Guest Star: Julian "Cannonball" Adderly; Story: D. C. Fontana; Teleplay: Herman Miller; Director: Barry Crane.

Traveling musicians meet up with Caine as they search for a magical cave.

Kung Fu: The Legend Continues (1993) [TV series]

Main Cast: David Carradine as Kwai Chang Caine, Chris Potter as Peter Caine; Executive Producer: Michael Sloan; 88 × 44 min.; Warner Bros. Television; Color.

Modern-day sequel to the original series. The grandson (David Carradine) of the original Kwai Chang Caine and his son Peter Caine (Chris Potter) are reunited fifteen years following a fire that destroyed the Shaolin Temple in California where they both lived.

"Gunfighters" (3:06) [WW]

Air date: February 27, 1995; Guest Cast: Clint Walker as Cheyenne Bodie, James Drury as Deacon, Clu Gulager as Deputy Clay Hardin, Robert Fuller as McBride; Story: Michael Sloan; Director: Jon Cassar.

Kwai Chang Caine travels through time to the Old West where he exchanges places with his grandfather Kwai Chang Caine. This offbeat episode marks the return of Clint Walker as Cheyenne Bodie and features former *The Virginian* stars James Drury and Clu Gulager.

"Cool Ride" (4:11) [WW]

Air date: September 30, 1996; Guest Cast: James Drury as Dr. Frieze, David Hewlett as Dr. Nickie, William Campbell as Wolfe, Deborah Duchene as Xenia, William Dunlop as Chief of Detectives Frank Strenlich, Belinda Metz as Detective Jody Powell; Writer: Phil Combest; Director: Jon Cassar.

Contemporary Western starring Drury as Dr. Freize, a carnival ride barker who happens to be the reincarnation of Deacon from "**Gun-fighters.**" Frieze uses mind control on chosen people who go on the ride and scares them to death. After their demise, he steals their souls to keep him alive.

Lansdale, Joe R. (1951–) [Comic book writer; Author]

Born in Gladewater, Texas, Lansdale began his writing career on *Mike Shayne's Mystery Magazine* before turning to horror, Westerns and adventure stories. His best-known comic book work includes stories for **Batman** and **Jonah Hex**. Apart from his Weird Western novels and stories, Lansdale continues to work in the mystery genre with a series of novels featuring Texas sleuths Hap Collins and Leonard Pine.

Selected works: *Dead in the West* (1983), *The Magic Wagon* (1986), *Savage Season* (1990), *Mucho Mujo* (1994), *Bad Chili* (1997), *The Bottoms* (2000), *A Fine Dark Line* (2002).

Lansdale and Truman's Dead Folks [Graphic novel; WW]

First publication: June 2004; Story: **Joe R. Lansdale**; Art: Tim Truman; Publisher: Avatar.

A bounty hunter must contend with zombies after he captures his prey.

"Lantern in the Sky" [Pulp fiction; WW]

Author: **Lon Williams**; Character: **Lee Winters**; *Real Western Stories* (June 1955)

Two strangers in a tavern claim to be reincarnations of the same famous poets.

Lash LaRue [Comic book character]

A comic strip character based on the popular Western film actor.

"The Case of the Supernatural" [WW]

First publication: *Six-Gun Heroes* #13 (March

Lash LaRue in "The Case of the Supernatural" from *Six-Gun Heroes* #13 (March 1952). Art by Doug Wildey. © 2009 AC Comics/Nightveil Media, Inc. Used with permission.

1952); Art: Doug Wildey; Publisher: Fawcett Publications.

When a skeptical Lash LaRue travels to Carson Gulch to investigate deaths attributed to a vampire, he is amazed to discover vampires really do exist.

The Last Crusaders [RPG book; WW]

Author: Shane Lacy Hensley; First publication: 1998; Setting: **Deadlands: Hell on Earth the Wasted West**; Publisher: Pinnacle Entertainment Group.

Secrets of the men and women of the righteous order of the Templars revealed. Includes the Wasted West adventure "The Destroyer."

The Last Guardian [Novel; SFW]

Author: **David Gemmell**; First publication: London: Random, 1990.

The last guardian, Jon Shannow the pistoleer, must close the portal of time between past and present to stop immeasurable evil from being unleashed. But to accomplish this, Shannow travels through the City of Beasts and the realm of the Dark Queen to find and take possession of the Sword of God.

See: **Jerusalem Man; Bloodstone: A Jon Shannow Adventure**

The Last Sane Cowboy and Other Stories [Graphic novel; WW]

First publication: April 2007; Story-Art: Daniel Merlin Goodbrey; Publisher: AiT/Planet Lar.

Anthology of Weird Western stories, including ones about a man who bleeds scorpions, talking horses, a girl who can smell the future and a cowboy scorpion.

El Latigo en las Momias Asesinas (1980) [Film; Mexico; WW]

Premiere: October 2, 1980; Main Cast: Juan Miranda as El Latigo, Rosa Gloria Chagoyán, Marcko D'Carlo; Executive Producer: Lic. Rafael Perez Grovas; Story: Ángel Rodríguez; Producer-Director: Roberto Rodríguez; 82 min.; Novelty Internacional Films S.A.., Películas Latinoamericanas S.A.; Spanish; Color.

El Latigo fights a group of killer mummies who target a beautiful girl and her family in this third film in the series.

El Látigo contra Satanás (1979) [Film; Mexico; WW]

Premiere: October 4, 1979; Main Cast: Juan Miranda as El Latigo, Noé Murayama, Yolanda Ochoa, Rubén Rojo as Padre; Executive Producer: Paco del Busto; Producer: Roberto Rodríguez; Story: Alfredo B. Crevenna, Roberto Rodríguez, Ramón Obón; Director: Alfredo B. Crevenna; 80 min.; Películas Latinoamericanas S.A.; Spanish; Color.

El Latigo clashes with Satan and his minions. Second film in the *El Latigo* series.

Latigo Kid Western [Comic book; WW]

"PARANORMAL GUNFIGHTER OF THE WEST"

First publication: 1988; Story: **Bill Black**; Art: Bill Black, **John Severin**; Publisher AC Comics.

In the late 1870s, young range rider Charlie Starrett discovers he has special abilities of mind over matter. Doc Marvel develops Starrett's paranormal powers as he travels the Old West with Marvel's medicine show. Charlie finally decides the time is right to venture out on his own and fights crime as the masked gunfighter, The Latigo Kid.

Guest stars include **The Black Phantom**, *Red Mask* and *The Durango Kid*, plus Steve McQueen as bounty hunter Josh Randall from the TV Western *Wanted Dead or Alive*. A mixture of Bill Black artwork and John Severin artwork from *Billy the Kid* creates a new story.

Black recalled, "Doc Marvel was a jab at Marvel Comics. Doc Marvel became Doctor Lieber, one of AC's vilest villains. He headed the Paragon Foundation and intended to live forever. He was named Lieber because **Stan Lee**'s real name is Lieber."

See: **Paragon**

Law Dogs [RPG book; WW]

Author: Steven Long; First publication: 1998; Setting: **Deadlands: The Weird West**; Publisher: Pinnacle Entertainment Group.

A guide to upholding the law and lawmen including The Pinkerton National Detective Agency, U.S. Marshals, U.S. Secret Service, Sheriffs and Texas Rangers. Includes the adventure "On Top of Old Skull Hill, All Covered in Blood" and a guide to the art of Hexslingers and Hexes.

Lee, Stan (1922–) [Comic book editor, writer, publisher]

Born in New York City, Stan Lee's first published work was the two-page text story "Captain America Foils the Traitor's Revenge" for *Captain America* #3 in May 1941. Although born Stanley Martin Lieber, he signed his work Stan Lee and set in motion a career that revolutionized the comics industry.

The cousin of publisher Martin Goodman's wife, Lee succeeded Joe Simon as editor of Timely Comics at the young age of 19 and entered the U.S. Army the following year, serving until the end of World War II in 1945. When he returned to Timely, the superhero titles were on a downward slide to cancellation. Horror, science fiction and Westerns took prominence. Lee provided plots for Timely's (now known as Atlas) various titles. The plots were then passed to the writers who created working scripts for the artists. This process became more flexible in the 1960s when Lee adopted the "Marvel Method" that involved the artist providing input at an earlier stage.

Although the majority of Western titles involved standard storylines, Lee did include fantastic elements that became increasingly weird when Atlas imploded due to weak sales and was succeeded by Marvel Comics. This period of transition proved a low point in Lee's career and he seriously considered leaving the industry. But he stayed and ushered in the "Marvel Age," turning the comic industry on its head with the co-creation of top-selling titles *Spider-Man* and the **Fantastic Four**.

The Western titles continued to be published but were largely ignored by a comic-reading public mainly interested in the trials and tribulations of Lee's new brand of "superhero with problems." By 1967 most of the remaining Western titles contained reprints with new cover art aimed at fooling the reader into thinking they were buying new stories. An attempt a reviving **Ghost Rider** failed.

In 1972 Lee was promoted to publisher and ultimately became chairman emeritus of Marvel Enterprises Inc. and executive producer of the motion picture productions. The expansion of Marvel into film and television has kept his creations alive but the Western characters *Kid Colt Outlaw*, *Two-Gun Kid* and *Rawhide Kid* have to date taken a back seat in film adaptations. In 2001 Lee, Gill Champion and Arthur Leiberman founded the production company POW! (Purveyors of Wonder) Entertainment Inc. to specialize in the new characters and franchises created by Lee.

Lee Winters [Pulp fiction character; WW]

Weird Western stories with a preternatural twist by **Lon Williams** featuring Deputy Marshal Lee Winters of Forlorn Gap and his horse Cannon Ball as they encounter all manner of strange happenings in the surrounding environs of Alkali

Lee Winters from **"Master of Indecision,"** *Real Western Stories* (April 1953).

Flats, Elkhorn Pass, Wild Cat Gulch, Black Fox Gap, Cow Creek, Goat Head Pass, Gallitena Gulch and Banshee Creek. The mature Winters is married to the beautiful young widow Myra. The stories were published throughout the 1950s in *Real Western Stories*.

Left for Dead (2007) [Film; Argentina; WW]

Premiere: September 8, 2007; Main Cast: Victoria Maurette as Clementine Templeton, Mariana Seligmann as Michelle Black; Producers: Kamel Krifa, Patricia K. Meyer; Story: Chad Leslie; Director: Albert Pyun; Sophia Productions; Color.

A vengeful demonic spirit traps a criminal and pursuing posse headed by Clementine Templeton in the Mexican ghost town of Amnesty.

Leftovers [RPG book; WW]

Author: Shane Lacy Hensley; First publication: 1998; *Deadlands: Hell on Earth* Dime novel series #1; Publisher: Pinnacle Entertainment Group.

Teller and Tasha attempt to stop a war between the norms and muties in the Wasted West.

Legend (1995) [TV series; SFW]

Hack dime novel writer Ernest Pratt (Richard Dean Anderson) is mistaken for the romantic hero he created, Nicodemus Legend.

The Bartok Steam-Powered Town and Country Quadrovelocipede and Electro-fulminators plus a pair of wings that Legend puts to good use are just a few of the various inventions of Hungarian scientist and genius Janos Bartok (John de Lancie), providing the series with science fiction and steampunk elements.

Premiere: April 18, 1995; Main Cast: Richard Dean Anderson as Ernest Pratt, John de Lancie as Janos Bartok, Mark Adair-Rios as Huitzilopochtli Ramos, Jarrad Paul as Skeeter; Creators: Bill Dial, Michael Piller; Executive Producers: Michael Greenburg, Michael Piller; 60 min.; Gekko Film Corp., United Paramount Network (UPN); Color.

Season One

Birth of a Legend (1:01); Mr. Pratt Goes to Sheridan (1:02); Legend on His President's Secret Service (1:03); Custer's Next to Last Stand (1:04); The Life, Death, and Life of Wild Bill Hickok (1:05); Knee-High Noon (1:06); The Gospel According to Legend (1:07); Bone of Contention (1:08); Revenge of the Herd (1:09); Fall of a Legend (1:10); Clueless in San Francisco (1:11); Skeletons in the Closet (1:12)

The Legend of Ghostwolf (2005) [Film; WW]

Premiere: July 19, 2005; Main Cast: John Weathers as Sarge, Hugo Perez as Jalisco; Producer-Story-Director: Shane Scott; 84 min.; Color.

When Jalisco and renegade soldiers search for Confederate gold in the Tonkawa gold mine, they encounter the monstrous guardian.

The Legend of Joe Moon [Comic book; WW]

First publication: March 2008; Story: Gonzalo Ventura; Art: Manuel and Leonardo Silva; Publisher: Pit Brothers Productions.

Horror Western featuring Clint Eastwood lookalike Joe Moon, a bounty hunter who transforms into a werewolf. Described by the publisher as "The first Spaghetti Lycanthro-Western."

Legend of the Phantom Rider (2002) [Film; WW]

Premiere: 2002; Main Cast: Denise Crosby as Sarah Jenkins, Robert McRay as Blade/Pelgidium, Angus Scrimm as Preacher; Producers: Alex Erkiletian, Hans Rodionoff, Tod Swindell; Story: Robert Ray; Director: Alex Erkiletian; 100 min.; Rolle's Range Farm Productions; Color.

Blade brutally murders Sarah Jenkins' husband and son and hold a town hostage until the mysterious supernatural phantom rider known as Pelgidium appears on the scene to exact revenge.

Legends of the DC Universe [Comic book; SFW]

"The Trail of the Traitor" #20–21 (September-October 1999); Editor: Mike Carlin; Story: Steven Grant; Pencils: Mike Zeck; Inks: Klaus Janson.

The red-skinned *Green Lantern* Abin Sur tracks intergalactic warlord Traitor to Arizona territory in 1882 and encounters racial prejudice from the local townsfolk.

Legion of Super Heroes (2006) [Animated TV series]

The Adventures of teenage super-heroes from 1,000 years into the future.

"Unnatural Alliances" (2:07)

Air date: November 17, 2007; Voice Cast: Jeff Black as **Terra-Man**, Phil Morris as Imperiex, Madison Davenport as Abel, Yuri Lowenthall as Kell-El, Kari Wahlgren as Duo Damsel, Michael Cornaccia as Bouncing Boy, Bumper Robinson as Star Boy, Adam Wylie as Brainiac 5; Producers: James Tucker, Linda

M. Steiner; Story: Keith Damron; Director: Brandon Vietti; 20 min; Kids' WB; Color.

Terra-Man and his robotic bounty hunters from the 41st century travel to the past to search for young orphan Abel, who holds the key to his future existence.

The Lemonade Kid [Comic book character; WMW]

First appearance: *Bobby Benson's B-Bar-B Riders* #1 (1950); Art: **Bob Powell**; Publisher: Magazine Enterprises, Parkway Publishing Company. AC Comics.

His shirt is golden and his twin sixguns are steel blue! His drink is lemonade...

Tex Mason is a busy man. As foreman of B-Bar-B Ranch he is guardian to orphan Bobby Benson. But unknown to all, he is also a security officer for the F.B.I. who fights crime as the Lemonade Kid.

The Lemonade Kid featured weird and unusual characters including a criminal known as The Spider who dressed in a spider outfit and caught his enemies in webs. Bob Powell provided the artwork for the 13-issue run in *Bobby Benson's B-Bar-B Riders* with **Gardner Fox** and Powell providing the majority of the stories.

"THE CLUTCHING CLAWS OF TERROR" [WMW]

First published: *Bobby Benson's B-Bar-B-Riders* #13 (February 1952); Art: Bob Powell; Publisher: Magazine Enterprises.

When archeologists discover a cave which houses ancient petrified Indians and the gold and jewels of their civilization, a winged, clawed "creature" which guards the treasure attacks and kills them. But the "creature" is just a fake created by thieves so they can take the treasure for themselves.

This was the only story to feature Bobby Benson and Lemonade Kid together.

Life with Snarky Parker (1950) [Children's TV series; Comic book; WW]

1. Premiere: January 9, 1950; Creators: Bill and Cora Baird; Producers: Bill and Cora Baird, Frank Fazakas; Director: Yul Brynner; 15 min.; CBS Television Network; b/w.

Marionette Western set in the Old West town of Hotrock. Deputy Sheriff Snarky Parker and his horse Heathcliffe attempt to rid Hotrock of villainous Ronald Rodent.

2. Comic book
First publication: August 1950; One issue; Publisher: Fox Feature Syndicate, Inc.

Sheriff Snarky's attempt to return hidden gold dust to a cave in the hills results in an encounter with Gordon the Ghost and the dastardly Nolan.

Light the Fuse ... Sartana Is Coming (1971) [Film; Italy-Spain; WW]

U.S. release title for *Una Nuvola di polvere ... un grido di morte ... arriva Sartana*.

The Lemonade Kid in "Webs of Doom!" from *Bobby Benson's B-Bar-B Riders* #4 (November-December 1950). Story by Gardner Fox, art by Bob Powell. © 2009 AC Comics/Nightveil Media, Inc. Used with permission.

The Lemonade Kid in "The Webs of Doom!" page 1. Story by Gardner Fox, art by Bob Powell. © 2009 AC Comics/Nightveil Media, Inc. Used with permission.

The Lightning Warrior (1931) [Film serial; WMW]

Premiere: 1931; Main Cast: Rin Tin Tin as Rinty, Frankie Darro as Jimmy Carter, George Brent as Alan Scott, Pat O'Malley as Sheriff A. W. Brown, Georgia Hale as Dianne; Producer: Nat Levine; Story: Ford Beebe, Wyndham Gittens, Colbert Clark; Directors: Armand Schaefer, Ben Kline; 250 min.; Mascot Pictures Corporation; b/w.

A cloaked figure known as the "Wolf Man" is terrorizing a community and stirring Indian unrest against settlers. Rin-Tin-Tin's final serial.

Chapter Titles: 1. *The Drums of Doom*; 2. *The Wolf Man*; 3. *Empty Saddles*; 4. *Flaming Arrows*; 5. *The Invisible Enemy*; 6. *The Fatal Name*; 7. *The Ordeal of Fire*; 8. *The Man Who Knew*; 9. *Traitor's Hour*; 10. *The Secret of the Cane*; 11. *Red Shadows*; 12. *Painted Faces*.

Lilly the Witch (2003) [Animated TV series; Germany-Ireland]

An enchanted book allows Lilly to travel through time with the help of Hector the pint-sized dragon. But she must keep the magical book a secret to protect it from evildoers. Based on the series of books by Knister.

"Lilly in the Wild West" (1:03) [SFW]
Air date: September 7, 2004; 25 min.; Magma Films Ltd., Trixter Film, Vivatoon; Color.

Traveling back in time to prove there were girl sheriffs in the Old West, Lilly is asked to be the new sheriff and to capture the gang that has kidnapped Hector.

Liminal States [Novel; WW]

Author: Zak Parsons; First publication: New York: Citadel Press, 2012.

New Mexico Territory, 1874. Gideon Long has been involved in an affair with Old West officer Warren Groves' wife, Annie. Long and Groves cross paths and discover a pool with magical restorative powers that allows a person to cheat death. The pool also creates duplicates of the pair. With the power of resurrection at their disposal the pair continues into the 1950s and beyond. But in the process they have empowered the pool, which has its own agenda.

Little Gods [Book Anthology; WW]

Author: Tim Pratt; First publication: Canton OH: Prime Books, 2003.

This collection of four poems and fifteen tales of fantasy and horror includes the Weird Western "Bleeding West." This short story about good and evil spirits in the Old West was originally published in *Deep Outside* in August 2001.

Little House on the Prairie (1974) [TV series]

Main Cast: Michael Landon as Charles Ingalls; Karen Grassle as Caroline Ingalls, Melissa Gilbert as Laura Ingalls, Matthew Laborteaux as Albert Quinn Ingalls, Lindsay Sydney Greenbush as Carrie Ingalls, Katherine MacGregor as Harriet Oleson, Richard Bull as Nels Oleson. Alison Arngrim as Nellie Oleson, Jonathan Gilbert as Willie Oleson.

"The Lake Kezia Monster" (5:19) [WMW]
Air date: February 12, 1979; Guest cast: Hermione Baddeley as Kezia Horn; Executive Producer: Michael Landon; Story: John T. Dugan; Director: Michael Landon; 60 min.; Ed Friendly Productions, National Broadcasting Company (NBC); Color.

When Mrs. Oleson decides to foreclose on Kezia Horn's property for non-payment of property taxes she purchases it. Laura and Albert Ingalls and their friends decide to scare Mrs. Oleson into returning the elderly woman's home by creating a lake monster.

"The Werewolf of Walnut Grove" (6:14) [WMW]
Air date: January 7, 1980; Guest Cast: Tod Thompson as Bartholomew Slater Jr., Sandy Ward as Bartholomew Slater Sr., Patricia Donahue as Mrs. Slater, Lucy Lee Flippen as Eliza Jane Wilder; Executive Producer: Michael Landon; Story: John T. Dugan; Director: William F. Claxton; 60 min.; Ed Friendly Productions, National Broadcasting Company (NBC); Color.

When bully Bartholomew Slater intimidates schoolmarm Miss Wilder to the point where she sees leaving Walnut Grove as her only option, Laura and Albert devise a plan. Albert poses as a werewolf to scare the bully into submission, but the plan backfires and it is left to student power to finally make Slater see the error of his ways.

"Little Sisters of Eluria" [Short story; WW]

Author: **Stephen King**; First publication: *Everything's Eventual: Five Dark Tales*; Publisher: 2002.

Roland Deschain wanders alone on the trail of the Man in Black following the fall of Gilead and slaughter of the Gunslingers at the Battle of Jericho. In the ghost town of Eluria situated in the Desatoya Mountains Roland encounters a lame dog, a drowned boy, the tinkling of bells and a group of mutants who attack him. When Roland stirs into consciousnesses he is surrounded by the Little Sisters of Eluria. But the female healers are far from sisters of mercy and closer to sisters of death.

King's short story is a prequel the first volume

of his *Dark Tower* series **Dark Tower: The Gunslinger**.

A Little Time in Texas [Novel; SFW]

Author: Joan Johnston; First publication: Silhouette Desire, 1992.

Angela Taylor, rescued from renegades by a Texas Ranger in 1864, is now trapped in modern-day America, surrounded by people who don't believe she is from the past.

Lobo Elseworlds [Comic book; SFW]

"A Fistful of Bastiches" Annual #2 (1994); Editor: Dan Rasplar; Publisher: DC Comics.

Anthology of Western strips in the DC Elseworlds Universe.

Lois and Clark: The New Adventures of Superman [TV series]

Main Cast: Dean Cain as Clark Kent-Superman, Terri Hatcher as Lois Lane.

Adventures of Superman, a.k.a Clark Kent, and his life at the *Daily Planet* with Lois Lane, Jimmy Olsen and Perry White.

"Tempus Fugitive" (2:18) [SFW]

Air date: March 26, 1995; Guest Cast: Don Swayze as Jesse James, Joshua Devane as Frank James, Terry Kiser as H.G. Wells, Lane Davies as Tempus; Story: Jack Weinstein, Lee Hutson; Director; James R. Bagdonas; 60 min.; Warner Bros.; Color.

Author H.G. Wells prevents Tempus from killing **Superman** as a child when he travels back in time to the Old West of 1866 while Lois Lane and Clark Kent time travel to 1966 where they meet Frank and Jesse James.

Lone [Comic book; SFW]

First publication: September 2003; Story: Stuart Moore; Art: Jerome Opena, Alberto Ponticelli, John Wycough; Six-issue mini-series; Publisher: Rocket Comics-Dark Horse Comics.

Legendary gun-for-hire Lone must save the post-apocalyptic town of Desolation from zombie mutants.

The Lone Ranger (1966) [Animated TV series; WW]

Premiere: September 10, 1966; Voice cast: Michael Rye as The Lone Ranger, Shepard Menken as Tonto; Executive producer: Arthur A. Jacobs; 27 × 30 min; Lone Ranger Productions, Jack Wrather Corporation; Color.

THE LONE RANGER (2013) © 2013

The Lone Ranger (2013), starring Johnny Depp as Tonto (Walt Disney Pictures, Jerry Bruckheimer Films).

Although based on the familiar radio, television and film character, this animated series introduced a Weird Western perspective. The dark atmosphere of the episodes with plots involving ghosts, witches, vampires, monsters, devils and villains such as Doctor Destructo and Puppetmaster showed influences of the TV series *The Wild, Wild, West* that was popular at the time.

Season One

The Trickster/Crack of Doom/The Human Dynamo (1:01); *Ghost Riders/Wrath of the Sun God/Day of the Dragon* (1:02); *The Secret Army of General X/The Cat People/Night of the Vampire* (1:03); *Bear Claw/The Hunter and the Hunted/ Mephisto* (1:04); *Revenge of the Mole/Frog People/Terror in Toyland* (1:05); *Black Mask of*

Revenge/The Sacrifice/Puppetmaster (1:06); *Valley of the Dead/Forest of Death/The Fly* (1:07); *A Time to Die/Ghost Tribe of Comanche Flat/Attack of the Lilliputians* (1:08); *Circus of Death/The Brave/Cult of the Black Widow* (1:09); *El Conquistador/Snow Creature/The Prairie Pirate* (1:10); *Man of Silver/Nightmare in Whispering Pine/Sabotage* (1:11); *Mastermind/The Lost Tribe of Golden Giants/Monster of Scavenger Crossing* (1:12); *The Black Panther/Thomas the Great/Island of the Black Widow* (1:13)

Season Two

Premiere: September 9, 1967

Paddle Wheeling Pirates/A Day at Death's Head Pass/Mad, Mad, Mad, Mad Scientist (2:01); *The Kid/Stone Hawk/Sky Raiders* (2:02); *The Man from Pinkerton/Tonto and the Devil Spirit/Deadly Glassman* (2:03); *Black Knight of Death/Taka/Fire Rain* (2:04); *The Secret of Warlock/Wolfmaster/Death Hunt* (2:05); *Terrible Tiny Tom/Fire Monster/The Iron Giant* (2:06); *Towntamers, Inc./Curse of the Devil Doll/It Came from Below* (2:07); *The Trickster/Crack of Doom/The Human Dynamo* (2:08); *Mister Happy/Birdman/Doctor Destructo* (2:09); *Mister Midas/Black Arrow/The Rainmaker* (2:10); *Flight of the Hawk/The Avenger/Battle at Barnaby's Bend* (2:11); *Puppetmaster's Revenge/Reign of the Queen Bee/Kingdom of Terror* (2:12); *Quicksilver/The Legend of Cherokee Smith/The Day the West Stood Still* (2:13); *Border Rats/The Lash and the Arrow/Spectre of Death* (2:14)

The Lone Ranger (2013) [Film; WW]

Premiere: July 3, 2013; Main Cast: Armie Hammer as John Reid/Lone Ranger; Johnny Depp as Tonto; William Fichter as Butch Cavendish, Tom Wilkinson as Latham Cole, Ruth Wilson as Rebecca Reid, Helena Bonham Carter as Red Harrington; Screenplay: Justin Haythe, Ted Elliott, Terry Rossio; Producer-Director: Gore Verbinski; 149 min.; Walt Disney Pictures, Jerry Bruckheimer Films; Color.

An aged Tonto recalls his days with John Reid and how Reid became the masked man following the massacre of Texas Rangers, including Reid's elder brother Dan, by infamous outlaw Butch Cavendish. When Reid is rescued after being left for dead by Cavendish and his men he regains consciousness in a grave dug by his rescuer, Comanche spirit warrior Tonto. Reid, now calling himself The Lone Ranger teams up with Tonto as they track down Cavendish and become involved in a web of corruption.

Artist Kirby Sattler licensed his work to be adapted for the film. "It just so happened Sattler had painted a bird flying directly behind the warrior's head. It looked to me like it was sitting on top. I thought: Tonto's got a bird on his head. It's his spirit guide in a way. It's dead to others, but it's not dead to him. It's very much alive."—Johnny Depp—*Entertainment Weekly* (April 22, 2012).

Reviewers were generally critical of the film. *The New York Times* critic A. O. Scott (July 2, 2013) stated: "This is an ambitious movie designed as a popcorn throwaway, nothing less than an attempt to reinvigorate and make fun of not just its source but also nearly every other western ever made. In trying to balance grandiosity with playfulness, to lampoon cowboy-and-Indian clichés while taking account of a history of violence, greed and exploitation, it descends into nerve-racking incoherence."

Richard Corliss of *Time Magazine* (July 2, 2013) added: "Even if it worked, the movie probably wouldn't connect with the worldwide mass of moviegoers because … it's a western. The films that have borrowed from that genre were smart enough to add space ships, giant monsters and a palette more colorful than Monument Valley brown."

The film's tortured stop-start production history and inflated budget of $215 million placed pressure on the film to have a strong opening weekend at the box-office. Bad reviews and a lukewarm response from audiences resulted in a weak $29,210,849 opening and a major loss for Walt Disney.

Lone Ranger and Tonto [Comic book; WW]

First publication: August 1994; Story: **Joe R. Lansdale**; Art: Tim Truman, Rick Magyar; Four-issue mini-series; Publisher: Topps Comics.

Lansdale's unique Weird Western spin on the classic characters involving stolen cursed Aztec artifacts.

The Lone Rider in Ghost Town (1941) [Film; WMW]

Premiere: May 16, 1941; Main Cast: George Houston as Tom Cameron/The Lone Rider, Al "Fuzzy" St. John as Fuzzy Jones, Alaine Brandes as Helen Clark, Alden Chase as Robert Sinclair, Edward Peil Sr. as Dennis Clark, Budd Buster as "Moosehide" Larsen; Producer: Sigmund Neufeld; Story: Joseph

O'Donnell; Director: Sigmund Newfield; 64 min.; Producers Releasing Corporation; b/w.

Robert Sinclair and his gang use a supposedly haunted ghost town as a base for their gold mining operations.

Lone Star and the Kansas Wolves
[Novel; WW]

Author: Wesley Ellis; First publication: New York: Jove, October 1982.

On the dusty Kansas plains Hungarian immigrants Jessica Starbuck and martial arts master Ki, meet a foe that has followed them to Starbuck land in America. Jessica seeks revenge on the cartel who murdered her father, while Ki protects Jessica and her Starbuck empire from both man and werewolf.

"Lone Star Planet" [Magazine fiction; SW]

Authors: H. Beam Piper, John J. McGuire; First publication: *Fantastic Universe Science Fiction*, Vol. 7, No. 3, March 1957

A junior diplomat is assigned to a planet of Texans with dinosaur-sized cattle.

> They had found Capella IV, a Terra-type planet, with a slightly higher mean temperature, a lower mass and lower gravitational field, about one-quarter water and three-quarters land-surface, at a stage of evolutionary development approximately that of Terra during the late Pliocene. They also found supercow, a big mammal looking like the unsuccessful attempt of a hippopotamus to impersonate a dachshund and about the size of a nuclear-steam locomotive. On New Texas' plains, there were billions of them; their meat was fit for the gods of Olympus. So New Texas had become the meat-supplier to the galaxy.
> See: *A Planet for Texans*

"Lone Star Traveler" [Short story; SFW]

Editors: William F. Nolan, William K. Schafer; First publication: *California Sorcery: A Group Celebration*; Abingdon MD: Cemetery Dance, 1999.

A time traveler visits Texas in 1910 in an attempt to save the life of an important person from the year 2060.

Lone Stars: The Texas Rangers [RPG book; WW]

Author: Christopher McGlothlin; First publication: 2001; Setting: *Deadlands: The Weird West*; System: Classic and D20; Publisher: Pinnacle Entertainment Group.

Guide to the Confederated States organization Texas Rangers.

Longarm and the Golden Ghost (# 302) [Novel; WMW]

Author: Tabor Evans; First publication: New York: Jove Books, 2003.

In Tascosa, West Texas Longarm investigates a mysterious murderous Conquistador who is spooking the locals with his suit of golden armor and ghostly appearance.

Longarm and the Haunted Whorehouse (#284) [Novel; WMW]

Author: Tabor Evans; First publication: New York: Jove Books, 2007.

Marshal Long goes undercover as Buck Crawford and heads to Animas Point to investigate reports of a haunted house of ill repute.

U.S. Deputy Marshal Custis Long alias Longarm works out of Denver, Colorado in the 1880s. First published in 1978 and penned by various authors under the name Tabor Evans, the series came to a conclusion in December, 2014.

Longarm and the Hell Riders (#345) [Novel; WMW]

Author: Tabor Evans; First publication: New York: Jove Books, 2007.

While investigating train robber Dog McCluskey Longarm learns of marauders who are terrorizing locals with their fiery heads. Longarm must seek the truth behind the Hell Riders.

Longarm and the Tabor Legend (#143) [Novel; WMW]

Author: Tabor Evans; First publication: New York: Jove Books, 1990.

The legend of Wild Bill Longley surfaces again when Marshal Long investigates the death of a fellow lawman. Rumors circulate that the killer is Wild Bill himself or his ghost.

Longarm and the Talking Spirit (#305) [Novel; WW]

Author: Tabor Evans; First publication: New York: Jove Books, 2004.

Longarm consults a Ute spirit in his quest to find the murderer of the Indian maiden Blue Quail Singing.

Longarm and the Vanishing Virgin (#245) [Novel; WMW]

Author: Tabor Evans; First publication: New York: Jove Books, 1999.

Longarm investigates a bail-bond outfit whose business revolves around voodoo and murder.

Longarm and the Voodoo Queen (#228) [Novel; WW]

Author: Tabor Evans; First publication: New York: Jove Books, 1997.

U.S. Marshal Long goes undercover to investigate the death of a Deputy Federal Marshal in the swampland of New Orleans. He uncovers a smuggling ring and voodoo at work in the form of a Cajun beauty and a voodoo doll made in the likeness of the murdered Deputy.

Longarm and the Wendigo (#4) [Novel; WMW]

Author: Tabor Evans; First publication: New York: Jove Books, 1979.

The Blackfoot Indians believe the Great Devil known as Wendigo is stalking their reservation in Montana and leaving a trail of blood and corpses. Marshal Custis Long has his own theories about the gruesome deaths.

Longarm on a Witch-Hunt (# 279) [Novel; WMW]

Author: Tabor Evans; First publication: New York: Jove Books, 2002.

On the trail of Bull Stennett and his gang hiding in a valley at the foothills of the Bighorn Mountains, Marshal Long is told by locals that the valley is haunted by witches who pose by day as the bewitching Crawford sisters.

"Long Live the King" [Pulp fiction; WW]

Author: **Lon Williams**; Character: **Lee Winters**; First publication: **Real Western Stories** (April 1955).

Deputy Marshal Lee Winters is puzzled when a strangely dressed man calling himself King Kiff-Wiff rides into town on an enormous black hog. Is he a ghost or the reincarnation of an ancient Egyptian pyramid builder?

Lord of Thunder [Novel; Juvenile: SW]

Author: **Andre Norton**; First published: New York: Harcourt, Brace & World Inc., 1962.

The tribes of Arzor join the Norbies as they journey into the uncharted country beyond the mountains known as the Blue. The **Beast Master** and Storm must follow them into the forbidden country to prevent the Arzor from suffering a horrible fate.

The second novel featuring exiled Native American Indian **Hosteen Storm.**

Lost Angels [RPG book; WW]

Authors: Matt Forbeck with John Goff, Paul Beakley; First publication: 1998; Setting: **Deadlands: The Weird West**; Publisher: Pinnacle Entertainment Group.

Sourcebook for the post–Devil's Tower City o' Lost Angels, California, and the havoc and destruction caused by Reverend Grimme and his cannibal cult. Includes the adventure "The Heart o' the Matter."

Lost Colony: Book Two: The Red Menace [Graphic novel; WW]

Author: Grady Klein; First published: 2007; Publisher: First Second.

In wintertime, Indian hater Sherman Krutch arrives on the island where existing Red Menace hysteria is further fueled by plans to build an army of Indian-fighting robots.

Set on a mysterious island in the mid–1800s, the book series examines 19th century America through parody.

Lost in Space (1965) [TV series]

The adventures of the Space Family Robinson and their attempts to find a way to return to Earth after becoming lost in space.

"West of Mars" (2:11) [SW]

Air date: November 30, 1966; Main Cast: Guy Williams as Prof. John Robinson, June Lockhart as Maureen Robinson, Mark Goddard as Major Don West, Billy Mumy as Will Robinson, Angela Cartwright as Penny Robinson, Marta Kristen as Judy Robinson, Jonathan Harris as Dr. Zachary Smith/ Zeno; Guest Cast: Lane Bradford as Pleiades Pete, Allan Melvin as Enforcer Claudio, Mickey Manners as Dee; Producer: Irwin Allen; Story: Michael Fessier; Director: Nathan Juran; 60 min; 20th Century–Fox Television, CBS, Irwin Allen Productions; Color.

Dr. Zachary Smith (Jonathan Harris) is mistaken for his lookalike, intergalactic gunslinger Zeno.

"Lost Paradise" [Pulp fiction; SW]

Author: **C. L. Moore**; First publication: Weird Tales (July 1936).

A stranger with a mysterious package reveals his past to **Northwest Smith** as Smith journeys through time and space to the moon of Seles and an encounter with Baloise the Beautiful and three gods who feed on death.

Love in Vein: Twenty Original Talesof Vampiric Erotica [Book anthology]

Editor: Poppy Z. Brite; First publication: New York: HarperPrism, 1994.

Features the Vampire Western "**Do Not Hasten to Bid Me Adieu**" by Norman Partridge.

"Lucky Larribee" [Pulp fiction; WW]

Author: **Max Brand**; First publication: Serialized in *Western Story Magazine* (4/2/32–5/7/32).

A lazy youngster named Larribee loves to play cards and drink at the local saloons. When his father sends him to live with his cousin's family Larribee's life is given a purpose when he first sets eyes on a magnificent blue stallion named Sky Blue. He has never been tamed, but owner Dan Gurry wants his horse broken so he can race him. Offering a partnership in the horse to anyone who can ride him Larribee is up to the challenge.

Meanwhile Larribee has become an enemy of the son of Major Ransome who wants revenge for being humiliated. After Larribee succeeds in riding Sky Blue, Josiah Ransome sets a burr under the saddle and the horse speeds off into the distance. A distraught Larribee sets off in pursuit, aided by Dan Gurry and Colonel Pratt. But they soon discover the Cheyenne, Crows and Pawnees have also spotted Sky Blue and want the impressive horse for themselves. Following a fearsome fight with Indians Larribee is accepted into the Cheyenne tribe as a blood brother to chief Shouting Thunder.

"The Sky People have this in their hands," said the Cheyenne. "They know who is finally going to ride Sky Blue."

Recovering his health, Larribee continues the pursuit of the magical Sky Blue with the help of Shouting Thunder and his former companions. But the trail proves to be deadly for some and Larribee feels he is being pushed forward by powers beyond his reason. "He was in that dreamy world of the mystic to which Shouting Thunder had introduced him… His own will was not enlisted. It was an extraneous force that pushed him onward relentlessly over rough and smooth."

Brand's story of Larribee's obsessive love for a horse and the ability for that love to transform him touches on the mystical in the beliefs of Shouting Thunder that clearly influence Larribee and serve to motivate him in times of self doubt.

Lucky Luke [Comic book; Belgium]

1. First appearance: *Le Journal de Spirou*, December 7, 1946; Creator: Morris (Maurice de Bevere); Story: Rene Goscinny. Publisher: Dupuis.

Capable of shooting a gun faster than his own shadow, lanky cowboy Lucky Luke, his intelligent chess-playing horse Jolly Jumper and incredibly stupid dog Rantanplan fight crime in the Old West.

Primarily a parody of the Old West featuring historic characters such as the Daltons, Jesse James and Billy the Kid, *Lucky Luke* incorporated Weird Western themes in the short-lived Italian live-action TV series and French animated TV series.

Although Lucky Luke has enjoyed long-lasting success in continental Europe, he hasn't captured the imagination of the British or American public to the same extent.

2. TV series; Italy; [WW]
Premiere: 1991; Main Cast: Terence Hill as Lucky Luke, Nancy Morgan as Lotta Legs, Fritz Sperberg as Averill Dalton, Ron Carey as Joe Dalton, Bo Greigh as Jack Dalton; Producers: Lucio Bompani, Rey Atalia; Story: Lori Hill, Carl Sautter, Doug Molitor; Directors: Terence Hill, Ted Nicolaou, Richard Schlesinger; Paloma Films, Reteitalia; Italy; 8 × 60 min; Color.

Short-lived Italian Western series with elements of fantasy, based on the long-running comic book character.

Season One (Weird Western episodes):

"Magia Indiana" (Grand Delusions) (1:02); Director: Terence Hill.

Lucky Luke witnesses the townsfolk of Daisy Town attending his own funeral.

"Il Treno Fantasma" (Ghost Train) (1:04); Director: Ted Nicolaou.

A gold prospector's fanciful stories of a ghost train are treated with scorn until people begin to disappear in front of their eyes.

"Una Notte di Mezza Estate a Daisy Town" (Midsummer) (1:06); Director: Terence Hill.

A gypsy's love potion causes the person who drinks it to fall in love with the first person he or she sees. But confusion follows when the towns-folk fall in love with the wrong person.

See: **Les Nouvelles Aventures de Lucky Luke**

Lynch [Novella; WW]

Author: Nancy A. Collins; First publication: 1998; Publisher: Cemetery Dance Publications.

The life of former desperado Johnny Pearl is shattered when a psychotic cavalry officer slaughters his wife and their unborn child. Pearl is left hanging from a tree until the arrival of a medicine wagon driven by the weird Dr. Mirablis and his traveling companion, the giant Sasquatch.

Macabre Western [Comic book; WW]

First appearance: 1971; Art: **Bill Black**, **Dick Ayers**; Publisher: Paragon Publications.

This title featured the first Magazine Enterprises **Ghost Rider** reprints under the new title **Haunted Horseman**. *Macabre Western* lasted two issues and included the classic Dick Ayers *Ghost Rider* strips "The Devil Deals in Death," "The Living Head," "The House on Skull Mountain" and "The League of Living Dead" and the horror strip "A Web for a Wedding Dress." The second issue also featured **Red Mask** in "Face of Death" by Frank Bolle.

The original Ghost Rider name couldn't be used because Marvel Comics owned the copyright with the publication of their version of *Ghost Rider* in February 1967. Bill Black, creator of *Macabre Western* and the re-titled Ghost Rider name Haunted Horseman, stated, "**Vincent Sullivan** protested Marvel's use of the name *Ghost Rider* but lost since Magazine Enterprises was out of business by the 1960s."

See: *Paragon Western Stars*

MacGyver (1985) [TV series]

Refusing to carry a gun, secret agent Angus MacGyver (Richard Dean Anderson) relies on ingenuity and resourcefulness to outwit his opponents.

"SERENITY: (5:12) [WW]

Air date: January 8, 1990; Main Cast: Richard Dean Anderson as MacGyver, Dana Elcar as Pete Thornton; Guest Stars: Teri Hatcher as Penny Parker, Cuba Gooding Jr. as Billy Colton, Robert Donner as Milt Bozer, Michael des Barres as Murdoc; Executive Producer: Stephen Downing; Story: Stephen Kandel; Director: William Gereghty; 45 min.; Henry Winkler/John Rich Productions, Paramount Television; Color.

MacGyver falls asleep and finds himself in the town of Serenity in the Old West. When he awakes, he is confused. His dream was so vivid it felt as if it really happened. When he spots a pocket knife with a bullet hole lying next to him, he recognizes it as the same knife that saved his life in his dream.

"MCGYVER'S WOMEN" (6:08) [WW]

Air date: November 12, 1990; Main Cast: Richard Dean Anderson as MacGyver, Dana Elcar as Pete Thornton; Guest Stars: Wil Calhoun as Jesse James, Russell Hamilton as Billy the Kid; Traci Lords as Jenny, Marshall R. Teague as Logan, Dale Wilson as Sundance; Executive Producer: Stephen Downing; Story: Stephen Kandel, Lincoln Kibbee; Director: Michael Preece; 45 min.; Henry Winkler/John Rich Productions, Paramount Television; Color.

In his dreams, MacGyver revisits the Old West town of Serenity where he meets Jesse James and Billy the Kid.

Mad Amos [Short story anthology; WW]

Author: Alan Dean Foster; First publication: New York: Ballantine Books, 1996.

Mountain man Mad Amos Malone and his crossbreed horse-unicorn Worthless encounter dragons, headless Indian spirits and a South Pacific island shaman in this collection of ten short stories.

Mad at the Moon (1992) [Film; WW]

Main Cast: Mary Stuart Masterson as Jenny Hill, Hart Bochner as Miller Brown, Stephen Blake as James Miller, Daphne Zuniga as Young Mrs. Miller, Eleanor Baggett as Older Mrs. Miller, Fionnula Flanagan as Mrs. Hill, Pat Atkins as Mrs. Russell; Executive Producer: Michael Jaffe; Story: Martin Donovan, Richard Pelusi; Director: Martin Donovan; 98 min.; Republic Pictures; Color.

Jenny Hill's mother (Flanagan) disapproves of her daughter's love for outlaw James Miller and arranges a marriage to young frontier farmer Miller Brown. Jenny's unhappiness is compounded when she discovers her husband turns into a werewolf every full moon.

Mad Max: Fury Road (2015) [Film: SFW]

Premiere: May 15, 2015; Main Cast: Tom Hardy as Max Rockatansky, Charlize Theron as Imperator

Furiosa, Nicholas Hoult as Nux, Hugh Keays-Byrne as Immortan Joe, Josh Helman as Slit, Nathan Jones as Rictus Erectus, Zoe Kravitz as Toast the Knowing, Rosie-Huntingdon-Whiteley as The Splendid Angharad; Executive producers: Bruce Berman, Graham Burke, Christopher De-Faria, Steven Mnuchin, Iain Smith; Story: George Miller, Brendan McCarthy, Nico Lathouris; Director: George Miller; 120 min.; Kennedy Miller Productions, Village Roadshow Pictures, Warner Bros.; 3-D; Color.

Immortan Joe and his "war boys" sons are in pursuit of Imperator Furiosa who has seized the heavily armed War Rig truck, along with Immortan's harem of breeding wives. Joining "war boy" Nux in pursuit is "Mad Max" strapped to the front of his car, a prisoner of Immortan Joe who is keeping Max alive as a reluctant blood donor for Nux.

A.O. Scott of *The New York Times* (May 14, 2015) stated: "The themes of vengeance and solidarity, the wide-open spaces and the kinetic, ground-level movement mark "Fury Road' as a western, and the filmmakers pay tribute to such masters of the genre as John Ford [and] Budd Boetticher."

The Irish Times (May 13, 2015) also acknowledged the Western influence. "George Miller has delivered the goods. There is some unhappy news. Too much of the action is rendered through computer graphics. Tom hardy is not quite what we hoped he would be. But *Fury Road* remains a post-apocalyptic western of the highest order."

Mad Max: Fury Road (2015), starring Tom Hardy as Max Rockatansky and Charlize Theron as Imperator Furiosa (Kennedy Miller Productions, Village Roadshow Pictures, Warner Bros.).

The prelude mini-series to the film *Mad Max: Fury Road* sees Imperator Furiosa planning the liberation of Immortan Joe's harem of wives, captive in the bio-dome of the Citadel.

Mad Max: Fury Road—Furiosa [Comic book; SFW]

First publication: June, 2015; Story: George Miller, Nico Lathouris, Mark Sexton; Art: Tristan Jones, Tommy Lee Edwards; Publisher: Vertigo.

Mad Max 2: The Road Warrior (1981) [Film; Australia; SFW]

Premiere: December 24, 1981; Main Cast: Mel Gibson as "Mad" Max Rockatansky, Virginia Hey as Warrior Woman, Bruce Spence as Gyro Captain, Max Phipps as The Toadie, Emil Minty as the Feral

Kid, Mike Preston as Pappagallo, Vernon Wells as Wez; Story: Terry Hayes, George Miller, Brian Hannant; Producer: Byron Kennedy; Director: George Miller; 94 min.; Kennedy Miller Productions, Color.

In a post-apocalyptic world of warring gangs competing for scarce gasoline reserves, Max Rockatansky strikes a deal with the natives of a besieged outpost to supply him with gas in return for a tanker to transport their gasoline reserves to safety.

Madame Tarantula [Comic book character; SFW]

First appearance: *Tigress Tales*, 2001; Creator: Mike Hoffman; Publishers: Antimatter Hoffman International, Eye Bank Comics.

Osimvah's father and aunt were murdered by the Apache Indian tribe who then raised the orphaned child as their own. Osimvah was eventually returned to the white people by Apache Curled Fingers when she was a young woman.

Madame Tarantula. **Artwork © Mike Hoffman. Used with permission.**

Capable of kindness and cruelty in equal measure depending on the circumstances, Madame Tarantula (the Apache translation of Osimvah is tarantula) has amazing regenerative powers with DNA replete in nanites that can restore limbs and heal wounds within seconds.

She lives her life as an outcast in the American New West of AD 4077 where she wanders between mining towns encountering Bioautomatonic drones from the feared Twilight Agency, indirectly responsible for the destruction of Earth's environment, and prospectors searching for radiumite with the help of robots.

Mike Hoffman describes his creation:, "I wanted to adapt traditional Western themes specifically to allow freedom in designing landscapes, flora and fauna, robots and other characters. Artistically, it was an exploration of odd, unusual shapes. My conception of Madame Tarantula probably owes something to actress Tura Satana as I later produced a comic book on her."

The Magic Wagon [Novel; WW]

Author: **Joe R. Lansdale**; First publication: Garden City NY: Doubleday, 1986.

Orphaned youngster Buster Fogg travels through Texas on a Magic Wagon with the mummified body of Wild Bill Hickok and a wrestling chimpanzee.

Lansdale's first novel mixes the traditions of the Western with eccentric characters and supernatural landscapes.

Magico Vento [Comic book character; Italy; WW]

First appearance: *Magico Vento* #1, July 1997; Creator: Gianfranco Manfredi; Publisher: Sergio Bonelli Editore.

When former soldier Ned Ellis is wounded in an explosion, the Lakota shaman who nurses him back to health believes him to be a messenger from the Great Spirit. With his new identity of Magico Vento he lives between the world of man and the world of magic and the spirits. The metal shrapnel lodged in his brain has destroyed all of his memories but allows him to foresee the future. His enemies include the secret association known as the Black Vault and demonic creatures Iktomi, the Demon of Deception, predatory monster Windigo, the animal- and human-devouring Beast and the winged creature Vultur.

Creator Gianfranco Manfredi has stated that Magico Vento was inspired by actor Daniel Day-

Madame Tarantula in "Ghosts of the Second Empire" from *Madame Tarantula: The Black Mariah Magazine* #1 (October 2004). Story and art © Mike Hoffman. Used with permission.

Lewis, whose rugged features express "intelligence and sensitivity."

"The Man on the Ground" [Pulp fiction; WW]

Author: **Robert E. Howard**; First publication: *Weird Tales* (July 1933)

Cal Reynolds and Esau Brill have "carried their mutual hatred into manhood." Now the bitter rivals are facing each other among the Texas hills at rifle range. Their hatred for each other engulfs them as they exchange shots.

"Through the opened lips gushed a tide of blood, dyeing the damp shirt. And like a tree that sways and rushes suddenly earthward, Esau Brill crashed down among the mesquite grass and lay motionless."

The feud is finally over but Cal Reynolds is shocked to find another body laying next to Brill.

"And as he gazed, an awful familiarity made itself evident... In one brief destroying instant he knew he was looking down at his own lifeless body. And with the knowledge came true oblivion."

The Man with No Eyes (2001) [TV pilot; SFW]

Premiere: October 2001; Main Cast: Mel Stewart as Stranger, Tania Gonzalez as Claire, William Bassett as Cleetus, Lidia Pires as Rebecca, Michael Yavnielli as Domingo; Producer: Tavin Marin Titus; Story: Tim Cox, David Goodin; Director: Tim Cox; 21 min.; USA Networks, Exposure Studios, Sci-Fi Channel; Color.

An alien gunslinger seeks vengeance in the Old West.

Manifest Destiny [Comic book; WW]

First publication: November 2013; Creator-Story: Chris Dingess; Art: Matthew Roberts; Publisher: Image-Skybound.

May, 1804. President Thomas Jefferson commissions Meriwether Lewis and William Clark, along with enlisted men, and a volunteer army consisting of convicts looking for pardons, to explore the new frontier wilderness and clear the way for the expansion of the United States. But they are ill prepared for the eerie and deadly landscapes and beasts they encounter.

Creator Chris Dingess describes *Manifest Destiny* as, "A colonial adventure into the untamed, monster-filled American West."

Manitou [Comic book character; WW]

First appearance: **Ghost Rider** #1 (February 1967); Publisher: Marvel Comics.

A Native American Indian God of unlimited powers replaces the Great Spirit as ruler of the Anasazi.

Mantoka, Maker of Indian Magic [Comic book character; WW]

First publication: *Funny Pages* #34 (January 1940);

Story: Richard Bruce; Art: Jack Cole; Publisher: Centaur Publications.

Aged medicine man Great Bird passes on the ancient secrets of magic to his son Mantoka, who uses them to escape the clutches of a ruthless mine owner exploiting Indian labor. Mantoka's amazing skills include turning his body to stone, vaporizing, swelling his body to twice its normal size, freezing water and trapping miners' souls in rats.

La Marca de Satanás (1957) [Film; Mexico; WW]

Premiere: December 12, 1957; Main Cast: Luis Aguilar, Crox Alvarado, Jaime Fernández, Pascual, García Peña, Flor Silvestre; Producer: Luis Manrique; Story: Ramón Obón; Director: Chano Urueta; 94 min.; Universal; Spanish; b/w.

Mexican horror Western. Re-edited third chapter from the *Headless Rider* serial.

See: *El Jinete sin Cabeza*, *La Cabeza de Pancho Villa*

Marshal Law [RPG book; WW]

Authors: John R. Hopler, Angel Leigh McCoy; First publication: 1996; Setting: *Deadlands: The Weird West*; Publisher: Pinnacle Entertainment Group.

Gamemaster screen and adventures. Includes two adventures: "This Harrowed Ground" by John R. Hopler and "Ghost Riders in the Sky" by Angel Leigh McCoy.

Marshal's Handbook [RPG book; WW]

Author: Shane Lacy Hensley; First publication: 1999; Setting: *Deadlands: The Weird West*; Publisher: Pinnacle Entertainment Group.

Gamemaster's guide to the world of Deadlands. Includes the adventure "Comin' 'Round the Mountain."

"The Martian Agent, A Planetary Romance" [Short story; SPW]

Author: Michael Chabon; First publication: *McSweeney's Mammoth Treasury of Thrilling Tales* # 10 (2002).

Alternate history story where rebel George Armstrong Custer fails in his mutiny against Queen Victoria and the British continue to rule the colonies. Two young brothers, Franklin and Jefferson Drake, flee from their father's enemies in post Civil-War America but are soon captured and placed in St. Ignatius Boys' Home. Uncle Thomas Mordden, an inventor and aeronaut, comes to their rescue and fills their minds with talk of moon travel.

"Martian Quest" [Pulp fiction; SW]

Author: **Leigh Brackett**; First publication: *Astounding Science Fiction* (February 1940)

A traditional Western plot is transferred to a Martian environment when a mysterious stranger is met with hostility and distrust by a farming community in the Martian desert.

In true Western fashion, the stranger redeems himself by saving the community from destruction. This short story marked the beginning of Leigh Brackett's distinguished writing career.

The Marvel Family [Comic book]

The adventures of Captain Marvel, Captain Marvel Jr. and Mary Marvel.

"THE MARVEL FAMILY BATTLE CHIEF THUNDERCLOUD"

Chapter One: "Redskin Vengeance"; Chapter Two: "The Pow-Wow of Peril"; Chapter Three: Terror on the Warpath" [WW]

First publication: #83 (May 1953); Story: Otto O. Binder; Art: Kurt Schaffenberger; Publisher: Fawcett Publications.

Three-chapter story featuring Chief Thundercloud, Dull Tomahawk and Chief Bloody Tomahawk fighting Captain Marvel, Captain Marvel Jr. and Mary Marvel.

"Mary Margaret Road-Grader" [Short story; SFW]

Author: Howard Waldrop; First publication: *Orbit 18*, edited by Damon Knight; New York: Harper, 1976

Post-apocalyptic Western where Native Americans have regained dominion over their land.

The Masked Marvel [Comic book character; WW]

First publication: *Gunsmoke—Blazing Stories of the West* #1 (April-May 1949); Publisher: Western Comics Inc., Youthful Publications.

Mild-mannered Chet Fairchild, son of oil millionaire Colonel Carlton Fairchild, originally adopted the menacing persona of the green skull-faced Masked Marvel to prove the innocence of his friend Slim Crane, falsely accused of murder.

The back-up strip in *Gunsmoke—Blazing Stories of the West* was primarily a Weird Menace Western with the skull mask designed to instill

The Masked Marvel in "The Blood-Sucker of Banta Gulch" from *Gunsmoke* #15 (October 1951). Art by Tony Tallarico. © 2009 AC Comics/Nightveil Media, Inc. Used with permission.

fear into criminals. But the Masked Marvel did include genuine Weird Western horror tales.

"Phantom Devils of Laredo"
First publication: *Gunsmoke* #11 (February 1951)
When the Masked Rider discovers local towns-folk dead through fear with "The Mark of the Devil" branded on their foreheads, he learns of a curse placed on Laredo by Indians two hundred years earlier.

"The Bloodsucker of Banta Gulch"
First publication: *Gunsmoke* #15 (October 1951); Art: Tony Tallarico.
The residents of Banta Gulch are terrorized by a blood-sucking monster that can only be killed by a stake through its heart.

"The Beasts of Horror"
First publication: *Gunsmoke* #16 (January 1952)
The Masked Marvel's life is threatened by beasts summoned by a deranged Indian medicine man.
A modern ancestor of the Masked Marvel appeared in *Femforce* #133's "Day of the Dead" (2005).

The Masked Rider (1919) [Film serial; WMW]

Premiere: May 1919; Main Cast: Harry Myers as Harry Burrel, Ruth Stonehouse as Ruth Chadwick, Paul Panzer as Pancho, Marie Treador as Ma Chadwick, Edna M. Holland as Juanita, Robert Taber as Santas, Boris Karloff; Executive Producer: Patrick Sylvester McGeeney; Producer: William Steiner; Story: Aubrey M. Kennedy; Director: Aubrey M. Kennedy; 15 episodes; William Steiner Productions, Arrow Film Corporation; Silent; b/w.
Mexican cattle rustler Poncho's (Paul Panzer) attempts to drive a Texan ranching family out of the border country result in Pancho being tortured and his hands crushed by the ranchers. The Masked Rider, his face completely covered, serves as a go-between delivering messages from the vengeance-seeking Pancho to the ranchers.
This was a "lost" 15-episode serial until 21 reels of 35mm tinted nitrate footage were found in the fall of 2003. This early serial is notable for its graphic violence and scenes of torture. The promotion for Chapter 6, *Pancho Plans Revenge*, stated, "See the miracle which prevents the arms of Ruth from being torn from their sockets. At the word of command, the horses start in opposite directions and Ruth faints at the first pull on

her wrists. Watch and wait for this episode." Boris Karloff appears (his first surviving film appearance) as a roughneck Mexican in a saloon in Chapter 2.
Chapter titles: 1. *The Hole in the Wall*; 2. *In the Hands of Pancho*; 3. *The Capture of Juanita*; 4. *The Kiss of Hate*; 5. *The Death Trap*; 6. *Pancho Plans Revenge*; 7. *The Fight on the Dam*; 8. *The Conspirators Foiled*; 9. *The Exchange of Prisoners*; 10. *Harry's Perilous Leap*; 11. *To the Rescue*; 12. *The Impostor*; 13. *Coals of Fire*; 14. *In the Desert's Grip*; 15. *Retribution*.

Master Comics [Comic book]

Anthology title featuring the adventures of Captain Marvel Jr., Master Man, Bulletman, Minute-Man, Hoodoo Hannigan and Balbo, the Boy Magician; who depends on his stage magician skills to deceive, startle and confuse his enemies. At his side is his African-American business partner John Smith. Unlike most black comic book characters of the era, Smith was written as intelligent and articulate. The strip ran from issue #33 (December 1942) through issue #47 (February 1944).

"Heap Big Magic" [WMW]
First publication: #47 (February 1944); Art: Bert Whitman; Publisher: Fawcett Comics.
Balbo, the Boy Magician, confronts an evil Indian shaman in the American West.

The Master Gunfighter [Comic book character; WW]

First appearance: *All-Star Western* #19 (June 2013); Creators: Justin Gray, Jimmy Palmiotti, Staz Johnson; Publisher: DC Comics.
Former rodeo performer Cody Barrow became the vampire and werewolf hunter known as Master Gunfighter after his family was attacked by vampires and he was forced to kill them. Although bitten by his vampire sister before her death, Barrow was unaffected, except for the ability to smell the presence of vampires.

"Master of Indecision" [Pulp fiction; WW]

Author: **Lon Williams**; Character; **Lee Winters**; *Real Western Stories* (April 1953).
Lee Winters encounters the disembodied voice of a ghost on his journey home to his wife.
There were always haunts in a place like this. Winters had half-expected to tie in with a ghost

or two on this winding cliff-lined road, but he hadn't expected to get his daylights scared out. He didn't see anything; he just heard a voice that came out of a wall of solid rock. It was a spook's voice, of course, for only a spook could live within a crackless, holeless cliff.

Matsumoto, Leiji (1938–) [Comic book artist]

Born in 1938 in Kurumé, on the island of Kyushu, Japan, Leiji Matsumoto is best known for his work on *Captain Harlock*, **Ginga Tetsudô Three-Nine** and **Gun Frontier** which he explored in both manga and animated versions.

Following his first published work in *ShÉnen Manga* at the age of age 15, his work appeared in shojo magazines aimed at girls. His first science fiction manga, *Sexaroid*, was published in 1968.

In 1971 Matsumoto created the popular manga series *Otoko Oidon* and in 1973 the World War II *Senjo Manga* series later known as *The Cockpit* in 1973. Matsumoto entered the world of anime in 1974 as character and conceptual art designer on *Space Battleship Yamato*, later released in the U.S. as *Star Blazers*.

In 2000 he began work with the French house duo Daft Punk on their album *Discovery*. The animated videos and soundtrack were edited together to create the 2003 animated feature *Interstella 5555: The Story of the Secret Star System*.

Matty's Funnies with Beany and Cecil (1962) [Animated TV series]

Alternative title for **Beany and Cecil**.

Max Mercury [Comic book character; SFW]

First appearance: *National Comics* #5 (November 1940); Publisher: Quality Comics, DC Comics.

Max Mercury began life as **Quicksilver**. An unremarkable imitation of DC Comics' *The Flash*, he entered comic book limbo when his strip was discontinued in 1949. In January 1995 (*The Flash* #97) he re-emerged as Max Mercury, a superhero with a history dating back to the 1860s when he was a scout with the U.S. Cavalry. After an Indian shaman granted him the power of speed, he was known as Ahwehota. Mercury has adopted numerous aliases on his travels through time, including Windrunner and Whip Whirlwind. The name Quicksilver was dropped

by DC Comics because a Marvel superhero of that name exists.

McCain's Memories [Novel; SFW]

Author: Maggie Simpson; First publication: New York: Silhouette Books, 1997.

Defense attorney Lauren Hamilton's latest client is accused killer Jon McCain. But Hamilton has one major hurdle to overcome before convincing the jury of her client's innocence: He happens to be a cowboy from 1877. This Western fantasy romance was published as part of the *Silhouette Intimate Moments* series.

McCarthy, Cormac (1933–) [Author]

Born in Providence, Rhode Island, McCarthy spent his childhood in Knoxville, Tennessee. His first novel *The Orchard Keeper* in (1965) won a Faulkner Award, but despite recognition from literary circles his work was ignored by the general public. The violent Western **Blood Meridian** (1985) finally brought him some attention but he would have to wait until 1992 and the publication of the first novel in his Border Trilogy, *All the Pretty Horses*, to make the breakthrough into greater public awareness. He has solidified his reputation with subsequent novels of merit including *No Country for Old Men* (2006).

Selected works: *The Orchard Keeper* (1965), *Outer Dark* (1968), *Blood Meridian* (1985), *All the Pretty Horses* (1992), *The Crossing* (1994), *Cities of the Plain* (1998), *The Road* (2006).

Medicine for the Dead (Children of the Drought book 2) [Novel; WW]

Author: Arianne "Tex" Thompson; First publication: Oxford, UK: Solaris, 2015.

Appaloosa Elim braves the wastelands with Dulei Marhuk's funeral party headed for the holy city of Atali'Karah. But monsters and magic await Elim, Vuchak and Weisei on their journey.

Men with Steel Faces (1940) [Film; SFW]

Premiere: May 2, 1940; Main Cast: Gene Autry as Gene Autry, Frankie Darro as Frankie Baxter, Betsy King Ross as Betsy Baxter, Dorothy Christy as Queen Tika, Wheeler Oakman as Argo, the High Priest, Warner Richmond as Rab, Muranian Ray Inventor, Smiley Burnette as Oscar; Producer: Nat Levine; Story: Hy Freedman, Gerald Geraghty, Wallace MacDonald, John Rathmell, Armand Schaefer; Directors: Otto Brower, B. Reeves Eason; 70 min.; Mascot Pictures; b/w.

Re-edited feature version of the serial *The Phantom Empire* (1935).

See: *Radio Ranch*

Merkabah Rider: Have Glyphs Will Travel [Novella; WW]

Author: Edward M. Erdelac; First publication: Santa Rosa, CA: Damnation Books, 2011

The third volume in the Merkabah Rider series continues with "The Long Sabbath," where Rider and his companion Kabede are being pursued across the desert by a horde of walking corpses led by three former members of the Rider's religious order who have defected to Adon's cause. In the second novella, "The War Shaman," the Rider attempts to convince the Chiricahua Apache to refuse the dark offer of the supreme Native American shaman Misquamacus, who has allied himself with dark powers in order to destroy the white man. "The Mules of the Mazzikim" features Nehema, the succubi and the Rider's attempt to rescue her. In "The Man Called Other" the Rider finally comes face-to-face with the object of his long quest for revenge and in "The Fire King Triumphant" the Rider travels to Tombstone to decipher the contents of the Sheardown letters and uncover Adon's plans to bring the Great Old Ones into the world.

Erdelac's final volume was the self-published *Merkabah Rider: Once Upon a Time in the Weird West* (2013). In the year 1882, Adon has gathered together an army of fallen Hasidic mystics and dark allies including skin walkers, necromancers, an undead gunslinger, Lilith the Queen of demons and the Angel of Death. The Rider and Kabede fight Adon with their own forces for good including Faustus Montague, an angelic being from another universe, a young with, an alien entity from the dawn of time and a preacher who is part steam engine and part man.

Merkabah Rider: Tales of a High Plains Drifter [Novella; WW]

Author: Edward M. Erdelac; First publication: Santa Rosa; CA: Damnation Books, 2009.

Four novella-length stories tell the tale of the Merkabah Rider, son of an Ashkenazi grocer in San Francisco. The Rider, who hides his true name to prevent coming under the influence of malevolent spiritual forces, is a Hasidic Jewish gunslinger and survivor of an ancient order of mystics called the Sons of the Essenes, who is scouring the demon haunted American Southwest of the 1880s for his murderous renegade teacher Adon. During his search he encounters a possessed sharpshooter, a vengeful conjure man, a bordello of succubi and a cult of Molech worshippers. The Rider is capable of astral travel and can see beyond everyday reality with the help of "Solominic seals mystically embossed" on his blue spectacle lenses.

Erdelac combines Jewish mysticism, demonology and religion with a hint of H. P. Lovecraft and Marvel Comic's *Dr. Strange* in the first of four books on the **Merkabah Rider**.

Merkabah Rider: The Mensch with No Name [Novella; WW]

Author: Edward M. Erdelac; First publication: Santa Rosa, CA: Damnation Books, 2010.

The Merkabah Rider continues his quest to track down his former mentor Adon in this second volume of four stories. In "The Infernal Napoleon" he confronts half-demons known as the shedim, born to a succubus who had sex with a human. "The Damned Dingus" sees the Rider encountering the walking dead who have been stripped of flesh by a creature lurking in the tunnels of a cave in Elk Mountain, near Las Vegas. Apache Indians are disappearing in the depths of night in "The Outlaw Gods" and in "The Pandemonium Ride" the Rider descends into hell, where he seeks help from the Adversary.

Author Erdelac populates his fictional universe with real-life historical characters Doc Holliday, Dave Rudabaugh, Dave Mather and Hoodoo Brown giving an air of authority to the supernatural proceedings.

Meteor Monster (1958) [Film; SFW]

This original working title of *Teenage Monster* was adopted for the television release.

Mighty Joe Young (1949) [Film; WW]

Premiere: July 27, 1949; Main Cast: Terry Moore as Jill Young, Ben Johnson as Gregg, Robert Armstrong as Max O'Hara, Douglas Fowley as Jones, Nestor Paiva as Brown, Denis Green as Crawford, Lora Lee Michel as Jill Young as a young girl; Producers: John Ford, Merian C. Cooper; Story: Ruth Rose; Director: Ernest B. Schoedsack; 94 min.; RKO Radio Pictures; b/w.

Promoter Max O'Hara persuades Jill Young to move her giant pet gorilla from Africa to his night

Mighty Joe Young (1949), starring Terry Moore as Jill Young, Ben Johnson as Gregg and Robert Armstrong as Max O'Hara (RKO Radio Pictures).

club "The Golden Safari" in Hollywood. But the move has disastrous consequences.

Willis H. O'Brien received an Academy Award for Best Special Effects. O'Brien's assistant Ray Harryhausen did the majority of the stop-motion animation. Scenes of cowboys on horseback attempting to rope and capture Mighty Joe Young foreshadow similar scenes in the cowboy-dinosaur features *The Beast of Hollow Mountain* (1956) and *The Valley of Gwangi* (1969). Both films would be based on Willis O'Brien scripts.

The Mighty Marvel Western [Comic book; WW]

First publication: 2006; Five-issue mini-series; Publisher: Marvel.

An umbrella title for a series of five Western adventures with a Weird Western flavor. The titles in order of publication are *Outlaw Files*, *Western Legends*, *Two-Gun Kid*, *Kid Colt and the Arizona Girl* and *Strange Westerns Starring The Black Rider*.

Miner's Massacre (2003) [Film; WW]

U.S. DVD release title for *Curse of the Forty-Niner*.

The Miracle Rider (1935) [Film serial; SFW]

Premiere: April 12, 1935; Main Cast: Tom Mix as Tom Morgan, Joan Gale as Ruth, Charles Middleton as Zaroff, Jason Robards as Carlton, Edward Earle as Christopher Adams, Producer: Nat Levine; Screenplay: John Rathmell, Maurice Geraghty; Story: Barney Sarecky, Wellyn Totman, Gerald Geraghty; Directors: B. Reeves Eason, Armand Schaefer; 306 min.; Mascot Pictures Corp.; b/w.

Zaroff and his gang terrorize Indians with a remote controlled plane in order to gain access to the rare explosive mineral X-94 found on their land. Tom Mix made his exit from the big screen in this Western serial with science fiction elements.

Chapter titles: 1. *The Vanishing Indian*; 2. *The Firebird Strikes*; 3. *The Flying Knife*; 4. *A Race with Death*; 5. *Double-Barreled Doom*; 6. *Thundering Hoofs*; 7. *The Dragnet*; 8. *Guerilla Warfare*; 9. *The Silver Band*; 10. *Signal Fires*; 11. *A Traitor Dies*; 12. *Danger Rides with Death*; 13. *The Secret of X-94*; 14. *Between Two Fires*; 15. *Justice Rides the Range*.

Mirage [Comic book character; WW]

A code name of *New Mutants* member **Danielle Moonstar**.

See: **Psyche**

The Misadventures of Clark and Jefferson [Comic book; SFW]

First publication: 2007; Creators: Jay Carvajal, Marc Borstel; Four-issue mini-series; Publisher: Ape Entertainment.

In 1875 Sagebrush, Arizona, Sheriff Clark and Deputy Jefferson fight ravenous aliens with an appetite for livestock and humans.

The Misadventures of Clark & Jefferson—Hairy Things [Comic book; WW]

First publication: January, 2010; Story: Jay Carvajal; Art: Marc Borstel; Three-issue mini-series; Publisher: Ape Entertainment.

In the Old West four unlikely friends stumble upon a remote town deep in the Colorado Rockies where Bigfoot lurks, waiting to attack. But when two of the friends are taken by cannibals hungry for fresh flesh the two remaining form an unlikely alliance with Bigfoot to try and rescue their friends held captive in a church.

The Missing (2003) [Film; WW]

Premiere: November 26, 2003; Main Cast; Tommy Lee Jones as Samuel Jones, Evan Rachel Wood as Lilly Gilkeson, Cate Blanchett as Maggie Gilkeson, Jenna Boyd as Dot Gilkeson, Eric Schweig as Chidin, Steve Reevis as Two Stone, Ray McKinnon as Russell J. Wittick, Val Kilmer as Lt. Jim Ducharme; Executive producer: Todd Hallowell; Producers: Brian Grazer, Daniel Ostroff, Ron Howard; Story: Ken Kaufman; Based on the novel "The Last Ride: by Thomas Eidson; Director: Ron Howard; 115 min.; Columbia Pictures, Revolution Studios; Color.

New Mexico, 1866. In a premise that has echoes of John Ford's The Searchers (1956) Lilly Gilkeson is kidnapped by Apaches. Maggie Gilkeson and the father she despises for abandoning her reluctantly team up to try track down and rescue Lilly. Chidin, the vicious leader of the renegade Apaches who also possesses mystical powers, is heading toward Mexico where Lilly and other kidnapped girls will be sold into slavery.

The film was a box-office failure with an opening weekend of $10,833,633 and subsequent theater sales failing to recover the $60 million budget.

The New York Times (November 26, 2003) film critic Elvis Mitchell stated: "Nearly 50 years after John Ford's 'Searchers' we have arrived at a point in film history when the movie industry can offer a less sophisticated version of the same material."

Missionary Man [Comic strip; UK; SFW]

First publication: Judge Dredd Megazine #2.29, May 1993; Creators: Gordon Rennie, Frank Quitely; Publisher: IPC Magazines, Titan.

The introductory story "Salvation at the Last Chance Saloon" established an Old West atmosphere for this post-apocalyptic strip set in the mutant-filled Cursed Earth of former North America. Preacher Cain has rejected Texas City's corrupt government and dispenses his own law in radiation-filled frontier towns with the help of a Bible and guns.

A Modern Day Western: The Sanchez Saga (1997) [Film; SFW]

Premiere; 1997; Main Cast: Charles Cullen as Reno Sanchez, Ken Tignor as Sheriff Jesse Lobo, Patrick Cooper, Donna Albano; Story-Producer-Director: Charles Cullen; 108 min.; Cullen Studios; Color.

West Texas, 1884. About to be hanged, outlaw Reno Sanchez drinks a bottle of tequila as a last request. As he chews on the worm at the bottom of the bottle he finds himself traveling forward in time to modern-day America where he is pursued by fellow time traveler Sheriff Jesse Lobo, who is on a journey to Nashville and Country & Western stardom.

Monsters, Muties, and Misfits [RPG book; WW]

Authors: Robin Laws, Charles Ryan, Paul Sudlow, Rob Vaux, Joseph Wolf, John Hopler; First publication: 1999. Setting: **Deadlands: Hell on Earth**; Publisher: Pinnacle Entertainment Group Inc.

Sourcebook and bestiary for the Hell on Earth role-playing game.

Moon Zero Two (1969) [Film; SW]

Premiere: October 20, 1969; Main Cast: James Olson as Capt. William H. Kemp, Catherina von Schell as Clementine Taplin, Warren Mitchell as J.J. Hubbard, Adrienne Corri as Elizabeth Murphy; Screenplay-Producer: Michael Carreras; Story: Gavin Lyall, Frank Hardman, Martin Davison; Director: Roy Ward Baker; 100 min.; UK; Hammer Film Productions, Warner Bros.-Seven Arts; Color.

In 2021, the moon is frontier territory in the colonization of space. Lunar salvage pilot Bill Kemp helps Clementine Taplin (Catherina von Schell) discover the truth behind the disappearance of her brother Wally, a prospector on the far side of the moon. Originally marketed as "The First Space Western" the movie was budgeted at a large $1,000,000. It failed at the box-office.

Moore, C. L. (1911–1987) [Author]

Born in Indianapolis, Indiana in January 1911, Catherine Lucille Moore acquired a taste for fantasy books thanks to a childhood of chronic bad health. The year 1933 saw the publication of her first **Northwest Smith** story for *Weird Tales*. Moore adopted the asexual C. L. Moore moniker to avoid the restrictions and prejudices towards female writers in the science fiction genre. Although the plots of her pulp stories were often repetitive, Moore's descriptive, imaginative and sensual style ensured that the Northwest Smith series attracted a popular following.

In 1938 Moore married science fiction author Henry Kuttner, often working in collaboration with him on projects. She turned to television in the 1950s, providing scripts for Warner Bros. TV productions such as *Maverick*, *Sugarfoot* and *77 Sunset Strip* (under her married name Catherine Kuttner) and the *Twilight Zone* episode "What You Need" (as Lewis Padget). Moore retired from writing in 1963 following the death of her husband and her re-marriage. She died on April 4, 1987 after a long struggle with Alzheimer's disease.

Selected works: Fiction series: *Jirel of Joiry* (1934–1969); *Keeps* (1943–1947); *Northwest Smith* (1933–1981); Science fiction novels: *Earth's Last Citadel* with Henry Kuttner (1943); *The Mask of Circe* with Henry Kuttner (1948); *Doomsday Morning* (1957).

More Wild, Wild West (1980) [Telefilm; SFW]

Premiere: October 7, 1980; Main Cast: Robert Conrad as James West, Ross Martin as Artemus Gordon, Jonathan Winters as Albert Paradine II, Rene Auberjonois as Capt. Sir David Edney, Victor Buono as Dr. Henry Messenger, Emma Samms as Mirabelle Merriwether; Executive Producer: Jay Bernstein; Story: William Bowers, Tony Kayden; Director: Burt Kennedy; 94 min.; CBS Television; Color.

Secret Service agents West and Gordon attempt to stop a mad scientist, who can make himself invisible, from taking over the world. Following this telemovie, plans were being made to resurrect *The Wild Wild West* TV series with Robert Conrad and Ross Martin when Martin died of a heart attack on July 3, 1981, at the age of 61.

Morningside Fall (*Legends of the Duskwalker* book 2) [Novel; SFW]

Author: Jay Posey; First publication: Nottingham, UK: Angry Robot, 2014.

Wren is the governor of Morningside, but others within the Council want him dead and he is forced to flee with his mother Cass and trusted allies. Seeking shelter at the border outpost Ninestory, they find it infested by the human hunting Weir.

Followed by *Dawnbreaker*.

The Mysterious Traveler (1943) [Radio series]

The chilling voice of Maurice Tarplin as the Mysterious Traveler narrated each episode with stories ranging from science fiction to horror to crime.

"Behind the Locked Door" (205) [WW]

Air date: May 24, 1949; Story-Producers-Directors: Robert A. Arthur, David Kogan; 25 min.; Mutual Broadcasting System.

Two modern-day archaeologists discover a cavern entrance behind a landslide in the Vermillion cliffs along the Colorado River. Clearing the rubble and exploring the cavern, they discover skeletons, the arrow of a Navajo Indian and remains of over forty wagons from a wagon train. They learn that pioneers of 1849 were forced to retreat into this cave by attacking Indians who then sealed the entrance. The Indian guide's warning of "evil being asleep in the cave' comes true when he is found clawed to death. The two archaeologists are left alone in complete darkness and in total fear of the terrors that await them in the cavern. This memorable episode creates an atmosphere of dread and apprehension.

Mystery in Space [Comic book]

Award-winning anthology science fiction title from DC Comics.

"Jesse James—Highwayman of Space" [SW]

First publication: *Mystery in Space* #2 (June-July 1951); Editor: Julius Schwartz; Story: Robert Kanigher. Art: Carmine Infantino, Joe Giella.

The Knights of the Galaxy pursue a space outlaw who is inspired by Jesse James of the American Old West and adopts his name and crime tactics to rob the people of Gala.

"Cowboy on Mars" [SW]

First publication: *Mystery in Space* #6 (February-March 1952); Editor: Julius Schwartz; Story: Manny Rubin; Art: Jim Mooney.

A cowboy, accidentally transported to Mars, makes the best of his situation by entering a

Martian rodeo and acting as a lawman in rounding up outlaws.

"EARTHMAN, GO HOME" [SW]

First publication: *Mystery in Space* #44 (June-July 1958); Editor: Julius Schwartz; Writer: Otto Binder; Art: Carmine Infantino, Bernard Sachs.

A space trader is greeted with hostility on a distant planet as a Martian receives similar treatment on his first journey to Earth. The space trader parallels an American Old West trapper trading with Native American Indians.

Mystery Mountain (1934) [Film serial; SFW]

Premiere: December 3, 1934; Main Cast: Ken Maynard as Ken Williams, Verna Hillie as Jane Corwin, Sid Saylor as Breezy Baker; Producer: Nat Levine; Story: Ben Cohen, Armand Schaefer, B. Reeves Eason, Sherman L. Lowe, Barney A. Sarecky; Directors: Otto Brower, B. Reeves Eason; 223 min.; Mascot Pictures Corp.; b/w.

In this twelve-part serial, railroad detective Ken Williams attempts to capture vigilante and master of disguise "The Rattler." Also known as "The Menace of the Mountain," the strangely disguised Rattler protects hidden gold in a secret cave filled with weird electronic weapons.

Chapter titles: 1. *The Rattler*; 2. *The Man Nobody Knows*; 3. *The Eyes That Never Sleep*; 4. *The Human Target*; 5. *Phantom Outlaws*; 6. *The Perfect Crime*; 7. *Tarzan the Cunning*; 8. *The Enemy's Stronghold*; 9. *The Fatal Warning*; 10. *The Secret of the Mountain*; 11. *Behind the Mask*; 12. *The Judgment of Tarzan*.

"Mystery of the Hollow Rock" [Pulp fiction; WW]

Author: **Lon Williams**; Character: **Lee Winters**; *Real Western Stories* (August 1954).

Legend had it that Indians had turned a man into stone. Deputy Marshal Lee Winters, however, scoffed at such nonsense. Yet, whatever had happened to Danny Sobo—and that intense-looking stranger with whom he had left Bogannon's saloon, a night ago?

Mystic Brand; or Frank Reade Jr. and His Overland Stage Upon the Staked Plains; The [Dime novel; SPW]

Author: "Noname" (**Luis Senarens**); *Frank Reade Library* #54 (September 30, 1893).

Natas: The Reflection (1983) [Film; WW]

Main Cast: Randy Mulkey as Steve, Pat Bolt as Terry, Nino Cochise as Smohalla, Bob Cota as the Killer; Executive Producers: Jack Dunlap, Peggy Dunlap; Story-Director: Jack Dunlap; 90 min; Arizona West Film Productions Inc.; Color.

A reporter's quest for the demon Natas takes him to a 200-year-old Indian shaman and an Old West ghost town full of zombie cowboys. Actor Nino Cochise, who claimed to be the grandson of legendary Chiricahua Apache chief Cochise, died one year after filming was completed at the age of 110.

The Native Star (*Venificas Americana* book 1) [Novel: SPW]

Author: M. K. Hobson; First publication: New York: Spectra-Ballantine Books, 2010.

It is 1876 and Emily Edwards is a witch with a problem. Mail-order is ruining her patent magic business. In order to survive she decides to cast a love spell on Lost Pine's richest lumberman Dag Hansen only to see the spell backfire and to make matters worse an enchanted artifact embeds itself in her hand. She flees the small Sierra Nevada settlement of Lost Pine pursued by warlocks who want the magical stone for themselves.

Accompanying Emily on her journey to San Francisco's Barbary Coast and cross-country by rail and biomechanical flying machine to Philadelphia is New York City warlock Dreadnought Stanton. Assigned by the Mirabilis Institute to study and educate the residents of Lost Pine in the art of magic, Stanton's pompous and arrogant manner hides a dark past.

Warlock Captain John Caul, is a Maelstrom, a member of President Grant's secret army of blood sorcerers. He will go to any extreme, including torture and death, in his attempts to retrieve the artifact for the U.S. government. Along the way Emily's romance blossoms as she learns more about the politics of magic and the warlocks and of how the magical stone is connected to her past.

Followed by the sequel, *The Hidden Goddess* (Venificas Americana Book 2).

Near Dark (1987) [Film; WW]

Premiere: October 7, 1987; Main Cast: Adrian Pasdar as Caleb Colton, Lance Henriksen as Jesse Hooker, Bill Paxton as Severen, Jenny Wright as Mae, Jenette Goldstein as Diamondback; Executive Producers: Edward S. Feldman, Charles R. Meeker; Story: Kathryn Bigelow, Eric Red; Director: Kathryn Bigelow; 94 min; F/M; Color.

In this contemporary horror Western, Caleb Colton is seduced by a beautiful vampire (Wright) and abducted by her family. Now trained in the art of vampirism, he is forced to kill for blood.

The New Adventures of Superboy [Comic book]

"SUPERBOY WHO NEVER WAS" [SFW]

First publication: #23 (November 1981); Story: Cary Bates; Art: Kurt Schaffenberger, Dave Hunt; Publisher: DC Comics.

The origin of **Terra-Man** finds Clark Kent in exile in the Old West as he puts his super-powers to good use fighting the reptilian alien known as the Collector. Kent learns he cannot run away from his responsibilities as Superboy and returns to the 20th century.

See: *Superboy*

The New Mutants [Comic book]

The adventures of a group of teenage mutants under the tutelage of Professor Charles Xavier.

"DEATH HUNT" [WW]

First published: #18 (August 1984); Story: Chris Claremont; Art: Bill Sienkiewicz; Publisher: Marvel Comics.

Danielle Moonstar summons and confronts the Demon Bear that has been haunting her dreams.

"SIEGE" [WW]

First published: #19 (September 1984); Story: Chris Claremont; Art: Bill Sienkiewicz; Publisher: Marvel Comics.

Recovering in the medical center from injuries suffered during her fight with the Demon Bear, the New Mutants prepare to defend Moonstar from more attacks. But The Demon Bear teleports Moonstar and the New Mutants to the dimension known as the Badlands

"BADLANDS" [WW]

First published: #20 (October 1984); Story: Chris Claremont; Art: Bill Sienkiewicz; Publisher: Marvel Comics.

In the dimension known as the Badlands, the Demon Bear transforms Tom Corsi and Sharon Friedlander into hostile Native American Indians. The New Mutants eventually defeat the Demon Bear. Moonstar discovers that her parents weren't killed but were enslaved by the Demon Bear.

"WAY OF THE WARRIOR"

First published: #41 (July 1986); Story: Chris Claremont; Art: Jackson Guice, Terry Austin; Publisher: Marvel Comics.

Moonstar confronts death in the form of an Old West gunslinger as Pat Roberts fights for his life in the frozen Rockies.

Nickel Children [Short Film; SPW]

Premiere: May 12, 2010; Main Cast: Easton Lee McCuiston as Jack, Jeremy Snowden as the Sheriff, Amanda Bailey as Captain Anastasia, Brian J. Lowry as Dr. Montague; Story-Director: Kevin Eslinger; 16 min; Color.

Children are kept captive in chicken wire cages as gambling "stock" waiting to perform for adults. Performances take the form of dances, where young girls are taken as property by victorious gamblers, or bloody and violent fights to the death. But a boy named Jack has a defiant spirit that grows stronger after being whipped for winning a fight and is aided in escaping his captors by airship captain Anastasia.

"Night of the Cooters" [Short story; SFW]

Author: Howard Waldrop; First publication: *Omni* Vol. 9 #7 (April 1987); Publisher: *Omni Magazine*.

A Texas sheriff fights Martian invaders out of H.G. Wells' *The War of the Worlds*.

Night of the Lepus (1972) [Film: WW]

Premiere: October 4, 1972; Main Cast: Stuart Whitman as Roy Bennett, Janet Leigh as Gerry Bennett, Rory Calhoun as Cole Hillman, DeForest Kelley as Elgin Clark, Paul Fix as Sheriff Cody; Producer: A. C. Lyles; Screenplay: Don Holliday, Gene R. Kearney; Based on the novel "The Year of the Angry Rabbit" by Russell Braddon; Director: William F. Claxton; 88 min.; Metro-Goldwyn-Mayer (MGM); Color.

In this often laughable modern day Western set on an Arizona ranch, ranch owner Cole Hillman takes measures to control an outbreak of rabbits. Zoologist Roy Bennett attempts to curb the rabbit population with hormone and genetically mutated blood injections on test subjects. But his efforts prove to be disastrous when one of the injected rabbits escapes and begins to breed. Giant rabbits with a taste for blood rampage through the ranch and beyond as they attack and kill anything in their path, including humans.

Night Rider [Comic book character; Comic book; WW]

See: **Ghost Rider**

Night Train [RPG book]

Author: John Goff; Art: Paul Daly, Jeff Lahren, Ron Spencer, Richard Taylor; First publication: 1997; *Deadlands: The Weird West* #3 Dime Novel series; Publisher: Pinnacle Entertainment Group.

Undead gunslinger Ronan Lynch rides into Varney Flats just in time to greet the sinister Night Train.

Nighthawk [Comic book character; WW]

1. First appearance: *Western Comics* #5 (September-October 1948); Creators: Robert Kanigher, Charles Paris; Publisher: National Periodical Publications.

The evolution of the Western masked crime-fighter known as Nighthawk into a superhero is convoluted and a prime example of the tangled history of many traditional cowboy characters from the 1940s. DC Comics had the choice of letting their old Western characters ride into the sunset or make them relevant to a contemporary readership rooted in superheroes, science fiction and fantasy. Nighthawk began as a traditional masked cowboy strip in *Western Comics*. A traveling handyman man named Hannibal Hawkes moonlighted as Nighthawk with the help of his black stallion Nightwind, two six-shooters, a lasso and bullwhip. In later adventures he teamed up with orphan Jim Peyton.

Nighthawk was retired in 1960 but returned as the reincarnation of ancient Egyptian Prince Khufu. Hannibal Hawkes eventually reincarnated as Carter Hall, alias **Hawkman,** bonding with his former lover **Cinnamon**, reincarnated as Shiera Sanders, alias **Hawkgirl**. He also joined **Bat Lash** and **El Diablo** as a member of the **Rough Bunch**.

2. A mercenary not connected to the original Nighthawk who appeared with Robin in the *Pulp Heroes* story "The Law West of Gotham."

Night's Children: Red Trails West [Comic book]

First publication: December 1994; Creator: Wendy Snow-Lang; Publisher: Millenium Publications.

Vampire Western. Part two of a *Night's Children* three-part mini-series.

No Graves on Boot Hill (1968) [Film; Italy; WW]

U.S. release title for *Tre croci per non moiré.*

Noble Metals [Novella; SPW]

Author: L.A. Witt; First publication: Hillisborough, N.J.: Riptide Publishing, 2014.

Robert Belton has resorted to prostitution in Seattle after gambling away money to stake his claim in the Klondike gold fields. Dr. John Fauth, a scientist-engineer and one of Belton's customers, entices Belton to join him on his trek to Alaska to gather the precious platinum required for his inventions. Aiding them on their travels is an eight-legged, steam powered mechanical luggage carrier.

Northwest Smith [Pulp fiction character; SW]

First appearance: *Weird Tales*, November 1933.

A smuggler, gun-runner and exile from Earth working outside of the law with self-interest and self-preservation as his main motives, Northwest Smith was originally envisioned as a Western genre character by creator **C. L. Moore**.

The influences of pulp masters **Edgar Rice Burroughs** and H. Rider Haggard are evident in the various exotic locales throughout the solar system visited by Northwest Smith. Moore blends many elements including the hardboiled, cynical private eye and Old West gunslinger to create a Western anti-hero in a science fiction setting.

She looked a second time at that face, its lean, leathery keenness and the scars that ray-guns had left, and the mark of knife and talon, and the tracks of wild years along the spaceways.—"**Black Thirst**" (1934).

Norton, Andre (1912–2005) [Author]

Born in Cleveland, Ohio, Alice Mary Norton knew she stood a greater chance of success in the male-dominated world of science fiction if she adopted a male pseudonym. Her first novel was published in 1934 but she continued to work as a librarian, bookstore owner and reader at Gnome Press until 1958 when she turned to writing full-time.

The theme of the exiled Native American making a new world for himself in a hostile environment was explored in her **Beast Master** novels. She is also remembered for her work on the *Witch World* series which ran to 35 novels.

Selected works: *The Prince Commands* (1934), *The Beast Master* (1959), *The Sioux Spaceman* (1960), *Lord of Thunder* (1962), *Witch World* (1963).

Les Nouvelles Aventures de Lucky Luke
(2001) [Animated TV series; France]

Premiere: September 16, 2001; Voice Cast: Antoine de Caunes as Lucky Luke, Eric Legrand as Jolly Jumper; Stories: Jean-François Henri, Jean-Luc Fromental; Producer: Marc du Pontavice; Director: Olivier Jean Marie; 52 × 26 min.; Dargaud Marina, FTVI, Xilam, France 2, France 3: Color.

"GHOSTS AND BAGPIPES" (1:19) [WW]

Air date: February 3, 2002

Staying at a castle, Lucky Luke is in the middle of a feud between the Irish population of O'City, the Scottish McCloud clan who live in the nearby castle and the Black Cloud Indians. The phantom of Bloody Laird complicates matters further.

"DO YOU BELIEVE IN MARTIANS?" (1:30) [SFW]

Air date: November 3, 2002

A strange light appears in the night sky above Nothing Gulch and a cow vanishes from its herd. The townsfolk have one explanation ... Martians!

"THE BEAST OF ALABAMA" (1:32) [WW]

Air date: April 28, 2002

In Alabama, the farmers believe their sheep are being devoured by a mysterious monster. Lucky investigates but is hindered by a self-appointed monster hunter.

"THE UNDEAD DALTONS" (1:42) [WW]

Air date: September 29, 2002

Once the Daltons are mistakenly declared dead, they pose as phantoms and embark on a crime spree. But a genuine phantom may exist in a ghost town where Joe is hiding out from Lucky.

Nova Phase [Comic book; SW]

First publication: 2014; Story: Matthew Ritter; Art: Adam Elbahtimy; Publisher: SLG Publishing.

Veronica Darkwater has ambitions to be, "a space race, or a bounty hunter, or an intergalactic trader, or a Universe renowned fencer." When she meets Fred "Quick Draw" Gunnard she decides to cash in on the bounty on his head with the help of her lucky coin. With the bounty money Veronica hopes to hop the next spaceship but the lucky coin becomes a target of armed soldiers in gold armor.

This light-hearted Space Western is illustrated in the style of an 8-bit video game.

Una Nuvola di polvere ... un grido di morte ... arriva Sartana (1971) [Film; Italy-Spain; WW]

Premiere; 1971; Main Cast: John Garko [Gianni Garko] as Sartana, Susan Scott [Nieves Navarro] as Belle Manassas, Piero Lulli as Grandville Fuller, Massimo Serato as Sheriff Manassas, Dan van Husen as Deputy Sheriff; Producers: Eduardo Manzanos Brochero, Luciano Martino; Story: Eduardo Manzanos Brochero; Screenplay: Eduardo Manzanos Brochero, Tito Carpi, Ernesto Gastaldi; Director: Anthony Ascott [Giuliano Carmineo]; 99 min.; Copercines, Cooperativa Cinematográfica, Devon Film; Color.

A convoluted storyline revolving around stolen gold, counterfeit money and cross and double cross includes some bizarre gadgets: a church organ that Sartana converts into a lethal machine gun–type cannon and a mechanical Indian head named Alfie which transforms into a gun and a deadly bomb.

"Nymph of Darkness" [Pulp fiction]

Authors **C. L. Moore** with Forrest J Ackerman; First publication: *Fantasy Magazine* (April 1935)

Northwest Smith encounters an invisible naked Venusian girl named Nyusa trying to evade pursuers on the Ednes waterfront. Smith discovers she is the daughter of The Darkness who is worshipped by underground dwellers known as the Nov. Nyusa's desire to escape the dark side and embrace her mother's humanity is under threat from the Nov who want her to be part of their ritual of dark worship. Northwest Smith becomes entangled in her plight and faces difficult choices.

Oblivion (1994) [Film; SW]

Main Cast: Richard Joseph Paul as Zack Stone, Andrew Divoff as Redeye/Einstein, Musetta Vander as Lash, George Takei as Doc Valentine, Julie Newmar as Miss Kitty, Meg Foster as Stell Barr, Isaac Hayes as Buster; Executive Producer: Charles Band; Story: Charles Band, Peter David, Mark Goldstein, John Rheaume, Greg Suddeth; Director: Sam Irvin; 94 min.; Full Moon Entertainment; Color.

Following the death of his father at the hands of the reptilian Red Eye, Zack Stone, becomes the reluctant sheriff of the alien outpost Oblivion.

Oblivion 2: Backlash (1996) [Film; SW]

Main Cast: Richard Joseph Paul as Zack Stone, Maxwell Caulfield as Sweeney, Andrew Divoff as Redeye/Einstein, Musetta Vander as Lash, George Takei as Doc Valentine, Julie Newmar as Miss Kitty, Meg Foster as Stell Barr, Isaac Hayes as Buster;

Executive Producer: Charles Band; Story: Charles Band, Peter David, Mark Goldstein, John Rheaume, Greg Suddeth; Director: Sam Irvin; 83 min.; Full Moon Entertainment; Color.

Bounty hunter Sweeney finds the task of taking seductive outlaw Lash into custody more complicated than he bargained for when he discovers she won a Derconium mine in a game of cards.

Sequel to *Oblivion*.

Oddworld: Stranger's Wrath [Video game; WW]

Release date: January 25, 2005; Third and first-person perspectives; Platform: Microsoft Xbox; Developer: Oddworld Inhabitants; Designer: Lorne Lanning; Publisher: Electronic Arts.

A bounty hunter referred to as Stranger travels across the Old West tracking valuable bounty in the form of Outlaws and encountering the violent Clakkerz and amphibian Grubbs in the Mongo River Valley. His weapon choice is the double-barrel crossbow complete with live ammunition in the form of thudslugs, stunkz, boombats and bees.

In Sekto Springs, upstream from the Mongo River Valley, Mr. Sekto has dammed the river to sustain his water bottling company and hunted the centaur-like Steef to near extinction. He now collects the remaining rare Steef heads and awaits the bounty to be delivered. The Stranger, a Steef himself, suddenly becomes the hunted. The Stranger learns that Sekto is an Octigi who stole water and fish from the Grubbs.

The goal of the player is to earn enough "moolah" (bounty money) to acquire ammunition, crossbows and various upgrades. The Stranger will die if the health bar is fully depleted.

Oky Doky Ranch (1949) [Puppet series; WW]

Main Cast: Rex Trailer; 15 min; b/w.

Revised format for *The Adventures of Oky Doky*, the twice weekly show starring cowboy puppet Oky Doky and cowboy star Rex Trailer.

"Old Garfield's Heart" [Pulp fiction; WW]

Author: **Robert E. Howard**; First publication: *Weird Tales* (December 1933).

Despite never appearing to age a day past fifty, Jim Garfield's seemingly far-fetched claims are mocked by the townsfolk of 1930s Lost Knob, Texas.

"I can't die," old Jim gasped, "Not so long as my heart is in my breast. Only a bullet through the brain can kill me… Yet it ain't rightly mine, either. It belongs to Ghost Man, the Lipan chief. It was the heart of a god the Lipans worshiped before the Comanches drove 'em out of their native hills."

"I was dead as a man can be. My heart was sliced in two, like the heart of a butchered beef steer."

"All night Ghost Man did magic, callin' my ghost back from spirit-land… He took out what was left of my mortal heart and put the heart of the god in my bosom."

Old Jim Garfield asks Doc Blaine to promise to remove his eternal beating heart from his body should he get shot in the head and die. When that time finally arrives the Doc keeps his promise.

"There in the doorway he stood, tall, dark, inscrutable—and Indian warrior… Silently he extended his hand, and I dropped Jim Garfield's heart into it."

The Indian vanishes like "a phantom of the night, and only something that looked like an owl was flying, dwindling from sight, into the rising moon."

Omega Chase [Comic book; SFW]

First publication: 2007; Creators: Keith Dallas, Julio Molina Muscara; Publisher: Th3rdworld.

Mack Baron has cloudy memories of being an officer on a galactic starship and an archer in medieval Europe. But he has enough present-day problems maintaining law and order as the sheriff of an Old West town where a horde of zombie gunslingers want him dead.

On Gossamer Wings [Novella; SW]

Author: James R. Strickland; First publication: Colorado Springs, CO: Copperwood Media, 2011.

In an alien landscape resembling the Old West an aphasic teenage girl named Natalie Bishop cannot speak but can understand mathematics to a genius level and thanks to an empathy with the Thingmakers is able to locate the drumlins required to make a zero-point energy flying machine. On learning of her plans an agent from the Bitspace Institute seeks to control the flying machine technology.

Strickland's novella was published as part of a

"Copperwood Double" with another Drumlins universe story *Drumlin Circus* by Jeff Duntemann.

On the Far Side of the Cadillac Desert with Dead Folks [Novel; SFW]

Author: Joe R. Lansdale; First publication: Arvada, CO: Roadkill Press, 1991.

Wayne the bounty hunter pursues and captures murderer Calhoun in the post-apocalyptic Cadillac Desert infested with zombies and littered with remnants of Chevrolets and Cadillacs. As they travel to Lawtown where Wayne will collect his bounty on Calhoun they meet a group of nuns and Brother Lazarus who controls the zombies through a bolt in their head.

On the Far Side with Dead Folks [Graphic novel; SFW]

Story: Joe R. Lansdale; Art: Timothy Truman; First publication: Urbana, IL: Avatar Press, 2004.

Adaptation of Lansdale's *On the Far Side of the Cadillac Desert with Dead Folks*.

Once Upon a Time in Hell (*Heaven's Gate* trilogy #2) [Novel; WW]

Author: Guy Adams; First publication: Oxford; Solaris, 2013.

Wormword is a town that travels through time and space and comes to rest for one day only every hundred years. And on that one day the living can escape death by traveling through a portal to Heaven. Each time the location is different but today, September 21, 1889, Wormwood has come to rest in an obscure part of the American Midwest.

The journey to Wormword has proved deadly for many as the remaining pilgrims finally reach their destination. They are greeted by a blond-haired man in a suit and waistcoat named Alonzo who acts as their guide to the beyond. The portal that once offered the promise of Heaven is replaced with the realities of the underworld as Elwyn Wallace finds himself traveling through Hell.

One Night in Sixes (*Children of the Drought* book 1) [Novel; WW]

Author: Arianne "Tex" Thompson; First publication: Oxford, UK: Solaris, 2014.

When half-breed Appaloosa Elim and young white companion Sil Halfwick fail to sell a herd of horses for their ranch boss Sil suggests they travel to the border town of Sixes to sell the horses. But Sixes is in forbidden territory with stories of shape shifters and animal gods who roam in the dead of night.

Followed by the further adventures of Appaloosa Elim in *Medicine for the Dead*.

OneeChanbara [Video game series; Japan; WW]

First release: 2004; Developer: Tamsoft; Platform: PlayStation 2, Xbox 360, Wii.

Aya, the bikini- and scarf-wearing Japanese cowgirl, fights her estranged half-sister Saki, who wants Aya's heart to bring her dead mother back to life. Zombies and other undead creatures add to the weird mix in this successful series of video games that includes *Zombie Zone, Zombie Hunters, Bikini Samrai Squad* and *Bikini Zombie Slayers*. A combination of American Western, Japanese Samurai and horror genres.

OneeChanbara: The Movie (2008) [Film; Japan; WW]

Main Cast: Otoguro Eri as Aya, Nakamura Chise as Saki, Hashimoto Manami as Reiko; Screenplay: Yôhei Fukuda, Yasutoshi Murakawa; Director: Yôhei Fukuda; 80 min.; Geneon Entertainment; Color.

Aya's scarf and bikini accompanies her cowgirl hat and boots as she defends her city against zombies in this film based on the popular PS2 game series.

Randall Larson writing for *Cinefantastique* (July 13, 2009) stated: "It's kind of a mixture of Leone and Miike and Romero and Tarantino without their budget or wit; it's an entertaining and likeable samurai-bikini-zombie-killing movie that plays out rather well."

See: *Chanbara Beauty*

The Outcasts [Comic book strip; France; SFW]

English title for *Les Persecutes*.

Out in the Black [RPG book; SW]

Authors: Tracy Hickman, Laura Hickman; Based on the motion picture screenplay by Joss Whedon (*Serenity* role-playing game); First publication: Margaret Weis Productions Ltd., 2006

An adventure for the *Serenity* role playing game, set in Frisco, a lawless mining town in the 'Verse.

Out of the Night [Comic book]

Supernatural anthology title that ran to seventeen issues between February 1952 and November 1954.

"Frozen Ghost" [WW]

First publication: #8 (May 1953); Editor: Richard Hughes; Art: Al Camy: Publisher: American Comics Group.

A lake is haunted by the vengeful ghost of an Indian chief with a deadly frozen touch.

Out of the Unknown (1965) [TV series; UK]

Science fiction and fantasy anthology series conceived by Sydney Newman, head of BBC's drama department. *Out of the Unknown*, which ran to 49 episodes between 1965 and 1971, was a mixture of original screenplays and adaptations of stories by science fiction authors, including Isaac Asimov, J.G. Ballard, Ray Bradbury, John Brunner, Robert Sheckley, Clifford Simak, Frederick Pohl and John Wyndham.

"The Fastest Draw" (2:09) [SFW]

Air date: December 8, 1966; Cast: Ed Begley as Amos Handworthy, Annette Carell as Emma Bowles, James Maxwell as Peter Stenning; Story: Larry Eisenberg; Adaptation: Julian Bond; Producer: Irene Shubik; Director: Herbert Wise; 50 min.; UK; BBC TV; b/w.

Obsessed by the memory of his U.S. marshal grandfather, Amos Handworthy builds an android gunslinger to test his skill as a gunfighter. Adapted from the Larry Eisenberg short story.

See: *The Fastest Draw*

Outland (1981) [Film; SW]

Premiere: May 21, 1981; Main Cast: Sean Connery as Marshal W.T. O'Niel, Peter Boyle as Sheppard, Frances Sternhagen as Lazarus; Executive Producer: Stanley O'Toole; Story-Director: Peter Hyams; 112 min.; Ladd Company; Color.

Marshal W.T. O'Niel investigates the mysterious deaths of workers on a mining colony on Jupiter's moon Io.

Outlaw Files [Comic book; WW]

First publication: June 2006; Stories: Michael Hoskin, Stuart Vandal, Ronald Byrd, Jeff Christiansen, Sean McQuaid, Mark O'English, Anthony Flamini, Madison Carter; Publisher: Marvel.

A collection of tales from the files of the Phantom Rider. Featured are the Phantom Rider, Black Rider, Tex Dawson, Gunhawk, *Kid Colt*, Masked Raider, Outlaw Kid, *Rawhide Kid*, Steam Rider and *Two-Gun Kid*.

See: *The Mighty Marvel Western*

Outlaw Star (1998) [Anime; Japan; SW]

U.S. release title for *Seihou Bukyou Outlaw Star* which premiered on January 15, 2001.

Outlaws (1986) [TV series; SFW]

Premiere: December 28, 1986; Main Cast: Rod Taylor as Sheriff Jonathan Grail, William Lucking as Harland Pike, Richard Roundtree as Isaiah "Ice" McAdams, Charles Napier as Wolfson Lucas, Patrick Houser as William Pike, Christine Belford as Deputy Maggie Randall; Creator: Nicholas Corea; 1 × 120 min, 11 × 60 min.; Universal TV; Color.

Season One [SFW episodes]

"Outlaws" (1:01)

Air date: December 28, 1986; Guest Star: Shannen Doherty; Story: Nicholas Corea; Director: Peter Werner.

The Pike gang and former gang member Sheriff Grail travel through time from 1886 to 1986 after lightning strikes them in a graveyard. Trapped in 1986 Houston, the sheriff and outlaws form the Double Eagle Detection Agency.

"Tintype" (1:02)

Air date: January 3, 1987; Story: Deborah Dean Davis; Director: Don Chaffey.

Harland Pike falls for a woman who is the image of his lost love from the Old West

"Primer" (1:03)

Air date: January 10, 1987; Story: Bruce Cerui; Director: Frank Orsatti.

When illiterate Billy Pike attends classes to learn to read, he encounters thugs working a protection racket.

"Orleans" (1:04)

Air date: January 17, 1986; Story: Nicholas Corea; Director: Phil Bondelli; Guest Star: Denny Miller.

Isaiah "Ice" McAdams attempts to recover buried cash he hid in 1886 but faces opposition from a descendant of his slave owner from the 1880s.

"Madril" (1:06)

Air date: February 7, 1987; Guest Stars: Lew Ayres, Claudia Christian; Story: Nicholas Corea; Director: Alan J. Leui.

A millionaire has plans to convert the Old West ghost town of Madril into a shopping mall. But the former sheriff of Madril in the Old West, Jonathan Grail, encounters unexpected trouble when an elderly resident recalls Grail shooting his father almost a century earlier.

"Potboiler" (1:07)

Air date: February 28, 1987; Guest Star: Marshall Teague; Story: Timothy Burns; Director: Frank Orsatti.

A western historian's curiosity is aroused when he notices the striking resemblance between a photograph of the Pike Gang taken in 1885 and the founders of the Double Eagle Detection Agency.

"Pursued" (1:08)

Air date: March 7, 1987; Guest Star: Robin Dearden; Story: Robert Heverly; Direct: Phil Bondelli.

Hired to locate the daughter of a dying ex-mobster, Jonathan Grail and the outlaws think of the loved ones they left behind in 1886.

"Hardcase" (1:10)

Air date: March 28, 1987; Story: Timothy Burn, Nicholas Corea; Director: Frank Orsatti.

A rebellious kid on the run reminds Billy Pike of himself at the same age when he turned to crime back in the Old West. He attempts to make certain the youth doesn't follow his same path.

"Birthday" (1:12)

Air date: May 2, 1987; Story: Timothy Burns; Director: Nicholas Corea.

With their ranch under siege, Grail recalls how he first met Wolfson Lucas. In a neat twist to the final episode in this short-lived series, footage from the TV Western series *Oregon Trail* is included in the flashback sequence. Like this episode, *Oregon Trail* also starred Rod Taylor and Charles Napier.

The Outpost [Novel; SW]

Author: **Mike Resnick**; First publication: New York: Tor, 2001.

A group of colorful characters including Three-Gun Max, Reverend Billy Karma, Hurricane Smith, Catastrophe Baker, Cyborg de Milo, Bet-A-World O'Grady, Sitting Bull and Crazy Horse exchange stories at the Outpost tavern on the planet Henry II, situated on the edge of a black hole. But an impending alien invasion forces them to pursue the invaders before their favorite bar is just another memory.

Overland Stage Raiders (1938) [Film; WW]

Premiere: September 20, 1938; Main Cast: John Wayne as Stony Brooke, Ray "Crash" Corrigan as Tucson Smith, Max Terhune as Lullaby Joslin, Louise Brooks as Beth Hoyt, Anthony Marsh as Ned Hoyt; Associate Producer: William Berke; Story: Bernard McConville, Edmond Kelso; Screenplay: Luci Ward; Director: George Sherman; 55 min.; Republic Pictures; b/w.

Modern-day Western with a Greyhound bus transporting a shipment of gold substituting for the "Overland Stage" of the title. Parachuting cowboys add to the weird mix. The 18th feature in Republic Pictures' *Three Mesquiteers* series starring John Wayne one year before he attained international stardom via *Stagecoach* (1939).

Owlwoman [Comic book character: WW]

First publication: *Super Friends* #7 (August 1977); Creators: E. Nelson Bridwell, Ramona Fradon; Publisher: DC Comics.

Cherokee Wenonah Littlebird is an American Indian from Oklahoma with night vision, superior tracking and navigation skills, heightened senses and the ability to glide on air currents. Owlwoman is a member of the international law enforcing Global Guardians.

The comic book *Super-Friends* was based on the Hanna-Barbera animated series of the same name.

Ozark [Comic book character; France; SFW]

First publication: *Mustang* #54 (1980); Story: Jacques Lennoz; Art: Franco Oneta; Publisher: Editions Lug.

Wa-Tan-Peh's sacred amulet gives Lakota Indian Russell Red Horse a.k.a. Ozark the ability to communicate telepathically with his cosmic-powered horse Mustang, who represents the mystic power of the Lakota tribe. Able to see through illusions and lies with the "Light of Kelios," Ozark protects himself from the evil forces of the supernatural with the Shield of Kronan. His enemies include the extra-dimensional entity Typho, the mad Dr. Kain and the alien invaders Gronz, whom he combats with the help of the Magic Circus troupe that has also been granted powers by the amulet.

Following the death of the Magic Circus members, Ozark's search for the seven gems known as

The mysterious "Preacher" appears as if in answer to the prayers of a young girl who asks for help for a strip-mining community at the mercy of Coy LaHood.

Eastwood's film shows influences of *Shane* (1953), ***Django il Bastardo*** and his previous Western ***High Plains Drifter***. The supernatural origin of Eastwood's character in both *Pale Rider* and *High Plains Drifter* is purposely left ambiguous.

The late film critic Roger Ebert (June 28, 1985) stated: "He may indeed be the pale rider suggested in the title, whose name was death, but he may also be an avenging spirit, come back from the grave to confront the man who murdered him. One of the subtlest things in the movie is the way it plays with the possibility that Eastwood's character may be a ghost, or at least something other than an ordinary mortal."

Ozark, "Le Disciple." Story by J.M. London, art by J.J. Dzialowski. © Mosaic Multimedia. Used with permission.

the Hand of Shivar leads him to the sorcerer Maleficus and goddess Shakti. Ozark returned in *Zembla Special* #154–55 in 2001, followed by an ongoing series in *Fantask* in 2002.

Pale Rider (1985) [Film; WW]

Premiere: June 28, 1985; Main Cast: Clint Eastwood as Preacher, Michael Moriarty as Hull Barret, Carrie Snodgress as Sarah Wheeler, Richard Dysart as Coy LaHood, Christopher Penn as Josh LaHood; Executive Producer: Fritz Manes; Story: Michael Butler, Dennis Shryack; Director: Clint Eastwood; 116 min.; Malpaso Company; Color.

El Pantano de Las Ánimas (1957) [Film; Mexico; WW]

Premiere: September 5, 1957; Main Cast: Gaston Santos as Gaston, Manola Saavedra, Pedro de Aquillon, Manuel Donde, Sara Cabrera; Producer: Alfredo Ripstein Jr.; Story: Ramón Obón; Directors: Rafael Baledón, Stim Segar; 75 min.; Alameda Films; Spanish; Color.

Cowboy detective Gaston, his horse Moonlight and assistant Squirrel Eyes hunt for a swamp monster responsible for killing the local townsfolk. K. Gordon Murray had further scenes filmed for the U.S. release in 1965. A low-budget mixture of the Western, horror, comedy and musical genres.

See: *The Swamp of the Lost Monster*

Paragon [Comic book character; SFW]

First appearance: *Captain Paragon* #1 (1970); Story-Art: **Bill Black**; Publisher: Paragon Publications, AC Comics.

Charlie Starrett first develops the paranormal ability of mind over matter with the help of Doc Marvel while adopting a new identity as Old West gunslinger Latigo Kid. But an encounter with Samuel Lieber, a pioneer in para-psychological studies, leads down the path of learning and discovery to domination, manipulation and experimentation. The end result is immortality, invulnerability, flight and super-strength as Charlie Starrett becomes Lieber-controlled government agent Captain Paragon in World War II.

Freed from Lieber's control by adversary the Black Shroud, Starrett remains in suspended animation until aliens from the planet Rur awaken him. Forming the paranormal group the Sentinels of Justice, Paragon finally defeats the Black Shroud and eventually marries **Femforce** member MS. Victory.

See: *Latigo Kid Western*

Paragon Western Stars [Comic book; WW]

First appearance: 1976; Art: **Dick Ayers**; Publisher: Paragon Publications.

This title continued the numbering from **Macabre Western** and featured the **Haunted Horseman** strip "Play of Death."

Pariah [Comic book character; WW]

First appearance: *Incredible Hulk* #268 (February 1981); Creators: Bill Mantlo. Sal Buscema; Publisher: Marvel Comics.

In the year 1871, a gunslinger is possessed by the Spirits of the Stone after digging into sacred Indian burial ground in Whispering Wells.

Pariah, Missouri [Graphic Novel; WW]

First publication: July 2013; Story: Andres Salazar; Art: Jose Pescador; Publisher: Decade Brothers Studio–SE Studios.

Pariah, Missouri is a riverboat boom-town and a haven for the unscrupulous. The charismatic Hy Buchanan works undercover as a foppish cheat, and creates a rag-tag team to uncover corruption and evil. Set on the supernatural frontier of 1857, Pariah Missouri is a western that leans on mysticism and folk-magic.

Pariah, Missouri Roleplaying Game Sourcebook [RPG; WW]

First publication: 2014; Story: Andres Salazar; Art: Jose Pescador; Publisher: SE Studios Everything is included to play *Pariah, Missouri* using Savage Worlds, FATE or Hero systems. Features stats, history, maps and all the information to plug in the game system of the player's choice.

Peace Party [Comic book; SFW]

First issue: May 1999; Creator: Rob Schmidt; Publisher: Blue Corn Comics.

Following a car crash, two modern-day Pueblo Indians receive special powers from an ancient Indian spirit and a mission to protect the Earth.

Peacemaker [Novel; SFW]

Author: Marianne De Pierres; First publication: Nottingham, UK: Angry Robot, 2014.

In a future Australia Virgin Jackson is the senior ranger in the "Wild West" themed Birrimun Park. Helping her in her duties is U.S. Marshal Nate Sixkiller, the grandson of a legendary Native American lawman. After Jackson witnesses a murder in the Park her world takes strange twists and turns with involvement in a local gang war, drug runners, attacks by crows and the return of the paranormal eagle Aquila, previously seen during her troubled youth.

Peacemaker: An Arcane West Novel [Novel; WW]

Author: K. A. Stewart; First publication: New York: InterMix Books, 2014.

Caleb Marcus is a Peacemaker in the Old West frontier. But he faces new problems in the small Western town of Hope. Children are being robbed of their magical powers and earthquakes are becoming a regular occurrence. And there's something not quite right about the local land baron who runs the school.

Penny Dreadful (2014) [TV series]

The series title refers to the 19th century British publications that were the equivalent of the American Dime Novels. The episodes feature fictitious characters from celebrated novels of the era including Dorian Gray, Dr. Victor Frankenstein and his monster, Mina Hark and Abraham Van Helsing. Also featured is a continuing Weird Western character who is introduced in the premiere episode.

"Night Work" [WW]

Premiere: May 11, 2014; Main Cast: Timothy Dalton as Sir Malcolm Murray, Eva Green as Vanessa

Gunslinger Ethan Chandler (Josh Harnett) hides a secret life as werewolf Ethan Lawrence Talbot in *Penny Dreadful* (2015).

Ives, Harry Treadaway as Dr. Victor Frankenstein, Josh Harnett as Ethan Chandler; 60 min.; Creator-Story: John Logan; Executive producers: Pippa Harris, John Logan, Sam Mendes; Director: J.A. Bayona; Showtime Networks, Sky, Desert Wolf Productions, Neal Street Productions; Color.

Ethan Chandler was born in 1857 and served as a soldier in the U.S. Cavalry, fighting in the American Indian Wars. He later toured with a traveling circus as a gunslinger. In 1891 Colonel Brewster's Wild West Show and Emporium of American Curiosities visits London. Chandler meets medium and clairvoyant Vanessa Ives and agrees to work as her armed escort as they attempt to recover Sir Malcolm Murray's daughter from a group of vampires.

In later episodes we learn that Ethan Chandler is in fact Ethan Lawrence Talbot, a human-wolf hybrid.

People of the Talisman [Novel; SW]

Author: **Leigh Brackett**; First publication: New York: Ace Books, 1964.

Expanded version of "**Black Amazon of Mars.**" The alterations are extensive, including a different conclusion.

See: *The Secret of the Sinharat*

Perdition's Daughter [RPG book; WW]

Authors: Shane Lacy Hensley, Hal Mangold; First published: 1996; **Deadlands: The Weird West** #1 Dime Novel series; Publisher: Pinnacle Entertainment Group.

This 100-page *Deadlands* dime novel includes a novella by Shane Lacy Hensley and an adventure set in Derry's Ford by Hal Mangold.

Les Persecutes [Comic book strip; France; SFW]

First appearances: *Special-Kiwi* #114, *Special-Rodeo* #115, *Kiwi* #462 to 467 (1987); Art: Raffaelle Paparella: Publisher: Éditions Lug.

Tawa, Edgar, young Milos, the eccentric Prof. MacKenzie, the villainous Sgt. Crumb and Corporal Buchet encounter the advanced underground civilization of the Riis in the Old West.

See: *The Outcasts*

Petticoat Planet (1996) [Film; SW]

Main Cast: Troy Vincent as Steve Rogers, Elizabeth Kaitan as Delia Westwood, Leslie Kay Sterling [Lesli Kay] as Sheriff Sarah Parker, Betsy Lynn George as Lily; Story: Matthew Jason Walsh; Director: Ellen Cabot [David DeCoteau]; 78 min.; Full Moon Entertainment, Castel Film, Romania; Color.

Astronaut Steve Rogers crashlands on a planet with an Old West theme inhabited solely by sex starved cowgirls. Soft-core Space Western set in Puckerbush Gulch.

"Phantom Cargo" [Pulp fiction; WW]

Author: **Lon Williams**; Character: **Lee Winters**; **Real Western Stories** (December, 1953)

Deputy Marshal Lee Winters has strange, eerie experiences on his ride through haunted Alkali Flats.

The Phantom City (1928) [Film; WMW]

Premiere: December 23, 1928; Main Cast: Ken Maynard as Tim Kelly, Eugenia Gilbert as Sally Ann Drew, James Mason as Joe Bridges, Charles Mailes as Benedict; Story: Adele Buffington; Producer: Harry Joe Brown; Director: Albert S. Rogell; Charles R. Rogers Productions-First National Pictures; 65 min.; Silent; B/W.

In the deserted mining town of Gold City, a mysterious Phantom warns Tim Kelly to stay clear of the gold mine. Kelly has inherited a share of the mine from his late father but others have ideas about taking the gold. Footage from this film was re-used in the 1932 remake **Haunted Gold**.

The Phantom Empire (1935) [Film serial; SFW]

Premiere: February 23, 1935; Main Cast: Gene Autry as Gene Autry, Frankie Darro as Frankie Baxter, Betsy King Ross as Betsy Baxter, Dorothy Christy as Queen Tika, Wheeler Oakman as Argo,

NAT LEVINE *presents* **Gene AUTRY** *in* **'THE PHANTOM EMPIRE'**

MASCOT SERIALS

"BLAZING THE TRAIL"   CHAPTER *4*   *PHANTOM BROADCAST*

The Phantom Empire (1935) film serial starring Gene Autry, Betsy King Ross, and Frankie Darro (Mascot Pictures).

the High Priest, Warner Richmond as Rab, Muranian Ray Inventor, Smiley Burnette as Oscar; Producer: Nat Levine; Story: Hy Freedman, Gerald Geraghty, Wallace MacDonald, John Rathmell, Armand Schaefer; Directors: Otto Brower, B. Reeves Eason; 245 min.; Mascot Pictures; B/W.

Twelve-part serial starring Gene Autry in a unique mix of the singing cowboy and science fiction genres. The ancient civilization of Mu, located beneath Autry's Radio Ranch, is threatened by speculators buying the Muranian supply of radium. Autry attempts to save the people of Mu and protect his Radio Ranch. The lead role was originally planned for Ken Maynard but he was replaced due to conflicts with producer Nat Levine. The serial was also released in condensed feature film format as *Men with Steel Faces* 1940) a.k.a. *Radio Ranch*.

Chapter titles: 1. *The Singing Cowboy*; 2. *The Thunder Riders*; 3. *The Lightning Chamber*; 4. *Phantom Broadcast*; 5. *Beneath the Earth*; 6. *Disaster from the Skies*; 7. *From Death to Life*; 8. *Jaws of Jeopardy*; 9. *Prisoners of the Ray*; 10. *The Rebellion*; 11. *A Queen in Chains*; 12. *The End of Murania*

Phantom of the Horse Opera [Animated theatrical short; WW]

1. Premiere: October 1961; Theatrical series: *Woody Woodpecker*; Story: Dalton Sandifer; Animation: Les Kline, Ray Abrams; Director: Paul J. Smith.

Woody Woodpecker encounters ghosts in Spooksville, Arizona.

2. See: *Beany and Cecil*

The Phantom of the Range (1936) [Film; WMW]

Premiere: November 28, 1936; Main Cast: Tom Tyler as Jerry Lane, Beth Marion as Jeanne Moore, Sammy Cohen as Eddie Parsons; Producer: Sam Katzman; Story: Basil Dickey; Director: Bob Hill; 57 min.; Victory Pictures Corp.; B/W.

Seeking a new life, Jerry Lane buys a ranch that

locals claim is haunted by the Phantom Rider. After Lane discovers a stash of money hidden on the ranch, he comes face to face with the Phantom Rider and a gang of thieves.

The Phantom of the West (1931) [Film serial; WMW]

Main Cast: Tom Tyler as Jim Lester, William Desmond as Martin Blaine, Frank Lanning as Francisco Cortez, Dorothy Gulliver as Mona Cortez, Tom Santschi as Bud Landers; Producer: Nat Levine; Story: Wyndham Gittens, Ford Beebe, Ben Cohn; Director: D. Ross Lederman; 172 min.; Mascot Pictures; B/W.

Ten-part early talkie Western serial starring Tom Tyler as Jim Lester, attempting to uncover the truth behind his father's death and the identity of "The Phantom." This mild Weird Menace Western takes on an added weird twist when the identity of The Phantom is revealed to be a character who was in the same saloon scene as The Phantom, therefore being in two places at the same time.

Chapter titles: 1. *The Ghost Riders*; 2. *The Stairway of Doom*; 3. *The Horror in the Dark*; 4. *The Battle of the Strong*; 5. *The League of the Lawless*; 6. *The Canyon of Calamity*; 7. *The Price of Silence*; 8. *The House of Hate*; 9. *The Fatal Secret*; 10. *Rogue's Roundup*

Phantom Pistoleer [Novel; WW]

Author: Tom West; First publication: New York: Ace Books, 1960.

"His ghost packed a .45."

Published with *The Challenger* by Giles A. Lutz in the Ace Double Western series with dos-a-dos binding.

The Phantom Rider (1936) [Film serial; WMW]

1. Premiere: July 6, 1936; Main Cast: Buck Jones as Buck Grant, Marla Shelton as Mary

The Phantom Rider (1936), a film serial starring Buck Jones as Buck Grant, Marla Shelton, Diana Gibson, Harry Woods and Eddie Gribbon (Serials Incorporated, Universal Pictures).

Grayson, Diana Gibson as Helen Moore, George Cooper as Spooky; Producer: Henry MacRae; Story: Basil Dickey, Ella O'Neill, George H. Plympton, Henry MacRae; Director: Ray Taylor; 258 min.; Serials Incorporated, Universal Pictures; B/W.

An eerie night rider in white, The Phantom Rider, fights outlaws who intend to drive rancher Mary Grayson off her land.

Chapter titles: 1. *Dynamite!*; 2. *The Maddened Herd*; 3. *The Brink of Disaster*; 4. *The Phantom Rides*; 5. *Trapped by Outlaws*; 6. *Shot Down*; 7. *Stark Terror*; 8. *The Night Attack*; 9. *The Indian Raid*; 10. *Human Targets*; 11. *The Shaft of Doom*; 12. *Flaming Gold*; 13. *Crashing Timbers*; 14. *The Last Chance*; 15. *The Outlaw's Vengeance*

2. Premiere: January 26, 1946; Main Cast: Robert Kent as Dr. Jim Sterling/The Phantom Rider, Peggy Stewart as Doris Shannon, LeRoy Mason as Fred Carson, Chief Thundercloud as Chief Yellow Wolf, George J. Lewis as Blue Feather; Producer: Ronald Davidson; Story: Albert DeMond, Basil Dickey, Jesse Duffy, Lynn Perkins, Barney Sarecky; Directors: Spencer Gordon Bennet, Fred C. Brannon; 167 min.; Republic Pictures; B/W.

Dr. Jim Sterling poses as the Indian god "The Phantom Rider" to help an Indian tribe deal with crooked Indian agent Fred Carson.

Chapter Titles: 1. *The Avenging Spirit*; 2. *Flaming Ambush*; 3. *Hoofs of Doom*; 4. *Murder Masquerade*; 5. *Flying Fury*; 6. *Blazing Peril*; 7. *Gauntlet of Guns*; 8. *Behind the Mask*; 9. *The Captive Chief*; 10. *Beasts at Bay*; 11. *The Death House*; 12. *The Last Stand*

3. Comic book character; WW
First appearance: **Ghost Rider** #56, May 1981; Creators: Michael Fleisher, Don Perlin; Publisher: Marvel Comics.

Archaeologist Hamilton Slade becomes possessed by his ancestors Carter and Lincoln Slade after discovering a burial urn containing their ashes.

Phantom Town (1999) [Film; WW]

Premiere: February 16, 1999; Main Cast: Belinda Montgomery as Mom, Jim Metzler as Dad, John Patrick White as Mike, Taylor Locke as Arnie, Lauren Summers as Cindy; Executive Producers: Donald Kushner, Peter Locke, Charles Band; Story: Benjamin Carr; Director: Jeff Burr; 130 min.; Kushner-Locke Company, Castel Films, Canarom Films; Color.

While searching for their missing parents, three kids come across the Old West town of Longhand, inhabited by zombie cowboys and body snatchers.

Pink Panic (1967) [Animated theatrical short; WW]

Premiere: January 11, 1967; Story: John W. Dunn; Director; Hawley Pratt; 6 min.; DePatie Freleng Enterprises, Mirisch Corporation; Color.

The Pink Panther encounters ghosts, skeletons and an Old West sheriff when he stays at the Dead Dog Hotel on a stormy night.

Pistol for a Hundred Coffins (1968) [Film; Italy-Spain; WW]

U.S.A. release title for **Una Pistola per cento bare**.

Una Pistola per cento bare (1968) [Film; Italy-Spain; WW]

Premiere: August 24, 1968; Main Cast: Peter Lee Lawrence as Jim "The Kid" Slade, John Ireland as Douglas, Gloria Osuna as Marjorie, Eduardo Fajardo as Chavel, Piero Lulli as Texas Corbett, Raf Baldassarre as Verdugo; Producer: Ennio Girolami; Story: Eduardo Manzanos Brochero; Director: Umberto Lenzi; 83 min; Copercines, Cooperativa Cinematográfica, Tritone Cinematografica; Color.

A tale of a man seeking revenge on the gang who murdered his parents becomes a Western horror movie anticipating the slasher genre of the 1980s as a group of lunatics escape from an asylum and sets their sights on the townsfolk. The lunatic rampage sequence has been compared to Edgar Allan Poe's *The System of Doctor Tarr and Professor Feather* by Italian film critic Federico de Zigno.

Pitch Black (2000) [Film; SW]

Premiere: February 18, 2000; Main Cast: Van Diesel as Richard B. Riddick, Radha Mitchell as Carolyn Fry, Cole Hauser as William J. Johns, Claudia Black as Sharon "Shazza" Montgomery, Keith David as Abu "Imam" al-Waid; Executive producers: Ted Field, Scott Kroopf, Tony Winley; Screenplay: David Twohy, Ken Wheat, Jim Wheat; Director: David Twohy; 109 min.; PolyGram Filmed Entertainment, Interscope Communications, USA Films; Color.

Stranded on a parched planet, Riddick and the crew of a commercial transport ship must overcome deadly nocturnal creatures that are ready to make their entry during the imminent month-long eclipse.

Roger Ebert of the *Chicago Sun-Times* (February 18, 2000) stated: "Clever, done with skill, yet lacking in the cerebral imagination of the best science fiction. How sad it is that humans travel countless light years away from Earth, only to find themselves inhabiting the same tired generic conventions. By the end of the movie, however, I was wondering if the trip had been necessary; most of the plot could be ported into a Western or a swashbuckler with little alteration."

Pitch Black was followed by *The Chronicles of Riddick* (2004) set on the planet Helion Prime where he battles the menace of the Necromongers. **Riddick** (2013) returns him to his Space Western roots.

The Place of Dead Roads [Novel; SW]

Author: **William S. Burroughs**; First publica-tion: New York: Holt, Rinehart, and Winston, 1984.

Gay gunslinger Kim Carsons and the outlaw gang Wild Fruits travel across space and time to fight aliens while attempting to create a society where homosexuality is legal. The second book in Burroughs's *Western Lands* trilogy is described as a "fantasized autobiography" by Burroughs' biographer Ted Morgan.

A Planet for Texans [Novel; SW]

Authors: H. Beam Piper, John J. McGuire; Publisher: New York: Ace Books, 1958.

Originally published as **"Lone Star Planet"** in *Fantastic Universe Science Fiction*, Vol. 7, No. 3, March 1957.

Planetfall (2005) [Film; SW]

Main Cast: Heidi Fellner as Lux Antigone, Charles Hubbell as Lieutenant Jerik; Producers: Michael J. Heagle, Troy Antoine LaFaye, Matt Saari; Story: Matt Saari, Michael J. Heagle; Director: Michael J. Heagle; 90 min.; Car School Film-O-Rama; Color.

Low-budget space spaghetti Western about female bounty hunters searching for an elusive psychedelic drug.

Portlandtown: A Tale of the Oregon Wyldes [Novel; WW]

Author: Rob DeBorde; Fits publication: New York: St. Martin's Griffin 2012

Astoria is a town of secrets, where the legendary Hanged Man, who once survived a hanging, is buried in the cemetery along with his red handled Colt Walker gun that never needs reloading and makes whoever owns it want to shoot to kill. Joseph Wylde's father-in-law, former U.S. Marshal James Kleberg, shot to death the Hanged Man ten years ago. Now his grave has become the target of small-time outlaws who sell his preserved corpse to a circus, but of more interest is a book found in the grave. A book of black magic filled with spells that can make the dead walk again. The Hanged Man is now a revenant zombie, capable of speech with a great desire to locate his missing gun and those responsible for his death—primarily the retired U.S. marshal, who now lives with Joseph Wylde and his family in Portland.

Posse Impossible (1977) [Animated TV series segment; WW]

First appearance: *Hong Kong Phooey* episode "Comedy Cowboys" (December 21, 1974); Voice cast: William Woodson as The Sheriff, Daws Butler as Deputy Duke/Deputy Stick, Chuck McCann as Deputy Blubber; Executive Producer; William Hanna.

A group of bumbling cowboy lawmen led by Slipshod Sheriff help keep law and order in Saddlesore. This segment of The C.B. Bears is primarily a comedy with some Weird Western situations.

Big Duke and Li'l Lil (1:01); *Trouble at Ghostarado* (1:02); *The Not So Great Train Robbery* (1:03); *The Alabama Brahma Bull* (1:04); *The Crunch Bunch Crashout* (1:05); *One of Our Rivers Is Missing* (1:06); *Sneakiest Rustler in the West* (1:07); *Bad Medicine* (1:08); *Busting Boomerino* (1:09); *Roger the Dodger* (1:10); *Riverboat Sam, the Gambling Man* (1:11); *The Invisible Kid* (1:12); *Calamity John* (1:13)

The Postman (1997) [Novel: Film; SFW]

1. Author: David Brin; First publication: New York: Bantam Book, 1985.

In a post-nuclear America, society is divided into various isolated communities. When Gordon Krantz wears the uniform of a dead mailman, people assume he's really a mailman and see him as a symbol of hope. Krantz goes along with the deception but in the process he actually begins to deliver mail and to effect contact between communities. As he travels further West to Oregon, he encounters fanatical survivalists and a community controlled by surviving technology in the form of Artificial Intelligence. But is this also a deception?

2. Film

Premiere: December 25, 1997; Main Cast: Kevin Costner as the Postman, Will Patton as Gen. Bethlehem, Larenz Tate as Ford Lincoln Mercury, Olivia Williams as Abby; Original novel: David Brin; Screenplay: Eric Roth, Brian Helgeland; Producers: Steve Tisch, Jim Wilson, Kevin Costner; Director: Kevin Costner; 177 min.; Tig Productions, Warner Bros. Color.

In 2013, following a nuclear holocaust that wipes out America, an individual (Costner) decides to deliver undelivered mail taken from a dead mailman. This simple feat is viewed as an act of rebellion against the neofascist army of the Holnists run by General Bethlehem and a symbol of hope for the future.

This box-office flop, with an estimated budget of $80 million and a worldwide gross of only $27 million, ditched much of the source material from David Brin's novel. The Western frontier theme is explored in a post-apocalyptic landscape as the mailman encounters "new" communities and increased hostility on his ill-defined, almost accidental quest of restoring America.

While far from satisfied with the film, Brin declared, "They rescued the 'soul' of the central character, making *The Postman* once again a story about a reluctant hero, a liar who slowly comes to realize his own value, and the importance of hope."

San Francisco Chronicle film critic Peter Stack (December 25, 1997) commented: "The movie goes on interminably, awkwardly mixing a post-holocaust world with a clunky Western staged in pinewood mountains. What emerges is a simplistic melodrama of mushy patriotism, stilted romance and hollow morality."

The New York Times critic Stephen Holden (December 24, 1997) stated: "'The Postman' knows no restraint. Every scene is played to the hilt for its mythic, tear-jerking potential, and after a while the accumulated sentiment begins to curdle. The dialogue, a numbing succession of western-movie clichés, is spoken with a cartoon-balloon emphasis that makes it all the more phony."

Pow-Wow Smith [Comic book character]

The adventures of Sioux Indian Pow-Wow Smith first appeared in *Detective Comics* #151 (January 1949) as a back-up strip to *Batman & Robin* before switching to *Western Comics* in 1954 starting with issue #43. When the title folded in 1961, Pow-Wow Smith became one of DC Comics' forgotten Western characters until the re-launch of *All-Star Western* in 1970. Early *Detective Comics* stories illustrated by Leonard Starr featured Smith as a deputy sheriff. He would later become Sheriff of Elkhorn.

"The Return of the Fadeaway Outlaw" [WMW]

First publication: *Western Comics* #73 (January-February 1959); Story: **Gardner Fox**; Art: Carmine Infantino; Publisher: DC Comics.

The Fadeaway Outlaw seems to disappear before Pow-Wow Smith's eyes. Actually, the Outlaw is just an accomplished escape artist who vanishes with the aid of an underground tunnel and secret passages.

"Menace of the Magic Arrows" [WW]

First publication: *Western Comics* #75 (May-June 1959); Story: Gardner Fox; Art: Carmine Infantino; Publisher: DC Comics.

A criminal invents an arrow that he believes can cause harm by striking a person's shadow.

Powell, Bob (1916-1967) [Comic book artist]

Born Stanley Robert Pawlowski in Buffalo, New York, Powell found his first work at the Eisner & Iger studio. (The studio provided complete comic books for various publishers including Fiction House, Timely, Fox and Quality). Powell learned his trade on a variety of titles including *Blackhawk* and *Sheena* and worked with Will Eisner on *The Spirit, Mr. Mystic* and *Lady Luck.*

Powell formed his own studio following military service in World War II and freelanced for Magazine Enterprises where he provided artwork for the first 13 issues of **Bobby Benson's B-Bar-B Riders** which included the strips **Lemonade Kid** and **Red Hawk**. His work was also featured in ME's **Best of the West**, **Straight Arrow**, *Strong Man, Thun'Da, Cave Girl, Africa, The Avenger, I'm a Cop, Jet* and *American Air Forces*. Harvey Comics also provided Powell with a regular source of income throughout the 1940s and 1950s with work on various titles including *Man in Black, Black Cat* and *Chamber of Chills.*

After time spent freelancing for Atlas Comics in the 1950s, Powell briefly became part of the "Marvel Age of Comics" in the 1960s with short stints on *Giant-Man, Human Torch,* **Daredevil** and the *Hulk.* His work away from comics included pencils in the early 1960s on the controversial *Civil War News* and *Mars Attacks* trading cards for Topps.

When cancer claimed him in 1967, he was art director at *Sick*, the satirical-humor magazine.

Preacher [Comic book; WW]

First appearance: 1995; Creators: Garth Ennis, Steve Dillon; Story: Garth Ennis; Art: Steve Dillon, Glenn Fabry; Publisher: DC-Vertigo.

Possessed preacher Jesse Custer wanders across America in search of God. The stories often touch on Western themes as Custer's travels take him into the Texas town of Salvation where he demands the sheriff's job.

Preacher: Saint of Killers [Comic book; WW]

First appearance: August 1996; Creators: Garth Ennis, Steve Dillon; Story: Garth Ennis; Art: Steve Pugh; four-issue mini-series; Publisher: DC-Vertigo.

Following the death of his wife and family, a former scalp hunter-bounty hunter is filled with hatred and the desire for revenge. After his own death, he is named "Saint of Killers" by the Angel of Death when a bargain is made for him to return to Earth to collect the souls of those who died by violence. A *Preacher* comic book spin-off.

Precious Metals [Novella; SPW]

Author: L.A. Witt; First publication: Hillsborough, N.J: Riptide Publishing, 2014.

Set in the same steampunk universe as *Noble Metals* this novella features different characters. Joseph Starling journeys to the Klondike in the hope of finding the men who murdered his older brother,

beat him to a pulp, stole their mining machine. Unable to work the machine without Joseph they are holding his younger brother hostage. Joseph, along with Constable Paul Benson of the North-West Mounted Police, make their way to the airship station through treacherous terrain.

The Presto Kid [Comic book character; WMW]

First appearance: *Red Mask* #51 (September 1955);

The *Presto Kid* in "The Floating Renegade" from *Red Mask* #54 (1957). Story by Gardner Fox, art by Dick Ayers. © 2009 AC Comics/Nightveil Media, Inc. Used with permission.

Creators: **Gardner Fox, Dick Ayers**; Publishers: Magazine Enterprises; AC Comics.

After his family is murdered in an Indian raid, the orphaned Jeff Grant vows never to use a gun or a rifle. Jeff is befriended by traveling magician Doc Cromwell, but his newfound happiness is shattered when Doc is murdered by a masked bandit. Jeff notices the scar on the bandit's wrist and vows to bring him to justice.

Many years later, Grant, who now owns a blacksmith shop in Red Gulch, sees that his latest customer has a scar on his wrist. The meek and mild-mannered Jeff adopts the guise of the Presto Kid and catches the murderer using magic tricks he learned from Doc Cromwell.

The Presto Kid continues to use his mastery of stage magic to fool outlaws and criminals into believing he has supernatural powers. But as meek Jeff Grant he receives disdain from the attractive Molly Blane, who views him as a coward.

This replacement strip for **Ghost Rider** in the **Red Mask** comic book ran to four issues. AC Comics resurrected the character through reprints including a new story in **Best of the West** #6, "Six Gun Showdown" by **Bill Black** it also featured **Durango Kid**, Red Mask and **Black Phantom**. John Nadeau and Dick Ayers provided the art.

Pretty Deadly [Comic book; WW]

First publication: 2013; Story: Kelly Sue DeConnick; Art: Emma Rios; Publisher: Image.

In the Old West a man named Mason marries Beauty, a girl he has loved since they were children. But the mentally unstable Mason is overcome with fear that he may lose her to another man and imprisons her in a stone tower. The young woman begs for Death to release her from her loneliness. Death answers Beauty's request but falls in love with her. Before she dies Beauty gives birth to Death's child, who claims the child's soul, while releasing Beauty's soul. The woman who comes to be known as Deathface Ginny is raised by Death as a reaper of vengeance and a hunter of sinful men.

Prey [Video game; SW]

Release: July 11, 2006; Developer: Human Head Studios, Aspyr Media, Venom Games; Platform: PC, Mac, Xbox 360; Publishers: 2K Games, 3D Realms.

Cherokee Domasi "Tommy" Tawodi leads an uneventful life as a garage mechanic, living on an Indian reservation until Earth becomes the target of an alien predator that feeds on humans.

Tommy's reservation becomes a prime target as members of his Cherokee Nation are abducted, along with himself and his girlfriend Jenny. The spirit of his grandfather tells Tommy he must learn to get in touch with his ancestral and spiritual heritage to survive. A spiritual hawk guides Tommy as he seeks to save Jenny, his tribe and the Earth from destruction by the aliens aboard the spaceship Sphere.

Priest [Comic book; Korea; WW]

First appearance: 1998; Creator-Story-Art: Min-Woo Hyung; 15 volume; Publisher: Daiwon C.I.-Tokyopop.

A priest sells his soul to Belial in return for the power to exact vengeance on those who destroyed his life and to seek redemption for releasing the fallen angel Temozarela.

His journey takes him across the Old West where he seeks to destroy Temozarela and his legion of twelve fallen angels. This manwha (comic book) was inspired by the computer game **Blood**.

Priest (2011) [Film; SPW]

Premiere: May 6, 2011 [UK]; Main cast: Paul Bettany as Priest, Karl Urban as Black Hat, Stephen Moyer as Owen Pace, Lily Collins as Lucy Pace, Madchen Amick as Shannon Pace, Maggie Q as Priestess, Christopher Plummer as Monsignor Orelas, Brad Dourif as Salesman, Cam Gigandet as Sheriff Hicks; Story: Cory Goodman; Based on the graphic novel series by Min-Woo Hyung; Director: Scott Stewart; 87 min.; 3D; Screen Gems; Color.

The animated introduction to the film sets up the premise. "There has always been man and there have always been vampires. Since the beginning the two have been locked in conflict. Facing extinction, mankind withdrew behind walled cities under the protection of the church. And then the ultimate weapon was found—the priests. Warriors with extraordinary powers trained by the church in the art of vampire combat." But the priests were so successful they were disbanded after the vampires were placed on reservations. The church considered the vampire problem over and the priests irrelevant. But their state of denial was hiding the truth. Vampires still roamed free.

The film abandons the graphic novel source material substituting a Steampunk style world for the Old West and transforming a demon possessed priest who witnesses the murder of his

Priest (2011), a film starring Karl Urban as Black Hat (Screen Gems).

adopted sister into a vampire hunting priest (Paul Bettany) tracking down his 18-year-old niece (Lily Collins) who has been kidnapped by a large group of vampires. Joining him on his quest is Lucy's sweetheart Sheriff Hicks (Cam Gigandet). Monsignor Orelas (Christopher Plummer) views belief in vampires as heresy and sends four priests to stop "Priest" and Hicks. Meanwhile, Lucy is in the hands of Black Hat, a human-vampire hybrid.

Reviews and audience reaction was lukewarm. *Variety* film critic Leslie Felperin stated (May 8, 2011): "Not exactly an unholy mess… Pic manages to blend many disparate looks and genres, from oaters via the 'Mad Max' pics to 1968's 'Witchfinder General,' yet it still feels oddly anonymous." Mark Olsen of the *Los Angeles Times* (May 14, 2011) said: "Even with all the various parts and pieces going into its structure, it feels bare-bones—the differentiation between the dystopian future-cities and the dust-bowl hinterlands never creates the tension it should, and a fistful of crucifixes that become throwing stars is as deep as the theology gets."

Priest was filmed with an estimated budget of $60 million and grossed $78 million worldwide.

A Princess of Mars [Novel; SW]

Author: **Edgar Rice Burroughs**; First publication: Chicago: A. C. McClurg, 1917.

The first novel in the Barsoom trilogy. Hiding from an Apache attack in Arizona, **John Carter** finds himself on Mars (Barsoom), where he is captured by the green Martian warriors of Thark. Winning the admiration of his captors, Carter rises to chieftain but isn't allowed to leave the city. He eventually joins forces with fellow captive Dejah Thoris, beautiful princess of Helium, and his female guardian Sola in an effort to escape the city of Thark.

See: "**Under the Moons of Mars**," *The Gods of Mars*

The Prisoner (1967) [TV series; UK]

When a secret agent (Patrick McGoohan) hands in his resignation, he is drugged and made a prisoner in a Mediterranean-style village on a remote island.

"LIVING IN HARMONY" (1:13) [WW]

Air date: January 14, 1968; Main Cast: Patrick McGoohan as The Prisoner/Number Six; Alexis Kanner as The Kid, David Bauer as The Judge/Number Two, Valerie French as Kathy; Story: Ian L. Rakoff,

Cover of *A Princess of Mars* by Edgar Rice Burroughs (1917). Dust jacket art by Frank Schoonover.

Patrick McGoohan as Number 6 in *The Prisoner's* "Living in Harmony" episode (1:13, 1967).

David Tomblin; Producer-Director: David Tomblin; 52 min.; Everyman Films, ITC; Color.

This unusual episode is an Old West version of the weekly series with Number Six as a sheriff handing in his tin star and gun in the revised opening title sequence. He is attacked on his way out of town and awakens in the town of Harmony, which is controlled by the Judge. The conclusion follows the familiar formula of Number Six trapped once again in the Village. CBS originally banned the episode in 1969 because of its depiction of drug use.

"The Problem with Mermaids" [Short story; WW]

Author: Ken Rand; First publication: *Faeries #3*, 1999.

Lucky Nickel Saloon patron Tom Murphy introduces his friends in the saloon to his new love: a mermaid from the local circus. But first he has to contend with her shotgun toting father. See: *A Spider Poor Cowboy Rapt and Wide Lemon*

Psych (2006) [TV series]

Main cast: James Roday as Shawn Spencer, Dule Hill as Burton "Gus" Guster, Timothy Omundson as Carlton Lassiter, Maggie Lawson as Juliet O'Hara, Kirsten Nelson as Karen Vick, Corbin Bernsen as Henry Spencer.

Shawn and his childhood friend Gus own the detective agency Psych and work on cases for the Santa Barbara Police Department as dubious psychics.

"HIGH NOON-ISH" (4:03) [WMW]
Air date: August 21, 2009; Guest cast: James Brolin as Hank Mendel, Jim Beaver as Stinky Pete Dillingham, Brent Sexton as County Sheriff Becker; Executive producer: Steve Franks; Writer: Kell Cahoon; Director: Mel Damski; 44 min., USA Network, NBC (National Broadcasting Corporation), Color.

When Old Sonora Town, an Old West theme attraction, is threatened with closure, Carlton Lassiter enlists the services of Shawn and Gus to uncover the truth behind recent strange events and deaths. They discover a secret gold mine and the legend of the Ghost Rider that supposedly haunts the town.

Psyche [Comic book character; WW]

The original code name of **Danielle Moonstar** of the *New Mutants*.

See: **Mirage**

El Pueblo Fantasma (1965) [Film; Mexico; WW]

Premiere: February 5, 1965; Main Cast: Rodolfo de Anda, Fernando Luján, Julissa; Producers: Francisco Gomez Gonzalez, Enrique Rosas Priego; Story: Alfredo Ruanova; Director: Alfredo B. Crevenna; 80 min.; Estudios América; Spanish; B/W.

A gunfighter maintains his fast draw status by turning his victims into vampires.

Pulp Heroes [Comic book; WW]

First publication: 1997; Publisher: DC Comics.

A series of comic book annuals under various umbrella titles including *Weird Western Tales*. A tribute to the pulp magazine genres of the past including Young Romance, Suspense Detective, My Greatest Adventure and Tales of the Unexpected. Each title had a distinctive cover painting in the style of the pulp artists of old.

"WEIRD WESTERN TALES" TITLES:

Adventures of Superman Annual #9

"TERROR OF THE SIERRA MADRE"
First publication: September 1997; Story: John

Rozum; Art: Enrique Alcatena; Publisher: DC Comics.

An alien released from life-term imprisonment does battle with Superman Blue.

"THE RETURN OF SAGANOWAHNA"

Story: Mike W. Barr; Art: Dale Eaglesham, Scott Koblish.

Superman Blue must stop a Native American who is utilizing the powers of **Super-Chief** to force an Indian tribe into selling their land to make way for a gambling resort.

"THE JOURNEY OF THE HORSEMAN"

Story: Paul Grist; Art: Enrique Villagra.

An alien attempts to save the Earth.

Hitman Annual #1

"A COFFIN FULL OF DOLLARS"

First publication: October 1997; Story: Garth Ennis; Art: Carlos Ezquerra (Part 1 & 3), Steve Pugh (Part 2); Publisher: DC Comics.

Hitman Tommy Monaghan and partner "Natt The Hat" Walls must overcome the super-human speed of the gunman Manko, Sheriff Halliday and gang leader Santiago to gain possession of a coffin full of stolen money buried in a Texan cemetery. This modern Weird Western pays homage to Italian spaghetti Western director Sergio Leone.

Impulse Annual #2

"SHOWDOWN"

First publication: 1997; Story: Willaim Messner-Loebs; Art: Craig Rousseau, Barbara Kaalberg; Publisher: DC Comics.

Impulse and Max Mercury come to the aid of **Vigilante** as he confronts opposition to his plans to transform Mesa City into a "Dude Ranch of the Future."

"THUNDER IN MESA CITY" CH. 2: "LIGHTNING STRIKES AGAIN"

Story: Tom Peyer; Art: Anthony Castrillo, Sam Glanzman.

In the Old West of 1881, **Max Mercury** alias Windrunner meets Johnny Tane before he became Johnny Thunder.

Robin Annual #6

"THE LAW WEST OF GOTHAM"

First publication: 1997; Story: Chuck Dixon; Art: Eduardo Barreto; Publisher: DC Comics.

Robin teams up with **Nighthawk** and **Pow-Wow Smith** to help defeat the Trigger Twins, Tad

and Tom, whom they track to an Old West Theme Park in the environs of Gotham City. The story also features Huntress, Shotgun Smith and Paige Willingham alias Tonya Trigger. The Nighthawk and Pow-Wow Smith featured in this story are not related to the classic heroes from DC Comics history.

Purgatory (1999) [Telefilm; WW]

Premiere: January 10, 1999; Main Cast: Sam Shepard as Sheriff Forrest/Wild Bill Hickok, Eric Roberts as Blackjack Britton, Randy Quaid as Doc Woods/Doc Holliday; Executive Producer: David A. Rosemont; Story: Gordon Dawson; Director: Uli Edel; 94 min.; Rosemont Productions, TNT; Color.

An outlaw gang discovers the town of Refuge is actually the spiritual way station of Purgatory.

I Quattro dell'apocalisse (1975) [Film; Italy; WW]

Premiere: August 12, 1975; Main Cast: Fabio Testi as Stubby Preston, Lynne Frederick as Emanuelle "Bunny" O'Neill, Michael J. Pollard as Clem; Story: Francis Brett Harte, Ennio De Concini; Director: Lucio Fulci; 104 min.; Coralta Cinematografica; Color.

An Italian horror spaghetti Western tale of torture, brutality and a madman who sees and speaks to dead people.

See: *Four of the Apocalypse*

Queen Emeraldas (1998) [OVA; Japan; SFW]

Voice Cast: Reiko Tajima as Emeraldas, Megumi Hayashibara as Hiroshi Umino, Hirotaka Suzuoki as Eldomein; Animation: Oriental Light and Magic; Screenplay: Mugi Kamio; Director: Yuji Asada; Bandai Visual; 4 × 30 min.; Creator: Leiji Matsumoto; Original video animation; Color.

Emeraldas roams the galaxies in the distinctive *Queen Emeraldas* starship complete with skull and crossbones insignia, fighting for the oppressed and haunted by the memory of her lost love.

Departure; Release date: May 6, 1998.

Emeraldas visits Planet Daibaran, a wasteland with an Old West–style frontier town populated by various gunslingers. Coming to the aid of adolescent orphan Hiroshi Umino, she becomes involved in a shootout with the leader of the Afressians, Colonel Eldomain.

Eternal Emblem; Release date: October 7, 1998.

Eldomain kidnaps Horishi and the townspeople of Daibaran in an attempt to force Emeraldas into battle.

Two further OVAs were released in 1999: *Friendship* (August 6, 1999) and *Siren* (December 18, 1999).

"Queen of the Martian Catacombs" [Pulp fiction; SW]

Author: **Leigh Brackett**; First publication: *Planet Stories* (Summer 1949); Publisher: Love Romances, Inc.

Eric John Stark avoids prison by working as a mercenary for Kynon in a war in the Martian Drylands. He also becomes a double agent for his mentor Simon Ashton, leader of the Earth Police Control. When he meets Kynon's queen, he learns of her secret in the city of Sinharat.

This first appearance of Eric John Stark was followed by "**Enchantress of Venus**" (Fall 1949). *Queen of the Martian Catacombs* was extended into the novel *The Secret of Sinharat* in 1964.

"Quest of the Starstone" [Pulp fiction; SW]

Authors: **C. L. Moore** with Henry Kuttner; First publication: *Weird Tales* (November 1937).

Jirel, warrior maid of Joiry, gains possession of the magical jewel known as the Starstone. **Northwest Smith**, initially hired by Franga to retrieve the jewel, changes sides and helps Yarol and Jirel defeat the warlock.

Both men stood on the spongy ground with feet braced, bodies balanced in the easy tautness which characterizes the gunman, hands light on their weapons, eyes very steady, very deadly.

The Quick & the Dead [RPG book; WW]

Authors: Shane Lacy Hensley, John Hopler; First publication: 1997; Setting: **Deadlands: The Weird West**; Publisher: Pinnacle Entertainment Group.

The original setting book for *Deadlands: The Weird West* includes the reference guide "Tombstone Epitaph's Guide to the Weird West."

The Quick and the Undead (2006) [Film; WW]

Premiere: February 2, 2006; Main Cast: Clint Glenn as Ryn Baskin, Nicola Giacobbe as Hans Tubman, Parrish Randall as Blythe Remington; Producers: Clint Glenn, Gerald Nott; Story-Director: Gerald Nott; 90 min.; Nott Entertainment; Color.

A virus is turning the population into the living dead. Bounty hunter Ryn Baskin kills zombies and cuts off their fingers for the bounty money. But when an outlaw gang betrays him, he has more than zombies on his mind as he seeks revenge.

Quick Draw El Kabong (1999) [Animated film short; WW]

Air date: 1999; Story: Dave Berg; Director: George Evelyn; Wild Brain Productions, 2 min.; Cartoon Network, Color.

Masked vigilante El Kabong alias Quick Draw McGraw saves a Mexican village of skeleton townsfolk from the resident "Bad Guy" in this revisionist take on the Hanna-Barbera character.

Quick Gun Murugan (2008) [Film; India; WW]

Premiere: April 15, 2008; Main Cast: Rajendraprasad as Quick Gun Murugan, Shanmugha Rajan as Gun Powder, Ashwin Mushran as Dr. Django, Rambha as Mango Dolly; Executive Producers: Junaid Pandrowala, Kumud Radhika Shahi; Story: Rajesh Devraj; Director: Shashanka Ghosh; Phat Phish Motion Pictures; Color.

Surreal Western spoof featuring a reincarnated karmic cowboy cow protector in modern India in a battle of vegetarianism vs. non-vegetarianism.

Quicksilver [Comic book character; SFW]

First appearance: *National Comics* #5 (November, 1940); Publisher: Quality Comics, DC Comics.

The first incarnation of **Max Mercury**.

Radio Ranch (1940) [Film; SFW]

Alternative title for **Men with Steel Faces**.

Rain o' Terror [RPG book; WW]

Author: Anthony Ragan; First publication: 2000; Setting: **Deadlands: The Weird West**; Publisher: Pinnacle Entertainment Group.

Fineas Von Landingham's airship has been stolen together with his new "doomsday device." But nobody has a clue who stole it.

Rakar [Comic book character; France; WW]

First appearances: *Zembla* #60; *Special-Zemba* #23 (1968); Story: Franco Frecura; Art: Ivo Pavone.

1. Costumed avenger with the secret identity of a Lakota chief who fights to preserve law and

Page from *Rakar*. Story by Franco Frecura, art by Ivo Pavone. © Mosaic Multimedia. Used with permission.

The Rangers
[Comic book characters; WW]

First appearance: *Incredible Hulk* #265 (November 1981); Creators: Bill Mantlo, Sal Buscema, Publisher: Marvel Comics.

A superhero group that includes the Weird Western characters **Phantom Rider**, **Red Wolf**, **Texas Twister** and **Shooting Star**. They initially formed after defeating super-villain Corruptor and also featured in *West Coast Avengers* #8 and *Civil War* #7.

See: **Ghost Rider**

Rango (2011) [Animated film; WW]

Premiere: March 4, 2011; Voice Cast: Johnny Depp as Rango-Lars, Isla Fisher as Beans, Alfred Molina as Roadkill, Timothy Olyphant as Spirit of the West, Abigail Breslin as Priscilla, Ned Beatty as Mayor, Bill Nighy as Rattlesnake Jake. Ray Winstone as Badd Bill, Harry Dean Stanton as Balthazar, Claudia Black as Angelique; Executive producer: Tim Headington; Story: John Logan, Gore Verbinski, James Ward Byrkit; Director: Gore Verbinski; 107 min.; Paramount Pictures, Nickelodeon Movies, Blind Wink Productions, GK Films; Color.

A wandering chameleon in search of an identity adopts the name Rango when he comes across the Old West town of Dirt. Impressing the locals when he succeeds in killing an aggressive giant hawk Rango is appointed Sheriff and is tasked with solving the drought problem. Rango

order in the Old West, alongside Briton Piquefouille and Pawnee Casanova.

2. This modern-day descendent of the 19th century Rakar possesses superhuman strength, senses, speed, reflexes, and stamina. Francis White River served in the U.S. Army Marines Corps before his resignation. He is a member of the super-team Hexagon.

Rango (2011), an animated film starring the voice talents of, from left, John Cothran Jr. as Elgin, Blake Clark as Buford, Stephen Root as Doc, Johnny Depp as Rango, Ian Abercrombie as Ambrose, Isla Fisher as Beans, and Alex Managuan as Spoons (Paramount Pictures, Nickelodeon Movies, Blind Wink Productions, GK Films).

soon discovers he's not cut out for the job and leaves town. But he regains his sense of purpose and destiny when he encounters the Spirit of the West, who tells him, "No man can walk out on his own story." Adopting the persona of Spirit of the West, who bears a striking resemblance to Clint Eastwood's "the Man with No Name," Rango defeats gunslinger Rattlesnake Jake and his rapid-fire gatling gun. And when he discovers the tortoise Mayor has been hoarding the water he restores it to the thankful townsfolk of Dirt.

Todd McCarthy of *The Hollywood Reporter* (March 1, 2011) remarked: "The dusty cards of the Old West are reshuffled into a winning hand in *Rango*, a madly clever animated sagebrush saga with style and wit to burn."

Rapunzel's Revenge [Juvenile book; WW]

Authors: Shannon and Dean Hale; Illustrator: Nathan Hale; First publication: New York: Bloomsbury, 2008.

Rapunzel, using her long red hair, escapes her enclosed world joins forces with an outlaw named Jack and his goose. Together they encounter magic in the territory of Gothel's Reach as they search for Rapunzel's mother, who is being held captive by the witch Gothel.

An updated version of the classic fairy tale in comic book form, set in a mythical landscape based on the American West.

Rascals, Varmints & Critters [RPG book; WW]

Authors: Tim Beach, Hal Mangold, etc.; First publication: 1998; Setting: **Deadlands: The Weird West**; Publisher: Pinnacle Entertainment Group.

Bestiary for *Deadlands: The Weird West*.

Rascals, Varmints & Critters 2: The Book of Curses [RPG book; WW]

Author: John Goff; First publication: 2000; Setting: **Deadlands: The Weird West**; Publisher: Pinnacle Entertainment Group.

The second bestiary for *Deadlands: The Weird West* includes profiles of Dracula, Frankenstein, and Springheel Jack.

Ravenous (1999) [Film; WW]

Premiere: January 24, 1999; Main Cast: Robert Carlyle as Col. Ives/F.W. Colqhoun, David Arquette as Pvt. Cleaves, Guy Pearce as Capt. John Boyd, Jeffrey Jones as Hart, Jeremy Davies as Toffler, John Spencer as General Slauson; Story: Ted Griffin; Director: Antonia Bird; 101 min.; ETIC Films, Twentieth Century–Fox; Color.

In the aftermath of the Mexican-American war of 1847 a Scottish traveler named Colqhoun finds refuge from the snow at Fort Spenser in the Sierra Nevadas. He tells Commanding Officer Hart, disgraced U.S. Army Captain John Boyd and others a tale of being trapped and snowbound in a cave with the evil Colonel Ives who resorted to eating human flesh. But when Hart decides to lead a search party to the cave to apprehend Col. Ives he comes to the grim realization that Colqhoun was the sole survivor and must have butchered and eaten everyone himself. A deranged Colqhoun kills everyone in the search party except Boyd who himself is forced to eat human flesh to survive.

Some time later Colqhoun returns to Fort Spenser posing as Colonel Ives. Only Boyd recognizes him and knows of their shared secret lust for flesh and of the Indian legend that says a man who eats human flesh steals their spirit and his hunger becomes insatiable as he becomes stronger. A showdown between the ravenous Colqhoun and Boyd, who resists his urge for flesh, becomes inevitable.

Variety film critic Todd McCarthy (January 25, 1999) concluded: "In its final stretch, tale becomes a watered-down, bloodied up frontier version of Faust and Mephistopholes. The story is at least strange enough to engage the interest, but Griffin's script is ultimately sophomoric and Bird's direction develops little tension or mystery as to what's going on or what will happen."

Ravenstorm [Comic book character; WW]

"Ghost Town"

First publication: *Marvel Two-in-One* #14 (March 1976); Story: Bill Mantlo; Art: Herb Trimpe, John Tartaglione; Publisher: Marvel Comics.

Demon spirit Kthara takes possession of the reanimated Jedediah Ravenstorm, a part Cherokee who had previously cursed the townsfolk of Lawless, Arizona, at the gallows one hundred years ago.

Rawhide Kid [Comic book; WW]

First appearance: *Rawhide Kid* #1, March 1955; Creators: **Stan Lee**, Bob Brown; Publisher: Atlas Comics–Marvel Comics.

1. The original Atlas Comics title was a standard Western comic book title lasting 16 issues before cancellation in September 1957.

2. Stan Lee and Jack Kirby provided *Rawhide Kid* with a back-story when the title was revived by Marvel Comics in August 1960. He started life as Johnny Clay before taking the surname of his adoptive father Texas Ranger Ben Bart following his parents' massacre by Cheyenne Indians. When Ben Bart was killed by outlaws, Johnny vowed to exact revenge. Although he decided on a life of helping others in trouble, he quickly gained an unjust reputation as an outlaw.

Weird Menace villains included an outlaw named Raven who dressed in a maroon bird costume and jumped on his victims from a great height; Red Raven, who was similar to Raven but learned to glide on the air currents; skilled athlete and gymnast The Rattler who dressed from head to foot in a green reptile costume; and pickpocket Bullet-Proof Man, who swapped live bullets for blanks and was considered invulnerable by his opponents.

Weird Western storylines:

"The Living Totem" [WW]

First publication: #22 (June 1961); Story: Stan Lee; Art: Jack Kirby, **Dick Ayers**.

The giant Living Totem, a hostile extraterrestrial whose spaceship crashed to Earth, is buried underground by Native Americans. A silver mine foreman accidentally releases him during mining operations. Now he plans to regain control of humans.

"The Ape Strikes" [SFW]

First publication: #39 (April 1964); Story: Stan Lee; Art: Dick Ayers.

When a trained gorilla exhibits human skills such as accurately firing a rifle, the Rawhide Kid begins to suspect that mad scientist Dr. Karlbad's brain has been transplanted into the ape.

"When the Scorpion Strikes" [SFW]

First publication: #57 (April 1967); Story: Larry Lieber; Art: Larry Lieber, John Tartaglione.

When Matt Cody humiliates apothecary Jim Evans in front of his girlfriend the latter seeks revenge by adopting a secret identity as the Scorpion and creating pellets that paralyze his victims.

See: **Ghost Rider**

3. The original Rawhide Kid was reduced to a dime novel creation in the 2000 mini-series *Blaze of Glory*.

4. In 2004, the five-issue mini-series *Rawhide Kid: Slap Leather* provided Rawhide Kid with a new homosexual persona.

The Rawhide Terror (1934) [Film; WMW]

Premiere: 1934; Main Cast: Art Mix as Al, Edmund Cobb as the Sheriff, Bill Desmond as Tom Blake, William Barrymore as Brent, Tommy Bupp as Jimmy Brent; Producer: Denver Dixon (Victor Adamson); Story: A. V. Anderson (Victor Adamson), Jack Nelson; Director: Jack Nelson, Bruce Mitchell; 52 min.; Security Pictures; B/W.

A phantom killer terrorizes the townsfolk of Red Dog, leaving behind his calling card, a strip of rawhide with the inscription "Remember ten years ago." This re-edited first part of an aborted serial was marketed as the first horror Western.

Co-written and co-produced by the eccentric Victor Adamson who was renowned for his two-day shoots, extremely low budgets and his hiring of near-incompetent crew members.

Razored Saddles [Book anthology; WW]

Editors: **Joe R. Lansdale**, Pat LoBrutto; Illustrations: Rick Araluce; First publication: Arlington Heights IL: Dark Harvest, 1989.

Anthology of horror, science-fiction and contemporary Western stories: *Black Boots* by Robert R. McCammon, *Thirteen Days of Glory* by Scott A. Cupp, *Gold* by Lewis Shiner, *The Tenth Toe* by F. Paul Wilson, *Sedalia* by David J. Schow, *Trapline* by Ardath Mayhar, *Trail of the Chromium Bandits* by Al Sarrantonio, *Dinker's Pond* by Richard Laymon, *Stampede* by Melissa Mia Hall, *Razored Saddles* by Robert Petitt, *Tony Red Dog* by Neal Barrett, Jr., *The Passing of the Western* by Howard Waldrop, *Eldon's Penitente* by Lenore Carroll, *The Job* by Joe R. Lansdale, *I'm Always Here* by Richard Christian Matheson and " by Chet Williamson.

Real American #1 [Comic book character; WMW]

First appearance: *Daredevil Comics #2* (August 1941); Creator: Dick Briefer; Publisher: Lev Gleason Publications.

> Jeff Dixon, full-blooded Indian and prominent lawyer, becomes the Bronze Terror in order to save his people from the wicked, cruel and corrupt vermin that are oppressing them.

Following the framing of his father for murder, Apache lawyer Jeff Dixon adopts a new, terrifying persona that includes a skull-mask for himself and his gray stallion.

Real Western Stories [Pulp magazine; WW]

First publication: December 1949; Publisher: Columbia Publications.

Real Western Stories began life as *Real Western Magazine* in January 1935. It was initially published by Ace Books and edited by A. A. Wyn; Robert W. Lowndes became the editor when Ace Books was taken over by Columbia Publications.

The title changed to *Real Western Stories* in December 1949 and lasted until April 1960. In February 1959 it became a digest-size magazine. One-hundred-thirty-five issues were published between 1935 and 1960. The title is remembered today for featuring the Weird West adventures of **Lee Winters** by **Lon Williams**.

The Reavers of Skaith [Novel; SW]

Author: **Leigh Brackett**; First publication: New York: Ballantine Books, 1976.

On a brutal, lawless planet, a betrayed **Eric John Stark** plans to bring freedom to the oppressed people of Skaith and make his escape. The final book in the Skaith trilogy.

See: *The Ginger Star*; *The Hounds of Skaith*

Red Country [Novel; WW]

Author: Joe Abercrombie; First publication: New York: Orbit, 2012.

Searching for two missing siblings, Shy South, her spineless old stepfather Lamb and two oxen venture into the lawless Far Country on their journey to the gold fever mining town of Crease. Their journey becomes one of self discovery as hidden, dark pasts are confronted and uneasy alliances are formed with soldier of fortune Nicomo Cosca and his weak lawyer Temple.

David Barrett of *The Independent* (UK) wrote: "Abercrombie has attempted something quite audacious—he's essentially written a Western in the style of one from Clint Eastwood's classic period, but set it in an epic fantasy world. And, darn if he doesn't pull it off. *Red Country* reads like neither a Western nor a fantasy novel, but something new, fresh and exciting."

Red Dead Redemption: Undead Nightmare [Video game; WW]

Release date: October 26, 2010; Writers: Dan Houser, Michael Unsworth; Senior Animation Specialist: Abraham Ahmed; Platform: PlayStation 3, Xbox 360; Developer: Rockstar San Diego-North; Publisher: Rockstar Games.

In this *Red Dead Redemption* expansion pack,

retired outlaw John Marston searches for a cure for a zombie plague that has spread throughout the Old West. His quest takes him to Mexico and the cause of the plague—a stolen ancient Aztec mask. Marston returns the mask and stops the zombie plague, but dies a few months later. The plague returns when Seth Briars steals the Aztec mask and John Marston becomes the latest member of the undead.

The player operates in an open world environment with zombie encounters in the form of the undead, zombie animals, hideouts and graveyards. The "Dead Eye" gunslinger can attack hordes of zombies with multiple shooting targets. There is also an online multiplayer mode that allows up to 16 players to take part at once.

Red Dwarf (1988) [TV series; UK]

Dave Lister finds himself marooned in space three million years in the future as the last remaining human survivor of the mining ship Red Dwarf. But he soon discovers he isn't alone in this BBC-TV comedy series.

"GUNMEN OF THE APOCALYPSE" (6:03)
Airdate: October 21, 1993; Main Cast: Chris Barrie as Rimmer-Dangerous Dan McGrew, Craig Charles as Lister-Brett Riverboat, Danny John-Jules as Cat-The Riviera Kid, Robert Llewellyn as Kryten-Sheriff, Jennifer Calvert as Loretta, Dennis Lill as Simulant Captain-Death, Robert Inch as War, Dinny Powell as Famine, Jeremy Peters as Pestilence; Executive producers-Story: Rob Grant, Doug Naylor; Director: Andy De Emmony; 30 min.; BBC-TV; Color.

Cyborgs called Simulants infect the spaceship Starbug with a computer virus as it heads towards a deadly collision with a volcanic planet. Searching for a solution Kryten enters a Virtual Reality environment but finds himself threatened by "The Apocalypse Boys" in an Old West town. Rimmer, Lister and Cat link to an AR console and a Western video game to enter Kryten's "reality" to fight the virus with a showdown.

Red Hawk [Comic book character; WMW]

First appearance: **Straight Arrow** #2; Art: **Bob Powell**; Publisher: Magazine Enterprises.

Set in an early American West, the adventures of Cheyenne brave Red Hawk featured many Weird Menace tales including:

"THE FANGED KILLER" [WMW]

First publication: Straight Arrow #18 (October 1951)
A disguised Comanche who lives among wolves has the power to command them to attack hunters and steal their furs.

"CLAWS OF DEATH" [WMW]
First publication: Straight Arrow #27 (October 1952)
A panther woman creates the illusion of her transformation into a black panther.

"THE FLYING HORROR" [WMW]
First publication: Straight Arrow #31 (June 1953)
An Indian tribe is convinced that the legendary Pa'aka the flying cat woman has come to life. But unknown to them, the Cheyenne woman known as Featherfoot is exploiting their fears with an outfit of feathered wings, claws and a fearsome mask.

"THE BEAR STICK" [WMW]
First publication: Straight Arrow #33 (October 1953)
Singing Doe, believed to dead following an attack by the Sioux, is painted in phosphorescent paint by Red Hawk to trick his friend Wolfpaw into thinking she is a ghost.

"LANDS BEYOND THE SUNSET" [WMW]
First publication: Straight Arrow #36 (April 1954)
A medicine man promises paradise in the Indian version of Heaven known as "The Happy Hunting Grounds." But it is all a scam to steal wampum. Indian Zombies feature in one panel.

"CANYON BEAST" [WW]
First publication: Straight Arrow #39 (October 1954)
A dinosaur menaces the Cheyenne after it hatches from a prehistoric egg and grows to huge proportions.

Bob Powell provided the art for the entire 54-issue run in Straight Arrow. Powell also illustrated Red Hawk in his one-issue solo title in 1953 and in **Bobby Benson's B-Bar-B Riders**.

Red Larabee, the Gunhawk [Comic book character]

First appearance: **Wild Western** #15 (April 1951); Art: Joe Maneely; Publisher: Atlas Comics.

Vowing to avenge the murder of his father, Preston Hardwick assumes the identity of Red Larabee. Complete with bulletproof vest, he uses his gunfighting skills to battle crime and bring killers to justice. His ten-issue run in *Wild Western* included two Weird Western stories.

"THE ALTAR OF QUAPULTEC" [WW]

First publication: *Wild Western* #20 (February 1952); Art: Chic Stone.

Aztecs living in the heart of a Sierra Madre volcano guard a golden key that can alter history and offer Red Larabee as a sacrifice to their gods.

"LEGION OF THE DEAD" [WW]

First publication: *Wild Western* #22 (June 1952); Art: Chic Stone.

Four executed murderers return from the dead.

Red Mask [Comic book character; Comic book; WW]

1. First appearance: *Tim Holt* #20 (November 1950); Creators: Ray Krank, Frank Bolle; Publisher: Magazine Enterprises.

Tim Holt adopted the alter ego Redmask to fight crime in issue #20 of his own title. The change in direction allowed for more colorful and offbeat characters including a lady with attitude who would eventually become his partner, the **Black Phantom**.

2. First publication: #42 (June-July 1954); Publisher: Magazine Enterprises.

Red Mask continued the numbering of its predecessor *Tim Holt* when it changed titles in June 1954. The comic book continued to publish **Ghost Rider** until issue #50 with **The Presto Kid** replacing it until the final issue #54 in September 1957.

Red Plains Rider [Comic book character, Podcast character; SW]

First publication: August, 2013; Story: Ben Acker, Ben Blacker; Art: Lar deSouza, Evan Larson, Evan Shaner; Publisher: Archaia Entertainment.

Born on Earth, the *Red Plains Rider* was found abandoned on Mars and raised by Martians. Following failed relationships with **Croach the Tracker** and **Sparks Nevada** "Red" married **Cactoid Jim**. That relationship also failed and ended in divorce. "Red" is renowned for her sharpshooting skills and tough demeanor as she delivers her own brand of justice on the red plains of Mars.

Published as part of a comic strip anthology collection inspired by the popular live audio theater show and podcast, **The Thrilling Adventure** *Hour* where Busy Phillips and Annie Savage play the character.

Red Prophet: The Tales of Alvin Maker [Comic book; SFW]

First publication: March 2006; Creator: Orson Scott Card; Publisher: Marvel Comics, Dabel Brothers Publishing.

A six-issue adaptation of Orson Scott Card's *Red Prophet: Tales of Alvin Maker* series. This alternate history of the American frontier involves the magical world of young Alvin Maker, a witness to history (the war between the red men and whites) along the Mizzipy River.

Red Ryder and the Secret of Wolf Canyon [Novel; WMW]

Author: S. S. Stevens; First publication: Racine, WI: Whitman, 1941.

Ranchers are being slaughtered in Wolf Creek. As Red Ryder and his Indian sidekick Little Beaver arrive in town the attacks and deaths continue and soon Red Ryder becomes the target of a monster wolf. Are werewolves at large or is it all a tactic to kill and scare away ranchers?

S.S. Stevens is a pseudonym for acclaimed *Red Ryder* artist Fred Harman, who drew the syndicated newspaper strip for 26 years.

Red Wolf [Comic book character; WW]

1. First appearance: *Marvel Spotlight* #1, November 1971; Creators: **Gardner Fox**, Syd Shores; Publisher: Marvel Comics.

The first incarnation saw Red Wolf as an adopted Cheyenne named Johnny Wakeley in the late 1800s. Raised by white foster parents who were brutally murdered by Native Americans, Wakeley was granted the power of the late warrior Red Wolf by the Cheyenne spirit god Owayodata.

2. First appearance: *The Avengers* #80, September 1970; Creators: Roy Thomas, John Buscema; Publisher: Marvel Comics.

Following the murder of his family, William Talltrees swears vengeance on the murderers and is visited by Owayodata, who passes on the power of Red Wolf to a new generation.

The second incarnation of Red Wolf alias William Talltrees was published 14 months before the complete story of his first incarnation was revealed.

Redblade [Comic book character; WW]

"Strange on the Range"

First appearance: *Marvel Fanfare* #49 (February 1990); Story-Art: Alan Weiss; Publisher: Marvel Comics.

Marvel's regular characters Dr. Strange, Nick Fury and Dum Dum Dugan traveled through time to feature in this one-off appearance by Chief Redblade of the Huachaqua Apaches. Redblade seeks revenge on the white man by using his mystical powers as a medicine man to transform himself into a giant beast.

Reed, Ishmael (1938–) [Author]

Born in Chattanooga, Tennessee, and raised in Buffalo, New York, Reed co-founded the underground newspaper *The East Village Other* in 1965. His first novel, *The Free-Lance Pallbearers*, was published two years later. A move to California and a teaching position at the University of California at Berkeley followed. Reed is an accomplished African-American author who challenges literary conventions and standard views of American culture and society.

Selected works: *The Free-Lance Pallbearers* (1967), **Yellow Back Radio Broke-Down** (1969), *Mumbo Jumbo* (1972), *Flight to Canada* (1976), *Reckless Eyeballing* (1986), *Japanese by Spring* (1993).

El Regreso del Monstruo (1959) [Film; Mexico; WW]

Premiere: August 12, 1959; Main Cast: Luis Aguilar as El Zorro Escarlata, Tere Velazquez as Young Lady, Jaime Fernandez as Sergio; Producer: Luis Manrique; Story: Luis Manrique, Antonio Orellana, Fernando Osés; Director: Joselito Rodríguez; 63 min.; Filmadora Méxicana S.A.; Spanish; B/W.

El Zorro Escarlata confronts a Frankenstein-like monster and a talking skeleton.

Renegade (2004) [Film; France; WW]

U.S. release title for **Blueberry: L'Expérience Secrète.**

Resnick, Mike (1942–) [Author]

Five-time Hugo Award-winning author Mike Resnick was born in Chicago, Illinois. He began his, prolific career in 1964 writing numerous "adult" novels under a pseudonym. Resnick has written over 50 science fiction novels and more than 175 short stories. His books can be divided into various fiction series including *Tales of the Galactic Midway*, *Eros*, *The Chronicles of Lucifer*

Jones, *Widowmaker*, *Oracle* and *Galactic Comedy*. Many include Western genre influences.

Selected works: *The Soul Eater* (1981), *Sideshow* (1982), **The Best Rootin' Tootin' Shootin' Gunslinger in the Whole Damned Galaxy** (1983), *Eros Ascending* (1984), *Adventures* (1985), **Santiago: A Myth of the Far Future** (1986), *Paradise* (1989), *Soothsayer* (1991), **The Widowmaker** (1996), **The Outpost** (2001)

The Return of Santiago [Novel; SW]

Author: **Mike Resnick**; First publication: New York: Tor, 2003.

Danny Briggs is a small-time thief with a mission to resurrect the legend of Santiago, outlaw of the Inner Frontier. Together with sidekick Virgil Soaring Hawk, he chronicles the exploits of the new legends of the Inner Frontier in his search for Santiago.

See: **Santiago: A Myth of the Far Future**

The Return of the Indian [Juvenile novel; Film; WW]

Author: Lynne Reid Banks; First publication: Garden City NY: Doubleday, 1986.

Fearing the consequences of Little Bear becoming trapped in the world of "giants," Omri entrusts his mother with the magical key to the cupboard. But temptation overcomes Omri and he uses the key once again only to discover Little Bear has been badly wounded in the Indian Wars. Omri must save his Indian friend and his village from destruction.

Sequel to **The Indian in the Cupboard.**

Revelation Trail (2013) [Film; WW]

Premiere: April 12, 2013; Main Cast: Daniel Van Thomas as The Preacher, Daniel Britt as Marshal Edwards, Robert Valentine as Samuel Beard, Jordan Elizabeth Goettling as Isabelle; Executive producer: David L. Gibson; Story: John P. Gibson, Daniel Van Thomas; Blake Armstrong; Director: John P. Gibson; 108 min.; Living End Productions, Extra Life Media, Entertainment One; Color.

This low budget production is set in the early 1880s where a Preacher joins forces with the Marshal of an Old West frontier town in a fight against the undead.

Richfield Presents Rockets and Range Riders [Comic book; SFW]

First publication: May 1957; Art: Alex Toth; Distributor: Richfield Oil Corporation.

As a family watches a rocket test in the American West, the grandfather recalls his time as a prospector in the Old West when gunslingers stole his gold and he was left with common borax. His grandson explains that Borax is now called Boron and is invaluable in the manufacture of rocket fuel. The father reminds them both that Boron is used in gasoline produced by Richfield Oil Corporation.

One-shot 16-page educational giveaway comic book to promote Boron gasoline.

Rick Montana [Comic book character; SW]

First appearance: *Tales From the Edge* #1 (June 1993); Creator: David J. Spurlock; Publisher: Vanguard Productions.

Space cowboy Rick Montana is lost in time and space as he protects the galaxy from evil forces with the help of his curvaceous sidekick Cindy. Montana has been described as a cross between John Wayne, Han Solo and Mal Reynolds. His *Tales from the Edge* comic strip adventures were later reprinted in *Space Cowboy* (2001).

Ricochet Rabbit & Droop-a-Long (1964) [Animated TV series]

Voice Cast: Don Messick as Ricochet Rabbit, Mel Blanc as Droop-a-Long; Stories: Tony Benedict, Warren Foster, Dalon Sandifer; Hanna-Barbera Productions; 23 × 7 min.; Color.

Animated tales of Sheriff Ricochet Rabbit of Hoop 'n' Holler and his deputy Droop-a-Long Coyote. Originally a segment of *The Magilla Gorilla Show* before moving to the series *Peter Potamus* for the second season.

"Mostly Ghostly" (2:05) [WW]
Air date: October 9, 1965; Directors: William Hanna, Joseph Barbera.

When Ghost Town Gus robs a stagecoach, Ricochet and Droopy enlist the aid of Great Granddaddy Richochet's ghost to capture the mischievous spirit.

"Space Sheriff" (2:11)[SFW]
Air date: November 20, 1965; Directors: William Hanna, Joseph Barbera.

Ricochet and Droopy travel to Mars to help the Martians battle the monster known as Gruesome Grock. Richochet defeats him with the help of his Super-Squelch bullets but on his return to Earth he discovers Gruesome is the new sheriff.

Riders of the Whistling Skull (1937) [Film; SFW]

Premiere: January 4, 1937; Main Cast: Bob Livingston as Stony Brooke, Ray "Crash" Corrigan as Tucson Smith, Max Terhune as Lullaby Joslin, Mary Russell as Betty Marsh, Yakima Canutt as Otah, Chief Thunder Cloud as High Priest; Producer: Nat Levine; Story: Oliver Drake, Bernard McConville, John Rathmell. Based on characters created by William Colt MacDonald; Director: Mack V. Wright; 58 min.; Republic Pictures; B/W.

The Three Mesquiteers' search for missing scientists and the lost Indian city of Lukachuke takes them to Whistling Skull, a rock formation resembling a human skull. The fourth movie in Republic Pictures' *Three Mesquiteers* series features an Indian mummy restored to life and idol-worshipping Indians.

Riddick (2013) [Film; SW]

Premiere: September 6, 2013; Main Cast: Van Diesel as Riddick, Jordi Molla as Santana, Matt Nable as Boss Johns, Katee Sackhoff as Dahl, Dave Bautisa as Diaz, Karl Urban as Vaako, Bokeem Woodbine as Moss, Raoul Trujillo as Lockspur; Executive producers: Mike Drake, Samantha Vincent, George Zakk; Screenplay-Director: David Twohy; 119 min.; One Race Productions, Radar Pictures, Riddick Canada Productions; Color.

Two groups of mercenaries compete for the bounty and head of Riddick on a hostile planet. But a deadly oncoming storm, lethal predators and the ingenuity of Riddick himself stand in their way.

R. L. Stine's Haunting Hour: The Series (2010) [TV Series]

Anthology horror-fantasy series.

"Coat Rack Cowboy" (3:20) [WW]
Air date: November 9, 2013; Guest cast: Frankie Jonas as Ethan, Rowen Kahn as Brett, Juan Riedinger as John "Mad Dog" McCoy, Peter Benson as Dad; Series based on *The Haunting Hour: Don't Think About It* and *Nightmare Hour* by R.L. Stine; Story: Jack Monaco; Director: James Head; 23 min.; Haunting Hour Productions; Color.

The spirit of Old West gunslinger John "Mad Dog" McCoy returns to life when his hanging tree is cut down in the present day. A shootout with the young boy of the household has unexpected results when McCoy is faced with the consequences of his actions from over a century ago.

Ringo, It's Massacre Time (1970) [Film; Italy; WW]

U.S. release title for ***Giunse Ringo e ... fu tempo di massacro***.

El Río de las Ánimas (1963) [Film; Mexico; WW]

Premiere: February 13, 1964; Main Cast: Joaquín Cordero as Leonardo Moncada, Alma Delia Fuentes, Andrés Soler; Story-Director: Juan José Ortega; 95 min.; Productora Fílmica México; Spanish; B/W.

A fire spirit warns of impending danger in this Mexican horror Western.

Rio Kid [Comic book character; Italy; WW]

International name for ***Il Cavaliere del Texas***.

Ripclaw [Comic book character; WW]

First appearance: *Cyberforce* #1, 1992; Creator: Marc Silvestri; Publisher: Top Cow Productions.

American Indian Robert Berresford discovers his true heritage when a shaman introduces him to the spirits of his ancestors. After they tell him of his future destiny as leader of the Indian nation, he learns of his real name Robert Bearclaw and discovers his ability to shape shift his hands into bear claws. Bearclaw is captured by Cyberdata who surgically removes his hands and replaces them with cybernetic replacements that he can also transform into bear claws.

Bearclaw alias Ripclaw converses with the spirit world of his ancestors and is often surrounded by ghosts asking to be avenged for their deaths.

R.I.P.D. [Comic book; SFW]

First publication: October 1999; 4-part mini-series; Creator-Story: Peter Lenkov; Art: Lucas Marangon, Randy Emberlin; Publisher: Dark Horse Comics.

Nick Cruz is murdered by an unknown assailant. Now thanks to the R.I.P.D. (Rest in Peace Department) he is offered the opportunity to find his killer, even if it takes him to Hell and back. Helping Cruz is Old West Sheriff Roy Powell who has been tracking murderers for the last century.

R.I.P.D.: City of the Damned [Comic book; SFW]

First publication: November, 2012; 4-part mini-series; Story: Jeremy Barlow; Art: Tony Parker; Publisher: Dark Horse Comics.

This prequel to ***R.I.P.D.: Rest in Peace Department*** (2013) features Roy Pulsipher confronting his past in the Old West in a story described by the publisher as "Cowboys versus demons in the Wild West."

R.I.P.D.: Rest in Peace Department (2013) [Film; SFW]

Premiere: July 17, 2013; Main cast: Jeff Bridges as Roycephus "Roy" Pulsipher, Ryan Reynolds as Nick Walker, Kevin Bacon as Bobby Hayes. Mary-Louise Parker as Mildred Proctor, Stephanie Szostak as Julia Walker, James Hong as Grandpa Jerry Chen (Nick Walker's avatar), Marisa Miller (Roy Pulsipher's avatar); Producers: David Dobkin, Peter M. Lenkov, Neal H. Moritz, Mike Richardson; Story: David Dobkin, Phil Hay, Matt Manfreddi; Based on *Rest in Peace Department* by Peter M. Lenkov; Director: Robert Schwentke; 96 min.; Dark Horse Entertainment, Original Film, Relativity Media, Universal Pictures; Color.

The Rest in Peace Department partners murdered detective sergeant Nick Walker with United States Marshal and former American Civil War soldier Roycephus "Roy" Pulsipher. Walker's Boston police partner Bobby Hayes killed him after Walker decided stealing gold while on duty wasn't a good idea. And while Walker's task in the afterlife is to gather souls who won't move on, Walker is obsessed with avenging his murder. In their investigations Walker and Roy have human avatars on earth. Walker is an old Asian man, while Roy attracts wolf whistles as a sexy female model.

The film failed to recover its $130 million budget after receiving negative reviews. Stephanie Merry of *The Washington Post* (July 19, 2013) declared: "The comic book–based 'R.I.P.D.' is a dud that squanders a decent cast and succeeds neither as the comedy nor the action film it purports to be."

The Rise of Ransom City [Novel; SPW]

Author: Felix Gilman; First publication: Tor Books 2012.

In an alternate history America the people of the Gun and the people of the Line each fight to become the dominant force. The Gun invokes terror and fear with their demon-possessed guns that grant them supernatural powers and the Line, with the aid of Engine spirits, continues to build factories and enslave the people.

Part scam-artist, part inventor Harry Ransom

has created the Ransom Process, a process that produces light, heat and magnetism and appears to attract spirits. His invention attracts both the Line and the Gun who both see the potential for increased dominance and control. In this sequel to *The Half-Made World* author Felix Gilman recounts Ransom's story in the form of autobiography as we are introduced to various characters he meets on his travels as he searches for investors.

River o' Blood [RPG book; WW]

Author: John Goff; First publication: 1998; Setting: **Deadlands: The Weird West**; Publisher: Pinnacle Entertainment Group.

Location book for the Mississippi River and New Orleans adventure "Trouble A-Brewin.'"

The Road to Hell: Devil's Tower 1 [RPG book; WW]

Authors: Paul Beakley, John Hopler; First publication: 1998; Setting: **Deadlands: The Weird West**; Publisher: Pinnacle Entertainment Group.

Adventure set in the City o' Gloom, Salt Lake City. The posse of heroes must discover who is killing the scientists working for Professor Darius Hellstromme. The first part in the Devil's Tower trilogy.

See: **Heart o' Darkness: Devil's Tower 2; Fortress o' Fear: Devil's Tower 3**

Road Warriors [RPG book; WW]

Author: John Hopler; First publication: 1998; Setting: **Deadlands: Hell on Earth**; Publisher: Pinnacle Entertainment Group.

Vehicle and highways of *Hell on Earth* location sourcebook. Includes the adventure "Hell Riders."

The Roaring Whispers (2007) [Film; Australia]

Premiere: September 2007; Main Cast: Dave W. Phillips as Clem, Sari Sheehan as Charlotte; Executive Producers: James Barahanos, Sean Phillips, Sylvia Phillips; Story: Dave W. Phillips, Michael Zadro; Director: Dave W. Phillips; 65 min.; Barahanos Productions; Color.

A hit-man, a "dead" girl and a young man attempt to bring down a huge corporation that is draining the world's natural resources. This low-budget film was described by director Phillips as containing elements of *Mad Max* and *Django*.

Robotika [Comic book; SFW]

First publication: December 2005; Creator-Art: Alex Sheikman; Story: Alex Sheikman, David Moran; Publisher: Archaia Studios Press.

Elite bodyguard corps member Niko must recover a stolen invention that has the potential for untold harm in the wrong hands. Set on the fringes of civilized society where chaos and violence are the order of the day, this title is a blending of the Old West, science fiction, cyberpunk, steampunk and Japanese samurai tales.

Creator Alex Sheikman stated, "I grew up in the Soviet Union and as a kid was fascinated by the American Westerns. 'Freedom' was what

Poster of *Robotika*. Artwork by Alex Sheikman. © 2009 Alex Sheikman. Used with permission.

Robotika strip by Alex Sheikman. © 2009 Alex Sheikman. Used with permission.

those movies shouted to me. As I grew up and got exposed to spaghetti Westerns and later on to the samurai epics that inspired them I started to understand the complex story ideas that were explored in these tales. *Robotika* is my attempt to re-visit the hero's journey that the Westerns describe so well and by combining the eastern and the Western themes, I invented a whole new genre ... the Sushi Western."

Rocket Robin Hood (1966) [Animated TV series; Canada]

The space adventures of Rocket Robin Hood and his Merry Men in the year 3000.

"Jesse James Rides Again" (1:08) [SW]

Air date: November 12, 1967; Voice Cast: Ed McNamara as Rocket Robin Hood; Director: Shamus Culhane; 22 min.; Trillium Productions, Krantz Films, Grantray-Lawrence Animation; Color.

On a hunting expedition, Rocket Robin and Will Scarlet encounter an elderly descendant of the Old West outlaw Jesse James. With the help of his rocket-powered horse, Jesse James robs from the rich and keeps it for himself. Rocket Robin Hood arranges for the descendant to hold up a fake Interplanetary Stagecoach but complications ensue.

The episode is divided into three acts—"Jesse James Rides Again," "The Slowest Gun in the Universe" and "The Big Heist."

Rod Serling's Night Gallery (1970) [TV series]

Anthology series of tales of science fiction, horror and fantasy, hosted by Rod Serling.

"Dr. Stringfellow's Rejuvenator" (2:28) [WW]

Air date: November 17, 1971; Main Cast: Forrest Tucker as Dr. Stringfellow, Murray Hamilton as Snyder, Don Pedro Colley as Rolpho; Producer: Jack Laird; Story: Rod Serling; Director: Jerrold Freedman; 50 min.; Universal Television; Color.

Dr. Stringfellow, peddler of fake medicinal cures, becomes the victim of his own unscrupulous nature when a young woman dies.

"The Dark Boy" (2:30) [WW]

Air date: November 24, 1971; Main Cast: Elizabeth Hartman as Mrs. Judith Timm, Michael Baseleon as Tom Robb, Michael Laird as Joel Robb, Steven Lorange as Edward Robb;; Producer: Jack Laird; Original story: August Derleth; Teleplay: Halsted

Welles; Director: John Astin; 50 min.; Universal Television; Color.

Judith Timm's new teaching job in Montana is disturbed by the figure of youngster Joel Robb who, she learns, died two years earlier. Halsted Welles switched the original story's New England location to Montana in his teleplay.

"The Waiting Room" (2:51) [WW]

Air date: January 26, 1972; Main Cast: Steve Forrest as Sam Dichter, Lex Barker as Charlie McKinley, Buddy Ebsen as Doc Soames, Jim Davis as Abe Bennett, Albert Salmi as Joe Bristol, Gilbert Roland as The Bartender; Producer: Jack Laird; Story: Rod Serling; Director: Jeannot Szwarc; 50 min.; Universal Television; Color.

A notorious group of gunslingers meet endlessly in a saloon as they relive their final gunfights for eternity.

Rogue Angel: Teller of Tall Tales [Comic book; SFW]

First comic book publication: February 2008; Creator: Randall Toy; Story: Barbara Randall Kesel; Art: Renae De Liz; Publisher: IDW Publishing.

Five-issue miniseries based on the series of books starring Annja Creed, archaeologist, cable show co-host and heir to Joan of Arc's mystical sword. Her research leads her to the Old West town of Virginia City in search of a manuscript that could alter Mark Twain's public reputation.

El Rojo (1966) [Film; Italy-Spain; WW]

Main Cast: Richard Harrison as El Rojo, Nieves Navarro as Consuelo, Peter Carter [Piero Lulli] as Lasky, Mirko Ellis as Cochise, Rita Klein as Pamela, Raf Baldassare as Ramon; Executive Producer: Tonino Sarno; Story: Roberto Amoroso, Leo Colman [Leopoldo Savona], Mike Mitchell, Rate Furlan; Director: Leo Colman [Leopoldo Savona]; 82 min.; Petruka Films, Ramo Films; Color.

El Rojo seeks vengeance on four hired guns who slaughtered his family. A violent tale of retribution is given a Weird Western twist with the inclusion of Black Bart, a character with a scarred and disfigured face hidden behind a clay mask in the style of the Phantom of the Opera. A metallic cybernetic voice adds to the weird quality of the character.

The Rook [Comic book character; Comic book; SFW]

1. First appearance: *Eerie* #82, March 1977;

Creator: Bill DuBay; Publisher: Warren Publishing.

Scientific industrialist Restin Dane has a penchant for dressing as an Old West gunslinger as he travels through time in the Time Castle, a machine that resembles a rook chess piece. He arrives at many destinations both future and past, including the Old West, in *Eerie* issues #82 thru 85.

In a story arc featuring villainous Sheriff Gat Hawkin, Dane arrives in Chancellorsville, Arizona, in 1874 and discovers a hidden mine shaft complete with alien scientific artifacts, located beneath his headquarters in present-day 1977. Wanting the Time Castle for himself, Hawkin critically wounds Dane. Bishop Dane, whom Restin Dane first met as a youngster at the Alamo, takes control of the Time Castle, traveling to the future to bring aid to Restin Dane in the form of the cavalry. Restin realizes he has been saved from a premature death by his great-great-grandfather, Bishop Dane.

Following his regular appearances in *Eerie*, Dane was promoted to his own comic book in 1979. It ran to 14 issues.

2. The character was revived and updated by Harris Comics in November 1994 in the three-issue mini-series *Chains of Chaos* before graduating to his own short-lived title in June 1995. Restin Dane a.k.a. The Rook now travels through the reality flow, a stream of energy that connects all dimensions and times. With his body acting as a host to a parasitic second skin of Chaotic armor, he combats the shards of Chaos in alternate realities, including the Old West.

A Rope of Thorns (*Hexslinger* book #2) [Novel; WW]

Author: Gemma Files; First Publication: Toronto: ChiZine Publications, 2011.

The Reverend Asher Rook, hexslinger, founds a town where magicians can live in peace. But Rook is consort to lxchel, a resurrected Mayan goddess and sacrificial victim Chess Pargeter seeks revenge with the help of Ed Murrow, Pinkerton agent turned outlaw.

Rory Randall the Singin' Cowboy [Comic book character; SFW]

First publication: *Prime Cuts* #1 (January 1987); Creator: Mitch Manzer; Publisher: Fantagraphic Books.

"Treasure of the Lost Empire"

The underground city of Vizania is ruled by evil dictator Namron, who plots to kidnap Rory Randall. Humor strip influenced in part by the 1930s Gene Autry film serial *The Phantom Empire*.

Roswell 1847 (2007) [Film: SFW]

Premiere: November 29, 2007; Main Cast: Norman Lovett as Alein, Kimberley Palmer as Medicine woman, Gabrielle Amies as Gabby, William Cheney as Sheriff Cheney; Executive producer: Geoff Eyers; Screenplay-Director: Ian Paterson; 86 min.; Cheney Films, Superteam Films; Color.

In 1847 a group of English settlers in search of Free Land end up in the old west and Roswell, New Mexico. They soon learn it is a frontier town with secrets.

Roswell, Texas [Web comic, Graphic Novel; SW]

First publication: 2006; Story: L. Neil Smith, Rex F. May; Art: Scott Bieser; Publisher: Big Head Press.

Science fiction Western set in an alternative timeline where Texas never joined the United States and Davy Crockett survived the Alamo to pursue a career in politics. Texican President Charles A. Lindbergh orders his friend "Wild Bill" Bear and a group of Texas Rangers to investigate reports of a flying saucer crash in Roswell in 1947.

Originally published as a serialized online comic strip before publication as a graphic novel in June 2008.

Rotten [Comic book; WW]

First publication: June, 2009; Story: Mark Rahner; Art: Dan Dougherty; Publisher: Moonstone.

The year, 1877. William Wade, secret agent for President Rutherford B. Hayes is assigned, along with partner J.J. Flynn, to travel the Old West to investigate reported outbreaks of the living dead.

The Rough Bunch [Comic book characters; SFW]

First appearance: *Guy Gardner: Warrior* #24 (September 1994); Creator: Beau Smith; Publisher: DC Comics.

The Rough Bunch, comprised of **Nighthawk**, **Cinnamon**, **El Diablo**, **Scalphunter**, **Pow-Wow Smith**, Strongbow, **Bat Lash**, Johnny Thunder, Madame .44 and Matt Savage, first gathered as a group to fight super-villain Extant and his time-zombies in the Old West of 1879.

Cover of *Roswell, Texas*. Story by L. Neil Smith and Rex F. May, art by Scott Bieser. © 2009 Big Head Press. Used with permission.

The Ruff & Reddy Show (1957) [Animated TV series]

The first television series from Hanna-Barbera featured a smart kitten named Ruff and a slow-witted dog named Reddy. It was filmed at the height of popularity of the TV Western and therefore included some Western-themed episodes. Stories were serialized over a 12- or 13-episode story arc in four-minute segments. Texas outlaw twins Killer and Diller featured in various storylines throughout the run of the series with one story arc involving a haunted gold mine.

"Spooky Meeting at Spooky Rock" (3:14) through "Tailspin Twins" (3:26) [WW]

Airdate: January 9, 1960–February 6, 1960; Voice Cast: Don Messick (Ruff, Professor Gizmo, Diller), Daws Butler (Reddy, Killer); Executive Producers: William Hanna, Joseph Barbera; 30 min; Hanna-Barbera Productions; Color.

Killer and Diller follow Ruff, Reddy and Professor Gizmo to Superstition Mountain and the haunted Lost Dutchman gold mine. In the mine they encounter Schultz, the ghost of the Lost Dutchman. As Killer and Diller load the gold, Schultz the ghost unloads it but finally agrees to give the cowboy outlaws his gold. Killer and Diller exit the mine in gleeful anticipation of wallowing in their new wealth. But Schultz has the last laugh as the ghostly gold disappears before their eyes.

Rustlers' Rhapsody (1985) [Film; WW]

Premiere: May 10, 1985; Main Cast: Tom Berenger as Rex O'Herlihan, Patrick Wayne as Bob Barber, Marilu Henner as Miss Tracy, Andy Griffith as Colonel Ticonderoga, Fernando Rey as Railroad Colonel, Sela Ward as Colonel's Daughter; Executive Producer: Jose Vicuna; Story-Director: Hugh Wilson; 88 min.; Impala, Paramount Pictures; Color.

A black-and-white singing cowboy (Berenger) suddenly finds himself in a color Western movie involving Italian cowboys and a cattle baron (Griffith).

Sabata (1969) [Film; Italy; WW]

U.S. release title for *Ehi amico ... c'è Sabata, hai chiuso!*

Saber Riders and the Star Sheriffs (1987) [Animated TV series; SW]

Premiere: September 14, 1987 Studio Pierrot, World Events Productions; 52 × 30 min.; Color.

Space Western featuring Saber Rider and the Star Sheriffs of Cavalry Command as they enforce law and order along the New Frontier with the aid of their robot-transforming spaceship *Ramrod*. The Outriders from the Vapor Zone

Dimension provide the conflict in this series adapted for an American audience from the original Japanese series *Sei Jushi Bismarck*.

Season One

Star Sheriff Round Up (1:01); Cavalry Command (1:02); Jesse's Revenge (1:03); Iguana Get to Know You (1:04); Little Hombre (1:05); The Greatest Show on the New Frontier (1:06); Little Pardner (1:07); Brawlin' Is My Callin' (1:08); Wild Horses Couldn't Drag Me Away (1:09); Castle of the Mountain Haze (1:10); Oh Boy! Dinosaurs! (1:11); Four Leaf Clover (1:12); The Highlanders (1:13); What Did You Do on Your Summer Vacation? (1:14); Jesse Blue (1:15); Showdown at Cimarron Pass (1:16); The Saber and the Tomahawk (1:17); All That Glitters (1:18); Sole Survivor (1:19); Legend of the Santa Fe Express (1:20); Snake Eyes (1:21); Famous Last Words (1:22); Sharpshooter (1:23); The Monarch Supreme (1:24); Gattler's Last Stand (1:25); Dooley (1:26); The Hole in the Wall Gang (1:27); The All Galaxy Grand Prix (1:28); Snowblind (1:29); Tranquility (1:30); Bad Day at Dry Gulch (1:31); Snowcone (1:32); Sneaky Spies (1:33); Stampede (1:34); The Challenge (1:35); The Challenge (1:36); Born on the Bayou (1:37); April Rides (1:38); The Walls of Red Wing (1:39); Jesse's Girl (1:40)

Season Two

The Amazing Lazardo (2:01); I Forgot! (2:02); Lend Me Your Ears (2:03); Born to Run (2:04); Legend of the Lost World (2:05); The Rescue (2:06); Eagle Has Landed (2:07); Cease Fire (2:08); Alamo Moon (2:09); The Nth Degree (2:10); Who Is Nemesis? (2:11); Happy Trails (2:12)

Sabrina the Teenage Witch (1996) [TV series]

The adventures of Sabrina Spellman, who learns she is a witch on her 16th birthday.

"WILD, WILD WITCH" (4:19) [WW]

Air date: March 31, 2000; Main Cast: Melissa Joan Hart as Sabrina J. Spellman/The Petulant Kid, Caroline Rhea as Hilda Spellman, Beth Broderick as Zelda Spellman; Guest Star: Richard Riehle as Jedediah; Creator: Nell Scovell; Story: Sheldon Krasner, David Saling; Director: Sheldon Bull; 30 min.; Warner Bros. Television; Color.

Sabrina, grounded for her constant complaining about rules in her life, is magically transported to an Old West town governed by numerous rules. Appointed sheriff, Sabrina soon discovers that abolishing the very rules she was complaining about can cause chaos.

Salem's Daughter [Comic book; WW]

First publication: April 2009; Creators: Joe Brusha, Ralph Tedesco; Art: Caio Menescal, Eric Basaldua; Publisher: Zenescope Entertainment.

Gunslinger Braden Cole is looking for revenge after the mysterious Darius killed Braden's wife and son. Meanwhile Darius is looking to recruit a young woman named Anna Williams. Anna is a witch with unique powers that go back to the Salem witch trials in 1692. Braden Cole seeks to protect her from the evil Darius.

The story of Anna Williams was told in the story arcs The Awakening and The Haunting.

"The Salt Wagons" [Pulp fiction; WW]

Author: **Lon Williams**; Character: **Lee Winters**; *Real Western Stories* (August 1955).

Deputy Sheriff Lee Winters confronts ancient Greeks and Persians in Alkali Flat.

He had never liked to cross Alkali Flat at night, for it was a haunted region then. But as its ghosts were late in coming out—usually appearing near midnight—he had thought to reach Alkali and cross it before its worst denizens were astir. But here was something different from anything he'd ever seen or heard of in any sort of place.

The Sam Plenty Cavalcade of Action Show Plus Singing! (2008) [Webseries; SFW]

Premiere: March 10, 2008; Main Cast: Drew Massey as Sam Plenty, Jeffrey Cannata as Doom Rider, Marie O'Donnell as Queen Verbosa, Victor Yerrid as Bob Choppy, Allan Trautman as Professor August Weadle; Creators: Paul Rugg, Mitch Schauer; Jim Henson Company; Color.

This science fiction-adventure-comedy-musical show is influenced by singing cowboy Gene Autry and his film serial *The Phantom Empire*.

The online serial "Sam Plenty in Underdoom" begins with Part 3 in a move reminiscent of the TV series *Cliffhangers*. Singing cowboy Sam Plenty takes over Plenty Ranch following the death of his father at the hands of a mutant. But Sam's life on the ranch is disturbed by denizens of the center of-the-earth world of Underdoom and the nefarious Queen Verbosa and her Doom Riders.

"SAM PLENTY IN UNDERDOOM" WEBISODES:

Test of Doom (Part 3); *Explosion of Doom* (Part 4); *Purification of Doom* (Part 5); *March of Doom* (Part 6); *Hat of Doom* (Part 7)

Samurai Western [Video Game; WW]

Release date: January 1, 2005; Voice Cast: Masato Amada as Gojiro Kiryu, Osamu Hosoi as Rando Kiryu, Steve Blum as Ralph Norman/Gunman 4, Jennifer Hale as Anne Barret/Child 1/Gunman 3; PlayStation 2; Developer: Acquire; Publisher: Spike Co. Ltd., Atlus USA, 505 Game Street (UK)

Gojiro Kiryu, a samurai, arrives in the Wild West to find and kill his brother Rando, but soon becomes entangled in fighting a ruthless tycoon named Goldberg who is leaving behind a trail of ghost towns.

Santiago: A Myth of the Far Future [Novel; SW]

Author: **Mike D. Resnick**; First publication: New York: Tom Doherty Associates, 1986.

Bounty hunter Sebastian Nightingale Cain alias The Songbird tracks the elusive legend known as Santiago across the Inner Frontier. Ambitious freelance journalist Virtue McKenzie, shady art collector The Jolly Swagman, fellow bounty hunter The Angel and Santiago admirer Moonripple join the search.

See: *The Return of Santiago*

Sarah Rainmaker [Comic book character; SFW]

First appearance: *Stormwatch* #8 (March 1994); Creators: Jim Lee, Brandon Choi, J. Scott Campbell; Publishers: Image Comics, Wildstorm.

Apache-born Sarah Rainmaker first noticed her powers while on the San Carlos Reservation in Arizona. She can harness the unusual abilities of nature, including controlling the weather, water and lightning bolts, and glide on air currents. **Ripclaw** helped her escape the clutchesof a group known as the Keepers but he failedto protect her from the government-backedInternational Operations and their Project:Genesis.

The *Gen 13* comic book series emphasizes her sexuality in a good-girl art manner and introduces conflict within the group concerning her bisexual nature.

"Satan's Bondage" [Pulp fiction; WW]

Author: Manly Banister; First publication: *Weird Tales* (September 1942)

The *Weird Tales* cover blurb describes the tale as "A Werewolf Western." One of the first combinations of horror and Western genres.

"Satan's Wool Merchant" [Pulp fiction; WW]

Author: **Lon Williams**; Character: **Lee Winters**; *Real Western Stories* (February 1953)

Winters swung his horse around. What he saw gave him a shiver; it was no wonder, he thought, that sight of its shadow had caused Cannon Ball to throw a fit. Here on horseback before him was a thing that passed as human, yet looked like something out of a collection of horrors. He was a man with long legs, a short, thick torso, and a small, barely-visible head—to all appearances utterly neck-less and half-imbedded between chunky, broad shoulders.

Savage: Vampire Hunter in the Badlands [Comic book; WW]

First publication: 1996; 5 issue mini-series; Creator-Story: R. A. Jones; Art: Ted Slampyak; Publisher: Caliber Comics.

Abandoned by his parents at birth, Christian Savage was raised by Father Liam O'Toole who lost his life when Savage dabbled in the occult. Now Savage is visited by the ghost of Father O'Toole who offers him advice.

Stoker, Colorado, in the 1870s. Christian Savage enters the No-Chance Saloon. With heightened paranormal senses vampire hunter Savage fires silver bullets blessed with holy water and notched with the sign of the cross. Vampire Ezra Dane orders the townsfolk to slay Savage and deliver his living heart, but Savage has an even greater threat to contend with in the evil Kronos.

Scalphunter [Comic book character]

First appearance: *Weird Western Tales* #39 (March-April 1977); Creators: Sergio Aragones, Joe Orlando; Publisher: DC Comics.

Abducted as a child and raised by Kiowa Indians, Brian Savage a.k.a. Scalphunter returned to white society as an adult and was appointed sheriff of Opal City. Although he possessed no special powers he did move in weird circles including coming into contact with the secret occult society known as the Tuesday Club and teaming up with fellow Weird Western characters **Jonah Hex** and **El Diablo**.

In December 1899, Savage was shot in the back by Jason Melville, a member of the Tuesday Club. His passing marked the end of an era but his spirit lived on in the reincarnated form of Opal City policeman Matt O'Dare.

Scalps (1983) [Film; WW]

Premiere: December 1983; Main Cast: Richard Hench as Randy/Black Claw, Frank McDonald as Ben Murphy, Jo-Ann Robinson as D.J., Carol Sue Flockhart as Louise Landon, Forrest J Ackerman as Prof. Trentwood; Story: Fred Olen Ray, John Ray, T. L. Lankford; Producer: T. L. Lankford; Director: Fred Olen Ray; 82 min.; American Partnership; Color.

Ignoring a warning to stay away from Black Tree, a group of archaeology students come under attack from Indian demons.

"Scarlet Dream" [Pulp fiction; SW]

Author: **C.L. Moore**; First publication: *Weird Tales* (May 1934)

For **Northwest Smith**, a shawl bought at the Lakkmanda Markets of Mars leads to a meeting with a young, attractive female and a journey into an enticing and dangerous dream dimension for. He soon feels trapped in a living landscape that includes vampiric grass and an unknown scarlet entity that feeds on the people.

Scout [Comic book character; SFW]

First published: December 1985; Creator: Timothy Truman; Publisher: Eclipse Comics.

Apache Indian Emanuel Santana is driven by his spirit guide as he fights an oppressive government in a an America stripped of resources by its former allies.

Screaming Eagle [Graphic Novel; WW]

First Published: 1998; Story: Scott Deschaine; Art: Mike Roy; Publisher: Discovery Comics.

The spirit of a young Indian boy merges with an American eagle after they are both shot by trappers. The revived boy names himself Screaming Eagle and sets out to defend his people in their fight with the white men.

This was the final work of veteran comic book artist Mike Roy. Roy was well known for his work on the Native American Sunday strip *Akwas* in the 1960s.

Se incontri Sartana prega per la tua morte (1968) [Film; Italy-France-West Germany; WW]

Premiere; August 14, 1968; Main cast: John Garko [Gianni Garko] as Sartana, Klaus Kinski as Morgan, Fernando Sancho as Jose Manuel Mendoza, Wil-liam Berger as Lasky; Producer: Aldo Addobbati; Story: Adolfo Cagnacci, Luigi De Santis, Fabio Piccioni; Director: Frank Kramer [Gianfranco Parolini]; 95 min.; Paris Étoile Films, Parnass Film; Color.

A stagecoach robbery leads to a series of grisly murders with the notorious Lasky gaining possession of a strongbox of cash. Sartana seeks the truth behind the robberies and decides on his own version of justice.

The mysterious figure of Sartana as directed by Parolini is on the surface a gunslinger with no past, a "Man With No Name" clone. But his character hints at an avenging spirit of death. Sartana creator Gianfrancro Parolini is quoted as saying that Sartana is a cross between James Bond and the comic strip character Mandrake the Magician.

Se sei vivo spara (1967) [Film; Italy; WW]

Premiere: May 3, 1967; Main Cast: Tomas Milian as Stranger, Raymond Lovelock as Evan, Roberto Camardiel as Mr. Sorrow; Story: Franco Arcalli, María del Carmen Martínez Román, Giulio Questi; Producer-Director: Giulio Questi; 117 min.; Italian; GIA Società Cinematografica, Hispamer Films; Color.

A half-breed outlaw (Milian), left for dead and restored to life by Apaches, seeks revenge. This surreal spaghetti Western features an amoral anti-hero wandering through a landscape of extreme violence and degradation.

See: *Django Kill—If You Live, Shoot!*

Seasons of the Reaper [Comic book; WW]

First publication: 2005; Story: Rômulo Soares; Art: Ivan Cha; Publisher: Speakeasy Comics.

An Indian hunting party rescues a boy from certain death following the slaughter of his parents. The Indians decide to raise him but sense something unsettling about the boy. For he is Death and all who have wronged him will have their souls taken.

The Secret Adventures of Jules Verne (2000) [TV series; Canada-UK]

In an alternative Victorian era, the young Jules Verne teams up with Phileas Fogg, British spy Rebecca Fogg and his valet Passepartout as they strive to keep their secrets safe from the League of Darkness.

"The Ballad of Steeley Joe" [SPW]
Air date: July 26, 2000: Main Cast: Chris Demetral as Jules Verne, Michael Praed as Phileas Fogg, Francesca Hunt as Rebecca Fogg, Michel Courtemanche as Passepartout; Guest Stars: Mario Diamond as Steeley Joe, Kent McQuaid as Jesse James, Josh Byer as Frank James, Minor Mustain as Sheriff Jim Downey, Jonathan Walker as Samuel Clemens, Dixie Seatle as Lily Ledoux; Creator-Story: Gavin Scott; Director: Gabriel Pelletier; 60 min.; Filmline International Inc., Talisman Crest; Color.

Apache Wells is under threat from local outlaws until Jules Verne, Phileas Fogg, Rebecca Fogg, Samuel Clemens, Passepartout and Lily Ledoux restore order with the help of a metallic robot gunslinger named Steeley Joe.

The Secret Empire (1979) [TV serial; SFW]
See: *Cliffhangers*

Secret of Haunted Mesa [Juvenile novel; WW]
Author: Phyllis A. Whitney; First publication: Westminster Press, Philadelphia PA, 1975.

Jenny learns of Indian warrior spirits when she becomes friendly with a local Indian boy while staying with her family at Haunted Mesa Ranch.

Secret of San Saba : A Tale of Phantoms and Greed in the Spanish Southwest [Graphic novel; SFW]
First publication: February, 1986—*Death Rattle* #1; Story-Art: Jack Jackson; Publisher: Kitchen Sink Press.

Faraone natives worship a silver "Cosmic Slug" that fell from the sky in the Southwest desert lands. When the natives are conquered by the Apaches, European missionaries learn of the silver slug and seek to possess it for its potential wealth—but the spirits of the dead protect it.

Originally published as the six-part "Bulto: The Cosmic Slug" in the Kitchen Sink comic book *Death Rattle*.

The Secret of Sinharat [Novel; SW]
Author: **Leigh Brackett**; First publication: New York: Ace Books, 1964.

Expanded version of "**Queen of the Martian Catacombs**" with minor changes to the final chapters.

See: *People of the Talisman*

The Secret of the Indian [Juvenile novel; WW]
Author: Lynne Reid Banks; Illustrator: Ted Lewin; First publication: New York: Doubleday 1989.

Patrick travels back in time to the Old West while Texas cowboy Boone and his girlfriend are stuck in the present day. On his return journey from the Old West, Patrick brings back a cyclone that has disastrous effects.

See: *The Key to the Indian*

Secret Six [Comic book; WW]
First publication: October 2010; Story: Gail Simone; Art: Jim Calafiore; Publisher: DC Comics.

"Six Guns Blazing!" #24 [WW]
In a corrupt Old West mining town the Secret Six fight deadly gunslinger Slade Wilson (Deathstroke), hired by Junior to lead an assault on the town. Scandal Savage serves as Sheriff with Bane as her deputy. **Deadshot** is a hired gunman, Catman the "Man With No Name" character type, Ragdolls the town fool and Jeanette the hooker.

Sei Jushi Bismarck (1984) [Animated TV series; Japan; SW]
Premiere: October 7, 1984; Voice Cast: Bin Shimada as Richard Lancelot, Kazuhiko Inoue as Bill Wilcox; Animation Studio: Studio Pierrot; Producers: Yousi Nunokala, Yoshitaka Suzuki; Director: Masami Anno; 51 × 30 min.; NTV; Color.

The solar system is under attack from the Deathcula. Shinji Hikari from Japan, Bill Wilcox from America, Richard Lancelot from Scotland and Marianne Louvre from France join forces to fight the phantom-like menace.

The original version of **Saber Rider and the Star Sheriffs**.

Seihou Bukyou Outlaw Star (1998) [Anime; Japan; SW]
Original air date: January 9, 1998; Creator: Takehito Ito; Director: Mitsuru Hongo; Sunrise Inc.; 26 × 23 min.; Color.

Gene Starwind and his young business partner Jim Hawking are the owners of the highly advanced prototype Outlaw Star spaceship. The self-proclaimed Outlaws traverse the space between the Federation and the illegal Pirate clans on the edge of the galaxy in search of the mysterious Galactic Leyline. Joining them on their quest is bio-android Melfina, catgirl Aisha Clanclan and female assassin "Twilight" Suzuka.

Season One

Outlaw World (1:01); *The Star of Desire* (1:02); *Into Burning Space* (1:03); *When the Hot Ice Melts* (1:04); *The Beast Girl Ready to Pounce!* (1:05); *The Beautiful Assassin* (1:06); *Creeping Evil* (1:07); *Forced Departure* (1:08); *A Journey of Adventure! Huh?* (1:09); *Gathering for the Space Race* (1:10); *Adrift in Subspace* (1:11); *Mortal Combat with the El Dorado* (1:12); *Advance Guard from an Alien World* (1:13); *Final Countdown* (1:14); *The Seven Emerge* (1:15); *The Demon of the Water Planet* (1:16); *Between Life and Machine* (1:17); *The Strongest Woman in the Universe* (1:18); *Law and Lawlessness* (1:19); *Cats and Girls and Spaceships* (1:20); *Grave of the Dragon* (1:21); *Gravity Jailbreak* (1:22); *Hot Springs Planet Tenrei* (1:23); *Cutting the Galactic Leyline* (1:24); *Maze of Despair* (1:25); *Return to Space* (1:26)

See: **Outlaw Star**

Senarens, Luis (1863–1939) [Dime novel author]

Born in Brooklyn, New York, Senarens is reported to have sold his first story to *Boys of New York* in 1877 at the age of 14. Taking over from departing **Harry Enton** on the **Frank Reade Jr.** series, Senarens worked under the pseudonym "Noname." He wrote Reade Jr. stories from 1882 until 1899 for *Boys of New York, Happy Days* and the *Frank Reade Library*. Other pseudonyms he adopted include Ned Sparling and Police Captain Howard. Following his retirement from the Frank Reade Jr. series, Senarens became managing editor of Tousey Publications from 1902–1923.

Senarens' work has been criticized for being poorly written, sadistic, imperialist and racist toward Native Americans, African-Americans, Irish-Americans, Jews and Mexicans. He has also been credited with creating the groundwork for the birth of science fiction as a legitimate genre.

Selected works (series): Frank Reade Jr., **Tom Edison Jr., Jack Wright**.

Sensation Comics [Comic book]

Superhero anthology title.

"Wonder Woman Tames the Wild West" [SFW]

First publication: #87 (March 1949); Story: Robert Kanigher; Art: Harry G. Peter; Publisher: DC Comics.

Travelling back in time to the Old West town of Twin Peaks in 1849 to discover why her name appeared in a diary, Wonder Woman encounters the villainous Jabez Dexter.

Seraphim Falls (2006) [Film; WW]

Premiere: September 13, 2006; Main Cast: Liam Neeson as Colonel Morsman Carver, Pierce Brosnan as Gideon, Angie Harmon as Rose, Anjelica Huston as Madame Louise; Producers: Bruce Davey, David Flynn; Story: David Von Ancken, Abby Everett Jaques; Director: David Von Ancken; 115 min.; Icon Productions, Samuel Goldwyn Films; Color.

The pursuit across the Old West of former Union captain Gideon by Colonel Morsman Carver of the Confederate Army becomes a story of revenge and forgiveness with a supernatural twist.

Stephen Holden of *The New York Times* (January 26, 2007) commented: "Late in the game 'Seraphim Falls' takes a fatal turn into the ridiculous. On the way to their final confrontation, Gideon and Carver each encounter lone symbolic figures who seem to have been awaiting their arrival, each offering a vaguely Satanic bargain … tossing such hallucinatory curveballs into the movie this near the end may look like a stroke of avant-garde brilliance, but it's really an act of cowardice."

Serenity [Film; RPG Game; SW]

1. Premiere: September 30, 2005; Main Cast: Nathan Fillion as Mal, Jewel Staite as Kaylee, Gina Torres as Zoe, Adam Baldwin as Jayne, Summer Glau as River; Executive Producers: Christopher Buchanan, David Lester, Alisa Tager; Story-Director: Joss Whedon; 119 min.; Universal Pictures; Color.

Following the Unification War, many Independents drift away from Alliance control and struggle to survive in the 'verse. This film sequel to the short-lived TV series **Firefly** takes place a few months after the events of the TV series. River Tam is pursued by an assassin for the Alliance who must kill her before she discloses government secrets hidden deep within her brain.

In an interview with BBC News (October 7, 2005) director Joss Whedon discussed the crossing of two genres, science fiction and the Western, in **Serenity** and **Firefly**. "They think it's going to be big hats, and it's going to be hokey. The fact of the matter is that I think the two are intrinsically related, because it's the final frontier—and

Serenity (2005), starring Summer Glau as River Tam and Nathan Fillion as Malcolm "Mal" Reynolds (Universal Pictures).

what's exciting about frontier life is the physicality of it. That's something we're losing in the Internet age. So for me, the Western and science fiction belong together."

Peter Bradshaw of *The Guardian* (October 6, 2005) said: "Here is a sci-fi action picture with more energy in its little finger than 'Revenge of the Sith' had in its whole bloated body. Whedon is a movie-making force to be reckoned with."

A film series had been planned but box-office performance was below expectations. *Serenity* earned $38.9 million worldwide on a $39 million budget. Plans for future films were scrapped. Despite its popularity Whedon's creation primarily attracted a loyal niche audience.

2. Role playing game; Author-Designer: Jamie Chambers; Based on the motion picture screenplay by Joss Whedon; First publication: Margaret Weis Productions Ltd., 2006.

See: **Out in the Black**

Serenity Adventures [RPG book; SW]

First publication: Margaret Weis Productions Ltd., 2008

Collection of tales for use with the *Serenity* role playing game and the Cortex System game rules.

Ghosts of the Rebellion by James Davenport; *The Best Things Get Better with Age* by Alana Abbot; *Freedoms Flight* by Ted Reed; *Seven Arks of Cibola* by Billy Aguiar; *Mother Load* by James M. Ward

Serenity: Better Days [Comic book; Graphic novel; SW]

First publication: March, 2008; 3 issue mini-series; Story: Joss Whedon, Brett Matthews; Art: Will Conrad, Jo Chen; Publisher: Dark Horse Comics.

A heist promises riches for the crew of Serenity but the capture and torture of a crew member places those riches in peril.

Serenity: Float Out [Comic book; SW]

First publication: June, 2010; One-off; Story: Patton Oswalt; Art: Patric Reynolds; Publisher: Dark Horse Comics.

Three stories featuring Wash, the late pilot of Serenity.

Serenity: Leaves on the Wind [Comic book; Graphic novel; SW]

First publication: January, 2014; 6 issue mini-series; Story: Zack Whedon; Art: Georges Jeanty, Karl Story, Fabio Moon; Dan Dos Santos; Publisher: Dark Horse Comics.

The official follow-up to the film sees the "most wanted" crew of Serenity come out of hiding after Zoe is captured. And the lure of money proves too much for Jayne as he returns to a cold reception.

Serenity: The Shepherd's Tale [Graphic novel; SW]

First publication: November, 2010; Story: Joss Whedon, Zack Whedon; Art: Chris Samnee, Steve Morris; Publisher: Dark Horse Books.

The story of Shepherd Books' life before he met Mal Reynolds and the Serenity crew.

Serenity: Those Left Behind [Comic book; Graphic novel; SW]

First publication: July, 2005; 3 issue mini-series; Story: Joss Whedon, Brett Matthews; Art: Will Conrad, Adam Hughes; Publisher: Dark Horse Comics.

A scavenger mission leads the Serenity crew into a trap with covert-operatives the Blue Gloves.

Serenity RPG: Big Damn Heroes Handbook [RPG book; SW]

First publication: September, 2009; Authors: Cam Banks, Jennifer Brozek, Jim Davenport, Nathan Rockwood, Clark Valentine, Tony Lee, Jason Durall; Publisher: Margaret Weis Productions Ltd.

Handbook supplement to the **Serenity RPG Game** includes additional rules.

The 7 Faces of Dr. Lao (1964) [Film; WW]

Premiere: March 18, 1964; Main Cast: Tony Randall as Dr. Lao, Merlin the Magician, Pan, Medusa, The Abominable Snowman, Apollonius of Tyana, Serpent; Barbara Eden as Angela Benedict; Novel: Charles G. Finney; Screenplay: Charles Beaumont; Producer-Director: George Pal; 100 min.; Metro-Goldwyn-Mayer; Color.

The townsfolk of frontier town Abalone, Arizona, flock to a traveling carnival and learn truths about their own strengths and weaknesses. Tony Randall plays seven different characters. He also appears as a member of the audience at the carnival.

Loosely based on the novel **The Circus of Dr. Lao** (1935) by Charles G. Finney.

Howard Thompson, film critic for *The New York Times* (July 23, 1964) declared: As directed and produced by George Pal, it is heavy, thick, pint-sized fantasy, laid on with an anvil. As the focal point, got up in seven different guises with accents to match, Tony Randall is excruciatingly coy and simpering. Mr. Randall is, in fact, the cutest thing to hit the screen since Shirley Temple. Obviously, he knows it, too."

Seven Mummies (2006) [Film; WW]

Main Cast: Matt Schulze as Rock, Billy Wirth as Travis, Billy Drago as Drake, Cerina Vincent as Lacy, Danny Trejo as Apache; Executive Producers: Richard E. Ragsdale, Robert M. Turner; Story: Thadd Turner; Director: Nick Quested; 90 min.; Talmarc Productions; Color.

Seven mummified Jesuit priests protect the treasure they buried in an Old West town.

When the townsfolk discover their riches, the mummies are awakened and turn them into vampires. Six runaway convicts hear of the legend from an Apache shaman and decide to check out the town and treasure for themselves.

Seven Soldiers [Comic book; WW]

First publication: #0 (April 2005); Story: Grant Morrison; Art: J.H. Williams III; Publisher: DC Comics.

"Weird Adventures Part 1: "Shelly and the Super-Cowboys"

A bored and frustrated Shelly Gaynor, the granddaughter of the original Whip, seeking new challenges, arranges a meeting with Greg Saunders alias the **Vigilante**.

"Weird Adventures Part 2: Big Time Country"

The Vigilante invites Gaynor to join a revived Seven Soldiers team consisting of I, Spyder, Gimmix, Boy Blue and Dyno-Mite Dan. Their first mission is to track down the giant spider of Miracle, which he first encountered in the Old West of 1875.

"Weird Adventures Part 3: Midnight at Miracle Mesa"

After successfully destroying the spider with a mixture of silver bullets and freezing spray, the team find they have walked into a trap and are attacked by the leader of the Sheeda Army, Nehbuh-loh, and his troops. Only one member will survive.

7th Dimension [Radio show; UK]

BBC Radio anthology show featuring science fiction, fantasy, horror and supernatural stories.

"Shambleau"

Original broadcast: April 21, 2007; Narrator: Elizabeth McGovern; Producer: Gemma Jenkins; 3 × 30 min.; BBC Radio 7.

Three-part narration of the **C.L. Moore** story featuring **Northwest Smith** and his encounter with a mysterious woman on Mars.

See: **2000x: Tales of the Next Millennia**

Severin, John (1921–2012) [Comic book artist]

Born in Jersey City, New Jersey, in 1921, John Powers Severin began his career in comic books following service in the U.S. Army. Early work for Prize Comics included the Western *American Eagle*. From 1953 until 1955 he worked for EC Comics and achieved recognition for his artwork on the war titles *Two-Fisted Tales* and *Frontline Combat*.

Following the close of EC, Severin worked for Atlas-Marvel on Western titles including *Ringo Kid*, **Rawhide Kid** and **Kid Colt Outlaw**. A partnership with fellow artist **Dick Ayers** began in 1967 on the Alley Award-winning *Sgt. Fury and His Howling Commandos*. He also contributed to Warren's short-lived but acclaimed war title *Blazing Combat* in the 1960s as well as Warren's horror titles **Creepy** and *Eerie*.

Severin has enjoyed a long career and was still working into his eighties on the Weird Western title **Desperadoes** and an updated *Rawhide Kid* and as cover artist for an issue of **Shaolin Cowboy** in 2007. His detailed style has served him well throughout his career and is particularly suited to the war and Western genres where he has flourished.

Sex and Death in Television Town [Novel; WW]

Author: Carlton Mellick III; Publisher: Portland, OR; Eraserhead Press, 2005.

A gang of hermaphrodite gunslingers known as the Crawler Gang fleeing from black demons head for the haven of Telos on a living worm train. Joining them is a silent gunslinger named Jesus Christ, newlyweds Random and his skeletal bride Typi and a snake-skinned nymphomaniac samurai with Stegosaurus spikes down her spine who can see into the future whenever she has sex. Arriving in Telos the motley group encounter people with televisions for heads who communicate through channel surfing. Nymphomaniac Cry and gunslinger Jesus seek to divide and conquer the people with a mixture of sex and death in this satirical Bizarro Western.

The Shadow of the Storm [Novel; SFW]

Author: Kurt R. A. Giambastiani; First publication: New York: New American Library, 2003.

One Who Flies of the Cheyenne Alliance, son of United States President George Armstrong Custer, is leader of the resistance against U.S. and European treatment of the Cheyenne in this alternate history series. The third novel in the *Fallen Cloud Saga*.

See: *From the Heart of the Storm*

Shadow on the Sun [Novel; WW]

Author: Richard Matheson; First publication: New York: M. Evans, 1994.

When two mutilated bodies are discovered on the outskirts of Picture City a peace treaty between the Apache and the U.S. government is put in jeopardy. Government agent David Boutelle suspects the Apache but Billjohn Finley, the Bureau of Indian Affairs agent who brokered the peace treaty has his own suspicions. As Finley and Boutelle investigate the gruesome deaths they come to realize a supernatural evil may be at play.

The Shadows, Kith and Kin [Book anthology; WW]

Author: **Joe R. Lansdale**; First publication: Burton MI: Subterranean Press, 2007.

This collection of nine short stories includes the Weird Western stories "Deadman's Road" and "The Gentleman's Hotel," the latter featuring the eternally damned gunslinger Reverend Jebidiah Mercer from **Dead in the West** as he confronts a walking corpse and werewolves.

Shadows Through Time [Novel; WWR]

Author: Madeline Baker; First publication: Akron, OH: Cerridwen Press, 2009.

Kelsey St. James is a 21st century girl with no interest in the Old West. But when she steps through a time portal Kelsey finds herself transported to the Old West town of Grants Crossing where she meets a half-breed gambler. T. K. Reese is wanted by the law and has promised himself never to fall in love again after he blamed himself for the murder of his wife. But the attraction between Kelsey and Reese stretches across time and space.

Shaman's Tears [Comic book; WW]

First published: May 1993; Creator: Mike Grell; Publisher: Image Comics.

After learning of his mystical powers from Indian shaman Grey Hawk, troubled half-Sioux Joshua Brand becomes the protector of the Earth as Stalking Wolf.

"Shambleau" [Pulp fiction; SW]

Author: **C. L. Moore**; First publication: *Weird Tales* (November 1933).

Space adventurer and outlaw **Northwest Smith** confronts the ancient myths of the Gorgon and Medusa when he befriends an alluring alien girl. Moore successfully weaves themes of eroticism, sensuality, fear of the unknown and disgust into a compelling story.

Had Northwest Smith, the famous outlaw of the spaceways, been able to foresee the future, he would not have shielded the frightened, scarlet-clad girl from the wild mob pursuing her through the narrow streets of Lakkdarol, Earth's latest colony of Mars. "Shambleau! Shambleau!" the crowd cried with loathing and disgust, but Smith drove them off with his blaster and took the exhausted girl to his quarters. There was no hair upon her face—neither brows nor lashes; but what lay hidden beneath the tight scarlet turban bound around her head?

See: *2000x: Tales of the Next Millennia*

Shambleau and Others [Pulp fiction collection; SW]

Author: **C. L. Moore**; First publication: New York: Gnome Press, 1953

The first collection of four **Northwest Smith** stories in one volume: "Shambleu" (1933), "**Black Thirst**" (1934), "**Scarlet Dream**" (1934) and "**The Tree of Life**" (1936).

Shaolin Cowboy [Comic book; SFW]

First publication: 2004; Creator-Story: Geoff Darrow; Art: Geoffrey Darrow; Publisher: Burlyman Entertainment.

A former Shaolin monk with a bounty on his head wanders through a post-apocalyptic landscape with his talking mule.

This ultra-violent, surrealistic comic book with little plot, minimal dialogue (the Wachowski brothers providing dialogue for the mule) and detailed quality artwork has received critical praise.

Shattered Coast [RPG book; WW]

Authors: Zach Bush, John Goff, John Hopler, James Maliszewski, Gareth Skarka; First publication: Setting: **Deadlands: Hell on Earth The Wasted West**; Publisher: Pinnacle Entertainment Group.

Location book for the Great Maze. Includes an adventure of the Cult o' Doom.

She-Hulk [Comic book]

Old West lawyer Matt Hawk a.k.a. **Two-Gun Kid** joined the pages of *She-Hulk* in 2006 beginning with issue #4 and concluding with issue #7.

"New Kid in Town" [SFW]

First publication: #5 (April 2006): Story: Dan Slott; Art: Juan Bobillo, Marcelo Sosa; Publisher: Marvel Comics.

Traveling through time to present-

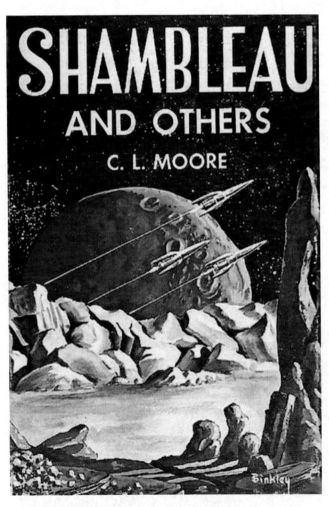

First edition dust jacket for *Shambleau and Others* by C.L. Moore (1953).

day America, Matt Hawk alias Two-Gun Kid becomes the latest member of She-Hulk's law firm.

She Returns from War [Novel: WW]

Author: Lee Collins; First publication: Long Island City, NY: Angry Robot, 2013.

After English heiress Victoria Dawes loses her parents to a vicious attack by supernatural hounds she travels to Albuquerque, New Mexico, to hire the services of monster hunter Cora Oglesby. Her quest leads her to Navajo skin walker Anaba and a journey of self discovery where she learns of her own supernatural gifts.

Shiloh Falls (2007) [Film; WW]

Premiere: December 1, 2007; Main Cast: Art LaFleur as Sheriff John Gaffney, Brad Greenquist as Dalton, Ellie Araiza as Mary, Esteban Louis Powell as Cole; Executive Producers: Philip Bligh, Roddy Mancuso, Bruce Randolph Tizes; Story: Art Lafleur, Adrian Fulle, Gregory Littman, Roddy Mancuso; Director: Adrian Fulle; 90 min.; Radio London Films; Color.

When the Dalton Gang are tracked to the town of Shiloh Falls by Sheriff John Gaffney,he has to contend with a stranger with supernatural powers before he can bring them to justice.

"The Shomer Express" [Short story; WW]

Author: Edward M. Erdelac; First publication: *Trigger Reflex: Tales of the Monster Hunter II* (2011); Publisher: Pill Hill Press.

This **Merkabah Rider** short story features the Rider guarding the desecrated corpse of a Jewish train passenger's deceased mother. The Rider senses inhuman forces at work as the train heads west through desert terrain.

Shooting Star [Comic book character; SFW]

First appearance: *Incredible Hulk* #265 (November 1981); Creators: Bill Mantlo, Sal Buscema; Publisher: Marvel Comics.

Texas-born Victoria Starwin began her career as a rodeo performer, renowned for her double act with fellow rodeo star **Texas Twister**. Her equipment includes a pair of guns that shoot star-shaped "bullets" capable of causing paralysis.

Shooting Star's Weird Western credentials include being possessed by a demon who assumed her identity. She served as a member of **The Rangers**.

The Shotgun Arcana [Novel; WW]

Author: R. S. Belcher; First publication: New York: Tor, 2014.

The Old West cattle town of Golgotha, Nevada is inhabited by strange and unnatural townsfolk and more are headed their way. In this sequel to *The Six-Gun Tarot* thirty-two savage killers and the corrupt angel Raziel and his insane cannibal

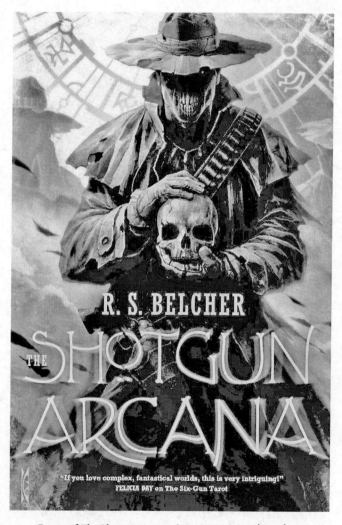

Cover of *The Shotgun Arcana* by R. S. Belcher (2014).

disciples are drawn by a shattered skull inhabited by the spirit of murder. A showdown in the Nevada frontier town that attracts the supernatural and evil forces will decide its fate and those of its colorful townsfolk.

The Sign of the Wolf (1931) [Film serial; WW]

Premiere: May 1, 1931; Main Cast: Rex Lease as Tom, Virginia Brown Faire as Ruth Farnum, Harry Todd as John Farnum, Jack Mower as Butch Kohler, Al Ferguson as Winslow, Josephine Hill as Pearl, Edmund Cobb as Prince Kuva; Producers: Harry Webb, Flora E. Douglas; Story: Carl Krusada, Elizabeth Burbridge; Directors: Harry Webb, Forrest Sheldon; 10 chapters, 194 min.; Metropolitan Pictures Corp.; B/W.

An explorer in India discovers radioactive chains that transform sand into jewels. On his return to the American West, he and his daughter become the target of criminals and a religious sect that considers the chains as sacred.

Contemporary Western featuring Indian fakirs, automobiles and cowboys on horses.

Chapter Titles: 1. *Drums of Doom*; 2. *The Dog of Destiny*; 3. *The Wolf's Fangs*; 4. *The Fatal Shot*; 5. *The Well of Terror*; 6. *The Wolf Dogs*; 7. *Trapped*; 8. *The Secret Mark*; 9. *Tongues of Flame*; 10. *The Lost Secret*

Silent Tongue (1994) [Film; WW]

Premiere: February 25, 1994; Main Cast: Richard Harris as Prescott Roe, Alan Bates as Dr. Eamon McCree, Dermot Mulroney as Reeves McCree, River Phoenix as Talbot Roe, Sheila Tousey as Awbonnie, Jeri Arredondo as Velada McCree; Producers: Ludi Boeken, Carolyn Pfeifer; Story-Director: Sam Shepard; 102 min.; Belbo Films; Color.

When Talbot Roe's half-breed wife Awbonnie dies in childbirth, he refuses to leave her corpse. Awbonnie appears to Roe as a ferocious ghost urging him to release her spirit by destroying her dead body but in his grief he ignores her plea.

Silver Deer [Comic book character; WW]

First appearance: *Fury of Firestorm* #27 (September 1984); Story: Gerry Conway; Art: Rafael Kayanan, Rodin Rodriguez; Publisher: DC Comics.

Native American shaman Silver Deer and **Black Bison** entrance Firehawk's father, Senator Walter Reilly, to return the land to her people. But Firestorm and Firehawk have plans to thwart them.

Silver on the Road [Novel; WW]

Author: Laura Anne Gilman; First publication: New York: Saga Press, 2012.

Working as the left hand of an equal opportunities devil, 16 year-old Isobel weaves her magic west of the Mississippi.

SilverHawks (1986) [Animated TV series; Comic book; SW]

1. Animated TV series.
Premiere: September 8, 1986; Voice cast: Larry Kenney as Bluegrass, Bob McFadden as Cmdr. Stargazer, Earl Hammond as Mon-Star, Maggie Wheeler as Melodia, Peter Newman as Mumbo Jumbo, Pete Cannarozzi as Copper Kid; Executive producers: Arthur Rankin Jr., Jules Bass, Lee Dannacher, Masaki Ihzuka; Animation director: Itaru Saito; 65x23 min.; Rankin-Bass Productions, Pacific Animation Corp.; Lorimar-Telepictures, Warner Bros. Television; Color.

In the year 2839 Commander Stargazer relays an S.O.S. to Earth following an intergalactic penal breakout. Mon-Star, universal public enemy number one is free and gathering a group of the most dangerous criminals in the Galaxy of Limbo. Stargazer wants the help of the SilverHawks to tackle the terror of Limbo. "Super androids with the minds of men," the cybernetic team known as the SilverHawks are led by Quicksilver. Lt. Colonel Bluegrass is second-in-command and guitar picking ace pilot of the transport and fighter craft, the Mirage. Wearing his cowboy hat and red bandana the cybernetically enhanced Bluegrass can control the Mirage craft from a distance using his guitar. Unlike the other SilverHawks Bluegrass doesn't have retractable wings but operates from within his detachable cockpit.

Season One

The Origin Story (1:01); *Journey to Limbo* (1:02); *The Planet Eater* (1:03); *Save the Sun* (1:04); *Stop Timestopper* (1:05); *Darkbird* (1:06); *The Backroom* (1:07); *The Threat of Dritt* (1:08); *Sky-Shadow* (1:09); *Magnetic Attraction* (1:10); *Gold Shield* (1:11); *Zero the Memory* (1:12); *The Milk Run* (1:13); *The Hardware Trap Pt. 1* (1:14); *The Hardware Trap Pt. 2* (1:15); *Race Against Time* (1:16); *Operation Big Freeze* (1:17); *The Ghost Ship* (1:18); *The Great Galaxy Race* (1:19); *Fantascreen* (1:20); *Hotwing Hits Limbo* (1:21); *The Bounty Hunter* (1:22); *Zeek's Fumble* (1:23); *The Fighting Hawks* (1:24); *The Renegade Hero* (1:25); *One on One* (1:26); *No More Mr.*

Nice Guy (1:27); *Music of the Spheres* (1:28); *Limbo Gold Rush* (1:29); *Countdown to Zero* (1:30); *The Amber Amplifier* (1:31); *The Savior Stone* (1:32); *Smiley* (1:33); *Gotbucks* (1:34); *Melodia's Siren Song* (1:35); *Tally-Hawk Returns* (1:36); *Undercover* (1:37); *Eye of Affinity* (1:38); *A Piece of the Action* (1:39); *Flashback* (1:40); *Super Birds* (1:41); *The Blue Door* (1:42); *The Star of Bedlama* (1:43); *The Illusionist* (1:44); *The Bounty Hunter Returns* (1:45); *The Chase* (1:46); *Switch* (1:47); *Junkyard Dog* (1:48); *Window in Time* (1:49); *Gangwar Pt. 1* (1:50); *Gangwar Pt. 2* (1:51); *Sneak Attack Pt. 1* (1:52); *Sneak Attack Pt. 2* (1:53); *Moon Star* (1:54); *The Diamond Stick-Pin* (1:55); *Burnout* (1:56); *Battle Cruiser* (1:57); *Small World* (1:58); *Match-Up* (1:59); *Stargazer's Refit* (1:60); *The Invisible Destroyer* (1:61); *The Harder They Fall* (1:62); *Uncle Rattler* (1:63); *Zeek's Power* (1:64); *Airshow* (1:65)

2. Comic book.
First publication: August, 1987; Story: Steve Perry; Art: Mike Witherby, Howard Bender, Jim Sanders III, Fred Fredericks; Publisher: Marvel-Star Comics.

The comic book based on the animated television series and Kenner toy line ran to seven bimonthly issues.

Silverload [Video game; WW]

Release date: 1995; Third-person perspective (POV); Developer: Millennium Interactive Ltd.; Publisher: Psygnosis Limited.

Silverload, once a booming mining town, has become a storm-ridden ghost town. Some claim the town is cursed because the mine was built on sacred Indian tribal land. Local children are going missing in the town and a bounty hunter has been hired to track them down. If he succeeds, the secret of Silverload will be revealed.

The Simpsons (1989) [Animated TV series]

"THE LASTEST GUN IN THE WEST" (13:12) [WW]

Air date: February 24, 2002; Guest voice: Dennis Weaver as Buck McCoy; Creator: Matt Groening; Executive Producers: James L. Brooks, Matt Groening, Sam Simon; Story: John Swartzwelder; Director: Bob Anderson; Guest; 30 min.; 20th-Century–Fox Television, Gracie Films; Color.

Bart and Lisa Simpson attempt to revive the career of former cowboy film star Buck McCoy by persuading Krusty the Clown to put Buck on

his show. In one scene we see a film poster of one of Buck McCoy's old starring roles in "Wyatt Earp Meets The Mummy."

"TREEHOUSE OF HORROR XIII"—"THE FRIGHT TO CREEP AND SCARE HARMS" (14:01) [WW]

Air date: November 3, 2002; Story: Brian Kelley; Director: David Silverman.

In the second Halloween episode, a visit to the cemetery prompts Lisa Simpson to start a campaign to ban guns in Springfield. But a gun-free Springfield encourages Billy the Kid and his zombie Hole-in-the-Ground gang to rise from their graves and create havoc with their gunslinging ways.

Sinbuck [Comic book; WW]

First publication: 2005; Story: David Barbour, Joe Vigil; Art: Tim Vigil, Joe Vigil; Publisher: Broken Halos.

Sequel to ***Gunfighters in Hell*** featuring Anna Sinbuck as the only surviving member of The Maleficent Seven. After discovering that the damned souls of her former partners are now imprisoned in the Cartagra Soul Cage, she decides to find the key to release them.

Sioux Me (1939) [Animated theatrical short; WW]

Premiere: September 9, 1939; Story: Melvin Millar; Animation: Herman Cohen; Supervision: Ben Hardaway, Cal Dalton; 7 min.; Leon Schlesinger Studios; Color.

An Indian chief asks a rain dancer to help end a drought. Meanwhile the chief's son buys weather pills which results in chaos.

Merrie Melodies short adapted from *Porky the Rain Maker* (1936) where the story centered around a farm.

The Sioux Spaceman [Novel; SW]

Author: **Andre Norton**; First publication: New York: Ace Books, 1960.

Kade Whitehawk, Amerindian of the Northwest Terran Confederation, is sent to a planetary trading post on Klor where the native Ikkinni are enslaved with collars that can kill. Whitehawk is touched by the plight of the Ikinni and has a plan to win their freedom from the tyrant Styor race.

Sir Edward Grey Witchfinder: Lost and Gone Forever [Comic book; WW]

First publication: February, 2011; 5-issue mini-series; Story: Mike Mignola, John Arcudi; Art: John

Severin, Mike Mignola; Publisher: Dark Horse Comics.

The Old West town of Reidlynne, Utah, 1880. Occult investigator Sir Edward Grey arrives in town searching for Lord Adam Glaren, a member of the Heliopic Brotherhood of Ra, dedicated to the secret teachings of the mysterious Larzod. Grey encounters a town whose church has been claimed by the devil and hostile locals who force him out of Reidlynne. But that is just the start of his supernatural troubles as he encounters a werewolf, a cowboy zombie shootout, a ferocious stone dog and Eris the witch.

Sir Edward Grey first appeared in *Hellboy* (October 2009).

Six-Gun Gorilla [Pulp fiction character; UK; WW]

First appearance: *The Wizard* #850 (March 18, 1939); 15-issues; UK; Publisher: D.C. Thomson.

Bart Masters purchases a gorilla from a sailor named O'Neil in San Francisco. Masters names the gorilla after the sailor and together they work Masters' Dragonfly Gold Mine in the Boulder Hills of Colorado. Master's gold has attracted the attention of the Strawham Gang and one night Masters and O'Neil come under attack while asleep in their log cabin. Masters is shot dead and O'Neil wounded as the gang divides the gold between the four of them. The wounded gorilla's sorrow turns to rage as he realizes Masters is dead. O'Neil picks up the scent of the killers.

"His keen eyes noticed something on which his dead master was half-lying. It was the revolver-belt and gun-holster. The six-shooter was as yet undrawn."

O'Neil takes target practice to improve his gun skills until he feels confident enough to track the killers.

"A strange grimness seemed to possess him. Tucked in his belt was the soiled handkerchief that he had picked up from the floor of the cabin. His nostrils dilated as he sniffed at it, then he turned suddenly towards the west and hurried up

TWO Great Free Gifts Inside For YOU!

Six-Gun Gorilla in The Wizard #850 (March 18, 1939). The Wizard © D.C. Thomson & Co. Ltd., Dundee, Scotland.

the trail which the four killers had taken. The Six-Gun Gorilla had started on its journey of vengeance. A new terror was loose!"

In addition to their strip titles, D.C. Thomson published boys' papers featuring illustrated text stories. *Adventure*, *Wizard* and *Rover* were later joined by *Skipper* and *Hotspur* in the 1930s to comprise the "Big Five."

Six-Gun Gorilla [Comic book; SFW]

First publication: June, 2013; 6-issue mini-series; Story: Simon Spurrier; Art: Jeff Stokely; Publisher: BOOM! Studios.

Blue is a former librarian who is thrust into the 22nd century parallel world named "The Blister," a new frontier, colonized by humans for its fertile land and natural resources. But the frontier is a lawless land in the throes of a civil war. Blue finds himself lost in the war zone pursued by the Rebel WarParty, pedal bike bandits and BXF soldiers. Meanwhile a rogue gunslinger battles a sadistic bounty hunter named Auchenbran. But this is a gunslinger with a difference. He is a bio-surgically modified silverback gorilla who loves using his huge six-guns and teams up with Blue, who seeks to return a mysterious "locket" to earth.

Creator Simon Spurrier re-imagined D.C. Thomson's **Six-Gun Gorilla** for his Sci-Fi Western spin on the character.

Six Gun Samurai [Comic book; WW]

First publication: July 2005; Story: Sean J. Jordan, Mike S. Miller; Art: Harold Edge, Sean J. Jordan; Six-part mini-series; Publisher: Alias Enterprises, LLC.

The disfigured Six-Gun Samurai and his mentor Tetsuya travel across the Old West to find the teenager's only living relative, his father. On their journey they meet Annabelle Rose, who is hunting for the Japanese gang who murdered her parents and left her for dead.

Six Guns & Sorcery [RPG book; WW]

First publication: 1996; Senior Editor: Mark Schumann; Setting: *Castle Falkenstein*; Publisher: R. Talsorian Games Inc.

Tom Olam returns to America in 1876 and on the Great Plains finds four colossal men with narrow glowing eyes slaughtering the inhabitants of an Indian village. This is an alternate history America where the Great Plains is home to the Indian Twenty Nations Confederation, Sam Houston is in his seventh term as president of the Republic of Texas and the United States is run in secret by the Freemasons.

The sourcebook for the world of *Castle Falkenstein*.

Six-Gun Snow White [Novel; WW]

Author: Catherynne M. Valente; First publication: Burton, Michigan: Subterranean Press, 2013.

A Nevada cattle baron forces the Crow people to hand over the beautiful Gun That Sings to him in marriage. When she dies in childbirth her half-breed daughter is hidden from public view until Mr. H remarries eleven years later. But the child's

Cover of *Six-Gun Snow White* by Catherynne M. Valente (2013).

stepmother taunts her half-breed heritage and names her Snow White as she attempts to "civilize" her. The abused Snow White flees her prison-like home on her horse Charming but is pursued by a Pinkerton detective, employed by her stepmother to return her heart. In the town of Oh-Be-Joyful Snow White finds solace when seven female outlaws befriend her. But her trials are not over in this re-imagining of the Snow White fairy tale set in the Old West.

The Six-Gun Tarot [Novel; WW]

Author: R. S. Belcher; First publication: New York: Tor, 2013.

The Old West cattle town of Golgotha, Nevada is inhabited by strange and unnatural townsfolk. The Sheriff still bears the mark of the noose around his neck and a store owner talks to the head of his departed wife, who talks back. The homosexual Mormon mayor Harry Pratt raises a magical sword by the power of his faith and a secret group of female assassins are the descendants of Lilith. There is fifteen-year-old Jim Negrey who owns a magical jade eye and wanders alone through the 40-Mile Desert with his horse Promise. The doubting angel Biqa is also Golgotha's richest man MalachI Bick who runs the saloon and brothel. Clay Turlough has brought back to life his best friend Auggie's now undead former wife Gerta with the help of a demonic worms serum. And finally there is an Indian skinwalker "son of a coyote" named Mutt who is central to the story.

Overlooking Golgotha is an abandoned silver mine that is ready to unleash an evil that threatens the future of not only Golgotha but all of Creation. The Great Wyrm awaits the unfortunate townsfolk of Golgotha.

Six Reasons Why (2008) [Film; Canada; SFW]

Premiere: July 15, 2008; Main Cast: Dan Wooster as The Nomad, Colm Feore as The Preacher, Mads Koudal as The Sherpa, Jeff Campagna as The Criminal, Matthew Campagna as Milton Joyce; Executive Producers-Story-Directors: Jeff & Matthew Campagna; 88 min.; Campagna Brothers Independent Productions, Interflix; Color.

A nomad, a criminal, an entrepreneur and his family servant wander the Badlands fighting for their territory in a future that has reverted to an Old West–style society.

The Sixth Gun [Comic book; TV series pilot; RPG; WW]

1. Comic book
First publication: May 2010; Story: Cullen Bunn; Art: Brian Hurtt; Publisher: Oni Press.

Six cursed guns from the dark days of the American Civil War give supernatural powers to their owners. The First strikes with ungodly force. The Second spreads Perdition's flames. The Third kills with a flesh-rotting disease. The Fourth summons spirits of the people it has slain. The Fifth grants eternal youth and has the ability to heal even a fatal wound. But the cost to the wielder of the gun is a thirst for the life energy of the gun's victims. The long-lost sixth and most powerful gun has come into the hands of a farmer's daughter Becky Montcrief and is sought by those who will kill anyone, including Becky, to obtain the mystical gun. But shady gunslinger Drake Sinclair aims to stop them in their tracks.

2. TV series pilot
Not broadcast: 2013; Main cast: Michael Huisman as Drake Sinclair, Laura Ramsay as Becky Montcrief, Graham McTavish as Silas Hedgepath, Elena Satine as Missy Hume, Brad Leland as Constantine, Pedro Pascal as Special Agent Ortega, Aldis Hodge as Agent Mercer; Executive producers: Carlton Cuse, Eric Gitter, Ryan Condal, Andy Bourne; Story: Cullen Bunn, Ryan Condal, Brian Hurtt; Director: Jeremy Reiner; 60 min.; Universal Television, NBC (National Broadcasting Corporation); Color.

This failed pilot based on the hit comic book series, was slated as a 6-episode mini-series for NBC Universal's SyFy Channel.

3. Role-Playing game
Release date: 2015; Writer: Cullen Bunn; Art: Brian Hurtt; Publisher: Pinnacle Entertainment Group.

A **Deadlands** Savage Worlds tabletop roleplaying game featuring characters *from* **The Sixth Gun** and **Deadlands** Weird West. It includes two short adventures written by Scott A. Woodard. **The Sixth Gun: The One-Hand Gang** is set in Blue Springs, Nebraska. Billy Abernathy, in possession of the Fifth Gun, and his gang—relic hunters and members of the Sword of Abraham—are robbing the First Security Bank.

The Sixth Gun: Circle The Wagon opens as night falls in New Mexico. The posse discovers three dead skin walkers along with the corpse of a bounty hunter. In a nearby wagon lies wanted murderer Randolph P. Tibbots holding the Fourth Gun in his hand. He is still alive.

The RPG game also includes a six-part adventure **The Winding Way** that serves as a prequel to **The Sixth Gun** comic book series. Also new Edges and Hindrances, guns and gear, rules for sorcery and voodoo, creatures, artifacts, locales and various rogues and scoundrels are included.

The Sixth Gun RPG Companion [RPG book; WW]

First publication: 2015; Story: Scott Woodward, Cullen Bunn; Art: Brian Hurtt; Publishers: Pinnacle Entertainment Group, Oni Press.

Includes the **Deadlands-Sixth Gun** crossover adventure **Fractured Frontiers** where two halves of a powerful relic are separated and dropped into parallel realities. Plus two Creature Features, *The Great Wyrms* and *Giselda the Grey Witch* and the comic prologue *Tall Tale of a Sixth Gun*.

Skeleton Dancer [Novel; WW]

Author: Alan R. Erwin; First publication: New York: Dell, 1989.

Vampire Apache Indians haunt a West Texas cave.

Skeleton Hand in Secrets of the Supernatural [Comic book]

This short-lived supernatural and horror anthology title was one of American Comic Group's less successful efforts with a short run of only six issues.

"Black Dust" [WW]

First publication: #4 (March-April 1953); Editor: Richard E. Hughes; Art: S. Cooper; Publisher: American Comics Group (ACG).

A cowboy and cowgirl are attacked by dust that has formed into an evil black dust creature.

Skeleton Man (2004) [Telefilm; WW]

Premiere: March 1, 2004; Main Cast: Casper Van Dien as Staff Sgt. Oberron, Michael Rooker as Captain Leary, Sarah Ann Schultz as Lt. Scott, Jackie Debatin as Sgt. Cordero; Story: Frederick Bailey; Director: Johnny Martin; 89 min.; Nu Image Films; Color.

A Native American Indian from the past stalks a group of Special Forces agents.

Skin Trade: A Historical Horror (Book #1) [Novel; WW]

Author: Tonia Brown; First publication: Jonesboro, AK: Permuted Press, 2015.

It is 1870 and the Great Undead Uprising has devastated the western frontier and destroyed the Indian Nations. Samantha Martin decided to move west when the people were fleeing to the safety of the east. Now she finds herself working as a trapper and skinner of zombies under the pretense of being a male in order to escape her past. Ultimately she wants to escape the Badlands but keeping up the pretense of being a male and denying her femininity is proving to be a dangerous masquerade.

Skinners [RPG book; WW]

Author: Lester Smith; First publication: 1999; Setting: *Deadlands: The Weird West*; Publisher: Pinnacle Entertainment Group.

A haunted Mississippi riverboat provides the setting for a tale featuring Ronan Lynch and a group of flesh skinners.

A Skull Full of Spurs: A Roundup of Weird Westerns [Book anthology; WW]

Editors: Jason Bovberg, Kirk Whitham; First publication: Fort Collins, CO: Dark Highway Press, 2000.

A collection of thirteen short stories taking place in the Weird West. Stories by Brian Hodge, Jack Ketchum, Richard Lee Byers, Edward Lee, Yvonne Navarro, Adam-Troy Castro, Rick Hautala, M. Christian, Lawrence Walsh, Nancy A. Collins, Richard Laymon, Michael Heck and Robert Devereaux feature a cowboy who cannot be killed, an extremely slow moving bullet, a confrontation with an angel and a hanged ghost out for revenge.

The Slayer (The Legend Chronicles book 2) [Novel; SPW]

Author: Theresa Meyers; First publication: New York: Kensington Publishing, 2012.

Sheriff Winchester Jackson of Bodie, California is a reluctant vampire and demon hunter. But even he knows vampires are meant for slaying and not co-operating with. Alexandra Porter is a vampire-in-distress who wants Winn to return with her to Transylvania. With both of them having a mutual interest in recovering the stolen piece of the Book of Legend they must learn to trust each other.

Sliders (1995) [TV series]

Main Cast: Cleavant Derricks as Rembrandt "Crying Man" Brown, Jerry O'Connell as Quinn Mallory, Sabrina Lloyd as Wade Welles, John Rhys-Davies as Prof. Maximilian Arturo, Kari Wuhrer as Capt. Maggie Beckett; 88 × 60 min.; St. Clare Entertainment, Universal TV, Studios USA Television; Color.

A group of companions travel through a portal to parallel universes with alternate realities and slide between worlds in an attempt to return home.

"The Good, the Bad and the Wealthy" (2:04) [SFW]

Air date: March 22, 1996; Guest Stars: Jamie Denton as Jack Bullock; Story: Scott Miller; Director: Oscar L. Costo.

The Sliders emerge in a world of gunslingers, poker games and gunfights in a modern corporate society.

"Way Out West" (4:18) [SFW]

Airdate: March 26, 1999; Guest Stars: Reiner Schone

as Kolitar; Marshall R. Teague as Sheriff Redfield; Story: Jerry O'Connell; Director: David Peckinpah.

Framed for murder by gunslinger "Mr. K" (Schone), Quinn and Rembrandt face the hangman's noose in an Old-West style Earth.

Slocum and the Bear Lake Monster (#204) [Novel; WW]

Author: Jake Logan; First publication: New York: Jove Books, 1996.

Laughter and mockery turns to the lure of money and a pretty face when a rich professor and his sexy assistant offer Slocum a large pile of money to prove the legend of the Bear Lake Monster is genuine.

The hero of each book is John Slocum. The former Confederate soldier and rider with Quantrill's Raiders lost his family home to a money-hungry judge after the Civil War. After killing the judge and burning his home to the ground Slocum ventured West to evade the law and is now a gunfighter roaming the Old West who has tried his hand at numerous jobs.

The *Slocum Westerns* series began in 1975 and totaled 430 titles with the final book published in December 2014. Originally published by Playboy Press the adult oriented stories featured an average of three explicit sex scenes per book placed between the Old West plots. Author Jake Logan is a pen name for a number of different ghost writers who worked on the title. The series occasionally wandered into Weird Western territory.

Slocum and the Beast of Fall Pass (#420) [Novel; WMW]

Author: Jake Logan; First publication: New York: Jove Books, 2014.

Slocum hunts a creature that has badly mauled two men. Is it someone or "something"?

Slocum and the Big Timber Terror (#428) [Novel; WW]

Author: Jake Logan; First publication: New York: Jove Books, 2014.

When a heavy snowstorm traps Slocum and his Appaloosa in Oregon's Cascade Range he searches for shelter among the pine trees but is shocked to discover "hovering a good eight feet off the ground were two glowing green eyes, a good hand's length apart and angled inward, as if whoever it was were filled with a seething rage" accompanied by a "guttural, screeching howl" and

a "powerful, slaughterous smell." The nightmarish local legend may have just paid Slocum a visit.

Slocum and the Indian Ghost (#96) [Novel; WMW]

Author: Jake Logan; First publication: New York: Berkley Books, 1986.

John Slocum comes to the aid of a wealthy widow who believes an Indian is haunting her parlor.

Slocum and the Invaders (#182) [Novel; SFW]

Author: Jake Logan; First publication: New York: Berkley Books, 1994.

In Arizona Territory, with a murderous gang pursuing him, Slocum meets an astronomer and his attractive female assistant. But events take an unexpected twist when Slocum discovers he is dealing with creatures from the planet Mars.

Slocum and the Presidio Phantoms (#318) [Novel; WW]

Author: Jake Logan; First publication: New York: Jove Books, 2005.

Ghosts called "haints" are affecting the soldier's morale in the Presidio and Slocum is called upon to help with the problem.

Slocum and the Spirit Bear (#407) [Novel; WW]

Author: Jake Logan; First publication: New York: Jove Books, 2013.

Ed Warren offers John Slocum a job protecting a small wagon train heading to the Rockies and Colorado mines in the hope of making their fortunes. But Spirit Bear and his band of supernatural creatures protect the land and attack the wagon train, threatening death if they continue on their journey. Slocum must stop Spirit Bear if they are to make it to the Colorado mines.

Slocum and the Witch of Westlake (#362) [Novel; WMW]

Author: Jake Logan; First publication: New York: Jove Books, 2009.

The townsfolk of Westlake fear the strange woman known as Minh is a witch. But John Slocum is more interested in her physical charms than her otherworldly charms.

Slocum on Ghost Mesa (#270) [Novel; WW]

Author: Jake Logan; First publication: New York: Jove Books, 2001.

John Slocum comes to the aid of passengers stranded in the desert after their stagecoach breaks down. But one of the passengers is murdered in the dead of night by something inhuman Slocum realizes his six-gun may not be enough to protect himself and the passengers.

Smallville (2001) [TV series]

Main Cast: Tom Welling as Clark Kent, Erica Durance as Lois Lane, Alison Mack as Chloe Sullivan, Justin Hartley as Oliver Queen/Green Arrow, Cassidy Freeman as Tess Mercer.

The adventures of Clark Kent as a teenager in Smallville and a young man in Metropolis, working for *The Daily Planet*.

"Shield" (10:02) [SFW]

Air date: October 1, 2010; Guest Cast: Keri Lynn Pratt as Cat Grant, Michael Shanks as Hawkman-Carter Hall, Sahar Biniaz as Shayera Hall, Bradley Stryker as Deadshot, Ted Wittall as Red Flag, Jessica Parker Kennedy as Plastique; Story: Jordan Hawley; Director: Glen Winter; 42 min.; Tollins/Robbins Productions, The CW Television Network; Color.

When reporter Cat Grant substitutes for Lois Lane who is on assignment in Egypt, she becomes the alleged target of **Deadshot**, but Red Flag has actually hired Deadshot to kill the Blur a.k.a. Clark Kent.

"Collateral" (10:12) [SFW]

Air date: February 4, 2011; Guest Cast: Alaina Huffman as Dinah Lance/Black Canary, Bradley Stryker as Deadshot, Ted Whittall as Red Flag, Lori Triolo as Lt. Trotter; Story: Jordan Hawley; Director: Morgan Beggs; 42 min.; Tollins/Robbins Productions; Miller Gough Ink, DC Entertainment, Smallville Films, Warner Bros., The CW Television Network; Color.

Clark Kent, Lois Lane, Oliver Queen and Dinah Lance all believe they have been tortured by Chloe Sullivan who is now under suspicion of being a traitor. But it is all a virtual reality illusion whose false reality can only be shattered by breaking through the virtual mirage into reality. Helping Chloe is Rick Flag's Suicide Squad, including **Deadshot** who she has blackmailed into working for her.

Smith & Robards [RPG book; WW]

Author: John Hopler; First publication: 1997; Setting: **Deadlands: The Weird West**; Publisher: Pinnacle Entertainment Group.

Book of mad science gear and technology. Includes the adventure "The Crucible."

Smoking Guns (1934) [Film; WMW]

Premiere: June 11, 1934; Main Cast: Ken Maynard as Ken Masters, Gloria Shea as Alice Adams, Walter Miller as Dick Evans, Harold Goodwin as Hank Stone, Bob Kortman as Biff; Producer: Ken Maynard; Story: Nate Gatzert, Ken Maynard; Director: Alan James; 62 min.; Ken Maynard Productions Inc., Universal Pictures; B/W.

Ken Masters escapes to the swamplands of Louisiana. Framed for murder, this unintentionally funny Western, which concludes in a haunted house, marked the end of Maynard's career at Universal.

Smonk: A Novel [Novel; WW]

Author: Tom Franklin; First publication: New York: William Morrow, 2006.

On the run from a posse of vigilantes, 15-year-old prostitute and killer Evavangeline arrives in Old Texas, Alabama where she meets murdering rapist E.O. Smonk, who is also being pursued by lawman Will McKissick. In Old Texas the only child left alive is McKissick's 12-year-old son. Dead boys, all dressed in their Sunday clothes, fill the local church while the one-armed rabid preacher and dog Lazarus the Redeemer, assassins, witches and zombies make certain you'll never get bored in Old Texas.

Solar Boy Django [Manga; Japan; WW]

First appearance: September 2003; Story: Makoto Hijoka; Publisher: Shogakukan

Strip in *CoroCoro Comic*; Based on the Boktai game produced by Kojima Hideo.

Django's search for his brother Sabata takes him to the Dark Castle where he defeats the vampire "The Count" and comes to believe that vampire Luna holds the clue to the fate of Sabata.

Although this manga belongs to the vampire horror genre, the main characters are named after spaghetti Western gunslingers, thus giving this a Weird Western twist.

Something About a Sword [RPG book; WW]

Authors: Walter Hunt, Evan Jamieson, Richard Meyer; Setting: **Deadlands: Hell on Earth the Wasted West**; First publication: Pinnacle Entertainment Group.

The Posse must find the sword of a missing Templar in the ruins of western Wyoming.

But to reach the sword they must survive attacks from mutants, rad-priests and hippies.

"Song in a Minor Key" [Pulp fiction; SW]

Author: **C. L. Moore**; First publication: *Scienti-Snaps* (February 1940).

Northwest Smith reminisces about his lost youth on Earth and comes to the realization that his present exiled outlaw state was always his destiny.

South o' the Border [RPG book; WW]

Author: Steven Long; First publication: 1999; Setting: *Deadlands: The Weird West;* Publisher: Pinnacle Entertainment Group.

Location book for Mexico.

Space Cowboy [Juvenile book; SW]

Author: Justin Stanchfield; First publication: London: Usborne Books, 2008.

On the terra-formed planet of Aletha Three, cowboy Travis McClure and his female friend Riane investigate a genetically engineered predator that is stalking cattle and may soon get a taste for human flesh. Described by the publisher as "Alien meets the Wild West!"

Space Hawk: The Greatest of Interplanetary Adventures [Pulp fiction collection; SW]

Author: Anthony Gilmore [**Harry Bates**]; Illustrations: Nettie Weber; First book publication: New York: Greenberg, 1952.

First collection of three **Hawk Carse** stories in one volume: *Hawk Carse* (1931), *The Bluff of the Hawk* (1932), *The Return of the Hawk* (1942).

Space Rage (1985) [Film; SW]

Main Cast: Richard Farnsworth as Colonel, Lee Purcell as Maggie, John Laughlin as Walker, Michael Paré as Grange; Executive Producer: Peter McCarthy; Story: Morton Reed, Jim Lenahan; Director: Conrad E. Palmisano; 77 min.; Garwood Films; Vestron Entertainment; Color.

Space Western set on the Botany Bay penal colony on the mining planet Proxima Centauri in the 22nd century. A former cop (Farnsworth) attempts to maintain law and order when a dangerous prisoner (Paré) arranges a mass breakout.

Space Vulture [Novel; SW]

Authors: Gary K. Wolf, John L. Myers; First publication: New York: Tor, 2008.

On the planet Verlinap, galactic marshal Captain Victor Corsaire and colony administrator Cali Russell are captured by Space Vulture for auctioning to criminals with the highest bids.

An effort to recapture the spirit of the science fiction pulps and an homage to *Space Hawk* by *Roger Rabbit* creator Gary K. Wolf and Roman Catholic archbishop John L. Myers.

Space Western Comics [Comic book; SW]

First issue: October 1952; Publisher: Charlton-Capitol Stories.

The adventures of **Spurs Jackson** and his Space Vigilantes as they tackle alien invaders attempting to conquer Earth and the universe.

This title began life as *Yellowjacket Comics* in September 1944, followed by a change in title to *Jack in the Box* in October 1946. Under the editorship of Charlton Comics founders John Santangelo and Edward Levy, the title became *Cowboy Western Comics* in 1948 only to switch direction and become *Space Western Comics* in October 1952 starting at issue #40. *The Shadow* creator Walter B. Gibson provided scripts for the first issue under the new title. Six issues later, with declining sales, it returned to its original title and format and survived another eleven issues before its final incarnation as *Wild Bill Hickok & Jingles* in March 1958.

The title was an interesting attempt at crossing the Western, military and science fiction genres and included a bizarre two-issue story involving Spurs Jackson and his Space Vigilantes pursuing Adolf Hitler and his fellow Nazis to Mars and beyond.

Space Western stories of interest included:

"THE SAUCER MEN" #40 (October 1952); Story: Walter Gibson, Art: John Belfi.

When Spurs Jackson is invited to visit Mars by Martian prime minister Korok, he becomes a pawn in the overthrow of Queen Thula.

"THE GREEN MEN OF VENUS" #41 (December 1952); Art: Stan Campbell.

Vodor and his fellow Venusians threaten the Earth disguised as cactii thanks to their resemblance to the plant.

"SPURS JACKSON AND HIS SPACE VIGILANTES MEET THE SUN MASTERS" #42 (February 1953); Art: Stan Campbell.

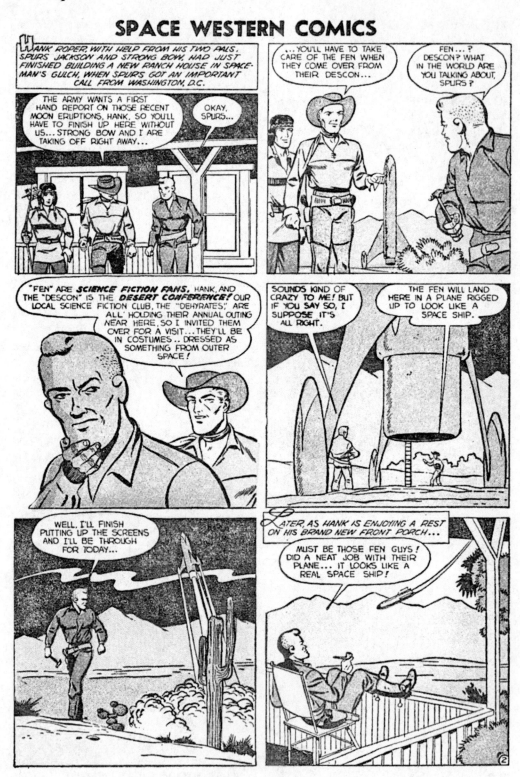

Interior of *Space Western Comics* #43 (April 1953), "The Battle of Spaceman's Gulch featuring Hank Roper."

The Sun is the target of the Sun Masters who want to drain it of energy.

"TRIP TO MERCURY" #43 (April 1953)

Strong Bow discovers that the ancient Aztecs fled the Spaniards in a rocket ship to Mercury and decides to follow.

"THE BATTLE OF SPACEMEN'S GULCH FEATURING HANK ROPER" #43 (April 1953)

When the U.S. Army attempts to repel the Artopod invaders from Neptune, they are met with light beams that cause their tanks and planes to disappear. The members of the science fiction club "Dehyrates" save the day when they spray the insect Artopods with insecticide and kill them. Spurs Jackson completes the job by blasting their spaceship.

"MADMAN OF MARS" (PART ONE) "TOMORROW THE UNIVERSE" (PART TWO), #44–45 (June-August 1953)

When hydrogen bombs from Mars hit Paris, Moscow, Honolulu, New York City and London, General Carpenter calls Spurs Jackson and his Vigilantes to Washington, D.C. where they are assigned to go to Mars to track the source of the bombs.

To their amazement Spurs, Strong Bow and Hank Roper come under attack from German Nazis when they arrive on the surface of Mars. They learn that Hitler and nine of his men escaped to Mars at the end of World War II. Hoping to capture Hitler, Spurs is told he escaped in a rocket soon after his arrival. Jackson and the Space Vigilantes track Hitler to an asteroid where one of Hitler's own men turns against Hitler and kills him.

"STRONG BOW MEETS THE STONE MEN FROM SPACE"

First publication: #44 (June 1953); Art: John Belfi

When Queen Thula of Mars visits Strong Bow and his Indian tribe in the Rainbow Desert, Arizona, the stone men of the planet Canis stir from 10,000 years of rest with the intention of taking over the Earth. Spurs Jackson comes to the rescue by dropping an atomic bomb on the rampaging Stone Men.

"SPURS JACKSON AND HIS VIGILANTES MEET THE MENACE OF COMET X" #44 (June 1953); Art: John Belfi.

With a comet on a collision course with Earth Spurs, Jackson, prime minister in the cabinet of Queen Thula, is asked if he can help. Spurs encounters old foes Vodor from Venus and Martian exile Korok who are controlling the comet and manages to save the Earth from destruction.

Sparks Nevada: Marshal on Mars
[Comic book character; SW]

First publication: August, 2013; Story: Ben Acker, Ben Blacker; Art: Lar deSouza, Evan Larson, Evan Shaner; Publisher: Archaia Entertainment.

Sparks Nevada, a marshal from Earth, rides his rocket steed righting the outlaw wrongs on Mars and upholding the law with his robot fists. With the help of Martian companion **Croach the Tracker** and the **Red Plains Rider** he pursues and confronts Wired Bill, John Steelhands and their robotic gangs.

Published as part of a comic strip anthology collection inspired by the popular live audio theater show and podcast, **The Thrilling Adventure Hour** where Marc Evan Jackson plays the character.

"A Spider Poor Cowboy Rapt and Wide Lemon" [Short story; WW]

Author: Ken Rand; First publication: *Faeries Magazine* #2, 2000.

A dead man walks into the Lucky Nickel Saloon. The hole from a .45 caliber bullet proves to be a severe hindrance when he tries to quench his thirst. And to make things worse, the regular patrons ban him from haunting the saloon.

See: **The Problem with Mermaids**

The Spider Woman Strikes Back (1946) [Film; WW]

Premiere: March 22, 1946; Main Cast: GaleSondergaard as Zenobia Dollard, Brenda Joyceas Jean Kingsley, Rondo Hatton as Mario; Producer: Howard Welsch; Story: Eric Taylor; Director: Arthur Lubin; 59 min.; Universal Pictures; B/W.

Contemporary horror in a Western ranch setting. A wealthy blind rancher (Sondergaard) is draining the blood from a young woman (Joyce) to feed her carnivorous plants in order to make a poison to kill cattle. By this means she intends to drive out the local ranchers so she can claim the land.

Gale Sondergaard was also featured in *Sherlock Holmes and the Spider Woman* (1944).

Spirit of Dawn [Novel; WWR]

Author: Samantha Byrnes; First publication: Freya's Bower, 2006.

A mystical frontier woman comforts the eldest male of his Navajo clan after his wife and child die of smallpox.

The Spirit of Thunder [Novel; SFW]

Author: Kurt R. A. Giambastiani; First publication: New York: ROC, 2002.

One Who Flies fights against his father President George Armstrong Custer's army as he helps the Cheyenne defy the oncoming railroad. Book two in the *Fallen Cloud Saga*.

See: *The Shadow of the Storm*

The Spirit Path [Novel; WWR]

Author: Madeline Baker; First publication: New York: N.Y. Leisure Books, 1993.

Lakota spiritual leader Shadow Hawk goes on a vision quest, traveling through time and space to the present day where he meets the beautiful Spirit Woman of his visions.

Commenting on the success of her Western romances despite the declining interest in the standard Western novel, Madeline Baker stated, "There's a difference between Western novels and Western romances. The women who read Western romances never seem to tire of them. I'm sure the fantasy aspect plays a big part in the success of time travel books, plus there's something compelling about the Indian way of life."

The Spirit Stalker [Novel; WW]

Author: Nina Romberg; First publication: New York: Pinnacle Books, 1989.

Corpses are turning up in East Texas. Caddo and Comanche Indian Meriam Winchester believe the deaths are the result of spirits working their evil through the killer. Only Sunny Hansen can tackle the evil, but she has greater fears for her safety from her abusive husband.

Spirit Warriors [RPG book; WW]

Author: John Hopler; First publication: 2000; Setting: *Deadlands: Hell on Earth the Wasted West*; Publisher: Pinnacle Entertainment Group.

Rules and histories for Native Americans, Shamans and Toxic Shamans who bargain with toxic spirits in the Wasted West.

Spoilers of the Plains (1951) [Film; SFW]

Premiere: February 2, 1951; Main Cast: Roy Rogers as Roy Rogers, Penny Edwards as Frankie Manning, Gordon Jones as Splinters, Grant Withers as Gregory Camwell; Story: Sloan Nibley; Director: William Witney; 68 min.; Republic Pictures; B/W.

Roy Rogers often appeared in Westerns set in the modern era complete with automobiles but with a traditional Western background including Western towns, sheriffs and horses. This movie features Rogers and his trusted horse Trigger fighting an oil pipeline blaze dressed in firefighting gear! A plot involving a rocket and satellites in space add to the strange mixture and defines this movie as an early example of a science fiction Western.

Spook Ranch (1925) [Film; WMW]

Premiere: September 20, 1925; Main Cast: Hoot Gibson as Bill Bangs, Ed Cowles as George Washington Black, Tote Du Crow as Navarro, Helen Ferguson as Elvira, Robert McKim as Don Ramies, Frank Rice as Sheriff; Story: Raymond L. Schrock, Edward Sedgwick; Director: Edward Laemmle; 60 min.; Universal Jewel, Universal Pictures, B/W.

Bill Bangs and his valet George Washington Black are arrested and placed in jail when the hungry pair steals food. The price of their freedom is to solve the mystery of a haunted house. Their investigations lead them to Don Ramies and his gang of outlaws who are attempting to find the location of a rancher's gold mine.

Spurs Jackson [Comic book character; SW]

First appearance: *Space Western Comics* #40; Publisher: Charlton—Capitol Comics.

Set in the 1950s "atomic age," the adventures of cowboy rancher Spurs Jackson and his Space Vigilantes appeared in *Space Western Comics*. Jackson owns Spaceman's Gulch Ranch in Arizona. Helping him run the ranch are his friends American Indian Strong Bow and Hank Roper. Jackson uses his skills as an electronics engineer to build a rocket ship that contains a light plane in the cargo hold. Together with Strong Bow and Roper, Jackson travels through the solar system and protects the Earth from invaders from Venus, Mars and Neptune.

Stageghost (2000) [Film; WW]

Premiere: 2000; Main Cast: Edward Albert as U.S. Deputy Marshal Coburn, Christopher Atkins as Matthew Bronson, Dana Barron as Renee Bloomer, John Vernon as Slim; Executive Producer–Story: Thomas Seiler; Director: Stephen Furst; 104 min.; Color.

After an empty bloodstained stagecoach arrives at a way station with the message "Give It Back," the locals are besieged by supernatural forces.

Star Trek (1966) [TV series]

Adventures of the crew of the U.S.S. *Enterprise* as it journeys through intergalactic space. Creator Gene Roddenberry described *Star Trek* as "*Wagon Train* to the stars" when pitching his original concept to the television networks.

"THE PARADISE SYNDROME" (3:03) [SW]
Air date: October 4, 1968; Main Cast: William Shatner as James T. Kirk, Leonard Nimoy as Spock, DeForest Kelley as Leonard H. McCoy, James Doohan as Montgomery Scott, Walter Koenig as Pavel Chekov; Guest Cast: Sabrina Scharf as Miranamee, Rudy Solari as Salish; Executive Producer: Gene Roddenberry; Producer: Fred Freiberger; Story: Margaret Armen; Director: Jud Taylor; 50 min.; Norway Corporation, Paramount Television; Color.

Captain Kirk loses his memory on the planet Amerind and is accepted into the local tribe, who are descendants of Native Americans from Earth. Falling in love with the beautiful Miranamee, Kirk must decide between the "idyllic life of the noble savage" and his duties as Captain of the U.S.S. *Enterprise* as his memory returns.

"SPECTRE OF THE GUN" (3:06) [SW]
Air date: October 25, 1968; Guest Cast: Bonnie Beacher as Sylvia, Rex Holman as Morgan Earp, Ron Soble as Wyatt Earp, Charles Maxwell as Virgil Earp, Sam Gilman as Doc Holliday; Story: Lee Cronin (Gene L. Coon); Director: Vincent McEveety; 50 min.; Norway Corporation, Paramount Television; Color.

The Melkots (aliens) transport the crew of the *Enterprise* to a recreation of Tombstone, Arizona, in 1881 and the shoot-out at the O.K. Corral.

Star Trek: Enterprise (2001) [TV series]

This prequel to *Star Trek*, set aboard the first starship *Enterprise*, explores the formative years of Starfleet.

"NORTH STAR" (3:09) [SFW]
Air date: November 12, 2003; Main Cast: Scott Bakula as Captain Jonathan Archer, Jolene Blalock as Sub-Commander T'Pol, Anthony Montgomery as Ensign Travis Mayweather, Dominic Keating as Lieutenant Malcolm Reed, Emily Bergl as Bethany, Steven Klein as Draysik, James Parks as Deputy Bennings, Glenn Morshower as Mac-Ready; Executive Producers: Rick Berman, Brannon Braga; Story: David A. Goodman; Director: David Straiton; Paramount Television, Braga Productions, Rick Berman Productions, 42 min.; Color.

Captain Archway and his crew encounter a human colony with an American Old West culture and discover that the colonists were originally slave labor for the Skagarans. But the humans have turned on the Skags and refuse them basic civil rights.

Star Trek: The Next Generation (1987) [TV series]

Sequel to *Star Trek* set in the 24th century.

"A FISTFUL OF DATAS" (6:08) [SFW]
Air date: November 7, 1992; Main Cast: Patrick Stewart as Captain Jean-Luc Picard, Brent Spiner as Lt. Commander Data/Frank/Eli/Henchman/Bandito/Annie, Jonathan Frakes as Commander William T. Riker, LeVar Burton as Lt. Commander Geordi La Forge, Michael Dorn as Lieutenant Worf, Marina Sirtis as Counselor Deanna Troi, Gates McFadden as Beverly Crusher; Guest Cast: Brian Bonsall as Alexander Rozhenko, John Pyper-Ferguson as Eli Hollander; Executive Producers: Michael Piller, Rick Berman; Teleplay: Robert Hewitt Wolfe, Brannon Braga; Story: Robert Hewitt Wolfe; Director: Patrick Stewart; 45 min.; Paramount Television; Color.

While acting as sheriff and deputy sheriff of Deadwood, Worf and his son Alexander meet multiple bad guy variations of Data in an Old West adventure on the holodeck.

"JOURNEY'S END" (7:20) [SW]
Air date: March 26, 1994; Guest Cast: Wil Wheaton as Wesley Crusher, Natalija Nogulichas Admiral Alynna Nechayev, Eric Menyuk asThe Traveller, Doug Wert as Jack Crusher, Tom Jackson as Lakanta, Ned Romero as Anthwara; Executive Producers: Michael Piller, Rick Berman. Jeri Taylor; Story: Ronald D. Moore; Director: Corey Allen; 45 min.; Paramount Television; Color.

Captain Picard is met with resistance when he attempts to relocate a Native American colony. Meanwhile, Wesley Crusher accepts an invitation from a Native Indian to undergo a vision quest.

Star Wars (1977) [Film; SW]

Premiere: May 25, 1977; Main Cast: Harrison Ford as Han Solo, Mark Hamill as Luke Skywalker, Carrie Fisher as Princess Leia Organa, Peter Cushing as Grand Moff Tarkin, Alec Guinness as Ben Obi-Wan Kenobi, David Prowse as Darth Vader, Anthony Daniels as C-3PO, Kenny Baker as R2-D2, Peter

Mayhew as Chewbacca; Executive Producer-Story-Director: George Lucas; 121 min.; Twentieth Century–Fox Film Corporation, Lucasfilm; Color.

Luke Skywalker gathers a group of allies in an attempt to rescue Princess Leia from the evil Darth Vader and to neutralize the planet-destroying Death Star.

With an initial budget of $11 million, the film produced a worldwide gross of over $775 million. Its major international box-office success led to a series of sequels and prequels including *The Empire Strikes Back* (1980), *Return of the Jedi* (1983), *Phantom Menace* (1999), *Attack of the Clones* (2002), *Revenge of the Sith* (2005) and *The Force Awakens* (2015).

The character of Han Solo carries on the tradition of space smugglers started by **Northwest Smith**. George Lucas said, "I always considered my films Westerns. What made the classic Westerns of guys like John Ford great was that the stories they told were so simple that they ended up being deeply resonant and inspiring."

The **Star Wars** franchise features many Western inspired gunslingers including, **Cad Bane**, Bulduga, Longo Two-Guns, Amaiza Foxtrain, Calo Nord, Uul-Rha-Shan, Boba Fett, Jango Fett and Gallandro.

Star Wars: The Clone Wars (2008) (Animated TV series) [SW]

Star Wars: The Clone Wars (2009), featuring Spaghetti Western inspired bounty hunter Cad Bane.

Voice cast: Corey Burton as **Cad Bane**; Executive Producers: George Lucas, Catherine Winder; 22 min.; Cartoon Network, TNT, Netflix; Color.

The Clone Army of the Republic fights Count Dooku's Separatist forces.

"Hostage Crisis" (1:22) [SW]

Air date: March 20, 2009; Story: Eoghan Mahoney; Director: Giancarlo Volpe.

Cad Bane and his team of fellow bounty hunters aim to take hostages at the Senate Building in exchange for crime lord Ziro the Hutt.

The first appearance of Cad Bane in the series.

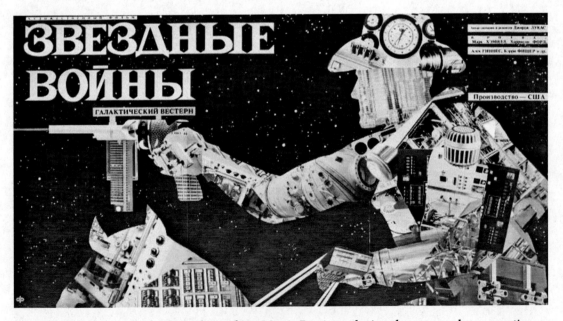

This film poster art for the 1990 release of *Star Wars* in Russia emphasizes the space cowboy connection.

Star Wars the Clone Wars: Battle Lines (Animated TV series) [SW]

"DECEPTION" (4:15)

Air date: January 20, 2012; Story: Brent Friedman; Director: Kyle Dunlevy.

Obi-Wan Kenobi fakes his own death and goes undercover as bounty hunter Rako Hardeen in an attempt to foil a plot to kidnap Chancellor Palpatine.

"FRIENDS AND ENEMIES" (4:16)

Air date: January 27, 2012; Story: Brent Friedman; Director: Bosco Nig.

Cad Bane, Moralo Eval and a disguised Obi-Wan are pursued by Anakin and Ahsoka.

"THE BOX" (4:17)

Air date: February 3, 2012; Story: Brent Friedman; Director: Brian Kalin O'Connell.

Bane, Eval and undercover Obi-Wan arrive at Serenno where bounty hunters are in competition to participate in a plot to kidnap the Chancellor.

"CRISIS ON NABOO" (4:18)

Air date: February 10, 2012; Story: Brent Friedman; Director: Danny Keller.

Undercover Obi-Wan Kenobi joins Count Dooku's plot to kidnap Chancellor Palpatine during the Festival of Light on Naboo. But Dooku intends to kidnap Palpatine himself.

Star Wars the Clone Wars: Republic Heroes [Video game; SW]

Release date: October, 2009; Third-person action-adventure game; Developer: Krome Studios; Publisher: LucasArts.

Players take part in key events leading into Season Two of the TV series. The Galactic Republic pursues the mysterious bounty hunter **Cad Bane** and the Skakoan super-villain Kul Teska. Players fight as Jedi Knights and Clone Troopers in over 30 missions.

Star Wars the Clone Wars: Rise of the Bounty Hunters (Animated TV series) [SW]

"HOLOCRON HEIST" (2:01) [SW]

Air date: October 2, 2009; Story: Paul Dini; Director: Justin Ridge

Cad Bane is hired by Darth Sidious to steal a valuable Jedi holocron from the vault of the Jedi Temple. He is assisted by techno-service droid Todo 360 and shape shifting bounty hunter Cato Parisitti.

"CARGO OF DOOM" (2:02) [SW]

Air date: October 2, 2009; Story: George Krstic; Director: Rob Coleman.

Unable to open the holocron and access the Kyber memory crystal that stores the records of all Force-sensitive infants in the galaxy, Bane requires the assistance of a Jedi He captures Jedi Knight Anakin Skywalker's Padawan Ashoka Tano and forces Skywalker to unlock the holocron.

"CHILDREN OF THE FORCE" (2:03) [SW]

Air date: October 9, 2010; Story: Henry Gilroy, Wendy Meracle; Director: Brian Kalin O'Connell..

Darth Sidious sets Bane and fellow nefarious travelers the task of kidnapping Force-sensitive children to train as Sith spies. But Bane is captured by Anakin and Ashoka and his mind probed before Obi-Wan Kenobee and Mace Windu. He escapes the Jedi Masters by trapping them on his hideout Black Stall Stallion.

Star Wars the Clone Wars: Secrets Revealed (Animated TV series) [SW]

"EVIL PLANS" (3:08)

Air date: November 5, 2010; Story: Steve Mitchell; Director: Craig Van Sickle.

C-3PO is abducted by Cad Bane to extract information about the Senate building. When his efforts fail he kidnaps R2-D2 for the information and discovers a plot designed by the Hutt families is in progress to free Ziro Desilijic Tiure out of Republic custody on Corusant.

"HUNT FOR ZIRO" (3:09)

Air date: November 12, 2010; Story: Steve Mitchell; Director: Steward Lee.

Bane and his crew of bounty hunters frees Ziro the Hutt from the high-security Detention Center. The Hutt Council are after information from Ziro concerning a journal that details the criminal activity of the Hutt families. Ziro escapes the Council with the help of his former lover Sy Snooties and they track the journal to the secret grave of Ziro's father. But Snooties turns on Ziro and kills him. She is a bounty hunter-for-hire and passes the journal to her client, Jabba the Hutt.

Stark and the Star Kings [Pulp fiction collection; SW]

Authors: Edmond Hamilton, **Leigh Brackett**; First published: Royal Oak MI: Haffner Press, 2005.

On Mars, **Eric John Stark** is summoned by the Lord of the Third Bend to combat an unknown force that is devouring all the energy in the solar system and beyond. His mission takes him 200,000 years into the future to join forces with the Star Kings.

The only collaboration between husband and wife Hamilton and Brackett combines Brackett's Eric John Stark and Hamilton's Star Kings in one adventure. The story, originally intended for Harlan Ellison's *Last Dangerous Visions*, remained unpublished until 2005. It was published as part of a collection of stories by Hamilton and Brackett that includes "**Queen of the Martian Catacombs**," "**Enchantress of Venus**" and "**Black Amazon of Mars**."

Steam Man [Comic book; SPW]

First publication: October, 2015; 5-issue mini-series; Story: Mark Miller based on Joe R. Lansdale's "**The Steam Man of the Prairie and the Dark Rider Get Down**"; Art: Piotr Kowalski; Publisher: Dark Horse.

In an alternative Old West steam powered giant robots tackle Martian invaders and killer albino apes. The giant metal Steam Man with the help of his monster hunter operators appears to be in control until a vampire spoils the fun and threatens the apocalypse.

"The Steam Man of the Prairie and the Dark Rider Get Down: A Dime Novel" [Short story; SPW]

Author: Joe R. Lansdale; First publication: *The Long Ones*; Publisher: Necro Publications, 1999.

A posse drives a steam man across the Old West in pursuit of the Dark Rider and his trained ape men. The Dark Rider is H.G. Well's time machine traveler who has upset the space-time continuum and is now a vampire. The Morlocks from Wells' story are now talking apes in Lansale's journey into torture, cannibalism and sex.

Steampunk [Comic book; SPW]

First publication: 2000; Story: Joe Kelly; Art: Chris Bachalo; Publisher: Cliffhanger-Wildstorm.

Steampunk fantasy title set in Victorian England involving time travel, robotics, immortality and the Old West.

Steam World Dig [Video game; SPW]

Release date: August 7, 2013; Platform: Nintendo 3DS; Developer: Image & Form; Publisher: Image & Form.

The player controls Rusty, a steam-powered mining robot who is exploring the mine left to him by the mysterious Uncle Joe in the Western mining town of Tumbleton. As Rusty digs deep into the mine he uncovers secrets, puzzles, hidden passages, rare ores, traps and foes. Precious ores are exchanged for cash to enable Rusty's standard mining tools to be upgraded as the game progresses. Defeating enemies leads to access to valuable water pools, lighter fuel and health. Loss of health results in a return to town, loss of half your money and the ore in your possession. Progress takes Rusty ever deeper into the mine and closer to uncovering the unexplored Old World.

Steampunk Cthulhu : Mythos Terror in the Age of Steam [Short story anthology; SPW]

First publication: June, 2014; Editors: Brian Sammons, Glynn Owen Barrass; Publisher: Chaosium Inc., Hayward, CA.

This anthology collection includes the story "The Reverend Mister Goodworks and the Yeggs of Yigg," that author Ed Erdelac describes as "a prequel spin-off which directly ties into **Merkabah Rider: Once Upon a Time in the Weird West**."

The Reverend Mister Goodworks also known as Reverend Shadrach Mischach Abednego Carter was a train engineer, who after a horrific crash, is partially reconstructed with steam engine parts and becomes a battling preacher dedicated to the destruction of evil.

The Reverend encounters a distressed Mexican woman fleeing across the desert at night who begs him to kill her and her unborn twins. But the Reverend refuses and finds himself delivering two vicious serpent-human hybrids.

Stinger [Novel; SFW]

Author: Robert R. McCammon; First published: 1988; Publisher: New York: Pocket Books.

The citizens of a remote Texas town find themselves in the middle of a pursuit involving an alien bounty hunter and his prey. When the townsfolk decide to aid the pursued, Stinger the bounty hunter envelops the town in a force field and searches for his prey using replicant copies of the townspeople with one major adaptation: They possess razor blade teeth and metal claws.

Stingray Sam (2009) [Film; SW]

Premiere: January 2009; Main Cast: David Hyde

Pierce as Narrator, Cory McAbee, Joshua Taylor, Crugie, Willa Vy McAbee, Caleb Scott, Frank Swart, Jessica Jelliffe; Executive Producer: Bobby Lurie; Story-Director; Cory McAbee; BNS Productions; B/W.

Space convicts Stingray Sam and the Quasar Kid must rescue a young girl captive in return for their freedom. A musical Space Western mini-series.

Stormshadow [Comic book character; France; SFW]

First publication: *Jeunesse-Selection* #1, *Pim Pam Poum* #16 (early 1960s); Creator: Emilio Uberti; Publisher: Editions Lug.

The character started life as Stormalong, a mysterious cloaked do-gooder operating in Louisiana in the 19th century.

Stormshadow sketch. Creators Emilio Uberti and Jean-Marc Lofficier. © Mosaic Multimedia. Used with permission.

Stormshadow—real name Sturmaloon—is the shaman of the Twilight People of Avalon, a race of alien shapeshifters and "monsters." Stormshadow's natural form is that of a dragon whose powers include shapeshifting, a form of teleportation, and considerable arcane knowledge.

In 1844, Stormshadow helped the Texan crimefighter **Drago**. Later, he found the descendents of Gal, who now lived in America under the name "Damon." During the late 19th century, Storm-shadow spent some time in Louisiana as "Stormalong," the Ghost of the South.

Editor Jean-Marc Lofficier, recalling the evolution of Storm-shadow, stated, "I decided to revamp-redesign the character in 2000 when I took over editing the line; I rechristened him Stormshadow and changed his design to look even more mysterious.

Straight Arrow [Radio show; Comic book; WMW]

1. Premiere: May 1, 1948; Main Cast: Howard Culver as Steve Adams/ Straight Arrow, Fred Howard as Packy McCloud; Story: Sheldon Stark; Director; Ted Robertson; Don Lee Network, Mutual Broadcasting System. 294 × 30 min.

Steve Adams, the owner of the Broken Bow cattle spread, and his friend Packy McCloud awaken in a subterranean cave in Sundown Valley that shimmers with gold crystals. Standing in the glowing light that fills the cave is a golden Palomino. A Comanche bow, golden arrows, headdress and garments hang on a wall awaiting Adams. He confesses his Comanche Indian birth to Packy and tells him of the legend of a warrior who will be a savior of the Indians. Taking the bow, arrows, headdress and clothes, Adams become legendary Straight Arrow, riding his golden Palomino Fury bareback out of the cave with his war cry "Kaneewah, Fury!"

Sponsored by the National Biscuit Company (Nabisco), the show featured a few Weird Menace episodes.

"THE DEAD MAN SPEAKS" (episode #4)

Airdate: May 27, 1948; "The Haunted Desert" (episode #9) Airdate: July 1, 1948; "Hunter and Haunted" (episode #112) Airdate: September 20, 1949; "The Beast with Green Eyes" (episode #113) Airdate: September 22, 1949.

2. Comic book based on the National Biscuit Company (Nabisco) radio show (1948–1951). The Magazine Enterprises title featured many Weird Menace tales. Artwork for the entire 55-issue run was provided by Fred Meagher. The back-up strip **Red Hawk** featured art by **Bob Powell**. The writer(s) were uncredited but **Gardner Fox**, who wrote the newspaper strip, is credited by many sources.

"THE GHOST OF STRAIGHT ARROW" [WMW]
First publication: #5 (September 1950)
Straight Arrow scares outlaws into believing he has returned to life after they mistakenly think they have killed him.

"THE DEATH WARNING" [WMW]
First publication: #7 (November 1950)
Outlaws frighten Indians into abandoning their gold mine with an emaciated Osage disguised as an undead zombie-like monster.

"GHOST GANG" [WMW]
First publication: #11 (March 1951)
Lawmen are fooled by a gang of outlaws posing as ghosts from beyond the grave.

"THE VALLEY OF TIME" [WMW]
First publication: #11 (March 1951)
Straight Arrow and Packy discover the ancient lost city of Navalaya where human sacrifice still goes on in an Inca-style culture.

"THE DESERT DEMON" [WMW]
First publication: #19 (November 1951)
Outlaws construct a giant buffalo to terrify locals who believe it to be a supernatural creature.

"THE DEATHLESS ONE" [WW]
First publication: #25 (June 1952)
Lakota warrior Lone Elk longs for death but he is under a curse of immortality placed upon him by a medicine man. The zombie-like figure of Lone Elk finally sees hope when Straight Arrow finds a way to lift the curse.

"THE GHOST APACHES" [WMW]
First publication: #30 (April 1953)
When Straight Arrow attempts to capture Apache outlaws, they slip through his fingers like ghosts and disappear in front of his eyes. Straight Arrow is perplexed as to how he can apprehend Apaches who have learned to imitate desert mirages.

"THE MYSTERIOUS STRANGER" [SFW]
First publication: #30 (April 1953)
A mad scientist, a century ahead of his time, has an arsenal of lethal weapons including a gun that fires explosive bullets, an electric chair, a super bomb, germ warfare and tear gas.

"THE HAUNTED VILLAGE" [WMW]
First publication: #40 (December 1954)
Outlaws attempt to keep their hideout safe from the law by faking a "Headless Horseman" and ghosts.

"SECRET OF THE SPANISH SPECTERS" [WMW]
First publication: #40 (December 1954)
The gold lust of Spanish treasure drives a man to dress his two sons as ghostly Conquistadors.

"THE PAINTED MAN" [WMW]
First publication: #55 (March 1956)
Medicine man Many Dreams stirs unrest among the Kiowa with talk of magical visions of a Painted Man who will guide them. When Straight Arrow discovers the truth behind the Painted Man and his plans for war, he decides to provide his own Painted Man with a message of peace.

Strange Adventures [Comic book]

Science fiction anthology comic book from DC Comics.

"THE STAR OSCAR" [SFW]
First publication: #34 (July 1953); Story: Sid Gerson; Art: Frank Giacoia; Publisher: DC Comics.
An alien experiences the Hollywood film industry and turns himself into an exact copy of an actor in a cowboy film.

"THE MIRAGES FROM SPACE" [SFW]
First publication: #61 (October 1955); Story: Otto Binder; Art: Gil Kane, Bernard Sachs; Publisher: DC Comics.
Futuristic landscapes in the Mojave Desert turn out to be mirages from the planet Jupiter.
Gil Kane's cover artwork depicts an amazed cowboy seated on his horse looking toward the mirage of a space-age city. In the interior story, the cowboy has been replaced with a modern-day astronomer with suit and tie.

"THE MAZE OF MARS" [SFW]
First publication: #64 (January 1956); Story: Otto Binder; Art: Sid Greene, Joe Giella; Publisher: DC Comics.

An underground maze in the West connects with Mars.

The Strange Adventures of Rangergirl [Novel; SFW]

Author: Tim Pratt; First publication: New York: Bantam Books, 2005.

Marzipan "Marzi" McCarty writes a neo-western comic called *The Strange Adventures of Rangergirl*. She is also the night manager-barista of Genius Loci, a Santa Cruz coffeehouse where she hangs out with weird friends who worship strange gods. When the comic book characters come to life, an evil force that wants to destroy California is unleashed.

"The Strange Piper" [Pulp fiction; WW]

Author: **Lon Williams**; Character: **Lee Winters**; *Real Western Stories* (December 1956).

Lee Winters encounters the Greek god Pan while searching for a criminal in Gallitena Gulch.

Strange Suspense Stories [Comic book]

Horror anthology comic book.

"THE MAN WHO OUTDISTANCED DEATH" [WW]
First publication: #4 (December 1952); Art: George Evans; Publisher: Fawcett Publications.

Frustrated by being beaten by Indian Sam Whitecloud in every one of the fourteen cross-country marathons to date George Kerrik seeks to discover the truth being his almost supernatural athleticism. As Kerrik follows Whitecloud to his home he finds him chanting a tribal rite to his ancestors in full Indian ceremonial attire. Sam Whitecloud declarers himself as Seminole Chief Whitecloud Comatok as two glowing hands radiate on his back with an unearthly glow.

Further research in the University library confirms Chief Whitecloud Comatok is two-hundred-and-twenty years old. When Kerrick confronts Whitecloud with the facts Whitecloud declares, "Life is a race against death. But do not pursue these thoughts any further, youthful one!" Kerrick ignores his advice and later observes Whitecloud running away from a large, dark figure. Kerrick chases after Whitecloud but the figure gains on him. Death is literally chasing them

for their lives. Whitecloud sacrifices his life for Kerrick's as death touches Kerrick and leaves its deathly glow. Death will return to claim him in a race to the death.

Strange Tales [Comic book]

Anthology title, originally featuring tales of fantasy, horror and gigantic monsters before it transformed into a superhero title in October 1962.

"WHEN THE TOTEM WALKS" [WW]
First publication: #74 (April 1960) Art: Steve Ditko; Publisher: Marvel Comics.

When two escaped convicts seek refuge on an Indian reservation and proceed to threaten the Indians, they incur the wrath of the Totem who comes to life and chases them back to their prison.

Strange Westerns Starring the Black Rider [Comic book; WW]

First publication: October 2006; Story: Steve Englehart. Joe R. Lansdale; Art: Marshall Rogers, Rafa Garres.

In this revival of the 1950s Western character the **Black Rider**, mild-mannered Doc Masters has an alter-ego lurking on the streets of New York City. **Joe R. Lansdale** provides a Weird Western tale featuring a cursed weapon and Gunhawk stars in "Midnight Gun."

See: *The Mighty Marvel Western*

"Stranger at Gunnison's Camp" [Short story; WW]

Author: Ken Rand; First publication: *Oceans of the Mind*, 2006.

A Salt Lake City newspaper reporter is told of the Indian massacre of Captain Gunnison and his scout team in 1853 and the curse that followed. When a reporter realizes he's touched the cursed sextant, he can only wait and hope...

The Stranger's Gundown (1969) [Film; Italy; WW]

DVD release title U.S. for **Django il Bastardo**.

Strangeways: Murder Moon [Comic book; WW]

First publication: March 2008; Story: Matthew Maxwell; Art: Luis Guaragña; Publisher: Highway 62 Press.

Former army officer Seth Collins, traveling to

Silver Hand in response to a letter from his sister is attacked by a man-wolf creature.

Sugar Creek (2006) [Film; WW]

Premiere: November 7, 2006; Main Cast: Daniel Kruse as Adam Stanton, Rebecca Harrell as Christine, Dayton Knoll as Kane St. Clair, Robert Miano as Pete St. Clair; Story-Director: James Cotten; 95 min.; Dark Highway Films, MagniForge Entertainment, Pale Horse Productions; Color.

A barefooted Adam Stanton stands alone and confused in an Arkansas field in 1898. The mysterious Horseman will track him down and kill him and nobody will come to his aid, for they know the Shoeless Man has been visited by the Horseman and death awaits all who have lived beyond their time.

Sukiyaki Western Django (2007) [Film; Japan; SFW]

Premiere: August 31, 2007; Main Cast: Hideaki Ito as Gunman, Masanobu Ando as Yoichi, Koichi Sato as Taira no Kiyomori, Yusuke Iseya as Minamoto no Yoshitsune; Executive Producer: Toshiaki Nakazawa; Story: Takashi Miike, Masa Nakamura, Director: Takashi Miike; 121 min.; Dentsu Productions Ltd.; Color.

In a post-apocalyptic future, a gunslinger (Ito) faces the rival Heike Reds and Genji Whites clans feuding over gold in a remote mountain village.

The rival Red and White clans are compared with the historical "Wars of the Roses" with quotes from Shakespeare's *Henry VI* in this hybrid Japanese "spaghetti Western."

Jim Ridley of *The New York Village Voice* (August 27, 2008) commented: "Delivered entirely in phonetic English for unneeded additional derangement, the garbled, woozily recreated dialogue adds another layer of movie fetishism to whirling duster coats, blazing six-guns and Mexican stand-offs cribbed from Sergio Leone and Corbucci."

Sullivan, Vincent (1911–1999) [Artist; Editor; Publisher]

Vincent Sullivan will be remembered as the man who saw the potential in **Superman** and **Batman** and signed their creators to contracts at National Allied Publications later known as DC Comics). Sullivan was also a key figure in the early evolution of the Weird Western in comic books.

Born in Brooklyn, New York, on June 5, 1911,

Sullivan had ambitions of becoming a newspaper comic strip artist. His early work at National-DC Comics included the cover artwork for *Detective Comics* #1 in 1937 as well as writing, lettering and editing duties. Within a year Sullivan was editor of **Action Comics**. Two years later he quit National to join Charles McAdams and Frank Marky at the newly formed Columbia Comics.

Columbia Comics failed to live up to its early promise and in 1943 Sullivan decided to form a new publishing company named Magazine Enterprises.

The company published comic books in various genres including film-radio- and television-licensed titles, crime, adventure, jungle, humor and Westerns. With their Western strip The Calico Kid floundering, Sullivan decided to revamp the character by giving it a "supernatural" twist and a new name, **Ghost Rider**. A similar revamp occurred with *Tim Holt* when the amiable movie star suddenly became the *Red Mask*. The move from standard Western comic books to titles with added mystery and flair resulted in increased sales. The work of editor Ray Krank, artists **Dick Ayers**, Frank Frazetta, Fred Guardineer, Frank Bolle and **Bob Powell** and writers **Gardner Fox** and Carl Memling were an essential element of their success.

With the restrictive Comic Code and the rising popularity of television eroding comic book sales Magazine Enterprises folded in 1957 and Sullivan retired from the comic book industry.

Sunabozu [Manga; Anime; Japan; SFW]

1. First publication: *Comic Beam*, August 5, 1997; Story-Art: Usune Masatoshi; Publisher; Enterbrain.

2. Air date: October 4, 2004; Director: Inagaki Takayuki; 24 × 24 min.; Gonzo; Color.

In the nuclear-ravaged Great Kanto desert, Kanta Mizuno a.k.a. Desert Punk is a sex-obsessed mercenary, equipped with a Winchester Model 1897 rifle, who survives by hiring himself out to anyone willing to pay for his talents. But the desert is full of enemies including Rain Spider, a rival debt collector who collects not only money but souls. And the devious Junko Asagiri, "Vixen of the Desert," uses her huge breasts to great advantage with Mizuno.

Based on the manga by Usune Masatoshi.

Season One

(U.S. release titles): *The Demon and the Double D's* (1:01); *Rock, Paper, Scissors* (1:02); *Fire Dragon Kong* (1:03); *An Ace in the Sand* (1:04); *The Price of Water* (1:05); *Wandering Lust* (1:06); *Age Before Beauty* (1:07); *A Dog in Heat* (1:08); *All That Glitters* (1:09); *A Little Bit of Wisdom* (1:10); *Compromising Positions* (1:11); *A Change of Heart* (1:12); *Opposites Collide* (1:13); *Kosund: Fully Automatic* (1:14); *The Girl Next Door* (1:15); *A Load of…* (1:16); *Perv in Pursuit* (1:17); *Too Close for Comfort* (1:18); *Scratching the Surface* (1:19); *A Raw Deal* (1:20); *Successor of the Desert* (1:21); *Hidden Agendas* (1:22); *Voices in the Wind* (1:23); *The Demon Revealed* (1:24)

See: **Desert Punk**

Sundown Arizona [Comic book; WW]

First publication: July 2005; Creators: Jay Busbee, Ryan Bodenheim; Art: Jason Ossman; three-issue mini-series; Publisher: Arcana Studios.

New York Herald crime reporter Will Dalton and his brother Sheriff Clay Dalton search for the truth behind the brutal killing of preachers in Arizona territory in 1880.

Sundown: The Vampire in Retreat (1989) [Film; WW]

Premiere: May 18, 1989; Main Cast: David Carradine as Count Jozek Mardulak, Morgan Brittany as Sarah Harrison, Bruce Campbell as Robert Van Helsing, Maxwell Caulfield as Shane; Executive Producers: Dan Ireland, Jack Lorenz; Story: John Burgess, Anthony Hickox; Director: Anthony Hickox; 104 min.; Vestron Pictures; Color.

The town of Purgatory has a secret: two rival factions of vampires, one feasting on human blood, the other on synthetic bottled blood. But with a new family arriving in town the temptation for fresh blood is overwhelming. Bruce Campbell plays a descendant of the original vampire hunter Professor Abraham Van Helsing.

Sundowners: Ghost Town [Novel; WW]

Author: James Swallow; First publication: London: Scholastic, 2001.

The first in a series of adventures set in 1878 featuring gunslinger Gabriel Tyler, Native American shaman Jonathan Fivehawk, an evil force known as the Faceless and its servant, rail baron Robur Drache.

Sundowners: Iron Dragon [Novel; WW]

Author: James Swallow; First publication: London: Scholastic, 2001.

The search for Fivehawk's sister Eyes-Like-Amber leads the pair to Winterville where Drache is building a railroad that apparently leads to nowhere.

Sundowners: Showdown [Novel; WW]

Author: James Swallow; First publication: London: Scholastic, 2001.

The final showdown with Drache and the Faceless as warriors rise from the dead in an ancient battleground.

Sundowners: Underworld [Novel; WW]

Author: James Swallow; First publication: London: Scholastic, 2001.

Tyler and Fivehawk track Drache to the Burnt Hills mine and attempts to rescue family members held captive by Drache's minions.

"'Sunset' Wins" a.k.a. "Macdonald's Dream" a.k.a. "The Dream of Macdonald" [Pulp fiction; WW]

Author: George Owen Baxter a.k.a. **Max Brand**; First publication: *Western Story Magazine* (April 7, 1923).

Former Texas Ranger Gordon "Red" Macdonald has one thought in mind. To possess a horse named Sunset. But when his owner Rory Moore refuses to sell at any cost "Red" turns to crooked card sharp Jenkins to win Sunset at the card table. When Jenkins cleans out Moore and wins his beloved horse for Macdonald he gets cold feet and flees to Canada. But Moore catches up to Jenkins who tells Moore how Macdonald paid him to win Sunset. Now Moore is headed for a showdown with Macdonald.

Meanwhile Macdonald has been experiencing a vivid, recurring dream where he meets a young woman riding a bay mare in a landscape where a river tells him to turn back and the girl warns him not to approach, "that house behind the garden!"

"He had come into a ghostly land, with voices speaking from rivers and with roads on which familiar strangers journeyed."

Ignoring the girl's advice Macdonald enters the "great castle of a house" where he encounters all the men he has killed and is offered a glimpse of the future as he views Rory Moore dead in his coffin and the eerie sight of Moore's likeness merging to into the girl.

"They could not be more similar, save for what was drawn on a large and manly scale in Rory's dead face, was made small and exquisitely beautiful in the living face of the girl."

The dreams haunt Macdonald's waking hours and influence his future actions as he faces Rory Moore for one final shootout.

Frederick Faust, best known to readers as **Max Brand** wrote this short story under the pseudonym of George Owen Baxter. Faust's original title was altered to "**'Sunset' Wins**" by the editor of *Western Story Magazine*, but later restored to "Macdonald's Dream" by William F. Nolan for his collection *The Best Western Stories of Max Brand* (Dodd, Mead, 1981). Editor John Tuska in his Max Brand collection *The Black Rider and Other Stories* (G.K. Hall, 1996) claimed the original title was "The Dream of Macdonald."

Super-Chief [Comic book character; SFW]

1. First appearance: *All-Star Western* #117 (February-March 1961); Story: **Gardner Fox**; Art: Carmine Infantino; Publisher: DC Comics.

After Iroquois Indian Saganowahna, Flying Stag of the Wolf Clan, prays to the Great Spirit Manitou, he comes into contact with a radioactive meteorite which gives him super strength and the ability to leap great heights and distances for one hour at a time. Flying Stag became Saganowhana (or Super-Chief) in honor of Manitou and the magical meteor amulet he wears. The continued wearing of the amulet grants Super-Chief an extended life but it comes at the expense of greatly diminished mental powers over time.

Super-Chief's original strip only lasted three issues before *All-Star Western* ceased publication. He was later featured in 1870s storylines with fellow Weird Western characters including **Black Bison**, **Firehair** and shaman Wise Owl.

2. A Native American utilized Super-Chief's powers in "The Return of Saganowahna."

See: *Pulp Heroes*

3. First appearance: *52* #22 (October 2006); Story: **Geoff Johns**, Grant Morrison, Greg Rucka, Mark Waid; Art: Eddy Barrows; Publisher: DC Comics.

Ex-convict Jon Standing Bear gains possession of the meteor amulet after suffocating his grandfather at his request. But after Jon Standing is banished to another dimension, Flying Stag regains control of the amulet.

Super Spook [Comic book]

Adventures of a superhero ghost in the style of Casper the Friendly Ghost.

"Go West!" [WW]

First published: *Super Spook* #4, June 1958; Publisher: Ajax-Farrell Publications.

Super Spook meets Native American Indians, cowboys and the Haunted Horse in this humorous tale.

Superboy [Comic book]

The adventures of Superman as a youngster in Smallville.

"Super Boy Meets Super-Brave" [WW]

First publication: #41 (June 1955); Art: Curt Swan, George Klein; Publisher: DC Comics.

An American Indian boy's magical powers drain Superboy's strength.

See: *The New Adventures of Superboy*

Supergirl: Legends of the Dead Earth [Comic book]

"Shootout at Ice Flats" [SW]

First publication: *Supergirl Annual* #1 (April 1996); Story: Joe Lansdale, Neal Barrett Jr.; Art: Robert Teranishi, Stan Wooch; Publisher: DC Comics.

On Bonechill IV, 22,000 light-years west of nowhere herfs and humans co-exist. But one disgruntled herf wants a showdown with Ice Flats Sheriff Eileen P. Garrett. In preparation for the showdown Eileen is given a magical S pendant to wear to give that grants "strength to those who have the courage to believe."

Superman & Batman: Generations III [Comic book]

An Elseworlds series of Imaginary Tales.

"The 26th Century: Part Two" [SFW]

First publication: #8 (October 2003); Story-Art: John Byrne; Publisher: DC Comics.

Superman is thrown back in time to the Old West where he discovers a young Jonathan Kent is out for revenge on bounty hunter **Jonah Hex**. But events lead to Martha Clark being shot and losing any chance of having children in the future.

Superman Batman [Comic book]

"Absolute Power Chapter 3: When Time Goes Asunder..." [SFW]

First publication: #16 (February 2005); Story: Jeph

Loeb; Art: Carlos Pacheo, Jesus Merino; Publisher: DC Comics.

In an alternate modern-day Gotham City, the law enforcement team of Gotham Central Precinct 13 consists of **El Diablo**, **Bat Lash**, **Tomahawk** and **Cinnamon** who wears the costume of Madame .44.

Superman's Pal, Jimmy Olsen [Comic book]

The adventures of the young red-headed reporter for the *Daily Planet*.

"The Fastest Gun in the West" [SFW]

First publication: #3 (January-February 1955); Story: Otto Binder; Art: Curt Swan, Ray Burnley; Publisher: DC Comics.

Jimmy Olsen's latest assignment lands him in serious trouble with the local gunslinger in the modern-day Western town of Tumbleweed until Superman comes to the rescue.

This story resembles the *Adventures of Superman* episode "Bully of Dry Gulch" (3:10) broadcast September 24, 1955.

"The Feats of Chief Super-Duper" [SFW]

First publication: #14 (August 1956); Story: Otto Binder; Art: Curt Swan, Ray Burnley; Publisher: DC Comics.

Jimmy Olsen and Superman journey through the time barrier to the Old West, where Jimmy's control over nature earns him the respect of the Native Indians who make him their chief.

"The Gunsmoke Kid" [SFW]

First publication: #45 (June 1960); Art: Curt Swan, John Forte; Publisher: DC Comics.

Jimmy Olsen travels in time to the Old West where he is mistaken for the outlaw the Gunsmoke Kid and becomes part of the Jesse James gang.

Supernatural (2005) [TV series]

Main Cast: Jared Padalecki as Sam Winchester, Jensen Ackles as Dean Winchester.

Following the tragic and suspicious death of their mother in a fire, brothers Sam and Dean Winchester track supernatural forces, demons and their missing father as they travel across America in Dean's black 1967 Chevrolet Impala. When they eventually find their father he tells Sam and Dean that their mother was killed by a demon and the only way to kill him is with a special gun created by Samuel Colt.

"Frontierland" (6:18) [SFW]

Air date: April 22, 2011; Guest Cast: Misha Collins as Castiel, Jim Beaver as Bobby Singer, Sam Hennings as Samuel Colt, Matthew John Armstrong as Elias Finch, Scott Hylands as Judge Mortimer, Dean Wray as Sheriff, Michael Woolvett as Deputy; Creator: Eric Kripke; Story: Andrew Dabb, Daniel Loflin, Jackson Stewart; Director: Guy Bee; 60 min.; Warner Bros. Television, Wonderland Sound and Vision; Color.

Castiel sends Sam and Dean Winchester back in time to Sunrise, Wyoming, in March 1861 to meet Samuel Colt after they stumble across his journal in the Campbell library. They arrive in time to witness the hanging of Elias Finch for the alleged murder of his wife. On the gallows Finch makes a promise to those responsible for his death.

Finch returns on his promise when Judge Mortimer and the Sheriff are reduced to ashes at his deadly touch. Dean Winchester warns the deputy that he is the next on Finch's list and wants to use him as bait to destroy Finch who is the Phoenix. The ashes of the Phoenix can destroy Eve, the Mother of All supernatural beings. Meanwhile Sam tracks Colt to twenty miles out of town and acquires his demon killing gun. Dean is now prepared for a final showdown with Finch.

"Suspended Animation" [Pulp fiction; WW]

Author: *Lon Williams*; Character: *Lee Winters*; *Real Western Stories* (October 1956).

This was the strangest corpse anyone in Forlorn Gap had ever seen, for in the unfortunate's pockets was a note reading: "....*Please do not bury me. I am not dead.*"

The Swamp of the Lost Monster (1957) [Film; Mexico; WW]

U.S. release title for *El Pantano de Las Ánimas*.

Switching Well [Novel; SFW]

Author: Peni R. Griffin; First publication: New York: Margaret K. McElderry Books; Toronto: Maxwell Macmillan Canada; New York: Maxwell Macmillan International, 1993.

Two twelve-year-old girls, one living in 1891 and the other in 1991, exchange time and place through a magic well.

Tales from the Texas West [Book Anthology; WW]

Author; Michael Moorcock; First publication:1997; Publisher: Mojo Press.

A collection of short stories, essays and reviews from the acclaimed British writer includes the supernatural Western "The Ghost Warriors."

Tales from the Trails: Mexico [RPG book; WW]

Author: James Moore; First publication:1999; Setting: **Werewolf: The Wild West**; Publisher: White Wolf Publishing.

19th-century Mexico sourcebook for the World of Darkness. The final book for the short-lived *Werewolf: The Wild West* game.

Tales o' Terror: 1877 [RPG book; WW]

Authors: Steve Long, Christopher McGlothlin, John Hopler, Shane Lacy Hensley; First publication: 1998; Game: **Deadlands: The Weird West**; Publisher; Pinnacle Entertainment Group.

Updates the Player's Guide and **Marshal's Handbook**.

Tales of the Unexpected [Comic book]

Science fiction, mystery and horror anthology comic book from DC Comics.

"MENACE OF THE INDIAN ALIENS" [SW]

First publication: *Tales of the Unexpected #44* (December 1959); Art: Jim Mooney; Publisher: DC Comics.

Space Western adventure for Space Ranger alias Rick Starr where he encounters green-skinned, turtle-faced Indians living on a reservation on one of Saturn's moons. They tell Starr that American Indians befriended their ancestors after their spaceship crashlanded on Earth. Intrigued by the American Indians, the aliens adopted their culture when they returned to their home planet.

Teenage Monster (1958) [Film; SFW]

Premiere: January 8, 1958; Main Cast: Gil Perkins as Charles Cannon, Stephen Parker as Charles Cannon as a boy, Anne Gwynne as Ruth Cannon, Stuart

Teenage Monster (1958), **starring Gilbert Perkins as Charles Cannon alias the hairy killer and Anne Gwynne as Ruth Cannon (Marquette Productions Ltd.).**

Wade as Sheriff Bob Lehman, Gloria Castillo as Kathy North, Charles Courtney as Marv Howell; Story: Ray Buffum; Producer-Director: Jacques R. Marquette; 65 min.; Marquette Productions Ltd.; b/w.

A young boy (Parker) grows into an extremely hairy psychopathic killer (Perkins) after being exposed to the rays from a fallen meteorite in the Old West of the 1880s.

This mix of science fiction, horror and Western genres was influenced by the success of American-International's *I Was a Teenage Werewolf* (1957) starring Michael Landon.

See: *Meteor Monster*

Terovolas [Novel: WW]

Author: Edward M. Erdelac; First publication: San Francisco: Journal Stone, 2012.

Suffering the effects of Post Traumatic Stress Disorder, Professor Abraham Van Helsing is diagnosed with melancholic lycanthropea. Following his release from Jack Seward's Purfleet Asylum Van Helsing travels to Surefoot, Texas, to return the ashes and personal effects of Quincey Morris, a wealthy young Texan killed during the final battle with Dracula. During his train journey Van Helsing meets Madame Callisto Terovolas, a Greek lady of Arcadian descent who is traveling to Texas to wed a Danish cattleman. Although delighted with her company Van Helsing can't shake the feeling Madame Terovolas reminds him of Dracula's wife.

Initially the educated and refined Van Helsing feels like a fish out-of-water in Texas and is greeted with cold indifference by Quincy's brother, Coleman Morris. When Sheriff Turlough and ranch foreman Early Searls are found butchered and mutilated Van Helsing's thoughts turn to dark, melancholy imaginings that he fears might be the result of a returning dementia.

Set in 1891 after the events described in Bram Stoker's *Dracula*, each character is framed within individual entries from journals and papers.

Terra-Man [Comic book character; SFW]

1. First appearance: *Superman* #249 (March 1972); Creators: Cary Bates, Julius Schwartz; Publisher: DC Comics.

Abducted by an alien who accidentally killed his father in the American Old West town of Cripple Creek, Toby Manning was raised on an alien planet by the reptilian Collector. After Man-

ning killed the alien in retaliation for his father's death, he returned to Earth but ultimately roamed the galaxies as an interstellar outlaw. Cosmic cowboy Terra-Man owned an array of futuristic weapons based on models of the Old West including atomic energy and sonic wave guns. His chewing tobacco created illusions and the smoke from his cigars had the effect of suffocating his victims. He rode Nova the white winged space-steed.

2. First appearance: *Superman* #46 (August 1990); Creators: Jerry Ordway, Dan Jurgens, Dennis Janke; Publisher: DC Comics.

Tobias Manning alias Terra-Man is a modern-day environmentalist who has the power to create teleportation vortexes and power blasts with the help of his technologically enhanced body armor. Together with his team of Terra-Men—robots dressed as Western outlaws—Manning causes environmental chaos and destruction while professing his innocence. Terra-Man died at the hands of Black Adam.

3. A Terra-Man unrelated to the previous incarnations but retaining his cowboy persona made his entrance as a cybernetic bounty hunter from the 41st century on the animated TV series *Legion of Super Heroes* in 2007. Able to regenerate his metallic skeleton, he is part-living tissue, part-robot.

See: *Legion of Super Heroes*; *Superboy*

Terra the Gunslinger [TRPG game; Japan; SPW]

Release date: February 2001 (Japan); Design: Jun'ichi Inoue, FarEast Amusement Research [FEAR]; Publisher: Enterbrain, Gamefield.

For this game, set on the continent of Terra, players are passengers on the transcontinental railroad traveling to the Western frontier. Players choose between Gunslinger, Saloon Girl, U.S. Marshal and Preacher (among others) as they confront monsters known as the Dark. The game includes real-life Western characters Jesse James and Belle Starr.

Terra the Gunslinger: Gun Frontier [TRPG game; Japan; SPW]

Release date: August 2002 (Japan); Design: Jun'ichi Inoue, FarEast Amusement Research [FEAR]; Publisher: Enterbrain, Gamefield.

Sequel to *Terra the Gunslinger* with an increased choice of characters as they continue to fight the demon of the darkness. Player characters include Gunslinger, Rocket Ranger, Shaman, Dark Hunter, Samurai, Private Eye, U.S. Marshal, Preacher, Boys & Girls, Bounty Hunter, Summoner, Saloon Girl, Gambler, Lt. Engineer, Steam Mage, Automata, Writer, Immortal, Avenger, Boxer, Cross Fire and Paladin.

Territory [Novel; SFW]

Author: Emma Bull; First publication: New York: Tor Books, 2007.

Wyatt Earp uses magic and sorcery to achieve his goals in this alternate history of the figures and events at Tombstone's O.K. Corral.

"Emma Bull is *really* good." – Neil Gaiman

E M M A   B U L L

Author of WAR FOR THE OAKS

Cover of *Territory* by Emma Bull (2007).

Tex and the Lord of the Deep (1985) [Film; Italy; WW]

U.S. release title for *Tex e il Signore Degli Abissi*.

Tex Arcana [Comic book strip; WW]

First appearance: *Heavy Metal*, March, 1981; Story-Art: John Findley; b/w; Publisher: Heavy Metal.

Adult horror Western comic strip with a touch of humor set in Hangman's Corners, involving the Mysterious Woman in White, vampires, the undead, witches, demons and werecoyotes. The Old Claim Jumper introduces each story in this throwback to E.C. horror comic books of the 1950s and the Warren titles of the 1960s.

Tex e il Signore Degli Abissi (1985) [Film; Italy; WW]

Premiere: 1985; Main Cast: Giuliano Gemma as **Tex Willer**, William Berger as Kit Carson, Carlo Mucari as Tiger Jack, Isabel Russinova as Tulac, Riccardo Petrazzi as Lord of the Deep; Executive Producer: Enzo Porcelli; Story: Giovanni L. Bonelli; Director: Duccio Tessari; 90 min.; Radiotelevisione Italiana (RAI), SACIS; Color.

With the help of a demon god, American Indian tribes of the Sierra hope to join together and "build the new reign of the children of the sun," reclaiming their tribal lands from the white man.

Based on the characters from the Italian comic strip *Tex* by **Giovanni Luigi Bonelli**.

Tex Willer [Comic book character; Italy; WW]

First appearance: *Tex* #1, September 30, 1948; Creators: **Giovanni Luigi Bonelli**, Aurelio Galeppini [Galep]; Publishers: L'Audace, Sergio Bonelli Editore.

"The Great White Chief of the Navajos," Texas Ranger Tex Willer fights outlaws and corruption in the Old West of the 1880s. His short marriage to Lilith, the daughter of the late Navajo Indian chief Red Arrow, enables him to see both sides of any racial conflict. A staunch, upright hero in the mold of Gary Cooper, he encounters the dark side of the supernatural through his greatest enemy Mefisto and son Yama.

Former outlaw Tex Willer is the longest-lived character in Italian comic book history with his stories still being published in 2009. Creator Giovanni Luigi Bonelli originally planned to name him Tex Killer but agreed to a compromise and named him Willer instead. Although the strip started out as a traditional Western, it has incorporated many weird aspects through the years including witch doctor El Morisco, immortal Egyptian Rakos, alien invaders, ghosts, zombies, werewolves and the ancient philosopher's stone.

Texas Strangers [Comic book; SFW]

First publication: March 2007; Story: Antony Johnston, Dan Evans; Art: Mario Book; Three-issue series; Publisher: Image Comics.

In a weird Old West where magic and sorcery is the norm, the Free Nation of Texas is run by wizards, elves, goblins and monsters. Teenage twins Wyatt and Madara Houston encounter trouble and adventure as they attempt to dispose of their father's strange knife.

Texas Twister [Comic book character; SFW]

First appearance: *Fantastic Four* #1977 (December 1976); Creators: Roy Thomas, Geoge Perez: Publisher: Marvel Comics.

When Texas-born Drew Daniels was caught up in a tornado that hit a nuclear reactor, he discovered he had the ability to generate tornadoes at will. He teamed up with **Shooting Star** as a rodeo double act for Cody's Rodeo, joining **The Rangers** initially to help Rick Jones and *The Avengers* against the Incredible Hulk.

They Call Him Holy Ghost (1971) [Film; Italy-Spain; WW]

U.S. release title for *Uomo avvisato mezzo ammazzato ... parola di Spirito Santo*.

13 Chambers [Comic book; SFW]

First publication: September 2008; Creator: Christopher "mink" Morrison; Publisher: 12-Guage Comics.

Following Abraham Lincoln's death, President Jackson disbands a secret group of federal lawmen known as the 13 Marshals. The 13th Marshal is ordered to retrieve all 13 Territory Peace Keeper pistols and return them to Washington, D.C. for retirement. But a mining baron named York stands in his way.

Alternative history Western.

1313: Billy the Kid (2012) [Film; WW]

Premiere: June 1, 2012; Main Cast: Brandon Thornton as Billy the Kid, Jason Zahodnik as Whitecastle, Chelsea Rae Bernier as Lottie, Lance Leonhardt as Buck, Ryan Curry as Lloyd, Ryan McIntire as Doc Holliday, Kodi Baker as Uriel, Michael Hudson as Rabanne; Executive producer: Martin Hellman; Story: Moses Rutegar; Director: David DeCoteau; 72 min.; Phase 4 Films, Rapid Heart Pictures; Color.

The desert town of Hell's Heart in 1881. Billy the Kid assumes he's found a safe place to recover from his wounds but soon realizes he is in the sights of the supernatural Manitou who want the Kid for a trophy.

The Thirteenth Child (*Frontier Magic* book #1) [Novel; WW]

Author: Patricia C. Wrede; First publication: New York: Scholastic Press, 2009.

Young Eff Rothmer is a seventh daughter living in the shadow of her twin brother, Lan, a powerful double seventh son. As the "thirteenth child" she is frowned upon as having bad blood by her relatives and Uncle Earn claims she is a witch who has cursed his house. Eff is glad to see the back of Helvan Shores when her father accepts a position teaching magic at the Northern Plains Riverbank College in North Plains Territory. The move to Mill City at the edge of the Great Prairie on the Western frontier comes with new dangers in the form of magical creatures across the Great Barrier that threaten the homesteaders' settlements. The young Eff and her brother Lan attend classes in Avrupan, Aphrikan and Hijero-Cathayan magic and learn of the Great Barrier Spell that keeps the magical beasts at bay.

Thor [Comic book]

Adventures of Thor the mighty thunder god, son of Odin, lord of Asgard.

"Easy Money" [WW]

First publication: #370 (August 1986); Story: James Owsley; Art: John Buscema, P. Craig Russell; Publisher: Marvel Comics.

Card cheat Sundance is told by an old codger that if he will give a man on a white horse a claim check, he will receive one hundred dollars. Sundance knows the claim check must be worth more and decides to try his luck at poker instead when he is handed an enchanted deck of playing cards by god of evil Loki posing as an outlaw gang leader. Sundance is soon caught up in a battle for eternal youth involving Thor, Loki, a group of trolls and the golden apples of the goddess Idunn.

This story is a rare example of a Thor adventure taking place in the Old West.

See: *Black Panther*

Those Who Remain There Still [Novel; WW]

Author: Cherie Priest; First publication: Burton, MI: Subterranean Press, 2008.

In death Heaster Wharton brings the feuding Coy and Mander clans together to face a challenge like no other. They must recover his last will and testament from deep inside a cave, known as the Witch's Pit in the hills of Kentucky. Unknown to the clans Daniel Boone haunts the cave that harbors a monstrous winged beast with a deadly sharp beak. A century earlier, Boone confronted the beast whilst clearing a path through the Cumberland Gap and trapped it in the cave. But the beast still lives and the combined force of six Coys and Manders must put their feuding aside if they want to survive to retrieve Wharton's will.

Three (*Legends of the Duskwalker* book 1) [Novel; SFW]

Author: Jay Posey; First publication: Nottingham, UK: Angry Robot, 2013.

In a post-apocalyptic wasteland the lone gunman and bounty hunter known as Three helps a mother and her son flee mercenaries as the screaming, blue eyed, cybernetic, Weir advance upon the remaining human outposts of civilization.

Followed by *Morningside Fall*.

The Three Burials of Melquiades Estrada (2005) [Film; WW]

Premiere: May 20, 2005; Main Cast: Tommy Lee Jones as Pete Perkins, Julio Cedillo as Melquiades Estrada, Barry Pepper as Mike Norton, Dwight Yoakam as Belmont, January Jones as Lou Ann Norton; Story: Guillermo Arriaga; Producer-Director: Tommy Lee Jones; 121 min.; Europacorp, Javelina Film Company, Sony Pictures; Color.

When Pete Perkin's friend and illegal alien

ranch hand is found murdered he captures the killer, brutal border guard Mike Norton. After he exhumes Estrada's corpse from the wrong burial spot Perkins imagines his friend has revived as Perkins and Norton accompany the body across the border to grant him a proper burial. Estrada's killer has to face his hateful prejudices against Mexicans as he crosses into Mexico and interacts with the community. This modern day Western tackles the subjects of social isolation and alienation and deconstructs the mythology of the lone Western hero.

"The Three Fates" [Pulp fiction; WMW]

Author: **Lon Williams**; Character: **Lee Winters**; *Real Western Stories* (February 1958).

> Then he saw an object which caused his scalp to creep and his hat to become loose on his head. On a scraped-out shelf of earth bare bones had been assembled to form a human skeleton. Winters and his horse were of one mind then, but before thought could be translated into homeward action, an apparition appeared, three ghosts marching in step over this ancient mound's curved summit.

The Three Supermen of the West (1973) [Film; Italy-Spain; WW]

U.S. release title for *...e così divennero i 3 supermen del West*.

The Thrilling Adventure Hour [Graphic novel anthology; SW]

First published: August, 2013; Writers: Ben Acker, Bill Blacker; Art: Randy Bishop, Lar deSouza, Joanna Estep, Billy Fowler, Tom Fowler, Evan Larson, Chris Moreno, Natalie Nourigat, Joel Priddy, Evan "Doc" Shaner, Jeff Stokely; Publisher: Archaia Entertainment.

Comic strips based on the characters featured in the live audio theatre production and pod cast, including *Sparks Nevada*, *Marshal on Mars*, *The Red Plains Rider* and *Cactoid Jim, King of the Martian Frontier*.

The Thrilling Adventure Hour [Live audio theatre; Podcast; SW]

Premiere: March 2010; Venue: Largo at the Coronet; Cast: The WorkJuice Players: Paget Brewster, Craig Cackowski, Mark Gagliardi, Marc Evan Jackson, Hal Lubin, Annie Savage, Paul F. Tompkins, Jenny Wade, James Urbaniak, Autumn Reeser, Busy Philipps, John Ennis, Josh Malina, John DiMaggio, Samm Levine; Music: Acker & Blacker, Andy Paley

Orchestra; Creators-Scripts: Ben Acker, Bill Blacker; Director: Aaron Ginsburg.

The stage show and podcast features the continuing Space Western adventures of *Sparks Nevada: Marshal on Mars* and *Cactoid Jim, King of the Martian Frontier*. Recurring guests including Nathan Fillion (*Firefly*) as *Cactoid Jim*. Other notable guest stars have included Karen Gillan (*Doctor Who*), Dick Cavett, Emily Blunt, Amy Acker, Clark Gregg, Jeri Ryan, Weird Al Yankovic, Neil Patrick Harris and Joe Mantegna.

The Thrilling Adventure and Supernatural Suspense Hour [Live audio theatre; SW]

Premiere: March 2005; Venue: M Bar, Hollywood; Original cast: The WorkJuice Players: Dave (Gruber) Allen, Paget Brewster, Craig Cackowski, Mark Gagliardi, Marc Evan Jackson, Hal Lubin, Annie Savage, Paul F. Tompkins; Music: Acker & Blacker, Eban Schletter, Andy Paley Orchestra; Creators-Scripts: Ben Acker, Bill Blacker.

The stage show that takes the form of a vintage radio drama was initially inspired by Ben Acker and Bill Blacker's reading of their film script for the Space Western *Sparks Nevada: Marshal on Mars*. The anthology format incorporated different genres including super-heroes, science fiction, time travel, paranormal crime and the Space Western adventures of *Sparks Nevada*.

The Thrilling Adventure and Supernatural Suspense Hour ran for five years, concluding its performances at M Bar in January 2010. With its title shortened to *Thrilling Adventure Hour* performances resumed in March 2010 at Largo, a nightclub located in the former Coronet Theatre in Los Angeles.

Through Darkest America (*Isaac Asimov Presents* series) [Novel; SFW]

Author: Neal Barrett Jr.; First publication: New York: Chicago, Ill: Congdon & Weed in association with Davis Publications, 1986.

In a future America devastated by war Howie Ryder flees his family's Tennessee farm after his father is killed and his sister kidnapped. He meets up with outlaw gun runner Pardo, supplier of arms to both Loyalist and Rebel armies in the Civil War. Genetically altered humans known as "stock" and lacking intelligence or speech have replaced animal livestock and are the main food source. Ryder turns to "cattle" rustling as he struggles to survive in the harsh post-apocalyptic frontier.

This science fiction Western incorporates familiar Western themes in a post-apocalyptic setting. It was followed by a sequel *Dawn's Uncertain Light*.

"The Thunder-Rider" [Pulp fiction; WW]

Author: **Robert E. Howard**; First publication: *Marchers of Valhalla*: West Kingston, R.I.: Donald M. Grant, 1972.

Texan James Garfield recalls his past life as 16th century Comanche Iron Heart while undergoing a Native American rite.

Howard's Weird Western story was later "freely adapted" by Marvel Comics in the sword and sorcery setting of *Conan the Barbarian* # 65 in "Fiends of the Feathered Serpent" (August 1976).

Thunderbird [Comic book character; SFW]

First appearance: *Giant Size X-Men* #1 (May 1975); Creators: Len Wein, Dave Cockrum; Publisher: Marvel Comics.

Apache John Proudstar first displayed his mutant abilities of heightened senses, speed, stamina and strength as a teenager. His time as an X-Men member was tragically ended when he died in a plane explosion during his second mission. His brother James Proudstar (**Warpath**) exhibits similar enhanced powers.

Tiger Lily [Stage and book character; WW]

First appearance: *Peter Pan, or The Boy Who Wouldn't Grow Up*; Story: J . M. Barrie; First performance; December 27, 1904, Duke of York's Theatre, London.

Native Indian princess Tiger Lily is a supporting character in J. M. Barrie's three-act story of a boy refusing to become an adult. It is laced with Edwardian values and racist overtones in Barrie's characterization of the Native Indian Piccaninny tribe. Barrie based the tribe on Native American models. Some commentators have observed that Barrie represents the dominant white Anglo-Saxon culture that views native cultures as ignorant and violent and in need of educating and taming—the British Empire in Neverland.

After Peter Pan rescues Tiger Lily from the pirates, the Indians show their appreciation. The pigdgin-English of Tiger Lily sits uneasy with modern readers.

"Me Tiger Lily," that lovely creature would reply. "Peter Pan save me, me his velly nice friend. Me no let pirates hurt him."

She was far too pretty to cringe in this way, but Peter thought it his due, and he would answer condescendingly, "It is good. Peter Pan has spoken."

Other commentators view Tiger Lily as an example of an empowered female who is a leader of her tribe. Her beauty attracts the males of her tribe, whom she repels with her hatchet. The true object of her desire is Peter Pan. She is therefore a model of a modern female who controls her environment and refuses to be controlled by it.

In 1911, Barrie expanded the play into the novel, *Peter and Wendy*. Barrie's play and novel has been adapted on numerous occasions for stage and screen.

Tim Holt [Comic book; WW]

First issue:1948; Art: Frank Bolle, **Dick Ayers**; Publisher: Magazine Enterprises.

Based on the RKO "Cowboy Star of the Movies" Tim Holt, this title (which began as *Tim Holt Western Adventures*) evolved into one of the first Weird Western comic books with the introduction of **Ghost Rider** in issue #11. Holt's alterego *Red Mask* a.k.a. Redmask, debuting in issue #20, also found himself in occasional Weird Western storylines and with a new partner, **Black Phantom**. The final issues featured "3-D Drawings with No Special Glasses Needed."

Time Enough for Love, The Lives of Lazarus Long [Novel; SW]

Author: **Robert A. Heinlein**; First publication: Putnam, New York, 1973.

Lazarus Long reflects on his 2,256-year life as he longs for death in the year 4272. The novel consists of three novella-length stories including the Space Western-themed "The Tale of the Adopted Daughter" which recalls Long's days as a pioneer.

Time Rider: The Adventure of Lyle Swann (1982) [Film; SFW]

Premiere: December 11, 1982; Main Cast: Fred Ward as Lyle Swann, Belinda Bauer as Claire Cygne, Peter Coyote as Porter Reese, Richard Masur as Claude Dorsett, L.Q. Jones as Ben Potter; Producers: Lester Berman, Harry Gittes, Michael Nesmith; Story: William Dear, Michael Nesmith; Director: William Dear; 94 min.; Zoomo Productions; Color.

A champion off-road racer is transported back to 1877 when he accidentally crosses the radius of a time machine in the Mexican desert.

The Time Tunnel (1966) [TV Series]

Main Cast: James Darren as Dr. Tony Newman, Robert Colbert as Dr. Doug Phillips, Lee Meriwether as Dr. Ann MacGregor, Whit Bissell as Lt. Gen. Heywood Kirk, John Zaremba as Dr. Raymond Swain; Executive Producer: Irwin Allen; 60 min.; Kent Productions Inc.; Color.

Dr. Tony Newman and renowned physicist Dr. Doug Phillips become trapped in time, unable to return to the present, when the top secret government project the Time Tunnel malfunctions.

This simple plot device allowed for numerous variations on the theme of attempting to change historic events in the past or the future. The reliance on 20th Century–Fox stock footage and one-dimensional characterization doomed the series to first season cancellation.

"Massacre" (1:08) [SFW]

Air date: October 28, 1966; Guest Cast: Joe Maross as Gen. George Armstrong Custer, Christopher Dark as Crazy Horse, Lawrence Montaigne as Yellow Elk; Story: Carey Wilber; Director: Murray Golden.

Tony and Doug are unable to prevent the 1876 massacre of General George Armstrong Custer and his troopers at Little Big Horn.

"Visitors from Beyond the Stars" (1:18) [SFW]

Air date: January 13, 1967; Guest Cast: John Hoyt as Alien Leader, Byron Foulger as Williams, Jan Merlin as Centauri, Fred Beir as Taureg, Tris Coffin as Crawford, Ross Elliott as Sheriff; Story: Bob & Wanda Duncan; Director: Sobey Martin.

Silver-skinned aliens land in Mullins, Arizona, in 1885 with the intention of pillaging the Earth for its food supply. Doug becomes the slave of the aliens as they proceed to threaten the townsfolk with death if they don't hand over their food. Tony and the sheriff attempt to devise a plan to destroy the source of the aliens' power.

"Billy the Kid" (1:22) [SFW]

Air date: February 10, 1967; Guest Cast: Robert Walker Jr. as Billy the Kid, Allen Case as Pat Garrett, Pitt Herbert as Tom McKinney, Harry Lauter as Wilson, John Crawford as John Poe; Story: William Welch; Director: Nathan Juran.

Billy the Kid swears revenge on Doug for attempting to kill him in Lincoln County, New Mexico, during a jail escape.

Timespirits [Comic book; SFW]

First publication: October 1984; Story: Steve Perry; Art: Tom Yeates; Publisher: Epic-Marvel Comics Group.

Native American "Time Spirit" Cusick of the Tuscarora travels in time to trade items for souls. After collecting the souls in a turtle shell Cusick eventually releases them into the after-life. A mixture of fantasy, science fiction and religion, the comic book has gained latter-day recognition for a blue-skinned naked female in issue #7 who bears a striking resemblance to James Cameron's beautiful native girl Neytiri in *Avatar* (2009).

Timestalkers (1987) [Telefilm; SFW]

Premiere: March 10, 1987; Main Cast: William Devane as Scott McKenzie, Lauren Hutton as Georgia Crawford, Klaus Kinski as Dr. Joseph Cole, Forrest Tucker as Texas John Cody, John Ratzenberger as General Joe Brodsky; Executive Producers: Charles W. Fries, Milton T. Raynor; Screenplay: Brian Clemens; Story: Ray Brown, Brian Clemens; Director: Michael Schultz; 100 min.; Fries Entertainment; Color.

Dr. Joseph Cole spreads a path of destruction as he travels through time from the 26th century to 1980s America to the Old West of 1886. Scott McKenzie and Georgia Crawford chase Cole across time to stop him from altering history.

Tin Star [Video game; SFW]

Release date: 1994; Developer: Software Creations; Publisher: Nintendo; Platform: SNES.

Robot sheriff Tin Star and his sidekick Mo Crash try to maintain law and order in East Driftwood in the Ol' West. But Black Bart and his Bad Oil Gang have other ideas.

Tin Star Void (1988) [Film; SFW]

Alternative video release title for *Death Collector*.

Tin Swift: The Age of Steam (Book #2) [Novel; SPW]

Author: Devon Monk; First publication: New York: Roc, 2011.

Bounty hunter Cedar Hunter has located his long lost brother Will but finds they both share the Pawnee curse of the werewolf. Hunter is now searching for the weapon known as the Holder to keep the assorted refugees he has gathered alive. Witch Mae Lindon avenging her husband's murder and the three Madder Brothers who know the secret mechanisms of the Strange.

Followed by Book # 3 in the *Age of Steam* series, *Cold Copper: The Age of Steam*.

Tom and Jerry [Animated theatrical short]

Created by director John Foster and developed by artists George Stallings and George Rufel in 1931, Tom and Jerry were Mutt and Jeff types, one tall and lanky, the other short and round. Their animated adventures were often surreal and bizarre in content, including this Weird Western.

"Redskin Blues" (1932) [WW]

Premiere: July 23, 1932; Producer: Amadee J. Van Beuren; Directors: John Foster, George Stallings; 7 min; Van Beuren Studios, RKO Radio Pictures; b/w.

Tom and Jerry flee from hostile American Indians after their stagecoach is attacked. The pursuing Indians use their feathered headdresses to fly in formation as they attempt to capture Tom and Jerry on a cliff. Overweight Indians transform into sexy dancing girls and the captured Tom and Jerry are rescued by the U.S. cavalry, navy, air force and armored tanks.

Tom Arvis' Wayout West [Comic book; SFW]

First publication: 1995; Story-Art: Tom Arvis; Sureshot Comics.

In 1888, the dying gold town of Saddlestone, Nevada, is invaded by reptilian aliens.

Tom Edison, Jr. [Dime novel character]

Created by Philip Reade, a pseudonym for all house writers at dime novel publisher Street and Smith, Tom Edison Jr., the son of inventor Thomas Edison, is pursued by the Blue Mask alias Edison Jr.'s cousin Louis Gubrious. Attempting to recreate the success of **Frank Reade Jr.**, Street and Smith had limited fortune with the character; Edison Jr.'s adventures only lasted for two years. Edison Jr.'s dime novel adventures took him into Weird Western situations on occasion.

Tom Edison, Jr.'s Electric Mule; or, the Snorting Wonder of the Plains [Dime novel; SPW]

Author: "Philip Reade" (1892)

A parody of the popular **Frank Reade** series.

Tom Edison, Jr.'s Prairie-Skimmer Team; A Sequel to Tom Edison, Jr.'s Sky-Scraping Trip [Dime novel; SPW]

Nugget Library #110 (1891); Part two of a four-part novel.

Tom Edison, Jr.'s Sky-Scraping Trip; or Over the Wild West Like a Flying Squirrel [Dime novel; SPW]

Nugget Library #102 (1891); Part one of a four-part novel

Thomas Edison Jr.'s latest invention, a gas-propelled flying squirrel suit, has its uses as he confronts Indians and his evil cousin Louis Gubrious posing as the Blue Mask.

Tom Terrific (1957) [Animated TV series]

Youngster Tom Terrific lives in a treehouse and wears a magical funnel-shaped hat that enables him to transform into anything he wishes.

Tom Terrific was broadcast each weekday morning as part of the *Captain Kangaroo* show with each adventure consisting of five chapters.

"GO WEST YOUNG MANFRED" [5 CHAPTERS] [WW]

Air Date: 1958; Executive Producer: Bill Weiss; Creator-Director: Gene Deitch; 26 × 5 chapters × 5 min; Terrytoons, CBS; b/w.

Chapter One: Tom Terrific decides to head West with Mighty Manfred the Wonder Dog by transforming himself into a stagecoach. But when all they encounter is modern-day traffic, Tom becomes a clock and turns back time to the Old West.

Chapter Two: When Tom and Manfred see a wagon train being attacked by Indians, Tom changes his body into a cavalry bugle to scare the Indians away. Manfred pulls the remaining wagon to California.

Chapter Three: Tom turns into an eagle and searches for the gold that will allow them to enter the "Gateway to the West."

Chapter Four: Tom makes his return journey to the wagon by turning into the Pony Express, but Manfred is captured by Indians. Manfred impresses the Indians who make him their honorary Big Chief Sleeping Brother.

Chapter Five: Manfred says goodbye to his "Redskin brothers" and heads to California with Tom.

Tomahawk [Comic book; WW]

First appearance: *Star-Spangled Comics* #69 (June 1947); Creators: Joe Samachson, Edmund Good; Publisher: National Periodical Publications-DC Comics, Vertigo.

Indian-raised white man Tom Hawk works as a frontier scout in the American Revolutionary War with young sidekick Dan Hunter.

The stories took on a weird quality in the late 1950s with stories involving dinosaurs, cavemen, giant gorillas, giant robots, giant spiders, aliens and a journey to the moon.

The comic book did eventually move its locale to the Old West beginning with issue #131 featuring tales of Tomahawk's son Hawk and a change of title to *Son of Tomahawk*.

Tomazooma [Comic book character; SFW]

First appearance: **Fantastic Four** #80 (November 1968); Creators: **Stan Lee**, Jack Kirby; Publisher: Marvel Comics.

A giant robot, "Totem Who Walks," built by the Red Star Oil Company, poses as the Keewazi Indian Tribe's spirit-god, Tomazooma, in an attempt to control their oil-rich tribal land. Keewazi chief Silent Fox, grandfather of Wyatt Wingfoot, is fooled at first before he asks for the help of Wingfoot and the Fantastic Four.

El Topo (1970) [Film; Mexico; WW]

Premiere: December 18, 1970; Main Cast: Alejandro Jodorowsky as El Topo, Brontis Jodorowsky as Young Son of El Topo, Mara Lorenzio as Mara, Paula Romo as Woman in Black; Executive Producer: Roberto Viskin; Story-Director: Alexandro Jodorowsky; 125 min.; Producciones Panicas; Spanish; Color.

After rescuing Mara from a Mexican village strewn with mutilated corpses and livestock, gunfighter El Topo begins his quest to defeat the four master gunfighters of the desert. But his journey ends in betrayal and leads to near death and rescue by a group of deformed cave dwellers who seek to escape from their enforced exile. Digging a tunnel to release them, he discovers the neighboring town is full of sadistic religious fanatics. The freedom of the exiled misfits has come at a price.

Bizarre, violent, sexual, unsettling, mystical and ultimately incoherent Western that has been described as resembling "a home movie on acid." The film crosses multiple genres and borrows freely from Sergio Leone's spaghetti Westerns and Tod Browning's *Freaks*. Director called the character of El Topo "a man searching for spirituality and peace."

The film was introduced to American audiences by Beatles manager Allen Klein after John Lennon and Yoko Ono saw it at a midnight screening at the Elgin Theater and convinced Klein to secure *El Topo* for U.S. release.

Film critic Roger Ebert (January 28, 1972) commented: "Jodorowsky lifts his symbols and mythologies from everywhere: Christianity, Zen, discount-store black magic, you name it. He makes not the slightest attempt to use them so they sort out into a single logical significance. Instead, they're employed in a shifting, prismatic way, casting their light on each other instead of on the film's conclusion. The effect resembles Eliot's 'The Waste Land,' and especially Eliot's notion of shoring up fragments of mythology against the ruins of the post-Christian era."

The film remained out of circulation for thirty years due to hostilities between Jodorowsky and Klein but a reconciliation led to its 2007 re-release.

Touche pas à la Femme Blanche (1974) [Film; France-Italy; WW]

Premiere: January 23, 1974; Main Cast: Catherine Deneuve as Marie-Hélène de Boismonfrais, Marcello Mastroianni as George A. Custer, Michel Piccoli as Buffalo Bill, Alain Cuny as Sitting Bull; Producers: Jean-Pierre Rassam, Jean Yanne; Story: Rafael Azcona, Marco Ferreri; Director: Marco Ferreri; 108 min.; Films 66, Mara Films; Color.

A political satire as contemporary Western set in 1970s Paris, France, featuring General George Armstrong Custer, Buffalo Bill and Sitting Bull.

See: *Don't Touch the White Woman*

A Town Called Pandemonium [Short story anthology; WW]

Editors: Anne C. Perry, Jared Shurin; Illustrator: Adam Hill; First publication: London: Jurassic London, November 2012.

The town of Pandemonium sits in New Mexico Territory on the edge of the Anasazi lands and four days ride from the Texas border, surrounded by ravines, mountains and an inhospitable desert. Cattle baron Representation Calhoun rules the dying frontier mining town that is home to an odd assortment of characters, each with their own dark secrets.

The original soft cover shared world anthology features ten short stories that include elements of horror and the supernatural. The Café de Paris hardcover edition (2013) includes an extra story and interview with illustrator Adam Hill. Includes "Grit" by Scott Andrews and "Sleep In Fire" by Osgood Vance.

Trail of Darkness [RPG book; WW]

First publication: 2014; *Deadlands Tall Tales* #4; Protocol Game Series; Author: Jim Pinto; Art: Rick Hershey; Publisher: Pinnacle Entertainment Group.

A group of men and women are on the hunt for the black magician and cult leader who murdered their friend Caleb. They only have one clue to his identity and whereabouts. He is living in Bell Creek, a small settlement on the edge of the silver mines in Northern Nevada where he is posing as a holy man with members of his cult. A story role-playing game set in *Deadlands: The Weird West*.

"Trail of Painted Rocks" [Pulp fiction; WW]

Author: **Lon Williams**; Character: **Lee Winters**; *Real Western Stories* (February 1956).

Moonlight cutting into Tallyho Canyon through an eastward notch fell here with spotlight brightness. That which had caught his attention wasan arrow painted in scarlet at a height level with his face. Its sharp end pointed west. Winters stared at it in damp terror, for its paint was not dry. A breeze blew against it, and it quivered as clinging blood.

But that which paralyzed him was the appearance of a hand—a hand without a body. Like that of Belshazzar's palace Winters had heard of from Scripture it traced its message upon a wall. Winters observed with cold fascination. It wrote: *Go back, Winters. You are heading for worse than death. Speckled Bill.*

The Trailsman: Ghost Ranch Massacre (#157) [WW]

Author: Jon Sharpe; First publication: New York: Signet, 1995.

Skye Fargo must contend with Hopi Indians who believe ghosts roam the land and sky, a cattle baron with equal hatred for the white man and the Indian, and a magician and his two bewitching daughters. Fargo discovers a series of gruesome murders with Hopi signs on the victim's bodies when he attempts to clear his name after the Hopi blame him for the death of a Hopi Brave.

The Trailsman book series featured Skye Fargo adventurers published under the pen name Jon Sharpe between 1980 and the conclusion of the series in December 2014.

The Trailsman: High Country Horror (#256) [WMW]

Author: Jon Sharpe; First publication: New York: Signet, 2003.

Skye Fargo alias the Trailsman comes to the aid of a wagon train of clueless passengers stranded in the Lost River Mountains for the winter. But a legendary half-man, half-bear, insane creature known as the Lost River Lurker awaits in the darkness and only Fargo has the courage to face him.

The Trailsman: Shoshoni Spirits (#101) [WW]

Author: Jon Sharpe; First publication: New York: Signet, 1990.

Skye Fargo "blazes through a maze of redskin magic and savage murder" as he encounters a beautiful but lying woman named Melody Abbott who wants to find her husband and the fortune that disappeared during an attack by Indians.

Tre croci per non morire (1968) [Film; Italy; WW]

Premiere: November 23, 1968; Main Cast: Craig Hill as Gerry, Ken Wood [Giovanni Cianfriglia] as Reno, Evelyn Stewart [Ida Galli] as Dolores, Peter White [Pietro Tordi] as Paco; Story: Franco Cobianchi; Director: Willy S. Regan [Sergio Garrone]; 98 min.; G.V. Cinematografica; Color.

Three gunfighters are offered prison pardons if they can find the evidence to clear a landowner's son convicted rape and murder charges.

A conventional story receives a Weird Western twist when the ghosts of two dead partners make a final-reel appearance.

Tre pistole contro Cesare (1966) [Film; Italy-Algeria; WW]

Main Cast: Thomas Hunter as Whity Selby, James Shigeta as Lester Kato, Nadir Moretti as Etienne Devereaux, Enrico Maria Salerno as Julius Cesar Fuller, Femi Benussi as Tula; Producer: Carmine Bologna; Story: Carmine Bologna, Piero Regnoli, Enzo Peri; Director: Enzo Peri; 95 min.; Dino de Laurentiis Cinematografica, Casbah Film; Color.

Whity Selby learns of a gold mine in Laredo left to him by his late, estranged father. But two other Nadir Moretti men also claim mine ownership: Etienne Devereaux who claims to possess magical powers of magnetism and hypnotism, and the kung fu master Lester Kato.

When the three men discover they are half-brothers, they join forces to defeat town landlord Julius Cesar Fuller who claims their father's land and gold mine and from his castle residence imagines himself to be the incarnation of the famous Roman emperor.

A Tree of Bones (Hexslinger book #2) [Novel; WW]

Author: Gemma Files; First Publication: Toronto: ChiZine Publications, 2012.

Hexslinger Chess Pargeter, trapped in the underworld, sacrificed himself in Ixchel's name to restore the town of Bewelcome and now seeks revenge on his former lover "Reverend" Asher Rook. With the aid of Pinkerton detective turned outlaw Ed Morrow and young spiritualist Yancey Colder they face the demon known as the Enemy as they lay siege to Hex City.

"The Tree of Life" [Pulp fiction; SW]

Author: C. L. Moore; First publication: Weird Tales (October 1936).

In the Martian ruins of Illar, **Northwest Smith** meets a mysterious priestess who tells him of the being named Tharg whom she serves. Smith learns from the Tree People that Tharg is a hungry god who wants Smith as his next meal.

Tremors 4: The Legend Begins (2004) [Film; SFW]

Premiere: January 2, 2004; Main Cast: Michael Gross as Hiram Gummer, Sara Botsford as Christine Lord, Lydia Look as Lu Wan Chang; Executive Producers: Brent Maddock, S.S. Wilson; Story: Brent Maddock, S.S. Wilson, Nancy Roberts; Teleplay: Scott Buck; Director: S.S. Wilson; 101 min.; Stampede Entertainment; Color.

Rejection, Nevada, townsfolk defend their town against the graboid worm monsters in 1889.

Tremors 4: The Legend Begins : Dirt Dragons (2004) [Computer Game; SFW]

1. Special effects featurette included with the DVD release.

2. Flash computer shootout game based on the film *Tremors 4: The Legend Begins*. Concept and development by Allan Krahl for Stampede Entertainment.

Tribal Force [Comic book; WW]

First appearance: Summer 1996; Story: John Proudstar; Art: Ryan Huna Smith; Publisher: Mystic Comics.

A group of Native American superheroes, including Little Big Horn alias "Gabriel Medicine God" and Navajo law student Basho Yazza (who creates warriors from rock), oppose the U.S. government's plans to claim their reservation land.

This one-shot comic book has been described as a Native American *X-Men* by co-creator Ryan Huna Smith.

Trigun [Manga; Anime; Japan; SFW]

1. First appearance: 1995; Story: Yasuhiro Nightow; Art: Nightow; 21 chapters; Publisher: Tokuma Shoten.

On a distant barren planet, Vash the Stampede destroys cities. Insurance claim inspectors Meryl Strife and Milly Thompson must track him down and stop his rampage. Meanwhile, bounty hunters seek the $60 billion reward for his capture.

Originally appeared in *Shonen Captain*. Continued as *Trigun Maximum* in *Young King Ours* magazine in 1998. The story concluded in 2007 in Japan.

2. Animated TV series

Premiere: April 4, 1998; Creator: Yasuhiro Nightow; Story: Yasuhiro Nightow, Yosuke Kuroda; Animation: Mad House; Director: Satoshi Nishimura; Tokuma Shoten, JVC; 26 × 30 min.; Color.

Season One

The $$60,000,000,000 Man (1:01); *Truth of Mistake* (1:02); *Peace Maker* (1:03); *Love and Peace* (1:04); *Hard Puncher* (1:05); *Lost July* (1:06); *B.D.N.* (1:07); *And Between the Wasteland and Sky* (1:08); *Murder Machine* (1:09); *Quick Draw* (1:10); *Escape from Pain* (1:11); *Diablo* (1:12); *Vash the Stampede* (1:13); *Little Arcadia* (1:14); *Demon's Eye* (1:15); *Fifth Moon* (1:16); *Rem Saverem* (1:17); *Goodbye for Now* (1:18); *Hang Fire* (1:19); *Flying Ship* (1:20); *Out of Time* (1:21); *Alternative* (1:22); *Paradise* (1:23); *Sin* (1:24); *Live Through* (1:25); *Under the Sky So Blue* (1:26)

"The Trophy Hunters" [Pulp fiction; WW]

Author: **Lon Williams**; Character: **Lee Winters**; *Real Western Stories* (February 1955).

Lee Winter's, pursuit of Red Wolf is connected to a collection of human heads.

> With his robe, black hair, pointed beard and leering eyes, this stranger resembled Winters' boyhood concept of Satan. His speech suggested both cruelty and cunning. "You have an odd look about you, Officer Whoever-you-be, as if you doubted my reality."
>
> "Yeah?" said Winters. "If it concerns you, I'm Deputy Marshal Lee Winters of Forlorn Gap."
>
> "Ah! From that haunted, empty town, are you?..."

Tunnel in the Sky [Juvenile novel; SW]

Author: **Robert A. Heinlein**; First publication: New York: Scribner, 1955.

The class in "Advanced Survival" are stranded on an alien planet when the "gate" for their return to Earth is disrupted by a supernova. The young men and women are forced to form a pioneer colony to survive.

Originally titled *Schoolhouse in the Sky*, the book was completed in under two months in late 1954. Western themes are explicit in the new frontier storyline and the transformation of Rod Walker into Captain Walker, leading a wagon train on a strange planet.

Turok [Comic book character; Comic book; SFW]

1. First appearance: *Four Color Comics* #596, December 1954; Creator: Gaylord DuBois; Publisher: Dell Publishing Co, Inc.

Originally conceived as a pre–Columbian Native American, Turok and his companion (a.k.a. brother) Andar are trapped in a Lost Valley populated by dinosaurs which they refer to as "honkers."

Turok Son of Stone was published by Dell, Gold Key and finally Whitman until its final issue #130 in April 1982.

2. First appearance: *Magnus Robot Fighter* #12, 1992; Story: Faye Perozich, Jim Shooter; Art: Gonzalo Mayo; Publisher: Valiant.

Valiant revamped the character in 1992, placing the comic book in the American West of the 1860s and retitling him *Turok Dinosaur Hunter*. Exploring a cavern in the sagebrush desert near the Rio Grande, Kiowa Indian hunter Turok and his friend Andar discover the other-dimensional Lost Land populated by menacing bionic dinosaurs, including Mon-Ark who possesses near-human intelligence.

3. Acclaim Comics further revamped the character when they purchased Valiant and obtained the license to *Turok*. Acclaim expanded into a series of *Turok* video games that proved to be very popular.

Turok: Evolution [Video game; SFW]

Release date: August 2002; Developer: Acclaim Studios; Publisher: Acclaim Entertainment; Platform (original release): Xbox.

An origin story in which Tal'Set becomes Turok beginning in Texas in 1866. Tal'Set is fighting his enemy Captain Tobias Bruckner when they both fall into a rift located between Texas and the Lost Land.

"Twenty Notches" [Pulp fiction; WMW]

Author: **Max Brand**; Six-part serialization; First publication: *Western Story Magazine* (14 March–18 April, 1931).

While riding an empty freight car with two fellow tramps, a young handsome man known as the Sleeper learns of Trot Enderby and his old Colt gun that cannot miss its intended target. When the train approaches the vicinity of Enderby's house the Sleeper jumps the box car hoping to steal the gun from Enderby after befriending him.

The Sleeper knows Enderby is dangerous. His gun has killed twenty men and he has no intention of being the next notch on his gun. Waiting for his moment to steal the gun the Sleeper slides it from under Enderby's pillow as he sleeps and rides away.

"[I]t seemed to the Sleeper that there well might be some peculiar property of the weapon which gave it an uncanny power."

Enderby pursues the Sleeper to Alcalde but the sight of the old Colt in the young man's possession is enough to make him cut and run.

"There was only one person in the room who was not greatly surprised. That was the Sleeper. Yet, he too felt a ghostly tingle down his spine, for this was the authentification of the fable of the magic gun, of course."

But the twenty notch weapon possesses the power to transform a person in a way that says as much about the person as the gun. The Sleeper discovers the truth of this when he is asked to re-

cover the stolen stallion Ironwood from the treacherous Parmenter and his gang.

The Twilight Zone (1959) [TV Series]

1. Science fiction-fantasy anthology series hosted by Rod Serling.

"Mr. Denton on Doomsday" (1:03) [WW]

Premiere: October 16, 1959; Main Cast: Dan Duryea as Al Denton, Martin Landau as Dan Hotaling, Malcolm Atterbury as Henry J. Fate, Doug McClure as Pete Grant, Jeanne Cooper as Liz; Executive Producer-Story: Rod Serling; Producer: Buck Houghton; Director: Allen Reisner; 25 min.; Cayuga Productions, CBS Television; b/w.

Alcoholic Al Denton is desperate to beat the demon drink and return to the glory days as a renowned gunslinger. When Henry J. Fate arrives in town offering Denton a magical potion that will guarantee him gun fighting accuracy for ten seconds at a time Denton feels his prayers have been answered. But he finds himself caught in the same vicious cycle that drove him to drink before—until a fateful gunfight frees him from his past.

Serling's original draft "You Too Can be a Fast Gun" was a simple wish fulfillment fantasy about a retiring teacher who becomes a gunfighter with the aid of a magic potion.

"Execution" (1:26) [SFW]

Premiere: April 1, 1960; Main Cast: Albert Salmi as Joseph Caswell, Russell Johnson as Professor George Manion, Than Wyenn as Paul Johnson; Producer: Buck Houghton; Teleplay: Rod Serling; Based on an unpublished story by George Clayton Johnson; Director: David Orrick McDearmon; 25 min.; Cayuga Productions, CBS Television; b/w.

In 1880 Montana, cowboy Joseph Caswell has been found guilty of murder and sentenced to die by hanging. Just as he is about to meet his fate, Caswell awakes in New York City, 1960, face-to-face with time machine inventor Professor Mannion in his laboratory. History repeats itself as a confused and distraught Caswell kills again with a blow to Mannion's head. But Caswell becomes a victim of murder himself when petty thief Paul Johnson strangles him in a struggle for his gun and unwittingly escapes into the time machine. He finds himself back in November 1880 in the hangman's noose originally reserved for Caswell. Justice has been served across time.

Serling changed George Clayton Johnson's original ending where the killer from the past is returned to the hangman's noose after being killed in the present by a policeman.

"DUST" (2:12) [WMW]

Premiere: January 6, 1961; Main Cast: Thomas Gomez as Sykes, Vladimir Sokoloff as Gallegos, John Alonso as Luis Gallegos, John Larch as Sherriff Koch; Producer: Buck Houghton; Story: Rod Serling; Director: Douglas Heyes; 25 min.; Cayuga Productions, CBS Television; b/w.

A desperate father clinging to any hope for his condemned son Luis Gallegos is approached by a peddler named Sykes who sells him a bag of "magic dust" that he claims will make the townsfolk release his son.

"A HUNDRED YEARS OVER THE RIM" (2:23) [SFW]

Premiere: April 7, 1961; Main Cast: Cliff Robertson as Christian Horn, Miranda Jones as Martha Horn, John Astin as Charlie, John Crawford as Joe; Producer: Buck Houghton; Story: Rod Serling; Director: Buzz Kulik; 25 min.; Cayuga Productions, CBS Television; b/w.

Christian Horn, headed toward California from Ohio in 1847, searches for food and water for his wife , dying eight-year-old son and fellow travelers. Walking over the edge of a rim in the territory of New Mexico, he encounters a truck driving down the highway and accidentally shoots himself in the arm avoiding what he perceives as a monster. Coming across a local diner where his wound is treated Horn notices a calendar dated September, 1961.

In this episode, shot on location near Lone Pine, California, director Buzz Kulik and lead actor Cliff Robertson both agreed to abandon the traditional cowboy clothes in favor of authentic clothes worn by someone traveling East to West.

"THE GRAVE" (3:07) [WW]

Premiere: October 27, 1961; Main Cast: Lee Marvin as Conny Miller, Strother Martin as Mothershed, James Best as Johnny Rob, Lee Van Cleef as Steinhart, Richard Geary as Pinto Sykes; Producer: Buck Houghton; Story-Director: Montgomery Pittman; 25 min.; Cayuga Productions, CBS Television; b/w.

Hired gunman Conny Miller arrives in town to find his target Pinto Sykes has already been killed and is dead in his grave. Miller also learns that before he died Sykes vowed to reach up from his grave if Miller paid him a visit. When Johnny Robe and Steinhart bet Miller that he won't have the nerve to visit Sykes' grave Miller rises to the challenge. It is a decision he will regret.

"SHOWDOWN WITH RANCE MCGREW" (3:20) [WW]

Premiere: February 2, 1962; Main Cast: Larry Blyden as Rance McGrew, Robert Kline as TV Jesse James, Arch Johnson as Jesse James; Producer: Buck Houghton; Story: Rod Serling; Based on an original idea by Frederic Louis Fox; Director: Christian Nyby; 25 min.; Cayuga Productions, CBS Television; b/w.

Bungling, cowardly TV Western actor Rance McGrew comes face to face with the real Jesse James who becomes his agent in an attempt to bring some reality to McGraw's weekly TV series. A satire on the juvenile nature of TV Westerns of the period.

"Mr. Rance McGrew, a three-thousand-buck-a-week phony-baloney discovers that this week's current edition of make-believe is being shot on location—and that location is the Twilight Zone."—Rod Serling.

Serling transferred Frederic Fox's original concept of a modern-day cowboy suddenly finding himself in the Old West to a Hollywood TV actor encountering the person he portrays on screen.

"THE 7TH IS MADE UP OF PHANTOMS" (5:10) [SFW]

Premiere: December 6, 1963; Main Cast: Warren Oates as Corporal Richard Langsford, Ron Foster as Sergeant William Connors, Randy Boone as Pfc. Michael McCluskey, Greg Morris as Lt. Woodard; Producer: Bert Granet; Story: Rod Serling; Director: Alan Crosland Jr.; 25 min.; Cayuga Productions, CBS Television; b/w.

A three-man National Guard tank crew on maneuvers near Little Big Horn are time-transported from June 25, 1964 to June 25, 1876, the day of Custer's last stand against the Sioux nation.

"MR. GARRITY AND THE GRAVES" (5:28) [WW]

Premiere: May 8, 1964; Main Cast: John Dehner as Jared Garrity, J. Pat O'Malley as Gooberman, Norman Leavitt as Sheriff Gilchrist, Stanley Adams as Jensen, Percy Helton as Lapham, John Cliff as Lightning Peterson, Kate Murtagh as Zelda Gooberman; Producer: William Froug; Story: Rod Serling; Based on an unpublished story by Mike Korologos; Director: Ted Post; 25 min.; Cayuga Productions, CBS Television; b/w.

Happiness, Arizona, circa 1890. Jared Garrity is a traveling resurrector of the dead with accomplices all too ready to fool a gullible public into parting with their money. But when Garrity promises to bring back to life 128 of the deceased at midnight he instills fear in the community for nearly all of the departed about to return were violent in life. Con-man Garrity leaves town richer and happier not realizing he really does have the power to raise the dead.

"Exit Mr. Garrity, a would-be charlatan, a make-believe con-man and a sad misjudger of his own talents. Respectfully submitted from an empty cemetery on a dark hillside that is one of the slopes leading to the Twilight Zone"—Rod Serling.

2. *The Twilight Zone—Radio Dramas* (2007)

Main Cast: Stacy Keach as the Host; Producers: Carl Amari, Roger Wolski; 43 min.; Falcon Picture Group.

Nationally syndicated weekly radio show adaptations of episodes from the original *Twilight Zone* television series. The original scripts have been expanded from 23 minutes to 43 minutes.

"A Hundred Years Over the Rim":
Cast: Jim Caviezel; Vol. 3 [SFW]

"The 7th Is Made Up of Phantoms":
Cast: Richard Grieco; Vol. 5 [SFW]

"The Grave":
Cast: Michael Rooker; Vol. 6 [WW]

"Mr. Denton on Doomsday":
Cast: Adam Baldwin; Vol. 6 [WW]

"Showdown with Rance McGraw":
Cast: Chris McDonald; Vol. 7 [WW]

"Dust":
Cast: Bill Smitrovich; Vol. 9 [WW]

The Two Devils [Novel; SFW]

Author: David B. Riley; First publication: Pittsburgh PA: LBF Books; Las Cruces, NM: Hadrosaur Productions, 2004.

Wandering barber Miles O'Malley and his horse Paul travel through the Old West of the 1880s meeting fallen angels, the owl-headed Mayan god of death Ah Puch, aliens from Mars, demons and Nick Mephistopheles.

Two-Gun Kid [Comic book]

First publication: March 1948; Art: Syd Shores; Publisher: Timely-Atlas-Marvel Comics.

1. The first Western comic book published by Timely (Marvel Comics). In a storyline that would be repeated in other Marvel Western titles, Clay Harder is wrongly accused of murder and spends his life on the run from the law with his trusted horse Cyclone by his side.

2. Following the cancellation of the title in April 1961, *Two-Gun Kid* was revived by writer-editor **Stan Lee** and artist Jack Kirby in issue #60 (November 1962). The new version of *Two-Gun Kid* continued the numbering from the original title. Original *Two-Gun Kid* Clay Harder was reduced to a dime novel character as Matt Hawk (later to undergo a name change to Matt Liebowicz) became the "real-life" Two-Gun Kid.

Influenced by the success of the Marvel superhero titles, *Two-Gun Kid* soon included various super-villains including Chief Roaring Bear, The Panther, Purple Phantom and hypnotist Silver Sidewinder.

Weird Western storylines:

"Nothing Can Save Fort Henry" [WW]
First publication: #65 (September 1963); Story: **Stan Lee**; Art: **Dick Ayers**.

Disgraced doctor Major Dave Dixon decides to get revenge on Fort Henry by supplying Chief Roaring Bear with a potion that gave him and his stallion super-strength and super-size. But Dixon's eventual act of self-sacrifice saves the fort from destruction.

"The Purple Phantom" [WMW]
First publication: #68 (March 1964); Story: Stan Lee; Art: Dick Ayers.

Wearing a phosphorescent costume, Hunk Hondo poses as the ghostly Purple Phantom in his cattle-rustling raids.

The title was finally laid to rest in 1979 but Two-Gun Kid returned in a Weird West adventure in *Daredevil, The Man Without Fear* in 1985. Two-Gun Kid was also featured in *The Avengers*, *West-Coast Avengers* and *She-Hulk* where he traveled through time, and the limited series' *Two-Gun Kid: Sunset Riders* (1995) and *Blaze of Glory* (2000).

3. *Mighty Marvel Western* mini-series one-shot; First publication: August 2006; Story: Dan Slott, Keith Geffin; Art: Eduardo Barreto, Robert Loren Fleming, Mike Allred.

A present-day adventure with She-Hulk reminding Two-Gun Kid of a tale from his past involving cattle rustlers and monsters.

2000x: Tales of the Next Millennia [Radio show]

Premiere: 1999; Announcer: Robert Foxworth; Host-Consultant: Harlan Ellison; Executive Producers: Andy Trudeau, Stefan Rudnicki; Producer-Director; Yuri Rasovsky; 26 × 60 min.; NPR (National Public Radio), Hollywood Theater of the Ear.

Radio anthology series consisting of 49 30-minute plays celebrating the new millennium in fiction.

"SHAMBLEAU" [SW]
Original broadcast: *NPR Playhouse* (February 20, 2001); Story: **C.L. Moore**; Adaptation: Sarah Montague; Main Cast: Kristoffer Tabori as **Northwest Smith**, Ann Marie Lee as the Shambleau, George Murdock as Yarol; 30 min.

This radio dramatization of C.L. Moore's original story avoids narration in favor of dialogue.

See: *7th Dimension*

Two Tiny Claws [Novel; SFW]
Author: Brett Davis; First publication: Riverdale NY: Baen, 1999.

In this sequel to *Bone Wars,* paleontologist Barnum Brown searches for dinosaur bones in turn-of-the-century Montana but encounters aliens and Old West gunslinger Luther Gumpson.

See: *Bone Wars*

Uchū Kaizoku Kyaputen Hārokku (1978) [Anime; Japan]
Premiere: March 14, 1978; Director: Rintaro; Toei Animation; 42 × 25 min.; Color.

Based on characters created by **Leiji Matsumoto.**

In the year 2977, humans devote all their time and energy to leisure. Captain Harlock and the crew of the *Arcadia* become Earth's only hope against the alien Mazone.

"MY FRIEND, MY YOUTH" (1:30) [SW]
Taking refuge from the pursuing Mazone on Pirate Island, Harlock recalls his first encounter with Toshiro Oyama and **Queen Emeraldas** in an Old West–style town where Toshiro saved him from a hangman's noose.

UFO (1970) (TV series; UK)
Main Cast: Ed Bishop as Commander Ed Straker, Michael Billington as Colonel Paul Foster, Dolores Mantez as Lieutenant Nina Barry, Wanda Ventham as Colonel Virginia Lake.

In 1980 a secret military organization named SHADO (Supreme Headquarters Alien Defense Organization) is formed to defend the Earth from an alien invasion.

"MINDBENDER" (1:14) [SW]
Air date: January 13, 1971; Guest Cast: Al Mancini as Lieutenant Andy Conroy, Charles Tingwell as Captain Beaver James, Stuart Damon as Howard Byrne; Executive producers: Gerry Anderson, Reg Hill; Story: Tony Barwick; Director: Ken Turner; 50 min.; Century 21 Television, Incorporated Television Company (ITC); Color.

Hallucinations affect Moonbase and SHADO HQ when Lt. Andy Conroy is killed in an Old West shootout with Mexican bandits on Moonbase, another sees aliens and Cmdr. Straker thinks he's an actor in a television series about SHADO.

Undead or Alive (2007) [Film; WW]
Main Cast: James Denton as Elmer; Chris Kattan as Luke, Lew Alexander as Geronimo, Navi Rawat as Sue; Producers: Deborah Del Prete, David S. Greathouse, Gigi Pritzker; Story: Glasgow Phillips, Scott Pourroy; Director: Glasgow Phillips; Odd Lot Entertainment; Color.

Comedy Western about two robbers fleeing an undead sheriff and his zombie posse. When the two are captured by Geronimo's niece Sue, they have no idea she may their only salvation from Geronimo's "white man's curse."

Under a Harrowed Moon Part 1: Strange Bedfellows [RPG book; WW]
Author: Matt Forbeck; First publication: 1997; **Deadlands: The Weird West** Dime Novel #4; Publisher: Pinnacle Entertainment Group.

Under a Harrowed Moon Part 2: Savage Passage [RPG book; WW]
Author: Matt Forbeck; First publication: 1998; Setting: **Deadlands: The Weird West** Dime Novel #5; Publisher: Pinnacle Entertainment Group.

Under a Harrowed Moon Part 3: Ground Zero [RPG book; WW]
Author: Matt Forbeck; First publication: 1998; Setting; **Deadlands: The Weird West** Dime Novel #6; Publisher: Pinnacle Entertainment Group.

Crossover series of Dime Novels with **Werewolf: The Wild West**. Undead hero Ronan Lynch and company are coerced to join forces with a team of werewolves. They venture from the Weird West to the Savage West to track evil Dr. Hellstromme and save two worlds.

Under a Prairie Moon [Novel; WWR]
Author: Madeline Baker; First publication: New York: N.Y. Leisure Books, 1998.

When Kathy inherits a neglected family ranch, she sets about bringing it back to life, but is disturbed by feelings of someone watching her every move. The spirit of Dalton Crowkiller a Lakota half-breed from the 1870s, befriends her and they fall in love. Pleading for a second chance at love, Dalton and Kathy are transported back to the Old West where Dalton is alive in the flesh once again. But they both become aware that their time together may be limited and come to appreciate each day knowing it may be their last.

"Under the Moons of Mars" [Pulp fiction; SW]

Author: Norman Bean (**Edgar Rice Burroughs**); First publication: *The All-Story Magazine* Vol. XXII #2 (February-July 1912).

One of the first attempts at mixing the Western and Science Fiction genres. The first title, *My First Adventure to Mars*, was changed to *The Green Martians*. In the margin of the first page of his original manuscript, Burroughs wrote *Dejah Thoris Martian Princess?*, a title he would adopt when he mailed the half-completed 43,000-word manuscript to *Argosy* magazine on August 14, 1911.

The story was expanded to 65,000 words and serialized in *The All-Story Magazine* under the pseudonym "Normal Bean" which was printed "Norman Bean" due to a typing error. Burroughs sold serial rights for $400. He told the *Chicago Examiner*:

> I was very much ashamed of my new vocation ... It seemed a foolish thing for a man to be doing—much on par with a man dressing in a boy scout suit and running away from home to fight Indians.

Synopsis: At the close of the American Civil War, former Virginia Confederate officer John Carter is prospecting in Arizona when Apaches attack.

> The Indians discovered that I was alone, and I was pursued with curses, threats, arrows, and bullets! The facts that it is difficult to aim anything but curses and threats accurately by moonlight; that they were upset by the unexpected manner of my arrival; and that I was a rapidly moving target; saved me from their various deadly projectiles and permitted me to reach the shadows of the surrounding peaks. My horse was traveling practically unguided, and so it happened that he entered a shallow gully that led to the summit of the range and not to the pass that I had hoped would carry me to safety. However, I owe my life and my remarkable adventures to this turn in the road.

After hiding in a cave, Carter ventures out upon the desert landscape of Arizona and gazes up toward the planet Mars in the sky.

> As I stood thus meditating, I turned my gaze from the landscape to the heavens where the myriad stars formed a gorgeous and fitting canopy for the wonders of the earthly scene. My attention was quickly riveted by a large red star close to the distant horizon. As I gazed upon it I felt a spell of overpowering fascination—it was Mars, the god of war, and for me, the fighting man, it had always held the power of irresistible enchantment. As I gazed at it on that far-gone night it seemed to call across the unthinkable void, to lure me to it, to draw me as the lodestone attracts a particle of iron.
>
> My longing was beyond the power of opposition; I closed my eyes, stretched out my arms toward the god of my vocation and felt myself drawn with the suddenness of thought through the trackless immensity of space. There was an instant of extreme cold and utter darkness.

Inexplicably Carter finds himself on Mars where he is taken prisoner by six-limbed green giants on eight-legged mounts.

> I opened my eyes upon a strange and weird landscape. I knew that I was on Mars; not once did I question either my sanity or my wakefulness. I was not asleep, no need for pinching here; my inner consciousness told me as plainly that I was upon Mars as your conscious mind tells you that you are upon Earth. You do not question the fact; neither did I.

After meeting the beautiful Martian princess Dejah Thoris, they join forces in their fight for freedom and the future of Mars.

The six-part serial was collected to form the novel *The Princess of Mars* (A.C. McClurg & Co., October 10, 1917). The novel served as the first part of a trilogy that continued with *The Gods of Mars* and concluded with *The Warlord of Mars*. Burroughs' subsequent stories in the series didn't feature a specific Western setting or John Carter but showed the influence of different genres including Western pulp fiction of the era.

Unforgettable [Novel; WWR]

Author: Madeline Baker; First publication: New York: N.Y. Leisure Books, 2000.

Visiting the ghost town of Bodie in Northern California while on vacation, Shaye Montgomery encounters the ghost of handsome Old West gambler Alejandro Valverde, who was hanged for his crimes. Shaye eventually meets Alejandro in the flesh when she travels back in time and space to the boomtown of Bodie in 1880. But can she save him from being hanged?

Uninvited (1993) [Film; WW]

Main Cast: Jack Elam as Grady, Zane Paolo as Billy Ray, Ted Haler as The Priest, Jerry Rector as Winchester, Bari Buckner as Emma; Producers: David Kleinman, Shawn Coulter, Larry Kaster; Story-Director: Michael Derek Bohusz; 90 min.; Rush Hour Productions; Color.

Eight strangers searching for gold trespass on sacred burial grounds, disturbing the ghosts who then exact their revenge.

The Unity [RPG book; WW]

Author: Shane Lacy Hensley; First publication: 2002; Setting: **Deadlands: Hell on Earth The Wasted West**; Publisher: Pinnacle Entertainment Group.

Conclusion of the *Deadlands: Hell on Earth* main storyline.

Uomo avvisato mezzo ammazzato ... parola di Spirito Santo (1971) [Film; Italy-Spain; WW]

Cast: Gianni Garko as Spirito Santo, Victor Israel as The Preacher, Poldo Bendandi as General Ubarte, Cris Huerta as Carezza/Chuck, Jorge Rigaud [George Rigaud] as Don Firmino Mendoza, Pilar Velazquez as Juana Mendoza, Paul Stevens [Paolo Gozlino] as Samuel Crow; Producer: Luciano Martino; Story: Tito Carpi; Screenplay: Tito Carpi, Federico DeUrrutia, Giuliano Carnimeo; Director: Anthony Ascott [Giuliano Carmineo]; 94 min.; C.C. Astro, Lea Film; Color.

Spiriti Santo helps local revolutionaries in their war against General Ubarte with the help of a unique machine gun. In return he asks for their help in finding gold.

The film includes many Weird Western elements including a quasi-supernatural main character dressed in white with a dove on his shoulder, chickens who lay dynamite eggs and a sidekick with superhuman strength. The subsequent films in the series were standard Westerns.

See: *They Call Him Holy Ghost*

Urban Renewal [RPG book; WW]

Author: Lucien Soulban; First publication: 2000; Setting: **Deadlands: Hell on Earth**; Publisher: Pinnacle Entertainment Group.

The buildings of Junkyard contain squatters and creatures waiting to pounce from among the ruins.

The Valley of Gwangi (1969) [Film; SFW]

1. Premiere: July 25, 1969; Main Cast: James Franciscus as Tuck Kirby, Gila Golan as T.J. Breckenridge, Richard Carlson as Champ Connors; Producer: Charles H. Schneer; Story: William E. Bast; Director: Jim O'Connolly; 96 min.; Morningside Productions, Warner Brothers/Seven Arts; Color.

When a cowboy (Franciscus) enters Forbidden Valley to return a midget horse on the advice of gypsies, he encounters living dinosaurs. He decides to capture an Allosaurus to place in an ailing Wild West show. But when a rival releases the dinosaur, it creates a path of havoc and destruction in the local town.

Willis O'Brien's script *Emilio and Guloso*, later retitled *Valley of the Mist*, was optioned by producer Jesse Lasky in the 1950s but never went into production. The script would be adapted for *The Valley of Gwangi*.

Howard Thompson of *The New York Times* (September 4, 1969) stated: "The first half is strictly standard, filled with human intrigue and mischief. Only when the obviously animated beasts from the past get into the act, about midway through, does the picture perk up, in a craggy wasteland. See this one backward."

2. Comic book adaptation

First publication: *Movie Classics* #01-880-912, December 1969; Art: Jack Sparling; Publisher: Dell Publishing Co.

"The Valley of Spiders" [Short story; WW]

Author: H.G. Wells; Illustrator: Garth Jones; First publication: *Pearson's Magazine*, March, 1903.

Three men on horseback pursue a half-caste girl and her fellow fugitives across a valley and stumble across a nest of giant, aggressive and poisonous spiders.

"A long and clinging thread fell across his face, a grey streamer dropped about his bridle arm, some big, active thing with many legs ran down the back of his head. He looked up to discover one of those grey masses anchored as it were above him by these things and flapping out ends as a sail flaps when a boat comes about—but noiselessly.

He had an impression of many eyes, of a dense crew of squat bodies, of long many-joined limbs hauling at their mooring ropes to bring the thing down upon him."

H.G. Wells' short story doesn't specify dates or a country but the illustrations that originally accompanied the story when it was first published suggest a possible Spanish American setting in the early 19th century.

"The Valley of the Lost" a.k.a. "Secret of Lost Valley" [Short story; WW]

Author: Robert E. Howard; First publication: *Startling Mystery Stories* #4, Spring 1967.

The Reynolds-McCrill feud went back fifteen years when old Esau Reynolds stabbed young Braxton McCrill to death in the saloon at Antelope Wells. Now John Reynolds has walked into an ambush at the same saloon but manages to escape on a mustang as he heads into the Lost Valley. Pursuing him are Jonas McCrill and his four cohorts. Reynolds targets Saul Fletcher with his single-action .45 as he lays in wait in the thickets. Shot through the heart, Fletcher is laid to rest in Ghost Cave, renowned for being haunted. The Kiowas, who once lived in Lost Valley, had told tales of murder, vampirism and cannibalism. But Reynolds has no time for legends and enters the cave with one purpose—to take the .45 calibre cartridges from Saul Fletcher's belt. When Reynolds enters no corpse lies on the cavern floor, but he uncovers a secret door leading to a chamber and the sound of somebody approaching in the darkness of a tunnel. Suddenly the figure lunges at Reynolds. Saul Fletcher has returned from the dead and even greater terrors await Reynolds in the cave in the form of telepathic snake-people and reality transformed.

"The fringing shadows had moved out from the darkness at the base of the walls and drawn about him in a wide ring. And though at first glance they possessed the semblance of men, he knew they were not human. The weird light flickered and danced over them, and back in the deeper darkness the soft, evil drums whispered their accompanying undertone everlastingly. John Reynolds stood aghast at what he saw. It was not their dwarfish bodies which caused his shudder, nor even the unnaturally made hands and feet—it was their heads."

Reynolds' flees from the reptilian beasts and destroys the cave with dynamite—but the horrors and depravity he has witnessed prove too much for him and he ends his torment with a bullet to his temple. Jonas McCrill discovers his corpse and "wondered that his face should be that of an old man, his hair white as hoarfrost."

Sold to *Strange Tales Magazine* in April 1932, this story remained unpublished during Howard's lifetime when the magazine went out of business. It eventually saw publication in 1967.

Vampire Hunter D [Novel; Animated film; Video game; Manga; SFW]

1. Novel

Author: Hideyuki Kikuchi; Illustrator: Yoshitaka Amano; First publication: Japan: Asahi Sonorama, 1983; First English translation: Kevin Leahy; Milwaukie, OR: DH Press, 2005.

Doris Lang, daughter of a werewolf hunter, lives her eight-year-old brother Dan on the outskirts of Ransyla. The 10,000 year-old vampire known as Count Magnus Lee takes a bride every 100 years to ease the boredom of his existence. Doris is his latest target of his affections and D must rescue her. Meanwhile Greco, the spoiled son of the mayor of Ransylva has eyes for Doris himself, but Doris has fallen in love with her rescuer D who is half human-half vampire. His left hand is a symbiotic entity with a face who often irritates D and has powers of its own.

To date (2015) there have been 29 novels published in the *Vampire Hunter D* series.

2. Animated film

Premiere: December 21, 1985 (Japan); Executive producers: Shigeo Maruyama, Yutaka Takahashi; Screenplay: Yasushi Hirano; Based on *Vampire Hunter D Vol. 1* by Key animation: Hiromi Matsushita; Director: Toyoo Ashida; 102 min.; Production company: Ashi Productions, Studio Live; Distribution: TOHO, CBS Sony Group Inc.; Color.

In the year AD 12,090 vampires rule the Earth as the Nobility. The vampire hunter known as D rises to the challenge when he is hired by feisty Doris Lang to save her from the vampire lord Count Magnus Lee who has bitten Doris and desires her for his bride. D declares that killing the one who bit Doris will cure her infection. D is attacked by mutants and the Snake Women of Midwitch posing as sexy sirens on his way to face the Count in his castle. Doris falls for her rescuer D who is a conflicted dhampir, "the freak spawn of a vampire and human" as described by the Count's daughter Larmica who later discovers to her dismay that she shares a similar half-breed lineage. In the classic Western tradition D rides alone into the sunset at the conclusion.

Followed by *Vampire Hunter D: Bloodlust*.

3. Video game
Release date: September 25, 2000; Platform: Sony PlayStation; Developer: Victor Interactive Software; Publisher: Jaleco.

Based on the film *Vampire Hunter D: Bloodlust*. The player controls D as they track down the kidnapped daughter. Vicious enemies and lots of blood and gore await in this 3D graphics game with a M for Mature rating.

4. Manga
Title: *Hideyuki Kikuchi's Vampire Hunter D Volume 1*; First publication: November 14, 2007; Adaptation: Saiko Takaki based on the original story by Hideyuki Kikuchi; Art: Saiko Takaki; Publisher: Media Factory (Japan); Digital Manga Publishing (U.S.).

Ongoing manga series with the intention of adapting each volume of Hideyuki Kikuchi's novels.

Vampire Hunter D: Bloodlust (2000) [Animated film; SFW]

Premiere: August 25, 2000; Producers: Taka Nagasawa, Masao Maruyama, Mataichiro Yamamoto; Animation director: Hisashi Abe; Story-Director: Yoshiaki Kawajiri; Based on *Vampire Hunter D: Demon Deathchase* Vol. 3 by Hideyuki Kikuchi; 105 min.; Production company: Madhouse; Distribution: Nippon Herald Films (Japan), Urban Vision (U.S.); Color.

Vampire Hunter D is hired by the elderly Elbourne to save his daughter Charlotte from vampire Meir Link. Meanwhile the human vampire hunters known as the Marcus Brothers have been hired by Elbourne's son with the same task and instructions. If D or the brothers discover Charlotte has already been infected by Meir and turned into a vampire then she must be killed.

Vampire Wars: Battle for the Universe (2005) [Telefilm; Canada; SW]

DVD release title (U.S.) for *Bloodsuckers*.

Vampires (1998) [Film; WW]

Premiere: October 30, 1998; Main Cast: James Woods as Jack Crow, Daniel Baldwin as Anthony Montoya, Sheryl Lee as Katrina, Thomas Ian Griffith as Jan Valek, Maximillian Schell as Cardinal Alba; Producer: Sandy King; Screenplay: Don Jacoby; Based on the novel *Vampire$* by John Steakley; Director: John Carpenter; 108 min.; Largo Entertainment, JVC Entertainment Networks, Film Office, Spooky Tooth Productions, Storm King Productions, Columbia Pictures; Color.

Jack Crow is leader of a team of vampire hunters in New Mexico with the official seal of approval of the Vatican. Crow and his team must obtain the legendary Black Cross of Berziers. Valek, a former priest who is now a vampire is desperate to locate the Cross himself for the powers it possesses.

In an interview for *Dreamwatch Magazine* (November 1997) director John Carpenter stated he combined material from the original John Steakley novel plus two screenplays. "I went in my office and thought, "It's going to be set in the American Southwest and it's a Western—Howard Hawks. It's a little more like *The Wild Bunch* than Hawks in its style, but the feelings and the whole ending scene is a kind of replay on *Red River*."

Vanishing Riders (1935) [Film; WMW]

Premiere: July 3, 1935; Main Cast: Bill Cody as Bill Jones, Bill Cody Jr. as Tim Lang, Wally Wales as Wolf Larson, Ethel Jackson as Joan Stanley, Donald Reed as Frank Stanley, Budd Buster as Hiram McDuff; Producer: Ray Kirkwood; Story: Oliver Drake; Director: Bob Hill; 58 min.; Spectrum Films; b/w.

When outlaw Wolf Larson and his gang are hired for ranch work, they see the perfect opportunity for cattle rustling. But the ranch has a reputation for being haunted and ranch owner Joan Stanley exploits their fear of ghosts to bring them to justice.

Vanquish the Night [Novel; WW]

Author: Shannon Drake; First publication: New York: Silhouette Books, 1990.

A young Texas woman falls for an immortal but risks eternal damnation. Vampire Western published under the anthology title *Bewitching Love Stories*.

Vartàn [Comic book; Italy; WW]

First publication: 1969; Creators: Furio Viano, Sandro Angiolini; Story: Furio Viano, Paolo Ghelardini; Art: Sandro Angiolini; Publisher: Furio Viano Editore.

Nicknamed "l'indiana bianca" (the white Indian woman), Vartan—the daughter of a Sioux princess and an English lord—prefers to dress as an Indian girl.

The sexually adventurous blonde gunslinger Vartan was involved in the occasional supernatural adventure involving monsters and vampires during the 200-issue run of her comic book. Her name and looks were loosely modeled on those of French female singer Sylvie Vartan.

Vengeance of the Vapor [Comic book; WW]

First comic book publication: May 2007; Story: Sal Cipriano; Art: Jok; Publisher: Markosia Enterprises.

The mysterious masked and cloaked figure known as the Vapor takes on the Heavy Gang who have gained control of the former gold mining town of Tin Cup. A mix of spaghetti Western and masked vigilante.

The Vigilante [Comic book character; WMW]

First appearance: *Action Comics* #42 (November 1941); Creators: Mort Weisinger, Mort Meskin; Publisher: National Periodical Publications-DC Comics.

A contemporary Western featuring singing cowboy Greg Sanders [Saunders]. Following the murder of his father Sheriff Sanders during a stagecoach robbery, Greg moonlights as cowboy crimefighter The Vigilante, pursuing his prey on his motorcycle.

The Vigilante possessed no extraordinary powers but had great skill as an expert marksman, motorcyclist, horseman and musician. A member of the All-Star Squadron and the Seven Soldiers of Victory and an honorary member of the *Justice League of America*, Greg Saunders spent almost twenty years in the Old West of the 1800s in a revised history (retroactive continuity) of the Vigilante.

The comic strip was adapted into the 15-part Columbia Pictures serial *The Vigilante: Fighting Hero of the West*. To celebrate the achievement National Periodical Publications published a one-shot free souvenir issue of *Action Comics* featuring *The Vigilante* on the cover.

See: *Justice League Unlimited*; *Pulp Heroes*; *Seven Soldiers*

The Vigilante: Fighting Hero of the West (1947) [Film serial; WMW]

Premiere: May 22, 1947; Main Cast: Ralph Byrd as Greg Sanders, Ramsay Ames as Betty Winslow, Lyle Talbot as George Pierce, George Offerman Jr. as Stuff, Robert Barron as Prince of Aravania; Producer: Sam Katzman; Story: Lewis Clay, Arthur Hoerl, George H. Plympton; Director: Wallace Fox; 285 min.; Columbia Pictures; b/w.

Loosely based on the DC Comics character appearing in *Action Comics*. A Western film actor described as the "Prairie Troubadour" (changed from the comic book's radio singing cowboy) leads a secret double life as a government agent.

The Vigilante attempts to track down the nefarious X-1 and the rare "Tears of Blood" pearls that are believed to have a 1,000-year-old curse placed upon them.

Chapter titles: 1. *The Vigilante Rides Again*; 2. *Mystery of the White Horses*; 3. *Double Peril!*; 4. *Desperate Flight*; 5. *In the Gorilla's Cage*; 6. *Battling the Unknown*; 7. *Midnight Rendezvous*; 8. *Blasted to Eternity*; 9. *The Fatal Flood*; 10. *Danger Ahead*; 11. *X-1 Closes In*; 12. *Danger Rides the Rails*; 13. *The Trap That Failed*; 14. *Closing In*; 15. *The Secret of the Skyroom*

Viking [Comic book character; France; WW]

First appearance: *Bronco* #1 (1966); Art: Annibale Casabianca; Publisher: Editions Lug.

Viking a.k.a. Rothgar fights for justice with superhuman strength in the early days of the settlement of the New World.

Viking returned to comic books in 2001 in *Special-Rodeo* #170 when he teamed up with one of *Drago*'s ancestors. It was revealed that he was immortal and had traveled to America with Erik the Red.

Vincent Price Presents [Comic Book; WMW]

Horror anthology comic book.

"Soulless Sam" [WMW]

First publication: March, 2010; Story: Nick Lyons; Art: Juan Tomajok; Publisher: Bluewater Productions.

Emily attempts to start a new life with her son Peter after her husband is brutally murdered by psychotic gunslinger Soulless Sam, but Sam has other plans for them.

A Visit from an Incubus (2001) [Short Film; WW]

Main Cast: Anna Biller as Lucy McGee, Jared Sanford as the Incubus, Natalia Schroeder as Madeleine, Gerald "J.J." Johnson as Saloon Manager, Joe Babicki as Bartender; Story-Producer-Director: Anna Biller; 26 min.; Anna Biller Productions; Color.

Interior from *Viking* (1965). Art by **Annibale Casabianca**. © **Mosaic Multimedia. Used with permission.**

Lucy McGe, is transformed from a shy, nervous female into a self-confident Old West song-and-dance saloon girl following repeated nightly visits from a demonic incubus.

Voyagers! [TV series; SFW]

Main Cast: Jon-Erik Hexum as Phineas Bogg, Meeno Peluce as Jeffrey Jones. Creator-Executive Producer: James D. Parriott; 20 × 60 min.; James D. Parriott Productions, Scholastic Productions, Universal TV; Color.

The time-traveling adventures of former pirate Phineas Bogg and the Voyagers and their mission to correct the mistakes of history.

"BULLY AND BILLY" (1:03) [SFW]

Air date: October 24, 1982; Guest Stars: Gregg Henry as Theodore Roosevelt, Frank Koppala as Billy the Kid; Story: B. W. Sandefur; Director: Virgil W. Vogel.

Arriving in Santiago, Cuba, during the Spanish-American War, Phineas and Jeffrey discover the Spanish are winning and that Billy the Kid killed Theodore Roosevelt in 1880. They decide to travel to 1880 and the Old West to prevent the presidential assassination.

"BUFFALO BILL & ANNIE OAKLEY PLAY THE PALACE" (1:12) [SFW]

Air date: January 9, 1983; Guest Stars: Diane Civita (Cary) as Annie Oakley, Robert Donner as Buffalo Bill Cody, Lurene Tuttle as Queen Victoria; Story: Jill Sherman Donner; Director: Alan J. Levi.

Phineas and Jeffrey help Annie Oakley with her performance in Buffalo Bill's Wild West Show in England.

La Vuelta del Charro Negro (1941) [Film; Mexico; WW]

Premiere: June 18, 1941; Main Cast: Raúl de Anda as Roberto/El Charro Negro, El Chicote as El Chicote, Agustin Isunza as Emeterio, Gilberto Gonzalez as Doctor, Carmen Conde as Marta, Fernando Fernández as Fernando; Producer-Story-Director: Raúl de Anda; 92 min.; Producciones Raúl de Anda; Spanish; b/w.

In this modern Weird Western, Roberto a.k.a. El Charro Negro discovers that graves are being desecrated by body snatchers. His attempts to corral the culprits lead him to a mad scientist (Gonzalez) who is experimenting on bringing the corpses back to life in his laboratory located in an abandoned monastery.

Comic relief is supplied by El Chicote and Agustin Isunza reprising their roles from *El Charro Negro* (1941).

Wa-Tan-Peh [Comic book character; France; WW]

First appearance: *Special-Rodeo* (2003); Art: Luciano Bernasconi; Publisher: Semic Comics.

Spin-off series of **Ozark**. Wa-Tan-Peh is a young apprentice shaman to Ozark in the Old West.

The Walking Dead [Comic book; Television series; Novel; Video game; SFW]

Deputy Sheriff Rick Grimes is one of the few survivors of an epidemic that has wiped out mankind. When he awakes from a coma he must adapt to a new world where civilized society is just a memory and the undead roam the earth in search of human flesh. Searching for his wife and son he travels to a military evacuation zone in Atlanta but meets more hostility when a former partner attempts to murder him. Grimes decides to gather the remaining survivors and travel to safer territory but the new world of the undead is a hostile land and survival is a day-to-day proposition.

1. Comic book
Creators: Robert Kirkman, Tony Moore; Writer: Robert Kirkman; Art: Tony Moore, Charlie Adlard, Stefano Gaudiano; First publication: October, 2003; Publisher: Image Comics.

The Eisner Award winning comic book has received critical acclaim. "Through the blasted American landscape, Kirkman's comic conjures a vision of life and undeath that challenges the stereotypes about gender and identity while telling a quintessential Western tale about grit, determination, and survival."—Jeffrey A. Sartain, *Undead in the West II* (Scarecrow Press 2013): 250-251.

2. Television series.
Premiere: October 31, 2010; Main Cast: Andrew Lincoln as Rick Grimes, Steven Yeun as Glenn Rhee, Chandler Riggs as Carl Grimes, Norman Reedus as Daryl Dixon, Melissa McBride as Carol

Wa-Tan-Peh in "Le Totem." Story by Jean-Marc Laine, art by Luciano Bernasconi. © Mosaic Multimedia. Used with permission.

Peletier, Lauren Cohan as Maggie Greene; Creator: Frank Darabont; Based on the comic book series by Robert Kirkman and Tony Moore; 44 min.; American Movie Classics (AMC), Circle of Confusion, Valhalla Entertainment, Darkwood Productions; Color.

Many critics have compared the highly successful AMC TV series to the Western. Erin Overbey of *The New Yorker* (October 12, 2012) commented: "While it does feature the undead, the series actually draws on the iconography and mood of the Western, complete with a reluctant sheriff, a wilderness to be explored, and 'savages' to be fought…. It also does something quite daring with a largely forgotten genre, transforming the gunslinger myth of the Old West into a new parable for our time."

A companion TV series *Fear the Walking Dead* set in Los Angeles premiered on AMC August 23, 2015.

3. Novel

Thomas Dunne began publishing a series of novels based on the television series in October 2011, starting with *The Rise of the Governor* by Robert Kirkman and Jay Bonansinga.

4. Video game

Release date: April 24, 2012; Story: Sean Vanaman, Mark Darin, Gary Whitta; Designers: Sean Vanaman, Mark Darin, Jake Rodkin, Harrison G. Pink, Andrew Langley, Sean Ainsworth; Platforms: Ouya, PlayStation, Xbox; Developer-Publisher: Telltale Games.

This interactive drama, graphic adventure video game is based on the comic book series. The action takes place shortly after rise of the zombies and includes new characters created for the five-episode game.

In March 2013, *The Walking Dead: Survival Instinct*, an action first-person shooter video game that serves as a prequel to the TV series, was released by Terminal Reality-Activision.

Walking Wolf: A Weird Western [Novel; WW]

Author: Nancy A. Collins; First publication: Shingletown CA: Mark V. Ziesing, 1995.

Billy Skillet, a white man raised by Comanches, is traveling companion to a vampire cowboy and part-werewolf.

Walt Disney's Comics and Stories [Comic book]

This anthology title featured a *Zorro* comic strip based on the Disney TV series.

"GHOSTLY CONFESSION" [WMW]

First publication: #275 (August 1963); Publisher: Dell Publishing Co.

After Zorro saves an innocent man from execution, the real killer believes the man he framed has returned from the grave as a ghost to seek vengeance.

Wanted Across Time [Novel; WWR]

Author: Eugenia Riley; First publication: New York: Avon Books, 1997.

Annie Dillon, travels through time to 1885, where she is mistaken for outlaw Rotten Rosie and taken prisoner by bounty hunter Sam Noble.

Wanted Undead or Alive [RPG book; WW]

Author: Paul Rickert; First publication: 2001; GURPS Deadlands Dime Novel #2; Publisher: Steve Jackson Games.

Sean Bailey seeks revenge on those who caused his death. Bounty hunter Caleb Harling must stop him before Bailey's End becomes a literal ghost town.

The Warlords of Mars [Novel; SW]

Author: **Edgar Rice Burroughs**; First publication: Chicago: A. C. McClurg, 1919.

His quest to rescue his wife, princess Dejah Thoris, from the Temple of the Sun takes **John Carter** to the polar regions of the north and a defining battle.

The third novel in the Barsoom trilogy.

Warpath [Comic book character; SFW]

First appearance: *New Mutants* #16 (June 1984); Creators; Chris Claremont, Sal Buscema; Publisher: Marvel Comics.

James Proudstar, the brother of original **Thunderbird** John Proudstar, is an Apache who possesses superhuman speed, reflexes, strength and flight. His initial thirst for revenge over his brother's death led him to adopt the name Thunderbird but he soon realized that Professor Charles Xavier was not responsible for the death. After discovering his Apache tribe had been slaughtered on their reservation, he joined the **X-Force** to locate the killers.

The Warrior's Way (2010) [Film; WW]

Premiere: December 3, 2010; Main Cast: Jang Dong

The Warrior's Way (2010), starring Jang Dong Gun as Yang, left, and Nic Sampson as Pug (Rogue, Boram Entertainment).

Gun as Yang, Kate Bosworth as Lynne, Geoffrey Rush as Ronald Lynne, Danny Huston as Colonel Yang, Tony Cox as Eight-Ball; Executive producers: Evi Hong. Timothy White; Story-Director: Sngmoo Lee; 100 min.; Rogue, Boram Entertainment; Color.

After a Sad Flute assassin refuses to kill an infant warrior princess, the last of her clan, he places his name at the top of his own clan's death list. He takes the baby with him to America pursued by his own warrior clan. On the edge of the desert, lies a town full of broken people—Lode, the Paris of the West. The assassin Yang hides among a group of struggling circus performers, forming a special relationship with the knife throwing Lynne, while awaiting the final showdown with his fellow Sad Flute assassins.

This martial arts Western features the occasional nod to the Weird West in the surreal setting of Lode and the almost supernatural abilities of the Sad Flute assassins.

Waste Warriors [RPG book; WW]

Authors: John Hopler, Jay Kyle, Jason Nichols; First publication: 2000; Setting: *Deadlands: Hell on Earth The Wasted West*; Publisher: Pinnacle Entertainment Group.

Includes martial arts and combat rules for the Waste Warriors of Hell on Earth, plus a history of the final days of the Last War.

Wasteland [Comic book; SFW]

First publication: July 2006; Story: Antony Johnston; Art: Christopher Mitten; b/w; Publisher: Oni Press, Inc.

Surviving humans adapt to a desolate America one hundred years after the Big Wet enveloped the land and destroyed civilization. This post-apocalyptic series has been described as a cross between *Preacher*, *Mad Max* (1979), *Deadwood* (2004) and *Dune*.

"The Water Carriers" [Pulp fiction; WW]

Author: **Lon Williams**; Character: **Lee Winters**; *Real Western Stories* (August 1956).

Myra's books inspired in him nightmarish thoughts; even more disturbing were Forlorn Gap's empty, gaping houses, eerie noises and pervading loneliness. It seemed to him—especially when he rode alone—that he lived in a world where he did not belong, or in a time long departed.

This feeling of unreality sometimes made him think that possibly he had already died before some wanted monkey's smoking gun, and rode now as a ghost of his former self.

The Way of the Brave [RPG book;W]

Author: Fred Jandt with Paul Beakley; First publication: 2002; Setting: *Deadlands: The Weird West*; System: d20; Publisher: Pinnacle Entertainment Group.

The Native Americans of Deadlands d20 including Guardian Spirits, Sacred Objects and Secret Societies. Based on the *Deadlands: The Weird West* book *Ghost Dancers*.

The Way of the Dead [RPG book; WW]

Author: Fred Jandt with Lester W. Smith, Shane Lacy Hensley; First publication: 2002; Setting: *Deadlands: The Weird West*; System: d20; Publisher: Pinnacle Entertainment Group.

New powers for the Harrowed in the Weird West. Includes the adventure "Dark Canyon." Based on the *Deadlands: The Weird West* book *Book o' the Dead*.

The Way of the Gun [RPG book; WW]

Authors: Steven Long, Steven Walmsey with John Goff, Shane Lacy Hensley, John Hopler; First publication: 2001; Setting: *Deadlands: The Weird West*; System: d20; Publisher: Pinnacle Entertainment Group.

Weapon tips and maneuvers to become the fastest gun in the Weird West.

The Way of the Huckster [RPG book; WW]

Author: Fred Jandt; Based on original material by John Goff; First publication: 2001; Setting: *Deadlands: The Weird West*; System: d20; Publisher: Pinnacle Entertainment Group.

The haunted history of the huckster. Based on the *Deadlands: The Weird West* book *Hucksters & Hexes*.

The Way of the New Science [RPG book; WW]

Author: Lucien Soulban; Based on original material by John Hopler; First publication: 2002; Setting: *Deadlands: The Weird West*; System: d20; Publisher: Pinnacle Entertainment Group.

Elixirs and Mad Scientists. Based on the *Deadlands: The Weird West* book *Smith Robards*.

The Way of the Righteous [RPG book; WW]

Author: Fred Jandt; Based on original material by John Goff; First publication: 2003; Setting: *Deadlands: The Weird West*; System: d20; Publisher: Pinnacle Entertainment Group.

D20 class book for the Blessed characters of the Weird West plus the enemies of the faith. Includes the adventure "The Mission." Based on the *Deadlands: The Weird West* book *Fire & Brimstone*.

Weird Business [Comic book anthology; WW]

First publication: 1995; Editors: **Joe R. Lansdale**, Richard Klaw; Publisher: MoJo Press.

Twenty-three tales by fantasy, science fiction and horror authors including Robert Bloch, Roger Zelazny, Michael Moorcock, Nancy Collins, Howard Waldrop, Poppy Z. Brite and artists John Lucas, Omaha Perez, John Bergin, Miran Kim and Dave Dorman. Includes Norman Partridge's Weird Western strip **Gorilla Gunslinger**.

Weird Science [Comic book]

"Incredible Science Fiction Stories" comic book anthology from EC, "An Entertaining Comic."

"Bum Steer" [SFW]

First publication: *Weird Science* #15 (September-October 1952); Story: Albert B. Feldstein; Art: Joe Orlando; Publisher: EC.

A cowboy and his horse are spooked by a weird horse-like creature. They find themselves in a spaceship surrounded by other human passengers and are told they are guests on a journey to another world. On their journey the human guests are treated to excellent food and the company of beautiful "human" girls. But to his horror the cowboy finds himself lured by a girl to a slaughterhouse with humans strung up like cattle. He is the next in line for the slaughter in the human food chain.

The Weird, Weird West [Juvenile book; WW]

Authors: Johnny Ray Barnes Jr., Marty M. Engle; First publication: San Diego CA: Montage Publications, 1996.

An earthquake releases zombie gunslinger Clayton T. Motley from his grave and his first thought is for revenge. Two-hundred years ago, one of Shane Reece's ancestors shot Motley. He fled to a cave where he died, but the bullet possessed strange properties that had an unusual effect on Motley. Now Fairfield is his destination and Shane Reece is his target.

Book 16 of the *Strange Matter* children's book series.

The Weird Weird West: Marvel Super-heroes [RPG game; WW]

Release date:1989; Role-Playing Game; Design-Author: Ray Winninger; Publisher: TSR, Inc.

Dodge City, Kansas, 1871: Due to a temporal time slip, the armies of Napoleon Bonaparte, Genghis Khan, and Alexander the Great are engaged in battle with each other.

Thrown into the mix are Marvel super-villains Doctor Doom, Mysterio, Black Knight, Scorpion and Sandman plus dinosaurs, alien invaders, a Mark Twain android and Albert Einstein.

The Avengers find allies in **Ghost Rider,** *Two-Gun Kid*, *Kid Colt*, *Rawhide Kid*, **Texas Twister, Red Wolf** and **Shooting Star** to defeat the armies and return the Old West to normal.

The second in the three-part "Time Warp" series of adventures.

Weird West [Comic book; WW]

1. First publication: 1994; Creators-Story: Noel K. Hannan, Rik Rawling; Art: Rik Rawling, Tom Simonton, Derek Grey, John Weldind, Kevin Cullen; Three-issue mini-series; Publisher: FantaCo Enterprises Inc.

Hobo musician Johnny Tumbleweed and reluctant shaman Joseph Thunderhead are featured in this mini-series set in the Supernatural Disaster Zone (SDZ) of the southwestern United States, otherwise known as the Weird West.

In the year 2066, Chief John Rainsong of the Apache Nation leads his people across state lines into the SDZ and initiates a new Indian Nation in the Weird West.

2. [RPG game; WW] Authors: Andrew Hackard, Stephen Dedman; First publication: 2001; *GURPS Deadlands* series.

The American West in 1877 is populated with undead gunslingers, malevolent Indian spirits and the malicious Reckoners.

Weird Western Adventures of Haakon Jones [Book anthology; WW]

Author: Aaron B. Larson; First publication: Shelburne, Ontario: Battered Silicon Dispatch Box, 1999.

Leaving his farm in Minnesota, Haakon Jones encounters many weird adventures as he journeys throughout the American West and beyond.

A collection of 36 Weird Western stories featuring Jones and his sidekick Small Jumper, originally published in *Classic Pulp Fiction Stories,* *Double Danger Tales, Of Unicorns and Space Stations* and *Trails.*

Weird Western Tales [Comic book; WW]

1. First publication: #12, June-July 1972; Publisher: DC Comics.

Following the successful launch of *Weird War Tales* in September-October 1971, DC Comics decided to attempt the same format with their Western line-up. *Weird Western Tales* evolved out of *All-Star Western* and continued the numbering sequence of that title. The first issue featured **Jonah Hex, Bat Lash, El Diablo** and **Pow Wow Smith**. It became apparent that Jonah Hex was the most popular character in the comic book. His name soon dominated the covers and continued until his final issue #38 in February 1977. **Scalphunter** replaced him as the cover feature for the remaining 32 issues. The series had a respectable eight-year run before its final issue #70 in August 1980.

2. First publication: April 2001; Publisher: Vertigo.

Four-issue anthology mini-series includes the talents of Dave Gibbons, Rick Burchett, **Joe R. Lansdale,** Paul Gulacy, Bruce Jones and Peter Milligan.

Welcome to Blood City (1977) [Film; U.K.-Canada; WW]

Main Cast: Jack Palance as Frendlander, Keir Dullea as Lewis, Samantha Eggar as Katherine; Executive Producer: Stanley Chase; Story: StephenSchneck, Michael Winder; Director: PeterSasdy; 96 min.; Stanley Chase Productions, EMI; Color.

In a strange and unfamiliar Western town, a group of strangers discover the only way to survive is by killing each other.

"The Werewolf" [Pulp fiction; WW]

Author: **Max Brand**; First publication: *Western Story Magazine* (December 18, 1926)

After Christopher Royal flees from gunfighter Harry Main he is convinced of his own cowardice. His sense of fear only increases when he sees a phantom wolf and in defending himself kills his own dog instead. When Royal meets an ancient Cheyenne Indian who talks of werewolves his greatest fears are confirmed. Fears that are intensified when Royal discovers the lifeless body of the Indian with his throat ripped out.

Werewolf: The Wild West [RPG game; WW]

Release date: 1997; Designers: Justin Achilli, Ethan Skemp; Role-Playing Game; System: Storyteller; Publisher: White Wolf Game Studio.

This horror Western RPG game is the Savage West version of *Werewolf: The Apocalypse*. Players' roles include the Garou tribes Uktena, Wen-digo and Iron Riders who battle among themselves and with the minions of the Bane spirit, Storm Eater. The Umbral storms created by Storm Eater cause disease and destruction and within the Umbra spirits can break into the physical realm through the Broken Lands.

Werewolf: The Wild West: A Storytelling Game of Historical Horror [RPG book; WW]

First publication: 1997; Publisher: White Wolf Publishing.

"Werewoman" [Pulp fiction; SW]

Author: **C. L. Moore**; First publication; *Leaves II*, 1938.

Northwest Smith becomes a wolf-man working in unison with a green-eyed were-woman as they are pursued by an unseen menace and an ancient curse. A simple tale is told with imagination and style as Smith moves through a mystical inner and outer landscape.

WesterNoir [Comic book; UK; WW]

First publication: 2012; Story: Dave West; Art: Gary Crutchley, Roland Bird, Pedro Lopez; Graphic design: Andy Bloor; Publisher: Accent UK.

Former sheriff Josiah Black hunts supernatural creatures in the Old West. Adventures include encounters with a demon spawn family, Louisiana swamp men and demonic Mississippi mermaids.

Tales of WesterNoir features short stories that supplement the main series.

Western Gothic: Ballad of Utopia [Trade Paperback; WW]

First publication: July 2005; Story: Barry Buch-

Cover of *Western Gothic: The Ballad of Utopia* (July 2005). Story by Barry Buchanan, art by Mike Hoffman. © Barry Buchanan & Mike Hoffman. Used with permission.

anan; Art: Mike Hoffman; Publisher: Antimatter Hoffman International.

Collected stories from the **Ballad of Utopia** mini-series.

Western Legends [Comic book; WW]

First publication: July 2006; Story: Jeff Parker, Karl Kesel, Fred Van Lente; Art: Tomm Coker, Carmine Di Giandomenico, Homs, Jack Kirby; Publisher: Marvel Comics.

Three all-new tales. The first features **Hurricane**, the Fastest Man in the West, in a story of bounty hunters and revenge by Parker and Coker.

In the second story (by Kesel and Di Giandomenico), **Red Wolf** is put to the test by a group of hooligans. The final new story by Van Lente and Homs centers on Major Brett Saber, the Man from Fort Rango, leader of an unruly group of frontier soldiers. The Native Indians threaten their stronghold but a mythical man-beast menaces Saber, his soldiers and the Indians.

A reprint of the origin of the **Rawhide Kid** by **Stan Lee** and Jack Kirby completes the issue.

See: *The Mighty Marvel Western*

Western Tales of Black Rider [Comic book]

First publication: #28 (May 1955); Publisher: Atlas Comics.

This title, which continued the numbering from **Black Rider**, ran to four issues before continuing into *Gunsmoke Western*.

Western Tales of Terror [Comic book; WW]

First publication: November 2004; Publisher: Hoarse & Buggy Productions.

Black-and-white horror Western anthology title that ran to five issues and featured **Hector Plasm** in the first two issues.

"Hector Plasm in: Ghost Town"

First publication: *Western Tales of Terror* #1, November 2004; Story: Benito Cereno; Art: Nate Bellegarde.

Hector Plasm, Sinner and Saint must free the town of Lagos of its spectral gunslinger.

"Hector Plasm in: Skull Creek Reservation"

First publication: *Western Tales of Terror* #2, December 2004; Story: Benito Cereno; Art: Nate Bellegarde.

Contemporary Western tale about ghosts haunting a trailer.

Westward [RPG book; SPW]

Author: Peter Schweighofer; First publication: 2013; Publisher: Wicked North Games, LLC.

Described as a Steampunk Western, this cinematic OpenD6 role-playing game for 3 or more players is set in the distant future on the desolate and hostile planet Westward. After forming a colony in Capital City the human explorers and their families venture into the Badlands, where the outcast humans known as the Ferals lay in wait. With the technology of the Steamtech helping them stay alive, the players explore and navigate the new, wild frontier by air and land.

Westward Weird [Short story anthology: WW]

Editors: Martin Harry Greenberg, Kerrie Hughes; First publication: New York: Daw Books, 2012.

Thirteen original stories with Weird, Steampunk, Science Fiction or Space Western themes. Subjects include time travel in "Maybe Another Time" by Dean Wesley Smith; zombies threatening a steam punk mining community in "Lowstone" by Anton Strout; werewolves and an Indian shaman in "Lone Wolf" by Jody Lynn Nye; a man-eating chimaera in "The Flower of Arizona" by Seanan McGuire; the devil as a cattle rustler in "The Temptation of Eustace Prudence McAllen" by Jay Lake; a city in the sky, financed by Wild Bill Hickok is attacked by demons in "The Last Master of Aeronautical Winters" by Larry D. Sweazy; European vampires meet their match when they travel to the United States in "Coyote, Spider, Bat" by Steven Saus. Jeff Mariotte, J. Steven York, Jennifer Brozek, David Gerrold, Brenda Cooper, Kristine Kathryn Rusch and Christopher McKitterick also contribute stories.

Westworld (1973) [Film; TV series; SFW]

Premiere: November 21, 1973; Main Cast: James Brolin as John Blane, Richard Benjamin as Peter Martin, Yul Brynner as The Gunslinger; Producer: Paul N. Lazarus III; Story-Director: Michael Crichton; 88 min.; MGM; Color.

For $1,000 a day you can live your dreams in the adult amusement theme park Delos. But the fantasy soon becomes a nightmare world when the automated android Gunslinger in Western World begins to kill the patrons and pursues John Blane and Peter Martin through Medieval World.

Variety (1973) said: "Westworld is an excellent film, which combines solid entertainment, chilling topicality, and superbly intelligent serio-comic story values. Michael Crichton's original script is as superior as his direction."

2. Television series (2016).

Jonathan Nolan adapted Michael Crichton's original story for a 60 minute HBO TV series starring Ed Harris as "The Man in Black" and Anthony Hopkins as Dr. Robert Ford.

See: *Futureworld*

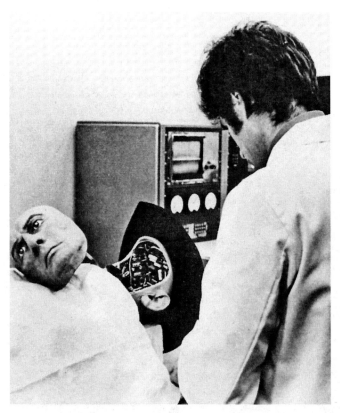

In *Westworld* (1973), The Gunslinger (Yul Brynner) is being cleaned by a Delos laboratory technician (MGM).

What's New Scooby Doo? (2002) [Animated TV series]

The adventures of the lovable Great Dane, Scooby-Doo who despite being a coward helps his gang of friends solve mysteries involving ghosts and all other things that go bump in the night.

"Go West Young Scoob" (3:02) [SFW]

Air date: February 5, 2005; Voice Cast: Frank Welker as Scooby Doo, Freddy, Casey Kasem as Shaggy, Mindy Cohn as Velma, Grey DeLisle as Daphne; Story: Ed Scharlach: Director: Chuck Sheetz; 30 min.; Warner Bros. Animation, Cartoon Network; Color.

The gang visits Cyber Gulch to see the Western robots when a power outage plays havoc with the robots circuitry and a group of renegade cowboy robots take control. But the robots feed on human energy to survive, placing everyone in mortal danger.

Whisky and Ghosts (1974) [Film; Italy-Spain; WW]

International release title for *Whisky e Fantasmi.*

Whisky e Fantasmi (1974) [Film; Italy-Spain; WW]

Main Cast: Tom Scott [Alberto Terracina] as Napoleone B. Higgins, Fred Harris [Fernando Arrien] as the Ghost of Davy Crockett, Maribel Martín as Rosy, Rafael Albaicín as Paco; Producer: Carlo Ponti; Story: Gianni Simonelli, Antonio Margheriti; Director: Anthony M. Dawson [Antonio Margheriti]; 105 min.; CIPI Cinematografica S.A., Compagnia Cinematografica Champion, Laser Films; Color.

The ghost of a drunk Davy Crockett attempts to help a traveling salesman (Scott) locate hidden treasure. Comically complicating matters are a group of Mexican bandits, a love interest and the ghosts of Johnny Appleseed and Pecos Bill.

A Whisper in the Wind [Novel; WWR]

Author: Madeline Baker; First publication: New York: N.Y. Leisure Books, 1991.

In the Black Hills of 1876, Cheyenne warrior Michael Wolf and Elayna share their love for each other across barriers of time and space.

Commenting on her work, Madeline Baker said, "I find the whole idea of time travel fascinating. The thought of sending a modern woman back in time, or bringing a man from the Old West to the future, just sounded like a lot of fun, plus it added an interesting twist to the plot. Fish-out-of-water stories are always popular, and my time travel romances are among my most popular books."

The White Buffalo (1977) [Film; WW]

Premiere: May 1977; Main Cast: Charles Bronson as Wild Bill Hickok/James Otis, Kim Novak as Mrs. Poker Jenny Schermerhorn, Will Sampson as Crazy Bull, Jack Warden as Charlie Zane, Clint Walker as Whistling Jack Kileen, Stuart Whitman as Winifred Coxy; Producer: Dino De Laurentiis; Screenplay: Richard Sale (based on his novel); Director: J. Lee Thompson; 97 min.; Dino De Laurentiis Company; Color.

When Wild Bill Hickok sees the vision of a large albino buffalo in a series of nightmares, he becomes obsessed with finding the beast and destroying it. He teams up with Crazy Horse who shares Hickok's obsessive quest but is searching for the buffalo and possession of its sacred white pelt so his dead child can find peace in heaven.

Whiz Comics [Comic book]

Superhero anthology title featuring the adventures of Captain Marvel, Ibis the Invincible, Spy Smasher, Dan Dare, Golden Arrow, Scoop Smith and Lance O'Casey.

"THE REDSKIN RIDDLE" [WW]

First publication: #27 (February 1942); Art: C.C. Beck; Publisher: Fawcett Publications.

Captain Marvel battles the death god of the Katonkas. Featuring Skull Face.

"AT BOYS' RANCH" [WW]

First publication: #103 (November 1948); Story: Otto Binder; Art: Pete Costanza; Publisher: Fawcett Publications.

When Billy Batson is told that Tom Boyd's Boys' Ranch is being attacked by the Black Buzzard Gang, he changes into Captain Marvel. The land lies on a valuable salt bed, and the gang members know it.

Wicked [Novel; WWR]

Author: Evelyn Rogers; First publication: New York: Love Spell, 2000.

An angel gives Cad Rankin one last chance to save his soul from damnation: clean up Rough Cut, Texas, or suffer the consequences of failure. When he meets the pure but sensual Amy Lattimer searching for her father, temptation and redemption meet head on.

The Wicked West [Graphic novel; WW]

First publication: October 2004; Creators: Todd Livingston, Robert Tinnell, Neil Vokes, Scott Keating; Publisher: Image Comics.

Cotton Coleridge, suspected of the murder of young Temperance Jones in the Texas town of Javer's Tanks, attempts to discover the supernatural secret behind her death.

The Wicked West Volume II: Abomination and Other Tales [Graphic novel anthology; WW]

First publication: November 2006; Story: Todd Livingston, Robert Tinnell, Neil Vokes, Scott Keating; Publisher: Image Comics.

Cotton Coleridge, cursed cowboy hunter of the undead, was introduced in *The Wicked West*. This anthology explores the reasons behind the curse and the character of Coleridge. The novella *Abomination* is followed by twenty-two short stories of the Weird West.

The Widowmaker [Novel; SW]

Author: **Mike Resnick**; First publication: New York: Bantam Books, 1996.

The adventures of bounty hunter Jefferson Nighthawk, the Widowmaker, and his various clones. Nighthawk has a terminal disease and one final mission: to defeat an assassin terrorizing the Inner Frontier.

The Widomaker Reborn [Novel; SW]

Author: **Mike Resnick**; First publication: New York: Bantam Books, 1997.

The clone of Jefferson Nighthawk is given the double task of rescuing a corrupt politician's daughter from the clutches of a rebel leader whom he must assassinate. But the daughter turns the mission on its head when she offers Nighthawk her father's fortune if he kills her father.

The Widowmaker Unleashed [Novel; SW]

Author: **Mike Resnick**; First publication: New York: Bantam Books, 1998.

Jefferson Nighthawk's terminal disease has been cured and his cryogenic sleep is over. He has aged while frozen in his slumber and he decides to retire. But the two Nighthawk clones have been keeping his deadly reputation alive by killing in his name. The Widowmaker realizes he has to face his enemies or else his retirement will be of the permanent kind.

See: *A Gathering of Widowmakers*

Wild [Novel; WW]

Author: Lincoln Crisler; First publication: Santa Rosa, CA: Damnation Books, 2011.

When Civil War veteran Colonel Albert Waters and his son Henry disappear from their El Paso, Texas, home Deputy Sheriff Kurt Kearney, the mysterious Matthias Jacoby and infamous New Mexico rancher, cattle rustler and outlaw Black Tom Catch search for clues. They find black magic and zombies along the trail.

Wild ARMs [Video game; SW]

Release date: December 20, 1996 (Japan); Role-Playing Game (RPG), 3rd Person Perspective; Developer: Media. Vision Entertainment, Inc., Sony Computer Entertainment (PlayStation); Executive Producer: Akira Sato; Publisher: Sony Computer Entertainment (SCEA).

The player controls 15-year-old ARMs weapons operator Rudy Roughnight and his companions, treasure hunter Jack Van Burace and apprentice mage Cecilia Lynne Adlehyde.

The group journeys through the landscape of Filgaia where they encounter robotic golems, an army of demons, the Quarter Knights and many other foes in their attempt to save the world from destruction.

Sequels: *Wild ARMs: 2nd Ignition* (1999), *Wild ARMs: Advanced 3rd* (2002), *Wild ARMs Alter Code: F* (2003), Wild ARMs: The 4th Detonator (2005), *Wild ARMs: The Vth Vanguard* (2006).

Wild ARMs: Advanced 3rd [Video game; SPW]

Release date: March 14, 2002 (Japan); Role-Playing Game (RPG), 3rd Person Perspective; Developer: Media. Vision Entertainment, Inc., Sony Computer Entertainment (SCEA). (PlayStation 2); Executive Producers: Akira Sato, Masatsuka Saeki, Fumiya Takeno; Publisher: Sony Computer Entertainment.

Four "Drifters" roam the desolate Old West–style landscape attempting to unlock the mysteries of an ancient prophecy. Opposing them are a group of scientists known as The Prophets and The Demons of legend.

Wild ARMs Alter Code: F [Video game; SPW]

Release date: November 27, 2003 (Japan); Role-Playing Game (RPG), 3rd Person Perspective; Developer: Media. Vision Entertainment, Inc., Sony Computer Entertainment (PlayStation 2); Publisher: Sony Computer Entertainment (SCEA), Agetec.

Enhanced update of *Wild ARMs* for Playstation 2 complete with 3D environments.

Wild ARMs: 2nd Ignition [Video game; SPW]

Release date: September 2, 1999 (Japan); Role-Playing Game (RPG), 3rd Person Perspective; Developer: Media. Vision Entertainment, Inc., Sony Computer Entertainment (PlayStation); Executive Producer: Akira Sato; Publisher: Sony Computer Entertainment (SCEA).

In this sequel to *Wild ARMs*, the Old West–style landscape of Filgaia is the same but the characters have changed. Nineteen-year-old Ashley Winchester, possessed by the demon Lord Blazer, leads the counter terrorist ARMS (Agile Remote Mission Squad) group consisting of Crest Sorceress in training Lilka Eleniak and former war hero turned bad guy Brad Evans in their battle against the terrorist organization known as Odessa.

Wild ARMs: The Vth Vanguard [Video game; SPW]

Release date: December 14, 2006 (Japan); Role-Playing Game (RPG), 3rd Person Perspective; Developer: Media. Vision Entertainment, Inc., Sony Computer Entertainment (PlayStation 2); Publisher: Sony Computer Entertainment.

Youngsters Dean Stark and Rebecca Streisand look upwards to see a giant arm of a golem falling from the sky. When they approach the arm, they find Avril, a young girl with no recollection of her life.

A journey begins across Filgaia to discover more about the little girl.

Wild ARMs: Twilight Venom (1999) [Anime; Japan; SFW]

Premiere: October 18, 1999–March 27, 2000; Animation: Bee Train; Directors: Itsuro Kawasaki, Koichi Mashimo; 22×30 min.; Color.

Famed gunslinger Sheyenne Rainstorm finds himself reborn in the body of a ten-year-old boy. Sorceress Loretta Oratio, Dr. Kiel Aronakus, vampire Mirabelle Graceland and genius Jerusha help Sheyenne search for his missing body and discover the secret behind the mysterious ARMs weapons.

Season One

"SLEEPING DIRTY" (1:01); Air date: October 18, 1999.

Loretta Oratorio and Mirabelle Graceland cross paths with young Sheyenne Rainstorm while attempting to steal the ARMS.

"ARMs CRAZY" (1:02); Air date: October 25, 1999.

Sheyenne searches for his real body while Mirabelle and Loretta attempt to steal from an ARMS collector.

"Desert Dragon Fantasy" (1:03); Air date: November 1, 1999.

Sheyenne, Kiel, and Isaac set out to rescue Machela from the Sand Dragon.

"The Faluna Bible" (1:04); Air date: November 8, 1999.

Sheyenne continues the search for his real body at the fortress library of Libra.

"Portrait of Lana" (1:05); Air date: November 15, 1999.

Sheyenne and Kiel look for Sheyenne's real body while attending the reading of the will of a deceased painter and meet up again with Loretta and Mirabelle.

"Affair of the Faraia Express" (1:06); Air date: November 22, 1999.

A train journey on the Faraia Express turns into a fiasco for everyone aboard.

"Someday My Robber Will Come" (1:07); Air date: November 29, 1999.

Loretta and Mirabelle seek to steal treasure from a convent.

"Mouth Wide Shut" (1:08); Air date: December 6, 1999.

Sheyenne, Kiel, Isaac, Loretta, Mirabelle and Jerusha become involved in a clan feud.

"The Slave of the Game" (1:09); Air date: December 13, 1999.

Sheyenne and Kiel attempt to find out more about the mysterious Queen of Hearts while Mirabelle tries to rescue Loretta from a life of slavery.

"Guilty or..." (1:10); Air date: December 20, 1999.

When a young girl saves Sheyenne, Kiel, and Isaac from an ambush, they promise to rescue the young girl's father from the baddies.

"No Home, No Body" (1:11); Air date: January 10, 2000.

Sheyenne, Kiel, and Isaac discover Sheyenne's hometown of Parskiarka is now underwater.

"Lie, Laila, Lie" (1:12); Air date: January 17, 2000.

Sheyenne prepares to rescue Laila from evil scientists, aware that she is a decoy and he is the real target.

"Lullaby of the Noble-Red" (1:13); Air date: January 24, 2000.

Sheyenne, Kiel and Isaac promise to return a baby girl to her parents. But Mirabelle, the father of the baby and a martial arts expert have different plans.

"Interview with the Ampire" (1:14); Air date: January 31, 2000.

The aging Count Ampire offers Mirabelle's family money in exchange for her hand in marriage.

"Natural Born Angel" (1:15); Air date: February 7, 2000.

Sybil tells Sheyenne she will reveal the location of his real body if she is safely escorted to the next town. But the journey isn't as simple as it sounds.

"Fatal Goddess" (1:16); Air date: February 14, 2000.

Sheyenne despairs over his repeated failure to locate his real body.

"Child at Heart" (1:17); Air date: February 21, 2000.

While recovering from memory loss, Sheyenne protects Dr. Clark from a female outlaw and her gang.

"The Day of the Bacchus" (1:18); Air date: February 28, 2000.

Kiel and Isaac join forces with assassin Golgol 30 to confront the men chasing Laila.

"Gone with the Smoke" (1:19); Air date: March 6, 2000.

Sheyenne, Kiel, and Isaac arrive at their final destination, to discover they are wanted.

"Faluna Struck" (1:20); Air date: March 13, 2000.

Sheyenne discovers that Kianu has been using Sheyenne's body.

"Once Upon a Time in Fargaia" (1:21); Air date: March 20, 2000.

Sheyenne duels with Kianu as centuries-old secrets are finally revealed.

"The Last of Sheyenne" (1:22); Air date: March 27, 2000.

The frustrated desires of a goddess result in the second coming of Twilight Venom.

Wild Bill Pecos [Comic book character]

Adventures of the marshal of Tombstone City, Wild Bill Pecos, and his deputy, Nuggets Nugent.

"THE RIDDLE OF THE PETRIFIED FOREST" [WMW]

First publication: *The Westerner* (1949); Art: Mort Lawrence; Publisher: Patches Publications.

Wild Bill Pecos and Nuggets Nugent investigate reports of ghostly sightings in Petrified Forest. To their amazement they discover the ghosts are albinos, "the last survivors of an ancient cave man tribe" living deep within the forest.

Wild Guns [Video game; SFW]

Release date: August 12, 1994; Third-person fixed viewpoint shooter (TPS); Developer: Natsume; Publisher: Natsume, Titus Software.

Wild Guns is a science fiction Western shooter from a third-person perspective. Annie hires bounty hunter Clint to help her seek revenge on the gang who killed a member of her family.

Levels of play include Carson City, Desolation Canyon, an armored train, a gold mine and an ammunition depot. Robots serve as adversaries.

Wild Horse Phantom (1944) [Film; WMW]

Premiere: October 28, 1944; Main Cast: Buster Crabbe as Billy Carson, Al "Fuzzy" St. John as Al St. John, Elaine Morey as Marian Garnet, Budd Buster as Ed Garnet, Kermit Maynard as Link Daggett; Producer: Sigmund Neufeld; Story: Milton Raison, George Wallace Sayre; Director: Sam Newfield; 56 min.; Producers Releasing Corporation; b/w.

Link Daggett and his gang are allowed to escape from prison so that Billy Carson can follow them through the labyrinths of supposedly haunted tunnels in the Wild Horse mine to recover stolen bank money.

Although the series of "Billy Carson" Westerns was set in the Old West, this feature begins with a 1940s prison break, complete with automobiles, before returning to an Old West setting.

Wild Times: Deathblow [Comic book; SPW]

First publication: June 1999; Story: Norman Partridge; Art: Tommy Lee Edwards; Publisher: WildStorm-DC Comics.

Western adventure starring gunslinger Michael Cray a.k.a. Deathblow in a tale about the passing of the Old West as an industrialist seeks to gain power at the turn of the century with his steam-controlled airplane.

Wild West [Pulp; UK; WW]

Alternate title for *Wild West Weekly*.

Wild West C.O.W. Boys of Moo Mesa (1992) [Animated TV series; SFW]

Premiere: September 13, 1992; Main Cast: Pat Fraley as Marshal Moo Montana, Jim Cummings as Dakota Duke/Sheriff Terrorbull/The Masked Bull/Skull Duggery, Jeff Bennett as Cowlarado Kid, Kay Lenz as Kate Cudster; Creator: Ryan Brown; Producer: Mitch Schauer; 26 × 30 min.; Greengrass, DiC, Ruby-Spears, King World, Gunther-Wahl Productions; Color.

A radioactive comet crashes into the Western desert, causing a huge mesa cloud that transforms the local cattle and animals into cowboys.

Season One

Another Fine Moo Mesa (1:01); *A Sheepful of Dollars* (1:02); *A Snake in Cow's Clothing* (1:03); *Bang 'em High* (1:04); *Bulls of a Feather* (1:05); *Dances with Bulls* (1:06); *Legend of Skull Duggery* (1:07); *School Days* (1:08); *Stolen on the River* (1:09); *The Big Cow Wow* (1:10); *Wedding Bull Blues* (1:11); *Westward, Whoa* (1:12); *Thoroughly Moodern Lily* (1:13)

Season Two

Billy the Kidder (2:01); *Boomtown or Bust* (2:02); *Circus Daze* (2:03); *Cow Pirates of Swampy Cove* (2:04); *How the West Was Shrunk* (2:05); *Night of the Cowgoyle* (2:06); *No Face to Hide* (2:07); *No Way to Treat a Lady* (2:08); *Skull Duggery Rides Again* (2:09); *The Cacklin' Kid* (2:10); *The Down Under Gang* (2:11); *The Fastest Filly in the West* (2:12); *The Wild West Pest* (2:13)

2. [Comic book] First publication: 1992; Creator: Ryan Brown; Publisher: Archie Publications.

3. [Arcade game] Release date: 1992; Designer: Ryan Brown; Platform: Shooter Scrolling; Publisher: Konami.

Wild West Companion [RPG book; WW]

Author: James Moore; First publication: 1998; Setting: *Werewolf: The Wild West*; Publisher: White Wolf Publishing.

Combination players and storytellers guide. Includes a history of the World of Darkness in the Savage West, a detailed description of the Storm Umbra and the Storm-Born creatures.

Wild West Weekly [Pulp; UK; WW]

First publication: 1938; Publisher: Amalgamated Press.

Although this U.K.-produced pulp featured predominantly standard Western stories it did venture into Weird Western areas at times with its regular characters The Phantom Sheriff and Willis Screever.

Weird Western stories featuring The Phantom Sheriff:

The Trail of the Robot Robber: First publication: January 7, 1938.

The Trail of the Iron Octopus: First publication: January 14, 1938.

The Trail of the Ten-Inch Cowboys: First publication: Vol. 2 #42.

Weird Western stories featuring Willis Screever:
Willis Screever's Cast-Iron Cowboy: First publication: Vol. 2 #41.

Wild Western [Comic Book]

First published: #3 (September 1948); Publisher: Atlas Comics.

Anthology title that continued the numbering from *Wild West*. The comic book included the occasional Weird Western story featuring **Black Rider**, **Red Larabee, the Gunhawk**, *Kid Colt* and *Two-Gun Kid*.

The Wild, Wild West (1965) [TV series]

Premiere: September 17, 1965; Main Cast: Robert Conrad as James T. West, Ross Martin as Artemus Gordon; Creator: Michael Garrison; Executive Producers: Philip Leacock, Michael Garrison; 104 × 60 min., 2 × 90 min.; CBS; b/w (Season One), Color.

1. A blend of James Bond, steampunk and science fiction set in the Old West of the 1870s, *The Wild Wild West* was an inventive series created by Michael Garrison. Robert Conrad starred as James T. West, a secret agent working for President Ulysses S. Grant. His companion was master of disguise, Artemus Gordon, played by Ross Martin. Their mission was to save America from evil scientists such as Miguelito Loveless, a 3'6" dwarf intent on death and destruction. Plots involved Loveless attempting to poison the world's water with LSD, a giant tuning fork designed to destroy the homes of the rich, deformed puppetmaster Zachariah Skull accusing West of murdering a marionette and a Doctor Faustina creating a robot double of West.

Working from their gadget-filled customized train car, West provided the action with his love of fighting and Gordon portrayed numerous characters with his love of disguises.

Season One [SFW episodes]

"THE NIGHT OF THE GLOWING CORPSE" (1:07)
Air date: October 29, 1965; Story: Henry Sharp; Director: Irving Moore.

The clues to the whereabouts of stolen radioactive franconium lead West and Gordon to a set of fingerprints found on the ankle of an attractive secretary.

"THE NIGHT THAT TERROR STALKED THE TOWN" (1:10)
Air date: November 19, 1965; Guest Stars: Michael Dunn as Dr. Miguelito Loveless, Richard Kiel as Voltaire; Story: John Kneubuhl, Richard Landau; Director: Alvin Ganzer.

West awakes in a ghost town populated by dummies and is imprisoned by Dr. Loveless, who has plans to create a perfect double to replace West.

"THE NIGHT OF THE HUMAN TRIGGER" (1: 12)
Air Date: December 3, 1965; Story: Norman Katkov; Director: Justis Addiss.

West and Gordon are sent to investigate a series of devastating earthquakes accurately predicted in threatening pamphlets warning of destruction.

"THE NIGHT OF THE HOWLING LIGHT" (1: 14)
Air Date: December 17, 1965; Guest Star: Sam Wanamaker as Dr. Arcularis; Story: Henry Sharp; Director: Paul Wendkos.

Evil scientist Dr. Arcularis (Sam Wanamaker) is turning his staff into near-zombies who obey his commands.

"THE NIGHT OF THE STEEL ASSASSIN" (1:16)
Air Date: January 7, 1966; Guest Star: John Dehner as Iron Man Torres; Story: Calvin Clements; Director: Lee H. Katzin.

Following an explosion that left him crippled, Civil War officer Colonel "Iron Man" Torres has reconstructed his body with steel. With superhuman strength, Torres seeks revenge on those who wronged him, including President Grant.

"THE NIGHT OF THE FLAMING GHOST" (1:19) [WW]
Air date: January 21, 1966; Guest Star: John Doucette as John Obedian Brown; Story: Robert Hamner, Preston Wood; Director: Lee H. Katzin

West tracks a man who claims to be abolitionist John Brown and says he cannot die.

"THE NIGHT OF THE PUPPETEER" (1:21) [SPW]
Air Date: February 25, 1966; Guest Star: Lloyd Bochner as Zachariah Skull; Story: Henry Sharp; Director: Irving Moore.

Crazed craftsman Zachariah Skull creates steam-powered life-size puppets for a mock courtroom in order to seek revenge on West and the Supreme Court justices who sentenced him to execution.

"THE NIGHT OF THE DRUID'S BLOOD" (1:24)
Air Date: March 25, 1966; Guest Stars: Don Rickles as Asmodeus, Rhys Williams as Dr. Tristam; Story: Henry Sharp; Director: Ralph Senensky.

Distinguished scientists are bursting into flames. West and Gordon discover that Amadeus and his evil assistant Dr. Tristam are killing them for the knowledge stored in the scientist's preserved brains.

"THE NIGHT OF THE BURNING DIAMOND" (1:26)
Air date: April 8, 1966; Guest Star: Robert Drivas as Morgan Midas; Story: Ken Kolb; Director: Irving Moore.

Investigating the puzzling case of the vanishing Kara diamond, West and Gordon discover that Morgan Midas is using an extract of distilled diamonds to enable him to move at super-speed and commit robberies.

"THE NIGHT OF THE MURDEROUS SPRING" (1:27)
Air date: April 15, 1966; Guest Star: Michael Dunn as Dr. Miguelito Loveless; Story: John Kneubuhl; Director: Richard Donner.

West suffers hallucinations as a result of a powerful drug that Dr. Loveless has created to pollute the water supply and cause mass killing across America.

"THE NIGHT OF THE SUDDEN PLAGUE" (1:28)
Air date: April 22, 1966; Story: Ken Kolb; Director: Irving J. Moore.

The townsfolk of Willow Springs have been paralyzed while the entire town has been stripped of cash. An evil professor is perfecting the paralysis drug to kill the entire population of San Francisco.

Season Two [SFW episodes]

"THE NIGHT OF THE RAVEN" (2:03)
Air Date: September 30, 1966; Guest Stars: Michael Dunn as Dr. Miguelito Loveless, Phyllis Newman as Princess Wanakee; Story: Ed Di Lorenzo; Director: Irving J. Moore.

West and Gordon enter the deserted town of Gravestown to rescue Chief War Eagle's kidnapped daughter Wanakee. The trail leads to their nemesis Dr. Loveless who shrinks West and Princess Wanakee to six inches in height, leaving them to fight a comparatively huge cat.

"THE NIGHT OF THE BIG BLAST" (2:04)
Air date: October 7, 1966; Guest Star: Ida Lupino as Dr. Faustina; Story: Ken Kolb; Director: Ralph Senensky.

Dr. Faustian and her mute servant Miklos bring a corpse, a look-like for Jim West, back to life. Faustina plans to have the duplicate West kill members of President Grant's cabinet and a look-alike Artemus kill the president.

"THE NIGHT OF THE RETURNING DEAD" (2:05)
Air date: October 14, 1966; Guest Stars: Sammy Davis Jr. as Jeremiah; Peter Lawford as Carl Jackson; Story: John Kneubuhl; Director: Richard Donner.

When West and Gordon confront a mysterious Confederate ghost rider, their bullets have no effect. The mysterious Jeremiah, a stable boy, claims to have power over animals and holds the key to the secret of the ghost rider.

"THE NIGHT OF THE FLYING PIE PLATE" (2:06)
Air date: October 21, 1966; Guest Star: Leslie Parrish as Morn; Writer: Daniel Ullman; Director: Robert Sparr.

When three green-skinned women claiming to be Venusians exit a spaceship that has apparently crashlanded and ask to trade their precious gems for gold to fuel their spaceship, West and Gordon sense confidence tricksters at work.

"THE NIGHT OF THE WATERY DEATH" (2:09)
Air date: November 11, 1966; Guest Star: Jocelyn Lane as Dominique; Story: Edward Di Lorenzo, Lew Garfinkle, Leigh Chapman; Director: Irving J. Moore.

West is shot with a dart from a blowgun by a woman dressed as a mermaid at the Mermaid Bar in San Francisco. He awakes aboard a gambling ship with a beautiful woman who screams they are being attacked by a fire-breathing sea dragon.

"THE NIGHT OF THE GREEN TERROR" (2:10)
Air date: November 18, 1966; Guest Star: Michael Dunn as Dr. Miguelito Loveless; Story: John Kneubuhl; Director: Robert Sparr.

West and Gordon, riding through a forest surprisingly devoid of life to meet with Indian chief Bright Star, are approached by a knight in armor and an armed group of "Merry Men" who take them to meet their leader, Robin Hood alias Dr. Loveless. Loveless is killing the food supply of the Indians with his poisonous gas and promises to feed them if they will accept him as their ruler. West and Gordon soon discover Loveless has more lethal plans for his gas.

"The Night of the Man-Eating House" (2:12)

Air date: December 2, 1966; Guest Star: Hurd Hatfield as Liston Lawrence Day; Story: John Kneubuhl; Director: Alan Crosland Jr.

West and Gordon, Sheriff Hollister and prisoner Liston Day rest at a deserted mansion haunted by the ghost of the prisoner's dead mother. A rejuvenated Liston Day plans to kill everyone in the state of Texas.

"The Night of the Lord of Limbo" (2:15)

Air date: December 30, 1966; Guest Star: Ricardo Montalban as Noel Bartley Vautrain; Story: Henry Sharp; Director: Jesse Hibbs.

Crippled Confederate colonel Vautrain travels back in time with West and Gordon to restore his legs and change the outcome of the Civil War by murdering General Grant.

"The Night of the Feathered Fury" (2:17)

Air date: January 13, 1967; Guest Star: Victor Buono as Count Carlos Manzeppi; Story: Henry Sharp; Director: Robert Sparr.

Count Manzeppi imprisons West in a giant bird cage and threatens him with torture unless he reveals the whereabouts of a toy bird. The bird contains the mystical Philosopher's Stone which transforms everything in its presence to gold during a full moon.

"The Night of the Brain" (2:21)

Air date: February 17, 1967; Guest Star: Edward Andrews as Mr. Brain; Story: Calvin Clements; Director: Lawrence Peerce.

West and Gordon receive newspapers with accurate reports of future deaths. They soon learn of Mr. Brain's plans to replace all the world leaders with doubles.

"The Night of the Deadly Bubble" (2:22)

Air date: February 24, 1967; Guest Star: Alfred Ryder as Captain Horatio Philo; Story: Michael Edwards; Director: Irving J. Moore.

Coastal destruction by massive tidal waves is being caused by giant undersea bubbles produced in the volcanic laboratory of Captain Philo.

"The Night of the Surreal McCoy" (2:23)

Air date: March 3, 1967; Guest Star: Michael Dunn as Dr. Miguelito Loveless; Story: John Kneubuhl; Director: Alan Crosland Jr.

Miguelito Loveless' latest invention is a device that allows people to move in and out of paintings. After successfully using a painting to steal a priceless jewel, Loveless plans to have the rulers of the world killed by placing assassins inside paintings.

"The Night of the Colonel's Ghost" (2:24) [WMW]

Air date: March 10, 1967; Guest Star: Roy Engel as President Ulysses S. Grant; Story: Ken Kolb; Director: Charles Rondeau.

Transporting President Grant to San Francisco, West and Gordon check out the town of Gibsonville but find it virtually deserted. A murder is blamed on the ghost of the father of Wayne Gibson but West and Gordon suspect that there is a more logical explanation.

"The Night of the Cadre" (2:26)

Air date: March 24, 1967; Guest Star: Don Gordon as General Titus Trask; Story: Digby Wolfe; Director: Leon Benson.

Titus Trask plans to implant a franconium crystal in the brain of West to gain access to President Grant and then implant a crystal in *his* brain. Controlling the president will allow Trask to become the first dictator of the United States.

"The Night of the Wolf" (2:27)

Air date: March 31, 1967; Guest Star: Joseph Campanella as Talamantes; Story: Robert C. Dennis; Director: Charles Rondeau.

After West is savagely attacked by a wolf, he learns of the mysterious Talamantes who has a power over wolves and is an expert in the study of werewolves.

Season Three [SFW episodes]

"The Night of the Undead" (3:21)

Air date: February 2, 1968; Guest Star: Hurd Hadfield as Dr. Articulus; Story: Calvin Clements Jr.; Director: Marvin Chomsky.

At a voodoo sacrificial rite, West is forced to shoot Tiny John in the heart but the man simply walks away. The next day Tiny John is found dead but his body mysteriously glows in the dark. Dr. Articulus is behind the strange happenings.

Season Four [SFW episodes]

"The Night of the Sedgewick Curse" (4:04)
Air date: October 18, 1968; Guest Stars: Jay Robinson as Dr. Maitland, Sharon Acker as Lavinia Sedgewick; Story: Paul Playdon; Director: Matrvin Chomsky.

In search of an eternal youth serum, Dr. Maitland has been conducting experiments on the Sedgewick family with the result of rapid aging and death before they reach the age of 40. Lavinia Sedgewick seeks eternal youth and the family inheritance.

"The Night of the Kraken" (4:06) [WMW]
Air date: November 1, 1968; Story: Stephen Kandel; Director: Michael Caffey.

When West and Gordon investigate a series of deaths by sea monsters, they discover a sinister plot to sink America's latest battleship.

"The Night of the Avaricious Actuary" (4:11)
Air date: December 6, 1968; Story: Henry Sharp: Director: Irving J. Moore.

West and Gordon investigate the mystery of palatial homes being destroyed by sound waves from a gigantic tuning fork and its connection to the Cyclops Insurance Company.

"The Night of the Spanish Curse" (4:14) [WMW]
Air date: January 3, 1969; Guest Star: Thayer David as Cortez; Story: Robert E. Kent; Director: Paul Stanley.

The townspeople of Soledad, New Mexico, are convinced they are being haunted by the ghosts of Cortez and his Conquistadors.

"The Night of the Winged Terror: Part 1" (4:15)
Air date: January 17, 1969; Guest Star: Christopher Carey as Tycho, Bernard Fox as Dr. Occularis/Jones, Jackie Coogan as Mayor Cecil Pudney; Story: Ken Pettus; Director: Marvin Chomsky.

Mayor Pudney destroys a new railroad bridge after seeing a raven. West investigates but remains mystified.

"The Night of the Winged Terror: Part II" (4:16)
Air date: January 24, 1969; Guest Star: Christo-

pher Carey as Tycho; Story: Ken Pettus; Director: Marvin Chomsky.

Tycho, a man with a big head, is in charge of a group of mad scientists who go under the collective name of Raven. When West is captured, he undergoes mind control programming to assassinate the Mexican Ambassador.

2. Comic book. First publication: June 1966; Publisher: Gold Key.

Based on the TV series. A second series of TV-based comic books was published in 1990 by Millennium Publications.

Wild, Wild West (1999) [Film; SPW]
Premiere: June 30, 1999; Main Cast: Will Smith as Captain James West, Kevin Kline as U.S. Marshal Artemus Gordon, Salma Hayek as Rita Escobar,

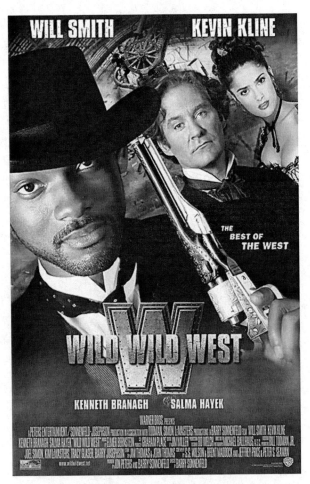

Wild Wild West (1999) a film starring Will Smith as Captain James West, Kevin Kline as U.S. Marshal Artemus Gordon and Salma Hayek as Rita Escobar (Warner Bros.).

Kenneth Branagh as Dr. Arliss Loveless, Musetta Vander as Munitia; Executive Producers: Barry Josephson, Tracy Glaser, Kim LeMasters, Joel Simon, Bill Todman Jr., Story: Jim Thomas, John Thomas; Screenplay: S.S. Wilson, Brent Maddock, Jeffrey Price, Peter S. Seaman; Director: Barry Sonnenfeld; 107 min.; Warner Bros. Pictures; Color.

Captain James West (Will Smith) and master-of-disguise Artemus Gordon (Kevin Kline) team up to thwart Arliss Loveless (Kenneth Branagh) from assassinating President Grant. The beautiful Rita Escobar (Salma Hayek) further complicates matters as West and Gordon contend with a gigantic steam driven metallic spider piloted by Loveless.

Based on the original television series. *Los Angeles Times* film critic Danny Biederman (July 2, 1999) was not impressed: "As enacted in the movie by Will Smith and Kevin Kline, the relationship between Jim and Artemus is marked by annoyance, irritability, disrespect, even name-calling. There's a "dumbing down" of the characters, leaving us with wild pranks and a juvenile spat over the proper density of a woman's breast. "TV's West and Gordon had neither the time nor the inclination for such foolishness, Suave and sophisticated, they maintained a good-natured sense of humor. This '99 model 'West' simply remains a shadow of the '65 classic. Unfortunately, for viewers uninitiated, this Will Smith opus gives the old show an undeserved bad rap."

The Wild, Wild West Revisited (1979) [Telefilm; SFW]

Premiere: May 9, 1979; Main Cast: Robert Conrad as James West, Ross Martin as Artemus Gordon, Paul Williams as Dr. Michelito Loveless Jr., Rene Auberjonois as Capt. Sir David Edney, Harry Morgan as Robert T. Malone, Jo Ann Harris as Carmelita, Trisha Noble as Penelope; Executive Producer: Jay Bernstein; Story: William Bowers; Director: Burt Kennedy; 96 min; CBS Television; Color.

James West and Artemus Gordon are called out of retirement to track down Dr. Michelito Loveless Jr. before he replaces President Grover Cleveland and leaders of England, Spain and Russia with doubles in his quest for world domination.

See: *More Wild, Wild West*

Wilder's Mate (*Bloodhounds* book 1) [Novel; WW]

Robert Conrad as James West in *The Wild, Wild West Revisited* (1979).

Author: Moira Rogers; First publication: Macon, GA: Samhain, 2011.

In the post–Civil War era of the Old West the Bloodhound Guild has been formed to combat the ever increasing menace of vampires. Wilder Harding is the creation of the Guild. A Bloodhound set with the task of hunting vampires. His latest assignment is the rescue of weapons inventor Nathaniel. Helping him is the inventor's apprentice Satira, a smart, beautiful young woman who was raised the charge of a Bloodhound. Now the new moon approaches when Wilder's sexual appetite will peak. He must rescue Nathaniel before his desire for Satira fogs his senses and threatens their blossoming relationship.

Williams, Lon (1890–1978) [Pulp fiction author]

Born, March 17, 1890, Lon Thomas Williams spent most of his life in Andersonville, Tennessee, working as an attorney. His short stories for **Real Western Magazine** included the supernatural Western adventures of **Lee Winters**, deputy sheriff of Forlorn Gap. His other continuing series, *Judge Steele*, was featured in *Western Action* magazine. The stories centered on Judge

Wardlow Steele of Flat Creek and his dealings with various criminal cases.

> Judge Steele tugged at his straw-colored mustache. When an innocent man was brought to trial for murder, only one conclusion could be drawn—namely, that he had been framed by some scoundrel lower than a snake. Possibility of such present villainy filled Steele with fury.—"The Finger of the Beast," *Western Action*, April 1955

Williams was also the author of several paperback novels, including *Hill Hellion!*, *Shack Baby* and *Hill Hoyden*.

Selected works (series): *Lee Winters*, *Judge Steele*.

The Winged Colt of Casa Mia [Juvenile book; WW]

Author: Betsy Cromer Byars; First publication: New York: Viking Press, 1973; Illustrated by Richard Cuffari.

Young Charles spends the summer at the Texas ranch of Uncle Coot, whom he idolizes from his life on the silver screen as a cowboy stunt man. A winged colt named Alado brings Charles and Uncle Coot to a new realistic understanding of each other.

Wings to the Kingdom [Novel; WW]

Author: Cherie Priest; First publication: New York: Tor, 2006.

Old Green Eyes is said to haunt and protect the dead at the Civil War battlefield in Chickamauga, Georgia. But when their unearthly protector departs the battlefield returns to Moccasin Bend the Civil War ghosts roam Chickamauga Battlefield and attempt to communicate with visitors. Eden Moore is a reluctant medium for ghosts who becomes involved after a paranormal TV team arrive to investigate the supernatural events at the battlefield.

This contemporary Southern Gothic novel, the second to feature Eden Moore is a follow-up to *Four and Twenty Blackbirds*.

Wishbone Cutter (1979) a.k.a. *The Shadow of Chikara* a.k.a. *Curse of Demon Mountain* [Film; WW]

Premiere: May 31, 1979; Main Cast: Joe Don Baker as Wishbone Cutter, Sondra Locke as Drusilla

Wishbone Cutter (1979), a "Witchcraft Western," starring Joe Don Baker as Wishbone Cutter, Sondra Locke as Drusilla Wilcox and Ted Neeley as Amos Richmond-Teach (AVCO Embassy Pictures, Fairwinds Productions Inc., Howco International Pictures Inc., Paramount Pictures).

Wilcox, Ted Neeley as Amos Richmond-Teach, Slim Pickens as Virgil Cane, Linda Dano as Rosalie Cutter, Dennis Fimple as Posey, Joy Houck Jr. as Half Moon O'Brian; Executive producer: Barbara Pryor; Writer-Producer-Director: Earl E. Smith; 114 min.; AVCO Embassy Pictures, Fairwinds Productions Inc., Howco International Pictures Inc., Paramount Pictures; Panavision; Color.

This "Witchcraft Western" which tells the "Chilling Indian Legend of Chikara and the Mountain of Demons" takes place at the end of the American Civil War in 1865. Confederate veteran Captain Wishbone Cutter, his half-breed companion Half Moon O'Brian and geologist Amos Richmond set out to locate diamonds hidden in a cave. But they are being followed and the great eagle spirit doesn't want the cave disturbed.

"With Forked Tongue" [Short story; WW]

Author: Ken Rand; First publication: *Talebones* #4, 1996.

Following a presidential rally, a PR man picks up a Native American hitchhiker in the Utah desert. The Indian tells the man of an ancient Indian curse that will bring a new meaning to the well-worn phrase "He speaks with forked tongue."

Wither [Novel; SW]

Author: Yolanda Sfetsos; Publisher: Cincinnati, OH: Samhein, 2009.

Colt Marshall is renowned across the galaxy for his horse roping skills. Now his pursuit of an escaped prisoner who may not be fully human leads him to the planet of his former lover.

"Wizard of Forlorn Gap" [Pulp fiction; WW]

Author: **Lon Williams**; Character: **Lee Winters**; *Real Western Stories* (April 1954).

In returning twilight he saw a form that might have been a man speeding northward, on foot. To his amazement that form rose and seemed to settle upon an invisible horse; seconds later this

"Wizard of Forlorn Gap" artwork from *Real Western Stories* (April 1954).

rider, or apparition, had disappeared into nothingness.

Wolf in Shadow [Novel; SFW]

Author: **David Gemmell**; First publication: New York: Ballantine Books, 1987.

Three hundred years into a new world order following the end of civilization, John Shannow searches for the holy city of Jerusalem and a new era of peace. But Abaddon, the Lord of the Pit, and his Hellborn army seek his death and the triumph of evil.

The first in a series of books featuring postapocalyptic gunslinger John Shannow, the Jerusalem Man.

See: *The Last Guardian; Bloodstone: A Jon Shannow Adventure*

The Woman Who Owned the Shadows [Novel; WW]

Author: Paula Gunn Allen; First publication: Splinters: San Francisco, 1983.

A woman leaves the New Mexico Indian reservation and a bad marriage behind her as she seeks a new life in San Francisco. But her new relationship and subsequent marriage falter with the death of her twin son. Divorce and attempted suicide follow. But a meeting with an old Indian woman gives her hope as she retraces her life and Indian ancestry through self-awareness and spiritual visions that link her with her past and present.

Wonder Woman [Comic book]

The adventures of Diane Prince alias Amazonian ambassador and Wonder Woman, Princess Diana.

"THE WINDS OF TIME PART 2: THE REDSKIN'S REVENGE" [SFW]

First publication: #17 (May-June 1946); Creator: William Moulton Marston; Story: Joyce Murchison; Art: Harry G. Peter; Publisher: DC Comics.

Wonder Woman and Steve Trevor journey back through time the 1840s and help

Native Americans get their revenge on cheating trader Silas Sneek.

"MYSTERY OF THE INDIAN TOTEM POLE" [SFW]

First publication: #47 (May-June 1951); Story: Robert Kanigher; Art: Harry G. Peter; Publisher: DC Comics.

Wonder Woman travels to the Old West from 1951 to discover why a totem pole bears her likeness.

See: *Sensation Comics*

Worms! [RPG book; WW]

Author: John Goff; First publication: 1999; *Deadlands: The Weird West* Dime novel #10; Publisher: Pinnacle Entertainment Group.

When Ronan Lynch bumps into Texas Ranger Hank Ketchum in Hilton Springs, Nevada, they join forces to combat Mojave rattlers.

Wounded Heart [Comic book character; France; SFW]

English title for the comic strip *Coeur Blessé*.

Wynonna Earp [Comic book; TV Series (2016); WW]

First appearance: December 1997; Creators: Beau Smith, Brad Gorby; Publisher: Wildstorm, Image Comics, Eclipse, IDW Publishing.

Wynonna Earp, great granddaughter of famous lawman Wyatt Earp and special agent for the U.S. Marshal Special Operations Unit, battles supernatural threats in the modern-day and the Old West.

X-Files (1993) [TV series]

Main Cast: David Duchovny as Special Agent Fox Mulder, Gillian Anderson as Special Agent Dana Scully

Two opposing FBI agents investigate the paranormal and become involved in government conspiracies.

"SHAPES" (1:18) [WW]

Air date; April 1, 1994; Guest cast: Ty Miller as Lyle Parker, Michael Horse as Sheriff Charles Tsanky, Donnelly Rhodes as Jim Parker, Jimmy Herman as Ish; Executive Producer: Chris Carter; Story: Marilyn Osborn; Director: David Nutter; 45 min.; Twentieth-Century–Fox Television; Color.

Cover of *Wynonna Earp* #1 (December 1997). Creators Beau Smith and Brad Gorby. © 2009 Beau Smith and Idea and Design Works, LLC. Used with permission.

A Montana Native American bloodline goes back to the era of Lewis and Clark, where a wolfman creature was illustrated in contemporary documents. When a similar creature is reported to be killing members of the local populace the police discover the body of a young Native American at the sight of the most recent attack. F.B.I. Agents Fox Mulder and Dana Scully investigate, gradually obtaining the cooperation of the suspicious, insular community. The Manitou is alive and well in 1994 in the form of a local Native American.

"FIRST PERSON SHOOTER" (7: 13) [SFW]

Air date: February 27, 2000; Guest Cast: Krista Allen as Jade Blue Afterglow/Maitreya, Dean

Haglund as Langly, Tom Braidwood as Frohike, Bruce Harwood as Byers; Chris Carter; Story: William Gibson, Tom Maddox; Creator-Director: Chris Carter; 45 min.; 20th Century–Fox Television, Ten Thirteen Productions; Color.

Virtual reality mixes with reality as Mulder and Scully investigate murders at a video game design studio where players are dying at the hands of the sexy game character. Mulder and Scully enter the virtual world of an Old West town to face a showdown with virtual gunslinger Maitreya.

X-Force [Comic book]

The militant mutant superhero title featured three Science Fiction Western characters: Apache *X-Force* member **Warpath,** Cheyenne *X-Force* member **Danielle Moonstar** and Externals member **Absalom.**

"THE YOUNG AND THE RESTLESS" #37 (AUGUST 1994) [SFW]
Story: Fabian Nicieza; Art: Paul Pelletier, Harry Candelario, Scott Hanna, Charles Barnett; Publisher: Marvel Comics.

Absalom recalls the time he was hanged for murder in the Old West of Wyoming and first discovered that he possessed mutant powers, including the ability to extend razor-sharp spines through his body.

"Q & A" #54 (MAY 1996)
Story: Jeph Loeb; Art: Adam Pollina, Bud LaRosa; Publisher: Marvel Comics.

Weakened by the Legacy Virus, Absalom loses his life when fellow External Selene drains his life force on the Rockefeller Center ice rink in New York City.

Xabungle a.k.a. *Sentou Mecha Xabungle* a.k.a. *The Bungler* [Animated TV series; Japan; SFW]

Air date: February 6, 1982; Animation; Tomonori Kogawa, Akihiro Kanayama; Directors; Yoshiyuki Tomino, Osamu Sekita, Iku Suzuki, Yasuhiro Imagawa; Production: Sunrise, TV Asahi; 50 × 25 min.; Color.

One of the earliest anime Science Fiction Westerns features Old West landscapes and towns populated with outlaws. The population of planet Zola believes they are descended from colonists from Earth but the truth is Zola is Earth. Purebred Innocents live inside a sealed dome, whilst the Civilian Underclass or Sand-Rats live in wilderness working as miners and traders. A huge robot called Walker Machine Xabungle is stolen by Civilian Jiron Amos who searches for the truth behind his father's death.

The serious sounding premise is given a lighthearted, approach with a bungling hero and humorous interaction between the characters and the robots. The 50 episode TV series was edited into feature length film, *Xabungle Grafitti,* in 1983.

Season One

I Live By Risking My Life (1:01); *We Got a Xabungle* (1:02); *Everyone's Got It Wrong* (1:03); *Why Do You Break the Law?* (1:04); *Three's A Crowd* (1:05); *What Are You Up To Jiron?* (1:06); *Those Who Believe Are Saved* (1:07); *Miss Never Misses* (1:08); *In the Field Blooms a Flower Named Maria* (1:09); *Brave Women Are Frightening* (1:10); *Chase Me! Chase Me!* (1:11); *The Many Mysteries of the Innocent* (1:12); *A Great Destruction Leaving Nothing Behind* (1:13); *Timp's Futile Resistance* (1:14); *Covered in Mud and Desperate* (1:15); *Sorrowful Energy* (1:16); *A Duel with Actors and Noh Theater* (1:17); *What's Wrong with Running Away From Home?* (1:18); *Take Flight Condor* (1:19); *Akon the Stud* (1:20); *Falling in Love, Being in Love* (1:21); *Rag Broken in Pieces* (1:22); *Rag Come Back To My Heart* (1:23); *A Fierce Death Machine! Flying Karas* (1:24); *A Big Battle of Two Reckless Fighters* (1:25); *Chaotic Battle with the Innocent* (1:26); *Sing the Song of the Warrior* (1:27); *The Innocent's Weakness* (1:28); *Even the Innocent Can Get Desperate* (1:29); *If They Get the Head, We're Done For* (1:30); *Manipulating a Woman's Heart* (1:31); *My Convenience is Your Convenience* (1:32); *Never Ending Troubles* (1:33); *Fatman's Feelings Fly Far* (1:34); *Military Unit Discovered* (1:35); *Special Sneaking Mission* (1:36); *A Kaleidoscope of Women* (1:37); *Dance, Elchi* (1:38); *Going Solo is No Go* (1:39); *Katakam, Ragged into Bits* (1:40); *End of Katakam* (1:41); *Greta Howls* (1:42); *Desperately Seeking Yop* (1:43); *Take Care, Sir Arthur* (1:44); *Stand Up to Face the Sun* (1:45); *Sir Arthur Does His Best* (1:46); *Awaken Elchi* (1:47); *Once and Future Sir Arthur* (1:48); *Showdown at X Point* (1:49); *Everybody, Run!* (1:50).

Yado [Comic book character; Italy; WW]

First publication: 1957; Story: G. L. Bonelli; Art: Francesco Gamba; Publisher: Sergio Bonelli Editore.

The son of a Piute witch doctor, Yado is sent into exile after he marries a white woman. Yado possesses powers of magic and the ability to talk with his coyote Kerr and stallion Hund. His energy is devoted to seeking revenge for the hostility his parents received.

Yasuhiro Nightow (1967–) [Comic book artist]

Born in Yokohama, Japan, Yasuhiro admits to having no formal art training and to learning his craft by copying manga artists such as **Leiji Matsumoto**, Rumiko Takahashi, Katsuhiro Ohtomo and Fumiko Takano. Abandoning his early career of selling apartments for Sekisui House, Yasuhiro became a professional comic artist at the age of 26.

He is best known for the creation of *Trigun* for *Shounen Captain* magazine and its subsequent anime adaptation.

The Year the Cloud Fell [Novel; SFW]

Author: Kurt R. A. Giambastiani; First publication: New York: New American Library, 2001.

Following the crash of the spy dirigible *A. Lincoln* in a thunderstorm over Unorganized Territory, President George Armstrong Custer's son is captured by the Cheyenne Alliance. One prophetic woman sees a future where Custer's son is at odds with his own father.

Book one of the **Fallen Cloud Saga** set in an alternative America of 1886.

See: *The Spirit of Thunder*

Yellow Back Radio Broke-Down [Novel; SFW]

Author: **Ishmael Reed**; First publication: 1969; Publisher: Doubleday: New York.

A traveling circus troupe, including the satanic African-American HooDoo gunslinger the Loop Garoo Kid and Zozo Labrique, a HooDoo mambo from New Orleans, arrives in the Western town of Yellow Back Radio.

A mix of HooDoo, Voodoo, Be-Bop and science fiction, this Western satire has been described as the first HooDoo Western.

Yogi's Space Race (1978) [Animated TV series]

Premiere: September 9, 1978; Executive Producers: William Hanna, Joseph Barbera; Directors: Ray Patterson, Carl Urbano; 90 min.; Hanna-Barbera Productions; Color.

This 90-minute animated show consisted of four segments including *Yogi's Space Race*, *Galaxy Goof-Ups* and **Buford and the Galloping Ghost**. The latter was broadcast as an independent series in 1979 despite the fact that the episodes originally aired on *Yogi's Space Race*.

Young Ones a.k.a. Bad Land: Road to Fury (2014) [Film; SFW]

Premiere: October 17, 2014; Main Cast: Michael Shannon as Ernest Holm, Elle Fanning as Mary Holm, Kodi Smit-McPhee as Jerome Holm, Aimee Mullins as Katherine Holm, Nicholas Hoult as Flem Lever, David Butler as Sam Lever, Robert Hobbs as Caleb Moore; Producers: Jake Paltrow, Michael Auret, Tristan Orpen Lynch; Writer-Director: Jake Paltrow; 100 min.; Subotica Entertainment, Spier Films, Screen Media Films; Color.

In a future U.S.A. where water is in scarce supply, Ernest Holm and his family live a harsh life as they struggle to survive on the parched land of the new frontier. A major new problem arrives in the form of his daughter Mary's new boyfriend Flem Lever when he makes moves on grabbing the Holm land for himself.

Henry Barnes of *The Guardian* (April 30, 2015) commented: "Jake Paltrow's repackaged sci-fi neo-western reeks of cheap knock off. In fact, it's a masterwork of getting by on the little you have. Jake Paltrow makes up for lack of budget with a surfeit of ideas. There hasn't been as convincing a sci-fi dustbowl story since the original Mad Max."

Yukon Terror [RPG; WW]

First publication: 2014; *Deadlands Tall Tales #3*; Protocol Game Series; Author: Jim Pinto; Art: Rick Hershey; Publisher: Pinnacle Entertainment Group.

The northern frontier of Alaska is home to strange creatures and horrors. A group of stranded strangers, taking shelter in an Alaskan cabin must survive the terrors lurking in the storm. A story role-playing game set in **Deadlands: The Weird West**.

Yuma Kid [Comic book character; Italy; WW]

First publication: 1953; Story: G. L. Bonelli; Art: Mario Uggeri; Publisher: Sergio Bonelli Editore.

Stranded by a sandstorm in the Gila desert, a youngster is rescued by Yuma Indians who take him into their care. Adopting the name Wind of Death, the Yuma Kid returns to his own world after hearing the prophecy of Wa-No-Tah, the witch who lives with her cougars in a cave.

"Yvala" [Pulp fiction; SW]

Author: **C. L. Moore**; First publication: *Weird Tales* (February 1936).

Northwest Smith and his Venusian friend Yarol become embroiled in an illegal slave trade when they are hired by an Irishman to discover the truth behind the myth of the beautiful sirens of Cembre.

> Lakkdarol is an Earthman's town upon Martian soil, blending all the more violent elements of both worlds in its lawless heart...

Zagor [Comic book character; Italy; WW]

1. First appearance: *Zagor* #1 (1961); Creator: Guido Nolitta [Sergio Bonelli]; Art: Gallieno Felli; Publisher: Sergio Bonelli Editore.

The lone survivor of a brutal attack by Abenaki Indians that killed his parents, Za-Gor-Te-Nay, the Spirit with the Hatchet, swears revenge. He later discovers that his father had also slaughtered the Abenaki, and comes to realize that violence only continues the cycle of hatred.

Zagor decides to devote his life to helping the oppressed from his base in the marshy forest of Darkwood. Pot-bellied Mexican sidekick Cico brings humor to a strip that mixes traditional Western adventure, horror and the weird.

2. (1970) [Film; Turkey; WW] Main Cast: Cihangir Gaffari as **Zagor**; Producer: Nami Dilbaz; Story-Director: Mehmet Aslan; Özdeyis Film; Color.

Film adaptation of the Italian comic book characters.

Zagor kara bela (1971) [Film; Turkey; WW]

Main Cast: Levent Cakir as **Zagor**, Yavuz Selekman, Muzaffer Temma, Sirri Elitas; Producer: Hasan Tual; Story: M. Nuri Seybi; Director: Nisan Hancer; Yerli Film; Color.

Film adaptation of the Italian comic book characters with Iranian actor Levent Cakir as Zagor.

Zagor kara korsan'in hazineleri (1971) [Film; Turkey; WW]

Main Cast: Levent Cakir as **Zagor**, Kazim Kartal as Kara Korsan, Kadir Savun as Fenerci; Producer:

Hasan Tual; Director: Nisan Hancer; Yerli Film; Color.

Based on the Italian comic book characters.

Zeke Deadwood: Zombie Lawman [Comic book; WW]

First published: Summer 2009; Story-Art: Thomas Boatwright, Ryan Rubio: Publisher: SLG Publishing.

Zeke Deadwood is a lone zombie lawman with a mission to clean up a western town from outlaws, but the townsfolk may find outlaws preferable to an undead sheriff coming to their rescue.

Zeppelins West [Novel; SFW]

Author: **Joe R. Lansdale**; First publication: Burton MI: Subterranean Press, 2000.

Alternate history novel featuring Buffalo Bill Cody's battery-powered head preserved in a jar of pig urine and whisky as Wild Bill Hickok, Annie Oakley and Sitting Bull travel on a zeppelin to Japan. Their mission is to rescue Frankenstein's monster and therefore learn the secret of reattaching Buffalo Bill's head to his body. This bizarre tale also includes the Tin Man, Dracula, Captain Nemo and Charles Darwin, among others.

Zombie Powder [Manga; Japan; SFW]

First appearance: *Weekly Shounen Jump* #34, 1999; Story-Art: Tite Kubo; 27 chapters; Publisher: Shueisha.

Powder Hunters Gamma Akutabi, C.T. Smith and John Elwood Shepherd seek the twelve "Rings of the Dead" that lead to the elusive, immortality-granting Zombie Powder in this action tale with clear Western influences. Due to weak sales, this action-orientated manga was cancelled before completion of the series.

Zombie Western: It Came from the West (2007) [Puppet animation; Denmark; WW]

Voice Cast: Niels-Peter Henriksen as Virgil, Tor Fruergaard as Indian, Kim Jeppesen as Eddie, Carsten Reinholdt as Jack; Producer: Soren Fleng; Story: Tor Fruergaard, Sissel Dalsgaard; Director: Tor Fruergaard; 17 min.; Happy Flyfish; Color.

Native Indians raise the dead and unleash zombies in response to the terrorizing Dark Butcher.

Zombie Western: The Legend of the Dark Butcher (2008) [Puppet animation; Spain-Denmark; WW]

Story: Juanjo Ramirez, Alby Ojeda; Directors: Tor Fruergaard, Juanjo Ramirez; 75 min.; Perro Verde Films, Happy Flyfish; Color.

Fourteen-year-old Virgil lives in an Old West saloon with his vicious, Indian-hating father. When his father slaughters an Indian family, he awakens an ancient curse and flesh-eating zombies rise from their graves seeking revenge.

Based on the 17-minute short *Zombie Western: It Came from the West*. First part of a proposed trilogy.

Zombieland (2009) [Film; SFW]

Premiere: October 2, 2009; Main Cast: Jesse Eisenberg as Columbus, Woody Harrelson as Tallahassee, Emma Stone as Wichita, Abigail Breslin as Little Rock, Amber Heard as 406, Bill Murray as Bill Murray; Executive producers: Ryan Kavanaugh, Rhett Reese, Ezra Swerdlow, Paul Wernick; Story: Rhett Reese, Paul Wernick; Director: Ruben Fleischer; 88 min.; Relativity Media, Pariah, Columbia Pictures; Color.

In a post-apocalyptic United States of Zombieland a shy, nerdy student joins forces with a Hostess Twinkie hunting, zombie obsessed, gun loving, snakeskin clothed cowboy and two streetwise sisters headed west to a rumored zombie-free colony in an amusement park. In an amusing cameo the group meet actor Bill Murray, one of the few survivors of the zombie apocalypse.

Traveling through a landscape where the security of civilization has been replaced with the remnants of a plague and the threat of being eaten alive or infected by zombies, this comedy-horror road trip film has Western influences in the character of Tallahassee and the westward journey across a hostile American landscape.

Zorro (1957) [TV Series]

The adventures of Don Diego de la Vega alias Zorro, masked champion of the oppressed. Disney's TV series featured traditional stories apart from "The Ghost of the Mission" which had a Weird Menace theme reminiscent of Western "B" movies from the 1930s.

1. "The Ghost of the Mission" (1:04) [WMW] Air date: October 31, 1957; Main cast: Guy Williams as Don Diego de la Vega/Zorro; Guest Cast: Britt Lomond as Capitan Monastario, Romney Brent as Padre Felipe, Jan Arvan as Don Ignacio Torres; Story-Director: Norman Foster; 30 min.; Walt Disney Productions; b/w.

Zorro spreads the rumor of a mad monk haunting a church where Torres is being held captive, then impersonates the "ghost" of the mad monk to enable Torres to escape from Monastario.

See: *Walt Disney's Comics and Stories*

2. Comic book
First publication: *Four-Color* #920 (June 1958); Art: Alex Toth; Publisher: Dell Publishing Co.

Adaptation of the TV episodes "Zorro Rides to the Mission" and "The Ghost of the Mission."

3. [Animated TV series; WW]
Air date: September 20, 1997; Voice Cast: Michael Gough as Don Diego/Zorro, Jeannie Elias as Isabela, Patrick Fraley as Don Alejandro, Tony Pope as Sgt. Garcia, Earl Boen as Capt. Montecero; 30 × 26 min.; Fred Wolf Films; Color.

The well-known story of Don Diego de la Vega alias Zorro in the West of the 1800s is injected with supernatural and steampunk elements in this animated TV series.

Season One

To Catch a Fox (1:01); *Sting of the Serpent-God* (1:02); *Night of the Tolchen* (1:03); *The Beast Within* (1:04); *The Enforcer* (1:05); *Two Zorros Are Better than One* (1:06); *Tar Pit Terror* (1:07); *A King's Ransom* (1:08); *The Pirates of San Pedro* (1:09); *The Anti Zorro* (1:10); *Valley of the Man-beast* (1:11); *The Revenge of the Panther* (1:12); *The Iron Man* (1:13)

Season Two

The Samurai and the Sorcerer (2:01); *The Poison Pen* (2:02); *Vision of Darkness* (2:03); *The Case of the Masked Marauder* (2:04); *Return of the Conquistadors* (2:05); *The Hunter* (2:06); *The Raiding Party* (2:07); *The Four Horsemen* (2:08); *The Nightmare Express* (2:09); *The Ice Monster Cometh* (2:10); *The Secret of El Zorro* (2:11); *The Nordic Quest* (2:12); *Adios, Mi Capitan* (2:13)

4. [Novel; WW]; Author: Isabel Allende; First Puplication: 2005; Publisher: HarperCollins.

A re-imagining of Zorro that incorporates elements of magic into the story. Born to a Indian Shoshone mother and Spanish military father, Diego is influenced by both worlds and sympathizes with the plight of the Native Americans.

Zorro Escarlata en la Venganza del Ahorcado (1958) [Film; Mexico; WW]

Premiere: December 11, 1958; Main Cast: Luis Aguilar as Luis, alias El Zorro Escarlata, Fernando

Fernández as Captain Orellana, José Eduardo Pérez as Riccardo Carrion, Irma Dorantes as Gloria Carrion, Pascual García Peña as Pascual; Producer: Luis Manrique; Story: Antonio Orellana, Luis Manrique, Fernando Fernández; Director: Rafael Baledón; Filmadora Mexicana; Spanish; b/w.

A Frankenstein-type monster with a witch for a mother is pursued by El Zorro Escarlata. Divided into three segments: "The Son of the Sorceress," "The Rope of the Hanged Person" and "The Secret of the Revived One."

Zorro: La Espada y la Rosa (2007) [TV series; Mexico]

Premiere: February 12, 2007; Main Cast: Christian Meier as Diego de la Vega/El Zorro, Marlene Favela as Esmeralda Sánchez de Moncada, Arturo Peniche as Fernando Sánchez de Moncada, Harry Geithner as Comandante Ricardo Montero de Avila, Andrea López as Mariángel Sánchez de Moncada; Story Executive: Humberto "Kiko" Olivieri; Executive Producers: Patricio Wills, Hugo León Ferrer; 122 × 60 min.; Telemundo-RTI Productions, Sony Pictures Television International, Zorro Productions Inc.; Spanish; Color.

This telenovela, set in California and Spain of the 1850s, includes popular elements of melodrama, romance and family intrigue but also explores supernatural themes such as mystical Indians, witches, an exorcist and demon possession.

Zorro's Fighting Legion (1939) [Film serial; WMW]

Premiere: December 16, 1939: Main Cast: Reed Hadley as Don Diego de la Vega/Zorro, Sheila Darcy as Volita, Carleton Young as Benito Juarez, Edmund Cobb as Manuel Gonzalez, William Corson as Ramon, Leander De Cordova as Governor Felipe; Screenplay: Ronald Davidson, Franklin Adreon, Morgan Cox, Sol Shor, Barney A. Sarecky; Producer: Hiram S. Brown Jr.; Directors: William Witney, John English; 212 min.; Republic Pictures; b/w.

Don Diego de la Vega attempts to discover the truth behind self-proclaimed god Don Del Oro, who is worshipped by the Yaqui Indians. Del Oro manipulates the superstitious Mexican villagers and dispatches his enemies with arrows of gold.

Chapter titles: 1. *The Golden God*; 2. *The Flaming "Z"*; 3. *Descending Doom*; 4. *The Bridge of Peril*; 5. *The Decoy*; 6. *Zorro to the Rescue*; 7. *The Fugitive*; 8. *Flowing Death*; 9. *The Golden Arrow*; 10. *Mystery Wagon*; 11. *Face to Face*; 12. *Unmasked*

Appendix I: Weird Westerns by Genre

Animated Film

BraveStarr: The Movie
Burst Angel: Infinity
Cowboy Bebop: Knockin' on
  Heaven's Door
The Good, The Bad and Huckle-
  berry Hound
Queen Emeraldas
Quick Draw El Kabong
Rango
Vampire Hunter D
Vampire Hunter D: Bloodlust
Zombie Western: It Came from
  the West
Zombie Western: The Legend of
  the Dark Butcher

Animated Television Series

The Addams Family
The Adventures of the Galaxy
  Rangers
Back to the Future
Batman: The Animated Series
Batman: The Brave and the Bold
Beany and Cecil
Beetlejuice
Birdman and the Galaxy Trio
BraveStarr
Buford and the Galloping Ghost
Burst Angel
El Cazador de la Bruja
Il Corsaro Cocco Bill
Cosmic Cowboys
Cosmo Warrior Zero
Cowboy Bebop
Coyote Ragtime Show
Desert Punk
Duckula

Eat-Man
Eat-Man '98
Felix the Cat
Futurama
Galaxy Express 999
Ginga Tetsudô Three-Nine
Grenadier
Gun Frontier
Gun X Sword
Justice League
Justice League Unlimited
Legion of Super Heroes
Lilly the Witch
The Lone Ranger
The Matty's Funnies with Beany
  and Cecil
Les Nouvelles Aventures de Lucky
  Luke
Outlaw Star
Posse Impossible
Ricochet Rabbit & Droop-a-Long
Rocket Robin Hood
The Ruff & Reddy Show
Saber Riders and the Star Sheriffs
Sei Jushi Bismark
Seihou Bukyou Outlaw Star
SilverHawks
The Simpsons
Star Wars: The Clone Wars
Sunabozu
Tom Terrific
Trigun
Uch Kaizoku Kyaputen Hurlock
What's New Scooby Doo?
Wild ARMs: Twilight Venom
Wild West C.O.W. Boys of Moo
  Mesa
Xabungle
Yogi's Space Race
Zorro

Animated Theatrical Short

The Backwater Gospel
Boos and Arrows
Boos and Saddles
Felix the Cat in Eats Are West
The First Bad Man
Phantom of the Horse Opera
Pink Panic
Sioux Me
Tom and Jerry

Authors

Bates, Harry
Brackett, Leigh
Brand, Max
Brautigan, Richard
Burroughs, Edgar Rice
Burroughs, William S.
Dorn, Edward
Ellis, Edward Sylvester
Enton, Harry
Gemmell, David
Heinlein, Robert A.
Howard, Robert E.
King, Stephen
Lansdale, Joe R.
McCarthy, Cormac
Moore, C. L.
Norton, Andre
Reed, Ishmael
Resnick, Mike
Senarens, Luis
Williams, Lon

Board Game

Deadlands: The Battle for Slaughter Gulch

Book Anthology

California Sorcery (see "Lone
 Star Traveler")
Custer's Last Jump and Other
 Collaborations
Dead Man's Hand: An Anthology
 of the Weird West
Dead Man's Hand: Five Tales of
 the Weird West
Deadman's Road
Little Gods
Love in Vein: Twenty Original
 Tales of Vampiric Erotica
Mad Amos
Night of the Cooters: More Neat
 Stories
Razored Saddles
The Shadows Kith and Kin
A Skull Full of Spurs: A Roundup
 of Weird Westerns
Tales from the Texas West
Weird Western Adventures of
 Haakon Jones

Book Character

Hosteen Storm
Tiger Lily

Book Series

Fallen Cloud Saga

Comic Book [titles featuring WW stories]

Action Comics
Adventures into the Unknown
The Adventures of Mendy and the
 Golem
All-New Booster Gold
All-Star Western
American Vampire: Second Cycle
Astonishing
The Avengers
Batman
Batman: The Return of Bruce
 Wayne
Best of the West
Black Panther
Black Rider
Blue Bolt Weird Tales of Terror
Bobby Benson's B-Bar-B Riders
Bonanza
Boris Karloff Tales of Mystery
Bulls-Eye

Buster Crabbe
Captain Marvel Adventures
Captain Marvel Jr.
Chambers of Chills
Creepy
Crux
Danger Girl
Daredevil the Man Without Fear
The Dark Tower: The Gunslinger
 Born
Dead in the West
Desperadoes
Desperadoes: Banners of Gold
Desperadoes: Buffalo Dreams
Desperadoes: Epidemic!
Desperadoes: Quiet of the Grave
Djustine: Tales from the Twisted
 West
Doc Frankenstein
Don Simpson's Bizarre Heroes
Dracula Lives
The Durango Kid
Fantastic Four
Femforce
Forbidden Worlds
Green Lantern
Gunsmoke: Blazing Stories of the
 West
Howdy Pardner
Journey into Mystery
Justice League of America
Justice League Unlimited
Kid Colt, Outlaw
Legends of the DC Universe
Lobo Elseworlds
Lucky Luke
The Marvel Family
Master Comics
Mystery in Space
The New Adventures of Superboy
The New Mutants
Omega Chase
Out of the Night
Paragon Western Stars
Pulp Heroes
Rawhide Kid
Rogue Angel: Teller of Tall Tales
Secret Six
Sensation Comics
She-Hulk
Skeleton Hand in Secrets of the
 Supernatural
Straight Arrow
Strange Adventures

Strange Suspense Stories
Strange Tales
Super Spook
Superboy
Superman & Batman: Genera-
 tions III
Superman Batman
Superman's Pal, Jimmy Olsen
Tales of the Unexpected
Thor
Tim Holt
Tomahawk
Two-Gun Kid
Vincent Price Presents
Walt Disney's Comics and Stories
Weird Science
Western Tales of Black Rider
Whiz Comics
Wild Western
Wonder Woman
X-Force
Zorro

Comic Book [Weird Western titles]

Aguila Solitaria
Alter-Nation
American Vampire
American Wasteland: Blood and
 Diesel
Bad Moon Rising
The Ballad of Sleeping Beauty
The Ballad of Utopia
Big Thunder Mountain Railroad
Billy the Kid's Old Timey Oddities
Bisley's Scrapbook
Bizarre Fantasy
Blazin' Barrels
Blood and Shadows
Bounty Killer
Brimstone
Caliber
Chains of Chaos
Champions of the Wild Weird
 West
Chickasaw Adventures
Colt the Armadillo
Contract
Copperhead
Cowboys & Aliens
Crawling Sky
Daisy Kutter: The Last Train
Dances with Demons
Dead Irons

Comic Book Artist

Comic Book Character(s)

The American Gun Club
Bat Lash
The Bird Man
Black Bison
Black Blaze
Black Crow
Black Phantom
Blackbow the Cheyenne
Buckaroo Banzai
Buckaroo Betty
Buzzard
Cactoid Jim, King of the Martian Frontier
Il Cavaliere del Texas
Cimarron
Cinnamon
Cocco Bill
Coeur Blessé
Coffin
Cowboy Gorilla
Cowgirls from Hell
Croach the Tracker
Danielle Moonstar
Dawnstar
Deadshot
Dick Demon
Doctor Saturn
Doctor Thirteen
Drago
El Diablo
Firehair
Flaming Star
Ghost Rider
Gorilla Gunslinger
Gunslinger Spawn
The Haunted Horseman
The Haunter
Hawkgirl
Hawkman
Hurricane
Jonah Hex
Judok
Lash LaRue
The Lemonade Kid
Magico Vento
Manitou
Mantoka, Maker of Indian Magic
The Masked Marvel
The Master Gunfighter
Max Mercury
Mirage
Night Rider
Nighthawk
Owlwoman

Ozark
Paragon
Pariah
The Phantom Rider
Pow-Wow Smith
The Presto Kid
Psyche
Quicksilver
Rakar
The Rangers
Ravenstorm
Real American #1
Red Larabee, the Gunhawk
Red Mask
Red Plains Rider
Red Wolf
Redblade
Rick Montana
Rio Kid
Ripclaw
The Rook
Rory Randall the Singin' Cowboy
The Rough Bunch
Sarah Rainmaker
Scalphunter
Scout
Shooting Star
Silver Deer
Sparks Nevada: Marshal on Mars
Spurs Jackson
Stormshadow
Super-Chief
Terra-Man
Tex Willer
Texas Twister
Thunderbird
Tomazooma
Turok
The Vigilante
Viking
Wa-Tan-Peh
Warpath
Wild Bill Pecos
Wounded Heart
Yado
Yuma Kid

Comic Book Writer

Bonelli, Giovanni Luigi
Bonelli, Sergio
Fox, Gardner
Lansdale, Joe R.
Lee, Stan

Comic Strip

American Gothic
Captain Ken
Coeur Blessé
Cowboy Bebop
The Demons
Fistful of Blood
Flesh
Frankie Stein: Time Traveller
Gun Frontier
Hector Plasm
Jed Puma
Missionary Man
The Outcasts
Les Persecutes
Red Hawk
Tex Arcana
Wounded Heart
Zombie Powder

Dime Novel

The Black Range; or, Frank Reade Jr. Among the Cowboys with His New Electric Caravan
Frank Reade and His Steam Horse. A Thrilling Story of the Plains
Frank Reade and His Steam Man of the Plains or The Terror of the West
Frank Reade and Sitting Bull; or, White Cunning versus Red
Frank Reade Jr. and His New Steam Horse Among the Cowboys; or, The League of the Plains
Frank Reade Jr. and His New Steam Horse in the Great American Desert; or, The Sandy Trail of Death
Frank Reade Jr. and His New Steam Horse in the Running Fight on the Plains
Frank Reade, Jr., and His New Steam Man or, The Young Inventor's Trip to the Far West
Frank Reade Jr. with His New Steam Horse in Search of an Ancient Mine
Frank Reade Jr. with His New Steam Man in Texas; or, Chasing the Train Robbers

Frank Reade Jr. with His New Steam Horse in the North West; or, Wild Adventures Among the Blackfeet

Frank Reade Jr. with His New Steam Horse; or, The Mystery of the Underground Ranch

Frank Reade Jr.'s New Electric Invention the "Warrior"; or, Fighting the Apaches in Arizona

Frank Reade with His New Steam Man Chasing a Gang of "Rustlers"; or, Wild Adventures in Montana

The Huge Hunter or The Steam Man of the Prairies

Jack Wright and His Electric Stage; or, Leagued Against the James Boys

Jack Wright and His Prairie Yacht

Jack Wright's Electric Prairie Car or, Hot Times with the Broncho Buster Part I

The Mystic Brand; or Frank Reade Jr. and His Overland Stage Upon the Staked Plains

Tom Edison, Jr.'s Electric Mule; or, the Snorting Wonder of the Plains

Tom Edison, Jr.'s Prairie-Skimmer Team; A Sequel to Tom Edison, Jr.'s Sky-Scraping Trip

Tom Edison, Jr.'s Sky-Scraping Trip; or Over the Wild West Like a Flying Squirrel

Dime Novel Character

Frank Reade & Frank Reade Jr.
Jack Wright
Tom Edison, Jr.

Dime Novel Magazine

Frank Reade Library

Film

Abraham Lincoln, Vampire Hunter
Abraham Lincoln vs. Zombies
The Adventures of Buckaroo Banzai Across the 8th Dimension

The Adventures of the Masked Phantom
After Sundown
Alferd Packer: The Musical
Alien Outlaw
Aliens in the Wild, Wild West
The American Astronaut
The Aurora Encounter
Avatar
El Anima de Sayula
El Ánima del Ahorcado contra el Latigo Negro
Back to the Future, Part III
Bad Land: Road to Fury
Bang Bang Kid
Battle Beyond the Stars
The Beast of Hollow Mountain
The Bells of Innocence
Big Calibre
Bill & Ted's Excellent Adventure
Billy the Kid Versus Dracula
Blood Trail
BloodRayne II: Deliverance
Blueberry: L'Expérience Secrète
Bodas de fuego
The Book of Eli
Border Phantom
Bubba Ho-Tep
Buon funerale. Amigos! ... paga Sartana
The Burrowers
La Cabeza de Pancho Villa
Cannibal! The Musical
Chanbara Beauty
El Charro de las Calaveras
Cold Harvest
Cowboy Zombies
Cowboys & Aliens
Cowboys vs. Dinosaurs
The Crimson Skull
Curse of the Forty-Niner
Curse of the Undead
The Dead and the Damned
Dead Man
Dead Noon
Dead Walkers
Dead West
Death Collector
Demoniaca
Derailed!
Desert Phantom
Devil's Crossing
The Devil's Mistress

Devoured: The Legend of Alferd Packer
Django il Bastardo
Django Kill—If You Live, Shoot!
Django Rides Again
Don't Touch the White Woman
Dove si spara di più
Dust Devil
Dynamite Warrior
... e così divennero i 3 supermen del West
E Dio disse a Caino
Ehi amico ... c'è Sabata, hai chiuso!
Empty Saddles
El Extraño hijo del sheriff
Four of the Apocalypse
From Dusk Till Dawn 3: The Hangman's Daughter
From the Earth to the Moon
Fury of Johnny the Kid
Futureworld
Gallowwalker
Get Mean
Ghost of Hidden Valley
Ghost Patrol
Ghost Rider
Ghost Riders
Ghost Town
Ginger Snaps Back: The Beginning
Giunse Ringo e ... fu tempo di massacro
Godmonster of Indian Flats
Greaser's Palace
Grim Prairie Tales
La Guarida del Buitre
A Gun for One Hundred Graves
Gunfighter
The Hanged Man
Haunted Gold
Haunted Ranch
Have a good funeral, my friend ... Sartana will pay
High Plains Drifter
His Brother's Ghost
If You Meet Sartana, Pray for Your Death
In Nome Del Padre Del Figlio e Della Colt
In the Name of the Father, the Son and the Colt
Inn of the Damned
Jesse James Meets Frankenstein's Daughter
El Jinete sin Cabeza

Los Jinetes de la Bruja
John Carter
Jonah Hex
Keoma
Khon fai bin
El Latigo contra las Momias As-
    esino [The Whip versus the
    Killer Mummies]
El Látigo contra Satanás [The
    Whip vs. Satan]
Left for Dead
The Legend of Ghostwolf
Legend of the Phantom Rider [Tri-
    gon: The Legend of Pelgidium]
Light the Fuse ... Sartana Is Com-
    ing
The Lone Ranger
The Lone Rider in Ghost Town
Mad at the Moon
Mad Max: Fury Road
Mad Max 2: The Road Warrior
The Man with No Eyes
La Marca de Satanás
Men with Steel Faces
Meteor Monster
Mighty Joe Young
Miner's Massacre
The Missing
A Modern Day Western: The
    Sanchez Saga
Moon Zero Two
Natas: The Reflection
Near Dark
Night of the Lepus
No Graves on Boot Hill
Una Nuvola di polvere ... un grido
    di morte ... arriva Sartana
Oblivion
Oblivion 2: Backlash
OneeChanbara: The Movie
Outland
Overland Stage Raiders
Pale Rider
El Pantano de Las Animas
Petticoat Planet
The Phantom City
The Phantom of the Range
Phantom Town
Pistol for a Hundred Coffins
Una Pistola per cento bare
Pitch Black
Planetfall
The Postman
Priest

El Pueblo Fantasma
I Quattro dell'apocalisse
The Quick and the Undead
Quick Gun Murugan
Radio Ranch
Ravenous
The Rawhide Terror
El Regreso del Monstruo
Renegade
Revelation Trail
Riders of the Whistling Skull
Riddick
Ringo, It's Massacre Time
El Río de Las Animas
The Roaring Whispers
El Rojo
Roswell 1847
Rustlers' Rhapsody
Sabata
Scalps
Se incontri Sartana prega per la
    tua morte
Se sei vivo spara
Seraphim Falls
Serenity
7 Faces of Dr. Lao
Seven Mummies
Shiloh Falls
Silent Tongue
Six Reasons Why
Smoking Guns
Space Rage
The Spider Woman Strikes Back
Spoilers of the Plains
Spook Ranch
Stageghost
Star Wars
Stingray Sam
The Stranger's Gundown
Sugar Creek
Sukiyaki Western Django
Sundown: The Vampire in Retreat
Swamp of the Lost Monsters
Teenage Monster
Tex and the Lord of the Deep
Tex e il Signore Degli Abissi
They Call Him Holy Ghost
1313: Billy the Kid
The Three Supermen of the West
Time Rider: The Adventure of
    Lyle Swann
Tin Star Void
El Topo
Touche pas à la Femme Blanche

Tre croci per non moiré
Tre pistole contro Cesare
Tremors 4: The Legend Begins
Undead or Alive
Uninvited
Uomo avvisato mezzo ammaz-
    zato ... parola di Spirito Santo
The Valley of Gwangi
Vampires
Vanishing Riders
A Visit from an Incubus
La Vuelta Del Charro Negro
The Warrior's Way
Welcome to Blood City
Westworld
Whisky and Ghosts
Whisky e Fantasmi
The White Buffalo
Wild Horse Phantom
Wild, Wild West
Wishbone Cutter
Young Ones
Zagor
Zagor kara bela
Zagor kara korsan'in hazineleri
Zombieland
Zorro Escarlata en La Venganza
    del Ahorcado

Film Serial

Deadwood Dick
The Lightning Warrior
The Masked Rider
The Miracle Rider
Mystery Mountain
The Phantom Empire
The Phantom of the West
The Phantom Rider
The Sign of the Wolf
The Vigilante: Fighting Hero of
    the West
Zorro's Fighting Legion

Graphic Novel

Anomaly
The Big Book of the Weird Wild
    West
Cocco Bill ja kummitukset
    [Comic album; Finland]
Dead West
Deadlands: Volume One: Dead-
    man's Hand
Deadworld: The Last Siesta

Far West

Gorilla Gunslinger: Meet Monjo...

Hong on the Range

Iron West

Lansdale and Truman's Dead Folks

The Last Sane Cowboy and Other Stories

Lost Colony: Book Two: The Red Menace

On The Far Side with Dead Folks

Pariah, Missouri

Screaming Eagle

Secret of San Saba: A Tale of Phantoms and Greed in the Spanish Southwest

Serenity: The Shepherd's Tale

The Thrilling Adventure Hour

Western Gothic: Ballad of Utopia [TPB]

The Wicked West

The Wicked West Volume II: Abomination and Other Tales

Juvenile Book

Billy the Ghost and Me

Blackfoot Braves Society: Spirit Totems

Bubba the Cowboy Prince: A Fractured Texas Tale

Calamity Jack

Dead Reckoning

Dragonfall 5 and the Space Cowboys

Escape from High Doom

Farmer in the Sky

Ghost Town at Sundown

Hank the Cowdog

Hong on the Range

The Indian in the Cupboard

The Key to the Indian

Rapunzel's Revenge

The Return of the Indian

Secret of Haunted Mesa

The Secret of the Indian

Space Cowboy

Tunnel in the Sky

The Weird, Weird West

The Winged Colt of Casa Mia

Novel

Across the Great Barrier

The Alloy of Law

The Angel and the Outlaw

Appaloosa Rising: or, The Legend of the Cowboy Buddha

Arizonan Kukka

The Arrivals

Bad Wind Blowing

The Beast Master

Beast Master's Ark

Beast Master's Circus

Beast Master's Quest

Becoming Coyote

The Best Rootin' Tootin' Shootin' Gunslinger in the Whole Damned Galaxy

Black Hills

Blood Meridian or The Evening Redness in the West

Blood Riders

Blood Rules

Bloodlands

Bloodstone: A Jon Shannow Adventure

Bone Wars

A Book of Tongues

The Buntline Special

Chase the Lightning

The Circus of Dr. Lao

The Clockwork Century

Cold Copper: The Age of Steam

Cowboy Heaven

Coyote Silk

Creeping Dread: The Fantastic Journals of Luther Henry

Crota

Dadgum Martians Invade the Lucky Nickel Saloon

The Damnation Affair

Dawnbreaker

Dawn's Uncertain Light

The Dark Tower: The Gunslinger

Dead in the West

Dead Iron: The Age of Steam

The Dead of Winter

Deadlands: Ghostwalkers

Devil's Engine

Devil's Tower

The Doctor and the Dinosaurs

The Doctor and the Kid

The Doctor and the Rough Rider

Doctor Who: The Gunfighters

Doctor Who: Peacemaker

The Drastic Dragon of Draco, Texas

Dreadful Skin

Dust of the Damned

The Earth Remembers

The Etched City

Fairy BrewHaHa at the Lucky Nickel Saloon

The Far West

The Fast Gun

A Feather in the Wind

Fistful of Feet

The Flight of Michael McBride

For a Few Souls More

For Texas and Zed

From the Heart of the Storm

Frontier Earth

Frontier Earth: Searcher

A Gathering of Widowmakers

The Ghost Flyers

Ghost Town: A Novel

The Ginger Star

Girl in Landscape

The Gods of Mars

The Golems of Laramie County

Good News

The Good, the Bad and the Infernal

Great Caesar's Ghost

Gunsmith: Bayou Ghosts

Gunsmith: The Ghost of Billy the Kid

Gunsmith: Magic Man

Gunsmith: The Valley of the Wendigo

Gunsmith: The Wolf Teacher

The Half-Made World

The Haunted Mesa

The Hawkline Monster: A Gothic Western

Heart of the Hawk

Heaven in West Texas

Hell Hole

Hell's Bounty

The Hidden Goddess

The Hounds of Skaith

The Hunter

I Travel By Night

In Blood We Trust

The Jerusalem Man

Karen Memory

The Last Guardian

Liminal States

A Little Time in Texas

Longarm and the Golden Ghost

Longarm and the Haunted Whorehouse

Novella

Poem

Pulp Fiction

Ghost Busters
Ghost Dancers
Ghost Towns
Ghost Train
The Good, the Bad, and the Dead
The Great Maze
The Great Rail Wars
The Great Weird North
GURPS Deadlands: Hexes
GURPS Deadlands: The Weird West
GURPS Deadlands: Varmints
Heart o' Darkness: Devil's Tower 2
Hell on Earth Reloaded: The Worm's Turn
Hell or High Water
Hexarcana
Horrors o' the Weird West
Horrors of the Wasted West
Hucksters & Hexes
Independence Day
Infestations
Iron Oasis
The Junkman Cometh
Killer Clowns
The Last Crusaders
Law Dogs
Leftovers
Lone Stars: The Texas Rangers
Lost Angels
Marshal Law
Marshal's Handbook
Monsters, Muties, and Misfits
Night Train
Out in the Black
Perdition's Daughter
The Quick & the Dead
Rain o' Terror
Rascals, Varmints & Critters
Rascals, Varmints & Critters 2: The Book of Curses
River o' Blood
The Road to Hell: Devil's Tower 1
Road Warriors
Serenity Adventures
Serenity RPG: Big Damn Heroes Handbook
Shattered Coast
Six Guns & Sorcery
The Sixth Gun: Circle the Wagon
The Sixth Gun: The One-Hand Gang
The Sixth Gun RPG Companion

Skinners
Smith & Robards
Something About a Sword
South o' the Border
Spirit Warriors
Tales from the Trails: Mexico
Tales o' Terror: 1877
Trail of Darkness
Under a Harrowed Moon Part 1: Strange Bedfellows
Under a Harrowed Moon Part 2: Savage Passage
Under a Harrowed Moon Part 3: Ground Zero
The Unity
Urban Renewal
Wanted Undead or Alive
Waste Warriors
The Way of the Brave
The Way of the Dead
The Way of the Gun
The Way of the Huckster
The Way of the New Science
The Way of the Righteous
Werewolf: The Wild West: A Story-telling Game of Historical Horror
Westward
Wild West Companion
The Winding Way
Worms!
Yukon Terror

RPG Games

Deadlands: Hell on Earth
Deadlands: Hell on Earth D20
Deadlands: Hell on Earth Reloaded
Deadlands: Lost Colony
Deadlands: Reloaded
Deadlands: The Great Rail Wars
Deadlands Tall Tales
Deadlands: The Weird West
Deadlands: The Weird West d20
Devil's Gulch
Diamond Gulch
Frag Deadlands [FPS]
Fudge: Deadlands
The Sixth Gun
Terra the Gunslinger [TRPG]
Terra the Gunslinger: Gun Frontier [TRPG]
The Weird Weird West: Marvel Superheroes

Weird West
Werewolf: The Wild West

RPG Magazine

Deadlands: The Epitaph

RPG Module

Hex: Escort to Hell

Short Film

Nickel Children

Short Story

"The Clockwork Sheriff"
"The Fastest Draw"
"Do Not Hasten to Bid Me Adieu"
"Drumlin Wheel"
"From Children's Reminiscences of the Westward Migration"
"Hart and Boot"
"Little Sisters of Eluria"
"Lone Star Traveler"
"The Martian Agent, a Planetary Romance"
"Night of the Cooters"
"Mary Margaret Road-Grader"
"Night of the Cooters"
"The Problem with Mermaids"
"The Shomer Express"
"A Spider Poor Cowboy Rapt and Wide Lemon"
"The Steam Man of the Prairie and the Dark Rider Get Down: A Dime Novel"
"Stranger at Gunnison's Camp"
"The Valley of the Lost"
"The Valley of Spiders"
"With Forked Tongue"

Short Story Anthology

Frontier Cthulhu: Ancient Horrors of the New World
Kaiju Rising: Age of Monsters
Steampunk Cthulhu: Mythos Terror in the Age of Steam
A Town Called Pandemonium
Westward Weird

Stage Play—Theater

Death Valley

The Thrilling Adventure and Supernatural Suspense Hour
The Thrilling Adventure Hour

Strategy Game

Bang! Howdy

Telefilm

Black Noon
Bloodsuckers
Copperhead
The Devil and Miss Sarah
Ghost Town
High Plains Invaders
Into the Badlands
More Wild, Wild West
Purgatory
The Sixth Gun
Skeleton Man
Television Pilot
Timestalkers
Vampire Wars: Battle for the Universe
The Wild, Wild West Revisited

Television Series

The Adventures of Brisco County, Jr.
The Adventures of Oky Doky
The Adventures of Superboy
The Adventures of Superman
Batman
Battlestar Galactica
Beyond Belief: Fact or Fiction
Bobby Benson and the B-Bar-B Riders
Bonanza
Captain Video and His Video Rangers
Captain Z-Ro
Charmed
Cimarron Strip
Cliffhangers
Defiance
Doctor Who
Earth 2
Fantasy Island
Fear Itself

Fear the Walking Dead
Fireball XL5
Firefly
Four Feather Falls
The Girl from U.N.C.L.E.
Highlander
Killjoys
Kolchak the Night Stalker
Kung Fu
Kung Fu: The Legend Continues
Legend
Life with Snarky Parker
Little House on the Prairie
Lois and Clark: The New Adventures of Superman
Lost in Space
Lucky Luke
MacGyver
Oky Doky Ranch
Out of the Unknown
Outlaws
Penny Dreadful
The Prisoner
Psych
R. L. Stine's Haunting Hour: The Series
Rod Serling's Night Gallery
Sabrina the Teenage Witch
The Secret Adventures of Jules Verne
The Secret Empire
Sliders
Smallville
Star Trek
Star Trek: Enterprise
Star Trek: The Next Generation
The Time Tunnel
The Twilight Zone
UFO
Voyagers!
The Walking Dead
The Wild Wild West
X-Files
Zorro
Zorro: La Espada y la Rosa

Video Games

Alone in the Dark: Ghosts in Town
Alone in the Dark 3

Back to the Future Part II & III
Badlands
Bang! Howdy
Blood
Blood II: The Chosen
Brave: The Search for Spirit Dancer
Darkwatch: Curse of the West
El Diablo's 'Merican Adventure
Fallout: New Vegas
God Hand
Gunman Chronicles
Gunman Clive
The Gunstringer
Oddworld: Stranger's Wrath
OneeChanbara
Prey
Red Dead Redemption: Undead Nightmare
Samurai Western
Silverload
Steam World Dig
Supernatural
Tin Star
Tremors 4: The Legend Begins: Dirt Dragons
Turok: Evolution
Vampire Hunter D
The Walking Dead
Wild ARMs
Wild ARMs: Advanced 3rd
Wild ARMs Alter Code: F
Wild ARMs: 2nd Ignition
Wild ARMs: The Vth Vanguard
Wild Guns

Web Comic

Cowboys & Aliens
Cowboys & Aliens: Worlds at War
Deadlands Reloaded: What a Man's Got to Do
Holliday Mountain Madness
The Sam Plenty Cavalcade of Action Show Plus Singing!
Web Series

Appendix II: Self-Published Titles

The increased popularity of self publishing and the e-book has seen an influx of Weird Western novels, novellas and comic books. I have included titles as of August 2015 that have generally received good reviews. Publishers are dominated by Amazon's CreateSpace although some authors have formed their own self publishing companies that are either distributed through CreateSpace, other self publishing platforms or through micro-small presses.

Books

Brackett Hollister: The Werewolf Pack: Author: Quentin Wallace

Brimstone Deep: Author: Laurian Smith

Burden Kansas: Author: Alan Ryker

Clockwork Legion (Series): Author: David Lee Summers

Close Encounters of the Old West: Author: Logan Hawkes

The Converted: Author: C. R. Hindmarsh

The Cowboy and the Vampire (Series): Author: Clark Hays

The Cowboys of Cthulhu: Author: David Bain

Coyote: The Outlander: Author: Chantal Noordeloos

Coyote's Trail: Author: Edward M. Erdelac

Cursed City: Where the Souls Are Worthless: Anthology

Custer's Run: Author: D. J. Curran

A Dead God's Wrath: Author: Rusty Carl

Dead or Alive: Author: William Harms

The Dead Sheriff: Zombie Damnation: Author: Mark Justice

Deadstock: Author: Ian Rogers

Doom Magnetic!: Author: William Pauley III

End Trails: Two Stories of the Weird West: Author: Andrew Leon Hudson

A Fistful of Horrors: Tales of Terror from the Old West: Author: Kevin G. Bufton

Flash Gold Chronicles (Series): Author: Lindsay Buroker

Ghosthunter: Author: Michael Saunders

The God Eaters: Author: Jesse Hajicek

Guns of Seneca 6: Author: Bernard Schaffer

The Hand of Osiris: Author: Frank Cavallo

Hellcat's Bounty: Author: Renae Jones

Hollywood Cowboy Detectives (Series): Author: Darryle Purcell

Horror at Cold Springs: Author: Michael Merriam

How the West Was Weird: Vol. 1-3: Editor: Russ Anderson Jr.

Hunting in Hell: Author: Maria Valonte

The Jesse James Archives (Series): Authors: Craig Gallant, C. L. Werner

Leather, Denim and Silver: Tales of the Monster Hunter: Editor: Miles Boothe

Lightning Wolves: Author: David Lee Summers

Long Horn, Big Shaggy: Author: Steve Vernon

Lost DMB Files Collection: Author: David Mack Brown

Moon Dance: Author: S.P. Somtrow

Nine Hours Till Sunrise: Author: Better Hero Army

Once Upon a Sixgun: Author: Nikki Nelson-Hicks

The Outlaw King (Series): Author: S.A. Hunt

A Pack of Wolves: Author: Eric S. Brown

The Shadow Town: Author: J. W. Bradley

The Shadow Trail: Author: J. W. Bradley

Showdown at Midnight: Editor: David B. Riley

Silver Bullets: Author: Laird Ryan States

The Sinner's Tale: Author: Zachary Ricks

Skin Medicine: Author: Tim Curran

Skull Moon: Author: Tim Curran

Sloughing Off the Rot: Author: Lance Carbuncle

Strange Tales of the Old West: Author: James "Doc" Manniken

Tom Horn vs. the Warlords of Krupp: Author: Glen Robinson

Trigger Reflex: Tales of the Monster Hunter II: Editor: Miles Boothe

Twisted Tumbleweed Tales: Author: Paul Victor Wargelin

Unicorn Western (Series): Authors: Sean Platt, Johnny B. Truant

Vampire Siege at Rio Muerto: Author: John W. Whalen

Walk the Sky: Authors: Robert Swartwood, David B. Silva

Welcome to Hell: An Anthology of Western Weirdness: Editor: Eric S. Brown

Wendigo Moon: Author: Priscilla U. McDaniel

The Wind Drifters (Series): Author: Guy Stanton III

The Work of the Devil: Author: Katherine Amt Hanna

Zombie West (Series): Author: Angela Scott

Comic books

Evercross: Publisher: Media Monsters

Hell West: Frontier Force: Creators: Frederic Vervisch, Thierre Lamy (Belgium)

Last Ride for Horsemen: Creators: Kevin La-Porte, Nathan Smith, Gavin Mitchell

The Leg: Creators: Van Jenson, Jose Pimienta (graphic novel)

The Legend of Oz: The Wicked West: Creator: Tom Hutchison

Lone Star Soul: Creator: Peter Colin Campbell

Next Town Over: Creator: Erin Mehlos

Pistoleras: Creator: Frank Candiloro

Quicksand Jack: Creators: Matt and Nick Long

Shepperton's Waltz: Publisher: Oort Cloud Comics

Steam West: Creator: Frederic Pham Choung (France)

Undertow: "The Organ Grinder": Publisher: 7th Wave Comics

Audio Drama

The Deadeye Kid: Creator: Julie Hoverson

Bibliography

Books and Periodicals

Ash, Brian, ed. *The Visual Encyclopedia of Science Fiction*. London: Trewin Copplestone, 1977.

Beahm, George. *The Stephen King Story*. Kansas City: Andrews and McMeel, 1991.

Black, Bill. *The Best of the West: The Westerns of Magazine Enterprises*. Longwood, FL: Paragon, 1995.

Bruschini, Antonio, and Federico de Zigno. *Western all'Italiana: 100 More Must-See Movies*. Firenze, Italy: Glittering Images, 2006.

_____, and _____. *Western all'Italiana: The Wild, the Sadist and the Outsiders*. Firenze, Italy: Glittering Images, 2001.

Clements, Jonathan, and Helen McCarthy. *The Anime Encyclopedia: A Century of Japanese Animation*. Berkeley, CA: Stone Bridge, 2015.

Collings, Michael R. *The Many Facets of Stephen King*. Mercer Island, WA: Starmont House, 1985.

Duncan, Randy, and Matthew J. Smith. *The Power of Comics: History, Form and Culture*. London: Bloomsbury Academic, 2009.

Franklin, Bruce H. *Robert A. Heinlein: America as Science Fiction*. New York: Oxford University Press, 1980.

Gerani, Gary, with Paul H. Schulman. *Fantastic Television*. Godalming, UK: LSP, 1977.

Giusti, Marco. *Dizionario del Western all'Italiana*. Italy: Arnoldo Mondadori Editore, 2007.

Goulart, Ron. *Great History of Comic Books*. Chicago: Contemporary, 1986.

Grossman, Gary H. *Saturday Morning TV*. New York: Arlington House, 1981.

Gunn, James. *Alternate Worlds*. Englewood Cliffs, NJ: Prentice-Hall, 1975.

Heinlein, Robert A., and Virginia Heinlein, ed. *Grumbles from the Grave*. New York: Ballantine, 1989.

Horn, Maurice, ed. *The World Encyclopedia of Comics*. London: New English Library, 1976.

Inge, M. Thomas. *Comics as Culture*. Jackson: University Press of Mississippi, 1990.

Kyle, David. *A Pictorial History of Science Fiction*. London: Hamlyn, 1976.

Miller, Cynthia, and A. Bowdoin Van Riper, eds. *Undead in the West: Vampires, Zombies, Mummies, and Ghosts on the Cinematic Frontier*. Lanham, MD: Scarecrow, 2012.

_____, and _____, eds. *Undead in the West II: They Just Keep Coming*. Lanham, MD: Scarecrow, 2013.

Miller, Cynthia, and Julie Anne Taddeo, eds. *Steaming into a Victorian Future: A Steampunk Anthology*. Lanham, MD: Scarecrow, 2012.

Morgan, Ted. *Literary Outlaw: The Life and Times of William S. Burroughs*. New York: Henry Holt, 1988.

Pascale, Amy. *Joss Whedon: The Biography*. Chicago: Chicago Review Press, 2014.

Pirani, Adam. *The Complete Gerry Anderson Episode Guide*. London: Titan, 1989.

Porges, Irwin. *Edgar Rice Burroughs: The Man Who Created Tarzan*. Provo: Brigham Young University Press, 1975.

Richetti, John, ed. *The Columbia History of the British Novel*. New York: Columbia University Press, 1994.

Robb, Brian J. *Steampunk: An Illustrated History of Fantastical Fiction, Fanciful Film and Other Victorian Visions*. Minneapolis: Voyageur, 2012.

Rottensteiner, Frank. *The Science Fiction Book: An Illustrated History*. New York: Seabury, 1975.

Silipo, Daniele, and Alessandra Sciamanna, ed. *Bizzarro Magazine "Weird, Weird West,"* vol. 2. Rome: Laboratorio Bizarro/Passenger, June 2012.

Slethaug, Gordon E. "*The Hawkline Monster*: Brautigan's "Buffoon Mutation." In *The Scope of the Fantastic: Selected Essays from the First International Conference on the Fantastic in Literature and Film: Culture, Biography, Themes, Children's Literature*. Edited by Robert A. Collins and Howard D. Pearle, III. Westport, CT: Greenwood, 1985. 137–45.

Weiss, Ken, and Ed Goodgold. *To Be Continued....* New York: Bonanza, 1972.

Wilt, David E. *The Mexican Film Bulletin.* College Park, MD, 2008.

Wright, Bradford W. *Comic Book Nation.* Baltimore: John Hopkins University Press, 2001.

Internet Sources

AC Comics. http://www.accomics.com

Adult Swim. www.adultswim.com

Anime News Network. http://animenewsnetwork. com

Atlas Tales. http://www.atlastales.com

Blue Corn Comics. http://www.bluecorncomics.com

Cinefania. http://www.cinefania.com

Classic Comic Books. http://mikegrost.com/comics. htm

Comic Book Resources. http://www.comicbookre sources.com

Comic Vine. http://www.comicvine.com

Cover Browser. http://www.coverbrowser.com

Dark Horse. www.darkhorse.com

DC Comics Database. http://dc.wikia.com

Don Markstein's Toonopedia. www.toonopedia.com

Galactic Central. http://www.philsp.com

Good Reads. http://www.goodreads.com

Grand Comic Book Database. http://www.comics. org

Internet Book List. http://www.iblist.com

Internet Movie Database. www.imdb.com

Kung Fu Episode Guide. http://kungfu-guide.com

Lambiek Comiclopedia. http://lambiek.net/home. htm

Max Brand. http://maxbrandonline.com

Moby Games. http://www.mobygames.com/home

Museum of Broadcast Communication. http://www. museum.tv

New General Catalog of Old Books and Authors. http://www.kingkong.demon.co.uk/ngcoba/ng coba.htm

Newsarama. http://www.newsarama.com/

19 Nocturne Boulevard. http://www.19nocturnebou levard.net

Old Corral. www.b-westerns.com

Project Gutenberg. www.gutenberg.org

RPG Geek. http://rpggeek.com

RPGnet. http://index.rpg.net

RPGNow. http://www.rpgnow.com/index.php

Serial Squadron. www.serialsquadron.com/index. html

Sinema Türk http://www.sinematurk.com/film_ genel/6915/Zagor-Kara-Bela

Space Westerns.com http://www.spacewesterns.com

Steve Jackson Games. http://www.sjgames.com

Television Heaven. www.televisionheaven.co.uk/four feather.htm

Television Obscurities. http://www.tvobscurities. com/articles/cliffhangers_2.php

Terence Hill. Com. http://www.terencehill.com/ mov_luckyluke_tv.html

Toonarific. www.toonarific.com

TV.com. www.tv.com

Visionary Comics. http://visionarycomics.com

Warrenverse. http://www.angelfire.com/zine2/war renverse

Weird West Emporium. http://weirdwestemporium. blogspot.com

Weird Westerns. https://weirdwesterns.wordpress. com

Whirligig. www.whirlygig-tv.co.uk

Wikipedia. www.wikipidia.org

WorldCat. www.worldcat.org

YouTube. www.youtube.com

Index

Numbers in **bold italics** indicate pages with photographs.